FULHAM OLD AND NEW

Being An

Exhaustive History of the Ancient Parish of Fulham

Volume I

by

Charles James Fèret

London
The Leadenhall Press, Ltd., 50, Leadenhall Street, E.C.

Simpkin, Marshall, Hamilton, Kent & Co., Ltd

New York: Charles Scribner's Sons, 153-157, Fifth Avenue
MDCCCC
(All Rights reserved)

[Above is a reproduction of the original 1900 title page]

Charles James Fèret

The cover shows a map of part of Fulham in 1741-45

Fulham Old and New,
first published in 1900,
is here republished by Michael Wood and FamLoc

FL

A FamLoc Book
Available in Print and eBook Format

Originally published 1900
This FamLoc Edition first published 2015
Copyright © 2015 Michael Wood
All rights reserved.

ISBN-13: 978-1518618581
ISBN-10: 1518618588

CONTENTS

Original Preface of 1900	Page v
FamLoc Preface	Page ix
List of Illustrations, Volume I	Page xi
Maps of Fulham, 1741-45	Page xvii
Chapter I: The Name "Fulham"	Page 1
Chapter II: The Manor of Fulham	Page 7
Chapter III: Boundaries of The Parish and of The Manor of Fulham	Page 22
Chapter IV: The River	Page 30
Chapter V: Agriculture and Trade	Page 39
Chapter VI: Population	Page 46
Chapter VII: Amusements	Page 48
Chapter VIII: Punishments	Page 52
Chapter IX: The Highways and Byways of Fulham	Page 62
Chapter X: Wintering of the Danes at Fulham	Page 67
Chapter XI: Fulham Ferry	Page 70
Chapter XII: A Bridge of Boats	Page 80
Chapter XIII: Old Fulham or Putney Bridge	Page 83

Chapter XIV: New Putney Bridge	Page 114
Chapter XV: The Old Town	Page 117
Chapter XVI: High Street (General)	Page 120
Chapter XVII: High Street (East Side)	Page 128
Chapter XVIII: High Street (West Side)	Page 174
Chapter XIX: High Street (Miscellaneous)	Page 198
Chapter XX: Burlington Road	Page 212
Chapter XXI: Church Row	Page 230
Chapter XXII: Fulham Church	Page 250
Chapter XXIII: Fulham Church: Its Monuments And Epitaphs	Page 359
Chapter XXIV: Fulham Churchyard	Page 470
Notes:	Page 521

ORIGINAL PREFACE OF 1900

This work, the outcome of many years of patient research, will, it is hoped, be found to furnish the reader with full and accurate information regarding the interesting Parish with which it deals.

"A system built upon the discoveries of a great many minds," says Dr. Johnson, "is always of more strength than what is produced by the mere workings of one mind, which, of itself, can do little. There is not so poor a book in the world that would not be a prodigious effort were it wrought out entirely by a single mind, without the aid of prior investigators."

To no one is the truth of this statement more evident than to the student of topography. His work may be original, but his facts must be mainly gathered from the records of those who have preceded him. To reduce to order a vast mass of matter drawn from the most heterogeneous sources, to test each statement, and to separate the wheat from the chaff, is a task of immense magnitude. Those alone who have undertaken to write biography or history can realise the arduous labours necessary to secure absolute correctness. The Author has often had to say with Boswell, "I have sometimes been obliged to run half over London, in order to fix a date correctly: which, when I had accomplished, I well knew would obtain me no praise, though a failure would have been to my discredit."

In dealing with such an enormous and varied mass of matter as that involved in the compilation of "Fulham Old and New," some mistakes are almost inevitable, but throughout the work the utmost care has been exercised to ensure accuracy. With this purpose in view, the Author has, wherever possible, consulted manuscript documents as original sources of information, and therefore the least likely to err. Many of these records have happily been the means of throwing much, new light upon the history of our Parish, and of bringing into connection with it the names of very many distinguished personages famous in the annals of our country.

It would be impossible to enumerate here a tithe of the

channels of information of which the Author has availed himself. The whole of the Court Rolls of the Manor of Fulham, commencing with the year 1382, have been carefully searched and have yielded a wonderful abundance of material of the deepest antiquarian interest. The accounts of the Churchwardens and Overseers of Fulham, dating from 1625, the Assessment and other Parish Books, preserved at the Fulham Town Hall, have all been explored. The Church Registers, beginning in 1675, have been fully examined. At the Probate Registry, the Public Record Office, the Bishop of London's Registry, the Ecclesiastical Commission, Lambeth Palace, Fulham Palace, the Guildhall, the Bodleian, the British Museum and numerous other places, very extensive searches have been made. Besides this, numberless original manuscripts, deeds, abstracts, letters, and other documents in private hands, have been consulted.

Nothing has been recorded upon mere surmise. In every instance in which historical facts have been given, the original authority for them has been sought out and examined, while the biographical notices of former residents have been culled from the most reliable sources. In many cases these notices have been supplemented by information furnished by the living representatives of the families concerned.

During the progress of this work the Author has been assisted to much information by old residents of Fulham, and by others who, in various ways, are connected with, or are interested in, the Parish. Among other kind contributors may be mentioned Lady Dilke, Lord Balcarres, His Excellency Sir Horace Rumbold, Bart., the Rev. W. C. Muriel, the Rev. J. S. Sinclair, Mr. A. Chasemore, Mr. G. Milner-Gibson-Cullum, the late Mr. C. E. Gildersome-Dickinson, Mr. John P. Hutchins, Mr. A. W. Stocken, Mr. Arthur Hussey, Miss Edith Harrison, Mrs. Lammin, Mrs. Roydhouse, Capt. George Merry, Mr. T. Aplin Marsh, Mr. F. W. Madden, Mr. F. G. Hilton Price, Mr. C. Mason, Mr. F. Manby, Col. Prideaux, Mr. John Rooth, Maj. General C. W. Robinson, Mr. T. E. Ravenshaw, Mr. R. F. Sketchley, Mr. D. Shopland, Mr. W. W. Watts, Lt. Colonel G. Hunter-Weston, Mr. J. A. Wild, Mr. A. Ballhatchet, Mr. G. E. Lloyd-Baker, the Rev. M. H. Boden, Mr. F. Hitchin-Kemp, Mr. J. Ravenshaw, the late Mr. D. McMinn, Mr. William Thatcher and Dr. Woodhouse.

On many etymological points the Author has been favoured with the opinion of the Rev. Professor Skeat, M.A., the distinguished Anglo-Saxon scholar.

The Author has to express his especial thanks to Canon Fisher, M.A., the late Vicar of Fulham, to Mr. Charles Griffin, an old resident of this Parish, to Mr. W. J. Harvey, and to Mr. S. Martin, of the Hammersmith Public Library, for the generous assistance which, throughout the work, they have at all times so readily accorded him.

CHARLES JAMES FERET.
Fulham, 1900.

The tower of Fulham Church, looking west,
showing moat in foreground.
From a drawing executed in 1835, signed "A. P.,"
preserved in the Vicarage "Faulkner."

PREFACE TO FAMLOC EDITION

For most of its history Fulham lay in the County of Middlesex, but, with the expansion of Greater London, it now forms part of the London Borough of Hammersmith and Fulham.

Fulham Old and New was first published in 1900. This Famloc Edition retains the three-volume format, and has been modified only slightly from Fèret's original:

A handful of typos have been corrected, and a small number of changes have been made to the punctuation, including indenting the quotations.

The original footnotes have been placed in an additional "Notes" chapter at the end of the book; the annotated text is underlined.

Those chapters having a common subject matter have been combined; e.g. the chapters "Fulham Church" and "Fulham Church (Continued)" have become the single chapter "Fulham Church."

The short number of entries in the original Errata page have been incorporated into the main text.

The List of Subscribers, those who paid upfront for the publication and so helped make it possible, has been moved to the end of Volume III.

Always bear in mind the book was originally published in 1900, and all mention Fèret makes of relative dates, such as "two centuries ago", "thirty years ago", etc within the main text are with reference to that publication date. Also, Fèret often refers to Queen Elizabeth - obviously Queen Elizabeth I.

The photographs have been digitally adjusted, but please bear in mind the quality of photographs in 1900. We will make some of the photographs and family trees available on the FamLoc website.

Some now-unusual words and contractions, etc used in *Fulham Old and New*:

Vizt. was used for "namely", "that is to say", and "as follows".
&c. is an older form of "etc."
Esq. is a contraction of Esquire, much used until fairly recently as a polite title appended to a man's name in the absence of any other title. Originally a member of the English gentry ranking below a knight.
Currency: The currency was Pounds, Shillings and Pence, abbreviated to £. s. d. There were twenty shillings to the Pound, and 12 pence to the shilling. In old records, 3d. (for example) was written as iij^d with a "j" replacing the final i, and the "d" as a superscript. There is also the superscript ^{li} for "pounds" in some of the quotations.
Area of Land: As well as acres, there were subdivisions of the rod and pole. These three were abbreviated to a, r, p.
Tombstones and memorials: Fèret uses the character "|" to differentiate separate lines on a memorial stone.

FAMLOC WEBSITE
Those wishing to find out more about Fulham local history and family history can visit FamLoc's website:

www.famloc.co.uk

- and navigate to the Fulham pages. Webpages can be added to continue the discussion of subjects in this book.

Finally, we would like to give our heartfelt thanks to Charles James Fèret, without whom much of the history of Fulham would have been lost.

Michael Wood, FamLoc, 2015.

LIST OF ILLUSTRATIONS IN VOLUME I

MAP OF FULHAM, 1741-45

CHAPTER I: THE NAME "FULHAM"
Arms of the See of London
Fulham, circa 1790

CHAPTER II: THE MANOR OF FULHAM
Fulham, from the "White Lion," Putney, 1783
Fulham, 1809
Fulham, from Putney

CHAPTER III: BOUNDARIES OF THE PARISH AND OF THE MANOR OF FULHAM
Fulham, circa 1805

CHAPTER IV: THE RIVER
A High Tide at Fulham in January 1877

CHAPTER V: AGRICULTURE AND TRADE
Fulham, 1750

CHAPTER VII: AMUSEMENTS
Fulham, 1750

CHAPTER VIII: PUNISHMENTS
Fulham, circa 1817

CHAPTER IX: THE HIGHWAYS AND BYWAYS OF FULHAM
First page of the oldest existing Poor Rate Assessment Book

CHAPTER X: WINTERING OF THE DANES AT FULHAM
A page from the old Parish Books

CHAPTER XI: FULHAM FERRY
Lease of Fulham Ferry, etc., William Moreton to Sir Ralph Warren, 12 Ap. 24 Hy. VIII

CHAPTER XII: A BRIDGE OF BOATS
Robert Devereux, Earl of Essex, General of the Parliamentary Army

CHAPTER XIII: OLD FULHAM OR PUTNEY BRIDGE
Fulham Bridge, 1742
Fulham Bridge, 1750
Fulham Bridge, from the Putney shore, circa 1760
Fulham Bridge, from the Putney shore, circa 1760
Fulham Bridge, from the Putney shore, circa 1799
Fulham Bridge, from the Putney shore, circa 1868
Fulham Bridge, from the Putney shore, circa 1868
Fulham Bridge, showing site of the landing stage of the old. Ferry, circa 1780
Fulham Bridge and Aqueduct, from the Putney shore

CHAPTER XIV: NEW PUTNEY BRIDGE
Putney Bridge, 1896

CHAPTER XVI: HIGH STREET (GENERAL)
Top of the High Street, 1894

CHAPTER XVII: HIGH STREET (EAST SIDE)
Fulham House, 1895
Jacob Tonson
Ranelagh House, garden view
Old houses on the site of Cowheard's Tenement
An ancient Fire-place in the old "Golden Lion," 1838
An ancient Fire-place in the old "Golden Lion," 1838
An ancient Fire-place in the old "Golden Lion," 1838
Marshall's Alley
Fulham Workhouse
High Street, east side
Four ancient tenements in Bear Street

CHAPTER XVIII: HIGH STREET (WEST SIDE)
The old "King's Head"
High Street, as seen from Holcroft's, from an oil painting by Mrs. Streatfield Baker
High Street, west side
High Street, west side, 1871
High Street, west side. just prior to the demolition of old houses in 1890
High Street, west side
The Grand Theatre, 1897
A corner in the Grand Theatre, 1897
The Grand Staircase
Backs of old houses, High Street, west side
Charles Hickman, Bishop of Derry
William Sharp, 1784
Granville Sharp, 1784
The Sharps on board their yacht off Fulham

CHAPTER XIX: HIGH STREET (MISCELLANEOUS)
An old cottage between the Moat and Bear Street, circa 1790

CHAPTER XX: BURLINGTON ROAD
Burlington Road, 1895
Burlington House School
Playground of Burlington House School
Playground of Burlington House School
Burlington House, shortly before demolition
Entrance to Fulham Convict Prison, 1895
Fulham Convict Prison
Cell No. 29, where Constance Kent was confined
The Chapel, Fulham Convict Prison
Plan of Sir Wm. Powell's Almshouses and adjacent property (originally Thomas Pyner's Messuage)
Burlington Gardens, 1895

CHAPTER XXI: CHURCH ROW
Fulham Vicarage, 1895
Miss Batsford's House
Sir William Powell's Almshouses, 1895

Site of Sir William Powell's Almshouses
Church Row, 1895

CHAPTER XXII: FULHAM CHURCH
In the Old Church
Tower of Fulham Church, looking west, 1835
The Ringing Chamber, 1894
Tower of Fulham Church, looking south, before the restoration of 1845
Interior of the Clock, 1894
Tower of Fulham Church, as restored by Mr. G. Godwin
Tower of Fulham Church, 1858
The Bell Loft, 1894
Tower of Fulham Church, looking west
Tower of Fulham Church, 1869
The Limpany Pew
The West Door
The South Door
Geometrical Elevation of Fulham Church, south side, from measurements by Mr. Upsden, Surveyor, 1797
Fulham Church, circa 1800, from the north-west
Fulham Church, south side, 1812
Fulham Church, circa 1820
Fulham Church, east end, 1836
Church Plate
Fulham Church, east end, circa 1850
North East view of Fulham Church, 1837
Old Fulham Church, east end
Old Fulham Church, west end
The Font, 1794
The old "Three Decker"
Fulham Church, south side, circa 1879
Fulham Church: Gallery plan, 1837
Fulham Church: Ground plan, 1837
Fulham Church: Elevation showing the addition to the North Front, 1840
Fulham Church, south side, 1895
The Blomfield Window, now in the South Transept

CHAPTER XXIII: FULHAM CHURCH: ITS MONUMENTS AND EPITAPHS
A defaced Monument formerly in Fulham Church, 1794
Supposed brass to the Rev. William Harvey, 1794
Supposed brass to Sir Sampson Norton, 1794
Monument to Sir Thomas Smith, 1896
Monument to Lady Margaret Legh, 1794
Monument to Lady Margaret Legh, 1895
Monument to William Payne and Jane his wife, 1794
Monument to Thomas Bonde, 1895
Monument to Katharine Hart, 1794
Monument to Katharine Hart, 1895
Monument to William Plumbe, 1896
Monumental brass to Margaret Svanders, 1896
Monument to William Earsby
Monument to John, Viscount Mordaunt, 1896
Monument to Thomas Winter, 1896
Supposed brass to Sir William Butts, 1794
Monument to Lady Dorothy Clarke and Dr. Samuel Barrow, 1896
Monument to Elizabeth Limpany, 1896
Plan showing the Positions of the Grave-Stones in the Old Church, before the Rebuilding in 1880-81

CHAPTER XXIV: FULHAM CHURCHYARD
Pathway through the Churchyard
South side of Fulham Churchyard, showing the old boundary wall, 1824
Plan of addition to Churchyard made in 1783
Plan of addition to Churchyard made in 1843
Fulham Churchyard, showing the path stopped up in 1868
West side of Fulham Churchyard, circa 1849
Plan of the Churchyard

Fulham Bridge. From an old print at the Hammersmith Public Library, inscribed "T. Preist, del. 1742."

Fulham Bridge. From an old print published by Henry Overton, circa 1750

Fulham Map 1741-45 (north west section)

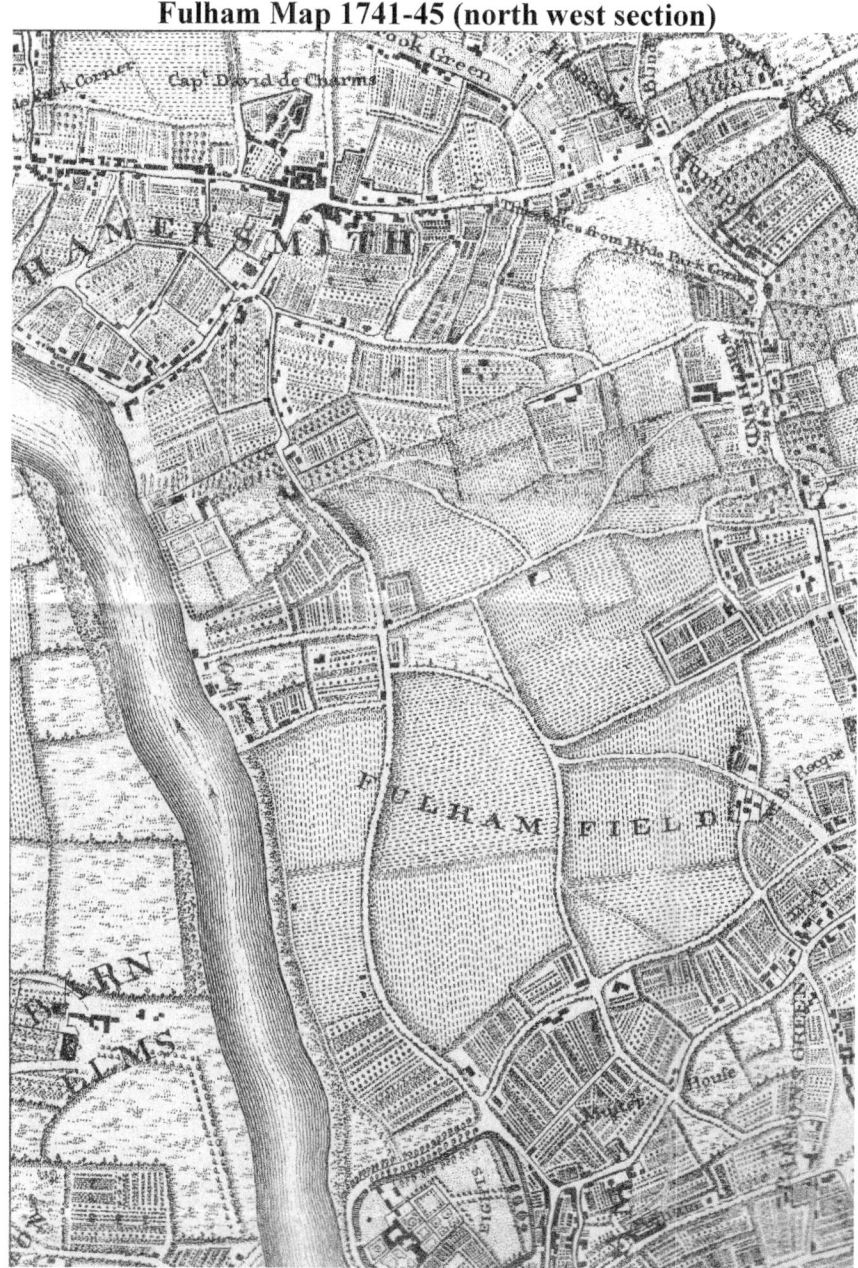

Charles James Fèret

Fulham in 1741-45 (north-east section)

Fulham in 1741-45 (south-west section)

Charles James Fèret

Fulham in 1741-45 (south-east section)

CHAPTER I: THE NAME "FULHAM"

The parish of Fulham is situated on the north bank of the Thames, in the hundred of Ossulstone in the county of Middlesex.

Before entering on a description of the parish, we propose to deal with the origin of the name "Fulham." Many speculations as to its meaning have been made by previous writers. John Leland, who flourished in the reign of Henry VIII, was the first to attempt its explanation. Towards the end of his poem, "Cygnea Cantio," he writes:

"Volucrum domus, Saxonicè Fulenham, vulgo, Fulham."
(The home of birds, in Saxon Fulenham, commonly Fulham)

Arms of the See of London

William Camden, the "father" of English antiquaries, in his "Britanniæ Descriptio" (1586-1607), also suggests "the house of fowls" as the meaning. John Norden, in his "Speculum Britanniæ" (1593-1598), while favouring the *Volucrum domus* theory, advances the startling proposition that the explanation may be *Volucrum amnis*, the "riuer of fowle."

William Somner, in his well-known "Dictionarium-Saxonico-Latino-Anglicum" (1659), expresses his belief that "Fullan-ham," the earliest form of the name, was so called from the marshiness of the place [à Loci uligine, ut opinor, derivatum]. John Bowack, in his "Antiquities of Middlesex" (1705), repeats the statements of Camden and Norden. Richard Newcourt, in his "Repertorium Ecclesiasticum Parochiale Londinense" (1708), gives the suggestions of Camden, Norden and Somner. Edward Lye, who revised Somner's "Dictionary" (published posthumously under the editorship of Owen Manning), adheres to Somner's explanation of "Fullan-ham" as "Cœnosa habitatio" or swampy homestead. The Rev. Daniel Lysons, in his "Environs of London" (1796), and Thomas Faulkner, in his "Historical Account of Fulham" (1813), repeat the definitions of Camden, Norden, Somner and Lye. Dr. Joseph Bosworth, in his "Anglo-Saxon Dictionary" (1836), translates "Fullan-ham" as "foul or dirty habitation." Sir Arthur W. Blomfield, in his lecture entitled "The Olden Times of Fulham," delivered in the Parish School-room, 27th June 1856, inclines to the belief that the name arose from the water fowl which once resorted hither. Mr. Thomas Crofton Croker, in his "Walk from London to Fulham" (1860), gives the suggestions of Camden and Norden.

Despite the favour in which the *Volucrum domus* theory has been held, it is quite impossible that Fulham can mean the "habitation of fowls." The objection to the explanation is two-fold. The Anglo-Saxon for a "fowl" (*avis, volucris*) is *fugl*, the genitive plural of which is *fugla*, so that, if the name meant the "habitation of birds," we should expect to find some such early form as "Fuglaham," but such a spelling has never been traced. Secondly, if such a form could be found, it would fail to account for the "n" in "Fullan-ham," the earliest known form of the name.

The only sure method of arriving at a correct interpretation of local place-names is to carefully examine the spellings current when Anglo-Saxon was a spoken tongue. The earliest known occurrence of the name is in a grant of the Manor to Earconuald, Bishop of London, the date of which is about the year 691, where the word is spelled "Fulanham." In the so-called Anglo-Saxon "Chronicle," under the year 879 (880), the name appears as "Fullanhamme" and "Fullanham." In the will of Bishop Theodred, circa 950, we have " Fullenham." "Fulenham" is another very early form. By the time of the Norman Conquest, the "an" (a suffix, as we shall presently see) had fallen away, and the name accordingly appears in the "Domesday Book" (1085-1086) as "Fuleham." For the next century or two we meet with such spellings as "Fuleham," "Fulleham," "Ffuleham," etc. In an instrument of Richard de Belmeis (Bishop of London 1108 to 1127 (?), the name is spelled Foleham, and in another by Richard of Ely (Bishop of London 1189 to 1198), it is written "Fuleham." In the Record Office is a deed, dated 1200, executed "apud Fuleham." About the time of the later Plantagenets, the prevailing forms of the name were, "Foleham," "ffoleham," "Folham" and "ffolham." Later again, we have "ffulham," "fullam," "fulham," "Falham," and finally "Fulham" as the settled orthography.

At the hands of foreigners the name assumes such extraordinary guises as phulham, foulan, foullemme, etc.

The leading forms may be thus arranged:

Fulanham	
Fullanham	
Fulenham	691 to 1066.
Fullenham	
Fuleham	
Fulleham	1066 to 1250.
ffuleham	
Folham	
Foleham	1250 to 1500.
ffoleham	
ffulham	
fullam	1500 to the present time.
Fulham	

These forms, of course, more or less overlap. Thus, the early chroniclers, such as Henry of Huntingdon, write Fulenham, etc.

The evolution from Fulanham to Fulham is perfectly natural and what we should expect. First, the case-ending "an" was softened to "en" and "e" and finally disappeared altogether. Then the dominant vowel "û" or "ou" was shortened, first to "ō" and then to the Modern English "u" or "ŏŏ" (as in "full") in accordance with the general laws of accent. The doubling of the initial letter, as in ffoleham, ffulham, etc., was simply a ready method of rendering the old scrip form for the capital "F," an elaborate letter not unlike two small f's partially super-imposed.

The word, then, with which we have to deal is "Fulanham." Divided into its constituent parts, this is simply "Ful-an-ham." The final syllable is the Anglo-Saxon *hām*, meaning a homestead or village community, a word which survives in "hamlet." *Ful* is, in all probability, the Anglo-Saxon for "foul," "miry" or "muddy," while *an* is a suffix denoting the dative case. In Anglo-Saxon it was customary to use place-names in this case. Of this practice there are hundreds of instances, such as the names "Fulanbroc" (Foulbrook, in Worcestershire), "Fulanea" (Fulney, in Lincolnshire), literally "foul-river," "Fulan-pit" (Fulpit, in Essex), etc.

"Fulham" thus signifies "foul-town," not exactly with the meaning which we now attach to the adjective "foul," but rather with the sense of "miry" or "muddy." The term *fūl* in Anglo-Saxon is almost invariably used in respect to the state of roads and fords, as is shown in the instances of the place-names above quoted. A generation or two ago the roads of Fulham were at times almost impassable on account of the collections of mud churned up by the market carts or deposited by the successive inundations of the river over the low-lying land. Pennant tells us that, when the Romans held sway in Britain, the land round by Westminster was mostly a flat fen, "which continued to beyond Fulham." Old residents of Fulham can still recall the days when the river washed up the High Street, and other low-lying parts of the " Town." Indeed, it was not till the Thames River (Prevention of Floods) Bill passed into law that the parish ceased to be periodically swamped by high tides. These late survivals enable us to form some slight idea of what must once have been the character of Fulham, when road making and land drainage were in their infancy, and when therefore the village must have lain a prey to the waters of the Thames whenever they rose above the low level of the soil.

One alternative to the "foul-town" derivation of "Fulham" is just possible. This involves the supposition that the village was founded by, or named after, a Saxon chieftain called Fulla. That Fulla was a real name seems to be indicated by the occurrence of Fullinga-dich in Kemble, where Fullinga is the genitive plural of Fulling, *i.e.* a descendant of Fulla. The form Fullanham (with two l's) favours this theory, and, if we had even traditional evidence connecting a Fulla with the parish, we might be justified in accepting this derivation. In that case "Fullan" would be the genitive of Fulla and Fullanham would simply mean "Fulla's home." The "l" is, however, by no means always doubled in the early spellings of the name. Though a word like *hām* frequently follows a personal name (while *fūl* generally goes with a natural feature, such as brook, bourne, etc.), it does not invariably do so. For instance, we have Newnham, i.e. *nēwan-hām* or "new home," where *nēwan* is an adjective in the dative case, precisely similar to *fūlan* in *fūlan-hām* or "foul-home."

Fulham would indeed be singular if it did not possess a tradition to account for its name. One does not hear much of it now, but down to within living memory the story was an article of faith with many of the simple village folk. Bowack, in his " Antiquities of Middlesex," was, we believe, the first to enshrine it in print.

Once upon a time, runs this legend, two weird sisters of gigantic stature, who lived on opposite sides of the river Thames, undertook to build the towers of two churches which stood near their respective dwellings, but, having only one hammer between them, and seeing that there was no bridge over the river, they were obliged to throw it across from one to the other as they wanted it. When the sister on this side required it, she would stand on the river's bank and shout across the water, "Sister, *full-home*," and her sister, with a dexterous cast, would deliver the hammer "full-home," as requested; and when she wanted it back again, she would shout out "Put nigh!" Now, as the hammer was required for every stone that was laid, it may easily be imagined that the amount of shouting that took place was considerable. At length, from the constantly reiterated cries of "Fulhome" and "Putnigh," the places were called by those names, and the church towers are still standing to prove the truth of the story! But, slow as the progress of the building must have been, it was destined to still further interruption, for, on one occasion, the Putney sister made an awkward throw and, in Bowack's quaint phraseology, the "hammer happened unfortunately upon its clawes and broke them." And now the pious work must have unavoidably stood still altogether, if, at this juncture, a gigantic blacksmith, who lived about two miles up the river, had not stepped in and, in the kindest manner, volunteered his services. His offer was accepted, and, in memory of his timely services, the place has ever since retained the name of Hammersmith!

Fulham, circa 1790. From a scarce engraving

It may be interesting to note that the only other place in the United Kingdom which bears the name of Fulham is a farm situated in the parish of Womersley, near Pontefract, owned by the Hawke family. Fulham House, as it is called, is about a mile from Womersley Station on the main road (called Fulham Lane), which crosses the line at a level crossing. The farm is in the extremity of Womersley parish. There are also ings or meadows near the house, called Fulham Ings. The following entry in an Elizabethan "Act Book," for the Deanery of Pontefract, now in the York Probate Registry, shows that the place must once have been of some importance:

1572-3 Jan. 18. There issued probate of the will of George Thompson nup' de ffulham.

No reliable information as to the origin of the name of this farm can be gathered.

CHAPTER II: THE MANOR OF FULHAM

The parishes of Fulham and Hammersmith, from time immemorial, formed a manor, the lords of which (with the exception of a brief period during the Interregnum) were the Bishops of London. Lysons, writing of the Manor, observes:

> "It is said to have been given to Bishop Erkenwald and his successors about the year 691, by Tyrhtilus, a bishop, with the consent of Sigehard, king of the east Saxons, and Coenred, king of the Mercians."

The authority for this statement is apparently the following passage in Wharton:

> Translationem etiam S. Erkenwaldi isto anno factam Adamus Murimouth memorat, qui tamen aliam celebriorem 1148, Nov. 14 minime prœtermisit. Huic latifundia in loco, qui dicitur Fulanham, sc. terram 50 manentium, cum consensu Sigehardi Regis East-Saxonum et Coenredi Regis Merciorum, Tyrhtilus Episcopus dedisse dicitur in vetusto Ecclesiæ Paulinæ Rotulo inter Thomæ Jamesii Collectiones MSS.
> - "Historia de Episcopis et Decanis Londinensibus," 1695, p. 18.

Translation:

> Adam Murimouth relates also the translation of St. Earconuald in this year (1148), nevertheless he has not omitted to make mention of another translation, still more celebrated, which took place 14 Nov. 1148. Tyrhtilus the bishop is said to have given large estates to him at a place called Fulham, to wit, land cultivated by fifty tenants, with the consent of Sigehard, king of the East Saxons, and Coenred, king of the Mercians, recorded in an ancient roll of St. Paul's Church among the Manuscripts Collections of Thomas James.

Lysons identifies "Tyrhtilus Episcopus" with Tyrhthel, who was consecrated second Bishop of Hereford in 688 and who was therefore contemporary with Bishop Earconuald, who occupied the see of London, from 675 to 693. No other bishop of this name is known.

To trace the origin of Manors, we must go back to a very remote antiquity. The name is Norman French and came in with the Conquest, but the institution is Saxon and existed for centuries prior to that event.

A manor was originally a freehold estate held by a lord or other great personage, who was, by long custom, entitled to maintain a tenure between himself and his "tenants," whereby a kind of feudal relationship was kept up between them.

Another name for the Manor, or barony, as it was sometimes called, was the vill, or villa, a name which seems to have been a survival of the times of Roman occupation, when the greater portion of the productive parts of Britain was divided into districts called villæ, or farms, cultivated under certain well understood conditions.

Broadly speaking, the Manor was divided into two parts: first, those portions of the estate which the Lord reserved for the use of his family and servants, known as the *terræ dominicales* or "demesne" lands, and secondly, those portions which, in return for certain specified services, the Lord, the *dominus manerii*, distributed among his tenants, originally known as lands held in villenage, and afterwards as copyholds.

In addition to these there were, in the Manor of Fulham, certain free lands, sometimes termed manors, sub-manors or manor farms. Such, for instance, were Wendon or Dowbeler's, Lane's, Rosamond's, Sandford's, Cofferer's, Wormholt and Paddenswick. Unlike the copyholds, which descended to the youngest son, the freelands went to the eldest. On admission to these freelands, the inheritors were required to do fealty to the Lord.

As to how these freelands originated we have no certain evidence. The ancient monasteries
and other religious houses held by what was termed "tenure in frankalmoigne." The exalted nature of the services they rendered freed them from all secular obligations except the *trinoda necessitas*, i.e. the maintenance of bridges, the building of castles and the repelling of invasions. As the Bishops of London were certainly responsible for the repair of the bridges in the Manor of Fulham, it seems fair to assume that they originally held by the tenure we have mentioned. Subsequently, by the general ordinance

adopted at Salisbury in the 17th year of William I, those who held manors in this way, being unable to render military services to the king, were compelled to enfeoff certain portions so that the required number of men might be forthcoming for the king's army. It is therefore probable that it was in this way that the Bishop of London came to divide up his Manor of Fulham.

Down to the passing of the Act known as "Quia Emptores" (18 Ed. I.), a new manor could easily be created or an old one divided, but that statute prohibited the creation of further manors. Hence the freelands or sub-manors within the Manor of Fulham must have owed their origin to a date anterior to this statute.

The description of the Manor of Fulham in Domesday occupies twenty seven lines. In the original most of the words are abbreviated. The extended text reads:

1. *Manerium*. In Fvleham tenet episcopus Londoniæ xl hidas.
2. Terra est xl carucatæ. Ad dominium pertinent xiii hidæ et ibi sunt iiij carucæ.
3. Inter Francos et uillanos xxvi carucæ et x plus possent fieri. Ibi
4. v uillani quisque i hidam et xiii uillani quisque de i uirgata
5. et xxxiiij uillani quisque dimidia uirgata et xxii cotarii de dimidia hida
6. et viii cotarii de suis hortis. Inter francigenas et quosdam burgenses
7. Londoniæ xxiij hidæ de terra uillanorum. Sub eis manent inter
8. uillanos et bordarios xxx unus. Pratum xl carucis. Pastura ad pecuniam
9. uillæ. De dimidio gurgite x solidi. Silua mille porcis
10. et xvii denarios. In totis ualentis ualet xl libris quando receptum
11. similiter Tempore Regis Edwardi L libris. Hoc Manerium fuit et est de episcopatu.

12. In eadem uilla tenet Fulcheredus de episcopo Londoniæ v hidas.
13. Terra est iii carucatæ. In dominio i caruca et i caruca uillanorum et tercia
14. posset fieri. Ibi vi uillani de dimidia hida iiij cotarii de octo
15. acris et iii cotarii. Pratum i boui. Pastura ad pecuniam uillæ.
16. Silua ccc porcis. In totis ualentis ualet Lx solidus quando
17. recepta similiter Tempore Regis Edwardi c solidis. Hanc terram tenuerunt ii sochemanni
18. homines episcopi Londoniæ fuerunt non potuerunt dare uel uendere absque
19. licentia episcopi tempore Regis Edwardi.

20. *Manerium*. In eadem uilla tenent canonici Sancti Pauli de rege v hidas
21. pro uno Manerio. Terra est v carucatæ. Ad dominium pertinent iii hidæ
22. et ibi sunt ii carucæ uillani ii carucas et tercia potest fieri. Ibi viij
23. uillani quisque de i uirgata et vii uillani quisque de dimidia uirgata
24. et vii bordarii quisque de v acris xvi cotarii et ii serui. Pratum
25. v carucis. Pastura ad pecuniam uillæ. Silua CL porcis. Inter totum
26. ualet viii libris quando receptum similiter Tempore Regis Edwardi x libris. Hoc Manerium
27. tenuerunt idem canonici Sancti Pauli in dominio tempore Regis Edwardi et est de uictu eorum.[*]

[*] This is the transliteration given by the Ordnance Survey Office. (Vacher & Sons.)

Translation:

Manor: In Fvleham the Bishop of London holds forty hides. The land is forty carucates. Thirteen hides belong to the demesne, and there are four ploughs there. Among the freemen and the villeins are twenty-six ploughs and ten more could be made.
Five villeins (have) each one hide there and (there are) thirteen villeins each with one virgate; and thirty-four villeins each with half a virgate; and twenty-two cottars with half a hide (jointly), and eight cottars with their own gardens. Among foreigners and certain burgesses of London (there are) twenty-three hides of the land of the villeins. Under these reside thirty-one villeins and bordars.
(There is) meadow for (the teams of) forty ploughs. (There is) pasture for the cattle of the vill. From half the river (there is derived) ten shillings. (There is) wood for one thousand hogs and (worth) seventeen pence.
With all its profits, it is worth forty pounds; the same, when received; in the time of King Edward, fifty pounds.
This Manor was and is belonging to the Bishopric.

In the same vill Fulchered holds of the Bishop of London five hides. The land is three carucates. In the demesne there is one plough, and there is one plough for the villeins, and a third could be made.
There are six villeins (with) half a hide and four cottars (with) eight acres, and three (other) cottars.
(There is) meadow for one ox. (There is) pasture for the cattle of the vill. (There is) wood for three hundred hogs.
With all its profits it is worth sixty shillings; the same, when received; in the time of King Edward, one hundred shillings.
Two socmen held this land: they were vassals of the Bishop of London. In the time of King Edward they could neither give nor sell it without leave of the Bishop.

Manor. In the same vill the Canons of St. Paul's hold of the King five hides as one manor.
The land is five carucates. Three hides belong to the demesne, and there are two ploughs there.
The villeins (have) two ploughs and a third can be made.
There are eight villeins each with one virgate; and seven villeins each with half a virgate, and seven bordars (each with) five acres; and sixteen cottars and two serfs.
(There is) meadow for (the teams of) five ploughs. (There is) pasture for the cattle of the vill. (There is) wood for one hundred and fifty hogs.
In the whole it is worth eight pounds; the same, when received; in the

time of King Edward, ten pounds.
The same Canons of St. Paul's held this manor in demesne in the time of King Edward, and it is for their support.

In order to gain a clear idea of the actual extent of these holdings, we must understand the meaning of the terms "hide," "carucate" and "virgate." The hide had no fixed limit, varying, in different localities, from 60 to 120 acres. The present total extent of Fulham and Hammersmith is rather over 4,100 acres, and there is no reason to suppose that the boundaries of the Manor of Fulham at the time of the Domesday Survey materially differed from those of the present parishes taken together. We are told that in Fulham the Bishop held 40 hides, that Fulchered held five hides of the Bishop and that the Canons of St. Paul's held five hides of the King. It is not altogether clear whether both the small holdings of five hides each are to be understood as additional to the Bishops manor of 40 hides. If so, the entire Manor would consist of 50 hides, and, assuming it to have been practically identical in area with Fulham and Hammersmith as they now exist, the Domesday hide for these parishes, would appear to have consisted of rather under 84 acres, instead of 100 acres, as is popularly supposed.

The carucate, again, was an indeterminate quantity. It was simply so much arable land as a plough (*caruca*), drawn by eight oxen, could annually till. In the Domesday Survey, it usually follows the measure of the hide, though at times its size varied according to the nature of the soil and the practice of husbandry in different parts.

The virgate, which is generally reckoned as the fourth of the hide, was the usual holding of the villein. Land, as a rule, was let by the Lord to his tenants in half acre strips, the villein's collection of these being designated his virgate or yardland. In Fulham, assuming that the yardland was the fourth of a hide, its size must have been about 21 acres.

The inhabitants or "tenants in villenage" of each manor were ranged in clearly-defined categories, the chief of which were the *villani*, the *bordarii*, the *cottarii* and the *servi*.

About the time of the Domesday Survey, the *villani* or villeins were by far the most important class of the tenants in villenage, comprising no less than 38 per cent. of the whole population.

Originally the statue of the villeins was very low. Under the thanes - the ruling military class in Saxon times - the villein was the servile cultivator of the soil to which he was attached. The Norman Conquest did not improve his condition. His new masters, the barons, took possession of the manors, while the villein himself remained exactly what he had been before. In respect to all except his lord, the villein was a freeman, but, in respect to his lord, he had no rights, except that he might not be killed or maimed or the women of his home ravished.

According to Sir Edward Coke, the *villani* or villeins obtained their name from the *villæ* or manors on which they worked. In Fulham, on the Bishop's manor, at the time of the Domesday Survey, there were five villeins who enjoyed the unusually substantial allowance of one hide, or as we compute, 84 acres, each, while 13 held the usual virgate or 21 acres each, and 34 only half a virgate or 10½ acres each. The holdings of some other villeins, who held under "foreigners and certain burgesses of London," are not particularized. On Fulchered's estate there were six villeins who held in common half a hide or 42 acres, while on that of the Canons of St. Paul's there were eight who held one virgate (21 acres) each and seven who held half a virgate (10½ acres) each. The Lord of the Manor furnished each of his villeins with a plank house, two plough oxen, a cow and six sheep. With this equipment he had to maintain himself and his family. He was compelled, when required, to work for the Lord, on his demesne, the rest of his time being devoted to his own holding. The lesser villeins, of whom there were 34 on the Bishop's lands at Fulham, were generally called half villeins from the fact of their owning only half of a virgate or yardland. These half villeins had only one plough ox apiece.

Under the Normans the system of villenage continued with but little alteration. In later times, however, the position of the villein materially improved. When the country grew into a settled condition and the lands held in villenage descended from father to son, in uninterrupted succession, the occupiers became entitled by prescription or custom to their holdings, so long as they performed the services required of them under their tenure, and according to the custom of the Manor. These customs were preserved and evidenced in the rolls of the Courts Baron in which they were entered. Tenants holding such lands, having nothing to show as title to their estates but the entries in these rolls, or copies of them, authenticated by the stewards or sub-stewards, came, in time, to be called tenants by copy of court roll, or copyholders. With the growth of copyhold tenure, villenage gradually died out.

Fulham, from the "White Lion," Putney. From a print at the Hammersmith Public library, inscribed "T. Dillon del. 1783."

Below the *villani* or villeins, came the *bordarii* or bordars, and the *cottarii*, cottars or cottiers. They belonged to a class which may, perhaps, be most conveniently designated cottagers. It is impossible to say what was the precise distinction between the bordars and the cottars, but, as they are separately mentioned in the Domesday Survey, it is evident that there must have been a difference. The holdings of both were similar. In Fulham, on the Bishop's lands, there were 22 Cottars who held half a hide jointly, equivalent to, say, 4 acres apiece, while eight possessed their own "gardens." There were also some bordars. On Fulchered's estate there were four cottars who, together, held 8 acres and three other cottars, the size of whose holdings is not mentioned. On the lands of the Canons of St. Paul's there were seven bordars who held 5 acres each, and 16 cottars of whose holdings no particulars are given. Together, the bordars and the cottars comprised about 32 per cent. of the whole population.

The servi, serfs or slaves, were the lowest order. Strictly

speaking, they can hardly be described as tenants in villenage at all. Seebohm remarks, "They seem to have held no land, and often to have been rather household thralls of the lord of the Manor than tenants in any ordinary sense of the Word." They were never a numerous body, and, at the time of the Domesday Survey, numbered only about nine per cent. of the population. In Fulham the only slaves of whom we hear were two on the small manor of the Canons of St. Paul's.

Besides the above classes we find, in connection with the Bishop's holding, reference made to freemen (*franci*), to foreigners (*francigenæ*) and to certain burgesses of London (*burgenses Londoniæ*) the precise numbers of whom are not stated. There can be little doubt that the "freemen" mentioned in line three of the above extract from the Domesday Survey were identical with the "certain burgesses of London" mentioned in line six. The expression "*inter francos et villanos*" is of very rare occurrence in Domesday. The "franks" were doubtless the holders of the freelands or sub-manors to which we have already referred. *Francigena*, according to Kelham, was a name applied to any person who could not prove himself to be an Englishman. It is, of course, impossible to say with certainty who were these "foreigners and certain burgesses of London," who placed themselves under the protection of the Bishop of London. It is probable that some of them, at least, were Jewish traders, whose descendants, a couple of centuries later, became quite numerous in the parish.

The readers of Domesday will be struck by the numerous references to plough teams. *Caruca* and *carucata* are terms of constant employment. The *caruca* was the plough and the team; the *carucata*, the team's tillage. The Domesday Book was designed as the nation's geld or tax book, and, as land was then practically the only taxable commodity, it is obvious why the compilers set out in such precise terms the actual and the possible extent of the tillage of each manor. No measurements of the land were taken, nor was such information essential for the purposes which the King had in view, since it was the amount of labour which was got, or which could be got, out of each manor, the "unit of enquiry," which formed the basis of assessment.

Tabulating the information in Domesday, we arrive at the following state of the tillage. On the Bishop's manor:

40 plough teams, *viz.*,

Land belonging to the demesne, 13 hides	4 ploughs
Land in the occupation of freemen and villeins	26 ,,
Land not yet turned to account	10 ,,
	40 ,,

On Fulchered's estate:

3 plough teams, *viz.*,

Land belonging to the demesne	1 plough
Land in the occupation of villeins	1 ,,
Land not yet turned to account	1 ,,
	3 ,,

On the manor of the Canons of St. Paul's:

5 plough teams, *viz.*,

Land belonging to the demesne	2 ploughs
Land in the occupation of villeins	2 ,,
Land not yet turned to account	1 ,,
	5 ,,

In the whole Manor of Fulham there were thus thirty-six plough teams in actual existence, while the land was, from a taxation standpoint, capable of further development to the extent of forty-eight plough teams.

In Domesday Book there are four principal descriptions of land: *terra, silva, pastura* and *pratum. Terra* was arable land, as distinguished from wood, meadow and common pasture. *Silva* is the usual term for wood. Everywhere in the Survey woodland is carefully entered, "not that the timber was at that time of great value," says Nichols in "Dissertation on Domesday Book,"

> "but principally on account of the acorns and beech-mast, which, when the country was in a very imperfect state of cultivation, had a degree of importance of which we can form a very inadequate idea at this time."

In the whole of Middlesex pannage is returned for 16,535 hogs. Here in Fulham we find that there was sufficient, on the Bishop's lands, for 1,000 hogs, on Fulchered's lands for 300 hogs, and on the Canons' land for 150 hogs, a total of 1,450 hogs, or about an eleventh of the whole county. Fulham was therefore comparatively rich in what was then regarded as by far the most valuable form of live stock. In the primitive times of which we are speaking, great difficulty was experienced in carrying cattle through the winter. Hence it was the custom to kill, in the autumn, whatever beef and mutton were required. The acorns and beech-mast, the "pannage" of Domesday, sufficed for the hogs, which constituted the staple food of the villeins and the poorer classes of the Manor.

Fulham. From a print at the Hammersmith Public Library, inscribed "T. Owen del. 1809."

The early Avisage Rolls of the Manor of Fulham furnish minute particulars of payments made by the tenants for the privilege of pannage, that is, of placing their pigs in the Lord's woods. In the Conqueror's time the Bishop's woods were, we are told, worth 17d. Three centuries later (in 1384), the Lord's woods produced for pannage no less than £3. 2s. 4½d. a year.

Many interesting facts are to be gathered from the Domesday record. On the Bishop's Manor proper, 113 persons are enumerated. Reckoning an average of five persons to a family, this would represent a population of 565. To this must be added the Bishop, his household, and the unenumerated foreigners and burgesses, perhaps another hundred. We shall probably not be far wrong if we set down the aggregate at about 700.

The reference to half the river being worth ten shillings per annum has been variously explained. The phrase used in Domesday is *de dimidio gurgite*. Baldwin translates it as "for half the stream," while, in the literal extension and English translation, published by Vacher & Sons (1862), we have "from half the weir." Ducange explains *gurges* as meaning a fish pool or weir. According to Bracton *gurges* was an artificial formation in the nature of a dam. As we shall presently show, the Lord of the Manor of Fulham was the owner of half the ferry between Fulham and Putney and of the fishery as far as his Manor bordered the Thames. On the whole it seems most probable that ten shillings per annum was roughly set down by the compilers of Domesday as the value of the river to the Bishop for both the moiety of the ferry and the right of the fishery which he enjoyed.

The value of the Bishop's Manor proper is set down at £40, but in the time of Edward the Confessor it had been £50. The decrease was probably due to the circumstance that, at the time of the Survey, only 30 out of a possible 40 ploughlands were worked. If £40 represent the value of the working of 30 ploughs, then £50 would represent the value of, say, 38 ploughs, so that the Bishop's Manor in King Edward's time must have been in a considerably better state of tillage.

We now come to the two small holdings of Fulchered and the Canons. The former is not, in the Domesday entry, termed a manor. Of Fulchered nothing whatever is known. Judging from his name, he was probably a Norman. He was evidently a new comer, for, in the reign of King Edward, the estate was held of the Bishop by two socmen who were the Lord's vassals, incapable of giving or selling it without his leave. Sochemanni or Socmanni were privileged villeins, who, though their tenures were absolutely copyhold, enjoyed an interest equal to a freehold.

On Fulchered's holding seventeen persons are enumerated. Averaging the families at five each, we have a population of 85. Including Fulchered's own household, we may perhaps estimate the total number of inhabitants here at 100.

Like the Bishop's Manor proper, Fulchered's holding had decreased in value since the time of King Edward. It had been worth £5 when probably the whole three ploughs, of which it was capable, were worked. If £5 represented the value of three ploughs, then the two which were in existence at the time of the Survey would be worth £3 6s. 8d., or, in round figures £3,
which is precisely the value at which the compilers assessed this estate in the Conqueror's time.

The position of Fulchered's holding it is impossible to determine with certainty. It is by no means improbable that it was mainly identical with the Manor of Paddenswick at Hammersmith.

The small Manor of the Canons of St. Paul's was held directly from the King. In King Edward's time it had been held by the same Canons. The Conqueror had not ejected them, though, from the neighbouring holding a Norman Bishop of London had apparently turned out the two Saxon socmen, the vassals of his predecessors.

Forty persons are enumerated in connection with the Canons' manor. Reckoning, again, an average of five to a family, we get a total population of 200. Like the other holdings, its value at the date of the Domesday Book had decreased. In King Edward's time, when its five ploughs were probably worked, it was worth £10. At the time of the Survey only four ploughs existed, which, at the same valuation, would represent £8, precisely the figure given in Domesday as the value of the holding in the Conqueror's time.

Fulham, from Putney. From an undated pen and ink sketch at the Hammersmith Public Library

The lands of the Canons were also within the Hammersmith division. St. Paul's, the dedication of the parish Church, the Chancellors, Chancellors' road, etc., are names which still suggest the association of the Canons and the Chancellors of St. Paul's with the place. A part of the Brandenburgh estate consisted of "Chancellor's lands." The old manor house known as Chancellors, formed a portion of the endowment of the stall held by the Chancellor of St. Paul's Cathedral. Chancellors' road, which connects the Fulham Palace Road with Queen Street, Hammersmith, crosses the site.

The total value of the Manor of Fulham was, in the time of Edward the Confessor, £65; at the date of the Survey it had sunk to £51.

The purchasing power of precious metals, weight for weight, was, at the time of the Survey, about fifteen times that of our own era. Taking, therefore, money at its present purchasing power, the Manor, in the time of the Confessor, was worth £975, and, in that of the Conqueror, £765 a year.

The Aula, Halla or Haula, was the hall or chief mansion house, the usual appendage of the Manor. The chief apartment at Fulham Palace, the ancient Manor House of Fulham, is still called the Bishop's Hall. Manor Hall, just over the boundary of Fulham, in Hammersmith parish, perhaps in name recalls the days when the Canons of St. Paul's were the lords of the little Manor mentioned in Domesday.

The chief officers of the Manor, the *præfecti* or *præpositi manerium* or *villarum*, included the reeve and bailiff, or steward, whose business it was to collect the rents, to levy distresses, to prevent trespasses, to keep the peace, and, generally, to do all the offices of equity and right between the Lord and his tenants. The *bedelli* or beadles, were the under bailiffs of the Manor.

The affairs of the Manor were regulated and controlled by two Courts known as the Court Leet and the Court Baron. The Court Leet (Anglo-Saxon *leth*, a territorial division) or View of Frankpledge, was a court of record, usually held, in Fulham, once a year, generally in April or May. It was usually presided over by the steward. The Court Baron was always held with the Leet, and also again about Michaelmas. It was composed of the freeholders of the Manor, presided over by the Lord or his steward. The presentments proper to each jurisdiction appear, from the existing Rolls, to have been much confused. Strictly speaking the Leet concerned itself with matters pertaining to the interest of the Crown and commonwealth, while the Baron confined its attention to the interests of the Lord and his tenants, but, judging from the Fulham Rolls, the jurors of the Leet often presented what should have been left to the homagers of the Baron and vice versa. The Court Baron was mainly concerned in surrenders by customary tenants, admissions and re-admissions, the infliction of fines, the redressing of misdemeanours and nuisances arising within the Manor, and the settlement of disputes as to property. Surrenders out of Court were presented at the ensuing Court. In Fulham the Lord seems to have enjoyed estrays and the goods of felons, but to have had no right in *felo de se* or deodands. Certain lands in the Manor were heriotable and these appear to have been freehold. The custom of Borough English, as in most Thames side manors, prevailed, i.e. upon a copyholder dying intestate, his customary land fell to the youngest son. In cases where there was only one son, he inherited. In default of male issue, the youngest daughter, or only daughter, took, and, where there was no issue, either male or female, the land fell to the youngest brother, or, in default, to the youngest uncle. The freeland, however, descended to the eldest son or brother, as at common law.

In pre-Reformation times the Courts were often held on Sundays. If the weather permitted, they were sometimes held in the open. In inclement weather they were held in the church or church porch. In later times they were usually held at the "King's Arms." Nowadays, the copyholders of the Manor transact what little business there is to be done at a meeting of the Court Leet and Court Baron held once a year at the "Windsor Castle," Hammersmith.

The earliest existing Rolls of the Manor of Fulham are of the time of Richard II. These are written on very narrow membranes, the details are meagre and the writing cramped and faded. Some of the Rolls of Edward IV are, however, beautifully written, and are as fresh as they were the day they were engrossed. The older Rolls are usually of parchment, though some, *tempo* Henry VIII, are on paper.

Since about 1680 the minutes of Court are entered in books. Down to 1725 the Rolls are in much abbreviated Law Latin, with here and there a Norman-French word.

In the pre-Reformation Rolls, the expression "Lordship of Fulham" bore a far wider signification than that of "Manor of Fulham," since the former included four distinct manors, viz.:

Fulham and Hammersmith
Zilling and Brayntford (Ealing and Brentford)

Acton
ffynchesle (Finchley)

While separate Courts Baron existed, held sometimes at Fulham and at others within the manorial jurisdiction concerned, the whole of the above four Manors were in one Court Leet or View of Frankpledge, which was always held at Fulham, as the head-quarters or *caput* of the Barony. Thus, for instance, Acton was in the Lordship of Fulham, implying that it was within the jurisdiction of that Leet.

Down to the time of Dr. Blomfield, the Bishop of London enjoyed the revenues of the following Manors: Fulham, Acton, Ealing, Ashwell, Drayton, Feering, Finchley, Greenford, Hanwell, Hornsey, Hadham, Kelvedon, Layndon, Stevenage, Stortford, Wickham, Rickmansworth and Paddington. At times, these are said to have amounted to over £16,000 a year.

The Lordship of the Manor of Fulham passed from the Bishop of London to the Ecclesiastical Commissioners on the 30th Dec. 1868, on the translation of Dr. Tait to the see of Canterbury.

CHAPTER III
BOUNDARIES OF THE PARISH AND OF THE MANOR OF FULHAM

Down to 1834, Fulham and Hammersmith formed a single parish, the two parts being respectively designated "Fulham-side" and "Hammersmith-side." In the year named an Act of Parliament was passed

> "For making the Hamlet of Hammersmith within the parish of Fulham, in the County of Middlesex, a distinct and separate parish, and for converting the perpetual Curacy of the Church of St. Paul, Hammersmith, into a Vicarage, and for the endowment thereof."

Since then the two divisions have existed as "distinct and separate" parishes, municipally governed, first by a Board of Highways, and then by the Fulham District Board of Works. By the Metropolis Management Amendment Act of 1885, this latter body was dissolved, 26th March 1886, the parishes of Fulham and Hammersmith being created corporate bodies under Schedule A of the Metropolis Local Management Act of 1855.

At the date of the Ordnance Survey (1873), the Parish of Fulham comprised:

Land: 1,692.692 acres
Water (ponds, etc.): 7.632 acres
Foreshore: 56.561 acres
Tidal water: 99.614 acres
Total: 1,856.499 acres

Now that the ponds at Parson's Green, Eelbrook, Gibbs Green, etc., are filled up, the "Land" may be more accurately set down at 1,700.324 acres.

Measured from north-east to south-west, the length of the parish is slightly over two miles two furlongs, while the width, along a line approximately in the direction of the Fulham Road, is about a mile and a half.

We will now take the boundaries of the parish, starting from its south-eastern corner.

The southern and western boundaries of Fulham lie through the centre of the channel of the River Thames at low water, the line extending from a point opposite the mouth of Chelsea Creek, to a corresponding one facing Haig's Distillery, about 100 yards south of Hammersmith Bridge.

The northern boundary, dividing Fulham from Hammersmith, first follows the line of the ancient watercourse called "le Perre," "Parre," or Parr Ditch, known in more recent times as the Black Bull Ditch, from an inn called the "Black Bull" which stood just to the west of it at the point where it crossed the Hammersmith Road. Starting from the Distillery, the course of the old ditch was easterly, running south of Chancellors' Road and north of Distillery Lane. Crossing what is now the Fulham Palace Road, it traversed the site of Yeldham Road, Wending its way in a north-easterly direction to the District Railway, the course of which it followed for a short distance. It then crossed the site of Margravine Gardens, to the northern end of Hammersmith Cemetery, and, recrossing the Gardens, it turned north at the junction of Great Church Lane with Deadman's Lane, and, running west of Gliddon Road, emerged in the Hammersmith Road opposite Brook Green. Bowack, in his "Antiquities of Middlesex " (p. 35), gives the following account of its origin:

> "When the inhabitants of Fulham and the inhabitants of Hammersmith did mutually agree to divide the parish, it was also agreed that a ditch should be dug as a boundary between them, it being the custom in those days to divide districts in this manner; whereupon a ditch was dug for the above purpose."

This ditch, which was the last to remain open in Fulham, was, in 1876, converted into a covered-in sewer.

The northern boundary of Fulham runs due east along the centre of the Hammersmith Road until it reaches the west end of Russell Road Bridge, opposite Portland Place.

On its eastern side Fulham was anciently bounded by a Creek or Ditch which rose in the vicinity of what is now Kensal Green

Cemetery and flowed southwards to the Thames. The Creek reached the northern boundary of Fulham at Counter's Bridge where it crossed the Hammersmith Road. From this point the Creek ran almost due south, dividing Fulham, first from Kensington, and then from Chelsea, finally entering the Thames just below Lacey's Point. The Creek itself bore no distinctive name common to its whole course. The portion between Fulham and Kensington was sometimes called Counter's Creek or Billingwell Ditch, and that between Fulham and Chelsea, the New Cut River, Chelsea Creek, or Bull Creek, the last designation being assigned to it from Bull Alley, which ran parallel with it.

In 1827, at an expense of about £40,000, the old Creek (or rather that portion of it which formed the eastern boundary of Fulham), was widened and formed into the Kensington Canal.

On 12th August 1828, the Canal was opened by Lord Kensington, who, accompanied by a number of friends, embarked in a barge at Battersea Bridge and proceeded up the Canal followed by several craft, laden with timber, coal, sand, etc., the first fruits of a speculation which was to end in failure. The Canal was 100 feet broad, and was capable of affording passage for vessels of 100 tons burden. The basin, which was at its northern end, just south of Counter's Bridge, was 400 feet long by 200 feet broad. The earnings of the Canal, from wharves, tonnage, etc., were estimated at £2,500 a year, but the actual receipts fell far short of this figure. It was about two miles in length.

Fulham, circa 1805. From a scarce engraving

In 1845 the West London Railway Company acquired the Canal for their "Extension." Its bed was accordingly drained and turned into a railway line. The ancient watercourse (except for a little piece at its mouth) was thus effaced as a parish boundary.

The time-honoured custom of "beating the bounds" goes back to a remote antiquity. Before the days of the Reformation the custom of perambulating the parish was certainly observed with great ceremony, and served the two-fold object of supplicating the Divine Blessing on the fruits of the earth and of preserving among the people a correct knowledge of the bounds of parochial and individual property.

With the advent of the Reformation, the ecclesiastical functions were reformed, and henceforward it became practically a civil custom, the main object of which was to keep in remembrance the exact limitations of the parish.

In Fulham the perambulation of the parish was usually made on Holy Thursday. The Vicar, with the parochial officers, a few of the more substantial inhabitants, followed by the boys from the parish school, would march in procession round the parish, the bounds of which the boys would strike with willow wands. At the conclusion of the proceedings, which sometimes occupied two days, a dinner was held, generally at the "King's Arms." The boys, who were not, of course, admitted to this, were regaled with bread, cheese and beer and presented with a new shilling each. In recent times it has been the custom for the boys simply to beat the land marks with their wands, but in less cultured days it was the practice to "bump" them, and even to whip them sharply, perhaps a primitive device for fixing in the memories of the lads - when they should become "substantial" inhabitants - the precise confines of the parish!

In the Court Rolls of the Manor are a few references to perambulations, or, rather, to boundary ways. In 1425, Nicholas Dixon, clerk, then the tenant of Sandford Manor, was presented for allowing his trees - doubtless along the creek - to overhang the processional way in the day of rogation (*via p'cessionale dietz regaconn*), while John Dansan was similarly presented for obstructing the processional way (*via p'cessionale*) "to the corner of Pesecroft." In 1450, at a View of Frankpledge, Sir Richard Cost, clerk, another tenant of Sandford Manor, was presented for his boughs hanging over the processional way at Mead Lane, a way down by the side of the creek leading to the Town Meads.

The years 1425 and 1450 were, no doubt, those in which the bounds had been beaten in Fulham, and consequently, the obstructions, etc., noted.
At a View in 1573, it was ordered:

> "That the boundaries between Ham'smyth and ffulham be sufficiently made before next Pentecost or 6s. 8d. forfeited."

Though the Parish Books commence in 1625, it is not till 1637 that we have any reference to the beating of the bounds in Fulham. In that year the Churchwardens

Payd for halfe ye perambulation dynner	16s. 0d.
payd for bread and beere for the boyes at Paines	3s. 0d.
payd for halfe this dinner at passing ye accounts	7s. 0d.

the other "halfe" being, of course, paid by the Churchwardens on Hammersmith side.

The cost of the dinner increased as years went on. Here are a few instances:

1638. Paid for perambulacon dinner	£1. 3. 6
1639. Pd. for p'ambulation dinner being the one halfe and for boyes	£1. 3. 6
1640. Pd. for p'ambulacon dinner	£2. 16. 10
1641. Pd. for p'ambulacon dinner	£2. 13. 11
1642. Pd. for p'ambulacon dinner	£1. 17. 0
pd. att that dinner for bread and beere for the Boyes	4. 0
1648. Expences att goeing the bounds of the Parishe	£1. 5. 3
1650. For Expences in goeing the Boundes of the Parish the last yeare	£2. 0. 9
1669. Paid for Perambulacon Dinner on holy Thursday last	£4. 1. 0

During the next few years the dinners became much more costly. At length, at a meeting of the Vestry, held on 6 May 1672,

> "Itt is Ordered for the future that there bee not expended at Perambulacon dinner more then tenn pounds on both sides the Psh."

The incidental expenses, connected with the beating of the bounds, are sometimes curious. In the accounts for 1711-12, the details are thus given at length:

" Spent on the boys goeing the Bowns upon the Rods	2.	3.	0
" For a Lam on the parembleation		16.	0
" Pd. for 8 grosse of Points and 550 wands	2.	17.	0
" Pd. for Bread, Chees and Bear for the boys	4.	3.	9
" Expended on the Road and at the Robing Hood	1.	10.	0
" Pd. the Wattermen and six men to go with the boyes		10.	0
" Paid for the Dinner	4.	12.	0
" Paid for Beere, Tobacco and Brandy		12.	0

The following is the return for 1740:

" Expenses in going the Perambulation	£4.	15.	6
" Paid the same day for a Dinner	£6.	3.	0
" ffor Points used the same day.	£1.	8.	0
" Paid Mr. Webb for bread &c. for the Boys		10.	0
" Paid for Wands on the aforesaid Acct		14.	0
" Paid six men for attendance		9.	0

In 1761 the details are as follows:

" Paid for Ribands Wans and men attending at going to the bounds of the parish . .	4.	7.	6
" Spent at the Swan on the same account	7.	6.	0
do. at the George	2.	10.	0
do. at the Robing Hood and for rolls and cheese	4.	0.	0

Other perambulations took place in 1752 and 1761.

From the above extracts it will be observed that the beating of the bounds was once an annual custom. Subsequently a septennial perambulation was adopted, for the gradual introduction of maps and the more settled character of the parish made an annual inspection of its boundaries unnecessary. In 1787 the "Sundry expenses at perambulating the bounds of the parish" amounted to no less than £38. 9s. 9d. On Holy Thursday in 1800 the bounds of Fulham were beaten. The "sundry expences" on this occasion totalled up to the enormous sum of £74 10s. viz.:

Mr. Bothomley for ribbons	20.	14.	6
Expences at Thom's at Shepherd's Bush	22.	8.	2
Paid Men and Boys for carrying the colours, etc.	1.	6.	6
Expences at the Swan, Walham Green, for breakfast, etc.	5.	15.	4
Expences at the King's Arms	24.	5.	6
	74.	10.	0

In 1811 the perambulation cost £56. 19s. 5½d., and in 1818, £58 13s. 7½d. The first perambulation after the separation of Fulham from Hammersmith took place on Ascension day, 1834. In recent times the custom of perambulating the parish has somewhat fallen into desuetude.

There are, in all, about 84 stones and other boundary marks fixed round the parish. The following detailed description of the boundaries of the ancient Manor of Fulham is given in the minutes of a Court General held 1st May 1650:

> "Item they present That ye Mannor of ffulham from ye New Cutt River wch runneth into ye River of Thames in Chelsey lotts and lyeth South East and is bounded by the River of Thames unto Chiswicke Townesend and returneth att ye end of ye Twigg Eight and takith in part of ye Twiggs Eight and soe cometh up ye land to ye West through a certeine yard belonginge to ye first house within ye parish of Chiswicke to ye great Road yt leadeth from London to Brenintford And then leadeth or extendeth into ye dwelling house of Samuell Hall and so to Stamford Brooke unto ye Comon Shore there and there taketh in pte of ye Common wthout ye Cottage lately built by Robt Grindee and returneth of from ye Common betweene ye lands in ye occupacon of John Simson and John Webb, all wch said lands held by ye said John Simson lyinge within ye Mannor of ffulham, from thence it cometh downe wth a certeine ditch before ye said severall mens lands unto ye Comon Shore wch lyeth betweene ye two meades ye one called Oatleys and thother called ye towne meade leadinge and belonginge to Acton all wch said meade called Oatleys are in ye said Mannor of ffulham from thence it extendeth downe Northward to a ditch lyinge betweene ye said Oatleys and a cmon ffeild knowne by ye name of South feild in ye pish of Acton from thence it extendeth alonge by ye afforesaid ditch betweene a pcell of land called ye Old ffields in ye occupacon of Wittia Vincent in ye pish of Acton and lyeth on ye north sides of Oatleys from thence it extendeth downe by a pikehill of Wm. Chalkhills ye Elder and from thence returneth to Acton Road betweene ye lands of Wittm Vincent in Acton aforesaid and ye lands of Wittm Chalkill afoesd which said lands of ye said Wittm Chalkill are wthin ye Mannor of ffulham and soe leadeth to Acton Roade to a bridge called Mile End bridge from thence by a ditch leadinge to East Acton lyeinge between ye lands in ye occupacon of Mr. Bernard on ye West and ye lands of Wm Chalkill and George Needler on ye East from thence it leadeth to old Oake lande lying in Acton pish and is divided by a ditch on ye East side of ye land to a Common called Old Oake in ye Mannor of Acton all ye land wthin ye Ditch beinge wthin ye Mannor of ffulham and soe it is sepated by a ditch leadinge betweene ye Comon of Old Oake on ye East and North and ye lane yt leadeth out of ye Old Oake to Holsdon Greene and is there devided by a ditch lyinge betweene ye same and ye

lands late of Ralphe Hartwell or his Assignes from thence it returneth eastward by a Greene lane leading towards ye roade yt goethe from Holsdon Greene to London and by ye land to a Cottage in ye occupacon of John Ledgingham ye grounds of ye South side of ye land beinge in ye Mannor of ffulham from thence it leadeth upon a straiteway and is devided by a comon Sewer betweene ye pish of ffulham East and cometh to a certeine bridge called Stanford bridge where ye pish of Kensington doth end and from Stamford bridge to ye River of Thames It is divided by ye new Cutt River lyinge betweene ye Mannor of ffulham on ye south west and pish of Chelsey on ye South East."

CHAPTER IV: THE RIVER

From very early times the fishery at Fulham, "<u>from Hamersmith Land's End to the Laystall</u>," belonged to the Manor. It was the custom of the Lord to lease the royalty of "fishing and free-fishing " to sundry persons, generally for a term of twenty-one years, on the condition that each year they gratuitously supplied his Lordship with three salmon and four hundred smelt, and, further, that they supplied him, when in residence at Fulham, with such fish as his domestics might require, at the current market rates.

The earliest indenture with which we have met, relating to the fishery, is dated 3 June 15 Charles II (1663). It is between Gilbert Sheldon, Bishop of London, and Sir Nicholas Crispe, knight, the owner of an extensive estate at Fulham. This indenture grants to Sir Nicholas:

> "The Royalty of ffishing and ffrefishing which the said Reverend Father hath or of right ought to have within the River of Thames by reason of such Charters of Royallty and Libertyes as the King's Most Noble progenitors have granted to the predecessors of the said Reverend Father or otherwise, howsoever, extending from Hamersmith Lands End and vnto the Laystall at ye end of the Meade being pcell of the Demeasnes of the said Reverend Father wthin the Mannor of ffulham and that in as large and ample manner as the said Reverend Father himselfe may in anywise take vse or enjoy the same to have and to hold the said Royalty of ffishing and frefishing before demised to the said Sr Nicholas Crispe his Executors, Administriters, and Assigns from ye making of these psents vnto the end of the terme of 20 and one years from thence next ensuing and fully to be compleate and ended, yielding and paying and delivering therefore yearly during the said terme to the said Reverend Father his Successors or Assigns at his Lordships Mannor in ffulham Three faire ffresh Salmons sweete and good (that is to say) one fresh Salmon at and upon ye ffeast of Pentecost comonly called Whit Sunday, another Salmon at and upon the Sunday next after the feast of Pentecost comonly called Trinity Sunday and another Salmon at and upon the feast day of ye Nativity of St. John Baptist then next following yearely dureing the said terme and ffower hundred Smelts to be delivered every yeare within the months of

ffebruary and March at London House. And if it happen the said yearely rent of 3 Salmon and 400 Smelts or any of them to be behinde and vnpayd by the space of 14 dayes over and after any terme of payment or delivery aforesaid in which the same ought to be payd according to the Intent and meaning of these psents That then the said Sr Nicholas Crispe shall from thenceforth every yeare yearely dureing the said Terme of 21 yeares pay and deliver vnto the said Reverend ffather his Successors and Assignes Six ffresh Salmons at ye tymes before expressed and the said Sr Nicholas Crispe for him his Executors Administrators and Assignes and every of them doth covenant promise and grant to and with the said Reverend ffather and his Successors by these psents That he the said Sr Nicholas Crispe his Executors Administrators and Assignes shall from tyme to tyme and at all tymes dureing the said Terme (at such tymes as his Lordp. shall reside at ffulham) afforde and serve his Lordp's servants to his vse such Salmon or any other ffish taken within the said River at such prices and Rates as he shall sell ye like to the ffishmongers of London without ffraud or deceite And as the like ffish may be bought for in ffishstreete at ye same tyme and the said Reverend Father doth for him and his Successors covenant promise and grant to and with the said Sr Nicholas Crispe his Exeeutors Administrators and Assignes and every of them by these psents That it shall be lawfull to and for the said Sr Nicholas Crispe his Executors Administrators and Assignes to have and take in and upon the shoare by the said river of Thames from Hamersmith Lands end to ye Laystall at the Meades end aforesaid free Liberty to walke and drawe their Netts and also to hang and drye their Netts upon the same shoares in places convenient And that in as ample manner and forme as at any tyme any other pson or psons farmeing the same ffishing heretofore had and vsed the same Liberty from ye said Reverend ffather."

In 1696 the fishery was leased to Mr. Timothy Lannoy and Mr. George Treadway who had purchased Sir Nicholas Crispe's estate. On 24 June 1700 a new lease was granted to Henry Shephard, John Shephard, Lawrence Shephard, John Pinckney and Robert Crowe "all of Chiswick, fishermen." On 11 Dec. 1724 the fishery was leased to John Borrow, fishmonger, of St. Martin's in the Fields. This appears to have been the last lease of the fishery ever made.

In 1763 Bishop Osbaldeston, in consequence of complaints made to him respecting the destruction of game within the Manor by unauthorized persons, appointed a gamekeeper in the person of one Thomas Bramley, junior. The document confirming this appointment proceeds:

> "And likewise we do hereby give and grant unto the said Thomas Bramley full power and authority to fish with the nets or otherwise in that part of the river of Thames belonging to our said Manor of Fulham from time to time and till such time as the said liberty of fishing there shall be demised or granted by us on lease to some person or persons as it has formerly been accustomed."

As London became more and more a commercial centre and the river was turned to business uses, the value of the "liberty" doubtless dwindled away, so that no further leasing was attempted.

In the olden time, the principal fish caught at Fulham were sturgeon, salmon, smelt, flounders, roach, dace, barbel, eels, shad, lampreys and lampern. Pike, trout and other kinds of fish were occasionally met with. Faulkner says that sturgeon were claimed by the Lord Mayor, who usually sent them to the King, the fishermen being entitled to a guinea for each fish. Barbel and eels used to be very plentiful.

It was long the practice to fish here for dace, bleak (*leuciscus alburnus*) and other small fish for the sake of their silvery scales, once largely used in the manufacture of artificial pearls. In the *Englishman* for Sunday 6 Sept. 1818 is the following account of this cruel trade:

> "Illegal fishing, for the furtherance of a curious purpose, has lately been discovered on the Thames. Regular fishermen, and large bodies of poachers, who 'swop' the Thames night and day, of all white fish for the sake of their scales merely. These are sold to Jews for manufacturing beads, in imitation of pearls; roach scales are sold at 21s. per quart; dace, 25s.; whilst for bleak 4s. 4d. a quart is the present market price in Duke's Place. The scales are torn off of them as fast as they are caught, and thus, often dreadfully mangled, they are tossed back into the water, to linger and die in torture."

Gorton, writing of Fulham in 1833, observes:

> "The fishery here is a source of some local profit; the principal fish taken are barbel, eels and lampreys, roach, dace, flounders and shad; the dace are chiefly valuable for their scales, which are used by the

Jews in the manufacture of false pearls."

As we have previously remarked, the Town of Fulham and the meadows adjacent to the river were in olden times subject to frequent inundations. The Parish Books abound with entries relating to payments made for clearing the water out of the Town. Thus, in 1716:

> "Paid Labourers a day to lett the water out of the Rodes: 3s. 0d.
> "Pd. Warren for Letting the Watter out of the Towne and cleaning the Churchway 5s. 0d."

In 1720:

> "Paid for letting out the water 6 days: 9s. 0d."

Such entries as these are almost endless, and show how frequent must have been the incursions of the river.

One of the highest tides ever known at Fulham occurred on 12 March 1774. The whole of the Town and the meadows facing Battersea Church, were, for some miles, entirely overflowed and considerable damage was done to the garden grounds and young plantations. Two West Country barges were, by the force of the current, carried out of the channel of the Thames and left in the fields. Some sheep in a field near the waterside were carried down by the stream and drowned. Boats were rowed in several gentlemen's gardens and the watermen landed their fares in the middle of the Town.

Another phenomenally high tide was that of 27 Feb. 1873. According to the *Standard*:

> "From Putney Bridge the water forced its way up High Street and Church Street, Fulham, to a considerable depth, and boats were rowed from the bridge to some way beyond Fulham Post Office, a distance of 150 yards."

On 20 March 1874 was a tide even higher than that of the preceding year. The grounds of Fulham Palace were inundated and much damage was done to some of the rooms and to the books in the Porteus Library. In the spring of 1875, five successive tides swept up the High Street, flooding all the houses as far as Holcroft's. Boats were rowed right up the street, bringing customers to the "Ship," the "King's Arms," the "Golden Lion," etc. A gentleman rowed his skiff over the Moat and looked into the windows of the Palace. Another occurred in 1877. In these periodic inundations, Fulham Church was a frequent sufferer. The inhabitants of the High Street used to board their doors to prevent the ingress of the water.

In 1875 the late District Board of Works carried out some important works in the neighbourhood of Fulham Bridge, raising the level of the approach road, the draw-dock, the landing-stage and plying-place. Since that date the inhabitants have been practically secured against the overflowing of the river.

A High Tide at Fulham in January 1877. From an illustration in the Pictorial World for 13 January 1877

Some remarkable frosts are recorded. A prolonged one occurred in the severe winter of 1740-41. A writer in the *London Evening Post* for Thursday 3 Jan. to Saturday 5 Jan. 1740, remarks:

"Several Painters have been induced from the odd Appearance which the Thames now makes, having on it many Islands, and forming Rocks and Mountains of Ice and Snow, to take sketches thereof, with Design to make a picture of so extraordinary a Winter Prospect."

Another great frost, which occurred in December 1788, is thus spoken of in the *Annual Register* for 1789:

"Hard Frost January 12, 1789.
The scene on the Thames is very entertaining. From Putney Bridge

upwards the river is completely frozen over and people walk to and from the different villages on the face of the deep. Opposite to Windsor Street (*i.e* Windsor Street, Putney) booths have been erected since Friday last and a fair is kept on the river. Multitudes of people are continually passing and repassing, puppet-shows, roundabouts and all the various amusements of Bartholomew Fair are exhibited. In short, Putney and Fulham, from the morning down to the dusk of returning evening is a scene of festivity and gaiety."

Bishop Porteus, who came to reside at Fulham in the winter of 1788, walked with Mrs. Porteus across the river to Putney.

The last great frosts occurred in February 1870 and January 1881.

From time to time a few curiosities have been found in the river at Fulham. Mr. A. Chasemore tells us that, in 1871, in sinking the cylinders for the new iron centre to the old Bridge, there were found a few old English tobacco pipes, some of the time of Queen Elizabeth, with stem and bowl almost the same thickness, an image of a bird roughly cast in lead, probably a Roman toy, and, further down, in the blue clay, the lower jaw of a wild boar. We gather from the *Archæological Journal* (vol. ii. p. 396, 1846) that there was then in the possession of a Mr. Hodgkinson of East Acton, a gold ring, engraved both on the interior and exterior with cabalistic characters, of about the middle of the fourteenth century. It was discovered in a creek of the Thames at Fulham. At a meeting of the British Archaeological Association on 11 Jan. 1860, Mr. Curle exhibited a Mauro-Spanish spur of iron which had been dredged up from the river at Fulham in October 1859. The broad flat shanks of this curious relic are described as straight and decorated with a zigzag band, while the ring-shaped ends were divided by a horizontal bar across their centres. At the back was a flat disc with a short neck, within which turned a rowel of seven points. It was considered to belong to the latter part of the sixteenth century.

With the exception of two small patches of brick earth in the neighbourhood of Fulham Road, there lies under the whole of Fulham a bed of sand and ballast varying in depth from ten to thirty feet. It is to this subsoil of gravel of the post pliocene or drift series that the general healthiness of the parish is largely due. Beneath the gravel lies the great bed of London clay, and, lower again, we come upon sandstone and greensand. Then, at a still greater depth, we reach the chalk strata. We cannot, perhaps, better illustrate the character of the tertiary beds which have been found in the parish than by appending the following four geological sections from borings which have been made in recent years for the purpose of sinking wells in different parts of Fulham. The four wells we have chosen, which are at points wide apart, are Mr. William Whiteley's well at his new Laundries and Cleaning Works, Mornington Park, West Kensington, the Fulham Union well, Fulham Palace Road, the Swan Brewery well, Fulham Road, and the well at Kops Brewery, Town Mead Road.

(I) MR. WM. WHITELEY'S WELL

	ft.	in.	ft.	in.
Dug Well				
Made Ground	5	0		
Gravel	8	0	13	0
Boring 11½ in.				
Blue Clay	8	0	21	0
Hard Blue Clay	87	0	108	0
Clay Stones	12	0	120	0
Hard Blue Clay	16	0	136	0
Light Sandy Clay	2	0	138	0
Blue Clay	14	0	152	0
Light Sandy Clay	36	0	188	8
Mottled Clay	25	0	213	0
Yellow Mottled Clay with pebbles	13	0	226	0
Dead Sandy Clay with pebbles	6	0	232	0

MR. WM. WHITELEY'S WELL (CONTINUED)

Mottled Sandy Clay	5	0	237	0
Hard Sandy Clay with pebbles	3	0	240	0
Very Hard Rock	1	0	241	0
Sandy Clay and pebbles	7	0	248	0
Dead Green Sand	7	0	255	0
Dead Green Sand and pebbles	5	0	260	0
Hard Green Sandy Clay, with pebbles	18	0	278	0
Chalk and Flints	19	0	297	0
Hard Chalk Rock	303	0	600	0

(2) FULHAM UNION WELL

	ft.	in.	ft.	in.
Dug Well				
Bottom of Brick shaft	10	6		
Boring				
Clean Washed Sand	7	10	18	4
Light Blue Clay	1	2	19	6
Light Blue Clay with pebbles	116	6	136	0
,, ,, very hard	16	0	152	0
,, ,, easier worked	28	0	180	0
,, ,, not so much stone	10	0	190	0
,, ,, lighter blue	4	0	194	0
Light Green Clay	2	0	196	0
,, ,, with red	22	0	218	0
Mottled Green Clay	4	0	222	0
,, ,, lighter	2	0	224	0
,, ,, darker	6	0	230	0
,, ,, lighter	5	0	235	0
Light Brown Clay	5	0	240	0
,, ,, with sand	29	0	269	0
Bed of Flints	1	0	270	0
Green Sandy Clay	1	0	271	0
Flints	2	6	273	6
Chalk, very flinty	4	3	277	9
,, water vein	4	9	282	6
Chalk	224	3	506	9

[The depths in the above boring are taken from basement floor line of the Fulham Union Workhouse, which is 8 ft. 3 in. below the general ground level.]

(3) SWAN BREWERY WELL

	ft.	in.	ft.	in.
Sand	6	0		
Blue Clay	119	0	125	0
Clay, various colours and with pebbles	100	0	225	0
Flints	1	0	226	0
Chalk	194	0	420	0

(4) KOPS BREWERY WELL

	ft.	in.	ft.	in.
Pit	5	0		
Ballast	14	6	19	9
Clay and Claystones	127	0	146	6
Shells and Mottled Clay	7	0	153	6
Mottled Clay	36	0	189	6
Clay and Ballast	7	0	196	6
Sandstone	2	0	198	6
Green Sand and Ballast	5	9	204	3
Ballast and Sand	2	3	206	6
Sandstone	8	6	215	0
Sand	27	0	242	0
Chalk and Flints	158	0	400	0

The natural level of Fulham is low. Many parts are below high-water mark, the average level being only a few feet above. In reference to its drainage, Fulham is therefore not favourably situated. The flow of the sewage, in consequence of the low level, is necessarily slow, and, on a fall of rain, there is always a tendency for the sewage from the higher districts around to cause a back flow into the parish sewers. In recent years, however, the London County Council and the local sanitary authorities have done much to remedy these defects in sanitation.

CHAPTER V: AGRICULTURE AND TRADE

Until comparatively recent years, Fulham has always been an agricultural district, devoted mainly to the cultivation of vegetables, fruit and flowers. Nearly the entire area of the parish was in the hands of market gardeners engaged in supplying the London market. Faulkner, in the second chapter of his history of Fulham, gives an excellent account of the state of agriculture in the parish, derived mainly, we believe, from information furnished to him by a well-known market gardener of his day, Mr. William Wilcox, of Parson's Green, a school-fellow of the historian.

Fulham. From an engraving by J. B. Chatelain, 1750.

Orchards were once very numerous in the parish, producing an abundance of strawberries, raspberries, currants, gooseberries, plums, pears and apples. Numbers of Shropshire girls would trudge to Fulham in the season to pick strawberries, and convey them into London. About midnight these girls, often numbering upwards of a hundred, would walk with the large baskets, weighing some 40 lbs., on their heads, filled with punnets of strawberries, and singing a tune that gave them a step to which to march.

In 1821 the market gardens and nurseries of Fulham numbered

nearly fifty, in 1853 they had decreased to twenty, while now only seven or eight survive.

The remarkable fecundity of the soil of Fulham was in a large measure doubtless due to the early Thames floods, which necessarily left rich deposits on the submerged lands. A favourite expression with the Rev. R. G. Baker was, "Oh! the richness of Fulham." From the husbandman's point of view this was perfectly true. For its rhubarb, its parsnips, its cabbages and its turnips, Fulham was, perhaps, without its rival among the western suburbs of London.

There is little to be said with regard to trade. Husbandry was the staple occupation of the people. In the oldest Church Registers, the occupation is sometimes appended to the name of a deceased person. By far the most frequent designations are those of " husbandman," "labourer," "gardener," and "waterman." Among others are: "cordwiner," "victualer," "coachman," "bricklayer," "surgeon," "weaver," "butcher," "tallow chandler," "malster," "brewer," "basket-maker," "farmer," "yeoman," "blacksmith," "serving man," "joyner," "carpinder," "wheelwright," "baker," "saylor," "button gilder," "a Turnys Clarke," "coller-maker," "plaistrer," "fruterer," perewigmaker," "ffishmonger," "barber surgeon," "plumer," "shoomaker," "working brewer," "whetster," "cloathworker," "working goldsmith," "wiardrawer," "schoolmaster," "barber," "hatter," "painter," "gold beatter," "turner," "glover," "a Pothecari," "brazier," "gouldsmith," "rnusisoner," and "distiller."

With most of the more important industries practised in the parish, we shall deal when we reach the parts more immediately concerned.

Under the manorial system the alehouses were well looked after. It was the annual custom, at the View of Frankpledge, to appoint two ale-conners or ale-tasters for Fulham, and two for Hammersmith. It was the duty of these officers to see that the beers sold were of good quality and the measures of the required capacities.

John Waymaker, at a View in 1415, was amerced 11d. for refusing to take the oath as ale-taster. In 1442 Peter Hopken and John Grene, the ale-tasters, were fined a penny each because they had badly executed their office. At the same Court, it was presented that Thomas Cherch, John Adam of Wenden-grene (Walham Green), Elizabeth Bertlet, Richard Naps and Richard Bedell, who were brewers of ale, had broken the assize. All innkeepers were obliged to place before their doors an ale-stake or ale-pole, whereby travellers might know the houses at which refreshments and lodging could be obtained. Agnes Jemys was, in 1436, fined 6d. because she

> "Has not placed a sign called an alestake outside her house although she has sufficient ale within her house to sell."

In 1478 John Aleyn was amerced 2d. because he would not expose his sign "called an ale-pole by which the King's lieges are unable to know where ale is to be sold." "Furthermore," we are told, "he will not suffer the said tasters to taste his ale or execute their office."

Roger Hawkyns, was, in 1526, required to make smooth "a pole called an ale-pole at his gate or forfeit 4d." The "White Horse" at Parson's Green, the "White Hart" at Walham Green, etc., retain their "ale-poles" to the present day.

At a Court General, held in 1551, the following regulation as to the sale of ale within the Lordship of Fulham was laid down:

> "All those who sell ale within this View to sell the same in one measure called a quart of ale for a halfpenny."

In 1658 it was ordered that:

> "Edward Dodd being chosen Ale Conner for ffulham, side hath not attended at the Cort Leet before the Steward of this Mannor to take his oath, therefore amerced xxs. [20 shillings]"

At the same time it was presented that:

> "Wm. Snell hath sold Beere in unlawfull measures called Black Jacks that is to say six Jacks at one penny a peece the same measure not conteyning a full quart, therefore he is amerced xl^s. [forty shillings]."

Thomas Harris was, in 1658, fined for selling beer without a license. The minutes of a Court Baron, held in 1658, record that

Edward Hall, a "Common Victualer," was fined five shillings because he abused the Homage and said they were "all knaues and fooles."

In the time of Elizabeth it was found needful to stringently enforce the laws respecting the licensing of taverns in Fulham. Thus, at a View in 1573, it was:

> "Ordered that Roland ffisher for Fulham Street and Joan Hill for Wendon Green shall be allowed to keep taverns (*cauponas*) because they have obtained licenses and sureties according to the Statute and that they shall not have more than two within this Lordship."

At the ensuing Court Baron the above order was confirmed with the addition "that there be no more taverns or drinking within this Lordship."

At a View in 1574 it was presented that:

> "Robert Lympenye of Fulham Street and Roger Bentley of Wandon Green keep taverns contrary to the order of last Court, wherefore they are amerced 13s. 4d. each."

The parish records contain numerous references to cases of drunkenness and to the orders issued to constables to keep watch on the doings of the frequenters of taverns. In 1632 the Churchwardens:

> "Received of Mr. Justyes Moylle for a fyne for one brott befor him and beinge drunke. 3s. 4d."
> "More received of Mr. Justyes Moylle for a ffyne for one beinge drunk and streckinge ye hedboroe. 6s. 8d."

Under the Commonwealth the laws against drunkenness, gambling and other offences were enforced with Puritanical zeal. The houses of parishioners were watched by informers who hunted up to the best of their ability every offender they could find. In 1652 the Churchwardens' Accounts record:

> "Given to 2 men as Informers to see who drew drinks after they were putt downe. 10s."

In 1723 the Churchwardens' Accounts record:

"To a distress warrant and serving it upon Mr. Day for Drawing Drink without a licence. 2s."
"Recd. for Thos. Days Drawing Drink without a licence. £1. 0s. 0d."

The question of Sunday drinking engaged the attention of the Fulham Vestry at a meeting on 8 July 1787, when

"It was resolved unanimously that it be recommended and this Vestry do earnestly recommend to the constable and headborough of this parish to be diligent and regular in searching the different public houses, particularly on Sundays, and if any shall be found where tipling is suffered during the time of Divine Service, or gaming or any other disorders or irregularities at any time, to give notice thereof to the magistrates resident in this parish to the intent that the persons keeping such houses may not be again licensed."

It was one of the old inns at Fulham which Mr. Samuel Shepherd, F.S.A., had in his mind when he wrote "Spring Buds," in 1844, where he sings

"Before an inn at Fulham stand,
With happy rustics round,
A small, but merry, village band,
Playing with cheerful sound."

Though little more than half a century has passed, the "happy rustics" and "the merry village band" have long since bidden us farewell.

The courts of the Manor also kept strict watch over the bakers. Thomas Cherche, "a common baker of bread," was, in 1442, amerced one penny because he had broken the assize. Bakers, who lived outside the Lordship of Fulham, were not allowed to supply bread to the Lord's tenants. Thus, in 1476, Robert West of Puttenhythe (Putney) and John Wykham of Westminster, described as "bakers of human food," were "in mercy iijd. each," because they had on two occasions sold within the Lordship and thus broken the assize. The following we quote from the "Middlesex County Records" (vol. i. p. 102):

"26 September 18 Elizabeth. - True Bill that, on the said day and at divers times before and afterwards, Rowland Fyssher, of Fulham co., Midd., baker, sold divers loaves called penny whyteloves and penny wheaten loves, each of them wanting assay to the quantity of eight ounces."

An entry in the minutes of a Court Leet, in 1657, runs:

"Thomas Pemberton, Baker 17 Ap. last within the jurisdiction of this Court did utter and put to sale one penny wheaten loaf wantinge of the just and dew weight or Assize of bread two ounces contrary to the Law, and therefore (we) do amerce him x^s..."

Edmund ffish of Fulham, baker, was, at the same Court, "amerced vijs. vijd." for short weight. The minutes further record:

"Alsoe Robert Blunstow of ffulham Baker the second day of December, one thousand six hundred fifty and Seaven within the jurisdiccon of this Court did utter and put to sale unto Edward Limpanie one penny white loafe wantinge of its just and due weight or assize of bread one quarter of an ounce. And also foure penny wheaten loafes wanting each of them of their just and due weight or Assize of bread three ounces and a quarter, amerced, vs."

The butchers, like the bakers, seem to have been a source of frequent trouble in various ways. The minutes of a Court General, in 1508, record that:

"John Robinson has sold flesh and taken excessive price wherefore in mercy ijd."

At the same Court Thomas Robinson, a butcher, was fined for over commoning within the Lordship. John Robinson, in 1509, suffered a further fine because he had

"cast the entrails of the beasts which he has killed on to the highway to the common nuisance."

In the minutes of a Court Leet in 1517, we read:

"Peter Carter is a butcher and has sold flesh unfit for food and has taken excessive gain, in mercy ijd.."

In the minutes of a Court, in 1658, we read:

"ffrancis Larkin being a Common Butcher did keep false weights in his shop to sell by, that is to say one seven pound weight wanting two ounces and one foure pound weight wanting an ounce and somewhat more and one or two pound weights wanting halfe an ounce to the annoyance of the people of this Commonwealth therefore he is amerced v^s."

CHAPTER VI: POPULATION

The first glimpse which we catch of the population of Fulham is in the grant of the Manor to Bishop Earconuald circa 691, at which period, we are told, the land was cultivated by fifty tenants. Estimating five persons to a family, this would give the population of the Manor of Fulham, at this early period, at about 250.

The Domesday Book furnishes the next clue to the number of the inhabitants. As we have already computed, the population of the Manor was then probably somewhere about 1000. At the Record Office are preserved certain Avisage Rolls temp. Richard II. The avisage, or avage, was a rent or payment made by the tenants of a manor for the privilege of pannage in the Lord's woods. In the whole Lordship of Fulham, in 1384, the pig keepers who paid rent to the Bishop numbered no less than 109.

From Roll 34, Chantry Certificates (Augmentation Office), I Edw. VI (1547-48), we learn that the parish of Fulham then contained "of howseling people," *i.e.* those capable of receiving the mass, "the number of ccccxliiij." (see 'Fulham Church').

In Fulham parish in 1625 the rated inhabitants numbered 109, representing a population of, say 545. In 1633 the rated inhabitants were 103, equivalent to, say, 515 people. The old Town or "Fulham Street," was the most thickly-populated part, then came North End, Walham Green and Parson's Green. In 1634 the rated inhabitants were:

ffulham streete:	45
Parsons Greene:	18
Pursers Crosse:	7
Wandon Greene:	22
Dawes Lane and the feildes:	4
North End	25
Total:	121

In 1640 the ratepayers numbered 129, and in 1641, 142. An assessment made in 1674 reveals the following distribution of the inhabitants:

"Fulham":	30
Beare Street:	37
Sow-gildrs Lane:	4
Parsons Green:	72
Dawes Lane:	26
Sand End:	12
Broom Feilde:	13
North End:	54
Crabtree Feild:	23
Total:	271

The population was therefore about 1,355. In 1724 we find the ratepayers totalled 445, equivalent to a population of about 2,225. Lysons states that the number of houses on Fulham side, in 1793, was 702, representing <u>a population of about 3,510</u>.

The census returns, since 1801, have been as under:

1801	. . . . .	4,428	1851	11,886
1811	. . . . .	5,903	1861	15,539
1821	. . . . .	6,492	1871	23,378
1831	. . . . .	7,317	1881	42,895
1841	. . . . .	9,319	1891	91,640

Under the Equalisation of Rates Act, the census was again taken on the night of Sunday, 29 March 1896, when it was found that the population of Fulham was 113,871, equivalent to 61 persons per acre.

CHAPTER VII: AMUSEMENTS

The amusements of the inhabitants of Fulham in ancient times were not always of the most harmless character. From the Court Rolls we learn that, in 1474, two men named Henry Halle and Thomas Fuller, who were

> "commonly wont to convey privately and to keep safe all in their houses and to play at '*talos*' (*i.e* dice) and other illicit games at a time when they ought not,"

were fined 6d. each. At a Court Leet, in 1475, John Aleyn of Westend (*i.e.* West End, Hammersmith), Thomas ffuller and John Aleyn, son of Roger Aleyn, were presented because

> "they are wont to play at '*talos*' and other illicit games and to sit up all night and sleep all day (*ac vigilare p' tota. noctem et dietum dormire*) and are not willing to serve or to work when required."

Accordingly, John Aleyn of Westend was fined 12d. and the other two 6d. each.

Bowls, always a popular game with Fulham men, were interdicted at a View in 1524:

> "No one inhabiting within this Lordship shall play at the game of bowls under penalty xjd."

Bishop Aylmer used to play at bowls in the grounds of Fulham Palace. In 1609 it was presented that:

> "Thomas Iles, gent., John Pulford, gent., Master Smith, Richard Burton, William Davis, Richard Springall, Master Longe, John Yates and divers others play at Bowles for their recreation Wherefore in mercy 6s. 8d. each."

In Puritan times a special licence had to be obtained from the Lords of the Council before a person could construct a bowling green. In 1656, Thomas Browne of Fulham petitioned

> "Lord Lawrence and the Council to erect and maintain a bowling green behind his house for the recreation of gentlemen."

At a Court General in 1507 the following presentment was made:

> "Alice, wife of Lewis Davy, keeps bad rule in her house and permits the servants of divers of the tenants to play at cards (*ad cardas*) and such like for the whole night to the common nuisance."

Quoits were once a favourite recreation among Fulham men. It is a curious circumstance that a word spelled "Fulhams," "Fullams" or "Fulloms" was long in use as a cant term to designate false dice. The late Dr. Brewer, in "Phrase and Fable," tells us that such dice were so called

> "From the suburb where the Bishop of London resides, which, in the reign of Queen Elizabeth, was
> the most notorious place for blacklegs in all England."

Dr. Brewer, unfortunately, does not inform us what is his authority for this sweeping charge, nor does he say whether the term arose because the dice were manufactured at Fulham, or merely because they were used there. A precisely similar explanation of the word occurs in the "Imperial Dictionary," in the "Encyclopædic Dictionary," and in other works of reference. It has, moreover, the support of Whalley, Gifford and Douce. In Webster's "Dictionary," "Fullam" or " Fulham" is defined as "An old cant word for false dice, named from Fulham where they were made," Nares, in his "Glossary illustrating English Authors," states that the term arose "probably from being *full* or loaded with some heavy metal on one side so as to produce bias which would make them give *high* or *low* as they were wanted." Nares found no proof in support of the conjecture that they were made at Fulham. It was not, he thinks, very likely that gambling flourished in "so quiet a village; nor would such a manufacture be publicly avowed." It will be observed that, while Nares identifies the first syllable of Fulhams or Fullams with the English "full," he fails to offer any explanation as to the second. Whatever may have been the way in which the name of our *quondam* village came to be used by playwrights and others to designate false dice, there can be little doubt that the cant term "Fulham" owed its origin to it.

Fulham. From an engraving by J. B. Chatelain, 1750

Fulhams were of two descriptions. Those intended to throw the high numbers (from 5 to 12) were called High Fulhams, and those intended to throw the low numbers (from 1 to 4), Low Fulhams.

Torriano, in his "Italian Dictionary," interprets *pise* by "False dice, high and low men, high Fullams and low Fullams." The word is not considered to be sufficiently vulgar to be excluded from Flugel's "German and English Dictionary" (ii. vols.) Johnson's "Dictionary" also includes it: the 1785 edition spells it "Fulham." Shakespeare has immortalized the word in the "Merry Wives of Windsor" (i. 3: 1598-99):

Pistol:
Let vultures gripe thy paunch! for gourd and fullam holds,
And "high" and "low" beguile the rich and poor.

Butler, in "Hudibras," uses the word in the sense of a sham: thus he speaks of the "fulhams of poetic fiction" ("Hudibras," pt. ii. canto I.) In his "Essay on Gaming" he has:

"Have their fulhams at command
Brought up to do their feats at hand."

The term was in common use among the playwrights of the Stuart period. Among these are G. Chapman ("Monsieur D'Olive "), Ben Jonson ("Every Man out of his Humour "), R. Simpson ("Nobody and Somebody"), W. Rowley ("A New Wonder, a Woman Never Vext"), T. Decker ("Bellman of London"), and T. Nash ("The Unfortunate Traveller"). In the "London Prodigal" is the following enumeration of false dice:

"I bequeath two bales of false dice, *videlicet*, high men, and low men, fulloms, stop cater traies, and other bones of function."

The account of Alsatia in the "Fortunes of Nigel" contains some interesting particulars as to this method of cheating at cards. In Douce's "Complete Gamester " (1676), are details as to how these dice were made. The Fulhams, Douce states, were chiefly made at Fulham. In a "Treatise on Dice Play" (1550), the word is spelled "fullans." This is, as far as we are aware, the earliest use of the term. The "*talos*" of the Court Rolls were doubtless identical with the "Fulhams" of the dramatists and poets.

CHAPTER VIII: PUNISHMENTS

The Court Rolls of the Manor and the records of the parish generally, contain a multitude of curious memoranda respecting infractions of the law. Though a somewhat black chapter in the history of the parish, the following brief selection of offences may not be without interest.

William Brother, at a Court Baron in 1393-94, was ordered to be distrained, because he had taken partridges and rabbits "from the Warren of the Lord of Fulham."

The following extract from the minutes of a Court General in 1422, shows that the Bishop of London enjoyed the property of felons within his Lordship:

> "One arrested on suspicion of felony was taken and delivered to the gaol of Neugate which had within this Lordship 4 pigs of the age of half a year, whereof 2 are in the custody of Edward Algar and 2 in that of John Vyrley, the which was arrested by William Wylmot after taking of the said felon and the same shall remain to the Lord if the said felon be found attaint and convicted."

The felling of timber, without the permission of the Lord, was a very common offence. Thus, in 1423, it was presented that:

> "John Pope is a common trespasser within the Lordship and has broken the hedges of the Lord and his tenants and cut down oaks and ashes to the prejudice of tenants."

Another case where the goods of the felon fell to the Lord of the Manor is reported by the Homage at a Court in 1424:

> "They present that a certain Ducheman, of whose proper name they are ignorant, on Wednesday next after Passion Sunday in the third year of King Henry abovesaid entered in the close and houses of Katherine Holmys at Acton within the Lordship of the Lord of Fulham and took thence feloniously and carried away ij craters (*i.e.* cups), masours (*i.e.* bowls, v spoons of silver of the price of xiijs iiijd, one purse with one noble of gold and 13½d. of silver in the same and one pair of shears for

a tailor, ij 'flameol' of thread (perhaps scarves or banners, comp. Lat. *flammeolum*), ij bead-prayers of black jet (geet) in one of which is a silver paternoster and in the other one crystal stone, and the same being taken in the Lordship of Fulham as a felon was delivered to the Compter of London. And moreover they say that they are as goods forfeited and are in the custody of John ---- the farmer of Fulham and Walter Mersh beadel there as goods forfeited to the Lord."

Thomas Brambell was, in 1442, presented because he had insulted the wife of William Here and drawn blood from her. In 1443 William Coteler cut down an acre of wood and underwood growing at "Colynnesfeld." In 1454. it was presented at a Court General that Nicholas Wakefield had insulted and made an affray upon John Brewer, "yresshman."

The goodwives of Fulham were often fined on account of their quarrels. The wife of John Holere was, in 1460, forced to pay 12d. because she was a common scold and perturber of the peace (*garulatrix et perturbatrix*) amongst her neighbours.

Loose women appear to have been remarkably numerous if one may judge by the frequency of entries relating to them. In 1461 Richard Mathew was forced to pay 20s. for being "a common receiver of harlots and suspected persons." In 1466 William Dyer was fined 6d. because he had made an affray on Thomas Sawyer "and blood from him drawn contrary to the peace of our Lord the King."

John Ben'sshe, in 1475, was fined for an affray with a dagger upon John Halle from whom he had drawn blood. At the same Court Katherine, the wife of Thomas Coxston, was declared to be a "common receiver of felons and felons' goods" and had "feloniously fled." In 1476 the following serious affray in Fulham was reported at a View:

> "R[d]. Sawyer has insulted and made an affray upon Robt. Tayllour and John Brambyll (Brambell) with one Normandy bill contrary to the peace of our Lord the King and the said Normandy bill remains in the custody of Robert Lovell to the use of the Lord."

At the same Court the Lord's beadle gave intelligence that Margaret Grenleff of Wandongrene, Margaret Benerssh and Margaret Blackwell of Berestrete were common breakers of the hedges of their neighbours. Margaret Blackwell, who was the wife of Thomas Blackwell, was evidently a ne'er-do-well, for, at a Court General in the same year, we find her amerced "iiijd" for stealing two partridges of the value of "vjd." Another, but less frequent offence was the ploughing up of boundaries so that the division between the fields of different tenants of the Bishop became effaced. In 1476, Nicholas Burton was presented for ploughing up 25 perches of a mere or boundary line between the lands called Belles and those of John Grove "so that the division of the lands is not known." At the same Court Joan Mitton was presented for being a common scold and scandalmonger (*garulatrix et scandalizatrix*). At a View, in 1487, John Colson was charged with keeping within his house at Fulham "a certain Margaret a whore" and with taking in "divers persons disposed to the common nuisance easily led." At the Court General held this year, Nicholas Hayward was also fined for keeping loose women in his house. At the same Court James Newman and Isabella his wife ("a common whore") were fined for helping and entertaining divers persons "contrary to the form of the statute." A presentment at a Court General, in 1484, runs:

> "The wife of Henry Sotyll, the wife of Thomas Parker, and the wife of John Ben'ssh, junior, are persons evil disposed and have stolen divers goods of their neighbours and hens and capons of the Lord in Fulham and Hammersmith and also other persons evil disposed and suspected have broken in the night into the houses of the said Lordship, stolen divers goods and the same they have supported to the great damage," etc.

At a Court General, in 1507, it was reported that John Wardell and Alice his wife, were loose characters who

> "receive and entertain suspected persons as well men as women, whom they permit to sit up the whole night to the common nuisance of all their neighbours contrary to the warning in that behalf made."

The female was further presented for receiving stolen goods:

> "The same woman bought one brass pot called a posnet with a handyll, of whom, unknown, which pot was stollen. Therefore it is ordered the

same to be seized to the use of the Lord and also one candelabrum and a woman's cap of white colour, of whom, unknown."

In 1508 the wives of John Tebold and James Style were fined 6d. each because they were "common quarrellers and scolds amongst their neighbours." For obstructing a common footway, leading from his dwelling to Fulham Church, John Kypping was, in 1514, fined " xxd."

The Court General, in 1516, heard a case of trespass brought by John Yong against William Day, who had by force (*vi et armis*), entered a close belonging to the complainant "in Berestrete" (*i.e.* High Street) and had trampled down and destroyed his herbage. A fine of 33s. was inflicted on Day. At the same Court John Beteryche, for an affray upon an unknown man and inflicting with his staff, a wound in his head, from which blood flowed, was amerced "xl^d." Roger Wilkynson, for an affray upon Richard Burton "with a hatchet upon his leg," was, in 1521, "in mercy iij^s iiij^d." The following appears among the minutes of a View in 1524:

"Thos. Olyuer and Alice his wife keep bad order in their house, viz., receive and entertain divers persons suspected, as well women as men to the common nuisance: to amend before next Court or forfeit xl^s."

At the Court General held this year, four tenants of the Lord were appointed arbitrators

"To hear and determine divers disputes and upbraidings, variations and discords between John Grene, smyth and Alice Oliuer, and they do promise faithfully to abide the arbitration and decisions of the said tenants under penalty that each who does not willingly obey shall forfeit 40s."

In 1545 a serious affray occurred between the servants of two prominent residents, William Yowe and Stephen Cleybroke. The particulars are thus recorded in the minutes of a Court General held in this year:

"Three men, whose names are unknown, servants to William Yowe, gent., on the 7 May 37 year of our now king at Fulham aforesaid by force of arms, to wit, with swords staves and shields as ordered by the said William, took a certain cow from the servants of Stephen Cleybroke, bailiff of the Lord there, which he had distrained and from the mercy of the Lord by strength and arms rescued and detained contrary to the custom wherefore the said William is in mercy iij^s iiij^d."

Further, Yowe was charged with impounding the cattle of Cleybroke. At the next Court, it was reported that:

"William Yeo, gent. has not withdrawn his action which he brought against Stephen Cleybroke in the Court of the Sheriff of Middlesex called the Sheriff's Turn as he was ordered at the last Court, wherefore he shall forfeit to the Lord, xls."

This heavy fine probably convinced Mr. Yowe, that the Lordship of Fulham was exempt from the jurisdiction of the Sheriffs Turn and capable of settling the quarrels of its tenants.

A curious case of uttering seditious words occurred at a meeting of the Court General in 1546. John Edgecum, we learn, was sitting with others in the Court "to deliver his verdict before Hugh Stewkeley," the deputy steward, when he

"Uttered and published these diabolical and malicious words in English, following, to wit, 'that he wold not belyue my lord Bishop of London's untreuthe nor his false bokes nor the said Hugh Stewkeley's sayings.'"

To appease Bonner and expiate his offence, poor Edgecum was amerced 20s.

In the minutes of a Court General, in 1553, it is recorded:

"Stephen Cleybrok keeps 2 fierce dogs (*canes agragarios*), called mastyves, which go in the king's highways in Ham'smyth to the grave danger and nuisance of the people of the king, frequenting the same ways both by day and night. Wherefore the same Stephen is ordered to keep his dogs secure in his house and not permit them to go in the ways aforesaid under penalty of 3s. 4d."

At a Court General held in 1565 it was announced that:

"One cloak (*pallia*), of the goods of Roger Barrett of felony suspected, has been taken within this Manor and now remaineth in the hands of

William Brasebridge."

John Snelling, at a View in 1574, was amerced 3s. 4d. for having

"drawn blood from Thomas Munnes and broken the Peace of our Lady the Queen."

The hedge breakers of Fulham got so bad that, in 1575, it was

"Ordered that all men within the parish having any tenements who after this break any hedges that then the same men shall be expelled from such and so many tenements for one quarter of a year after proof or forfeit 10s."

The following presentment was made at a View in 1576 :

"Henry Hilton has drawn blood upon one Richard Davies schoolmaster (*pedagogii scholæ*) upon two separate occasions, wherefore in mercy vjs viijd."

Lysons, quoting from the now lost Churchwardens' books, gives the following under date 1583:

"Paid to my Lords Pareter for bryngyng towe inquisitions, whereon was to enquire for those that absent themselves from the churche; and the other to enquire of those that be over the sea for religion . . . 8d."

The Middlesex County Records (vol. i., p. 163, 20 Aug. 27 Eliz.) furnish the following "True Bill against Isabella Potter (of Fulham), spinster for recusancy."

Recusancy was the obstinate refusal of a person to attend divine service in the Established Church. By I Eliz., c. 2, it was enacted that a fine of 12d. should be imposed on every one so absenting himself without reasonable cause. The statute was not repealed till 1844.

Thomas Hardinge and others were presented at a Court General, in 1611, because they

"have lodged certain vagrants in the night season that goe a begging to London in the daye tyme contrary to a payne made att the laste Court Leete."

In the minutes of a Court General, in 1658, we find the following:

> "John Harris sonne of Henry Harris c'taine pigeons in the Comon feild belonging to the Mannor did shoote and kill wth a certaine fouling peece therefore amerced x^s."

The annexed extracts from the Parish Books for 1654 and 1659 will give the reader some idea of the extent of the zeal of the Puritans prior to the Restoration of the Monarchy. They are in respect of fines enforced by the parish officers against certain persons for gambling:

Offences and transgressions done against the law (1654)

Ed. Sanders	10s. 0d.
Ed. Hall	10s. 0d.
Hen Barton	10s. 0d.
Rich Tingle	10s. 0d.
Jo^n Pighwise	10s. 0d.
Good. Ebswordes	3s. 0d.
Ed. Limpany	£2 0s. 0d.
Mihill. Salter	10s. 0d.
Ed. Arnold	5s. 0d.
Rowland Davies	10s. 0d.
Wm. Lone	10s. 0d.
Rich. Blackman his wife	5s. 0d.
Benja. Hamon	5s. 0d.
Will Bond	10s. 0d.
	£7 8. 0.

Transgressions and offences done against the law also for Breach of the Lords day, vizt. on ye -- day of Nouember, 1659.

Thomas ffoakes for Breach of ye Sabbath	10s. 0d.
B— H— for ye same offence	10s. 0d.
Edw. ffarmer for ye same offence	10s. 0d.
John Broomhall Barber for ye same ofence	10s. 0d.
Rich. Kirbey for ye same ofence	10s. 0d.
Rich. L— for ye same offence and for sufering vnlawfull games in his howse	£2 0s. 0d.
Off Edw ffarmer for playing there	6s. 8d.
Off Tho ffoake for playing there	6s. 8d.
Total	£5 3. 4.

Disbursed out of ye said monies, vizt.:

Paid Mr. Lisle at ye request of ye informer being ye moiety of his fine for gaming	£1 0s. 0d.
Paid John Broomhall Barber at ye request of ye informer ye moiety of Thomas ffoakes his ffyne for gameinge	3s. 4d.
Paid Edward ffarmer at ye request of ye informer ye moiety of his ffyne for gameinge	3s. 4d.
Paid Edward ffarmer for two warrants	2s. 0d.
Paid Richard Kirbey at ye request of ye informer out of ye fine for gameinge	6s. 8d.
Paid Thomas ffoake to buy waightes and measures for ye Mannour	18s. 0d.
Receipts in all	£5 3. 4.
Disbursed thereof	£2 13. 4.
Distributed	£2 10. 0.
wch was ye remainder.	

All wch summ and summs was disposed of and giuen to Christn poore people, following:

To Thom. Bennett, his wife hauinge been sick a long season	5s. 0d.
To widdow Norwood lying sick	6s. 0d.
To William Swift, hee and his whole family hauing been sick a long season	6s. 0d.
To Mary Harding to buy her shooes and stockings	5s. 0d.
To Widdow Bolcham very poore	5s. 0d.
To Geo Bedforde wife lying in child bed and beinge very poore	6s. 0d.
To Giles Woldridges wife beeng very poore	5s. 0d.
To Widdow Cox	5s. 0d.
,, ,, Barr	5s. 0d.
,, ,, Wheeler	2s. 0d.
	£2 10. 0.

The tenants of the Manor were not allowed to house lodgers or "inmates," except under certain restrictions imposed by the Homage. Some of the tenants appear from time to time to have compromised themselves by admitting to their houses persons of an obnoxious character. Over his tenant the Lord could exercise a large amount of control, but in the case of the tenant's lodger the Lord had no power except through his tenant. As the "inmates" rendered him no service, it was clearly not to his interest that they should exist in the Manor.

One of the earliest regulations made in regard to them was in 1573, when, at a Court Baron, it was resolved that "Every landlord who after this shall receive any inmate shall forfeit xs a month."

At the next Court occurred the first case of contravention of this rule:

> "Wm. Emesty keeps a sub-tenant called in English an inmate contrary to the statute wherefore he is amerced xs."

Many similar presentments occur. An order in 1577 reads:

> "And it is ordained and decreed by the whole Homage that after this no tenant of lands receive or admit into their houses or other tenements any labourer or other poor (man) without receiving a testimony of his honest conversation and the same to be delivered to the Constable of the parish of Fulham."

In 1605 it was ordered that

> "If any person or persons within this pishe shall receave into his or their service any woman or women being greate with childe or shall pmitt or suffer them or any of them to lodge in any of their Howses or barnes by meanes whereof any of the said women shall happen to be delivered of child within the said pish Then every suche pson or psons so receavinge hir or them shall keepe the child or children so borne in the said parishe and discharge the parishe thereof or els pay downe to the Churchwardens and Overseers for the poore for the tyme beinge toward the mayntenaunce and keepinge of the said child or children tenne poundes."

At a Vestry held 12 Feb. 1664-65, the following order was made:

> "It is ordered y^t notice bee giuen vnto all such psons as are owners of cottages vnder the vallue of eight poundes per annum, that they doe giue sufficient security to the Churchwardens and Ou'seers of the poore of this pish of ffulham for the tyme being to save and keepe harmless the said pish off all tennants that they shall take into their said cottages fforthwith; and such psons as refuse so to doe shalbee proceeded against accordinge to law, and y^t they doe acquitt the said pish of all damages and charges that may ensue."

Fulham. From an engraving, circa 1817

CHAPTER IX
THE HIGHWAYS AND BYEWAYS OF FULHAM

In times prior to the days of Vestries, the highways of the Manor were inspected at the annual View of Frankpledge, the Jurors of which had full power to deal with all matters relating to repair, maintenance, obstructions, etc. Thus, at a Court in 1460, one John Lawrence was fined for placing rubbish in "a certain water ditch," so that the right course of the water was "diverted and turned into the king's highway and the way submerged." In 1568 Peter Atkinson had to ay 6s. 8d. for grubbing up and carrying away trees in the queen's highway near his house.

Each owner of property, consisting of one or more ploughlands, was required to send his carts, drawn by oxen or horses, each in the charge of two men, to assist, generally during six days in the year, in the repair of the roads, in addition to which all the inhabitants, except the very poor, were required to contribute to the general assessment levied in respect to the maintenance of the highways and other public burdens. In 1575 one John Johnson was convicted on account of his failure to render the service required of him. The "Middlesex County Records" (vol i. p. 100), contain the following details of the case:

> "June, 18 Elizabeth. - True Bill that (due notice having been given publicly in the parish church of Fulham, on the Lord's Day next after the feast of Easter, that six certain days, viz., the 18th, 19th, 20th, 21st, 22nd, and 23rd days of June in the said year, were appointed for mending and repairing the highways of Fulham) John Johnson, of London, gentleman, having in his occupation one hundred and twenty acres of land, being a Plougheland and more, neither found nor sent any wain or cart, fitted according to the custom of the country with oxen, horses, or other cattle, two fit men, and fit necessaries for carting things for this purpose, either for the said six days or any one of them. G. S. P. R., Michaelmas 18 Eliz."

In 1605 it was ordered that:

"No man shall lay any soyle, mudd or Earthe in the streetes or in the kinges highway except he or they remove it wthin one moneth next after."

Fulham and Hammersmith had each its surveyor, an officer who had to be annually elected. When the surveyor took his view of the roads, a party of Vestrymen would generally accompany him. In the days of the Stuarts and long afterwards, journeying over the roads of Fulham was no light matter, and the bold man who undertook the task naturally required to renew exhausted nature at the wayside inns. In the year 1664 the clerk had to disburse 16s. "vpon acctt vpon viewinge the highwayes with the surveuour on ffulham side." The labours of the day were concluded by a dinner. On 4 July 1664, there was

"Pd for a dinner for the gent. and neighbors after viewing the highways ... £1 14 0."

In 1716 the surveyor on Fulham side commenced the keeping of a detailed account of his receipts and disbursements. This volume is entitled:

"A Booke For the Surveior only on Fulham side Beginning in the year 1716."

It contains a fund of curious entries tending generally to show how terrible must have been the state of the majority of the roads of the parish.

In 1725 Parliament passed an Act for repairing certain thoroughfares in the parishes of Kensington, Chelsea and Fulham, trustees being appointed for the management of what now became turnpike roads. At a meeting of the Fulham Vestry on 16 April 1726, it was resolved,

"in order to make a composition with ye Trustees of the turnpike for Kensington, Chelsea an (sic) Fulham, to give them forty pounds in money and work to repair all the roads in the sd. parish that lyes within the Act of Parliament for mending the said roads this present year."

In 1740 a further Act was obtained "for Enlarging the Term and Powers" granted by the Act of 12 Geo. I. By this the number of Trustees was increased and the tolls leviable were fixed as under:

For every Coach, Berlin, Landau, Chariot, Calash, Chaise or Chair	Drawn by six horses or other cattle	6d.
,, ,,	Drawn by four horses, etc.	4d.
,, ,,	Drawn by three horses, etc.	3d.
,, ,,	Drawn by less than three horses, etc.	2d.
For every Waggon, Wain, Dray or Cart or other Carriage	Drawn by six horses, etc.	6d.
,, ,,	Drawn by five horses, etc.	5d.
,, ,,	Drawn by four horses, etc.	4d.
,, ,,	Drawn by three horses, etc.	3d.
,, ,,	Drawn by less than three horses, etc.	2d.
For every Horse, Mare, Gelding, Mule or Ass, laden or unladen, and not drawing		1d.
For every Drove of Oxen or Neat Cattle		10d. per score.
For every Drove of Calves, Hogs, Sheep, or Lambs		5d. per score.

The Act exempted from toll coaches or other carriages belonging to the King or the Prince and Princess of Wales or any other member of the Royal Family, or any horses of his Majesty's Guards attending his Majesty, the Prince and Princess of Wales, or any member of the Royal Family.

The Hammersmith Road, from Counter's Bridge westwards to the Powder Mills near Staines, came under other Acts, passed 3 and 10 George I, the terms and powers of which were enlarged by a further Act, passed 11 George II.

The Surveyor's Book ceased in 1764, to be succeeded by a series of High Way Rate Books. Faulkner, in 1812, observes:

> "The roads in this parish were, till within the last half century, at times nearly impassable; it required two teams of horses to draw one cart; and it was usual for the gardeners to assist each other on the road to or from London."

The Turnpike Acts worked very badly in Fulham. The Trustees were ever on the alert to erect more bars, so as to increase their receipts, while the inhabitants chafed under the annoyance of having continually to pay toll on journeying along their high roads. In 1802 the Vestry successfully resisted the intention of the Trustees to erect four extra toll bars in the "Town of Fulham." At this time Fulham paid annually £23 to the Trustees as a composition for the repair of the roads, which were neither watered, watched, lighted nor paved, in spite of the fact that, some years previously, the inhabitants had consented to an additional toll on the promise of these advantages being imparted to Fulham as they had been to St. Margaret's, Westminster, St. George's, Hanover Square, Kensington, Chelsea, etc.

Matters slumbered on till 1830, when the Trustees again made a move to erect more turnpikes in Fulham. A deputation accordingly waited on the Commissioners of the Turnpike Roads, pointing out how greatly the parishioners of Fulham would consider themselves aggrieved by the erection of toll gates in the streets of their "Town," blocking them up in every outlet, intercepting and impeding the communications of the neighbourhood, and inflicting a tax upon it from which it had heretofore been entirely free. They did not, however, get much comfort, the Commissioners merely making notes of the objections urged, and informing the deputation that they would consider them privately.

The result was unsatisfactory. Further bars went up, including one at each end of Back Lane (Burlington Road), which was thus entirely blocked as far as vehicular traffic was concerned. In 1845 there was a still further addition made to the bars. Three years later the Vestry appointed a Committee to consider the best means of removing the turnpikes, but nothing was then accomplished. The gates and bars in the parish were now as under:

Toll House between Chaldon House and the Fulham Charity Schools.
Toll Bar (with hut) at the entrance to Fulham Park, by Elysium Row.
Toll Bar, Burlington Road, Holcroft's end.
Toll Bar, Percy Cross, towards Parson's Green.
Toll Bar (with hut) at south corner of Dancer's Nursery Ground, opposite Munster House.
Toll House (with clock) opposite the "Swan," Walham Green.

Toll Bar opposite Sussex House, Fulham Palace Road.
Toll Bar opposite the "Bell and Anchor" in the Hammersmith Road.

In 1863 the Metropolis Trust Commissioners introduced a Bill providing for the removal of toll gates and bars in the Metropolis, throwing the entire cost of the future maintenance of the roads on the parishes through which they passed. The Bill became law, and the obnoxious barriers were removed from Fulham and other parishes.

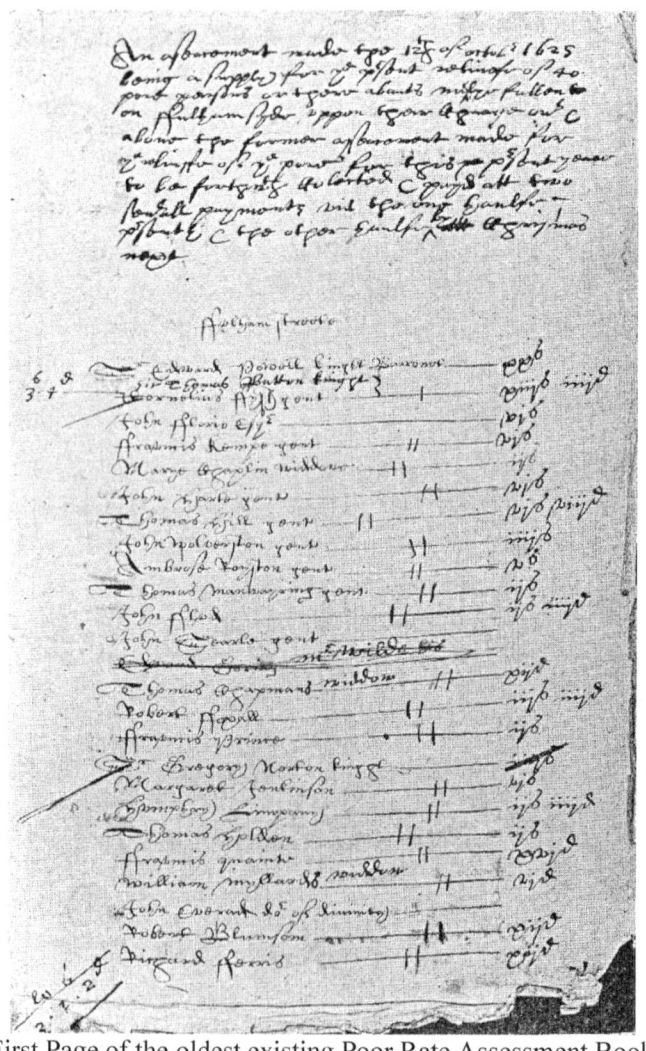

First Page of the oldest existing Poor Rate Assessment Book

CHAPTER X
WINTERING OF THE DANES AT FULHAM

With the exception of the grant of the Manor to Bishop Earconuald, circa 691, the first historical event recorded in connection with Fulham is the sojourn made here by the Danes in the winter of 880-81. Four years before, their chieftain, Guthrum, had landed at Wareham. Alfred, after a protracted struggle, forced the invaders back on Gloucester, but, reinforcements of the foe arriving, they reappeared at Chippenham, carrying all before them. In the spring of 878, the King gained a surprising victory over the invaders at Edington, but, though successful in the battle, Alfred knew only too well that his enemies had far too strong a hold upon the country for him to dream of any scheme of extermination. He therefore wisely directed his efforts towards a treaty with the Danes. In July 878, a solemn peace was effected at Wedmore, by which it was agreed that the Danes should be allowed to settle in the eastern portion of the island.

Guthrum, who was induced by Alfred to adopt the Christian faith, held loyally to his compact. In due course he and his followers repaired to East Anglia and for a while it seemed as if peace was in store for the kingdom. But Guthrum was himself quite unable to control his countrymen, who periodically descended, sometimes upon the English coast, at others on the neighbouring shores of the Continent.

It was in the winter of 880 that a great army of these "pagans," driven out of Flanders by Charles II, King of France, swooped down on England. Sailing up the Thames, the Vikings and their followers landed at Fulham where the horde went into winter quarters. It would be interesting to know how the army comported itself during its five or six months' stay in Fulham. The fact that the chronicles are silent on the subject points to the probability that the horde did not attempt any offensive action. They had had a severe struggle on the Continent, and, as they were contemplating a renewal of the war, it seems most likely that they bivouacked here merely for the purpose of tiding over the winter and recruiting their strength. All we know is that the invaders, in the spring of 881, accompanied by some of Guthrum's disaffected subjects, left Fulham for the Low Countries where hostilities were renewed.

The descent of the horde upon Fulham is thus recorded in the "Anglo-Saxon Chronicle":

> "An. DCCCLXXIX Hoc anno, profecti sunt pagani ad Cirenceaster de Cippanham, et ibi commorati sunt uno anno. Eodem item anno, in unum coacta est cohors paganorum, et (in hibernis) resedit apud Fullanhamme juxta Tamesin. Hoc anno discesserunt pagani de Cyrenceaster in Orientalem Angliam eamq(ue); terram incoluerunt ac diviserunt. Eodem etiam anno perrexerunt pagani, qui olim in Fullanham commorati fuerant trans mare in Franciam ad Gandavum et ibi manserunt uno anno."

Translation:

> A.D. 879. In this year the pagans set out for Cirencester from Chippenham and stayed there one year. In the same year, too, a body of the pagans drew together and sat down in winter quarters at Fulham on the Thames. In this year the pagans left Cirencester for East Anglia and occupied and divided the region. And in the same year the pagans, who had before sat down at Fulham, went over the sea by way of France to Ghent and remained there one year.

The story told in the "Anglo-Saxon Chronicle" is repeated and somewhat amplified by some of our early chroniclers. In the "Rerum Anglicarum Scriptores post Bedam," etc. (1601), are parallel passages by Henry, Archdeacon of Huntingdon, and Roger of Hoveden. The latter historian, in the place of "Fullanham," in the above passage from the "Chronicle," writes "in Insula Hame." This variation in the text is probably due to a misreading of the original manuscript, since it gives no sense.

The story of the landing of the Danes at Fulham is very similarly recorded by John Brompton and Simon of Durham in the "Historiæ Anglicanæ Scriptores," in the "Chronicle of Melrose," and in the "Chronicle" of Florence of Wigorn, etc. Why the marauders selected Fulham for their brief sojourn we can only surmise, and possibly quaint old Norden is not far out when he observes:

"The woodes and apt scytuation of the place for passage of water (no doubt) moved them thereunto."

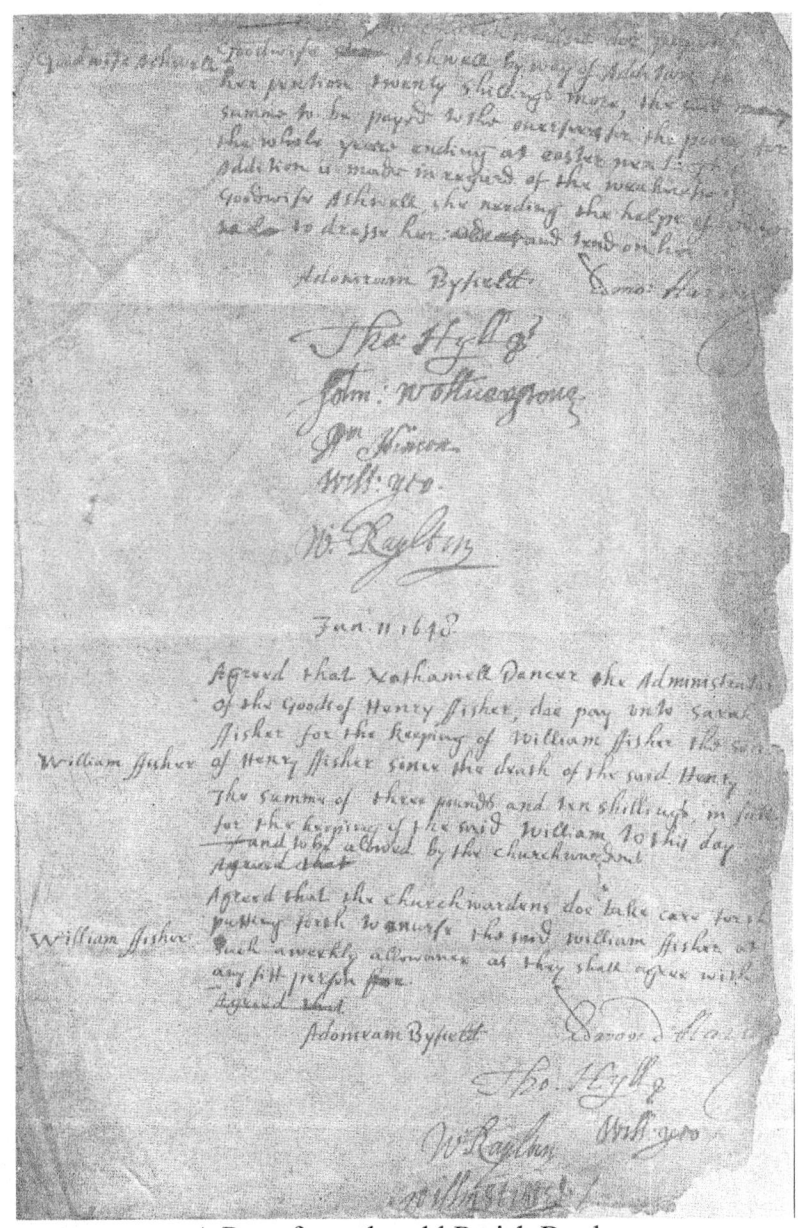

A Page from the old Parish Books

CHAPTER XI: FULHAM FERRY

Down to the building of the old Bridge, in 1729, the only communication between Fulham and Putney was by ferry. From the earliest times in the history of our parish we hear of the Ferry. It is, in fact, supposed by some that a regular ferry existed here at the time of the Conquest. The first direct allusion to it occurs in the "Rot. de Lib. ac de Misis et Præstitis," where we read:

"A° 11 Johann (A.D. 1210).
"In expñ Thom̄ Marescaƚƚ et duo hōum carettar̄ et septē eq°rū de garderoba morantiū cū ħnesio de garderob̄ p unā noctē ap̄d Kingeston̄ p p'ceptū dn̄i R ij.soƚ viij.d̄. et in passaḡ ħnesii de garderob̄ ap̄d Fuleħā j.d̄."

[*Translation*: In the expenses of Thomas Marescall and of two men carters and seven horses of the wardrobe remaining with the harness of the wardrobe for one night at Kingston, by order of our Lord the King, two shillings and eight pence; and in the passage of the harness of the wardrobe at Fulham 1d.]

Translation:

> In the expenses of Thomas Marescall and of two men carters and seven horses of the wardrobe remaining with the harness of the wardrobe for one night at Kingston, by order of our Lord the King, two shillings and eight pence; and in the passage of the harness of the wardrobe at Fulham 1d.

It is clear from the above entry that the harness of King John's horses was, in 1210, conveyed across the river at Fulham for the sum of a penny.

Eleanor of Provence, the unpopular queen of Henry III, on one occasion at least, hired the ferry boats at Fulham to convey across the river the harness of her own and her damsels' horses. An entry in the "Wardrobe Account," 36-37 Henry III [Carecta 1-14 reads:

> "1253. (The week ending) Sunday after the Assumption of the Blessed Mary (17 Aug.) Boats hired to carry the Queen and her damsels over the Thames at . . . mhe . . . (perhaps Lamheth, Lamb-heth, or Lambeth), 8d.; boats hired at Foleham, the same day, for the Queen's harness, 3d."

In the time of Edward I one Robert the Ferryman of Putney had the honour of conveying the royal household to and from

Fulham. In the Household Expenses of this king occurs the following passage:

> "Roberti Passatori de Puttenhethe passanti de Puttenhethe usque Fulham familiam et officia hospicii regis cum 2 bargiis ultra Thamesis per 2 dies mensis Marcii principio 4s. apud Westm."

Translation:

> To Robert the Ferryman of Putney, who conveyed from Putney to Fulham the household and servants of the King's Hospice with two barges across the Thames chiefly during two days of the month of March, 4s., at Westminster.

In the reign of Henry V the Ferry was in the hands of two men, Bartholomew East and John Wassingham, between whom a kind of partnership apparently existed. The old ferry boat having fallen into a dilapidated condition, the men quarrelled as to sharing the expense of the building of a new one. Eventually the matter was referred to arbitration. In the minutes of a Court Baron, in 1422, is the following account of the dispute:

> "Forasmuch as strife and discord were moved between Bartholomew Est of Fulham of the one part and John Wassingham of the same of the other part of and upon the keeping of the passage of Fulham aforesaid and concerning the making of the boat of the said passage, the parties aforesaid put themselves to stand high and low (ad standu in alto et basso) to the ordinance of John Cok, cordewaner, of Fulham aforesaid and of John Hyerde, smyth, of Hamersmyth in Fulham aforesaid nominated by the parties aforesaid And to stand to the order and arbitrament of the said John Cok and John Hyerde the parties aforesaid plighted their faith in the hand of Roger Pynchepole, John Partrych of Chelchehuth, John Danyell and others being present And if either of the parties aforesaid should refuse the order and arbitrament aforesaid that he should forfeit to the Lord of the Manor of Fulham aforesaid for the time being one hundred shillings Sterling which said John Koc and John Hyerde in presence of the aforesaid Roger Pynchepole, John Partrych and very many others on Monday after the quinzaine of Easter in the within written year of [King] Henry ordered and made their arbitrament as below as follows, namely That the aforesaid Bartholomew shall cause to be made afresh a new boat sufficient and fit for keeping the passage aforesaid before the feast of Holy Trinity

next ensuing And that the aforesaid John Wassingham should pay to the said Bartholomew on Monday the morrow of the feast of Holy Trinity half the cost and expense of the boat aforesaid And if the said John shall fail in his payment that the said Bartholomew may have and occupy the aforesaid boat entirely by himself And that the aforesaid John Wassingham or any one in his name shall in no wise intermeddle with the said boat but that he may have and occupy the old boat of the said passage by himself And that the said Bartholomew or any one in his name shall in no wise intermeddle with the said old boat except that now John Wassingham shall pay to the said Bartholomew 13 shillings and four pence for his share of the said old boat."

From very early times, the Ferry, with certain messuages attached thereto, was leased by the Bishop in moieties, each moiety being termed "half the passage." Bartholomew East's share, which had been previously held by one Thomas Brother, was, in the reign of Henry VII, in the possession of Sarre (*i.e.* Sarah) Cadman. Subsequently it was leased to Robert Barnaby and Alice his wife. On their deaths, the share passed to John Barnaby, their youngest surviving son, who, in 1550, was duly admitted. Immediately afterwards, however, he and his wife Joan, sold their interest in the Ferry to Hugh Stewkeley. On the death, in 1606, of George Stewkeley, his brother, Sir Thomas Stewkeley, knight, was admitted. Sir Thomas, in 1605, disposed of his share of the Ferry to Edmund Powell, in whose family it remained down to the time of Sir John Williams.

The other moiety of the Ferry was leased with the messuage known as Passor's. This half of the passage was long in the tenure of the Thurstons. In 1494 John Thurston, son and heir of Geoffrey Thurston, and Margery his mother (late wife of Geoffrey), made a compulsory surrender of their tenement called Passor's, together with "the moiety of the passage of the Ferry at Fulham." This forfeiture seems to have been due to their having allowed their property to fall into a ruinous state, for it was provided that if they paid £24 into Court together with the costs of

> "all repairs and other necessaries there in the meantime made and imposed by the said Lord upon the said tenement, passage and the Wharf,"

- the surrender was to be null and void.

Probably the Thurstons never recovered the property, for, a few years later, we find it in the hands of John Moreton. At a View in 1513 the jurors presented that John Moreton and John Young "ought to amend their banks near the Ferry." On the death of John Moreton, about 1518, his wife, Petronella, continued to enjoy the moiety of the Ferry. At a Court Baron, in 1520, Petronella being dead, William Moreton, of Moreton, co. Chester, son of Ralph Moreton (brother of John Moreton), as next of kin and heir, was admitted.

In 1532, William Moreton, son of the William Moreton just mentioned, leased for thirty years to Sir Ralph Warren the Ferry and its two boats, together with a tenement and a close. The endorsement of the lease is as follows:

> "ffulham Raylph Warren lease of a tenmt (tenement) etc. and a close, a pt (part) of the 2 ferry boats and ferry for 30 years. Rent £5 8s., and 12s. cheife rent. Signed Rd Utrede."

Lease of Fulham Ferry, etc.:
William Moreton to Sir Ralph Warren, 12 Ap. 24 Hy. VIII

The text is as follows:

"This Indenture made the xijth day of Aprill in the xxiiijth yere of the reigne of sou'aigne Lorde King Henry the viijth Betwene Willm Morton of Morton Halle in the pisshe (parish) of Asbury in the Countie of Chester, Gentilman, sone and heire of Willm Morton deceased on that oon (one) ptie (part) and Rauff Waren Citezein and Alderman of London on that other ptie Witnesseth that the said Willm Morton hath demised granted betaken and to ferme letten (an old legal phrase signifying letting by lease), and by these psents (presents or deeds) dimiseth granteth and betaketh and to ferme letteth to the said Rauff Waren alle that his Tent (tenement) wt (with) stable bern (barn) yerd (yard) orchard and Close of lond adioyning and other their app'tenncs (appurtenances) set (situate) lying and being in ffulham in the Countie of Midd together wt (with) alle his pt pp't and porcion of the two fferybootes (boats) and ffery at ffulhm aforsaid the whiche oon Thomas Waren there nowe holdeth and occupieth and alle other pfitts (profits) comodities and advauntages to the said Tent and ffery appteynyng or in anywise belonging the whiche were late of the said Willm Morton ffader of the said Willm or of any other psone (person) or psones seased to his vse To haue and to hold alle the said Tent and fferybootes and alle other the premisses wt (with) their app'tenncs (appurtenances) to the said Rauff Waren his executors and assignes in as large and ample man'r as the said Thomas Waren the same nowe holdeth ffrom the ffest (feast) of the Natiuitie of seint John baptist next comyng after the date of these psents vnto thend (the end) and terme of thirty yeres than (then) next ensuyng and fully to be completed, yelding therefore yerely during four the first yeres of the said terme to the said Willm Morton or his assignes a peper corne at the ffest of the Natiuitie of seint John baptist oonly if it be asked and nomore for that, that the said Rauff at the speciall instaunce and request of the said Willm Morton hath welle and truly consented and paide to the same Willm the some of twenty oon poundes and twelve shillinges stirlinge beforehand for the rent or fferme of the said Tent and ffery and other the p'misses during the said iiij yeres wherof and wherewt (wherewith) the said Willm Morton holdeth hym welle and truly contented, satisfied and paide and therof and eu'y pcell (parcel) therof he clerely aquyteth and vtterly dischargeth the said Rauff Waren, his executors and assignes by these pnts (presents), and yelding and paying therefore yerely during xxvj the last yeres of the said terme to the said Willm Morton his heires or assignes ffyve poundes and eight shillinges sterlinge at two termes of the yeres that is to witt at the ffeste of the birth of o^r (our) lord god and the Natiuitie of seint John baptist or w^{t}in (within) a moneth alwayes next ensuyng after either ffest of the said ffests by even porcons. And also the said Rauff Waren, his executors or assignes shall yeld and paye yerely during the said terme to the bisshyp of london twelve shillinges sterlinge for cheiff or quyte rent out and for the p'msses, and the said Willm Morton for hym his heires and executors coven'teth (covenanteth), and granteth to and w^t (with) the said Rauff Waren and his executors by these p'sents, that he the same Willm Morton his heires or assignes at his or their own ppre (proper) costes and charges alle the said Tent and ffyrybootes (ferry boats) and alle other the premisses wt their app'tenncs in alle things and by alle things welle and sufficiauntly shall repaire support susteyn and maynteyn and all the housing belonging to the same agenst wynde and rayne shall make defensable and the same shall newe make edifie and buyld as often and when as nede shalbe during the said terme of xxx^{ti} yeres, and rnoreou'r the said Willm Morton his heires and assignes at his or their like costes and charges shall pay and bere alle and eury other rentes and charges whatsoeu'r they be going and due to be paide and borne out, and for the said Tent and ffery and other the p'misses and therof and of eury pcell therof shall clerely acquyte discharge and save harmeles aswell the said Tent and ffery as the said Rauff Waren his executors and assignes by these p'snts. And if it fortune the said yerely rent of vli viijs (£5 8s.) during the said xxvj the last yeres of the said terme of xxxti yeres to be behynde vnpaide in pt or in alle by the space of a quarter of a yere ou'r or after any terme of payment therof above said in whiche it oweth to be paide and in the meane season it be of the saide Rauff his executors and assignes laufully asked That than (then) it shalbe leefull (lawful) to the said Willm Morton his heires and assignes into the said Tent (tenement) and other the p'misses to entre and distreyn and the distresses there so taken leefully (lawfully) to bere leade dryve and cary away and comande them to w^{t}holde (withhold) vntill the saide rente w^t (with) th' arrerages (the arrears) of the same if any such be to them be fully contented and paid and ffurdermore the said Willm Morton coventeth graunteth pmiseth and hym his heires and executors byndith to the said Rauff Waren and his executors by these p'snts that he the same Rauff his executors and assignes for the forsaid yerely rent of v^{li} viij^s (£5 8s.) to be paide in rnan'r and forme aboue rehersed shall peasably and quietly haue hold occupie and enioye alle the saide Tent and ffery other the p'misses wt (with) their app'tenncs wtout (without) any lett trouble vexacion hurt, or interupcion of the saide Willm Morton his heires executors or assignes and wtout (without) any laufull expulsion or putting out of any other p'sone or psones during the said terme of xxx^{ti} yeres and the said Rauff Waren for hym and his executors wolle (will) and graunteth by these p'sents that if the said Willm Morton and his heires welle and truly pforme obsrve fulfille and kepe alle and eu'y the covenntes grantes and p'misses abouesaide

whiche on his or their ptie ar (are) to be pformed obsrvd fulfilled and kept in man'r and forme aboue rehersed That than an obligacion of the date of these p'sentes wherein the saide Willm Morton is hold and bounde to the saide Rauff Waren in c^{li} (£100) sterlinge shalbe void and hadd for nought orels (or else) it shall stonde (stand) in full strength and vertue. In Witness wherof the saide pties to these indentures interchaungeably haue sette their sealle youen the day and yere aboue wryten.
Pr. me Wyllyam Moreton."

Thomas Warren, the heir of Sir Ralph, died in 1567. On his death Lady Johanna Warren, formerly Whyte, the widow of Sir Ralph, was admitted to "half of the passage of the ferrye there, called Fulham fferrye."

On her death, in 1572, the interest in the Ferry passed to her daughter, Lady Joan, wife of Sir Henry Cromwell. In 1583 precept was served on Sir Henry Cromwell and Hugh Stewkeley, his neighbour at the Ferry, "to make the Wharfe and stayers at the fferry."

On the death of Lady Joan Cromwell, her youngest son, Sir Philip Cromwell, was admitted. Sir Philip, in 1604, disposed of his right in the Ferry to Edmund Doubleday, who, in 1608, surrendered it to his own use and that of Margaret Caldwell, daughter of Lawrence Caldwell, vintner, by way of jointure for a marriage about to be solemnized between them. Edmund and Margaret Doubleday, in 1618, sold their interest in the Ferry to Thomas Hill. It subsequently passed to Thomas Hill, junior, and to Judith Hill, widow of the latter.

The admission of Judith Hill, widow, is thus recorded in the minutes of a Court General in 1650:

> "At this Court the Lord by his Steward, John Smith, Esq., granteth to Judith Hill, widow, by Richard Bomene, her attorney, half the Passage of the Ferry heretofore granted and allowed by the Lord of the Manor of Fulham and now used in and from Berestreet across the River Thames to the village of Putney in Surrey, to hold to the said Judith for life at the rent of 6s. 8d. at Michaelmas, and to carry the Lord, his chattles and cattles by day or night."

In 1651 Henry Hill (son of Thomas Hill), Joan his wife, Isaac Swifte, Margaret his wife and Elizabeth Hill surrendered their interest in the Ferry (after the death of Judith Hill) to Bennet Hamon conditionally on his paying 6s. Sd. yearly and

> "Passing and repassing the Lord his family or servants and all or any of them, their horses, coach or coaches, etc., and his and their cattle from time to time by night or day without demanding or receiving anything for the same services."

The Court Rolls contain several entries of regulations which were, from time to time, laid down for the management of the Ferry. In the minutes of a Court General, in 1606, is the following:

> "If any Waterman or his servaunts dwelling wth in the pish of ffulham shall cary over att or from ffulham fferie to Putney any person wthin the Mannr of ffulham or dwelling els where out of the Mannor and do not pay to the ferrieman for eu'y passenger dwelling wth in the Mannor a farthing and for euery passenger dwelling els where out of the Mannor a half penny he or they shall forfete and loose to the Lord for eu'y time so offending as aforesaid the some of iij^s iiij^d."

In the minutes of a Court General in 1608:

> "Wee present and finde by an auncient Custome wthin this Mannor that all the Inhabitants wthin this pishe hane beene alwaies heretofore carried ouer the Thames as theire occasions haue served betwixt ffulham and Putney by the fferriman there paying to the said fferriman a farthing for euery man or woman so carried ouer and for euery man and for his horse beeing of this pishe one ob (*i.e.* obolus, a half penny) and for euery straunger that dwelled out of the pishe one ob and for his horse and himself one penye And also wee doe further presente and finde that the like Custome hath beene heretofore vsed that when the said fferriemen haue not beene readye or that the passengers haue been disposed to goe ouer wth a payer of oares or a paire of skulles the owners or workmen in the said oares or skulles haue paid to the fferrymen or owners of the said fferries for the Inhitantes of this pishe so by them carried ouer a farthing apiece and for a straunger one half peny apiece."

And, again, in 1609:

> "Yf any wherryman or Waterman wthin this Mannor shall carry any pson or psons ouer the fferry from ffulham to Putney contrary to a

payne heretofore made not answering the fferryman his accustomed due wch is a farthing for eu'y inhabitant dwelling wthin the Mannor and a half penny for eu'y forayner dwelling out of the Mannor, he or they that so offendeth contrary to our Custome shall forfeite or loose to the Lord for euery such offence at euery time he or they offendeth ij^s vj^d."

The State Papers (Domestic) contain a warrant, dated 28 Dec. 1639, for payment to the ferrymen of the several ferries at Fulham, Richmond, Hampton Court and Shepperton for ferrying Charles I and his household over the Thames during a period of three years. The total amount paid was £93. 13. 0.

During the reigns of James I and Charles I the ferry boat at Fulham was in charge of one John Fludd, a noted character in his day. At a View in 1648 it was ordered

"That John Fludd and Thomas Munden tennants of the ferry boat at ffulham doe each of them provide a sufficient foot boate to convey passengers over the said fferry before the 24th of July next."

Under date 6 Sept. 1649, the "Expence Book of James Master, Esquire," contains the following:

"Sept. 6. For crossing ye water at Fulham & an horse 00. 01. 00." ("Arch. Cant.," vol. 15)"

Thomas Symonds, the heir of Sir John Williams, in 1719, sold his share of the Ferry to Daniel Pettiward of Putney.

The approach to the Ferry, on the Fulham side, was on the site of the draw dock, on the west side of the old Bridge. On the Putney side, the approach was by the opening to the ancient hithe at the lower end of Brewhouse Lane.

The passage of the river in the ferry boats was often attended by considerable danger. In rough weather the boats were sometimes driven down as far as Wandsworth before they could reach the Surrey shore. Archbishop Laud's servants were on one occasion crossing from Fulham to Putney when the ferry-boat capsized. Laud thus notes the incident in his "Diary," under date 18 Sept. 1633:

"I was translated to the archbishopric of Canterbury, the Lord make me able, etc. The day before, when I first went to *Lambeth*, my Coach, Horses and Men sunk to the bottom of the *Thames* in the Ferry Boat, which was over-laden, but, I Praise God, I lost neither Man nor Horse." (p. 49.)

CHAPTER XII: A BRIDGE OF BOATS

Before we deal with the history of old Fulham Bridge, it will, perhaps, be convenient if we pause here to speak of the celebrated "bridge of boats" which, in 1642, the Parliamentary forces threw across the river from Fulham to Putney.

This bridge, which was protected at either end by earthworks, spanned the river at a point about midway between Fulham Ferry and Broomhouse Dock. The precise site of its approach on the Fulham side is generally supposed to have been about facing Mulgrave House. Down to the early years of this century it was still plainly discernible. The fort on the Putney side remained intact until about 1845 when it was demolished.

The object of the Parliamentary Army, in throwing this pontoon across the river, was to intercept the Royal forces. The King, while initiating overtures for a truce, had made an advance on London. The Earl of Essex, hurriedly quitting the House of Lords, rode across the parks in the direction of the sound produced by the firing of the royal artillery. As he neared Brentford the Earl learnt, to his surprise, the trick which had been played. The King's nephew, Prince Rupert, closely followed by his uncle, had taken advantage of a November fog to attack Brentford, which they hoped to capture, after which he intended to press on to Hammersmith, where the Parliamentary train of artillery lay.

When Essex arrived on the scene, the royal troops had drawn off from Brentford and were quietly encamped just westward of the town. On 14 Nov. 1642, the Earl found himself at the head of an army of 24,000 men. For some hours the two forces faced each other on Turnham Green. While the Parliamentary commanders were debating as to what course they should take, Charles managed to withdraw his army to Kingston where he crossed the Thames. The Parliamentarians were disconcerted, for, as the royal army continued to hold Kingston Bridge, and as there was no other bridge on this side of London Bridge, there were no means of pursuing the King's force. In these circumstances Essex determined to bridge the river at Fulham by means of boats.

"Memorable Accidents" for 15 Nov. 1642 Contains the following announcement:

> "The Lord-Generall hath caused a Bridge to be built upon barges and lighters over the River Thames, between Fulham and Putney, to convey his Army and Artillery over into Surry, to follow the King's forces; and he hath ordered that forts shall be erected at each end thereof to guard it; but for the present the seamen with the long-boats and shallops full of ordnance and musketts lie there upon the river to secure it."

Robert Devereux, Earl of Essex, General of the Parliamentary Army.
From an old engraving

Again, in the "Perfect Diurnall" for 15 Nov. 1642, we read:

> "Tuesday, Information was given that his Majesty retreated from Brainsford with the Prince and Duke of York on Sunday about 12 of the clock, and that he had been at Kingston, the malignant party of that towne having let downe the draw Bridge, after the Parliament forces were marched away from thence, and that at his Majesties comming thither with his forces, he was brought into the towne with some expressions of joy, as the ringing of bells, and the like. And that his Majesty was going away again from thence to outlands, but the greatest part of his forces continue at Kingston, the Earl of Essex being also

marcht forwards after them towards Hounsloe: And that a bridge was making over the Thames, with flat bottom boates, from Fulham to Putney, that the Lo. Generals forces might march over the River into Surry and be ready to attend the Kings Forces upon all removes, and to prevent them going into Kent, for that it is feared they would endeavour to goe into that county, and try if they could possess themselves with some fort town, etc."

The Army of Lord Essex was, however, out-manoeuvred, for, before the bridge could be brought into use, the King withdrew to Oxford.

The Parish Books are unfortunately silent with regard to this bridge. How long it was allowed to remain we do not know.

In the summer of 1647 the King's Army advanced upon Uxbridge, when the opposing forces of the Parliament were billeted about Fulham and Putney. From "Perfect Occurrences" for 27 August 1647, we find that the major portion of the officers had quarters at Putney. At Fulham, Colonel Rainsborough was quartered at Major Rainsborough's, Col. Hammond at "Mr. Terries," Sir Hardres Waller at Mr. Hill's, Col. Scrope and Col. Tomlinson at Mr. Herbert's, Col. Twesleday and Col. Okey at Mr. John Wolverston's. Col. Porter at "Mr. Seares," and the Adjutant General of Foot at Mr. Snowe's.

Major Rainsborough is, down to 1650, given in the Parish Books as a rated inhabitant. "Mr. Terrie" was Mr. Geo. Tirrey, "Mr. Hill" was Mr. Thomas Hill, "Mr. Herbert" was, perhaps, Mr. James Herbert, and "Mr. John Wolverston" was Mr. John Wolverstone, all residents of Bear Street. "Mr. Seares" was probably Mr. Geo. Sayers.

CHAPTER XIII
OLD FULHAM OR PUTNEY BRIDGE

The first attempt made to connect Fulham with Putney by means of a permanent bridge was in 1671, when a Bill was introduced into the House of Commons to obtain powers for this purpose. The project met with strenuous opposition from the citizens and corporation of the City of London, and was laughed down in a debate which took place on the second reading of the Bill, which was lost, on a division, by 67 votes to 54. Fortunately, the substance of this curious but interesting discussion is preserved in Grey's "Debates." It is as follows:

"*Die Martis*, Ap. 4, 1671.
A Bill for building a bridge over the river Thames from Putney was read. On the motion that it be read a second time - MR. JONES (member for London) rose and spoke as follows:
'Mr. Speaker, - It is impossible to contemplate without feelings of the most afflictive nature the probable success of the Bill now before the House. I am sensible that I can hardly do justice by any words of mine to the apprehensions which not only I myself personally feel upon the vital question, but to those which are felt by every individual in the kingdom who has given this very important subject the smallest share of his consideration. I am free to say, Sir, and I say it with the greater freedom, because I know that the erection of a bridge over the river Thames at Putney will not only injure the great and important city which I have the honour to represent, not only jeopardize it, not only destroy its correspondence and commerce, but actually annihilate it altogether. (Hear, hear.) I repeat it in all possible seriousness, that it will question the very existence of the metropolis; and I have no hesitation in declaring that, next to pulling down the whole borough of Southwark, nothing can destroy more certainly than building this proposed bridge at Putney. (Hear hear.) Allow me, Sir, to ask, and I do so with the more confidence because the answer is evident and clear, how will London be supplied with fuel, with grain, or with hay if this bridge is built? All the correspondences westward will be at one blow destroyed. I repeat this fact boldly, because, as I said before, it is incontrovertible; as a member of this honourable House, I should not venture to speak thus authoritatively unless I had the best possible

ground to go upon, and I state, without the least fear of contradiction, that the water at Putney is shallow at ebb, and assuming, as I do, that the correspondences of London require free passage at all times, and knowing, as I do, that if a bridge be built there not even the common wherries will be able to pass the river at low water, I do say that I think the Bill one which only tends to promote a wild and silly scheme, likely to advantage a few speculators, but highly unreasonable and unjust in its character and provisions; because, independently of the ruin of the City of London, which I consider inevitable in the event of its success, it will effect an entire change in the position and affairs of the watermen, a change which I have no hesitation in saying will most seriously affect the interests of His Majesty's Government, and not only the interests of the Government, but those of the nation at large.'

MR. WALLER followed the honourable member for London, and gave it as his opinion that the erection of a bridge at Putney could not be considered as oppressive, even were a toll laid upon the bridge, because, said the honourable gentleman, 'those who dislike paying the toll may go by water, and so pay nothing. (Hear, and a laugh.) It seems to me, if it be a bad thing for Southwark it will be a good thing for Westminster, where the Court is, and where we are. (A laugh.) At Paris, Sir, there are several bridges - at Venice, hundreds. What then? Paris is not ruined, and Venice flourishes. I must say I think the opposition offered to this Bill shows considerable want of patriotism. No object in my mind can be more beneficial to the country than the extension of its resources, the multiplication of those avenues and approaches to the metropolis, by which the public wealth may be increased, and the national character elevated; no object in my mind is better calculated to extend the reputation of this country, or its mercantile advantages, than a *bridge over the river at Putney*. (Loud cheering.) Besides, Sir, if I may be permitted to make such an allusion, I think it by no means irrelevant to throw out, by way of observation, that the King cannot hunt in London; if the King wishes to hunt he must cross the water. This is a fact incontrovertible by gentlemen on the other side of the House, and a fact which I think well worthy our consideration; in short, I have no hesitation in saying that the measure of building a bridge over the river at Putney is one which independently of the advantages to which I have just cursorily alluded, cannot fail to be of the greatest utility and convenience *to the whole British nation*'

SIR THOMAS LEE, in a very excellent speech, expressed at some length his fears that the Bill was little better than a job, and that its object was to improve the value of the new buildings about the neighbourhood of the House of Commons. (Hear, hear, and a laugh.)

MR. SECRETARY TREVOR: 'I really am at a loss to understand why there is any serious opposition raised abstractedly to a bridge at Putney;

because, although Putney is further up the river Thames than London, honourable gentlemen who speak so warmly against the proposed bridge at the former place because it is likely to infringe upon the *vested rights* of the watermen might, by a parity of reasoning, contend that there ought to be no bridge at London.' (The Right Hon. Secretary sat down amidst continued cheers.)

SIR WILLIAM THOMPSON being loudly called for, rose and made the following speech: 'Sir, when a convenience has long been possessed, it grows, as it were, into a custom, and therefore the observations of the Right Hon. Secretary, with regard to London Bridge, do not, as it appears to me, at all apply to the romantic and visionary scheme of building a bridge over the river at Putney; one thing, indeed, may be well enough remarked upon in the right honourable gentleman's speech. He talks of the objections which might be made to London Bridge by those who oppose the imaginary bridge at Putney. It is true, that those who would support the one would annihilate the other, for if a bridge be raised at Putney, London Bridge may as well be pulled down. (Hear, hear.) Yes, Sir, I repeat it - because this bridge, which seems to be a favourite scheme of some honourable gentlemen whom I have in my eye - if this bridge be permitted, the rents necessary to the maintenance of London Bridge will be annihilated; and, therefore, as I said before, the bridge itself must eventually be annihilated also. But, Sir, this is not all. I speak affectionately of the City of London, and I hope I shall never be forgetful of its interests - (Hear, hear, from Mr. Jones) - but I take up the question on much more liberal principles, and assume a higher ground, and I will maintain it, Sir. London is circumscribed - I mean the City of London - there are walls, gates and boundaries, the which no man can increase or extend; those limits were set by the wisdom of our ancestors, and God forbid they should be altered. But, Sir, though these landmarks can never be removed - I say *never*, for I have no hesitation in stating that when the walls of London shall no longer be visible, and Ludgate is demolished, England itself shall be as nothing; yet it is in the power of speculative theorists to delude the minds of the people with visionary projects of increasing the skirts of the City so that it may even join Westminster. When that is the case, Sir, the skirts will be too big for our habits; the head will grow too big for the body, and the members will get too weak to support the constitution. But what of this, say honourable gentlemen; what have we to do to consider the policy of increasing the town while we are only debating a question about Putney Bridge? To which I answer, look at the effects *generally* of the important step you are about to sanction; ask me to define those effects *particularly*, and I will descend to the *minutiæ* of the mischief you appear prone to commit. Sir, I, like my honourable friend, the member for the City of London, have taken opinions of scientific men, and I declare it to be their positive conviction, and mine, that if the fatal bridge (I can find no other suitable word) be built, not only will quicksands and shelves be created throughout the whole course of the river, but the western barges will be laid up high and dry at Teddington, while not a ship belonging to us will ever get nearer London than Woolwich. Thus, not only your own markets, but your Custom House will be nullified; and not only the whole mercantile navy of the country absolutely destroyed, but several west-country bargemen actually thrown out of employ. I declare to God, Sir, that I have no feeling on the subject but that of devotion to my country, and I shall most decidedly oppose the Bill in all its stages.' (Hear, hear, hear.)

COLONEL STROUDE said that he approved of the motion of the bridge at Putney, although he must confess there appeared a somewhat too sanguine expectation of carrying a question of such importance on the part of its advocates.

MR. BOSCAWEN, before he came down to the House, could not understand what possible reason could be adduced in favour of a bridge at Putney; and now that he had heard the reasons of honourable gentlemen, he was equally at a loss to account for them. If there were any advantage derivable from a bridge at Putney, perhaps some gentleman would find out that a bridge at Westminster would be a convenience. Then other honourable gentlemen might dream that a bridge from the end of Fleet Market into the fields on the opposite side of the water would be a fine speculation; or who knew but at last it might be proposed to arch over the river altogether, and build a couple more bridges, one from the Palace at Somerset House into the Surrey marshes, and another from the front of Guildhall into Southwark. (Great laughter.) Perhaps some honourable gentlemen who are interested in such matters would get up in their places and propose that one or two of these bridges should be *built of iron*. (Shouts of laughter.) For his part, if this Bill passed, he would move for leave to bring in half a dozen more Bills for building bridges at Chelsea, and at Hammersmith, and at Marble-Hall Stairs, and at Brentford, and at fifty other places besides. (Continued laughter.) 'Now, Sir,' continued the honourable gentleman, 'some honourable gentlemen have talked of Paris and Venice as examples for us to follow. Why, Sir, Venice is built in the water, and if it were not for bridges there would be no streets. What has that to do with London? As to Paris, it is true there are many bridges, and what is the consequence? There is no use for watermen; and are we for our advantage, even admitting for argument's sake any to arise, to compromise the vested rights of the watermen? (Hear, hear, hear.) I, for one, say no; but when I say no upon this particular point abstractedly, I do not mean to say that I for one *alone* disapprove of the measure *in toto*. Neither the people of Middlesex nor of Surrey in the localities desire it, and I must say that at best it is a new conclusion to no end.'

MR. LOVE rose and said 'Sir, I feel myself called upon to say a few words upon this very important question, because I am authorised to state (which I feel it my bounden duty to do, after what has just dropped from the honourable gentleman who spoke last), that the present Lord Mayor is of a very different opinion from his immediate predecessor. (Hear, hear, hear.) I really speak nothing but the opinion of the worthy chief magistrate, when I say that if any carts go over Putney Bridge the City of London is *irretrievably ruined*. This, I have no hesitation in saying, is the matured opinion of the present Lord Mayor. (Hear, hear, hear.) Some honourable gentlemen who seem to think that the body of Thames watermen are nobodies - (Great laughter) - treat their vested rights with something very like contempt, and even those who condescend to consider the interests of that body with a little complacency tell you that the ferry in that part of the river encourages but very few hands. Now, Sir, that I deny. (Hear, hear.) I have procured a list of persons employed in the ferries at Putney, from which I can assert that very many watermen actually subsist upon the produce of the ferry there. (Hear, hear.) Now, Sir, there is another point to which I must speak. The projected bridge, I understand, is to be built of wood. (Much laughter.) Honourable gentlemen may laugh, but such is the fact; and although one honourable gentleman has just now humorously suggested iron as a material for bridge-building, it is - (Hear, hear) - if not less strange, not less true that it is proposed to build this visionary Putney Bridge of timber. (Hear, hear.) As to the possibility of the undertaking, I leave that to the projectors; but I presume timber wherewith a bridge across the Thames is to be built must be vast and large, and that the bridge must consist of many arches. If that be the case, I have no hesitation in saying that these pieces of wood, thick and numerous as they must be, will stop the tide altogether. (Hear, hear, hear.) And when the tide ebbs in the short space which intervenes between London Bridge and Putney, *there will never be sufficient water in the river to admit of the passage of the smallest boat*. (Hear, hear, hear.) I repeat, Sir, never after the tide ebbs will there be sufficient water for the smallest boat to row between London Bridge and Putney. In short, I state here, without fear of contradiction, that if the odious measure is carried, the river above London Bridge will not merely be injured by it, but *totally destroyed as a navigable river*.' (Hear, hear.)

SIR HENRY HERBERT next addressed the Speaker in the following words: 'Mr. Speaker, I honestly confess myself an enemy to monopolies. I am equally opposed to mad, visionary projects, and I may be permitted to say that in the late King's reign several of these thoughtless inventions were thrust upon the House, but most properly rejected. If a man, Sir, were to come to the bar of the House, and tell us that he proposed to convey us regularly to Edinburgh in coaches in seven days, and bring us back in seven days more, should we not vote him to Bedlam? Surely we should, if we did him justice. Or, if another told us that he would sail to the Indies in six months, should we not punish him for playing upon our credulity? Assuredly, if we served him rightly. Well then, Sir, here are persons proposing to build a wooden bridge over the Thames, in an unfrequented part of the country, and which they imagine, from the mere novelty of the speculation, we shall agree to. I say, Sir, suppose the matter worthy of discussion, it is of too great importance to be discussed in such a House as this. Why, Sir, there are not a hundred and fifty members present. What would our constituents say - what would the country at large say - if we decided a measure of such importance as the building a wooden bridge at Putney in so thin a house as this? I must think it would appear extremely strange to let this Bill go to a second reading after all we have heard so reasonably alleged against it.'

The cries of 'Question' here becoming very general, the House divided:

For the Bill   54
Against it   67

Majority against it   13."

Fulham Bridge. From an old print at the Hammersmith Public Library, inscribed "T. Preist, del. 1742."

Fulham Bridge. From an old print published by Henry Overton, circa 1750

For the next fifty-five years we hear of no further attempt to connect Fulham with Putney by means of a bridge. In 1722, however, the scheme was successfully revived. The actual circumstances of its resuscitation we do not know. There may, however, be some truth in a good story which is told about Sir Robert Walpole in connection with this matter. The prime minister, so the report goes, was one evening, about the year 1720, returning with his servant from Kingston where he had been in attendance upon the king (George I). Being anxious to get back to the House of Commons, he rode post haste to Putney, thinking to take the ferry there to Fulham. On his arrival, however, he found the ferry boat hauled up on the opposite shore, and no sign of a waterman. Sir Robert and his servant shouted till they were hoarse, but failed to attract attention. The ferrymen, Tories to a man, were carousing at the "Swan," and, it is somewhat uncharitably added, were enjoying in secret the discomfiture of their would-be passengers, who were eventually forced to reach town by another route. The incident is said to have determined Sir Robert to make a mental vow that a bridge should take the place of the ferry.

Another theory advanced to account for the erection of the bridge, is to the effect that Prince George of Wales, afterwards George II, often found great inconvenience in crossing by ferry when on his hunting expeditions to Richmond Park, and that he accordingly besought Sir Robert Walpole to exercise his influence in support of a Bill to build a bridge at Fulham.

Whatever the exact truth may be, we find that, at a Parliament held at Westminster on 9 Oct. 1722, and continued, with prorogations, to 20 Jan. 1725-6, a Bill was introduced for the building of a bridge across the Thames from Fulham to Putney. This Bill was read, for the first time, on 22 March 1724-25. On 30 March, and again on 2 April 1725, the Bill was discussed. On the latter date it was referred to a Committee, the petitions presented to the House to be heard by counsel, when the House considered the report of the Committee for the Bill and the report was read. The Bill, having passed the Commons, was sent up to the House of Lords, by whom it was approved, 24 May 1726. It received the sanction of his Majesty when he prorogued Parliament (12 George I, 8 June 1726).

The first meeting of the Bridge Commissioners was held at the "Swan," 26 July 1726. No less than sixty-eight noblemen and gentlemen attended. Amongst those present were the Duke of Grafton, the Duke of Newcastle, the Earl of Scarborough, Lord Onslow, Sir Robert Walpole, Sir John Stanley, bart., Sir J. Coleby, bart., Sir John Hobart, K.C.B., Sir R. Gough, Sir Thomas Jones, Col. Howard, Sergeant Birch, Col. Armstrong, Col. Paget, Sergeant Chapel, Charles Montague, Charles Dartiquenave, Surveyor of the Water and Gardens, Nicholas Dubois, master mason, Thomas Ripley, controller of His Majesty's works, William Kent, master carpenter, and Richard Arundel, surveyor of His Majesty's works. Mr. John Eden was appointed clerk. The following resolutions were carried:

> "That a humble petition be presented to His Majesty praying that he would be graciously pleased to grant letters patent, under the Great Seal, for the incorporation of the Commissioners and Trustees.
> That such a bridge be built as may supply the present exigency, and be useful for the building of a more substantial bridge as there may be occasion."

At the next meeting, held on 22 Aug. 1726, at the "Bull Inn," Putney, the Duke of Newcastle informed the Commissioners that the King had given directions for the preparation of a charter of incorporation. It was ordered that a survey of the river should be made, showing the places where a bridge might be erected.

Fulham Bridge, from the Putney shore, circa 1760.
From a print at the Hammersmith Public Library

The Committee considered three sites, viz. "(I) from Putney to Mr. Gray's land at Fulham, (2) from Brewhouse Lane, Putney, to Fulham Dock, and (3) from the east corner of Mr. Prettlewel's garden to the carpenter's yard at Fulham."

It was decided to select the first, where the width of the river between the banks was 780 feet, with 18 feet of water at high tides and 6 feet at low tides, giving an average of 13 feet on ordinary tides. Next, three designs for a bridge were submitted, the first by Mr. Thomas Ripley, the second by Mr. John Price, and the third by Mr. William Halfpenny. Further, a plan and a section of a bridge of boats, with the model thereof, was shown to the Committee, who were informed that such a bridge might be finished in about two months, would cost about £5,000 building and the repairs about £300 per annum. It is not stated by whom this plan, which was rejected, was submitted. It had doubtless been suggested by the pontoon made by Lord Essex in 1642.

The Committee finally decided to adopt Mr. Ripley's design, which was for a wooden bridge 23 feet in width and 780 feet in length, with a centre lock to have 17 feet of waterway above the highest tides.

The following three tenders for the erection of the Bridge were considered:

Mr. Thomas Hall: £7,500
Mr. Thomas Phillips: £6,698
Mr. John Meard: £6,650

Fulham Bridge. From an engraving published in the "Modern Universal British Traveller."

The Committee decided to accept the second. In consequence, however, of certain financial difficulties, it was found impossible, as the Act stood, to carry out the scheme. At a general meeting, it was resolved:

> "That it is the opinion of the Commissioners that the said Act of Parliament incapacitates all of the nobility and others of the trustees, although incorporated, to contribute to the work by any loan of money, or by purchase of any annuities, and that it cannot be expected the trustees will subject themselves to censure of Parliament and action at law upon the part of the said Act."

The Commissioners accordingly petitioned Parliament with a view to the amendment of the Act. After setting forth the cost of the compensations to be paid in respect to the abolition of the Ferry, the cost of the construction and maintenance of the Bridge, the annuities to be paid to the watermen, etc., the petitioners requested that they might be furnished with the powers of granting annuities in perpetuity or to assign the tolls to a contractor, and that, when incorporated, they should have power to lend or advance moneys without fear of any legal consequences; that they should be empowered to grant to any person or families a license to pass free of toll during their lives for such terms as should be agreed upon; and lastly that the Bridge might be free and exempt from all rates and taxes whatsoever, except those paid on incomes or profits.

The second Act, amending the first, was passed 1 George II (1727). The Commissioners, under the enlarged powers conferred by this Act, invited subscriptions in order to raise a capital of £30,000, on which dividends at the rate of 4 per cent. were to be paid, the tolls to be mortgaged for the repayment of the same. The following is the list of the original subscribers. Each of the gentlemen named subscribed £1,000 and was thus Proprietor of a thirtieth part of the bridge.

> The Right Hon. Sir R. Walpole, knt.
> The Right Hon. George Lord Carpenter.
> Sir Matthew Decker, bart.
> The Hon. Sir Charles Wager, knt.
> The Hon. Sir George Walton, knt.
> Joseph Andrews, Esq.
> Stephen Bisse, Esq.
> The Hon. Col. George Carpenter.
> William Cheselden, Esq., M.D.
> Thomas Cranmer, Esq., M.D.
> George Dowdeswell, Esq.
> William Genew, Esq.
> Burrington Goldsworthy, Esq.
> Edward Harrison, Esq.
> John Huggins, Esq.
> James Hustler, Esq.
> Edmund Jones, Gent.
> J. Kingsmill, Esq.
> Robert Mann, Esq.
> Thomas Martin, Esq.
> John Martin, Gent.
> Abraham Meure, Esq.

Captain Charles Molloy.
Henry Parsons, Esq.
Timothy Perry, Gent.
Thomas Phillips, Gent.
Thomas Ripley, Esq.
Edward Salter, Esq.
Captain Peter Solgard.
George Tilson, Esq.

These thirty shares were subsequently sold in moieties. After the passing of the Reform Bill, in 1832, they were further divided into eighteenths and twentieths to enable the possessor to hold votes for the counties of Surrey and Middlesex. The first meeting of the Proprietors was held at the Lottery Office, Whitehall, 27th Nov. 1728, when Admiral Sir Charles Wager was elected Chairman. At this meeting fresh models and designs were submitted. These included:

(1) The model and design for a timber bridge, by Mr. Thomas Ripley, previously offered to the Commissioners.
(2) A model and design for a stone bridge, by Mr. John Price, together with the model of a timber one.
(3) The design for a timber bridge, by Mr. William Halfpenny, previously offered to the Commissioners.
(4) A design for a timber bridge, by Mr. John Goodyear.
(5) A model of a bridge, by Captain J. Perry.
(6) Two designs for timber bridges, by Sir Jacob Ackworth.

These designs were referred to a Committee, who eventually reported in favour of one of the two sent in by Sir Jacob Ackworth. A Building Committee, consisting of Sir Charles Wager, Mr. John Huggins, Mr. Thomas Ripley, Dr. William Cheselden, and Mr. Thomas Phillips, was appointed. They presented a detailed report at a meeting held on the 22nd January 1728, when a model of the bridge was submitted by Mr. Thomas Phillips.

The following are the details of the estimate of cost prepared by Sir Jacob Ackworth:

		£	s.	d.
498 piles, 1½ loads in each pile, is 622½ loads, at £3 per load	. . . .	1,867	10	0
Driving the piles, at £2 each	.	996	0	0
609 loads of cubed timber and plank, at 2s. 6d. per foot, or £6 5s. per load .	.	3,806	5	0
Workmanship to do. at 1s. 6d. per foot, or £3 15s. per load	.	2,283	15	0
2,120 yards of paving with shells, clay, chalk, gravel and sandwich stone, at 7s. per yard	.	742	0	0
For gins, stages and barges	.	300	0	0
214 cwt. of wrought iron in shoes, for piles and nails, at 30s. per cwt. .	.	321	0	0
Painting	.	100	0	0
Making good the ground and works at the end of the bridge . . .	.	400	0	0
Two houses for the toll-gatherers	.	140	0	0
3,125 ft. of Portland stone and work, at 3s. per foot	.	460	0	0
For watchmen, candles, etc.	.	100	0	0
		11,516	10	0

Mr. Thomas Phillips, who constructed the Bridge, was carpenter to His Majesty King George II. According to the "Gentleman's Magazine," he died 15th August 1736.

The total cost of the Bridge, including that of the Bill, the approaches, purchase of rights, etc., amounted to £23,084. 14s. 1d.

Faulkner asserts that

> "The plan of this bridge was drawn by Mr. Cheselden, surgeon of Chelsea Hospital, who, in his profession, acquired the greatest reputation, and, by the skill displayed in this useful piece of architecture, in the has shown the affinity that exists among the sciences."

This statement, which altogether ignores Sir Jacob Ackworth, is somewhat incorrect. Mr. J. F. Wadmore writes in "Old Fulham Bridge":

> "A careful examination of the minutes of the earlier meetings of the Proprietors shows that, although Sir Jacob Ackworth's design for the bridge was selected, it was materially modified in execution, and its construction superintended by a Committee of eight of the Proprietors, of whom Mr. Ripley at one time, and Mr. Cheselden at another, appear to have taken the chief part... The interest shown by Mr. Cheselden in the construction of the brick arches and abutments, and arranging for the toll-houses, gave, no doubt, some colour to the statement made by Faulkner in his 'History of Fulham,' that Dr. Cheselden (then one of the leading surgeons of his time) gained his experience in architecture while practising as surgeon at Chelsea Hospital, which enabled him to design a bridge standing on so many wooden legs."

There is no doubt that Cheselden, who was an architect of no mean ability, rendered the Proprietors much practical assistance. This is evidenced by the fact that, at a meeting held on 2 July 1730, they passed the following resolution:

> "Resolved, as the bridge is built entirely according to a scheme and principles laid down by Mr. Cheselden, and as he has been very serviceable in directing the execution of the same, that the thanks of the Proprietors be given to him for the advantages which have been received from his advice and assistance, they being of opinion that no timber bridge can be built in a more substantial and commodious manner than that which is now erected."

Fulham Bridge, 1799. From a print at the Hammersmith Public Library

At the meeting held on 2 July 1730, the two following resolutions were also carried:

> "That a book be made with a draught and description of the bridge; that the same be done in such manner as Mr. Cheselden may direct, and that he be desired to advise with Mr. Ripley and Mr. Phillips about the same; that the whole expense do not exceed thirty guineas, and that no more books be printed than shall be for the use of the Proprietors.
> That Mr. Phillips well deserves a gratuity from the Proprietors for having been so expeditious, and having performed his work in such a substantial and workmanlike manner, and that he be presented with a piece of plate not exceeding the value of thirty guineas."

Mr. W. Eden, the secretary, was at the same time voted 100 guineas.

The settlement of the claims of those interested in the Ferry was a difficult matter. The Ferry, on the Middlesex side, was held of the Manor of Fulham, while that on the Surrey side was held of the Manor of Wimbledon. For their interests in the Ferry there were paid:

> "To the most noble Sarah Dutches dowager of Marlborough Lady of ye Manor of Wimbledon, For Her Grace's Interest in the Ferry from Putney to Fulham: £364 10 0.
> To the Rt. Rev. the Lord Bishop of London, Lord of ye Manor of Fulham, in right of ye Church. For his Lordships Interest in ye Horse Ferry from Fulham to Putney: £23 0 0."

In the case of the Manor of Fulham it was provided by the Act that the Bishop of London for the time being should for ever enjoy free passage over the Bridge for himself, his household at Fulham Palace, his horses, coaches, etc. Croker tells us in his "Walk" that passengers over the bridge were often much astonished at hearing the exclamation "Bishop!" shouted out by stentorian lungs of bricklayers, carpenters, and others, who might be going to the Palace, that being the password which carried exemption from toll.

Dr. Gibson, who was Bishop of London at the time of the erection of the bridge, was invited to furnish the Proprietors with a list of persons either attached to or having connection with the Palace, who were entitled to the "pass." From the Minute Book it appears that the following names were given:

> "My Lord Bishop, his lady and children; Dr. Bettesworth, brother-in-law to the bishop, his lady and children; Dr. Tyrwhit, son-in-law to the bishop, and his lady; his Lordship's chaplains, Drs. Cobden and Crow, with other officials, *viz.*, Mr. Skelton, register (*i.e.* registrar); Mr. Powlet, secretary; Mr. Thomas Powlet, receiver; Mr. Castilione, and sixteen domestics; five of Dr. Bettesworth's and a like number of Dr. Tyrwhit's, in all, thirty-four persons, the number of children not being mentioned."

Mr. Daniel Pettiward, Mr. William Skelton and Mr. Bennet Hamon Gotobed, joint tenants of the Ferry, were also compensated, receiving in all £8,000.

At the time of its extinction the average annual income yielded by the Ferry was about £400.

By the Act authorising the construction of the Bridge, the sum of £62 per annum was directed to be paid by the Proprietors, in perpetuity, to the churchwardens of Fulham and Putney, to be divided by them among the watermen, their widows and children, as a recompense to their fraternity for the loss of the Sunday ferry.

The Bridge was commenced about the end of March 1729 and completed in the remarkably short space of eight months. In the *Historical Register* for 31 March 1729, is the following:

> "The Workmen began to drive the Piles in the River of Thames, in order to the building of a Bridge from Putney to Fulham."

The *Weekly Journal*, or, *The British Gazetteer* for 19 April 1729, records:

> "The New Bridge that is building between Fulham and Putney, is begun in the Middle of the Thames, where the Great Arch of 28 Feet wide is to be erected, to be supported by 28 Piles, 14 of a Side. The Builders thought they should have driven the whole Number of Piles there by Saturday Evening, but could not exceed 19, the Ground proving harder than they expected; the Rammer for driving them is 1,500 Pound weight, and the Piles are forced in nine or ten Foot deep."

Fog's Weekly Journal for 9 August 1729, records:

> "The Bridge at Fulham goes on very fast, so that it is thought all the Piles will be driven by the latter end of September, and intirely finish'd by Christmas next. Many think it will be the finest Piece or Architecture of that kind, that ever was built. We are inform'd, that the Breadth of the River in that Place, when High water, is seven hundred feet."

The following is from *The Weekly Journal*, or, *The British Gazetteer* for 30 Aug. 1729:

> "The Bridge between Fulham and Putney is in such Forwardness, that the Scaffolds on which the Engines for driving the Piles are fix'd, are upon dry Ground at Low Water. The Stone and Brick work at the Ends

of the Bridge is almost completed.

A convenient Landing Place for the Ferry Boats, which are to be made use of till the Bridge is passable, is made at Brewer's Lane on the Putney side, and a Landing Place to answer the same is making below the Bridge on Fulham Side. And we hear that the Subscribers for Building the said Bridge being made acquainted with the Accident that happen'd to a Barge passing under the said Bridge, through the Carelessness of the Bargemen, consulted with several able and experienced Men of that Profession in Relation to the Navigation of the River; and by their Approbation and Advice, the said Subscribers have caused two more wide Passages or Openings to be made under the Bridge on Putney Side in the Channel or deepest Part of the River, through which the largest Barge may with Ease and Safety go through, the Position of the Bridge in that Place, answering exactly to the Ebbing and Flowing of the Tide. And as the Barges and Lighters have been used always to pass and repass that way, the said Bargemen are of opinion the Bridge will not in the least incommode the Navigation, otherwise than by obliging them to strike their Masts when passing under the same."

Fulham Bridge. From a photograph by Mr. H. Ambridge, 1868

The Country Journal, or, *The Craftsman* for 18 Oct. 1729, reports:

"Thursday the last Pile of the Bridge between Fulham and Putney was drove, the first being drove the 5th of April last. The Thames where the Bridge is built is about 800 Feet wide, and about 600 Feet of the Bridge is cover'd with Plank already; the Planks are Oak of four Inches thick, upon which is laid Loam four Inches deep, upon that Chalk six Inches, and on that, Gravel 10 Inches thick."

The erection of the Bridge was not unattended by mishaps. Three are thus reported in contemporary journals:

From *Fog's Weekly Journal*, 16 Aug. 1729:

> "The Barge that was sunk last Week by striking against the Piles that are drove for erecting a Bridge from Fulham to Putney, as she was going up the River, was last Saturday Morning weigh'd and carried up with the Tide to Barn Elms. She belonged to Mr. Thomas Haley, of Henly upon Thames, and was loaded with Rags, Soap, Sugar, Salt, Plums, etc. The Damage sustain'd in the whole, is computed at £200."

From *Fog's Weekly Journal*, 23 August 1729:

> "On Tuesday Morning about 8 o'Clock, a Barge laden with Timber from Hinman's, for the use of Putney Bridge, overset near Cuper's Stairs, when a Piece of Timber, of about 2 Tun weight, fell upon the neck of one John Somerton, which so miserably bruised him, that the Blood sprang out of his Nose and Mouth with great Violence, after the Surgeon had dress'd his Wounds, he was by Order of Mr. Philips the Carpenter, conveyed on a Bier to St. Thomas's Hospital, where his Life is despair'd of. At the same time another Labourer receiv'd a desperate Bruise on his Right Arm by the said Piece of Timber."

From the *Country Journal*, or, *The Craftsman*, 30 August 1729:

> "Last week some Workmen who were at Work on the New Bridge at Fulham, by Accident let a large Piece of Timber fall into the River, which happening to light upon a Twickenham Boat that was passing thro' the Lock at the same Time, struck the Head of the Boat short off, and split it quite through the Middle, but the Lives of six Men that were in it were saved by two Watermen, who seeing their Distress, went immediately with their Boat to assist them."

On 6 Oct. 1729 the Committee reported on the completion of the Bridge. In the following month four tollmen were engaged at a salary of ten shillings a week. Each man was provided with a coat, hat, staff and lanthorn.

At 9 a.m. on Friday, 14 Nov. 1729, the bridge was thrown open for the use of foot passengers. At a meeting at the Lottery Office, held on 13 Nov., the secretary, Mr. Eden, was ordered "to be at Fulham to-morrow morning at 9 of the Clock" to put the tollmen on their duty, and to give notice to the Churchwardens of both parishes to warn the ferrymen not to ply;

> "and that he do fix a Paper at each end of the Bridge giving Publick Notice of the Proceedings of ye Proprietors this Day relating to this Affair, and that he do Publish in ye News Papers an Account of the Toll as settled by Act of Parliament."

The following" appears in *Fog's Weekly Journal* for 15 Nov. 1729:

> "A Deed of Assignment of the Tolls of the Bridge, lately built between Fulham and Putney, was executed yesterday at the Lottery Office in Whitehall, by a great number of the Commissioners appointed by the Acts of Parliament, the Proprietors of the said Bridge, and the persons to whom the Tolls are assigned in Trust for the said Proprietors.
> Several Gentlemen have already rode over the Bridge on Horseback, all the covering is laid on except the Gravel, and the whole will be completed within a Fortnight.
> Colonel Armstrong, who lately made a survey of the Bridge at the desire of the Commissioners, at their last meeting, reported to them at their General Meeting held yesterday, that the said Bridge is built agreeable to the Directions in the Acts of Parliament; and that the same is performed in a judicious and workmanlike Manner, and in many Respects exceeding the Conditions of the Contract formally made between the said Commissioners and the Proprietors.
> The following pontage is to be paid for Passage over the New Bridge between Fulham and Putney, viz.:

		s.	d.
A Coach, Chariot, *etc.* drawn by six or more Horses		2s.	0d.
ditto by four Horses		1	6
ditto by less than four Horses		1	0
Every Wagon, Wain, Dray, Carr, Cart or Carriage, drawn by four or more Horses or Oxen		1	0
Every Horse, Mule or Ass, not drawing			2
Every Foot Passenger on Sundays			1
And every other Day			½
Every drove of Oxen or neat Cattle per score, and proportionable for greater or less numbers		1	0
Every drove of Calves, Hogs, Sheep, or Lambs per score, and proportionable for more or less			6

An account of the money arising by the tolls is to be given in to each House of Parliament once a year, within 20 days after the Opening of the Session.

There appeared in *Fog's Weekly Journal* for 22 Nov. 1729, and in some other newspapers, the following account of the crossing of the Bridge by the Prince of Wales:

> "The Same Day (Saturday 15 Nov.) his Royal Highness the Prince went to hunt in Richmond Park, and in going thither and returning back, passed over the new Bridge between Fulham and Putney in a Coach and six, with two other Coaches in his Retinue, attended by his Guards, which was the first Time of any Coaches passing over the same: And his Royal Highness was pleased to order five Guineas for the Workmen. It would appear, however, that an officer attending Lord Cobham's regiment of horse then quartered at Fulham to attend the King and Prince at such times as they may go over the bridge, requested that the Proprietors would allow both horse and foot to pass over the bridge without paying toll, in consideration of the sum of £15 paid yearly by His Majesty for the passage of the troops over the ferry. This was accordingly agreed to, but the secretary and toll-men were to take an account of the number so passing."

The Bridge was opened, for traffic generally, on Saturday, 29 Nov. 1729.

At a Court Baron in 1730, the following presentment was made in respect to an encroachment by the Proprietors:

> "We of the Homage present that the Proprietors of the new bridge between this town and Putney or some of them have caused to be taken in a piece of Wast ground on the west side of the entrance of the said bridge being parcel of this Manor of Fulham in prejudice of the rights of the said Manor and to the great hindrance of the waterman plying there and drawing up their boats as usual (vizt.) from north to south, next the entrance of the said bridge, 80 feet in length, from north to south facing the Swan ale-house, 64 feet in length, to the north abutting on the way leading to the said Swan ale-house 40 feet and on the south next the river of Thames 14 feet in breadth."

Old Fulham Bridge was 786 feet in length, or, measuring from gate to gate, 805 feet 6
inches. Its width between the parapets was 23 feet, divided into a carriage-way of 19 feet, and one foot-way of 4 feet. At the sides of the bridge were curious angular recesses to enable passengers to take refuge when vehicles were passing. The Bridge had a clear waterway of 700 feet. There were 26 openings or locks. The centre opening, which was the largest, measuring thirty feet, was known as Walpole's Lock.

There were two toll houses, a small one on the east side at the Putney end, and a large one, known as the Bridge House, at the Fulham end. The roof of the latter spanned the roadway. It included the residence of the manager, office and toll house. These were completed in March, 1730. The first meeting at the Bridge House was held on 8 Oct. 1730. The toll houses were built of red brick, but, in later times, were, with the exception of the roof, whitewashed over. On the tops of the toll houses bells were hung so that, in case of disorder, the toll men might go to each other's assistance. These two bells, which existed down to the demolition of the Bridge, were occasionally used for this purpose. They were also rung nightly when the day tollman went off and the night tollman came on duty.

On 29 Nov. 1729 it was ordered:

"That the collectors of the tolls have hats and gowns provided for them, which gowns are to be of good substantial cloth, of a deep blue colour and lined with blue stuff or shalloon. Also that they have staves with brass or copper heads, and that Mr. Mann [Clerk to the Proprietors] be desired to order and direct in what manner they shall be made and to provide ye same."

Doubtless in the early years of old Fulham Bridge the bells and the staves were often brought into requisition. Wimbledon and Putney Heath were then dreary and dangerous wastes, the resort of highwaymen and footpads.

The Minute Books of the Bridge Committee and the newspapers of the day furnish us with many curious details of violent scenes on old Fulham Bridge. A few instances may be noticed. The *London Evening Post* for Saturday 10 Jan. to Tues. 12 Jan. 1730 gives the following case:

"A few days since Robert Platt, a Waterman of Putney having insulted one of the Toll Collectors of the new Bridge there, was taken up by the Lord Chief Justice Raymond's Tipstaff, by virtue of a Warrant granted by his Lordship, upon the Oath of the said Toll Collector; and the said Platt is now confined in the King's Bench Prison in Southwark."

On 17 Nov. 1739 the Committee met in order to examine into a "riot and assault" committed by three officers of the Army, "on the persons of the tollmen belonging to the said bridge, by beating them in a most cruel and inhuman manner." At a subsequent meeting it was resolved, upon their making an apology and paying twenty guineas compensation, not to prosecute them "in consideration of their youth and the ruin that might follow in case of prosecution against them."

The following we quote from *The London Evening Post* for Sat. 6 Dec. to Tues. 9 Dec. 1740:

> "On Thursday last came on at the King's Bench Bar, at Westminster, the Trial of the Toll-gatherers of Fulham Bridge, for a violent assault, and abuse to the Hon. Miss Carylls, their servants and company, in coming over the said Bridge in July last, because they would not pay for more Horses than really belonged to them and their attendants and, the Matter being clearly proved the Jury found Haines, the chief offender then try'd, guilty of the said Assault particularly on Mr. Goolde; and being to be try'd the next day for another Assault and Battery upon Mr. Daniel Willmott of the Golden Cross at Charing-Cross, committed the same Day and Time in July last, his Counsel mov'd for Mercy till next Term to try whether he could make it up, and that he might be brought into open Court and ask Pardon of the Ladies and the company which the Ladies' chief Counsel, Mr. Kettlebey, came into, the rather as he believed the Ladies and the company's chief Aim was to make the Fellow an Example only for the Benefit of the Publick, and to the deterring all others from such Treatment for the future, for the Safety and Satisfaction of all Passengers who have occasion to travel that way."

On 9 Aug. 1752 the Committee

> "Paid Expenses at sending two Irish Fellows to Clerkenwell new jail for assaulting and Beating the Toll Man on his Duty on Sunday 9 July 12s. 6d."

On 25 January 1755 the Committee sanctioned

> "Expences at taking 2 Men before Justice Beaver and carring one of them to Bridewell that knocked James Merritt down and otherwise used him very ill 5s. 6d.

> "Paid the Constable for his Trouble in the above affair 5s. 0d.

On 8 Feb. 1755 the Committee

> "Paid Justice Beaver at Swearing self (*i.e.* the Clerk) and Toll Men, and his trouble in Committing one of the Persons to Bridewell that abused the Toll Men 5s. 0d."

In Oct. 1758 the Committee

> "Paid Mr. Thornton Constable for taking ye Man into custody that assaulted and Beat Brick on his duty 1s. 0d."

The Bridge House From a photograph by Mr. H. Ambridge, 1868

In the earlier years of the Bridge the takings amounted to about £40 per week. Some of the old Cash Books are preserved at the Fulham Public Library and others at the Public Record Office. The receipts are entered week by week, as paid in by the collectors. The journal Entry Books were kept by the tollmen. Here the receipts are entered day by day under the several heads "coaches," "chairs," "wagons," " horses," "mules," "asses," "foot passengers," "oxen," "neat cattle," "calves," "hogs," "sheep," "lambs," etc. On 8 Feb. 1740, there passed over Fulham Bridge 12 six-horse coaches, 3 four-horse coaches, 24 coaches drawn by less than four horses, 334 horses, mules and asses, 15 hogs, 1052 foot passengers, etc., the receipts for the day being £7. 12. 4½. Foot passengers paid a halfpenny each on week-days and one penny on Sundays. On Sundays the foot passengers enormously exceeded in numbers those on week-days. Thus, on the third Sunday in May 1742, 922 people crossed to Putney and 722 crossed to Fulham, while on the preceding Saturday the numbers were, respectively, 145 and 77. The accounts for 1752, the year in which the "new style" was adopted, show a jump from Wednesday 2 Aug. to Thursday 14 Aug. The King, who was in the habit of paying an annual composition of £100, was actually allowed a deduction of £1. 10s. in respect to the eleven days omitted from the calendar!

The Bridge House. From a pen and ink sketch made, shortly before demolition, by an inmate of Munster House Asylum

The receipts for the latter half of 1752 show:

Rec^d his Majesty's Composition money to the 17 of Jan.	£46 1 6
By eleven days deducted for the new stile	1 10 0
By poundage deducted as usual	2 8 6
	50 0 0

On 25 May 1767, when George III reviewed the Guards on Wimbledon Common, the receipts amounted to no less than £63. 10. 7. In later times, on exceptional occasions, the takings rose to as much as £100 in a day. Mr. Joseph Roe notes in his "Diary"

under date 4 July 1807:

> "Lord Spencer gave a Publick breakfast at Wimbledon this day and a great concourse of Nobility went over Fulham Bridge from Coaches and 6 to single Horses."

On 10 June 1811, when the Prince Regent (afterwards George IV) reviewed 28,000 men on Wimbledon Common, the amount taken exceeded £100. Another red-letter day was Saturday 20 July 1867, when the Sultan of Turkey (Abdul Aziz Khan) and members of the English Royal family, reviewed the Volunteers on the same Common.

One or two attempts were made to buy up and rebuild the old Bridge, but they failed. In 1851 an unsuccessful attempt was made to launch a company for the purpose of

> "Making and establishing and maintaining the bridge and pier and works . . . to be called by the name of the Putney and Fulham New Bridge and Pier Company or by such other name as may be adopted by the Provisional Directors."

Fulham Bridge, showing site of the landing stage of the old Ferry.
From a print published by Robert Sayer, circa 1780

The proposed capital was £80,000. An Act of Parliament was obtained to enable the promoters to carry out their plans. The Subscribers' Agreement, dated 29 Dec. 1851, shows subscriptions in the names of ten gentlemen, representing £64,500, the amount actually paid being £3,175. Nothing further is known as to the movement.

Originally the Bridge was lighted by oil lamps fixed on upright posts. These were removed in 1845, when gas was introduced. In 1870-72 the three central locks were removed, and in their place an iron span, 70 feet wide, was inserted. In the centre of old Fulham Bridge was an iron plate which marked the boundary line between Fulham and Putney. It bore the names of the churchwardens of the two parishes and the date 1873.

In 1870 the Bridge suffered material damage by collision. In 1877 the Metropolis Toll Bridges Act was passed, giving power to the late Metropolitan Board of Works to purchase and free from toll the bridges in the Metropolis, and to rebuild those of Battersea, Fulham and Hammersmith. On the 26 June 1880 the Prince of Wales declared the three bridges free of toll. In Nov. 1880, the necessary Parliamentary notices were given and plans deposited for the erection, by the Metropolitan Board of Works, of a new bridge between Fulham and Putney. Old Fulham Bridge was closed on 29 May 1886. The work of demolition was at once begun and completed before the close of the year.

Before we deal with the new Putney Bridge - for the name, Fulham Bridge, is nowadays never heard - we propose to give a few miscellaneous notes relating to the old structure. Where not otherwise described, the quotations are taken from the Cash Books:

1729. From *The London Evening Post*, for Thursday 25 Sept. to Sat. 27 Sept. 1729:

> "On Wednesday last a Barge upwards of 100 Foot long, with 37 Chaldron of Coals and other Goods, was sunk at the New Bridge at Fulham."

1730. From *The London Evening Post* for Sat. 24 Jan. to Tues. 27 Jan. 1730:

> "The Shares for the New Bridge at Fulham of £1,000 each, of which £740 is only paid in, have been sold for £1,000, and are now sold for 1,000 guineas per Share."

1733. Jan. 5. Subscribed towards ye New Organ that has been lately Erected in Fulham Church £10. 0. 0.

1742: In the minutes of a meeting, held at the Bridge, 11 Sept. is the following:

> "Mr. Bruce sent a Haunch of Venison, several Gentlemen who generally attend, were sent to, only the above mentioned came."

The "above mentioned" were five in number.

On 13 Aug., 1743:

> "It was agreed to take on Mr. Haines (tollman) again Tho' he had been Formally Discharg'd, he Promising he would Behave himself well, and endeavour to Correct his Passion and Heat which he owned he had been guilty of."

As Haines subsequently received a present of a guinea, it may be assumed that he kept his promise.

1749:

Mar. 30.	Paid for Whitewashing the Office and Toll Room	5s. 0d.
Apl. 1.	Paid the four toll Men and Mr. Grier their wages	£2. 11. 6.
Apl. 4.	Paid Mr. Adderly for a Cask of Oyl as p. bill and receipt	£3. 2. 0.
Apl. 4.	Paid for 10 penny Post Letters to Summon the Committee	10.
	Paid for a Quarter's Drawback due Lady Day last	8s. 8d.
	Paid the Higler a quarter's Ditto as p. bill on ye File	£1. 10. 4.

A higgler was one who carried provisions about for sale, a hawker. At the present day, in Kent, Sussex and elsewhere, the men who go round to the cottages and small farms, to buy up the ducks, hens, eggs, etc., to sell again, are known as higglers.

Apl. 10.	Paid half a year's Poors Rates to the Parish of Fulham	37. 10. 0.
	Paid Towards the Subscription of Epsom Races p. order of Ld. Carpenter	3. 3. 0.
Apl. 25.	Paid at Advertiseing a List of the Horses to run at Epsom	6. 0.
May 6.	Paid an Assistant Man at the Epsom Races	3. 6.
	Gave the Toll Men to Drink at the above Race Week	2. 6.
May 9.	Paid half a years Land Tax to the Parish of Fulham	£55. 0. 0.
May 27.	Paid Wateridge at Mr. Dowdeswell Morris and Lawes Surveying ye Bridge	1s. 0d.
June 9.	Paid the Window Tax for the year 1748	£1. 8. 0.
May —	Paid at three times Advertising the Breakfast at Putney Bowling Green House	6. 0.
	Paid at Advertising the Prince's Plate to be Row'd for, *etc.*	2. 3.

July 8.	Paid a Quarter's Drawback to yᵉ Higler for his Cart due Midsum last	£2. 2. 4.
July 9.	Paid for takeing up a Buckett that had lay 2 years in the Thames and very little ye wors	6d.
Aug. 5.	Paid for paint and painting both Toll Houses	£2. 10. 6.
Aug. 26.	Gave the Carpenters to Drink at Working at the Bridge this week	1. 6.
Aug. 29.	Paid for Russia Drabb to make 2 Night Toll Bedds	8. 0.
Sep. 16.	Paid Wateridge, etc. at takeing a Hundred pounds in Silver to the Bank	1. 0.
Oct. 7.	Paid for Chocolate at a meeting of yᵉ Committee	1. 0.
Oct. 31.	Paid for a night watch coate for the Toll Men	£2. 0. 0.
Nov. 2.	Paid at takeing out a Warrant for a Waterman for Working over on a Sunday	1. 6d.

The Sunday Ferry, it will be remembered, was abolished by the Act. There were frequent breaches of the law.

Dec. 30. Gave the Duke of Newcastle's Groom for his Christ. Box 10s. 6d.

1749-50

Feb. 16. Paid for a Box of Pounce. 9d.

1750

May 12. Paid for two new Bedticks and a pair of Blanketts for Mr. Madgwick and the Toll Men £2. 8s. 6d.
Dec. 31. Paid Expences for Horses and Servᵗˢ at the George at a meeting of the Committee 5s. 6d.

1750-1

Feb. 28. Paid Mr. Portman at Receiveing the King's Compn money 10s. 6d.

The Composition money was the payment of £100 annually to free his Majesty and his household across the bridge.

1751

Oct. 9. By an alowance to Ceely p. Order of the Committee for his Giving half a Guinea in Change instead of a sixpence 10s. 0d.

1752

Apl. 13. Gave the Tollmen to drink being the first £10 day 1s. 0d.

A £10 day was a rare occurrence, hence this curious custom.

July 29. Paid Mr. Anderson for the Milestone as p. bill, etc. £3. 4s. 0d.

The milestone stood at the foot of the Bridge: on it was fixed a lamp.

1753

Dec. 29. Gave the 3 Blind men being Fulham waits 1s. 0d.

1754

Oct. 8. a Leven (eleven) penny post letters to the Proprietors 11d.

1755

Dec. 31. Gave the two Blind Fiddlers 1s. 0d.

1757

The "Gentleman's Magazine" for January 1757, records:
"Sun. 9 Jan. One of the piers of Putney Bridge gave way, being pressed by the great load of ice against it, and sunk about four feet. A coach with four gentlemen in it was passing over it at the time, but received no other damage than being much frightened."

1758

Apl. - Paid John Carter for a Thousand of Printed papers for the Tollmen 5s.

1759

Oct. - Paid for a Night Watch coat for the Tollmen £1. 15s. 0d.

The picturesque old Bridge was a favourite subject with

artists. One of the best known paintings of it is that by Mr. G. F. Winkfield. In the Art Gallery of the Corporation of Manchester is an oil painting, 3 ft. by 4 ft., entitled "Old Putney Bridge," from the Fulham side of the Thames at low water, by Mr. C. Napier Hemy, purchased by the Corporation in 1883.

An account of the old Bridge would hardly be complete without the inclusion of a few of the more notable anecdotes which have gathered around its memory. Sir Arthur Blomfield, in his lecture on "The Olden Times of Fulham," repeats the following:

> "An amusing anecdote is related of a nobleman, who, not long after the erection of the bridge, was invited to the Palace by the Bishop. He drove down in his coach and six, and, finding that he had reached Fulham an hour earlier than he intended, he directed his coachman to drive backwards and forwards over the new bridge that he might enjoy the view from it, before proceeding to the Palace. His surprise may be imagined when he found he had to pay a good round sum for his amusement."

Each journey across, for a coach and six, was, as we have seen, half a crown. We are afraid this anecdote is a myth.

The following paragraph appeared a few years back in the "West London Observer":

> "A rather amusing occurrence took place at the toll-house of Fulham Bridge on Thursday night, the 24th inst. An elderly gentleman, who had partaken rather freely of the cup that not only cheers but also inebriates, wished to pass over the bridge, but strongly objected to pay the toll demanded of him, and was walking off, declaring his intention of not being victimized out of a halfpenny, when the tollman, as is his custom in such cases, finding he could not procure the required toll, took the gentleman's hat off his head instead, but discovering it to be rather heavy, turned it over, and on giving it a smart tap on the crown, out fell a splendidly glossy wig, which had come off with the hat. It is unnecessary to add that the gentleman, finding himself suddenly bald, immediately paid the toll, and amid the laughter of a small crowd, which by that time had collected, and heedless of the earnest entreaties to leave them a lock, quickly took his wig and hat and himself off."

One night, in the month of April 1842, Daniel Good, a coachman in service at Putney, hastily passed through the toll gate, throwing to the collector, as he went, a coachman's coat which he requested the man would keep till his return. Good never did return, for, in the words of Mr. C. H. Ross, when writing his biography, "he passed, later on, through Calcraft's hands, and was choked to death at Newgate." This was for the murder of his sweetheart, Jane Jones, in a stable in Putney Park Lane. It was while hurrying away from the scene of this crime that he threw his coat to the tollman.

The following anecdote we cull from Mr. Chasemore's "History and Associations of Old Fulham Bridge":

"A few years ago the bridge possessed a cat, which would watch under the bridge at low tide, and when she saw a fish, plunge into the water after it, and rarely miss her mark. One night she made her appearance in the toll-house, covered with mud, with an enormous eel twisted round her body, and her teeth firmly fixed in its head."

The site of the old Toll House is now a wharf belonging to the Fulham Vestry.

Fulham Bridge and Aqueduct, from the Putney shore.
From a photograph by Mr. H. Ambridge

CHAPTER XIV: NEW PUTNEY BRIDGE

The handsome stone Bridge, which now connects Fulham with Putney, was erected between the years 1882-86. It was built on the site formerly occupied by the <u>aqueduct of the Chelsea Waterworks Company</u>.

The new Bridge spans the river by five segmental arches. The width between the parapets is 44 feet, divided into a carriage-way of 25 feet, and two footpaths, each 9 ft. 6 ins. wide.

The centre arch has a span of 144 feet, with a rise of 19 feet 3 inches, and a headway of 20 feet above Trinity high-water mark. The arches on either side have spans of 129 feet, and headways of 17 feet, while the two shore arches have spans of 112 feet, and headways of 13 feet 9 inches.

The width of the river between the abutments is 700 feet, and there is a clear waterway under the arches of the Bridge of 626 feet. The entire structure is of granite. The quantity of stone employed in its construction was about 300,000 cubic feet, of which a portion was obtained from Cornwall and Aberdeen, and portions from the Prince of Wales's quarries in the former county.

On the Fulham side of the river a new rising approach was formed from High Street at its junction with Church Street, partly through the Vicarage garden and close to Fulham Church. The total length of this approach is 210 yards; its width is 50 feet, and its gradient 1 in 35.

On the Putney side a new approach was formed in a direct line from Putney High Street in lieu of the narrow and circuitous approach to the old Bridge. Its gradient is 1in 35, and its width varies from 52 to 70 feet. In consequence of the improved headway of the arches of the new Bridge, the approaches had to be carried to a higher level, and it was thus necessary to raise Windsor Street to meet the new approach from the High Street. At the foot of this approach a new draw dock from the river was formed, in place of the one previously existing adjacent to the old Bridge.

The contract for the whole of the permanent works for the new Bridge was let to Mr. John Waddell (now Messrs. Waddell and

Sons), of Edinburgh and London, for £240,433 19s. The Bridge was commenced in the summer of 1882.

The foundations of Putney Bridge are carried into the London clay to an average depth of about 24 feet below the bed of the river. To get in the foundations of the piers, a timber dam of single piles was first driven down to a depth of 37 feet below Trinity high-water mark, enclosing a space around the site of each pier. After the water was pumped out from this enclosure, wrought iron caissons were built up within the dam and sunk down to the intended depth of the pier foundations by excavating the ground from within them. Each caisson was formed with a double skin of wrought iron, with a space of 3 feet 6 inches between, and this was filled with concrete before lowering. Three of these caissons were sunk under each pier, and the spaces left within them were excavated, and after the caissons were sunk to the required depth, filled in solid with concrete, upon which the masonry of the piers was built.

Putney Bridge. From a photograph by Mr. T. S. Smith, 1896

The memorial stone was laid by the Prince and Princess of Wales on the 12 July 1884, on the west side of the southern abutment, and was bedded at a level of about 18 inches above Trinity high-water mark. It is inscribed:

"This stone was laid by their Royal Highnesses the Prince and Princess of Wales, 12th July 1884"

The Bridge was designed, and its erection superintended, by the late Sir Joseph W. Bazalgette, C.B., engineer, and Mr. Edward Bazalgette, assistant engineer. On Saturday, 29 May 1886, the Prince of Wales formally opened the new Bridge.

The Vestry of Fulham have, from 1 December 1887, maintained one half of the road and footways of Putney Bridge.

CHAPTER XV: THE OLD TOWN

Leaving the Bridge, we will now visit the "Old Town," starting on our journey at the south end of the High Street. From what we have said regarding the meaning of the name "Fulham," it is clear that the settlers who first inhabited and named the district were Anglo-Saxons. When or under what circumstances they came, we know not. As the landing of the Saxons at Ebbsfleet, near Sandwich, is recorded to have occurred in the year 449, and as the name "Fulanham" makes its first appearance circa 691, it is clear that the settlement must have been effected between these two dates.

Naturally, the first inhabitants dwelt by the river shore, where they founded their "town," a name which, singularly enough, is retained to the present day to designate the oldest part of the parish, the High Street and the adjacent thoroughfares. The Anglo-Saxon equivalent of "town" is *tún*, which primarily means a fence, a homestead or village (cf. týnan, to enclose). The old Town was, then, the little collection of tenements enclosed or fenced in, cut off from the neighbouring thickets and woods. Gradually, as the population increased, the Town was extended, roads were formed and other settlements made at greater distances from the river, such as Parson's Green, Walham Green, North End, etc.

Bowack, writing in 1705, gives, in his "Antiquities of Middlesex," the following description of the parish:

> "It seems at present to be in a declining and languishing condition, not but it boasts of a greater number of houses and inhabitants than was in it formerly; but the buildings are not so magnificent as those more antient nor is here the many honourable and worthy families at present which us'd to reside upon this spot. It has been much augmented in number of houses of late for the dwellings of the tradesmen and such as live by their labour; who are chiefly gardeners, farmers, husbandmen and watermen; not that it wants good edifices and considerable families to ennoble it as will appear by and by. The houses of the common people are commonly neat and well built of brick, and from the gate of the Queen's Road (*i.e.* the King's Road) run along on both sides of the

way almost as far as the church. Also from the Thames side into the Town (*i.e.* the High Street) stands an entire range of buildings; and upon the passage leading to the Church call'd Church Lane (*i.e.* Church Row) are several very handsome airy houses. But the buildings of this place run furthest toward the north, extending themselves in a street through which lyes the road a very considerable way towards Hammersmith (*i.e.* the North End Road), besides there are several other handsome buildings towards the east call'd the back lane (*i.e.* Hurlingham Road), and a great number of gardeners' houses centr'd in the several remote parts of the parish. This place being so conveniently seated both for passage of citizens and considerable persons, where (as at its neighbour Putney and several other villages upon the Thames) they are handsomely accommodated with good lodgings to the great advantage of the inhabitants."

Bowack further tells us that, though the Town was conveniently and pleasantly situated, it was, in the opinion of some, not very healthy, a "great part of the buildings standing upon a wet, moist sort of ground."

In spite, however, of Bowack's condemnation, Fulham was proverbial for its healthfulness. Persons used to come here to "take the air," such was its renown. The *London Evening Post* for Tuesday, 1 April to Thursday, 3 April 1740, contains the following:

"On Tuesday his Royal Highness the Prince of Wales took the Air about Fulham."

Bishop Porteus, in his "Brief Account of Three Residences" (1808), describes the village as a very indifferent one, ill-built and ill-inhabited. He adds:

"But the pretty cottages dispersed among the lanes and gardens around it, and still more the long range of handsome mansions stretching along the banks of the Thames, from the Episcopal Palace on the west to Lady Lonsdale's on the east, are very beautiful and desirable residences."

Norris Brewer, in his "London and Middlesex" (1816) observes:

"The village of Fulham consists of several streets, the principal of which is nearly half a mile in length. The domestic buildings have some variety of style; but, in the more populous parts, they are chiefly of a humble character, and many exhibit the low and mean mode of construction which prevailed in the time of the first James."

The Old Town, which has now lost most of its former characteristics, was anciently at a much lower level than it now is, a fact which can be attested by inspecting the ancient tenements still existing in the High Street, to enter which the visitor has to descend a few steps to reach the rooms, which were once level with the roadway.

CHAPTER XVI: HIGH STREET (GENERAL)

To trace the beginnings of the High Street, we must go back to very remote times, to days certainly anterior to the Conquest of England by the Normans, for its ancient appellation, Bear Street, affords evidence that the way must have been named when Anglo-Saxon was a living tongue.

Before proceeding to discuss the name or the early history of Bear Street, we may say a few words regarding its original course. Prior to the building of the old Bridge, Bear Street ran up from the river shore by the Ferry for a short distance north-easterly and then almost due north to the high ground by Colehill, where the way divided, one lane trending north-west to Hammersmith (*i.e.* the Fulham Palace Road) and the other almost due east to the village of Wandon or Walham Green (*i.e.* the Fulham Road). If we look at the map we shall see that Bear Street ran more or less parallel with the north-eastern and north-western reaches of the Moat of the Manor House and that its northern end, at Bishop's Avenue, was coterminous with the corresponding limit of that watercourse, which here turns south-westwards. Bear Street thus included what is now the southern portion of the Fulham Palace Road. When we come to consider the name "Bear Street," we shall see the significance of this circumstance.

When, in 1729, Fulham Bridge was built, that portion of the way, which lay between the river and Church Row, was designated Bridge Street, leaving Bear Street to consist of the remaining part.

About the close of the last century the name Bear Street died out. <u>The name High Street, which came into vogue</u>, was applied to the old thoroughfare between Church Row and Holcroft's, the remaining portion of Bear Street, northwards, being included in the old road to Hammersmith. When, in 1886, the new Bridge was built, somewhat to the westward of the old one, involving the demolition of the greater part of the western side of Bridge Street, in order to form the new approach, the name High Street was applied to the whole of the old thoroughfare, Bridge Street ceasing, in name, to exist.

Top of the High Street. From a photograph by
Mr. J. Dugdale, 1894

We will now deal with the etymology of the name "Bear Street." Various guesses at the origin of the name have been made. It has been popularly supposed that, in some way or other, the appellation was associated with "bear," the animal. Why, it has been urged, may not some Bishop of London, in days more barbarous than our own, have possessed a bear-pit in a secluded corner of his grounds abutting on the old High Street? A bear-garden was once situated at Bankside, close to the precinct of the Clink Liberty and very near to the Palace of the Bishop of Winchester. To the present day there exist, in witness of this fact, not only Bear Gardens, but also Bear Lane, in Southwark. Or, failing the discovery of the remains of a bear-pit in the grounds of Fulham Palace, why might not the thoroughfare have been indebted for its name to some ancient inn whose sign was "The Bear"? This is not an unknown mode of street nomenclature. Thus, for instance, there is the "Rampant Horse" at Norwich, and the whole street is called simply "Rampant Horse Street." Inns were often named from the badges of great men, whose retainers or late servants were perhaps the landlords. The "Bear" is well known as meaning "Warwick." Did the Earls of Warwick ever honour the High Street by their abode in it, or was there ever in it a hostelry styled "The Bear"? To all these conjectural questions a negative answer must be returned. No inn, no badge, no great family with a bear for a crest, can be found to account for the name.

Another suggestion has been made: can "Bear" mean "barley"? From very early times Fulham was famous for its inns. Ale-drinking was, we know, dear to our Saxon ancestors. May not therefore those of them who lived in Fulham have called the chief street of their Town "barley street" from the neighbouring fields of grain which they cultivated to produce their favourite beverage? In Anglo-Saxon a bear was *bera*, and barley was *bere*, both of which words, in Middle English, become *bere*, while, later still, both merge in *bear*. They cannot therefore be philologically distinguished. Fortunately, however, we are able, through the evidence afforded by the Court Rolls of the Manor, to set the origin of the name Bear Street completely at rest. A careful examination of these records has revealed an unknown and hitherto unsuspected orthography in the shape of "Bury Street."

We cannot, perhaps, better illustrate the change (1) from Bury Street to Bere Street and (2) from Bere Street to Bear Street, than by quoting from the Rolls the following instances of the use of the name between 1391, when it first appears, in the form Bury Street, and 1682, when Beare Street or Bear Street had become the recognized spelling of the name:

1391. Burystrete
1391-92. Berestrete
1393-94. Burystrete
1394. Burystrete and Berestret
1395. Burystrete
1397. Burystrete
1402. Burystrete
1404. Berestreet
1422. Berestret
1425. Burystret and Berestret
1443. Berestrete
1447. Berestret
1477. Berestret

1496. Berestrete
1507. Berestret
1513. Burystrete
1516. Berestrete
1517. Berestrete
1518. Burystrete
1519. Berestrete
1519. Burystrete
1523. Berestret
1523. Burystrete
1525. Berestrete
1526. Berestret
1552. Burystrete
1566. Berestrete
1567. Berestrete
1570. Barestrete
1572. Berestrete
1573. Berestrete
1574. Berestrete *alias* Burystrete
1577. Beerestrete
1578. Berestret
1606. Bearestreete
1625. Bearestreet
1629. Bearestreete
1645. Beerestreete
1657. Bearestreete
1659. Beerestreete
1661. Bearestreete
1665. Barestreete
1667. Barestreete
1682. Bearestreet

This list is instructive. Bury Street is, we clearly see, the most ancient form of the name, but, even towards the close of the fourteenth century, the orthography Bere Street had made its appearance, while, in the next hundred years, it altogether superseded the older spelling. In the sixteenth century, out of twenty-one quotations, the expiring form Bury occurs but six times, ceasing to be used at all after 1574. At first "Bere" was undoubtedly pronounced as a dissyllable, precisely like "Bury." Later on, when the meaning and the older orthography were falling out of men's minds, "Bere" became a word of one syllable. This is evident from the 1570 quotation of "Bare" Street, where, also, we see that the "r" was already influencing the vowel-change. The 1574 quotation of "Berestrete alias Burystrete" is valuable, since it conclusively proves that the two forms designated the same street, while, at the same time, it suggests to us that the amplification "alias Burystrete" was made by the scribe, not to show the then current spelling, but by way of preserving and of recalling to mind what was, even then, a form which had become practically obsolete. The transition from Bere to Bear was probably due to some popular or fanciful etymology at a date (circa 1606) when the original form of the name had become completely lost.

The question which therefore presents itself for solution is the meaning of Bury Street. As to this there can be no doubt. "Bury," originally a dative of the Anglo-Saxon *burh* or *burg*, meant, in very early times, a fort or an enclosed or fortified place. Then it came to mean a manor house or large farm, a sense in which it still survives in many place-names, such as Shrewsbury, Canterbury, Aldermanbury, Bury St. Edmund's, Hamburg, Bergen, Burgos, etc.

The reason for calling the main thoroughfare of our Town by the name of Bury Street is perfectly obvious. From the earliest time the Manor House has stood within the shelter of the ancient Moat. In those unsettled days, when the country had scarcely come to acknowledge a single ruler, there could have been little practical distinction between "fortress" or "castle," the primary sense of "bury" and "manor house" or "court," its subsequent meaning. What, then, could be more natural than that the one street of ancient Fulham, which ran contiguous to the north-eastern and north-western reaches of the Moat of the Manor House, should be named Bury Street, that is, the street which lay by the side of the Bury or Court House of the Bishop?

An alternative appellation for Bear Street was Fulham Street, but the latter name seems to have been sometimes used in a less restricted sense. Bear Street was the road from the Ferry to Bishop's Avenue, while Fulham Street virtually designated the whole of the old Town.

In the Court Rolls the name Fulham Street is rarely used. In the minutes of a Court held in 1520, occurs the expression "Berestrete formerly ffulhamstrete." In the old Parish Books the preference is given to Fulham Street, Bear Street being only occasionally used. The name Fulham Street does not occur after 1641.

The earliest mention of Bear Street occurs in the minutes of a Court General held in 1391. It reads:

> "At this Court Robert Elyes surrendered one Cottage with curt in Bvrystrete in length from the king's street which leads towards Wendenesgrene and the tenement of Thomas Webbe called folates tenement (*i.e.* Folase tenement) and in breadth from between a vacant place whereon the said Robert lately built on the south and the lands of William Edwyne otherwise called Cheseman on the north to the use of John Hunt of Potenhuth (Putney)."

In the minutes of a Court Baron, held in 1391-92, we read:

> "John Brother surrenders one cottage in Bere Strete which was formerly William Brother's and that Isabel Brother, mother of the said John, held to the use of Alice, daughter of the said John."

At a View, held in 1394, the Jurors made complaint with respect to a dunghill "in the king's highway at Berestret." Again, in 1397, the Jurors presented that "William Alderych has a dunghill at Burystrete."

At a View, in 1476, Thomas Coxston and Richard Brown were informed against for having cut and carried away, without license, "Wood growing upon the border of the moat ditch of Fulham in Berestret."

At this early period the few cottages which Bear Street boasted probably stood either on the east side of the thoroughfare or else down by the Ferry. On the west side, between the Moat and the street, was the "Lord's Waste." It was doubtless from this piece of open land that Coxston and Brown improperly possessed themselves of some of the Bishop's timber. In the same year John Yonge was fined for carrying away

> "Certain pieces of timber growing upon the customary lands of the Lord called Holdyngland in the tenure of Juliane James."

The offender, having duly submitted himself, was given

> "License to cut down divers pieces of timber of elm growing upon a toft of holdyng land at the end of Berestret which was formerly Norman's that he might be able to build with the same timber within this Lordship as much as pleaseth him."

In 1507 John and Jane Tylney were presented for having placed "dung in the highway in Berestret." In 1525 the Jurors at a View decreed that

> "None to remain within the Lordship in Berestrete who do not cast their refuse from their houses under penalty of xij^d."

In the same year it was ordered that

> "All the Inhabitants in Berestrete shall keep their pigs sufficiently ringed and yoked so that they do not grub up the lands of the Lord as before they were wont to do."

In 1571 the Court Baron ordered that no cottager should keep more than two pigs or forfeit 2d. for each pig in excess. In the following year this order was renewed, and it was further laid down that *no* tenant of the Manor should keep more than ten pigs or little pigs, under penalty of 2d. per pig.

In Close Roll 3-4 Philip and Mary we have another instance of the use of the alternative names Fulham Street and Bear Street. The entry reads:

> "8 Dec. 1556. John Bevill sells for £200 to Richard Buckland, haberdasher, of Paternoster Row, land in Beare Street *alias* Fulham Street, Fulham, which he bought of Ambrose Nicholas, salter, 7 Jan., 2 and 3 Phil. and Mar. (1555)."

At a View in 1570 the Jurors resolved that:

> "All persons after this who erect any dung hills against the Lord's Moat through Barestrete shall forfeit iij^s iiij^d."

The Waste of the Manor lying between Bear Street and the

Moat was, in course of time, let by the Lord for building purposes, but always with the proviso that each tenant should clean so much of the Moat as ran to the back of his land. Failure of this service involved a heavy fine and sometimes, even, the voidance of the grant. Thus, at a Court Baron held in 1657,

> "The Lord granted admittance to Benedict Smith, waterman, to a piece of waste land in Bearestreete in the Towne of ffulham and also of two houses by him thereon lately built upon condition he cleanse and scour part of the Lord's Moate lying neare and against the said houses or else the said grant to be void."

The Lord's Waste between the Moat and Bear Street was first generally built over about the time of the Commonwealth. In 1669 Joan Smith, widow, surrendered to John Storer a cottage "Built upon the Waist at the upper end of Beare Streete."

CHAPTER XVII: HIGH STREET (EAST SIDE)

We will now stroll along the High Street, commencing at the south end. Taking the east side first, we come, on our right, to the "Eight Bells," or "Ye Olde Eight Bells," as it is now called (No. 89, High Street). Anciently it was styled simply "The Bell." " 'The Bell,' " says Larwood, in his "History of Signboards" (p. 477), "is one of the commonest signs in England, and was used as early as the fourteenth century, for Chaucer says that the 'gentil hostelrie that heighte the Tabard' was 'faste by the Belle.' " At a Court Baron held in 1629 we find

> "License granted to John ffludd, gent., to let to farm one tenement called the Bell in Beare streete for 21 years to any person or persons of honest conversation."

The property then comprised "a cottage and a garden." The "Eight Bells" was doubtless so called to commemorate, in 1729, the increase in the peal in the tower of the Parish Church from six to eight bells. The first mention of the "Eight Bells" in the Highway Rate books occurs under the year 1771. It was from the "Eight Bells" that the old Saloon omnibuses used to run to London Bridge.

Just behind the "Eight Bells" is Putney Bridge and Fulham Station. It was opened for traffic 1 Mar. 1880, the extension of the District Railway from West Brompton to Fulham Old Town having been sanctioned by an Act passed in 1878.

Among the few historical houses which still survive in the parish, Fulham House (No. 87, High Street), takes a foremost place.

In ancient times a messuage lay here, covering the site of Fulham House and its neighbours, which bore the name of Passour's, Passor's or Passer's. The messuage was called after a family of the name of Passor who were living in Fulham in the time of Edward III. We gather from a later recital in the Court Rolls that in 1339, one Robert Passor surrendered to Richard

Passor and Margaret his wife a messuage and twelve acres of land near the waterside at Fulham. This, in conformity with the custom of naming holdings, would be called "Passor's tenement" or, briefly, "Passor's."

The ancient messuage extended along the east side of Bear Street from Fulham Ferry to the turning which led to Hurlingham Field, the Church Street of later times. Eastwards it was bounded by the demesne lands of the Lord. To this messuage belonged, as we have seen, a moiety of Fulham Ferry. The land attached to the tenement consisted of three acres and one rod. A detached portion, three acres in extent, enclosed in a croft known as Passor's Mead, or the Eyot, lay adjacent to the river. Of this portion we shall speak in our account of Willow Bank. Six acres of land at Colehill anciently also formed a portion of Passor's, making up the twelve acres referred to in the Court Roll of 1339.

Fulham House. From a photograph by Mr. J. Dugdale, 1895

From the Passors the tenement came into the possession of a family named Thurston. In 1397 it was in the occupation of John Thurston and Alice his wife. At a Court General in 1483 Geoffrey Thurston Was elected bailiff "in virtue of his tenement called Passours." He is often mentioned in the records of the Manor. His son, another John, made a compulsory surrender of Passor's in 1494.

Passor's was next in the possession of the Moretons or Mortons. About 1518 John Moreton died seized of the messuage. His wife, Petronella, dying in 1520, William Moreton of Moreton, co. Chester, son of Ralph Moreton (brother of John Moreton), was admitted. In 1521 this William Moreton surrendered Passor's to Ralph Warren, a merchant of the staple at Calais.

Sir Ralph Warren was the son of Thomas Warren, of London, fuller. In 1528 he served in the office of Sheriff, and, in 1536, was Lord Mayor of London. On the death of Sir William Bowyer, in 1543, he was again elected Lord Mayor for the remainder of Sir William's term of office. He was knighted, 18 Oct. 1547. In 1532 Ralph Warren obtained from William Moreton, son of the William Moreton above named, a further lease of Passor's, the tenement, at this time, being in the occupation of his son, Thomas Warren. Sir Ralph Warren died 11 July 1553 and was buried in the chancel of St. Swyth's Church in Cheapside. His marble tomb records that he had two wives, Dame Christian and Dame Joan.

Passor's apparently descended to his son, Thomas Warren, and Alice his wife. In 1567, Thomas and Alice Warren being then both deceased, Lady Joan or Johanna Whyte, wife of Sir Thomas Whyte and relict of Sir Ralph Warren, was admitted to Passor's in accordance with the terms of the will of her first husband.

Sir Thomas Whyte, Lady Joan's second husband, was a Merchant Taylor of London. He was the son of William Whyte of Reading, formerly of Rickmansworth. He founded St. John's College, Oxford, and was a great benefactor to the Merchant Taylors' School. He also established schools at Reading and Bristol. He was Alderman of Cornhill Ward, and was chosen Sheriff in 1547. He was Lord Mayor of London in 1553 and was knighted at Whitehall on 10 Dec. of the same year. His first wife Avice, whose surname is not recorded, predeceased him and was buried in the church of St. Mary Aldermary. His second wife, Lady Joan, the widow of Sir Ralph Warren, survived him. He died 11 Feb. 1566-67, aged 72. His will is dated 17 Mar. 1561-62. Lady Joan Whyte died in 1572.

Passor's now fell, in right of his wife, to Sir Henry Williams *alias* Cromwell, of Hinchinbrook, co. Huntingdon, who had married Joan, daughter of Sir Ralph Warren. Sir Henry Cromwell, by his wife Joan, had issue Robert Cromwell of Huntingdon, who married Elizabeth, daughter of Sir Thomas Stewart, kt. This Robert Cromwell was the father of Oliver Cromwell, the Protector. There are many traditions which, in one way or another, seek to connect Oliver Cromwell with Fulham. The residence of his grandfather, Sir Henry Cromwell, at Passor's, probably affords a clue to the origin of some of these stories.

Lady Joan Cromwell died 12 Oct. 1584. At a Court Baron, held in the April following, her death was reported but her heir was not known,

> "so a day was given for the Jurors to return a true verdict, viz., until 21 May next at the Palace of the Lord Bishop of London, or vjs viijd for each defaulter."

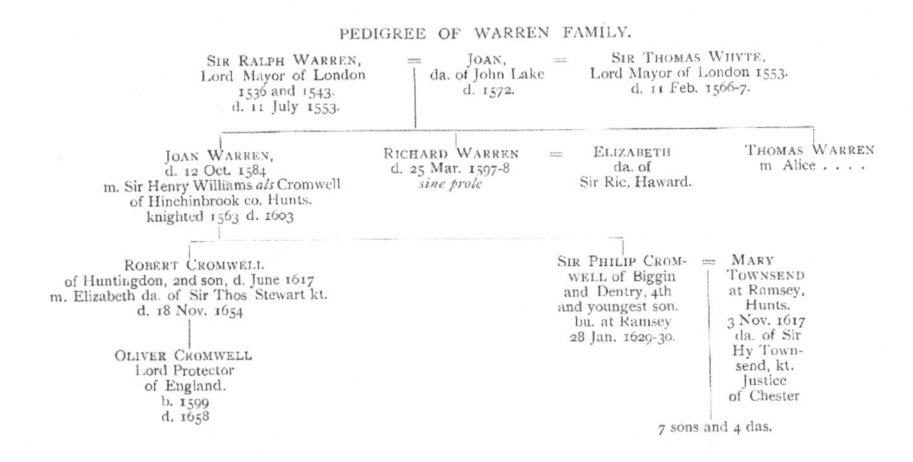

PEDIGREE OF WARREN FAMILY.

Sir Ralph Warren, Lord Mayor of London 1536 and 1543. d. 11 July 1553.	=	Joan, da. of John Lake d. 1572.	=	Sir Thomas Whyte, Lord Mayor of London 1553. d. 11 Feb. 1566-7.

Joan Warren, d. 12 Oct. 1584. m. Sir Henry Williams *als* Cromwell of Hinchinbrook co. Hunts. knighted 1563 d. 1603	Richard Warren d. 25 Mar. 1597-8 *sine prole*	=	Elizabeth da. of Sir Ric. Haward.	Thomas Warren m Alice ....

Robert Cromwell of Huntingdon, 2nd son, d. June 1617 m. Elizabeth da. of Sir Thos Stewart kt. d. 18 Nov. 1654	Sir Philip Cromwell of Biggin and Dentry, 4th and youngest son. bu. at Ramsey 28 Jan. 1629-30.	=	Mary Townsend at Ramsey, Hunts. 3 Nov. 1617 da. of Sir Hy Townsend, kt. Justice of Chester

Oliver Cromwell Lord Protector of England. b. 1599 d. 1658

7 sons and 4 das.

Sir Philip Cromwell, kt., the youngest son and heir of the Lady Joan Cromwell, succeeded to Passor's. In 1604 Sir Philip sold the estate to Edmund Doubleday, who, in 1618, disposed of Passor's to Thomas Hill, described as "citizen and writer of Court Letter (*i.e.* scrivener) of London."

Thomas Hill (or Hyll, as he invariably signed) resided at Fulham for a great number of years. In 1622 he held the office of Churchwarden. Very little is known concerning him. In the Guildhall Library are several indentures which show that he possessed property in Cornhill. In 1644 he surrendered his messuage in Bear Street to his own use for life with remainder to George Tirrey, Tirry, Terry or Terrie, who had married his only daughter Elizabeth. He died in 1650. The Churchwardens' Receipts for burials that year include

Mr. Tho. Hill 7s. 8d.

On the death of Thomas Hill, his property at Fulham was divided between his son, Thomas, and his daughter, Elizabeth, wife of George Tirrey.

Thomas Hill, junior, and his wife Judith, continued to reside at Passor's. On the death of Mrs. Judith Hill, about 1652, the property passed to Margaret and Elizabeth, the children of Henry Hill (son of Thomas Hill, junior) and Joan his wife. Margaret married Isaac Swifte, of Staple Inn, gent., and Elizabeth married William Cogan, of London, gent. In 1652, Margaret Swifte and Elizabeth Cogan sold their reversion in Passor's to Edith Roberts, widow.

On 6 April 1675 Mark Cottle, a London merchant, was admitted

> "To one heriotable messuage called Passers near the Ferry and one parcel of land called the Eight formerly the land of Edith Roberts, deceased, which Sarah Roberts, daughter of the said Edith Roberts, surrendered to the said Mark."

On 1 Nov. 1679 Cottle surrendered Passor's to the use of Theodosia Bucknor, who, in turn, surrendered it to Thomas Clements, of London, gentleman. In 1700 the property passed to Charles Clements, the youngest son of Thomas Clements, and in 1702 it was mortgaged to Thomas Dickens of the Middle Temple. In the following year Passor's and the Eyot became the property of Humphrey Hyde of London. In 1704 the estate was purchased by Richard Sanders, a brewer, who, in 1720, surrendered Passor's and "the Eyte" to "Jacob Tonson, citizen and stationer of London, and his heirs." Tonson's admission is dated 3 June 1720.

This famous bookseller and publisher was born in 1656. He was the son of a barber-surgeon in Holborn, who, at his death, left his two young sons £100 apiece. Both determined to become printers and booksellers. At the age of 14 Jacob was apprenticed to

Thomas Barnet, and, before he had served his time, he was admitted to the freedom of the Stationers Company and commenced business with his small capital at the Judge's Head in Chancery Lane. John Dunton, the bookseller, thus describes him:

> "He was bookseller to the famous Dryden, and is himself a very good judge of persons and authors; and, as there is nobody more competently qualified to give their (*sic*) opinion upon another, so there is none who does it with a more severe exactness, or with less partiality; for, to do Mr. Tonson justice, he speaks his mind upon all occasions, and will flatter nobody."

Jacob Tonson. From an old drawing

Tonson was much more than the publisher of Dryden and Pope. He was the first to popularise Milton's "Paradise Lost" and to bring Shakespeare's works before the general public. When he came to Fulham he must have been a very wealthy man. In 1724 he acquired New Close at North End, and in the same year was chosen to the office of the Lord's reeve. He died in 1736.

On his death, Passor's went to Samuel Tonson, his great nephew, youngest son and heir of his nephew, Jacob Tonson, the younger, who was the heir of Jacob Tonson, the elder, but who had predeceased him. Samuel Tonson, being under 21, his custody was granted to his elder brother, a third Jacob Tonson. The next holder of Passor's was Richard Tonson, who was here as late as 1773.

During the next fifty years there is little to record about Passor's. In 1804 the house was taken by Miss Mary Fleming who, with her sister, established a girls' boarding school here, called Fulham House School. The surviving sister resided here till her death, which occurred in 1828. Her ghost, it is said, still haunts the great cellars in the basement of the house. After the Flemings came the Loves, a trio of beautiful women known in their heyday as the "three Graces of Fulham." After the three Misses Love came, in 1838, the four Misses King, who, for nearly forty years, carried on a highly successful establishment. The house was, in 1877, purchased by the late Mr. Parkins Hammond Jones, who died here in 1892.

The exterior of this pleasant old house, which was built probably about the time of Queen Anne or George I, is familiar to most of us. The stone gateway is believed to be by Inigo Jones. Passing under this, and crossing the front garden, we find ourselves in the old hall, at right angles to which runs, throughout the width of the house, a spacious corridor. Along each of the upper floors extends a similar corridor, and even among the fine cellarage in the basement a similar arrangement is seen. Judging from the beautiful carving in most of the rooms, the panel-work, the mantel-pieces, etc., the house would seem to have been built for a wealthy family - not unlikely for Jacob Tonson. Like, however, a good many more notable houses, it fell on evil days. Twice, as we have seen, its occupants turned it to the purposes of a school. Pseudo-restorers, in their love of fine gilding and new paint, laid coat upon coat of colour on the beautiful carving with which the rooms abound, until at last the original work was almost obliterated.

The chief apartment of the house is a handsome room on the first floor, measuring 32 ft. 6 ins. by 22 ft. 6 ins., with a height of 16 ft. 6 ins. The mantel-piece is an elegant piece of work. The carving around the door of this room is, according to tradition, the work of Grinling Gibbons, whose flowers and foliage in wood possess almost the lightness of nature.

Fulham House is, as we have observed, alleged to be ghost-haunted. A writer in the *Fulham Chronicle* for 21 Sept. 1889, gives the following account of a search which he and Mr. P. H. Jones made for the mysterious visitor:

"Well armed, with three lights, we descended a flight of steps, which landed us in a long passage, on either side of which were cellar openings. We speculated upon the most likely spots which Miss Fleming's ghost would select for her dreary sojourn, but though I carefully examined every corner, I could perceive no being from the nether World. Whether our voices, or the lights we carried, drove the ghost from our ken, or whether it had at length forsaken its darksome home, I know not. At any rate, our search proved fruitless, and I think we returned from the vaults inclined to disbelieve in a tradition which Fulham folk have fostered for sixty years."

Mr. J. P. Norrington, formerly Surveyor to the Fulham Vestry, when staying, a few years ago, at Fulham House, encountered, as he was retiring to rest, the ghost of a man, habited in Vandyck costume. This ghost, which Mr. Norrington is perfectly certain he saw, is said to have been seen by other people.

Ranelagh House, garden view.
From a photograph by Mr. H. Ambridge

Ranelagh Lodge (No. 85, High Street) was named after the late Lord Ranelagh, its former owner. From 1807 to 1813 it was occupied by Joseph Neeld or Nield, a solicitor, head of the firm of Neeld, Fladgate and Young. He was the father of Joseph Neeld, M.P. for Chippenham, and of John Neeld, M.P. for Cricklade. From 1823 to 1829 it was the residence of the Rev. R. S. B. Sandilands. In later times, Ranelagh Lodge has been favoured by the medical profession. Here Dr. Joseph Holmes, a well-known physician, lived from 1830 to 1846. He was succeeded by Dr. George Tate in 1850, by Dr. Henry P. Freeman in 1853 and by Dr. Thomas Woodhouse in 1864. Ranelagh Lodge is now the property of the District Railway Company.

Little is known regarding the early history of Holland House (No. 81, High Street), now in the occupation of Messrs. J. S. Hodgkins and Co., Limited. At this house resided, from 1796 to 1816, the Rev. John Owen, M.A., lecturer at Fulham Church. Here also lived Mr. Robert Lapidge and his son, Mr. Edward Lapidge, the architect, whose name will be remembered in connection with Fulham Church. Some few years ago, in relaying the drainage, the workmen came upon an ancient door in the wall which divides this house from Ranelagh Lodge. The top of this door is still buried about 5 feet below the surface of the ground. Many old silver and copper coins were found here.

The site of Nos. 81-85 marks the position of an ancient cottage whose history went back to the time of Edward VI, when it was owned by the Barnabys. In the time of James I it was in the possession of Augustus Bullocke, Merchant Taylor of London, who, in 1626, sold it to Thomas Hill of Passor's.

The old tenements (Nos. 69 to 79A), just southwards of the "King's Arms", stand on the site of a once well-known house called Cowheard's tenement. Nothing can be definitely asserted as to the meaning of the name, which is variously spelt Coughierdis, Cowhyerdes, Cowherdes, Kowherdes, Cowherds, Cowheards, etc. In ancient times some ten acres of land in different parts of Fulham belonged to the tenement. In 1391 the Lord of the Manor granted to William Hunt, one of his tenants, "one vacant tenement of ten acres with appurtenances called 'Cough'deslond.' "

In the Court Rolls for 1419 mention is again made of the tenement called "Coughierdis." In the reigns of Henry V and VI the lands appertaining to this tenement were in the occupation of one Akermann. At a Court General, held in 1442, inquest was made by the Jurors as to the situation of "the parcell of Wareland called Cowhyerdeslond which is in the tenure of Akerman," with the result that they found that 1 acre 3 rods lay in "Berecroft" (*i.e.* Bearcroft), 2 acres upon "Colyshill" (*i.e.* Colehill), 3 acres in "Chirchehill," and 3 acres on the west side of Windmill Hill. In 1450 Richard Coppyng was admitted to Cowheard's. At a View, in 1470, it was presented that Coppyng had died seized of a "heriotable garden in ffulham called Cowherdes," when his youngest son, Thomas, was admitted.

Soon afterwards Cowheard's passed into the hands of John Cokeryk. In 1509 and 1512 "the heirs of John Cockeryke" were defaulters for Cowheard's. Sir Michael Dormer, citizen and alderman of London, was, for some years, the owner of Cowheard's, to which he was admitted in 1522. In the Court Rolls for 1550 there is a reference to "Coweherds tenement." In the margin facing the entry, in a later handwriting, are the words "Cowheards in Beerestreete." Subsequently, John Gresham held Cowheard's. In 1567 he surrendered it to William Smythe.

Old houses on the site of Cowheard's tenement.
From a photograph by Mr. J. Dugdale, 1895

For many years we hear little of the tenement. On 16 June 1666, Christopher Tomlinson, a London merchant, sold Cowheard's to Francis Larkin, butcher, of Fulham. On 10 December of the same year Larkin surrendered the property to his son, Miles Larkin, and Elizabeth Child. In this surrender it is described as

> "All that mansion house with appurtenances in the tenure of Valentine Clarke situated in Fulham abutting upon the road leading towards the Ferry Place there," etc.

This is the last we hear of Cowheard's, which, not unlikely, soon afterwards came down to make way for the old houses now standing. At the rear of No. 79 is another tenement, hidden from the street, and reached by means of a passage between No.79 and Holland House. Against the east wall of this tenement, which is numbered 79A, is the date 1668, composed of large iron figures. The brickwork of this side of the house was restored some years ago, when doubtless the old figures were re-affixed. They are now considerably spaced, and arranged in the following order:

1 6
6 8

As we do not hear of Cowheard's tenement after 1666, the date 1668 would very well suit for that of the building of the tenements which now stand on the site. In the scullery of No. 77 is a pump (dated 1787) the water from which is exceedingly pure and cool.

In the upstairs back room of this house, early in the century, lodged the "old coffin Woman," a little wizen-faced person regarded by many of her neighbours as a witch. Mrs. Owen, for such was her name, entertained a great dread of a pauper's burial, for in those days parish coffins were very bad. She, therefore, had her coffin made betimes, and stood it in a recess in her apartment. Every now and again she had it re-lined and oiled. This frequent oiling, in the end, made the coffin resemble a piece of bog oak. It is even said that she had shelves fixed across it so that she might use it as a cupboard. From No. 77, High Street, the "witch" moved

Fulham Old and New

to John's Place, and thence to other quarters. Finally, her increasing infirmities made it imperative that she should enter the Workhouse, but she declared she would never go there without her coffin. The Rev. R. G. Baker interceded in her case, and, by soft persuasion, induced her to go on the understanding that he stored her coffin in the loft over the coach house of the Vicarage! In the Union in the Fulham Palace Road, the old lady died some forty years ago, and was duly interred in the coffin which had been her companion for half a lifetime.

At the corner opposite the "King's Arms" was, in very early times, a cottage known as Kemp's or Kempe's, attached to which was a field known as Newcroft. In the reign of Edward III, Kemp's was the property of William de Colbrook, who was admitted about 1352. In 1415 Robert Cole surrendered Kemp's to John Danyell, "firmar de Fulham and Wormeholt," who, in 1429, sold it to William Rede. Next we find it in the occupation of a family named Edwen or Edwyn. Geoffrey Edwen, son of Robert Edwen, in 1444, sold Kemp's to john Cadman. We hear little more of Kemp's till 1518, when John Yonge was elected the Lord's bailiff for "Kemps in Berestrete." John Barnaby, the son of Robert Barnaby, in 1550, sold Kemp's to Thomas Cuttler, who shortly afterwards disposed of it to Stephen Cleybroke. Subsequently Kemp's came into the hands of Peter Maye who died in 1573, when his son William was admitted. Thomas Maye, in 1582, sold Kemp's to John Hilton of Putney. It was probably soon afterwards taken down.

On the site of Kemp's in Bear Street, at the north-west corner of Church Street (now the New King's Road), was built the house known as the "Nagg's Head." The first we hear of it is in the time of James I. It is narrated in the minutes of a Court General, held in 1614, that, on 6 June of that year:

> "William Thomas, of St. Martin in the Fields, co. Mid., gent., and Robert Thomas his son and heir apparent came to an Inn in Fulham called the Nagges heade and then and there surrendered by the hands and acceptance of Edmund Powell and Thomas Francis, gents., divers lands in Hammersmith," etc.

At a Court Baron, held in 1630, it was presented that

"Joseph Holden and his Tenant, Mr. Brisco at the Naggs head in Fulham shall before the 2 Feb. lay out a sufficient sinke under his house down to the Motte (Moat) in Bearestreete."

John Taylor, the Water Poet, in his "Catalogue of Taverns in ten Shires about London," 1636, mentions "The Nags head" at Fulham.

In the time of Charles II the old hostelry was the property of Sir William Powell. By his will, dated 2 Dec. 1680, Sir William devised, with other property, "that Capitall Inn called the Naggs head in ffulham" to his brother, Thomas Hinson, and to Christopher Plucknett, in trust for the support of the [Almshouses which he had founded in Back Lane](). It was then in the occupation of Humphrey Painter, innkeeper.

As we shall presently see, in speaking of John Dwight's house, John King was, in 1685, living "at the sign of the Naggs Head." A [manuscript "List of Taverns in London and Westminster and 10 miles round](),", compiled apparently between 1690 and 1698, contains the following:

"Taurons in ffullham
the nages head."

In 1713 we find Richard Osgood rated for the "Nagg's Head," and in 1726, his brother, Peter Osgood. Richard Osgood removed to Little Chelsea, where he died in 1747. Peter Osgood conducted the "Nagg's Head" for many years. By 1756 the house had apparently ceased to be an inn, and was subdivided into several tenements. In a lease to Christopher Gray, for 31-years, dated 20 Mar. 1756, the property is described as:

"All those three several messuages or tenements now or late in the several tenures or occupation of Samuel Webb, Samuel Lyse and Robert Inwood, all which said premises were formerly called or known by the name of the Nagg's Head Inne and formerly in the tenure or occupation of Peter Osgood. And also all that messuage or tenement now in the tenure or occupation of Charles Wale, Esq., lately erected on part of the ground belonging to the said Nagg's Head Inne, all which said premises are situate, standing and being in ffulham aforesaid, together with the Brewhouse, Barnes, Stables, Outhouses, Gardens, Yards," etc.

The subsequent history of the property presents no feature of interest. Among the records of the Powell Trustees, who still own the property, are numerous leases of the estate. Besides the site of the "Nagg's Head" Inn (formerly Nos. 1, 3, 5 and 7, Church Street and 65 and 67, High Street), the Powell Trust also included Nos. 39, 41, 43 and 45, High Street. Of these latter premises we shall presently speak. The whole of the houses on the "Nagg's Head" site were pulled down in 1895, when other and larger premises were erected.

In Bear Street, now marked by the site of 57a and 57b, High Street, stood the house of John Dwight, the celebrated potter, next door to the "Nagg's Head" inn. At a Court Baron, held 1n 1685, the Lord

> "Granted out of his hands to John Dwight, customary tenant of this Manor, a parcel of waist land lying before the house where the said John now dwells in Beare Streete between the house of John King at the sign of the Naggs Head towards the south and the house of widow Jackson (towards the north?) and the said John Dwight admitted."

It was at this house in Bear Street that John Dwight died in 1703, and his widow, Lydia Dwight, six years later. Here, too, lived, until his death in 1737, Dr. Samuel Dwight, their eldest surviving son.

No. 57, High Street is the "Golden Lion," last rebuilt in 1893. The original house was a Tudor building, but its history, prior to the present century, is an absolute blank. Judging from the character of its principal apartments, it must at one time have been a mansion, the residence of a well-to-do family. When, or under what circumstances, it became a tavern, we do not know.

The earliest notice of the "Golden Lion" inn is that supplied by Faulkner in 1812. He writes:

> "The public house in the High Street, known by the name of the *Golden Lion*, is the most ancient house in the town, and was built about the time of Henry VII, as appears from its corresponding style of building with that part of the palace built by Bishop Fitzjames.

The interior has undergone but little alteration, the wainscoting and chimney pieces being in their original state, and still in good preservation. In a room above stairs is a curious carved mantle-piece, and there are two staircases within the walls now blocked up."

Norris Brewer, in "London and Middlesex" (1816) gives a similar account. In Pinnock's "County Histories (Middlesex)" (1824), it is stated that:

"The inn called the Golden Lion is an ancient building of the time of Henry VII, which will repay curiosity for inspecting it."

A writer in the "Gentleman's Magazine," for June 1838, gives the following detailed account of the house, which had then been recently demolished:

"The Old Golden Lion Public House, which stood in the High Street, Fulham, and was pulled down in April 1836, presented a curious specimen of the architecture of the Tudor ages. The irregular form of the building had a picturesque effect; it was constructed in the usual manner of the period, being of brick to the first story and timber work and plaster above; the roof highly ridged and tiled. An entrance from the street opened into a small passage or hall, having the great stairs immediately facing the entrance door; the massive balusters and huge posts surmounted by lofty pinnacles, and the dim light from the small latticed window, gave a sombre appearance to this part of the edifice.
In a room north of the hall was discovered, at the north-east corner, on taking down the wainscot, the remains of a small winding staircase of brick and stone, which led originally to the upper part of the mansion: the low pointed arched doorway was about two feet six inches in width; these stairs immediately joined a large fire-place. In the apartment on the south side of the hall was a trap door, which opened on to a short flight of winding stairs leading into a vaulted cellar, well built of brick with courses of stone, having a recess on the north side; an arched doorway of stone faced a flight of stone steps leading to the back part of the building: this vault had not been used for many years, and was commonly known as 'Bishop Bonner's Dungeon.' The east view of the mansion presented a more irregular front than the west. The general character of the original structure was distinguished by long windows divided into numerous lights by massive mullions and transomes. An apartment on the principal story was of some interest; the obtusely pointed arched fire-place, enriched panelling of oak, and a bay window, together with its size, being larger than the other apartments, would

prove this to have been the grand room of the house. Heavy beams of chestnut crossed the ceiling - supported by a slender pillar - at the intersection. Some apartments, south of this principal room, had been disused for many years; the windows being partly blocked up. A room on the east side was wainscoted and panelled in a plainer style; a long window extended the whole length of the east end of the apartment, and a thick beam crossed the ceiling, supported at each end by rude pieces of timber. The fireplace was highly enriched by caryatid figures, and carved work of oak-foliage in low relief ornamented the stone mantle.

The fire-place in the apartment immediately under this on the basement floor was also much ornamented.

The upper rooms were exceedingly lofty and airy, the space usually divided off into lofts being open to the roof - showing the heavy beams and girders in all their rude simplicity; the windows small and near the roof, the doorways narrow and low, and formed roughly of un-planed board - opening by a wooden latch and spring."

Ancient fire-places in the old "Golden Lion."
From the "Gentleman's Magazine," June 1838

According to tradition the house belonged to Bishop Bonner, and was used by him for the confinement and punishment of obstinate heretics. "Bonner's Dungeon," mentioned by the writer in the "Gentleman's Magazine," was the Bishop's prison-house. Old residents will still tell you of a wonderful subterranean passage which led from the Bishop's Palace to the "Golden Lion." When, in 1836, John Faulkner pulled down the "Golden Lion," this underground passage was explored. Joe Hatch, the waterman, who at that time kept a little fish shop with a quaint bay window, next door to the "Compasses," went as far through the tunnel as he could go, and returned with a strange implement resembling a gridiron. This was at once proclaimed to be an instrument of torture on which Bonner had doubtless roasted his victims! Off this underground passage were found a number of cuttings or recesses, some 18 inches deep, filled with human skeletons. These, on being touched, crumbled away. There is no doubt that this passage under the High Street really existed, but it is, of course, impossible to say for what purpose it was originally formed. The explorers appear to have been unable to get any further than a point about underneath where the Fulham Gospel Hall now stands, on the opposite side of the road. When the brick sewer was made through the High Street, a considerable portion of "Bonner's Passage" was done away with.

An ancient fire-place in the old "Golden Lion."

Bonner's association with the "Golden Lion" is wholly traditional. It is quite feasible that he may have had some family connection with the house. From the "Visitation of Cheshire," 1580 (Harleian Soc. vol. xviii. p. 205), we learn that

> "Elizabeth ffrodsham (Boner) died at Fulham in K. E. 6 tyme during the imprisonment of [her son] Boner in the Marshalsey, who, notwithstanding, gave for her mourning coates at her death."

Possibly this Elizabeth ffrodsham, the Bishop's mother, may have resided at this mansion, which had not then, of course, degenerated into a village inn.

In July 1847, Mr. Crofton Croker read, at the meeting of the British Archaeological Association, held at Warwick, an ingeniously compiled paper "On the Probability of the 'Golden Lion Inn,' at Fulham, having been frequented by Shakespeare about the years 1595 and 1596." In it, Croker tells us that, when the old hostelry was taken down, a pipe, "of ancient and foreign fashion," was found behind the wainscoting of one of the rooms. The stem, he adds, was a crooked shoot of bamboo, through which a hole had been bored, and a brass ornamental termination (of Elizabethan pattern) formed the head of the pipe. "Why," he asks,

> "may not this have been the pipe of that Bishop of London (Fletcher), who had risen into Elizabeth's favour by attending Mary on the scaffold at Fotheringhay, and who, having fallen into disgrace in consequence of a second marriage at an advanced period of his life, sought, we are told, in the retirement of his house at Fulham 'to lose his sorrow in a mist of smoke,' and actually died there suddenly on the 15 June 1596, 'while sitting in his chair smoking tobacco'?"

Croker then points out that there lived in and about Fulham such men as John Florio, the translator of the "Essays" of Montaigne, John Norden, the topographer, John Fletcher, the playwright, Robert Burbage, a distant connection of Richard Burbage, Shakespeare's fellow actor, Joshua Sylvester, and Henry Condell, another fellow actor. The "Golden Lion," he presumes, "must have been, according to the custom of the times," frequented by these men, and, he thinks, there is reasonable presumption to suppose that "our immortal Shakespeare was also a member of this clique."

A writer in the "Gentleman's Magazine" for September 1847, commenting on Croker's paper, observes:

> "This composition was a very ingenious tissue of conjectural coincidences, spun out of the slightest possible materials. Its main thread was a presumption that John Fletcher, the poet, before the death of his father, Bishop Fletcher in 1596, and consequently before he was 20 years of age, was on intimate terms with Shakespeare and enjoyed his society at Fulham, where, instead of making themselves happy in the Bishop's hall, they preferred to repair to a public house. From the ruins of this house Mr. Crofton Croker had had the good fortune to recover a pipe which he suggests the Bishop himself may have left there as he is said to have died when smoking tobacco! For corroborative argument the author adduced these facts - that John

Norden, the surveyor, lived near Fulham in 1596, that Joshua Sylvester visited his uncle Plumbe at North End, and that Florio, the brother-in-law of Daniel, and Henry Condell, the actor, certainly resided at Fulham about 1625 - thirty years later. From this 'mass of facts,' asks Mr. Croker, who can doubt that the Golden Lion may have been frequented by Shakespeare? We do not, however, find that he advances any proof that the Golden Lion was in existence in the reign of Elizabeth, or, if it was, that it was the only tavern then at Fulham; or that the Palace was so full or so severe a household under the cloud-compelling Prelate that his son and his presumed friend Will were obliged to go elsewhere. The Golden Lion, which has formed the scene of these visions, was an old mansion perhaps of the reign of Elizabeth or her successor, but too handsomely fitted up for a village ale-house at that time. It was no doubt the residence of a rich citizen or Middlesex gentleman."

On the demolition of the old inn, the wainscotings were sold by the owner, Mr. John
Powell, to a Mr. Street, of Brewer Street, and they subsequently found their way to Southam House, near Cheltenham, the seat of Baron Ellenborough.

The old Fulham Volunteers used to keep their arms and accoutrements at the "Golden Lion." It was here that the parish officers frequently held the "Perambulation Dinner." It was, also, at the old "Golden Lion" that the Bachelors' Club held its meetings. Samuel Knight, nephew of John Knight of Walham Green, was the first member of the club married from it. For a long period the "Golden Lion" was the property of the Powells. From them it passed to Mrs. Ann Sophia Blake, and from this lady to the late Col. Edward Harwood, in whose family the property still remains.

By the "Golden Lion" a court leads through to Burlington Road. It is a private right of way.

Next to the "Golden Lion," perhaps on the site of Nos. 49 to 55, High Street, stood a once noted manufactory for the weaving of carpets and tapestries, established, in 1752, by Peter Parisot, a Frenchman domiciled in England.

Fifty years earlier some Walloons had set up at Fulham a small tapestry factory. In the Church Registers are the following references to it:

1699 William King Clarke at the Manufactori   bu. 2 Oct.
1700 Richard fflower, a weaver, from the Manufactori   bu. 9 Sept.

About this "Manufactori," however, no records now exist. Lysons gives the following details regarding Parisot's venture:

> "About the year 1753, Peter Parisot established a manufacture of carpets and tapestries at Fulham, where both the work of the Gobelines, and the art of dyeing scarlet and black, as then practised at Chaillot and Sedan, were carried on. Parisot had engaged some workmen from Chaillot, whom, at first, he employed at Paddington, but afterwards removed to Fulham, where the Gobeline manufacture had been already established, and where he had conveniences for a great number of artists of both sexes, and for such young persons as might be sent to learn the arts of drawing, weaving, dyeing and other branches of the work. Parisot's manufacture was particularly patronized by the Duke of Cumberland and countenanced by other branches of the royal family; but his goods were too expensive for general use, and the manufacture soon declined."

The Frenchman first comes into rating under the year 1753, his premises being thus assessed in the Rate books:

Mr. Peter Parrisot for his house and new school late Mr. Crofts: £4. 4.
He for Houses late King's, Dimock's and Leader's: £1. 4.
He for the House late Tiller's: 8s.
He for the dye house: 12s.

Parisot published an interesting little 24 paged pamphlet, dated "Fulham, April the 2nd, 1753," descriptive of his undertaking. Its title page runs:

> "An Account of the New Manufactory of Tapestry after the Manner of that at the Gobelines; and of Carpets after the Manner of that at Chaillot, etc., now undertaken at Fulham by Mr. Peter Parisot. London, Printed for R. Dodsley in *Pall Mall*; and sold by M. Cooper in *Pater Noster* Row, MDCCLIII."

The author commences by impressing on the nobility and the gentry of the kingdom the duty of being "the first to promote whatever tends to advance the Riches and Power of that Country from whence their own Property and their own Grandeur arise."

Then he proceeds:

"A Manufactory of Carpets, Tapestries and other House-Furniture, after the Manner of those of Chaillot and the Gobelins at Paris is now set on foot and carrying on at Fulham; upon which an attempt will be made towards founding an Academy of Drawing and Painting. There is also erected a Dye-House for dying Scarlet, after the Manner of the Dyers at the Gobelins; and Black as they do at Sedan."

Then Mr. Parisot invites his friends over to Fulham:

"As this undertaking was begun and has been carried on upon Views directly pointing to the Honour and Advantage of this Country, it seems proper that the Public should be informed of the Objects of it; which would have been done sooner but that I was afraid it might be said I was presenting them with bare Ideas only upon Paper. But now the work is in such Forwardness that anybody by taking the Trouble of going to Fulham may satisfy himself by what he will see already done and doing there as to what can be done in these new Manufactures; I am encouraged to lay the whole Design before the British Nation and to give them a faithful and particular Account of this great Undertaking."

With much elaboration, Parisot goes on to give what he terms "a short and very imperfect Sketch of these Manufactures," which he hopes "will afford sufficient Motives for encouraging this Nation to countenance and encourage" the venture started at Fulham, "and to induce the Government to give some Assistance towards its firm Establishment and Improvement." After giving some account of his negotiations with a couple of refugee weavers whom he met at Westminster, but who acted ungratefully towards him, and the first starting of the business at Paddington, Parisot continues:

"I had now got a competent number of foreign master-workmen when Chanse offer'd a much more commodious Situation for this Undertaking at Fulham. Many reasons concurred to induce me to fix there, but more especially the Convenience of the River and the great Number of spacious and commodious buildings, which I found there and fully answering my Purpose and which I came into Possession of upon reasonable Terms. Besides room for all the different Branches of the Manufactory, and which is enough for one hundred Master-Workmen, there will be sufficient and separate Convenience for the Women it is proposed to employ in Works relative to it, and which are suited to their Sex, such as that of Fine Drawing mention'd before, the preparing of the Wool and Silks for the Manufactures, etc. . . . By this Description - and it does not exceed Truth - it will be easily believed that an Establishment of this Extent cannot have been carried so far without considerable Expence. I think myself obliged to declare that this has with the greatest Munificence been supplied by [His Royal Highness the Duke](), as a Purchase for the Nation of the Advantage of this Manufactory. His Royal Highness from the same Motive and from his Love of these fine Arts, is pleased to continue his Benefactions in order to contribute to enable me to support the Weight of the Expence necessary for carrying on this Undertaking."

In conclusion Parisot pictures the various blessings which his new manufacture would inevitably confer. He remarks:

"This Establishment offers Employment to both Sexes; to the weakly as well as to the more robust; and some Parts of this Manufacture afford means of Help to many Families of the better Sort who are burdened with a numerous Female Offspring. No apprentices or young persons, who may be desirous to be instructed in any Branch of this manufacture will be received but such as are natural born Subjects of His Majesty, and they will be educated in the Protestant Religion."

As to the probable cost of his Wares, Mr. Parisot speaks in guarded terms:

"It will be impossible to give any general Ideas with regard to the Price for the Works of these Manufactures. That must depend upon the Designs and Patterns as well as the Degree of Fineness of the Works which may be chosen. Persons may also find their own Patterns for any Piece of Work in one or the other way. When these Points shall be settled the conditions will be agreed on before the Work shall be put in Hand, and it is not doubted but they will be as reasonable as for things of the same kind brought from France. There are to be seen at Fulham several Pieses now begun and in some Forwardness; and others already finished which may be purchased. I wish heartily that this

Establishment at Fulham of which I have here given an Account may be acceptable to the Nation and that it may give me an Opportunity of showing my zeal to serve the Country which by Choice I have made my own."

This little book, which is now exceedingly scarce, was reviewed at length in the "Gentleman's Magazine" for 1753 and 1754 and in other periodicals of the day.

The Duke of Cumberland appears for awhile to have most liberally financed the undertaking. Indeed, in contemporary literature it is sometimes spoken of as "the Duke's." George Bubb Dodington, who was at that time living at Fulham, notes in his "Diary," under date 8 Mar. 1753:

"We went to see the manufacture of tapestry from France, now set up at Fulham by the Duke. The work, both of the gobelins and of chaillot, called savonnerie, is very fine, but very dear."

The "Gentleman's Magazine" for Oct. 1753 records a visit paid to the Manufactory by the Princess Dowager of Wales, who is said to have expressed

"great satisfaction at the performance of the Sieur Parisot, the manager, and her design to encourage so national an undertaking."

Peter Parisot was a remarkable adventurer with an alias. He was, in reality, no other person than Pere Norbert, once a noted Capuchin, but subsequently a renegade priest, resident in this country. His character is amusingly sketched in the following extract from a letter, written by a M. Giuseppe Baretti to his brother. It is dated "Plymouth 18. iv. 1760."

"At 11 o'clock this morning I left Exeter, after having visited two manufactories, one of serge and the other for making that description of tapestry called in France, 'tapisseries de Gobelins,' after the name of the place where it is made in Paris. As to the Gobelin tapestry, the art of making it in its complete perfection was brought to England by a distinguished anti-Jesuit, the renowned Father Norbert, a French Capuchin whom Benedict XIV, himself an anti-Jesuit, permitted to live in England on condition that he went as a missionary converting the good souls who tasted his doctrines. Far from seeking to fulfil this duty, this honest monk has taken the liberty of secularizing himself (*a pris la liberté de se séculariser de sa propre autorité*) and has appeared under the name of M. Parisot. He has made himself director of a manufactory for this kind of tapestry. He has, by means of a voluntary subscription among the gentry and the well-to-do, succeeded in obtaining help to the extent of ten thousand pounds sterling. Of this I was assured at the time. This gentleman, shortly after his arrival in London, found means to pocket this sum (*d' empocher cette somme*). I have several times gone from this capital to Fulham to see his looms which might have procured him an honest livelihood had he exercised the least economy, but he was a spendthrift and possessed some eminent qualities - especially those two cardinal virtues known by the name of incontinence and vanity - so that he did not take long to run into debt; he became a bankrupt and took to his heels (fit banqueroute et prit la fuite!)"

If this story be true, Peter Parisot was hardly the philanthropist which his book would lead us to believe. M. Baretti, as a frequent visitor at the Manufactory at Fulham, was doubtless well acquainted with Parisot.

The "Nouvelles Archives de l'Art Francais," 1878, contain several letters which throw much light on the Manufactory at Fulham, the main industry at which was the weaving of velvet pile carpets. Among them is a letter, dated 19 Sept. 1752, from M. d'Isle to M. de Vaudieres, a nephew of Mme. de Pornpadour, containing a copy of a letter addressed from England by a workman at the Fulham Manufactory to his father in France, described as an "ouvrier des Gobelins." Another letter, dated 30 Aug. 1752, from Baptiste Grignon, is addressed "To Mr. Parizot in Foullemme Manufactory à London."

In 1755 Parisot removed from Fulham to Exeter, but his career was over. On 12 Jan. 1756, his entire stock, consisting of fifty-nine lots, was sold off at public auction. The front leaf of the little four page Catalogue, the only known copy of which is at the British Museum, reads:

"A Catalogue of the Entire Works of the Velvet, Woollen and Cotton Manufactory, Lately removed from Fulham to Exeter Under the immediate Protection of His Royal Highness the Prince of Wales consisting of a Variety of magnificent and beautiful Carpets, Chairs and Skreens, after the Manner of the Royal Manufactories at Chaillot, and the Gobelins at Paris. As likewise Of several fine Pieces of Cotton, in Imitation of Needlework, after the Manner of the Manufactory of Rouen Which will be sold by auction By Mr. Langford, At his House in the Great Piazza, Covent Garden, on Monday the 12th of this Instant, January 1756. . . . N.B. These Works having been first establish'd at Fulham in the Year 1750, several of the Pieces are manufactured by Natives of England, taken then as Apprentices, and instructed in these valuable Branches."

At the end of the Catalogue is the following note:

"N.B. A printed account in French and English of the rise and progress of this Manufactory, with Mr. Parisot' Address to the Public thereon, may be had at One shilling each, of Mr. Dodsley in Pall Mall, Mr. Lewis in Russel Street, Covent Garden, Mr. Baldwin in Pater Noster Row, and Mr. Woodfall at Charing Cross."

Some of the items in the Parisot Catalogue have noted against them the prices which they fetched. The highest, £64. 1s., was for

"A magnificent large Carpet 18ft. by 13ft. of a most elegant and beautiful design."

According to Faulkner, Parisot's premises were subsequently turned into a school, then into a playhouse, and, about 1770, were pulled down and houses erected on the site. No records, however, are extant to show that they were ever used as "a playhouse."

A noteworthy house in Bear Street was a tenement known as Goodriche's *alias* Symonds', which stood on the site now covered by the Fulham National Schools. The early history of the house is obscure. In the time of Queen Elizabeth it was the property of the Maynards, a family who enjoyed extensive holdings in Fulham.

For some years Goodriche's was the residence of John Hart, whose wife, Katherine, was buried in our Parish Church in 1605. His name regularly appears in the assessments down to 1635, when the clerk strikes out the Christian name "John" and inserts above it "Dr.", from which we may infer that Dr. Richard Hart, his son, succeeded to the property.

In 1640 Dr. Hart's name ceases and that of Alderman James Viccars, Vicars or Vickers takes its place. James Vickers was a successful London merchant. His will, dated 8 Oct. 1657, is a curious document. The following are the more important passages:

"I, James Vickers, late Alderman of London, now liueing att ffulham in the Countie of Middlesex, being aged Sixtie Eight yeares this Eight day of October Anno Domini 1657. To Mary my wife £3,000 and my house and furniture for life. Remainder to my sonnes Edward and William Vickers and their heirs. To my son Edward Vickers now in Lisbon £700 besides £700 which he has already. To my younger son William Vickers now apprentice in Cheapeside with Master Bidaught and Master Berknitte £1,800 to be paid him at his comeing out of his tyme; Provided that he hath the report of his Masters of a good Husband and noe waster. But if it shall happen that he shall prove a prodigall and a spendthrift then I order him but £1,300. To my Daughter Thurman besides what she hath received already for her wedding portion, £800.

Whereas I did some Eight yeares past bestowe my Daughter Anne Vickers unto a Wicked ungodly wretch John Hackett of London Dyer Sonne and heire to Richard Hackett of Dytton in the Countie of Surrey Esquire in marriage giueing her for a portion £1,500 in readie money and £200 laid out and for Cloathe and other expenses upon agreement and covenants that the said Richd Hackett should settle upon his sonne John Hackett and upon my daughter Anne Hackett and their heirs £300 per annum and £150 per annum jointure, which was perfected the monie paid and the marriage solemnized.

Now Soe it hapned that after he had three boyes liueing by her and he through his Lewd Courses being ingaged for diuers greate Summes for her ffather and his ffather for him and had wasted all and came to me and Complained he was worth nothing (which I admired at) and suddenlie after his ffather and he wickedlie ioynes and cutte of the entailment of three hundred a year settled upon my Grandchildren and paid theire debts with it soe farr as it would goe and afterwards sent my Daughter and her fower children home to me without a Bedd scarce to lie on and his ffather denying to alowe them two pence maintenance whoe had gone beyond them for theire whole Estate. And for his Sonne my Daughter's husband he is gonn a way from her for Ireland and there for ought I knowe meanes to reside. Now for my poore daughter whoe hath nothing to helpe her except my Bountie towards her may starue she and hers I doe order and bequeath that my Loueing Wife will continue her with he

Whereas it Pleased God to giue me my eldest Sonne John Vickers whome I bredd att Cambridge Bac. in Arts whoe behaued himselfe very prodigally stubborne and profuse soe high that the Universitie could not endure it and coming home to me upon his Submission which he promised should be faythfull and fervent I bound him Apprentice unto me to trade a Marchant into Rushia which was my former Life. And upon his ffaythfull promises I sent him ouer sea with a stock to the value of betweene two or three Thousand pounds hoping he would haue procured a greate Match but so it hapned that being not long setled (in) Russia with my Estate to the value of £1,300 he contrary to his protestations and dutie both to God and his ffather entred into marriage without my privitie unto a ffactor's Daughter there one Margery Osborne though I earnestly writt and sent unto him to the Contrarie yet he disobediently went on maryed and begott Boyes and afterwards wth weeping teares came over into England with his Wife and Children (the third tyme) and submitted himselfe unto me whoe had spent me there in Russia the summe of ffifteene hundred pounds att least in the space of three or fower yeares since his comeing over being reconciled with him upon his greate protestations I tooke a house and warehouse for him with a stock of one Thousand pounds to trade in to Russia where he had been bredd which he Quickly through his greate ill husbandrie and Lazines wasted all and fell to worse courses being disobedient unto me and not seeing my face in three yeares space but shifting and gitting into his hands what he could of mine especially one Great Summe of ffourteene hundred pounds which I tooke in his name but onlie in truste it being my owne Estate which I here he Challenges as his owne and hath Compounded for a quantitie the parties that it was none of mine and soe hath taken less then halfe the debt discharging the parties and hath sent me word that he will doe with a debt of fiue thousand pounds which is owing to me of a noble man being formerly taken in name as my eldest Sonne which God forgiue him for his greate disobedience. Now this I sett downe largely in my will to lett the world take notice that upon my reputation and in the presence of God I speak it That since he came from the Universitie of Cambridge he hath laid out of my purse one time or other aboue ffower Thousand pounds besides what he doth intend to have out of my fiue Thousand pounds debt which shall not trouble me in regard he is my Sonne hoping he will proue better after my decease soe now to my will what I giue him viz. 1st I require of him a general release from the beginning of the World to 1 Oct. 1656 and if he refuse I giue him £100 and soe farwell praying God to giue him better grace but if he do consent then I giue him 2 leases of certain houses in Bridewell Lane, etc.

My wife sole executrix and my son-in-law Master Nicholas Thurman shall be my executor. I give unto the writer of this my last will and testament John Gee parish Clerke of ffulham 40s. My Corps to be buried in St. Austins Watling St. London at the upper end of the Chancell near the bodies of my father and 3 Children. I order and will that Master Mathew ffowler now preacher of Hammersmith doe preach my ffuneral sermon and doe burie my Bodie after a Christian-like and decent buriall and give Christianlie Exhortation to the Auditorie."

In 1675 his sons, Edward and William Vickers, surrendered the property to George Grove, of London, merchant. In 1684 Edward Vickers, who was then residing at Colchester, surrendered Goodriche's *alias* Symonds', then in the occupation of John Lee, of the Inner Temple, to the use of Walter Thomas, "clerk." In the Vicar General's Books is the following record:

> "Thomas, Walter, of Fulham, co. Middlesex, clerk, bachelor, about 28, and Mary Butler of same, spinster, about 24, and at own dispose, at Fulham aforesaid, 4 Sept. 1677."

In 1687 we find Walter Thomas, "clerk," appointed the Lord's reeve for "Goodridge's." At a Court Baron held in 1708:

> "Walter Thomas, clerk, surrendered the heriotable messuage called Goodriches *alias* Symonds and the yardling lying before the said messuage and extending to the lane called Sowgelder Lane which messuage is situated in Beare St. in occupation of said Walter Thomas, to use of Sir Thomas Rawlinson, kt., and alderman of London and heirs and he admitted."

Sir Thomas Rawlinson was the eldest surviving son of Daniel Rawlinson of the "Mitre Tavern," Fenchurch Street, where he was born. In 1686 he was appointed Sheriff of London, by Royal Mandate of James II, he having been foreman of the jury which tried Alderman Cornish. In 1705 he became Lord Mayor of London. He was colonel of the White Regiment of Train Bands. At a Court, held 22 Sept. 1705, Sir Thomas was appointed President of Bridewell and Bethlehem Hospitals. In the year 1680 he married Mary, daughter of Richard Taylor, of the "Devil Tavern" in St. Dunstan's in the West, citizen and vintner of London. Sir Thomas, who died 2 Nov. 1708, was buried at St. Dionis. His Will, dated 20 Jan. 1700-1 (codicil 20 July 1707) was proved 12 Jan. 1708-9 (P.C.C. 18 Lane). In 1709, Tempest Rawlinson, his youngest son and heir, was admitted to Goodriche's.

Lady Rawlinson, the widow of Sir Thomas, in 1713, re-married, her second husband being Michael Lister. The following we take from Chester's "London Marriage Licenses":

"Lister, Michael, of St. Martin in the Fields, bachelor, 26, and Dame Mary Rawlinson of Fulham, Middlesex, widow, 50, in Berwick Street Chapel, in the Parish of St. James aforesaid, 30 May, 1713."

Tempest Rawlinson, described as "citizen and salter of London," died unmarried, 1 Jan. 1736-37, and was buried at St. Dionis on 7 Jan. His will, dated 18 Sept. 1733, was proved 11 Jan. 1736-37, by Honor, wife of John Starke of Epsom, merchant, sister of the testator.

In 1726 Tempest Rawlinson surrendered Goodriche's to his elder brother, Richard Rawlinson, of Gray's Inn, LL.D., the collector of the Rawlinson Manuscripts in the Bodleian Library at Oxford. Dr. Rawlinson, who was born in 1700, was a distinguished topographical antiquary. His best known works are the "Chief Historians of All Nations and their Works," 1728-30, "The English Topographer," 1720, and the "History and Antiquities of Hereford," 1747.

In 1752 Dr. Rawlinson obtained the consent of the Lord of the Manor to let all his property in Fulham for 21 years. Lysons states that, in 1754, Dr. Rawlinson, who died in 1755, bequeathed Goodriche's to the Principal of Hertford College, Oxford, and his successors, and adds, in a note, that he had originally left it to the Society of Antiquaries, but that, "in consequence of some disgust, revoked the devise."

After having remained for many years unoccupied, the ancient building was, in March 1794, pulled down. Faulkner, in 1812, observes:

"This site, after having laid (*sic*) waste for several years, for want of a sufficient title for building on, has been converted into gardens and is now occupied by Mr. James Wilson."

Subsequently Dr. Roy, of Burlington House School in Back Lane, laid out the piece of ground as a convenient approach to his establishment.

In 1861 the site was acquired for the extension of the Fulham National Schools. At midsummer that year Bishop Tait laid the foundation stone, and at the beginning of 1862 the school, which is the Boys' Branch, was formally opened. In 1897 the school was considerably enlarged, the yard in front being built over.

The site of the four houses, Nos. 39, 41, 43 and 45 High Street, to which we now come, though of no historic note, is interesting as forming a portion of the property left by Sir William Powell towards the maintenance of the Almshouses which, until 1870, stood in their immediate rear in Back Lane.

From the will of Sir William Powell, 2 Dec. 1680, we learn that, at that time, there stood here a messuage then in the possession of Thomas Pyner, carpenter. This property was left by Sir William to his brother, Thomas Hinson, LL.B. On Hinson's death the reversion went to Sir William's only daughter, Lady Mary Williams, wife of Sir John Williams, knight. Sir William devised the property, in trust, for her use, to Richard Powell, bencher of the Inner Temple, and Christopher Plucknett, of North End. On 2 April 1706, there was a second probate of the will of Sir William Powell by William Williams, son of Sir John Williams. In 1708, Sir John Williams and his son, William Williams, demised to Thomas Hinton (perhaps a son of Dr. Thomas Hinson),

> "All that messuage or tenement containing three lower rooms and a shed and three upper rooms with a little room over the shed and the staircase going up without the house and then late in the tenure or occupation of Thomas Pinor"

The subsequent dealings with the property, which became divided into four tenements, may be best gathered from the following notes of the title deeds:

19 July 1725 Thomas Hinton, carpenter, assigns to Alexander Stopford Catcott for £200 a lease which he obtained from Sir John Williams and William Williams, his son, in 1708, for 51 years from Lady Day at £7 rental.

13 May 1729. Release of the Equity of Redemption of four houses from Thomas Hinton to Alexander Stopford Catcott. £105 paid.

28 July 1729. Underlease granted by Alexander Stopford Catcott to John and Elizabeth Merry of one house on payment of £50 and 24s. per annum for 30 years.

30 April 1733. Lease renewed to Alexander Stopford Catcott for 36 years at expiration of lease in 1759 for fine of £21: rent £7.

22 Mar. 1766. New lease for 29 years to Martha, Augusta and Thomas Catcott, children of Alexander Stopford Catcott, deceased, for 29 years: rent £7. (The Rev. A. S. Catcott died in 1748: he left his leasehold property to his three young children equally. On 4 April 1766 the four tenements were purchased by a Mr. Harrison. In some unexplained way the above lease passed into the hands of Ann Webb of Hanwell, who, on 30 Dec. 1790, let the property to Samuel Webb for £20 per ann.)

10 Oct. 1792. Ann Webb gave up to the Trustees of the Powell's Almhouses the above lease for the sum of £50. (This purchase appears to have been made by the Trustees in pursuance of a scheme which they had in view for rebuilding the Almshouses in Back Lane, Mr. Nathaniel Chasemore having agreed to carry out this work in consideration of receiving from the Trustees a lease of the property which they had purchased of Ann Webb except such part as should be wanted to complete the erection of the new Almshouses.)

16 Jan. 1811. Confirmation of agreement made 12 Oct. 1792 with Nathaniel Chasemore to rebuild the Almshouses and to pay £50 fine (to reimburse the Trustees the sum paid to Ann Webb), and to expend £500 on the work of rebuilding, etc. This being done, the above lease was granted. Rent £7 for 40 years and £10 for 21 years.

8 Feb. 1854. Lease to Wm. Chasemore, son of Nathaniel Chasemore, for 21 years from 29 Sept. 1853; rent £42.

The grant of this lease eventually brought the Trustees of Sir William Powell's Charity into a most difficult position. Mr. William Chasemore, who died 1 Feb. 1865, sold the premises to a Mr. Dickinson, who took an assignment of the term granted by the lease. The latter then entered into possession or receipt of rents, and for some time duly paid the ground rent. Subsequently he mortgaged the premises, by way of underlease, to an assurance company. Failing to keep up his payments, the company proceeded against him. He left the country, and the company entered into possession, and continued to occupy the premises till 25 Mar. 1873. On the Trustees requiring the premises to be repaired, the company quitted them. For some time the property remained deserted and shut up. Eventually it was recovered on ejectment, and possession given to the Trustees by the Sheriff of Middlesex.

Out of the rent and profits of the Trust, Sir William Powell directed that the devisees should buy and provide for six poor men of the parish six coats and six pair of breeches, made of good English woollen cloth, and that they should, upon the feast day of the Nativity deliver the same in or at the church porch of Fulham unto the six poor men. In the succeeding year the devisees were required to make a similar gift to six other poor men of the parish. These twelve men were, in turns of six, to be annually the recipients of the charity.

The four houses were, in 1895, pulled down and the site is still (1899) vacant.

Where Rigault Road now enters the High Street was Marshall's Alley. It owed its name to a Mrs. Marshall who kept a greengrocer's shop (No. 35, High Street) at one corner of the turning. At the High Street end the alley, which passed under a house, No. 37, was only 3 ft. 3 in. wide. Eastward of a tenement erected over the alley by W. Chasemore in 1843, the passage widened to 13 feet. In 1898 the alley was abolished and the present road formed.

Marshall's Alley

Behind No. 27, High Street pieces of ancient brickwork have, on two or three occasions been dug up, showing that some very old tenement must have stood here.

The two small cottages, Nos. 21 and 23, High Street were built by Nathaniel Chasemore about the beginning of this century.

The old Parish Workhouse in the High Street occupied the site of the four houses on the east side Nos. 13, 15, 17 and 19. It was erected in 1775-76 to meet the growing needs of the parish. Down to the days of the Stuart kings, the population of Fulham was very sparse and the necessities of the "casual poor" were met by disbursements made by the Overseers. The Parish Books are crowded with entries relating to doles given to the sick, the lame and the halt, the aged and the poor, to penniless travellers, and to a thousand other descriptions of impotent persons. After awhile, the Overseers kept a list of the "pension poor," in other words, of the permanent residents of the parish who were unable to support themselves. With the growth of the population this out-pension system became cumbrous, costly and unworkable.

In 1731-32 the Vestry matured a scheme for renting a building in Bear Street to serve the purposes of a poor house. It so happened that a Mr. Robert Kirk was indebted to the parish £200. On 27 Dec. 1731 the Vestry ordered that this sum, with the interest due thereon, should be paid into the hands of the Churchwarden to be "applied to what use the parish shall think fit." On 17 Mar. 1731-32

> "It was ordered that the sum of two hundred pounds received of Mr. Kirk and now in the hands of Mr. Crornpton psent Churchwarden shall be applied to the use of a workhouse and for no other use whatever and shall for the present be put out upon the security of the Land Tax for the year 1732."

Shortly afterwards it was decided to rent some premises, the property of the Powell family, which had fallen vacant on the east side of Bear Street. On 19 April 1732,

> "It was unanimously agreed that the sum of twenty five pounds p. ann. be paid for certain tenements situate in the Town of Fulham, late in the occupation of Mr. John Whale, the property of Thomas Symonds, Esquire, to be applied to the use of a Workhouse, and that the rent shall

commence on Michaelmas Day next ensuing and shall continue for the space of eleven years."

Thomas Symonds was the son-in-law of Sir John Williams, himself the son-in-law of Sir William Powell.

On 13 July 1732, the Vestry appointed a Board of Trustees, eighteen in number, besides the Churchwarden and Overseers, to manage the affairs of the Workhouse and to

"Provide sufficient Household goods, Cloaths and Linnen for the said Workhouse and that the Linnen be mark'd with the letters F.P., so that they may not be taken away or embezled and that they take in such poor as have a right to and are in want of ye Parish's assistance there to be fed, lodg'd and cloath'd and that all such Poor as have their Health and Limbs be appointed to such sort of Work as they are fit for; and such proper Tools and Implements as are necessary to employ them be provided by the said Trustees for that purpose, and that no separate pensions be allowed to any person out of the House, but that the whole Collections for ye poor be apply'd towards the support of the House, the maintenance of the poor therein and other usual and necessary charges, and that where any of the Trustees hereunder nam'd shall happen to dye or remove themselves out of the said Parish, that then the vacancies shall be filled up by the parishioners in Vestry, and that the said Trustees or the major part of them now and for the time being do chuse a discreet, sober and sensible man to be Master of the said Workhouse, for the Welfare of the said House depends entirely on having a man capable to keep the accounts of the House so as to set down what Stores, Cloaths and other Goods are brought into the House, how they are disposed of and to whom, and to keep an exact Register of all persons taken into the House or dismissed from it and to receive and pay all ye monies for the service thereof, and that the said Trustees or the major part of them do chuse such women servants as they shall find occasion for and that a yearly account of all Receipts and Disbursements for the said Workhouse be laid before the Vestry within one month after Easter in every year, in order to be examin'd and passed by them and that such account be entered in a Book and sign'd by the Persons present at such Vestry."

About 1733 the Workhouse premises became the property of Mr. Richard Coope. Whether the "pension poor" did not take kindly to the new method by which the parish sought to care for them, we do not know, but the following entries are suggestive of popular discontent and resentment:

> 1733. Pd. Mr. Hearsom to cry the Workhouse windows when broke to make discovery thereof: 1s.

> 1735. Pd. Mr. Lovejoy for mending the windows of the Workhouse: 5s.

> 1735. Pd. for mending the Workhouse windows: 7s. 6d.

The Overseers' Books about this time contain some curious entries relative to the new Workhouse. The following are samples:

> 1734. Spent with a gentleman about taking a Girl out of the Workhouse: 1s. 6d.

> 1734. Carrying Widw. Harding to ye Workhouse in a cart: 1s. 6d.

> 1735. Paid Widow King for baking puddings: 1s. 6d.

At the rear of the Workhouse was a fruit garden, the produce of which was generally sold. In 1737 the Churchwardens

> Received for the Walnuts at the Workhouse: £1. 5s.
> Received for the Crop of Mulberries at the Workhouse: 9s.

The Workhouse soon filled with poor. As early as 20 May 1738, We find the Vestry ordering,

> "That Wm. Harding be allow'd a shilling a week to provide him a lodging till there is room for him in the Workhouse."

About 1743 the old Board of Trustees was abolished, and the management of the Workhouse handed over to a Committee to be annually elected. Things evidently did not work smoothly, for, on 28 May 1746, the Vestry decided to appoint

> "a separate and distinct Committee to examine and enquire into the management and state of the Workhouse of this parish and all particulars relating thereunto from 1732 to 1743 and from thence to the present time."

On 24 June of the same year the Committee's report was read at a meeting of the Vestry, assembled in the Belfry of Fulham Church. After the reading of this document it was

> "Ordered that Mr. John Hollis, Mr. James Dunn, and Mr. John Poole do go down to the Workhouse and bring up the poor that are able just as they be that the Vestry may see them."

A fresh Committee was appointed, and matters seem to have gone better for awhile. In 1749 the "parish officers" acquainted the Vestry that they had engaged a Mr. Brown to be Master of the Workhouse, "to which the parishioners had no objection." The following entries occur among the receipts for 1749:

> Received by a gold ring sold of (*sic*) a woman in ye Workhouse: 6s. 3d.

> Found in a woman's pockett when dead in the House: 3s.

In 1754 the Vestry decided on its first experiment in the matter of the employment of the inmates of the Workhouse. A new Master being wanted, Mr. Richard Atlee attended before the Vestry on 20 Dec. 1754 and offered his services gratuitously on the condition that he enjoyed the labour of the inmates. This novel scheme was accepted, and Mr. Atlee was chosen Master "till further orders," under the following curious proposals "delivered by himself":

> "I purpose to employ your poor in winding of silk and to take care of them in the manner following and for my trouble and care I shall expect the labour of the people for my constant salary.
> 1st. A particular account shall be kept of the concerns of the house and proper methods shall be taken to prevent people from making away with anything that belongs to the house.
> 2nd. Great care shall be taken to teach the children to read and to instruct them in the princepals of religeon agreable to the faith of the Church of England and every morning and evening prayers shall be read and likewise Grace before and after meat and the person I will put in as master shall attend the children at Church twice every Sunday if the weather permits.
> 3rd. Particular care shall be taken of the sick and the orders of the apothecary duly observed.

4th. House and poor shall be kept clean and the children shall be washed and combed every day, and proper time shall he given to the people to make and mend their linnen and likewise to mend their cloaths and stockens, and the people shall have their victuls in a proper time and in a decent manner and great care shall be taken that nothing shall be wasted or wanted.

5th. The people shall work from 6 o'clock in the morning til 6 in the evening during the summer season and in the winter only by daylight, and out of the sd. time they shall have one hour for dinner and half an hour for breakfast, and if any gentleman shall think any person or persons overworked, such person or persons shall never be required to work again.

(Signed) RICHD. ATLEE."

Mr. Atlee's *régime* at Fulham Workhouse was short lived. On 21 April 1755, the Vestry ordered:

"In consideration that Mr. Atley has not complied or perform'd his proposals and contract with the parish, that the Churchwarden and Overseers do give him ten days' notice for him or his agent to quit the said Workhouse."

And on 1 May following they ordered:

"That Mr. Atle be immediately discharged and that Jo. Fitch do succeed him as master of the said house under these following proposals (viz.), to take care that the poor be allway clean and decent, that all possible care shall be taken that nothing shall be embezeld or wasted, that the house shall be kept clean, the children read twice a day and catechized and go to Church every Sunday with the Master or Mistress attending them, that the people shall be employ'd in winding silk, to work from 7 o'clock in the morning til 6 o'clock in the evening dureing the sumer season and only be (*sic*) daylight in the winter, that for my salary and care I expect the people's labour.

(Signed) JOSEPH FITCH."

Mr. Fitch proved a satisfactory Master, for, on 12 May 1756, the Vestry reported that he and his wife had behaved well as Master and Mistress and were:

"Allways watchfull to procure masters and mistress's for the boys and girls who were fit to put out apprentices."

The earliest existing Workhouse Committee Book begins on 8 Aug. 1771, when there were in the House 7 men, 12 women and 19 children, a total of 38 persons.

The permanent Workhouse in the High Street was, as we have stated, erected in 1775-76 on a piece of ground the property of Mr. John Powell. The lease, which bears date 15 Aug. 1775, is made "between John Powell, Esq. of the one part, and David Russell, Jas. Preedy and John Webster," the Churchwarden and Overseers, on the other part.

The Workhouse was a substantial brick building. Facing the High Street the premises were enclosed by a wall, inside which was a narrow courtyard. The front door of the Workhouse opened directly into the central hall. The stairs leading to the upper floors were approached from passages to the right and left of the hall. The Workhouse had two wings, extending towards the back. The house consisted of two floors, the upper rooms being similar to the lower. In the front was a stone bearing the date of the erection and the names of the then Vicar, Churchwarden and Overseers. At the rear, in Back Lane, was an airing yard for the inmates.

Spinning, as an occupation for the inmates, was introduced into the Workhouse in 1785. The Overseers' Accounts for this year record:

> "Gave the people in the Workhouse when they first began the Spinning, etc.: 4s. 10d.
>
> Paid for 4 new Spinning Wheels: 10s. 2d."

In 1787 the Vestry considered the proposals of Messrs. Kilner and Company "for employing the poor in picking and cleaning cotton," but they came to the conclusion that, unless the Company could see their way to making a gift of £50 in return for the services rendered, they had better employ the old people in some other manner.

The Overseers in 1787

> "Gave the Beadle of the Royall Exchange for bringing home two girls that got out of the Workhouse 5s. 0d."

The Workhouse Committee Book contains the following curious entries about an orphan lad in the House:

8 Jan. 1788. "Ordered that Mr. Cobbett do take William Atkyns under his care for a month by way of trial previous to his instructing him (if, upon trial, he shall be found apt to learn) to play the violin."

5 Feb. 1788. "Mr. Cobbett reported to the Committee that he had, according to the order of the Committee of 8 of Jany. taken William Atkyns under his tuition and that he found him apt to learn and has no doubt but that in a reasonable time he will learn sufficiently to earn his livelihood.
Ordered that he continue to instruct him; that he do provide him with a violin to practice on at the expence of the parish not exceeding 12s. price. The terms agreed upon for teaching him are half a guinea for ten lessons and half a guinea entrance."

The lad could hardly have turned out the brilliant musician anticipated, for, nine years later (7 Nov. 1797), the Committee

"Ordered that William Atkyns be allowed one shilling a week."

Fulham Workhouse. After a memory sketch by Mr. C. Wilcox, 1897

In 1790 the Workhouse Committee decided to effect a change in the employment of the inmates and for this purpose formulated a scheme for carding and spinning. The accounts of the Overseers for this year include:

Expences: Mr. Castell, Mr. Faulkner and Mr. Gover going to Greenwich W. H. to inspect their works of Carding and Spinning, etc. when we were about to employ our own People in the same manner.	16s. 6d.
Gave the Master of the Workhouse for his information	5s. 0d.
Expences: Several journeys to town and treating with different persons about employing them	15s. 6d.
Sundry Expences for Wheels, etc. to set them to work, as per account .	£7 12 9
Paid Henry Wilkinson for instructing them	£1 19 0
Paid Mr. Gover for his superintendence being ⅛ part of the sum earned as by agreement with him	£4 15 6
	£16 4 3
Received for labour done by the poor in the Workhouse in Carding and Spinning Mop Yarn from 7 Dec. 1790 to the 7 July 1791	£28 13 0.

Dr. William Sharp, of Fulham House, in 1802, induced the Workhouse authorities to introduce inoculation for cow-pox into the House. The following extracts from the Committee Book, relating to a meeting held on 2 March 1802, are of interest:

> "Mr. Sharp represented to the Committee the very great benefits which had resulted from the adoption of Innoculation for the Cow Pox; and declared it was his opinion that it was by no means dangerous in itself; and as it was now proved almost beyond the possibility of a doubt effectually to prevent any person who had it from ever after having the small pox, which disorder has been lately very prevalent and destructive among the lower classes of people in this parish and its vicinity; he therefore recommended it to the consideration of the Committee which would be the best mode of inducing the vaccine Innoculation among the poor of this parish.
>
> <u>Mr. Bunnett</u> informed the Committee that he would undertake to innoculate those who would come to him for that purpose every Monday and Tuesday between the hours of nine and ten at his own house; or at Mr. Manning's at Walham Green between the hours of twelve and one.
>
> The Committee accepted Mr. Bunnett's offer and ordered the necessary steps to be taken to make the same generally known throughout the parish."

As late as 1806 "mopp yearn" was spun in the Workhouse.

Faulkner, however, in 1812, observes:

> "There has been no labour done in the house for many years; but at present, two gentlemen, Messrs. Jonas Hall and Charles Plaw, have obtained the consent of the parish officers to erect some machinery for cotton-spinning in part of the house; for the use of which, and the labour of the poor, the parish is to receive £50 *per ann.* while they continue to work; but it seems doubtful whether it will succeed, as there are very few men in the house capable of labour."

On 18 Feb. 1812 the Workhouse Committee considered the proposal of Messrs. Hall and Plaw and decided to allow them

> "to erect and make use of their machinery for the purpose of spinning cotton in the room on the left side of the Workhouse yard and make trial of such persons in the House as may be fit for Labor and can be spared for the space of three months."

The books contain no further reference to this scheme, which proved unsuccessful. During the later years of the existence of the old Workhouse, the only work done. by the inmates was the making of strawberry pottles, the demand for which was almost constantly in excess of the supply. Faulkner tells us that, in his day,

> "The poor have meat four days every week for dinner, and three days bread and cheese of good quality. For breakfast, they have milk-porridge five days, and the other two, bread and cheese, and the children bread and butter."

In 1836, the Vestry learnt with dismay that the Poor Law Commissioners proposed to join Fulham with some other parishes, converting the whole into a "Union," and at a meeting held it was unanimously resolved to petition against any such amalgamation. The Union, however, was to come, and, on Thursday, 4 Mar. 1847 the parishioners were called together to receive a report from the "Guardians of the Fulham Union relative to the erection of a new Union House."

The change was effected none too soon, for the old Workhouse had long ceased to afford adequate accommodation. In 1847 it was considered to be fitted for the reception of only 156 children or 104 adults, while, in the preceding winter, no less than 130 inmates had been lodged in the House.

The old parish Workhouse continued to be used down to 1850, when the new "Union" Workhouse in Fulham Fields, begun in 1849, was approaching completion. In the minutes of the Guardians for 24 Oct. 1850 is the entry of a letter from Mr. Hackman, the Vestry Clerk of Fulham, asking the Board's permission

"for the inhabitants of Fulham to give a substantial dinner to all the more respectable inmates (children included) of the Fulham Workhouse prior to their leaving that place."

High Street, east side. From a photograph by Mr. H. Ambridge

The Guardians assented and the poor folk bade farewell to their old home over a sumptuous repast. The removal of cases from the old parish poorhouse to the new Union was accomplished on Tuesday 26 Nov. 1850. From this date the old Workhouse in the

High Street remained unoccupied, although an abortive attempt was once made by some of the parishioners to convert it into twelve separate dwellings for the labouring classes. After standing empty for some ten years the premises, in 1860, were pulled down and the materials sold. Some of the walls of the washhouses belonging to the old Workhouse, behind No. 23, still stand.

Close to the Workhouse stood the Watchhouse or Cage, in olden times the parish lock-up for petty malefactors and vagrants. "Honest" John Phelps, the last man to remember the Cage which stood in Bear Street, described it as "a small out-house entered by means of a pair of iron doors."

In the Parish Books the entries referring to the Cage are very numerous. The following may be quoted in illustration:

1630

"ffor the burying of a boie that died in the Cage and stripping vii^d."

1632

"Pd. to John Yattes wife tht layd out for ye huryall of a poore gerle that died in the Cage in the toune 1s. 4d."

1648

"It. for a Woman brought abedd in the Cage 4s. 4d."

"It. for a Winding sheete for a poore woman that dyed in the Cage 3s. 6d."

"It. for 6 Trusses of straw for poore people in the Cage 3s."

In 1712 the Overseers

"Paid for necesaris for the woman that lay in the Cage £1 17s. 11d."

"Paid the Medwife for Laying the Woman in the Cage 5/-, and the Woman for nursing her 5/-."

"Gave the woman in the Cage by Mr. Ceny's [churchwarden] order 5s."

In 1713 the Overseers

> "Gave a souldier and his Wife that lay in the Cage 1s. 6d."

In 1715 the Overseers paid for:

> "A Truss of straw for a sick woman in the Cage and Provision 1s."

> "A Truss of straw for a poore man in the Watchhouse and Provesion 2s."

The ancient Cage was taken down in 1718. On 11 Feb. of this year there was

> "Paide for pulling downe the old Watchhouse 4s. 2d."

The Church Registers record in 1729:

> Cornelius out of the Cage buried 24 Dec.

At a Vestry held 26 Sept. 1751 Henry Goodwin, the Parish Constable, reported that the "Watchhouse or Cage" wanted "proper repairs to receive prisoners," when it was ordered that two of the local tradesmen should immediately do the work. In 1792 the better-to-do inhabitants of Church Row and the neighbourhood made a successful effort to secure the removal of the Cage to a less conspicuous position inside the walls of the Workhouse. At a Vestry, held 8 July 1792,

> "Mr. Chasemore produced an estimate for building a new cage or parish room within the Workhouse wall, next the street, which, together with the new wall to be erected in front of the cottages behind the present cage, amounts to the sum of £26, and the inhabitants of Church Row and the neighbourhood, having offered to raise among themselves the sum of 10 gs. [10 guineas, i.e. 10 pounds and 10 shillings] towards defraying the expense thereof, Resolved that Mr. Chasemore be directed to do the said works forthwith and that the parish will pay the residue of the expense exclusive of the ten guineas so to be Contributed by the inhabitants of the neighbourhood as above said."

Finally, in 1814, the Cage was re-erected at the rear of the

Workhouse in Back Lane. One of the very last persons confined in the Cage was a man named Parrett. Whilst here he committed suicide, and was buried in the cross roads by Munster House.

Continuing our walk along the east side of the High Street there is little else to call for mention. In the road facing No. 11, whilst making some connections with the sewer, in 1867, the workmen discovered a piece of solid red brickwork several feet in front of the building line, showing that some edifice must have stood there prior to the four old cottages which, until 1827, occupied this site. These four ancient tenements, which lay immediately to the north of Fulham Workhouse, certainly dated back to the time of George I and probably to a much earlier period. They were long in the possession of the Catcott family. In the year 1720 Mr. Alexander Catcott bought of Francis Gotobed

> "Four tenements (formerly but three) standing contiguous, adjoining to the south end of a messuage lately sold by Francis Gotobed to Robert Lympenny of fulham, Gent, and now in the tenure of Davis (wch last is a public house wth the sign of the rose) and extending from thence southward towards the river of Thames and abutting eastward on a Road called the back lane and westward on fulham town or the high road commonly called Beare Street."

These four houses were sold by Mr. Thomas Catcott in 1826, to the Commissioners of Roads. Of the "Rose" public house, which adjoined the last cottage, little is known.

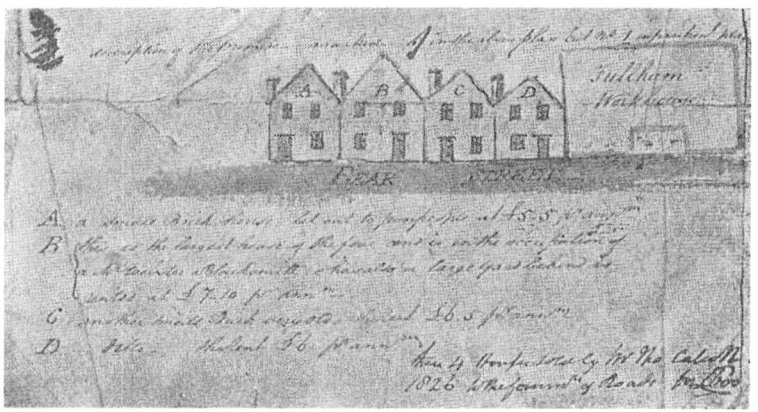

Four ancient tenements in Bear Street. From an original sketch plan in the possession of Mr. John Rooth

Just at the top, where the High Street joins Burlington Road, were several dilapidated little huts of a very old-world character. These were swept away when the present shops were built.

At the top of the Town, near the wall of Holcroft's, stood, until about sixty years ago, the Parish Stocks and Whipping Post. The first pair of Stocks were erected in 1523. At a View in 1523 we find the Jurors

> "Present that the Lord of the Manor ought to make a pair of Stocks within this Lordship."

The Bishop complied with the "presentment," but how long the Stocks lasted or in what part of the Lordship they were erected, we know not. By the time of Charles II they had apparently ceased to exist, for, at a Parish Vestry held on 1 May 1667, the following resolution was passed:

> "That the ow'seeres for the poore and constable doe for the future joyne in the reformacon of the Sabbath day and that a paire of Stockes and whippinge post bee erreeted by the Churchwarden and that it bee allowed by Assesmt."

A rate was levied to defray sundry expenses, including:

> "To errect a paire of stocks and whippinge post ffoure pounds."

In 1737 a new whipping post was set up. The apparatus consisted of an upright post, some seven feet high, from which hung a pair of iron manacles for fastening the wrists of malefactors. Attached to the post, and on either side of it, were the Stocks. Behind was a rough wooden bench on which the culprits were seated.

The Stocks were often used for the punishment of petty offenders whose misdoings were not sufficiently serious to bring them before the justices. At Fulham it was the custom to seat the culprits in the Stocks on Sunday mornings in order that persons returning from church might pelt them as they passed.

Adjoining the Parish Stocks was the Town Pump.

CHAPTER XVIII: HIGH STREET (WEST SIDE)

We will now take the West side of the High Street. Near the top stood the old "Kings Head." The present house, No. 12, which still bears the old sign, marks its site. The earliest reference to it occurs in the Court Rolls for 1695, when

> "John Shaw, of Fulham, victualler, surrendered one messuage called the 'King's Head' in Beare Street in the occupation of said John to use of himself for life, Remainder to Jane his wife."

In 1707 this John Shaw mortgaged the property to Richard Sanders, innkeeper. By his Will, dated 8 Jan. 1723-24, Richard Sanders devised all his estate to his daughter Sara, and his son James, who were, in 1724, admitted to the "King's Head." The history of this inn has been uneventful.

In 1883 a great improvement was made at the top of the High Street by the demolition of the old houses (Nos. 2, 4, 6, 8, 10 and 10a) which stood to the north of the "King's Head."

The old "King's Head." From a photograph by Mr. H. Ambridge

An interesting house still standing on the west side of the High Street, is No. 22, known in olden times as the Colehouse or Coalhouse, Coal Hole or Coal Cellar. It is, along with Nos. 50 to 72 (even numbers inclusive), the property of the Parish Church.

It was used by the parish officers for the storage of coal laid in by them for sale or distribution to the poor during the winter months. In 1637 the Churchwardens paid five shillings "for the measures for the colehouse." In the inventory of Church Furniture, etc., taken in 1670, there are, among other items enumerated, "one bushell, one half bushell, one shovell," with the explanation that "these last menc'oned are in the Colehouse." In 1640 the Overseers paid:

> "Itm. for one bushell of Coles dd". (*i.e.* delivered) to Thomas Woldreges his wife when she was shut vp by the appointment of Doctor Cluett 7d."

The wife of Thomas Woldrege had presumably caught the plague, and, in conformity with the rude custom of the age, had been "shut vp" in her house. Dr. Cluet was the Vicar. In 1638 the Churchwardens:

> "pd. for Priscilla at the Colehouse 2s. 6d."

> "pd. for the Coleman's child 3s. 6d."

On 20 Feb. 1647, the Vestry

> "Agreed that Mr. Stisted (the Churchwarden) doe take care of the scouring of the lord's moate by the Poores house in fulham street and that for that part of the ground behind the Colehouse next vnto the moate that in consideration of Mr. Woluerston his cleansing of the said moate along by the said ground he shall haue the vse of the said ground only he is to giue liberty at all times for the repair of the said Colehouse."

The "Poores house," where the parish officers kept necessaries for the relief of the poor, was further down Bear Street, on the site now occupied by the Church Houses, Nos. 50 to 72 (even numbers). In 1648 the Churchwardens paid:

"For Broomes, a Baskett and making cleane the Colehouse 2s. 2d."

In 1649 the accounts contain

"Item for Cleaning the Howse and Heauing in the Coales 3s. 4d."

"To the Bricklayer and to a labourer for work in tyling and mending the Colehouse 10s. 2d."

High Street, as seen from Holcroft's.
From an oil painting by Mrs. Streatfield Baker

In 1652 the Vicar and Churchwardens obtained from Col. Harvey, who was then the Lord of the Manor, a grant of the "Poores house" and the Colehouse, with two parcels of land belonging thereto, on the following conditions:

"Att a Vestrie Julie 15 1652
Whereas vppon ye Request of the Inhabitants it pleased the Lord of the Mannor Col. Edmond Harvey to make a graunt to the Minister and Churchwardens of a howse commonly called the poores house belonging to the pish as also one other howse called ye Cole howse together wth Two severall pcells of land therevnto belonging vppon the paymt of such quitt rent and pformance of other dew services That is to say To clense the Lords moate against the said severall howses a

> farre as the said howses and land extendeth, to its Auncient wideth and depth ffor the Tearme of J J (*i.e.* eleven) yeares from the 25th of March last past The Inhabitants doe gratefully accept of the same and doe herby order and agree that the said Rent be herafter paid and the said moate clensed as aforesaid by the Churchwardens for the time being who are herby authorized to pay the same as often as occasion requireth."

These two houses, with the two parcels of land attached, are, as we have said, now represented by the thirteen Church Houses (Nos. 22 and 50 to 72, High Street) above mentioned.

In 1654 the Churchwardens

Paid to Mr. Mead ffor 7 chaldron of Coles	£8. 13. 4.
Paid ffor ffreight for the ship p.	7. 0.
Paid ffor measureinge, filling, etc., as p. bill	2. 4.
Paid ffor cartage to the house	5. 10.
Paid ffor ffilling and Lainge vp	2. 0.
	£9. 10. 6.
Paid for deliuering the Coles to the poore att ffower severall tymes or dayes at 12d. p. diem	4. 0.

In the minutes of a Vestry, held 19 Nov. 1654, we read:

> "It is ordered that the Coales which are laid in for the poore this yeare shall bee sould out for 6d. the Bushell and the stock to bee maid good out of the rnonethly Collection gathered in the Church after Sermon."

And on 27 Nov. 1664:

> "Itt is ordered yt ffifty chaldron of coles now in the Colehouse shalbe sould att six pence p. bushell till such tyme they bee all deliuered and att such tymes and daies as the Churchwardens and Ouerseers shall appoint and the Churchwarden shall bee accountable for the money ariseing thereby and the persons hereunder named are to be desired to assist the Churchwarden yt is to say, Mr. Tho. Beauchampe, Mr. Tho. Willett, Mr. Anto. Nourse, Mr. Hen. Owen, and Mr. Edw. Limpany."

In 1669 the Churchwardens:

> "Paid for a new locke for the poores colehouse doore 3s. 0d."

Soon after this date the Colehouse ceased to be used for its original purpose. In 1704 it was leased to Richard ffullwood. Various other tenants followed. In 1787 "the house called the Coal house" was let to Mrs. Elizabeth Pattenden at a neat rent of 50s. per annum for a term of 40 years.

High Street, west side. From a photograph by Mr. H. Ambridge.

High Street, west side, in 1871.

We hear but little more of the "Poores house" mentioned in the extracts from the Vestry minutes for 1647 and 1652. When, in

1732, premises were rented on the east side of the High Street for the establishment of a regular workhouse, the "poores house" became useless, and, being very old, it was decided to take it down. On 10 June 1734 the Vestry agreed:

> "That the materials belonging to the old house situate in the middle of the Town, opposite the thoroughfare next to William Franklyn (*i.e.* Marshall's Alley), be forthwith sold to the best bidder and the money thence arising to he paid to Mr. William Souch present churchwarden and by him applied to the use of the parish."

On the 4. Oct. following the Churchwarden was empowered

> "to lett the ground whereon the old house stands opposite the Workhouse to Richard Watkins by the year at the rate of twenty shillings p. ann. to commence at Michaelmas last."

There can be little doubt that this old house, which the Vestry were about to demolish, and which was parish property, was identical with the "Poores house."

The Vestry, on 5 Dec. 1741, sold to Nathaniel Frankling for the sum of £2. 2s. the materials of "two old small tenements belonging to this Parish, situate in the Town, opposite the Workhouse," and agreed to let him occupy the ground on the payrnent of 20s. annually.

On a board in the porch of All Saints the Church Houses are thus described:

> "A House called the Coal House situate on the west side of Bear Street in the Town of Fulham let on lease to Mrs. Elizabeth Pattenden at £2. 10. 0 per annum.
> A Piece of Land with sundry Buildings thereon situate on the west side of Bear St. in the Town of Fulham let to Mr. Charles Young and Mr. Edward Hudnott at £10 per annum."

The Church Houses, which, at the beginning of this century, brought in only £12. 10s. a year, now produce rather over £300. An account of the Church lands, on which the Church Houses stand, is to be found in the report of the Charity Commissioners of 1835.

It is a little singular that a slip of land at the back of the

Colehouse does not belong to the Trustees of the Church Houses, but remains to the present day copyhold of the Manor of Fulham. In the will of Mrs. Elizabeth Pattenden, dated 30 Nov. 1814, this double description of tenure is specifically mentioned. This lady held the Colehouse and two other tenements in trust for John Hodsdon and his heirs. Mrs. Elizabeth Greenhill, only child and heiress of John Hodsdon, inherited under the will. Her youngest son, Henry Greenhill, succeeded to the copyholds, and, in 1873, sold his interest to Mr. Edward Goddard, of Chapel Street, Mayfair.

High Street, west side, just prior to the demolition of old houses in 1890.
From a pen and ink sketch by Mr. A. Beaver.

The Fulham Gospel Hall (No. 92), which marks the site of two ancient wood cottages, originated in the year 1868, when a few Christians, who resided in the neighbourhood, met at the house of one of their number to consider whether something could not be done to provide Gospel services on Nonconformist lines, of which the locality was then quite destitute. As a result of the conference, a committee was formed, consisting of members of various denominations. At first, temporary premises were taken at No. I7,

High Street. In 1879 the two cottages, of which we have spoken, were condemned by the authorities as being unfit for habitation, and, the site being offered on lease for building, it was secured and a hall, capable of seating about 250 persons, was erected at a cost of some £600. The new premises were opened in 1880.

High Street, west side.
From a photograph by Mr. H. Ambridge.

"The Compasses," an old-fashioned and straggling inn, was pulled down about 1860, when the present house (No. 94) was erected. Its history has been uneventful. In the Parish Books it is not mentioned until 1833.

Crossing from the corner of Church Row, leaving the approach to Putney Bridge on our right, we come to the Grand Theatre, erected in 1896-97. This handsome structure, which is on all three sides surrounded by roads, was designed by Mr. W. G. R. Sprague. The theatre is built in the classic style, of Portland stone and brick. At the main entrance, at the junction of the High Street with the approach road to Putney Bridge, is a gracefully-proportioned portico, semi-circular in shape, over which is a loggia. From the ground level a flight of steps leads to the entrance vestibule, constructed to complete the circle of which the portico forms one half. The inner vestibule has a fine domed ceiling, supported by marble columns with bronze capitals.

Leaving the vestibule, we enter the crush room, where the box offices are placed. The ceiling of this room is panelled out in a large oval centre, and the whole is decorated in an elaborate though chaste style. Here two marble staircases lead to the dress circle, while entrances to the stalls are on either side.

The Grand Theatre. From a photograph by Messrs. C. G. and A. C. Wright, 1897

The theatre is what is termed a two-tier house, the first row consisting of dress circle and balcony, and the second, of the gallery. On each side of the stage are four private boxes. A noteworthy feature of the theatre is the entire absence of columns, thus giving a perfect view of the stage from all parts of the house. In lieu of columns, support is obtained by iron girders fixed on the cantilever principle. Attached to the dress circle are a saloon bar, lounge and balcony. The decorations of the theatre are throughout executed in the style of Louis XIV. The auditorium provides the following seating accommodation:

Eight Private Boxes: 32
Stalls: 74
Dress Circle: 95
Pit Stalls: 102
Balcony: 135
Pit: 305
Gallery: 382
Total accommodation: 1,125

The centre panel of the ceiling is dome-shaped, with four medallions in mitres, filled in with painted subjects. The proscenium is very elaborately finished with open scroll-work and figures. The whole of the decoration is treated in delicate shades of cream and light terra-cotta, and all the ornamentation is richly gilded. The draperies are of a beautiful ruby colour. The act drop, which was painted by Mr. W. T. Hemsley, is novel and handsome.

A corner in the Grand Theatre. From a photograph by
Messrs. C. G. and A. C. Wright, 1897

The width of the auditorium is 60 ft. The stage, which is 76 feet wide by 43 feet deep, was constructed by Mr. E. Glacken. The proscenium opening is 30 ft. wide and 28 ft. high. The height from stage to grid is 56 ft. The whole building covers an area of 12,000 feet.

The theatre is absolutely fire-proof. For lighting purposes, both electricity and gas are available. The Grand Theatre, which was built by Messrs. W. Pattison & Sons, was opened on the evening of Monday, 23 Aug. 1897, when *The Geisha* was performed.

The Grand Staircase. From a photograph by Mr. Alfred Ellis

A famous mansion in Bear Street was Stourton House, more generally known as Fulham House or Fulham Hall. It stood on the west side, just northwards of the "Swan" inn. A portion of the site is now occupied by Cambridge House, No. 156, High Street, and the houses northwards. The approach to Putney Bridge covers most of the site.

From "London and Middlesex Fines," it appears that a messuage which lay here was, in 1397, sold by Richard Mede to "John Shirebourne, clerk." This John Shirebourne, who was Archdeacon of Essex, held the property down to his death in 1434. He was buried at Fulham. He was probably the son of William Shirebourne, or de Shirebourne, *alias* Ilberd, who held the rectory of Fulham from 1365 to 1413. Another John Shirebourne succeeded to the property. From Escheats, 17 Ed. IV, we learn that this John Shirebourne and others, in 1449, sold the messuage, consisting of a house and garden, valued at 3s. 4d. *p. ann.* to John, first Lord Stourton.

The Stourtons were an ancient West of England family. Sir John de Stourton, who acquired the property at Fulham in 1449, was the son of Sir William de Stourton. It is stated in Hoare's "History of Wiltshire" that

> "Sir John de Stourton was perhaps the most distinguished character of this ancient family, and to whom the estate at Stourton is indebted for many valuable privileges. He served his monarchs Henry V and VI with great ability in their foreign wars as well as in public capacities at home in his own county, for which services he was advanced in dignity, and was created a Baron, with other emoluments, anno 1448."

Backs of Of houses High Street west Side

From the "Cal. Inq. Post Mortem ", 2 Ed. IV (1462), we gather that "Joh'es Stourton de Stourton, miles," held in Fulham at the time of his death a "mess. cum gardin." By his wife, Margery, daughter of Sir John Wadham of Merefield, Som., kt., he had issue four sons and two daughters.

The eldest son was William Lord Stourton, the second baron. He was summoned to Parliament 9 Ed. IV (1469). He died 18 Feb. 1477-78, and was buried in the church at Mere, Wilts. From the

"Cal. Inq. Post Mortem", 17 Ed. IV (1477), we learn that "Willielmus Stourton de Stourton, miles," died possessed of the same messuage and garden at Fulham. <u>An entry in the Stourton Manuscript Book is to the same effect</u>. The second baron married Margaret, daughter and co-heiress of Sir John Chidiok of Chidiok, co. Dorset, kt., by whom he had three sons and three daughters.

John, the eldest son and heir, became the third Baron of Stourton. He was summoned to Parliament 20 Ed. IV (1480). The Stourton Manuscript Book records that he died 7 Oct. 1 Henry VII (1485). The "Cal. Inq. Post Mortem" fixes the date as 6 Oct. 1485. His will, dated 18 Aug. 1484, was proved 1 July 1493 (P. C. C. 24 Dogett). In it no mention is made of Fulham, though the testator directs that his feoffees shall distribute certain sums to charitable works for the health of his soul out of the Manors of Merston Bygot and Weston Bokeres (Frome, co. Dorset),

> "so always provided that Alianora Thorley have free annual possession without profits to the sum of xx^s."

This lady, there can be little doubt, was related to John Thorley, who was buried in Fulham Church in 1445. His daughter, Anne Stourton, who probably predeceased her father, was buried in Fulham Church. Katherine, the wife of the third baron, was the daughter of Sir Maurice Berkeley, of Beverstone, Gloucestershire. She died 25 June 1494. Hoare's statement that the third baron died without issue, is inaccurate, as he left a child, Francis.

Francis, the fourth Baron of Stourton, died in childhood, 18 Feb. 1486-87. The Stourton Manuscript Book records:

> "Fraunciscurn D'n'm Stowrton qui obijt infra etatum anno 3 Henr' Septimi."

William, who succeeded as fifth baron, was brother of John, the third baron. In the Court Rolls of the Manor of Fulham, this "Lord of Storton" is first mentioned in the minutes of a Court Baron in 1516, when he was returned as a suitor of the Court, but, being in default, *i.e.* not in attendance, was amerced "iij^d." The "Lord of Stourton" is again mentioned among the essoins at a Court Baron in 1518.

About this time William, the fifth baron, sold his estate at Fulham to Ralph (afterwards Sir Ralph) Warren, the owner of the messuage known as Passor's, which, as we have seen, lay on the east side of Bear Street and faced the property of the Stourtons. In 1519 we find "Ralph Waryn" doing fealty to the Lord of the Manor for "certain lands formerly William Stourton Lord of Stourton." The fifth baron died 17 Feb. 15 Henry VIII (1523-24). His will, dated 22 May 1522, was proved 16 March 1523-24 (P. C. C. 17 Bodfelde). He married Thomasine, daughter of Sir Walter Wrottesley.

For the next sixty years the history of Stourton, or Fulham House, is almost a blank, its story possibly merging for awhile in that of its neighbour Passor's.

In the time of Elizabeth a family named Cordell lived here. At a Court in 1580 a presentment was made for the repair of "the stayers" of the Ferry, at the bank of the Thames "near the house of Edward Cordell, Esq." On account of her abstention from church the wife of this Edward Cordell, in 1581, was caught within the meshes of the Act of Uniformity. The "Middlesex County Records," vol. i. p. 122, contain the following particulars of the case:

> 18th March 23 Elizabeth. - True Bill that (whereas it is enacted by a certain statute of Parliament of 23 Elizabeth, that every person over sixteen years of age, who should refrain from attending at church, chapel or some usual place of common prayer, against the tenor of a certain statute of the first year of her Majesty's reign For Uniformity of Common Prayer, and should be lawfully convicted thereof, should forfeit for each month, after the end of the said session of Parliament, in which he or she should so refrain, the sum of twenty pounds of lawful money) Elizabeth Cordell, wife of Edward Cordell, of Fulham, co. Midd., esq., and dwelling in the same parish, from the 18 March 23 Eliz. to 1st Oct. then next following refrained from attending divine service at the church of Fulham, and went to no other church, chapel or usual place of Common Prayer. G. S. P. R. Michaelmas, 23 Eliz.

William Cordell was a subsequent tenant. The next owner of Fulham House or Hall was that distinguished merchant trader, Thomas Winter, whose monument still adorns All Saints. In our account of his tomb, we have said all that is recorded of him. It is most likely that he built Fulham Hall on the site of what had been Stourton House. In the Parish Books his name first appears in 1650 and recurs down to his death, which took place 15 Jan. 1681-82. He left Fulham Hall to his widow, Ann, who, in 1688, became the wife of Charles Orby, and died in March 1689-90. On his wife's death, Thomas Winter directed in his will, dated 28 July 1679, that his Fulham property should go to Edward Winter, his nephew, son of his brother, Sir Edward Winter. In the event of his death without heirs male, the property was to go to Francis Winter, another brother of Thomas Winter, and, in default of heirs male, to Robert Pennington, who had married Joan Winter, sister of Thomas Winter. The Parish Books about this period are so incomplete that it is impossible to say who succeeded, but members of the Pennington family are known to have lived at Fulham.

At a Court Baron, in 1657, the following presentment was made:

> "Presented that it is not to damage or pr'judice of the tennantes of the said Mannor That the Lord of the said Manor grant unto Mathew Harwell, Michaell Wood and Robert Woolridge and their heirs certain parcels of the Waste lieing neere unto the fferry place on which is builded a house called ffulham Hall as alsoe one other parte of the Waste of the Lord lieing behind the said ffulham Hall on which is already laid the foundacon of foure houses. Whereupon the said Lord by Wm. Benson gent. his Steward and upon and by the Consent of the Homage and tennantes Hath Granted unto the said Mathew Harwell, Michaell Wood and Robert Woolridge and their heirs the parcells of ground and the Cottage thereon built and the said 4 houses to bee built on which is already laid the foundacons To the Use of the Watermen liveing or which shall hereafter live within the Towne and Towneshipp liveing in ffulham aforesd which are or shall bee contributors to the buildinge and repayreinge of the said prmisses and to such use and uses as shall be by the said Watermen of ffulham aforesd or the greater parte of them among themselves Articled and agreed upon and declared Provided alwaies and uppon condicon that if the said prmisses hereby granted shall at any time hereafter bee conurted (converted) or put on to any other use than as aforesd this surrender shall be void."

From this it would seem that the land adjacent to Fulham Hall, which stood on a portion of the Waste of the Manor, was, in perpetuity, to be allotted for tenements to three watermen of

Fulham, and that the foundations of four other houses for these men, on a piece of the adjacent Waste, were already laid. The entry, however, is somewhat ambiguous in meaning.

At a Court Baron in 1661, Matthew Harwell, Michael Wood and Christopher Harwell, watermen, were duly admitted to three "tenements." The four other houses, referred to in the foregoing minute, are now described as built. At a Court Baron in 1673 three trustees were appointed to manage the property. At a Court Baron in 1703, Fulham Hall is again referred to in connection with the watermen's trust, but unfortunately with the same doubtfulness of meaning.

The property next passed into the possession of a family named Gotobed, and we hear no more of the watermen. In 1706 Sarah Gotobed died seized of "four cottages in Bare St. and three tenements near ffulham fferry," and Bennet Hamon Gotobed, second son of Henry Gotobed, was admitted. These "three tenements" and "four cottages" represented the premises previously allotted to the Watermen.

Charles Hickman, Bishop of Derry

From about 1711 to 1713 Fulham Hall or House was in the occupation of Charles Hickman, Bishop of Derry. This learned prelate was educated at Oxford. In 1684 he was appointed domestic chaplain to Laurence Hyde, Earl of Rochester, Lord Lieutenant of Ireland. In 1702 he was promoted to the see of Derry. He married Anne, daughter of Sir Roger Burgoyne of Parson's Green and of Sutton, co. Bedford, bart. He died at Fulham, 22 Nov. 1713, aged 65, and was buried in the Chapel of St. Blaise, Westminster Abbey. Down to Faulkner's time the hatchment of Bishop Hickman still existed in the middle aisle of Fulham Church.

In 1716 Bennet Hamon Gotobed obtained permission to let all his customary lands and subsequently surrendered the four cottages adjacent to Fulham Hall to John Gibson and Elizabeth his wife, who, in 1729, surrendered them to the use of Jacob Tonson, junior. In 1742 he sold the cottages to Matthew Ramsey, who, in 1751, surrendered them to John Howe. At that date they had lately been increased from four to five.

In 1718 Thomas Ellis of St. Andrew's, Holborn, surrendered a portion of the Waste, described in the Court Rolls as bounded on the south by "a footway leading from ffulham fferry to the Bishop of London's Pallace," to the use of Mary Suffield of Portsmouth. In the following year this land passed into the possession of the Hon. Colonel George Howard, then the owner of Fulham Hall. In 1720 Col. Howard, who belonged to the noble house of the Howards, Dukes of Norfolk, sold the property to Lewis Vaslet.

Lewis or Louis Vaslet was a naturalized Frenchman. We first hear of him at Hampstead, where he kept a school from 1713 to 1716, among his pupils being Charles Hervey, younger son of John Hervey, first Earl of Bristol. In the latter year Vaslet came to Fulham. The Churchwardens' Receipts for 1716-17 include:

"Reed for Pewing Mr. Vasslett £1. 1. 6."

In Back Lane he founded the famous educational establishment known in later times as Burlington House School. Testard Lewis Vaslet, his son, died 21 Mar. 1730-31 and was buried at Fulham.

Lewis Vaslet married twice, first, Mary, daughter of Claude

Barachin, who died 10 Jan. 1704-5 and was buried in the churchyard of the Temple, and, secondly, Catherine, daughter of Charles Testard, who died 29 Apl. 1730. In the Church Registers the burial of the second wife is thus entered:

1730 - the wife of Mr. Lewis Vaslett . . . bu. 3 May.

Mr. Lewis Vaslet did not long survive his wife and son Testard, dying 12 June 1731. The Church Registers record:

1731. Mr. Lewis Vaslett bu. 16 June.

The will of Lewis Vaslet, dated 18 May 1731, was proved 18 June following by his daughter, Catherine (P.C.C. 166 Isham). The following is an extract:

> "I Lewis Vaslet of ffulham in the County of Middlesex, schoolmaster. Whereas I have with my late Loving wife Catherine's Consent by Indenture dated 15 Oct. 1720 settled my Dwelling House, gardens, stables and Coachhouse with the appurtenances in ffulham aforesaid, now I do devise to my son Andrew and his heirs for ever my Great House commonly called ffulham house by the Water Side in ffulham aforesaid which I bought of Colonel George Howard and lately in the occupation of Lady ffrances Buckingham and in the last place of Mr. James Powell together with three small tenements adjoining now in the occupation of Mr. Robert Gray, Mr. William Mallard and Mr. Anthony Hinton.
> To the Charity School of Fulham on ffulham side £20. To my daughter Catherine and her heirs all my copyhold that I bought of Thomas ffrewen, Esq., and all the buildings thereon and a stable under a Summer House in the occupation of Mr. Bartholomew Wimberley situate in Back Lane, ffulham, and a piece of land in the occupation of Mr. Robert Hester and Mr. Thomas Croft, clerk, and myself."

His children were Testard Lewis, who predeceased his father at the age of 25, Andrew and John Francis, Elizabeth, Ann and Catherine. The last married after her father's death, her first husband being John Noades or Nodes and her second, Oliver Edwards.

In 1728 we first find "The Lady Buckingham" rated for Fulham House. She resided here till 1736.

In the *London Evening Post*, for Saturday, Mar. 14 to Tuesday, Mar. 17 1741, appears the following advertisement for the letting of Fulham House:

> TO BE LETT
> AT FULHAM IN THE COUNTY OF MIDDLESEX
> A Compleat modern built Brick House, consisting of four Rooms on a Floor, with good Stabling for eight Horses, and Rooms over them for Servants, with two Coach houses, a very good Wash-house, Brew-house, Laundry, Cellaring, &c., two very good Gardens wall'd in, the one a Pleasure Garden and the other a Kitchen Garden, both planted and stocked with the best of Fruits, likewise an exceedingly fine shady Elm Walk, near a Quarter of a mile in Length.
> Enquire of Mr. Beauchamp, Carpenter in Fulham, near the same House.

Lord William Manners (1749) and Councillor Robert Bignal (1755-61) were subsequent occupants. In 1780 Fulham House became the home of William Sharp, brother of Granville Sharp, the distinguished philanthropist. They were the sons of Dr. Thomas Sharp, Prebendary of the Cathedrals and Collegiate Churches of York, Durham and Southwell, and grandsons of that sturdy churchman, John Sharp, dean of Norwich, whose preaching against Popery brought down on him the wrath of James II.

William Sharp, the elder son, became a London surgeon, practising at Guy's. For many years he lived in the Old Jewry. After a successful career he settled at Fulham, where he spent the last thirty years of his life. He died at Fulham House, 17 Mar. 1810. In the Church Registers is the following entry:

> 1810. William Sharp Esq. bu. 23 Mar.

Lysons states that William Sharp made considerable improvements upon his estate, "and built a beautiful cottage near the water side." This was Egmont Villa, built by William Sharp upon a site, acquired from the Bishop of London, to the west of the "Swan" inn.

In the "Gentleman's Magazine" for 1810 is a review of:

> "A Discourse occasioned by the Death of William Sharp, Esq., late of Fulham House, delivered in substance at Fulham Church, on Sunday 25

March 1810, by the Rev. John Owen, M.A."

William Sharp. From an engraving by C. Turner,
after a painting by J. Abbot, 1784.

William Sharp married Catherine, daughter of Mr. Thomas Barwick. This lady, after the death of her husband, continued to reside at Fulham House. Here, on 6 July 1813, died her brother-in-law, Granville Sharp, in his 79th year. In the Church Registers is the following entry:

1813. Granville Sharp, Fulham bu. 13 July, aged 79.

This eminent philanthropist was born in Durham, 10 Nov. 1735. He was apprenticed to a draper. In his spare time he taught himself Greek and Hebrew and obtained a position in the Ordnance Department. An accident determined his life. Chancing to meet a negro named Somerset who, being ill, had been turned adrift by his master, he took him under his care, and, on his recovery, obtained employment for him. Two years later Somerset was reclaimed by his old master. Sharp resisted the slave owner, and went deep into the law. In 1772 the great Somerset case was decided in the Court of King's Bench, the judges ruling that a slave could not be held in this country. So conscientious was Sharp, that, during the quarrel with the revolted American Colonies, he threw up his position in the Ordnance Department, sooner than assist in sending out war *matériel* to be used against a people with whom he sympathized.

He was one of the originators of the Association for the Abolition of Negro Slavery, and took a prominent part in founding the colony of Sierra Leone in Africa. He was the author of various works, the principal of which are "The Injustice, etc., of Tolerating Slavery in England," 1772, and "Uses of the Definite Article in the Greek Testament," 1798.

In Westminster Abbey, near Poets' Corner, is a marble tablet to the memory of Granville Sharp.

Granville Sharp. From an engraving by
C. Turner, after a painting by J. Abbot, 1784

In the grave of William and Granville Sharp lie the remains of Elizabeth Prowse, of Wickin Park, Northamptonshire, a married sister. In the "Gentleman's Magazine" for 1810 is a review of a "Discourse delivered in Fulham Church" in memory of this lady.

Mary, the daughter of William Sharp, married, in May 1800, Thomas John Lloyd-Baker, of Hardwicke Court, Gloucestershire. According to W. J. Pink's "History of Clerkenwell," Granville Square in that parish, planned in 1826 and completed in 1841, was first named Sharp Square, in compliment to the memory of the wife of Mr. Baker, the landowner. It now, of course, records the Christian name of her uncle, the abolitionist.

Mrs. Catherine Sharp, the widow of William Sharp, died at Fulham House, 9 Feb. 1814.

Mr. G. E. Lloyd-Baker, of Hardwicke Court, the great

grandson of William Sharp, possesses numerous records of the family. Amongst other things are William Sharp's Account Books, which are clear and interesting. The great family picture of the Sharps, considered to be Zoffany's masterpiece, is also at Hardwicke Court. This fine picture represents the Sharps in the stern of their yacht, holding a music party, a kind of entertainment for which they were famous. In the background are seen Fulham Church and the Cottage. George III and Queen Charlotte used to drink tea on this yacht while listening to the music. On one occasion the King enquired how they slept on the yacht, when William Sharp unfolded a sofa (still at Hardwicke Court) and made up a bed for him.

The Sharps on board their yacht off Fulham.
From the great painting by Zoffany, now in the possession of
Mr. G. E. Lloyd-Baker.

On Mrs. Sharp's death, Fulham House was, for a short while, tenanted by Sir Jarvis Clifton. In 1817 the house was taken by Mr. William Townsend, who died here, 30 June 1823. The last occupant of the famous old house was Mr. Townsend's sister, Mrs. Mary Barnard, widow of the Rev. Benjamin Barnard, prebend of Peterborough. She resided here from 1823 till her death, which occurred on 16 April 1842. She was buried by the side of her brother at Kensington.

In 1841 Fulham House was thus advertised for sale:

"Fulham: Particulars of sundry eligible Freehold, Leasehold, and small part Copyhold Estates, for investment and occupation, consisting of The Capital Freehold Family Residence called Fulham House, with coach houses, stabling, pleasure and kitchen gardens, etc., situate on the High Road and near to the Church at Fulham; two leasehold cottages, with gardens, adjacent, one (Thames Bank) let to W. H. Lane, Esq., the other (Egmont Villa) many years in the occupation of the late Theodore Hook, Esq., and two small tenements with gardens; also, two original shares and one quarter share in Fulham and Putney Bridge, giving votes for the counties of Surrey and Middlesex, which will be sold by auction by Messrs. Winstanley, at the Mart, on Thursday, Nov. 4, 1841, at 12 o'clock, in 8 lots."

The property was purchased by Mr. Henry Scarth, who, on Mrs. Barnard's death, in 1842, had the house demolished and the building materials sold.

Old Fulham House, which thus disappeared, in 1842-43, stood, secluded by high walls, in picturesque pleasure grounds and plantations, ornamented with cedar and other trees. On the ground floor was the dining-room, 26½ ft. by 17½ ft., with coloured walls, and windows reaching to the floor, opening into the garden. This apartment communicated by means of folding doors with the drawing-room, 17 ft. by 17 ft., a very fine room. On the same floor were the library, with an enriched ceiling, a small boudoir, etc. The hall had a handsome portico entrance supported by columns. The house was of red brick.

The site of Fulham House was leased to Mr. William Chasemore, Mr. J. Cambridge Faulkner and others for building purposes. Cambridge House, which may be regarded as the surviving representative of the ancient mansion, stands on what had been Mrs. Barnard's stable and coach house.

It was erected in 1843 by Mr. William Chasemore, who called it Holly House, there being then several exceedingly large holly trees growing there, one or two of which still remain. On going to live at Horsham, in 1854, he let it to Mr. W. H. Holland. A later tenant, Mr. Thomas Challis, who resided here from 1865 to 1869, renamed it Cambridge House, in allusion to an appointment which he held under the Duke of Cambridge. In 1877 the house was sold by Mr. W. Chasemore's trustees to Mr. Grant Macdonald.

On the old wall of Cambridge House, adjoining what were once the coal offices of Messrs. Downs and Co., were many names, cut by the watermen of Fulham. Mr. A. Chasemore, in his history of the old Bridge, records the following: Kelley (grandfather of the champion), I. W., 1771; G.W., 1773; 1775, G.K.; Rd. Rigg, 1776.

Some poor tenements, known as Pitman's Place or John's Place, were, in 1844, built on another portion of the site, just to the south of Fulham Church. John's Place was named after John Faulkner, the builder and owner. The path from underneath Putney Bridge, skirting the south side of Fulham Churchyard, is still known as John's Place.

CHAPTER XIX: HIGH STREET (MISCELLANEOUS)

A few other noteworthy houses, the actual sites of which are doubtful, remain to be mentioned. Folase or Folate's tenement stood in Bear Street in the time of the Plantagenets. Rose's tenement is mentioned in the Court Rolls from 1386 to 1540. Tebell's tenement, in the "Town of Fulham," was, in the time of James I, in the occupation of Sir Stephen Thornix, knight. It was long owned by the Powells. In 1649 Sir Edward Powell surrendered it to his heir, William Hinson alias Powell, and Katherine his wife, daughter of Dr. Richard Zouch. Dawbroke's tenement is referred to in the Rolls from 1385 to 1613. Cowper's tenement, on the east side of Bear Street, is mentioned from 1442 to 1551.

A tenement, evidently of much original importance, became known as 'The Anchor." In 1489 the site of this house was purchased of Sir Thomas Thwaites by Thomas Wyndowe, Wyndowt or Wyndout, and John Wynger, two London mercers. Thomas Wyndout, of St. Antholin's, was an alderman successively of the wards of Cripplegate and Coleman Street, and Sheriff of London and Middlesex in 1497. He died 1n 1499. He married Katherine, daughter of Thomas Norland, of Battle. In his will, dated 17 July 1499 (P.C.C. 4 Moone), executed 22 May 1500 and proved 1500-1, are the following references to Fulham:

> "and ij more of the said viij torchies I bequeth to the parish church of ffulhm in Midd."

> "The said Kat'yne my wife shall have during lief all my londes and tenements in the Towne and ffeldis of ffulhm co. Midd."

His widow, Katherine, married Sir Richard Haddon, kt., of St. Olave's, Hart Street, alderman and mercer of London, Sheriff of London in 1496, and Lord Mayor in 1506 and 1512. He died in 1516. Dame Katherine Haddon died in 1524. Her will, dated 21 Nov. 1524, proved 6 Feb. 1524-25 (P.C.C. 30 Bodfelde), contains the following bequests:

"To the Repacions of the pishe Church of ffulhm xx^s."

"To Kateryn Wyndowt all the stuffe of housholde that is and was at ffulhm as I left hit to hir fader."

An old cottage between the Moat and Bear Street, circa 1790.
From an original sketch plan in the possession of Mr. John Rooth

The property at Fulham went to Bartholomew Wyndout, only son and heir of Thomas, lord of the manor of Raddiswell in Great Hormead, co. Herts. Bartholomew Wyndout died 23 Aug. 1521, and was buried in the church of Great Hormead. His wife, Ann, survived him. Their only son, Richard, died in childhood. Their daughter Katherine, sole heiress, married, first, John de la Wood, and, secondly, Henry Hammond. In 1553 Ambrose Nicholas, citizen and salter of London, purchased of Henry Hammond his premises "in Bearestrete alias Fulhamstrete in Fulham."

Amongst the Ashmole Manuscripts in the Bodleian Library at Oxford (No. 1137, fol. 78) are, roughly sketched in pen and ink, the arms of Wyndout, Norland, Norton and one other. Beneath the four shields are the words:

"In the Hall windowes at the signe of the Anchor at Fulham, 4 Oct. 1666."

They were probably placed in the window about 1515, in which year Bartholomew Wyndout received a grant of the coat depicted.

Other Noteworthy Residents of Bear Street and the Neighbourhood

Sir Arthur Aston, the staunch Royalist, was the younger of the two sons of Sir Arthur Aston, kt., of Fulham, of which parish the younger Sir Arthur was probably a native. In the battle of Edgehill, he commanded the Dragoons. Charles I appointed him to the command of the garrison at Reading, and made him commissary-general of the Horse. Subsequently he succeeded to the command of the garrison at Oxford, where he broke his leg, the limb having to be amputated. No sooner had Charles II been proclaimed in Ireland, than Sir Arthur Aston took the command at Drogheda. Cromwell and his son-in-law, Ireton, at once proceeded to Dublin, capturing town after town. Drogheda was stormed on 10 Sept. 1649, the Protector himself fighting in the breach. The town fell, the inhabitants were put to the sword, while Sir Arthur was hacked to pieces and his brains beaten out with his wooden leg.

One "Master William Bennett" lived at Fulham, *temp.* Elizabeth and James I. He was a native of Clapcot, Berkshire, and is described as nephew (though more probably grandson) of Thomas Teasdale, the first scholar of the Free Grammar School at Abingdon, and one of its greatest benefactors. "Master William Bennett, of Fulham, in the County of Middlesex, gent," who had been educated at Abingdon School, left lands at Broad Blunsden and Weddell in Wiltshire for the perpetual relief and benefit of six poor children, born in the town of Abingdon, to be chosen from time to time by the Master and Governors of Christ's Hospital, to wear livery gowns and to be called "Master Bennet's poore schollars." His will is dated 29 Dec. 1608.

William Bennett died and was buried at Fulham, 19 Feb. 1608-9. In 1609 his bequest was duly carried out by his brother, Ralph Bennett, and his uncle, Thomas Teasdale.

That fine old navigator, Sir Thomas Button, had a house in Bear Street. Thomas Button was the fourth son of Miles Button, of Worlton, co. Glamorgan. In 1589 he entered the naval service. He served both in the West Indies and in Ireland. In 1612 he commanded an expedition in search of the North West Passage, exploring, for the first time, the coasts of Hudson Bay. New Wales recalls Button's nationality and Button's Bay, where he wintered, preserves his name. In the course of the next summer, Button succeeded in exploring the west coast of Hudson Bay. On the approach of autumn he returned home. We next find him made Admiral of the King's Ships on the coast of Ireland. About 1620 Admiral Button was knighted in Dublin by his kinsman, Sir Oliver St. John, the Lord Deputy. In 1624 he joined the Council of War, and in the following year became a member of the Commission appointed to inquire into the state of the Navy. It was perhaps about this period that he came to Fulham, as many letters, addressed by him from here, bear date 1625, 1626 and 1627. In his later years he was involved in disputes with the Admiralty about the non-payment of his pension and other matters. Some account of Sir Thomas Button will be found in Clark's "Glamorgan Worthies." His own "Journal" of his voyage to Hudson Bay is lost.

In the 1625 assessment, we find under "ffulham streete," "John Everad, Docr of Divinitye," rated to the poor at "vjs." The entry refers to Dr. John Everard, Evered, Everitt, or Everett, etc., a well-known mystic and divine, born about 1575, and educated at Cambridge. He was a man of wide learning, a neo-platonist in his early days, and a mystic to the last. He became a reader at St. Martin's in the Fields, in which capacity he preached, in Jan. 1618, a slanderous sermon regarding the Lord Mayor and aldermen. The Bishop of London compelled him to make a public apology. In the same year he published "The Arriereban," dedicated to Lord Bacon.

Dr. Everard was a keen opponent of the proposed marriage between Prince Charles, son of James I, and the Spanish Infanta. In March 1621 he was imprisoned in the Gatehouse, Westminster, for preaching against the alliance and enlarging on the cruelties of the Spaniards in the West Indies. The expression of his opinions several times led to his imprisonment, "some lord or other," on each occasion, begging his release. These appeals to the royal clemency led James I to exercise his wit. "Who is this Dr. Ever-out? his name shall be Dr. Never-out," observed the King. Everard left St. Martin's to become chaplain to Lord Holland. In 1636 he was charged with fatalism, antinomianism, and anabaptism, but, after being detained for some months, he was dismissed without a trial. He was soon in trouble again. Among the State Papers is the following order, dated Whitehall, 26 Nov. 1637, signed by

Archbishop Laud, Lord Keeper Coventry, Lord Treasurer Juxon, and Secretary Coke, and directed to Sir William Becher and Edward Nicholas, Clerks of the Council:

> "You are to repair to the dwelling of Dr. Everitt at Fulham and to seize all his papers and bring away such of them as may concern the State, according to such instructions as you have received, and all mayors, sheriffs and other His Majesty's officers and subjects whom it may concern are to be aiding unto you."

He was again prosecuted, Laud threatening to bring him to a morsel of bread because he could not make him stoop or bow before him. He was deprived of a living he held at Fairstead, in Essex, worth £400 a year, and in July 1639, was fined £1,000, but in the following June, when he read his submission on his knees in Court, he was released and his bonds were cancelled.

Dr. Everard did not long survive this degradation, dying at Fulham in 1640. Here, shortly before his death, he was visited by his friend, Elias Ashmole, the alchemist. In Ashmole Manuscripts 1440, fol. 204, in the Bodleian Library, is a prescription given to "Jo Everard at Fulham 7bris 16, 1640." It is full of cabalistic signs, of an almost unintelligible character. At folio 199 is a paper apparently relating to astrology. It concludes with the words:

> "Finished at Fulham on Sunday, August 9, 1640, by J. E., D.D." (i.e. John Everard, D.D.)

Dr. Everard was buried in Fulham Church. The Churchwardens' Accounts for 1640 show:

> "rec for buryall Dr. Evered in the Church 7s. 8d."

Sir Cornelius Fairmeadow lived near Bear Street from 1627 to 1638. The Churchwardens Accounts for the latter year contain:

> "rec. for a knell great bell Sr Cornelius ffarmadoe 5s."

He was knighted at Windsor, 25 Sept. 1628. From a presentment made at a Court held in 1641, we gather that the lands of "the heirs of Coreley ffayremeadowe, kt., deceased," lay east of

Bear Street and to the north of Churchfield, perhaps in the neighbourhood of Fulham Park. Nothing more is heard about the heirs of Sir Cornelius till 1642, when we find "the Ladie ffarmido" in possession. At a View in 1646 the Jurors present:

> "Wee order and payne the ladie ffayremeadowe for contynewing a sinke into the King's highway in ffulham whereby the passengers and neighbours are much annoyed, same to be stopped before the last of May."

The Rate books for 1648 show:

> "The Ladie ffarmedowe or her ten^t (tenement) 2s. 6d."

After this date the name ceases.

For the last five years of his life, John Florio, clerk of the closet to Anne, Queen of James I, resided at a house in Bear Street.

Florio, who was descended from the Florii of Sienna, was born in England about 1550. At the University of Oxford he taught the Italian and French languages, in the former of which he instructed Anne, the consort of James I. He also acted as tutor to Prince Henry, the King's son.

Florio is, perhaps, best remembered as the translator of the "Essays" of Montaigne. He was also the author of "Florio, his First Frutes, yielding Familiar Speech, Merrie Proverbes, Wittie Sentences, and Golden Sayings," 1575; "Florio, his Second Frutes, being 6,000 Italian Proverbes," 1591, and a "New World of Words: an Italian-English Dictionarie," 1595.

According to Anthony à Wood, Florio retired to Fulham, shortly before his death, on account of the plague. He possessed the lease of a house in Shoe Lane, but, after 1619, he seems to have kept to his retirement at Fulham. In the earliest existing assessment for the "pore of fulham-syde," under "ffulham streete," stands the entry,

> "John fflorio, Esqr. vj^s."

against which the clerk has made a marginal note "recd 2s. 6d.," which doubtless means that the poor lexicographer was unable to meet the full rate. In the next assessment, made 12 Oct. 1625, he is again assessed at "vjs." for his house in Bear Street, though he is stated to have died in Aug. or Sept. 1625. In the 1626 assessment we find

"fflorio M^ris v^id."

- without any amount against the name.

Florio, who died at Fulham, where he was buried, was a pedant, and, as such, became the butt of many literary men of his time. Shakespeare cruelly satirizes him in the person of Holophernes or Holofernes in "Love's Labour Lost," a schoolmaster who "speaks like a dictionary." The Italian doubtless raised the hostility of the playwrights by his wholesale condemnation of English dramas as "neither right comedies nor right tragedies, but perverted histories without decorum." Florio's sententious style may be judged from a letter, in Italian, which he addressed to Secretary Windebank. This effusion is dated Fulham, 9 Dec. 1619. In it Florio begs the Secretary to accept the fruit of his barren genius, if not as wine, yet as the juice of sour grapes. He sends him two pieces of "rubbish," of which he is the author, and which that blessed royal soul now in glory - Florio was referring to his late pupil, Prince Henry - often looked into. He proceeds to beg Windebank to add the salt of his benignity to the mass of flour and water which is prepared, to bring it into bread! He concludes by telling his correspondent that he is prevented from waiting on him by the bitter cold, the dirty streets and importunate old age.

Florio's will, which is dated 20 July 1625, and was proved 1 June 1626 (P.C.C. 97 Hele), is a singular document, which breathes a rare conjugal affection. The following is an extract:

> "I Jhon fflorio of ffulham in the Countie of Middlesex Esquire. To be buried at discretion of wife and executors.
> To my daughter Aurelia Molins the Wedding Ring wherewith I married her mother being aggreived at my very heart that by reason of my pouerty I am not able to leaue her any thing else.
> I giue and bequeath as a poore token of my love to my sonne in law James Molins a ffaire blacke velvett deske embroidered with seede pearles and with a siluer and Guilt inkehorne and dust box therin that

was Queene Annes.

To the right honourable my singulare and euer honored good Lord William Earle of Pembroke Lord Chamberlaine to the kings most excellent Maiestie and one of his royall counsell of state all my Italian ffrench and Spanish bookes as well printed as unprinted being in number about Three hundred and ffortie namely my new and perfect Dictionary as also my tenn Dialogues in Italian and English and my unbound volume of diuers written Collections and rapsodies, most heartilie entreating his Honourable Lordshippe (ass hee once promised mee) to accept of them as of a Signe and token of my seruice and affeccon to his honor and for my sake to place them in his Library eyther at Wilton or els at Baynards Castle at London humbly desiring him to giue way and favourable assistance that my Dictionarie and Diologues may bee printed and the proffitt thereof unto my wife.

Likewise to his noble Lordshippe the Coruine stone (as a iewell fitt for a Prince wch fferdinando the great Duke of Tuscanie sent as a most precious guift (among diuers others) unto Queene Anne of blessed memory the use and vertue wherof is written in twoe peeces of paper both in Italian and English being in a little box with the stone most humbly beseeching his honor (as I right confidently hope and trust hee will in charity doe if neede require) to take my poore and deere wife into his protection & not suffer her to bee wrongfully molested by any enimie of myne as also in her extremity to affoorde her his helpe good word and assistance to my Lord Treasurer that shee may bee paid my wages and the arrearages of that which is unpaid or shalbee behinde at my death.

Residue of goods to my wife Rose Florio most heartily greiving and euer sorrowing that I cannot guie or leave her more in requitall of her tender love, loving care, painfull dilligence, and continuall labour, to mee, and of mee in all my ffortunes and many sicknesses then whome neuer had husband a more loving wife, painfull nurse, or comfortable consorte. And I doe make institute, ordaine, appoint and name the right Reuerend ffather in God Theophilus ffeild Lord bishoppe of Landaffe and Mr. Richard Cluet Doctor in divinity Vicar and preacher of the Word of God at ffulham both my much esteemed dearely beloved and truely honest good frends, my Executors and overseers and to each of them for their paines an old greene veluett deske with a silver inke and duste box in each of them, that were sometymes Queene Annes my soueraigne mistrisse entreatinge both to accept of them as a token of my hearty affecon towards them and to excuse my poverty which disableth mee to requite the trouble paines and courtesie which I confidently beleeve they will charitably and for Gods sake undergoe in advising directing and helping my poore and deere wife in executing of this my last and unrevocable will and Testament, if any should bee soe malicious or unnaturall as to crosse or question the same.

As for the debts that I owe, the greatest and onelie is upon an obligatory writing of myne owne hand which my daughter Aurelia Molins wth importunity wrested from [sic] of about three score pound whereas the truth and my conscience telleth mee and soe knoweth her conscience it is but Thirty ffoure pound or thereabouts But let that passe since I was soe unheedy as to make and acknowledge the said writing I am willing that it bee paid and discharged in this fforme and manner My sonne in law (as my daughter his wife knoweth full well) hath in his hands as a pawne a faire Gold ring of mine with thirteene faire table diamonds therein enchased which cost queene Anne my Gracious Mistrisse seuen and fforty pounds starline and for which I might many tymes haue had fforty pounds readie money upon the said ring my sonne in the presence of his wife lent mee Tenne pound I desire him and pray him to take the overplus of the said Ring in parte of payment as also a leaden Ceasterne which hee hath of myne standing in his yard at is [sic] London-house that cost mee at a porte-sale ffortie shillings as also a siluer caudle cup with a couer worth about fforty shillings which I left at his house being sicke there desiring my sonne and daughter that their whole debt may bee made up they satisfied with selling the Lease of my house in Shoe-lane and so acquitt and discharge my poore wife who as yet knoweth nothing of this debt.

If my servant Artur -------- [sic] be with me at death my wife to give him such poore doubletts breeches hatts and bootes as I shall leave and therewithall one of my ould cloakes soe it bee not lyned with velvett."

The testator notes that this will is written "euery sillable" with his own hand and signed and sealed with seal of arms.

In 1629 Sir Edward Grevill came to reside in Bear Street. Sir Edward Grevill, of Milcote, co. Warwick, was the son of Lodowick Grevill, and Thomasine, daughter of Sir William Petrie, knt., his wife. In Dugdale's "Warwickshire" is a graphic account of the execution of his father, Lodowick, for an atrocious murder. On his father's death, Sir Edward rapidly got through the extensive family estates, which he was obliged to sell.

Sir Edward married Joan, daughter of Sir Thomas Bromley, Lord Chancellor. By her he had one son, John, who predeceased him, and seven daughters. He appears to have died about 1634, for in the following year the assessment is made out in the name of "The Lady Grivill." In 1636 the plague attacked Lady Grevill's house which was closed by the authorities and watched. The following extracts from the Parish Books tell their own melancholy tale:

> "pd. Osborne for two daies warding at the Ladie Grivills: 2s. 4d.
> pd. Henry Young for watching and warding at the same place: 4s. 3d.
> pd. Young for warding 3 weekes and fiue daies: £1 8s. 0d.
> pd. Kelly for watching two nights: 2s. 0d.
> pd. Nicholls for warding: 6d.
> pd. Elizabeth Jones and widowe Owyn for being at the Ladie grivills: £1 2s. 0d."

The sequel to this record may be gathered from the following line in the next assessment:

> "The Ladie Griuill dead . . . "

From the "Cal. Inq. Post Mortem" we learn that in 20 Ric. II (1396):

> "Thomas de Holand comes Kantiæ et Alesia uxor ejus"

held manors, or portions of manors, in several counties, including in

> "Fulham unum messuag' et 50 acre terr' ut de maner' de Fulham - Middx."

Sir Thomas de Holand or Holland, second Earl of Kent, of the name, was the second son of Sir Thomas de Holand or Holland, K.G., first Earl of Kent, of the name, by the Princess Joan Plantagenet, commonly called "the Fair Maid of Kent," daughter of Prince Edmund of Woodstock, Earl of Kent, youngest brother of Edward II. He was born circa 1352-55, and succeeded his father as Earl of Kent and Lord Wake of Lyddell in 1360. According to Froissart, he was knighted in 1367. By the marriage of his mother, the widowed Countess of Kent, with her cousin, Edward the Black Prince, he became half brother to Richard II. His will is dated Easter day 20 Ric. II. He died 25 Apl. 1396, and was buried at Westminster, 6 June 1396. He married, in 1364, Alesia, second daughter of Richard Fitzalan, Earl of Arundel, by the Princess Eleanor Plantagenet, daughter of Henry Earl of Lancaster, his second wife.

At a house in Bear Street lived, in the time of Charles I, Francis Kempe, attorney of the Common Pleas, etc. In the Fulham Rate books his name appears from 1625 to 1635. According to the pedigree of the Kempes in Harleian Manuscripts vol. 17 ("Visitation of London," 1633-35), he was the son of Francis Kempe of Little Hadham, Herts. He was the father of Leonard Kempe, M.A., Bartholomew Kempe, M.A., rector of Greyingham, co. Lincoln, and Henry Kempe of the Inner Temple, and of three daughters, Frances, Eliza Katherine, and Susan. The second daughter married Humphrey Shalcross of Fulham.

In the assessments for 1633, under "ffulham street," appears the name of "Captaine Kirke." In Col. Chester's "London Marriage Licenses" is the following entry:

"Kirke, David, of Fulham, Middlesex, Esq., bachelor, 34, and Sarah Andrewe, spinster, 21, daughter of Sir John Andrewe, of St. Giles in the Fields, Middlesex, Knight, who consents, --- at St. Bennet's, Paul's Wharf, London, 24 Apr. 1633."

Captain Kirke was knighted in the following year. He appears to have left Fulham in 1636.

In Bear Street resided Thomas Manwaring, where he died in 1639. The Churchwardens' Accounts for this year show:

"rec. for buryall and cloath (*i.e.* Hearse cloth) Manuring 10s. 2d."

His widow, Mrs. Elizabeth Manwaring, continued to reside in Bear Street. As late as 1657 we find "Elizabeth Mainwaring widow" fined fourpence at a Court Leet as a tenant in default. She was a sister of Sir Edward Powell of Munster House.

Sir Roger Martin lived at Fulham *temp.* Charles II and James II. The following entries occur in the Church Registers:

1680 Thomas son of Sir Roger Martine bu. 12 Nov.
1683 ffrancis son of Sr Roger Martin bu. 21 of Sept.
1685 Jermany son of Sr Roger Martin, a child bu. 26 of June.
1690 Mary dau. of Sr Thomas Marten bu. 6 May.

The Rate books show that, from 1647 to 1650, Charles Earl of

Nottingham resided at a house in the neighbourhood of Bear Street. In 1648 the Churchwardens received for pewage "of the Earle of Nottingham's servant" and of other persons, £1. 2. 6.

A Flemish family of the name Van Acker were settled at Fulham in the reign of Charles I. The first of these was Francis Van Acker or Ackere. In the State Papers (Domestic) is a letter, dated "in Fulham parish," 2 Nov. 1625, from Francis Van Ackere to Sir Robert Pye stating that he was not in any way able to advance the great sum of money solicited on a Privy Seal. In 1639 Nicholas Van Acker, believed to have been the son of Francis, James Butler and Prudence, his wife, all of Fulham, petitioned the King for letters of naturalization.

Sir William Walworth, Sheriff of London in 1370 and Lord Mayor in 1374 and 1380, lived at a house at Fulham. It was during his second mayoralty that Wat Tyler's rebellion occurred. Sir William probably died at Fulham. At a Court Baron, held in 1386, his death is thus presented:

> "Sr William Walleweche, kt., who held a tenemt and 5 acres in Fulham died since last Court."

His will, dated 20 Dec. 1385, was proved 24 Dec. 1385 (P.C.C. 1, Rouse). In it occur the following bequests:

> "To the rector of the church of ffulhm xx^s To the vicar of the same xx^s To the works of the said church xl^s To Ivo de ffulhm five marks and one of my robes."

Sir William, who was buried at St. Michael's, Crooked Lane, left a widow, Dame Margaret Walworth. In 1390 John Campden and others sold the reversion of the lands of Dame Margaret, after her death, to William Wickham, Bishop of Winchester, and others.

Miscellaneous Notes

The following miscellaneous notes relating to Bear Street follow in chronological order:

1429. The following entry occurs in the minutes of a Court Baron held in 1429:

> "Avice who was the wife of William Oxwyke in pure widowhood surrendered into the hands of the Lord of the Manor one Cottage with curtilage in Bury Stret in Fulham formerly of John Brothere parcel of Kernpes tenement to the use of Robert Eyre otherwise called Roberde Jamys To whom seizen was granted to have and to hold to him and his heirs by the rod by the Services and Customs, etc., under this condition, that if the said Avice have for the term of her life her dwelling in one lowermost chamber at the east end of the house called the fferehous (firehouse) with ffeer and flet (fire and house-room) in the same and part of the profit of the herbs growing in the curtilage there with free ingress and egress so often as she please that then this surrender shall remain in its strength and effect otherwise it shall be lawful for the said Avice by license of the Lord to re-enter into her former estate anything in this surrender to the contrary notwithstanding And the said Robert gave to the Lord for a fine for entry to have in the form aforesaid as appears And he did fealty."

This is an interesting entry. The widow's dower consisted of fire and lodging in her late husband's house as long as she lived, with the right to gather herbs in the garden. "Feer and flet" was once a common legal term. A "firehouse" was a house which contained at least one hearth and chimney, in other words, a permanent dwelling house.

1491. From the Court Rolls:

> "Nicholas Sturgeon should repair the wholf in Bairstrete before his gate."

1525. The Court Rolls for this year contain the first reference to the existence of "a common ditch in Berestret."

1552. The following, from the minutes of a Court General in 1552, is an early instance of default by fine of customary lands:

> "Robert Whyte, gent., has sold one garden to a certain John Brydges lying in Berestrete by fine levied in the King's Court to the prejudice of the Lord and his successors."

1625. From the Court Rolls:

> "Ordered that Humphrey Lympenie cause his Loame which Lyeth in ffulham street to the annoyance of the way to be removed before Michaelmas next or else to forfeit for every Load vj^s viij^d."

1633. In this year there were 35 persons rated under the head ffulham streete"

1640. From the Churchwardens' Accounts:

> "Itm. to a sicke woman of ffulham streete Aug 16 . . . 1s. 0d.

1666. In this year there were 31 persons assessed for property in Bear Street.

1684. At a Vestry held 4 June of this year:

> "It is this day ordered in Vestry that the widow Winslow doo hold ye peece of ground in Bearestre conteyneing about eight rodd now in her occupacon at ye yearely rent of twelve shillings vntill order from ye parish."

CHAPTER XX: BURLINGTON ROAD

We will now turn into Burlington Road. Doubtless from the occupation of some of its earlier inhabitants, the way was once known as Sowgelders Lane. In the Court Rolls the first mention of the lane by this name occurs under date 1578. In 1674 we find four persons assessed as follows:

"Sow-gildrs Lane
Mrs. Aurel Hicks vid. . . . 6s. 4d
Resident of fflorence . . . 0s. 0d.
Mr. Tho. Hooke . . . 4s. 6d.
S^r Wm Powell Baront . . . 15s. 0d."

Burlington Road From a photograph by Mr. J. Dugdale, 1895

The last mention of Sowgelders' Lane occurs under date 1728. In the olden times the lane was more generally known as the Back Lane, from its position in relation to Bear Street. In the Court Rolls for 1577 it is merely described as "a lane" to the east of Bear Street. It is not till 1613 that the name "the backe lane" occurs in these records. Sir William Powell, in his will, dated 1680, speaks of the Almshouses he founded as situated "in a certain Back Lane."

In the Parish Books it is not until 1713 that we come across the name "Back Lane."

East Side

On our right, just facing the wall of Fulham Pottery there existed, until a few years ago, a small *cul-de-sac* which rejoiced in the designation of Broomstick Alley.

A little way further down was the Fulham Academy, a famous school for boys, known, in its later days, as Burlington House School.

In 1728 Lewis Vaslet, a schoolmaster, obtained the property upon the surrender of Thomas Frewen of Cleybroke House. It consisted, at that time, of a messuage divided into two tenements together with "a stable under the summerhouse in the Back lane in Fulham now in the occupation of Mary Hickman widow."

We have previously spoken of Lewis Vaslet in our account of Fulham House. He seems to have been a pedagogue of the olden school, whose primary aim was to well ground his boys in Latin and French. He was the author of three works. The first, the third edition of which he dates "Ex ludo nostro Literario qui est Hampstediæ 6° Non Jul. 1713," is a small book on Latin accidence, followed by a string of trilingual exercises in the shape of proverbs and sayings in Latin, English and French. The book is cumbrously entitled

> "Nomenclator trilinguis, usitatiora rerum nomina continens in quo Praeter Genus & Declinationem Nominum, notatur etiam Syllabarum Quantitas Adjicitur Verborum & Adjectivorum Sylvula una cum Proverbiis Miscellaneis Ducentis & Duodecim. In Puerorum ngenuorum gratiam qui cum Latinis Gallica conjungunt. Editio Tertia Actior & Emendatior Londini [MDCCXIII]."

In 1723 Lewis Vaslet published an

> "Introduction à la connoissance des Antiquitez Romaines, traduites en partie d'un ouvrage Latin de Cellarius et en partie tirée des meilleurs auteurs, etc. La Haye, 1723."

In 1730, the year of his death, appeared,

"Emmanuelis Alvari Regulae de Syllabarum Quantitate, cultiores multo et auctiones quam ante editæ . . . et Lusus Poetici Opera et Studio. L. V. Lond., 1730."

The dedication has the signature as from "Fulham, e ludo nostro Literario 8° Id. Maii, 1730."

Burlington House School

On the death of Vaslet, another Frenchman, Nicholas Guillibeau, conducted the School in Back Lane. During his regime, he had among his pupils the young Lord Compton, the heir of the Earl of Northampton. In the possession of the Compton family is a remarkable collection of letters written by this old schoolmaster and his pupil between the years 1734 and 1737. The letters are chiefly addressed to the Countess (the lad's mother), whose replies, unfortunately, are not preserved. The series opens with a letter, dated 12 Oct. 1734, from Guillibeau to the Countess of Northampton, in which he writes:

"My Lord Compton continues, thank God, in very good health. His Lordsp presents his duty to my Lord and to your Ladysp and Services to the Ladies. Mr. Humes brought his Lordship's frock and Breeches this morning and the Hatter has also sent a Hatt."

On 5 Nov. 1734, Guillibeau writes to the Earl:

"His Lordship continues, thank God, in very good health, only his hollow Tooth has felt a little uneasy these 4 or 5 days, but since I have stopped the hole with a grain of Mastick it has been easyer."

The next is an undated letter, written apparently in August 1737, the handwriting being that of a child. It is from the boy to his mother. It runs:

"Madam I do not doubt the return of your Ladyship's birthday must give great delight to everyone that has the pleasure and happiness to be acquainted with you, surely then it must give inexpressible delight to me and my sisters, who are so much obliged to you for your love and tenderness towards us; I assure your Ladyship I most sincerely congratulate you of it, and heartily wish you may see a great many of them in health and prosperity. We have had some little rain since we came to Fulham, but I hope there has not been enough about Ashby to hinder you from riding out. We had a very good journey and found the roads exceeding (*sic*), but they were very empty, there being but very few travellers. Mr. Lee just called here, he said he was going to the Bishops, but whether he will dine there or not I cannot tell. Pray present my duty to Pappa and my service to my uncle, aunts and sisters together (with) my congratulations to them upon your Ladyship's birthday. I will now trouble you no longer, only beg that you will believe me to be, Madam, your most Dutyfull son,
James Compton."

Playground of Burlington House School

On 16 Aug. 1737, Guillibeau writes:

"My Lord Compton goes on in his Studys with Chearfulness. He found his form advanced in Martial and Horace . . . My wife and I return my Lord and your Lady^{sp} thanks and are very much obliged for the fine piece of venison and the Rabets your Lady^{sp} has been pleased to give us."

Again, on 3 Sept. 1737:

"My Lady, Lord Compton continues, thank God, in very good health. His Lordship drinks no Malt drink, the beer here, being newer than what he used to have at home, makes him dislike it, so I thought to mention this to your Ladyship because this is about the time your Ladyship used to order wine for his Lordship's use."

In less than another month, Guillibeau had bad news to convey to the Countess, for Dr. Isaac Lowndes was summoned to attend his Lordship. The letter, dated 13 Sept. 1737, reads:

"My Lady, my Lord Compton has caught a cold, which I hope will prove to be nothing but the Distemper that goes about . . . Early in the morning I sent for Mr. Lounds . . . He ordered his Lordship some of Gascoin's Powders every six hours."

Two days later, 15 Sept. 1737, the old time-serving pedagogue reassures the anxious Countess:

"My Lord Compton has, thank God, very well recovered."

The next day (16 Sept. 1737) the boy writes:

"Madam, I perceive myself now, I think, quite recovered of my little indisposition, bleeding at the Nose did me a great deal of good, for it bled a great deal Tuesday night and Wednesday. My master and I went last Sunday to see Lady How at Parson's Green, who has invited me to dine there some day. Colds are so frequent in London that hardly anybody escapes them, which is occasioned chiefly, I believe, by the uncertainty of the weather."

On 22 Sept. 1737, Guillibeau informs the Countess that he has written to Mr. Agutter, as requested by her Ladyship, for "three dozen of Red Port" for "my Lord Compton."

Another letter, dated "Fulham, 1st Oct. 1737," from

Guillibeau to the Countess, runs:

> "My Lady, my Lord Compton continues, thank God, in very good health, as all the boys in our School likewise do. We have had very wet weather for above six weeks, which made me send last week for a Matt for his Lordship's chamber to keep it clean, so that it may not want washing so often for fear his Lordship should not (*sic*) take Cold by the rooms not being thoroughly dry. His Lordship is much more in his chamber than formerly, writing his exercises."

Playground of Burlington House School

The last glimpse we catch of Guillibeau is in a letter, dated "Fulham, 8 Oct. 1737," addressed to the Countess, informing her that "his Lordship is making a Latin epistle in verse to send to the Consol (Charles Compton) by one of his schoolfellows who is going to Lisbon."

The lad was James, the eldest son of James 5th Earl of Northampton, who married Lady Ferrers. He predeceased his father.

The Rev. Thomas Croft continued the School in Back Lane. By far his most famous pupil was Thomas Pennant, LL.D., the distinguished naturalist and antiquary. In 1753, Mr. Peter Parisot rented at least a portion of the premises, including the "new school late Mr. Croft's." Subsequently, about 1757, the school was resuscitated under Mr. Edmund Day and continued by that gentleman's son. In 1767 the younger Day obtained a license to act as schoolmaster at the Parish School. In the Vicar General's Books is a copy of the license.

Burlington House, shortly before demolition.
From a photograph by Mr. J. Dugdale

From about 1787 to 1799 the School was in the occupation of the Rev. Dr. Rowley. In 1807 Mrs. Rowley sold the School to Mr. Robert Roy, who had kept a large scholastic establishment in Old Burlington Street, Piccadilly. It was, of course, during his proprietorship that the name Burlington House School first obtained. On the death of Mr. Robert Roy, in 1824, the School was continued and enlarged by his son, the Rev. Robert Roy, M.A. In 1827 the Rev. R. Roy obtained a lease of the whole site extending from Back Lane eastwards to Mrs. Carey's land (see "Fulham Road") and southwards to the New King's Road, with the exception of a strip of land at the south-west corner of the lane, belonging to the Bishop of London, and the site of the Gate House adjoining the New Kings Road. About this time the Rev. Dr. Roy succeeded in getting the name of the thoroughfare altered from

Back Lane to Burlington Road. In 1856 he enfranchised the site.

The Rev. Dr. Roy, on his retirement in 1840, let the school to Dr. Henry Laumann, who continued it till 1853. Subsequently Dr. Laumann moved to the Rectory House, Parson's Green. The following is a copy of a quaintly-worded prospectus issued by Dr. Laumann, illustrated with views of the School:

"BURLINGTON-HOUSE SCHOOL,
FULHAM, MIDDLESEX.
conducted by
DR. LAUMANN,
SUCCESSOR TO THE REV. ROBERT ROY, M.A.

"Young gentlemen are carefully instructed in the Latin and Greek Languages, Mathematics, English Literature, with the usual branches of a liberal education, preparatory to their introduction to the Public Schools, or to the Royal Military and East India Colleges. Those pupils who are intended for the Counting House are diligently prepared in Vulgar and Decimal Fractions, Exchange with Foreign Countries, Book-keeping, etc., etc.

The system pursued in this Establishment combines the most assiduous attention to the health and comfort of the Pupils, with an earnest solicitude to inculcate those sound religious and moral principles, which not only conduce so essentially to the formation of the character and disposition, but which also exercise so important an influence over their future conduct.

The Junior Department (for Pupils under nine years of age), which is under the immediate direction of Mrs. Laumann, and properly qualified female Assistants, is entirely separated from the Upper School; and, in consideration of their tender age, the Young Gentlemen are constantly under the superintendence of one of the Assistants, both in the bed chamber and during the hours of relaxation.

The house is airy and commodious, the School and Sleeping rooms are large, the Play-grounds and walks extensive, and situated on a dry gravelly soil.

Each young gentleman has a separate bed."

The grounds of Burlington House measured 3a. 3r. 9p.

In 1853 Burlington House and grounds were purchased by the Government for the purpose of erecting on the site a reformatory prison. Fulham Refuge, which was built by J. Dawson in 1856, on the site of the boys' cricket field attached to Burlington House

School, was originally designed as a reformatory home for young females. The most hopeful cases were selected from the criminal prisons with a view to their being permanently reclaimed.

Entrance to Fulham Convict Prison.
From a photograph by Mr. T. S. Smith, 1895

At the Fulham Refuge the young women were trained in laundry and other industrial occupations, and spent here, as a rule, the last two or three years of the terms for which they had been sentenced. For the younger convicts there was a school in the prison. Sir Joshua Jebb, in his capacity as Director General of Convict Prisons, took a keen interest in the institution, the inmates of which were affectionately known as "Jebb's pets." After a while the Fulham Refuge was turned into an ordinary Convict Prison, the establishment being enlarged to hold about 400 prisoners.

Facing the main entrance in Burlington Road was the Chapel (pulled down in 1897), where the Protestant inmates attended Divine worship. From the Chapel a covered-in way led to a large room used as a Roman Catholic Chapel. The prison premises occupied three sides of a square. The cells were ranged in tiers round the several blocks, access being gained by means of staircases which communicated with narrow galleries running round the floors. In No. 29 Constance Kent was confined for the murder of her little half-brother, Francis Savile Kent, at Road, Somerset, on the night of 29-30 June 1860. In addition to the ordinary cells there were three "preliminary cells," to which prisoners were first relegated, and four "penal cells," which were used in cases of extra punishment. From these latter the light could be totally excluded.

Fulham Convict Prison.
From an old print in the "Illustrated London News."

Cell No. 29, where Constance Kent was confined.
From a photograph by Mr. J. Dugdale

The prison premises also included a hospital with quarters for the medical staff, a laundry, etc. Burlington House, which was bought with the site, was used as the officers' quarters. In the grounds stood the old gateway which formerly faced the house. Fulham Prison ceased to be used in 1888, "short term" sentences having materially reduced the amount of accommodation needful for female convicts.

In addition to Constance Kent, Madam Rachel and Mrs. Gordon-Baillie may be mentioned as convicts who served at Fulham Prison.

The Chapel, Fulham Convict Prison.
From a photograph by Mr. J. Dugdale

After remaining empty for a few years, the site was, in 1893, sold for a building estate. Shortly afterwards the greater part of the premises were demolished, Burlington House itself coming down in 1895. The ground is now covered with small houses.

Rigault Road, which formed the northern boundary of Fulham Prison, marks the site of a noted fruit garden. Passing a little row of cottages, we come to Northampton Place, or Mawby's Buildings, as it was once better known. The houses on the north side were built in 1825 by Mr. S. Mawby, a native of Northampton, whence the name. Mawby is best remembered in Fulham as the originator of the first local omnibus - the "Paul Pry," which ran between old Fulham Bridge and Charing Cross, the fare for which journey was 1s. 6d. In pre-Mawbian days the coaches to town charged 2s. 6d. each. Mawby was a self-made man, who came to London without even the proverbial shilling in his pocket.

The houses on the south side of Northampton Place were built by Mr. Potter without back windows, so that the residents could not overlook the grounds of Dr. Roy's establishment.

West Side

At No. 2, on the west side, lived Richard Green, the last surviving toll-man of Fulham Bridge. Here he died on 15 Aug. 1897, aged 75. Nos. 10 to 20, Burlington Road mark the site of the rear of the old Workhouse premises. Where No. 10 stands was the old Cage, removed here from the High Street in 1814. It was in this lock-up that "Captain" Corder, a notorious housebreaker - one of the last footpads on the London Road - was confined. The Cage was removed about fifty years ago.

A little further south, on the site where the Burlington Road Lecture Hall stood until a few years ago, were Sir William Powell's Almshouses, founded in the reign of Charles II. The precise date of the foundation of this charity cannot be ascertained. An almshouse certainly existed in Bear Street long before the time of Sir William Powell. Scattered through the Court Rolls are two or three references to it. At a View, held in 1573, Michael Dormer was ordered

> "to cart away (*abcarior*) his dunghill at the Almshouse before Pentecost or forfeit . . . iij^s. iv^d."

It is very possible that the origin of Sir William Powell's charity may be enshrined in the following presentment, for the appointment of fresh Trustees, made at a Court General in 1667:

> "At this Court it is presented that, on 11 Dec. 1666, Thomas Cranke, son and heir of Thomas Cranke of Fulham, yeoman, deceased and last surviving trustee of two parcels of the Waste and a cottage thereon erected, as appears by roll of Court of --- Oct. 1620, surrendered all his title into the hands of the Lord to the said tenement, containing rooms for four poor widows of the parish, situate in Beare Streete to use of

William Powell, knight and bart., Rcd. Stevenson, vicar of Fulham, Henry Elwes, Esq., Thos. Beauchampe, John Shercroft, Wm. Dodd, Jno. Plucknett, gent., John Earsbey, John Burton, senior, Wm. Dauncer, and the said Thos. Cranke, inhabitants of Fulham, to hold to the use of the Poor of Fulham for ever."

The Churchwardens' Disbursements for 1669 include:

"Paid Wm. Williams bricklayer for repairinge Almes how: 10s. 11d."

In his will, dated 2 Dec. 1680, Sir William devised, in trust, to Richard Powell and Christopher Plucknett

"All that parcell situate lying and being in a certain Back Lane in the parish of ffulham, whereon there is now erected and built a certain messuage or tenement, divided into twelve rooms, and inhabited by twelve poor women, together with all outhouses, buildings, gardens and other accommodation thereunto belonging, or therewith used and enjoyed."

In support of this charity Sir William Powell left (I) the messuage in the possession of Thomas Pyner and (2) the inn called the "Nagg's Head," both situated in Bear Street. The Almshouses and the messuage of Thomas Pyner formed one block.

Sir William died without leaving any regulations for the government of his charity. After the death of Richard Powell, the surviving Trustee, the heir-at-law could not be found. In these circumstances it was deemed advisable to commit the charity to the trust of the Vicar and parish officers, under whose care it remained until the Charity Commissioners framed a Scheme in 1870.

By his will, dated 7 Apl. 1723, Sir John Williams, son-in-law to Sir William Powell, gave Fan Mead in the Town Meadows towards the sustenance of the Powell Trust. The terms of this bequest are as follows:

"I give and bequeath the Meadow called ffan Mead in the parish of ffulham in the County of Middlesex to the Vicar Churchwardens and Overseers of the poor of the said Parish of ffulham towards the repairing the Almeshouse in ffulham which Sr William Powell my wifes ffather built for twelve poore women and if there happens to be any remains out of any of the Rents of the said Meade or Tenements given by the said Sr William Powell after the annual Charge of Clothes for six poor men and six poor women and of Coales and bread to the twelve poor women that then and in that case the residue of the Rents aforesaid shall be equally divided between twelve poor women and twelve poor men and soe, as often as there remains any of the rents after the usual yearly allowances and repairs are done paid and defrayed."

In 1792-93, the Almshouses, which had fallen into a dilapidated state, were rebuilt. The Churchwardens' Accounts for this period contain the following item:

"Pd. for Lodging the Alms Women while their Houses were Rebuilding £18. 6. 8."

The contract for this was let by the Trustees (the Rev. G. Jepson, Vicar, and William Bryon, Churchwarden) to Nathaniel Chasemore. By an agreement or memorandum, dated 12 Oct. 1792, Mr. Chasemore covenanted

"To erect and build and completely finish for them within nine months at his own costs and charges 12 new alms houses with Pallisadoes in front agreeably to a plan and estimate made for that purpose and under the inspection and controul of them and of their surveyor,"

subject to the Trustees granting him, on certain specified terms, a lease of the houses at the rear of the Almshouses (see "Thomas Pyner's Messuage").

The Rev. R. G. Baker, in his "Fulham Benefactions," in speaking of this arrangement between the Trustees and Mr. N. Chasemore, observes with quiet humour:

"This agreement was duly performed on both sides. But, it is to be regretted, that too liberal an use was made of the old materials in building the new Alms-Houses, in consequence of which a considerable expense has been subsequently incurred in putting them into proper repair. It appears, however, that the sum of about £350 was laid out by Mr. Chasemore in erecting them, which, added to the £500 laid out on the demised premises and the £50 paid to Ann Webb, makes a total of about £900 for the consideration of his lease."

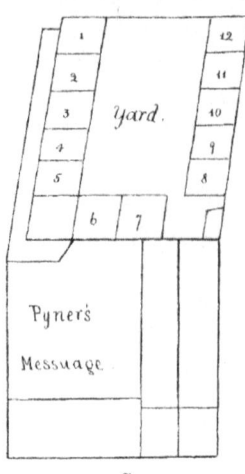

Plan of Sir Wm. Powell's Almshouses and adjacent property (originally Thos. Pyner's Messuage)

In 1868, the Almshouses having once more fallen into decay, it was decided to make an effort to obtain the sanction of the Charity Commissioners to rebuild them on a more airy and cheerful site, adjacent to Fulham Churchyard. It was pointed out to the Commissioners that the old Almshouses had only one small room to each, that the dwellings themselves were ill-ventilated and below the level of the road, and that they were constantly requiring repair. Early in the following year (1869) the Commissioners gave their sanction to the proposal of the Trustees. In 1870 the old Aimshouses were sold by auction. The following is a copy of the announcement of the sale:

> "Fulham Town. Particulars and Conditions of Sale of a compact freehold consisting of 12 cottages brick built and tiled, situate in Back Lane, Fulham, and known as Powell's Alms Houses, being very central, and having a frontage of 64 ft. 4 in. and a depth of 75 ft. containing an area of about 5,000 square feet. Mr. Edward Taylor has been favoured with instructions from the Trustees of 'Powell's Charity' to sell by auction on Tuesday, 5th of July 1870, at the 'Compasses Tavern,' High Street, Fulham, at 2 o'clock punctually, etc."

Burlington Gardens. From a photograph by Mr. J. Dugdale, 1895

The new Almshouses, erected on the site adjoining the Churchyard, are described in our account of Church Row.

A little further south we come to a row of picturesque old cottages, running at right angles to Burlington Road, known as Burlington Gardens. From this point to the wall of Fulham Pottery, there is nothing which calls for comment.

Some few years ago, when the deep sewer was laid in Burlington Road, there was found, at a depth of about four feet, a paved way in the centre of the road, made of large stones like lapstones used by cobblers. This shows what must have been the low level of the original lane, which, in later times, was above that of the High Street.

Other Noteworthy Residents

Henry Condell, one of Shakespeare's fellow actors, had a "country house" in Back Lane. In the assessments for 1625, we find "Henry Cundale, gent," rated to the poor at "iiijs." In 1626 and 1627 his name again appears. In the latter year he died. In 1627-28 John Wolverstone was licensed

"To demise one cottage in the occupation of Widow Condell and near the lands of the said John in Back Lane in ffulham to the said Elizabeth Condell for . . . years."

The number is illegible. In 1628 we find the "widdowe Cundall" assessed for the cottage. Mrs. Condell lived on at the house down to 1635.

Henry Condell was one of the ten principal comedians who performed in Ben Jonson's *Every Man in his Humour* in 1598, and in *Every Man out of his Humour* in 1599. With Shakespeare and Richard Burbage, he was a member of the company called the "Lord Chamberlain's Men." In May 1603, when this company was formally enrolled as the "King's Servants," Condell's name figures as sixth in the list. He became "a partner in the profits" of the Globe Theatre, built by the brothers Richard and Cuthbert Burbage, and he also enjoyed a share in the profits of the Blackfriars Theatre.

In a new patent granted to the company, 27 Mar. 1618-19, Condell's name appears immediately after those of John Heminge and Richard Burbage, and when, in 1625, Charles I renewed the company's privileges, his name appears second in the list. Shakespeare, Richard Burbage, Condell and Heminge were great friends. In his will, dated 5 Mar. 1615-16, Shakespeare bequeaths 26s. 8d. to "my fellowes, John Hemynges, Richard Burbage and Henry Cundell . . . to buy them ringes." In 1623 Heminge and Condell published the first collected edition of Shakespeare's plays.

Condell, in the earlier part of his career, lived at a house in the parish of St. Mary, Aldermanbury. About 1625 he gave up the stage, and soon afterwards sought retirement at Fulham. About this period there was a severe outbreak of the plague in London. Thomas Decker, the dramatist, ridiculed the fleeing and awe-stricken fugitives in a satire entitled "A Rod for Run-aways." This elicited an anonymous reply called "Run-aways' Answer," which was inscribed, "To our much respected and worthy friend, Mr. H. Condell, at his country house at Fulham." The writers of this "Answer" assert that they have been unjustly assailed by Decker, and that they left London on a professional tour, and not out of any fear of the pestilence. They add that Condell, whom they wish to appoint as arbitrator in the dispute, entertained them royally before their departure.

Henry Condell died at Fulham in December 1627, and was interred in the church of St. Mary the Virgin, Aldermanbury, on the 29th of that month. On 15 July 1896, a monument of red granite was unveiled in the churchyard of St. Mary the Virgin, to the memory of Henry Condell and John Heminge.

In the reign of James I, Robert Jenkinson of Townley, Lancashire, and Fleet Street, resided in Back Lane. His first wife was Bridget, widow of a Mr. Whinyard of London, and third daughter of his uncle, Anthony Jenkinson, the well-known oriental traveller and ambassador to the Czar Ivan the Terrible. His second wife, Margaret Carleill, was the daughter of Anthony Burbage, and widow of Lawrence Carleill, who died in 1597.

Robert Jenkinson was buried at St. Dunstan's in the West, 2 Dec. 1617. His widow, Mrs. Margaret Jenkinson, is rated for her house in Back Lane down to 1637, when she sold it to John Robinson. The house eventually passed into the possession of Charles, Earl of Peterborough. In the old "Register Book" is the following record of a gift by Robert Jenkinson:

"Mr Robert Jenkenson sornetymes dwelling in the Parishe of Fulham gave by worde of mouth the summe of Twentie poundes for the use of the Poore of the sayd parishe, which accordinglie was payd."

Robert Jenkinson, son of Robert and Bridget Jenkinson, was knighted at Theobalds, 30 April 1618. He was the ancestor of the Earls of Liverpool. He died in 1645.

CHAPTER XXI: CHURCH ROW

Church Row, which extends from the south-west corner of the High Street to the north-east entrance to the Churchyard, is an old and interesting place. The houses along the terrace, on the northern side, are very suggestive of the olden time, presenting now, probably, much the same appearance as they did to Bowack, when, in 1705, he wrote:

> "Upon the passage leading to the Church, called Church Lane, are several very handsome, airy houses."

Church Row, or Lane, as it was sometimes termed, ranks amongst the very oldest of the bye-ways of the parish. More than five hundred years ago a passage existed here. On the south side of this way stood the Vicarage. No houses then bordered the north side, from which, doubtless, an uninterrupted view of the great ditch or Moat of the Manor House was obtainable.

Facing the primitive Vicarage and adjacent to the Churchyard lay a garden which had, from time immemorial, belonged to the Lord of the Manor. The site of this garden is now represented by Sir William Powell's Almshouses and the piece of land to the west which was added to the Churchyard in 1843. This garden of the Bishops of London bore (as far as the difficult scrip in the Court Rolls can be deciphered) the name of Godeyereshauyll. The meaning of the first part of this word is clearly Gode-yeres, the genitive case of Godeyer, the old spelling of Goodyear. Owing to the uncertainty of the orthography of the latter part of the word, it is difficult to state its meaning. Possibly it may be *havyll*, signifying "property" (*cf.* the verb to *have*).

In 1392 Bishop Braybroke granted this garden to one John Hunt, with the stipulation that a passage, 12 feet in width, extending from the Churchyard to the bridge known as Church-bridge, should be preserved to himself and his successors. This interesting grant, made at a Court General, held 12 Dec. 1392, runs in the following terms:

> "The Lord grants to John Hunt one garden called Godeyereshauyll near the Churchyard of Fulham, reserving to the Lord and his successors one way in length from the gate of the Churchyard aforesaid to the footbridge beyond the great ditch (magnā fossam) of the Lord Bishop there and in breadth xij feet the which said garden called Godeyerhauyll has been a long while in the hands of the said Lord and of his predecessors, as by the rolls of this Manor will appear, to hold by the rod according to the custom."

In this 12 foot way we can see the first beginnings of the still narrow little row which runs from the High Street to the gates of the Churchyard.

The Homage, at a Court General held 22 May 1561, ordered that no person should in future dig soil in "the way leading to the Church" under a penalty of 20s. In the Court Rolls, Church Row is not mentioned by name till 1648. In the Parish Books the name comes into use in 1650.

As the reader will already have gathered, there existed, at the entrance to Church Row, a bridge which crossed the open ditch which ran down Bear Street to the river. In the Court Rolls for 1442 we read:

> "Alice Brother has accroached to herself, to her lands, one parcel of land at Cherchebregge, in length 8 perches, and in breadth 2 feet, Wherefore she is amerced vj^d."

In 1448 John Bunch sold "one toft at the end of Churchbregge" to William Salvat.

In 1447 the Jurors at a View presented that the bridge called "Cherchebregge" should be repaired by the Lord. Again, in 1455, the Lord was called upon to repair "Chyrchebregge in Berstret." In the Court Rolls for 1523 Sir Michael Dormer was granted

> "one parcel and one toft where was formerly a building at the end of the bridge of Churchbrygge in ffulham."

In more recent times the repair of the Churchbridge was chargeable to the parish. Thus, in 1642, the disbursements of the Churchwardens include:

"pd. for mending the Church bridg 8s. 0d."

An assessment in 1650 included the cost of "repairing of the Bridge in the Church Row." Again, in 1652, the assessment made includes "the repayring of the Bridge in the Church Row." In 1649 the Churchwardens paid:

> "For clensing the soyle under the bridge going to church and for raking the weeds of eleven rods of the Towne ditch . . . 12s. 6d."

In ancient days Church Row seems always to have been a semi-private way which, on Sundays, was barred across at the foot of the Churchbridge, to prevent vehicular traffic from disturbing the congregation at their devotions in the Church. At a Vestry meeting held in April 1656, it was

> "Order'd and agreed that the Surveyors for the high roads shall cause to be sett vp two substantiall posts with a crosse barr at the end of ye Bridge passing into ye Church Row according as anciently hath beene accustomed to ye Intent that hereafter noe coaches be sufered to passe along fro thence to ye Churchyard on ye Lords days wch of late hath beene very offensive and dangerous to ye people as they have been comminge fro the Church in that narrow passage or way."

At a meeting of the Vestry, held in 1666, the following similar resolution was passed:

> "Itt is ordered that a substantiall post & lock bee put vpp at the churchbridge to prevent the passage of Coaches Carts and Carriages into the Church rowe from spoilinge & breakinge vpp the pavement & to prevent other mischeife & nucencies that may happen; and that the Churchwarden doe see the same done accordingly."

On 1 May 1667, the Vestry made a rate for sundry expenses, including "to repair the Church bridge, three pounds."
At a Vestry, held 28 Feb. 1680-81,

> "Itt is agreed that whereas ye Churchbridge is att present out of repair, that forthwith the same be amended the one halfe at the charge of the pish, the other halfe at the charge of Willim Saunders who is at present

an inhabitant in the Church Row."

In 1716 the Churchwardens

"Pd. Warren to clean the Church Bridg 2. 0."

In 1780 the Surveyor paid two men a guinea "for cleaning the Sewer at the Church Bridge." After this we hear no more of it. When the Town Ditch was bricked in, the need for a bridge of course ceased.

In August 1894 an interesting discovery was made by some workmen in the employ of the Fulham Vestry. In excavating a trench at the entrance to Church Row, immediately facing the Church Room, the men came upon a very hard substance, which they had considerable difficulty in breaking to allow of the introduction of the pipes they were laying. Upon the earth being more completely removed, a wall of old Kentish ragstone, precisely similar to that forming the Church Tower, was found. It was situated at a depth of between 5 and 6 feet beneath the level of the present roadway. This block of rubble masonry was laid in lime mortar and was well put together. There is little doubt that this was one of the abutments of the old Churchbridge. Unfortunately the cutting was hurriedly refilled, without any careful examination of the "find" having been made.

South Side

On the south side of Church Row, close to the Churchyard, stands Fulham Vicarage, a plain, flat-fronted house, with red-tiled roof. The stucco front was added early in the present century.

A vicarage house, on this site, existed at a remote period. It is mentioned in the Court Rolls of the Manor of Fulham as early as 1430 in connection with the cottage called Goodriche's, which stood opposite to it. Similar references to it occur in the Rolls for 1495, 1508 and 1546. In the Report of the Commissioners concerning the Augmentation of Livings, 1647-1658, we find it stated:

"The Viccaridge house wth Orchards and garden is worth Sixteene pounds p. Ann."

The precise date of the erection of the oldest part of the present Vicarage is unknown.

The tiled roof and the red brickwork of this portion point to the first half of the last century. A Vicarage house is indicated in Rocque's Map of 1741-45. The Rev. William Cole, in his account of his visit to Fulham Church, on 20 April 1758, observes:

"The Vicarage House is an exceeding handsome new built Brick House standing close to the Church Yard, on the North East corner and has a good Garden running to the Thames, the Wall of which by the Road going to the Bridge on the Thames between Fulham and Putney and very near it, is just now built of Brick by Mr. Cumberland."

Fulham Vicarage. From a photograph by Mr. J. Dugdale, 1895

Cole, whose slipshod English is sometimes difficult to understand, was, of course, mistaken about the garden of the

Vicarage running "to the Thames," although it is literally true that the Thames at flood tide occasionally ran to the garden! On such occasions the houses in Church Row itself have been under water, with their cellars flooded to a depth of four feet or more. The "Wall" alluded to by Cole, on the east side of the Vicarage grounds, subsequently gave place to a row of houses and workshops, which formed the west side of the northern end of Bridge Street. These were swept away when the new Bridge was built.

Originally the Vicarage was only a four-roomed cottage. The wing along the Churchyard was added at an unknown date. The Rev. William Wood, in 1812, and the Rev. R. G. Baker, in 1834, carried out extensive alterations in the Vicarage. The former built a large addition at the back. The latter re-faced the front of the house and entirely remodelled the interior.

The portion added at the back of the house, with its semicircular windows, comprises a sitting-room on the ground floor and a bed-room on the first floor. On each side of the fire-place in the dining-room is a collection of theological books bequeathed to the Vicarage by Mr. R. R. Wood, of Italian Villa, Hurlingham Road, a great friend of Mr. Baker. There is a manuscript catalogue of the library, compiled by the Rev. R. G. Baker, partly annotated. The private library is to the left of the hall; to the right is the parish room. The handsome staircase runs centrally through the house.

The grounds of the Vicarage, before the curtailment occasioned by the diversion of the new Bridge, measured 1a. 1r. 26p. The garden once boasted some enormous trees, in which the crows used to build nests. Some of the trees and shrubs here were propagated from the celebrated arboretum at Fulham Palace. Against the walls of the houses in Bridge Street grew some fine pear trees. This part of the grounds, separated from the lawn by a hedge, was used as a vegetable garden.

Near the north-east corner of the Vicarage grounds stands the Church Room, built in 1885, by the late Vicar, the Rev. F. H. Fisher, at his own cost. The site had previously been that of the Vicarage stables. It is the private property of the Vicar for the time being.

Towards the south-east corner of Church Row, with an

opening from Bridge Street, was once a group of cottages, called, from the familiar object in their centre, "Pump Court."

"16 Dec. Paid a Man sitting up to watch the broken Drain at the end of Pump Court, Candle, Beer, etc., 2s. 0½d."
- Highway Rate-book for 1774.

North Side

We will now deal with the north side of Church Row. The site of Sir William Powell's Almshouses marks the position of a somewhat handsome house, known in its later years as No. 10, Church Row. It was erected in 1750 on the site of a still more ancient building. When John Hunt, in 1392, received a grant of the Bishop's garden in Church Row, there was apparently no cottage standing upon the ground. It is not until some forty years later that we hear of a house bearing the name of Goodriche's or Godriche's, doubtless so called from its first tenant. At a Court Baron, held in 1430, we learn that:

"William Reyngnold out of Court surrendered one cottage with curtilage called Gooclriches otherwise called Godericheshawe situate opposite the Vicarage of Fulham with a certain parcel of land adjacent upon the ditch west of Fulham Churchyard to the use of Henry Wakefield and Isabell his wife."

Subsequently Goodriche's came into the possession of Robert Lovell, the Lord's beadle. On his death it passed to his widow, Joan Lovell, who, in 1495, surrendered it to Richard Hill, Bishop of London. The Bishop immediately placed in possession of Goodriche's his servant, one Richard Vaughan.

It next came into the hands of William Boteler, Buttler, or Butler, serjeant-at-arms to Henry VIII. In 1508 he surrendered it to the Rev. George Trevelyon and Humphrey Trevelyon, his brother.

The Trevelyons held Goodriche's till 1517, when they re-surrendered it to William Butler, who, in 1521, disposed of the tenement to Robert Pakyngton, a London mercer. For many years it remained in the possession of the Pakyngtons. John Pakyngton, of London, mercer, sold Goodriche's to William Maynard, of London, mercer. Subsequently it was in the occupation of

Evangelist Maynard, his brother. In 1576 he obtained license to let Goodriche's for three years to John Challoner, a wealthy merchant.

In his will, proved 4 Mar. 1606-7, Challoner states that if the Company of Haberdashers will repay the sum of £8. 6s. owing to him, they shall have a piece of plate and 40s. for the hire of their barge if they come to attend his funeral at Fulham. The aged poor there received £5. The Rev. Peter Lillie, the Vicar of Fulham, was to receive ten shillings and a mourning gown for preaching the funeral sermon. In the minutes of a Court Baron, held in 1607, it is entered:

> "Died John Challoner, gent., seized of customary lands in the occupation of Joan Challoner, widow, and Richard Challoner, gent., his youngest son and next heir."

At the next Court Baron it was reported that Joan Challoner had erected seven cottages "near Fulham Churchyard."

Later, we find Goodriche's in the occupation of the Saris or Sears family, a member of whom, Capt. John Saris, is buried in Fulham Church. It was next the property of John Smith, a leatherseller of London, who, in 1641, mortgaged Goodriche's to James Vickers or Viccars, who also held Goodriche's *alias* Symonds' in Bear Street. During the occupation of the house by the Vickers family, the old name of Goodriche's died out. James Vickers himself resided at his house in Bear Street, Goodriche's, in Church Row, becoming the residence of his son, John. On the death, in 1657, of James Vickers, his grandson, James Vickers, aged 13, son of his son John Vickers, and Mary Vickers, widow of James Vickers, were admitted to the house in Church Row. In 1674 this James Vickers, "of London, merchant," surrendered his messuage to John Hall, citizen of London.

In 1681 this messuage was granted by the Bishop to the use of Robert Limpany, who, in 1696, sold it to William Skelton.

According to Faulkner, William Skelton owed his rise in life to a singular incident. Skelton was, he tells us, originally a footboy in the service of Bishop Compton. In this capacity he was the means of detecting a cook who had mixed poison in some broth for the Bishop's table in order more speedily to obtain a legacy which his master had bequeathed to him. The fact being discovered, the cook was dismissed, while young Skelton, as a reward for his fidelity, was placed with an attorney. Whatever may be the truth of this story, it is certain that Skelton, in 1704, received the office of registrar to the Bishop of London. In the "Lræ. Patentes Dni. Epis. London. pro officio Registrarij" is preserved a copy of the appointment, which bears date 9 June 1704. It is signed "H. London." William Skelton died in July 1720, and was buried at Fulham. By his will, dated 11 July 1720, he devised his property to his wife, Prudence, who, however, died in June of the following year and was also buried at Fulham. Her will is dated 11 May 1721. On the death of Prudence Skelton, her son, William, was admitted to the messuage. In the Churchwardens' Accounts for 1720 is the following entry:

> "Receiv'd of Mr. Skelton as a fine for being excus'd from serving Overseer of the Poor *an.* 1720, £5."

In 1728-29 William Skelton took a prominent part in the movement for increasing the peal in the Parish Church from six to eight bells, two of which bear his name.

A singular advertisement relating to Mr. Skelton's dog appears in *The Country Journal*, or, *The Craftsman*, No. 167, for 2 August 1729. It reads as follows:

> "Whereas it was advertised in this Paper in April last, that there was lost from Fulham in the County of Middlesex, on the 22nd Day of that Month, a Liver-colour'd and white Pointing Dog, very nimble, who had on his Neck a Leather Strap, with a Brass Plate engraved, William Skelton, in Doctors'-Commons, which Dog, as since appears, was soon after delivered to Tho. Stringer, near Hanover-Square to return to the said Mr. Skelton; but by gnawing the Rope he was ty'd with, he got away from the said Stringer, and is not yet recovered. Whoever therefore brings the said Dog to the said Mr. Skelton, or the said Stringer in Oxford-Court in Tyburn-Road, shall receive Three Guineas Reward and no Questions asked."

William Skelton was also registrar of the Bishopric of London, to which office he was admitted on the death of his father. In 1750 he rebuilt his messuage in Church Row. He died 9 Nov. 1762, and was buried at Fulham. His son, yet another William, succeeded to the property. He died soon after and was buried at Fulham. In Fulham Churchyard there still exists a table tomb formerly inscribed to the memory of the Skelton family.

Miss Batsford's House. From an engraving after a water-colour drawing in the possession of Mrs. Elizabeth Cleasby.

When, in 1861, Mr. Walter Rye copied some of the inscriptions, a few fragments of the Skelton epitaph existed, but the stone was then fast peeling off. Not a letter can now be seen.

By the present generation the house of which we are speaking is best remembered as the home of the Batsfords. Mr. Edward Batsford was married to Frances Tolhurst at Fulham Church, 3 Feb. 1770. In 1778 he succeeded William Law as parish clerk and sexton. He died 4 Nov. 1800. Two of his daughters, Hester and Ann, for many years conducted here a very successful "seminary for young gentlemen." On Hester Batsford's death, in 1820, the school was continued by the surviving sister down to 1841. On Miss Ann Batsford's retirement, the house and garden came into the market. Bishop Blomfield, hearing that it was likely to be acquired as a private lunatic asylum, bought it out of his episcopal revenues. Pulling down the house in 1843, he gave a portion (33 perches) of the site to the Churchyard and allowed the Vicar the use of the remainder, rent free, as a garden of herbs.

On the death of Bishop Blomfield, the remainder of the site above referred to lapsed to the Ecclesiastical Commissioners. In 1868 the Trustees of Sir William Powell's Charity applied to this body with a view to the acquisition of a portion of the ground for the purpose of building thereon new Almshouses to take the place of the old premises in Burlington Road. The Trustees succeeded in purchasing the site for £200. The Deed of Conveyance bears date 28 Oct. 1869.

Sir William Powell's Almshouses.
From a photograph by Mr. J. Dugdale, 1895

The Almshouses were erected by Mr. W. Wigmore in 1869 in accordance with a design prepared by Mr. J. P. Seddon. The cost, including that of the site, amounted to about £2,900. The foundation stone was laid by the Rev. R. G. Baker on 15 May 1869.

The pretty Gothic *pensions* which face the Churchyard contain two rooms each, and afford accommodation for twelve inmates. The block terminates towards Church Row in an artistically designed tower. Against the first house is a tablet inscribed:

SIR W. POWELL'S ALMSHOUSES.

Founded 1680.

Rebuilt 1869.

God's Providence, Our Inheritance.

On the West front of the upper portion of the tower are sculptured the heads of "Faith," "Charity," and "Hope." Beneath are full length figures of "Miriam," "Anna," "Deborah," and "Dorcas," and, on the south front, "Ruth" and "St. Mary."

The small piece of garden at the rear of the houses remains the property of the Ecclesiastical Commissioners.

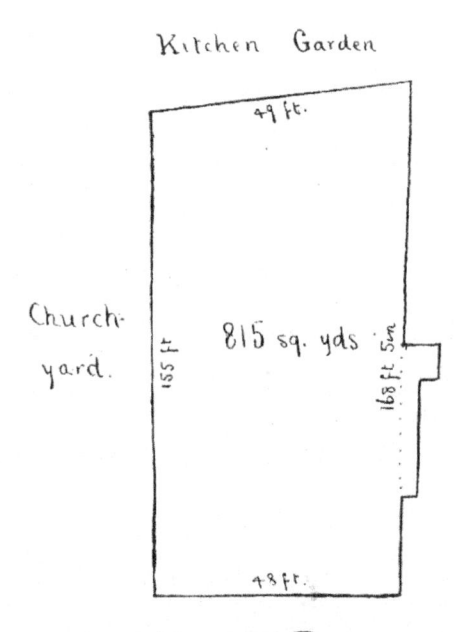

Kitchen Garden

99 ft.

Church-yard.

155 ft

815 sq. yds

168 ft. 5in

48 ft.

Church Row.

Site of Sir William Powell's Almshouses

One of the most noteworthy residents of Church Row was Robert Limpany, barber surgeon, who died here in 1735. The family had long been domiciled in the parish. As far back as 1573 a certain "Robert Lympeny" was re-elected "into his office." This was the same "Robert Lympenye" of Fulham Street, who, in 1575, was fined for keeping a tavern contrary to the order of the Court. In 1579 he was elected "constable of Fulham." His son, Humphrey Limpany, died in 1641. The Churchwardens' Receipts for that year include:

"rec. for knell and cloath Limpany 3s. 6d."

Edward, the son of Humphrey Limpany, married Margery Whiting of Fulham. He died 23 April 1662, aged 58. His widow, Margery, died 7 Dec. 1675. Both were buried in Fulham Church.

Edward and Margery Limpany had two sons, Edward and Robert. The former, Edward, first appears in the rating in 1664. On 9 April 1667 he was elected Overseer, and, on 13 April 1669, Surveyor of the Highways. His name disappears from the assessments after 1687.

The second son, Robert Limpany, was born in 1641. On 20 May 1672, the Faculty Office granted a license for his marriage with Isabella Cornish of Fulham. In the Court Rolls the name of Robert Limpany first comes into notice in 1665-6. On 4 Feb. of this year he was admitted to a cottage in Bear Street. On 4 April 1681, he was admitted to a messuage in Church Row, consisting of four (anciently two) cottages with orchards. These are now represented by Nos. 7, 8 and 9. Elizabeth, the only child of Robert and Isabella Limpany, baptized on 3 Feb. 1691-92, died on 10 Oct. 1694. She was buried in Fulham Church.

Robert Limpany was a great benefactor to Fulham Church and gave largely towards the cost of the repairs effected in 1686, when he held the post of Churchwarden. Bowack, who was Limpany's contemporary, asserts that his "estate was so considerable in the parish that he was commonly called Lord of Fulham."

At one time or other he held, in addition to about two-thirds of Church Row, several messuages in Bear Street (including the "King's Arms"), Holcroft's and Cleybroke's.

PEDIGREE OF LIMPANY FAMILY

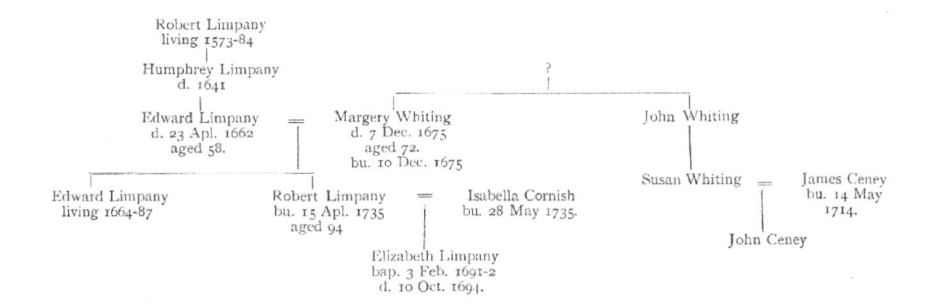

```
         Robert Limpany
         living 1573-84
                |
         Humphrey Limpany                              ?
            d. 1641                                    |
                |                                      |
    ┌───────────┴───────────┐                          |
    Edward Limpany  =  Margery Whiting         John Whiting
    d. 23 Apl. 1662    d. 7 Dec. 1675                  |
      aged 58.           aged 72.                      |
         |             bu. 10 Dec. 1675                |
    ┌────┴──────┬──────────────┐                 Susan Whiting = James Ceney
 Edward Limpany  Robert Limpany = Isabella Cornish               bu. 14 May
 living 1664-87  bu. 15 Apl. 1735  bu. 28 May 1735.                1714.
                    aged 94                                        |
                       |                                       John Ceney
                Elizabeth Limpany
                bap. 3 Feb. 1691-2
                 d. 10 Oct. 1694.
```

Limpany died, at the age of 94, at his house in Church Row, early in April 1735. His widow survived him but a few weeks. The Church Registers record:

1735. Mr. Robert Limpany bu. 15 Apl.
1735. Mrs. Isabella Limpany bu. 28 May.

Robert Limpany's will, dated 20 Nov. 1734, was proved 13 May 1735 (P.C.C. 105 Ducie). The following is an extract:

"I Robert Limpany of the parish of ffulham in the County of Middlesex Gent. To my wife Isabella Limpany all my real and copyhold and personal estate for ever. All my copyhold estate now in the possession of Mr. Eustice the Coachman together with my Warehouse thereto adjoining as also £40 Stock I have in the Stationers Company . . . All my ffreehold and copyhold estate situate in ffulham aforesaid beginning at Pools the Butchers down to Bagley's house that works with Mr. Dwight the Potter going down to the Water side in ffulham aforesaid unto Isabella Cotton Eldest Daughter of Thomas Cotton and her heirs for ever. All my ffreehold and copyhold at the upper end of the said Town of ffulham vizt the mansion house of Sr Edward ffruin's which I lately purchased together with Beauchamps house Lees and Davis house at the Rose unto Elizabeth Cotton youngest Daughter of Thomas Cotton and her heirs for ever and if said Isabella and Elizabeth Cotton die under 21 then I devise such estates to Limpany White son of Edmond White Esq and heirs for ever.

I devise all my copyhold now in the possession of Mr. Reynolds Mr. Simpson my sister Winch my own house that I now dwell in, Mrs.

Burbage, the widow Bakers and Mr. Wells situate in the Church Row in ffulham to my Nephew-in-Law Edmond White Esq and heirs for ever. To Katherine White his eldest daughter my 2 copyhold houses in possession of Mrs. Mead and Dents.

To Abraham Odell and his heirs all my copyhold in possession of the Widow Jones, Bignal, Tucker and Raisy. To John Ceney and heirs the 2 houses in possession of the Widow Whale All my copyhold at the Church Yard Stile of ffulham which is let in 5 tenemts unto Nurse Redman and her daughter Martha Lever and their heirs To my Maid Servant Dorothy Tripp and heirs all that copyhold in possession of Richard Whale Bricklayer.

I give and bequeath yearly and every year the sum of twenty Shillings to be paid unto the Organist of ffulham so long as the Organ shall be used and playd upon in the Parish Church of ffulham, and no longer, to be paid out of my Estate of the Kings Arms in ffulham aforesaid."

Codicil 17 Feb. 1734-35.

"I hereby revoke so much of the devise to the said Isabella Cotton as concerns my ffreehold and copyhold houses etc. in occupations of Mr. Emet, Mr. Reynolds, Mr. Phelps, Mr. Chubb, Mr. Peirce, Mr. Hester, and Simon Bagley, being the houses from Pump Court in ffulham towards the waterside and do devise same to Edmond White and his heirs. To Elizabeth Cotton and heirs my house in ffulham in occupation of Mr. ffranklin.

I further charge my house called the Kings Arms in ffulham with 40s. yearly to be layd out in 3d. loaves of bread to be distributed by the Church Warden and Overseers of the Poor of ffulham to the poor there immediately after Divine Service in the forenoon of the fifteenth of January if it be the Lords day or else on the next Lords day And also with the payment of any Sum not exceeding the rate of twenty shillings yearly for keeping in repair my Monument in ffulham Church All which moneys charged on the Kings Arms I appoint to be paid at Christmas yearly.

I also charge the Kings Arms aforesaid with the payment of 10s. yearly at Christmas to the said Churchwarden and overseers to be by them distributed in Wiggs and Ale on the first day of March yearly to the poor Children in the Charity School at ffulham.

I charge the estates devised by my will to Elizabeth Cotton with the annual payment of £3 at Christmas to be by the Churchwarden and Overseers of ffulham distributed in meat and drink as the bread."

In 1739 the inhabitants of Church Row included Mr. Samuel Ashhurst and Mr. Henry Holland. The former, with his wife Sarah and his son John, lies buried in Fulham Church. The latter was the father of Henry Holland, the famous architect, who himself resided in Fulham.

Of the houses which form the terrace on the north side of Church Row, all are ancient. The three oldest are Nos. 7, 8 and 9, though the others, Nos. 1 to 6, which lie a little back, with small forecourts, have also attained a respectable antiquity. The former are curious old places, abounding in wood partitions, cupboards large enough to sleep in, and ceilings supported by old fashioned beams. The latter also partake, in their internal arrangements, of much the same character.

For many years No. 8 was the residence of Mr. Richard Lester, who died 26 Feb. 1855, and lies buried with his first wife in the adjacent Churchyard.

No. 7, in 1811, was purchased by Mr. Joseph Roe, sergeant of his Majesty's Chapels Royal and house steward under Bishop Porteus. In the Chaplain's Room at Fulham Palace are preserved some of Mr. Roe's account books, kept by him as sergeant. A quaint "Diary," which he privately kept, from 1807 to 1812, is now in the possession of Mr. Robert Sindle, the present tenant of No. 8.

Elsewhere we have several times quoted from this interesting record. Here we may quote one or two things personal to the diarist. Bishop Porteus was by no means a saint in the eyes of his sergeant, but was ever ready to give his patronage where he was likely to receive a *quid pro quo*. Thus, under date 23 May 1808, Roe notes:

> "Dr. Ayreton died yesterday morning. Page and Evans has been after his place, he also held the place of Lutinist £41. 10. 0. pr anm a sinecure. The Bp ought to give this to his servants, but I fear unless he is a gainer by it, he will give it from them. I have had a pretty good experience of this, for it is certain I shod never have been Serjt of the Kings Chapel had not the Bishop been interested in it for I paid to his Order 1000£. I hope the World will know it."

Mr. Roe purchased No. 7, Church Row on his retirement from his stewardship, etc. His "Diary" abounds with voluminous details about the alterations which he carried out in his house and garden. The following are a few of the more noteworthy:

> "1811. 27 Sept. Paid this day into the Hands of Stirling Hodsal & Co.

£650 for a House in Church Rowe, Fulham, in trust to Cobb and Sheperd untill the title etc. is completed.
28 Sept. Was this day put into possession of the above house. Paid Parsons the Tennant 8. 8. 0. for trees shrubbs dung frame and three lights a copper Brick and Iron work and for the Bells, crunks pulls etc. as hung, and for all the Rubish left behind.
29 Sept. Sunday at Church and after dinner we went to Church row and God forgive me I weeded my Cabbage and Green Cale which was nearly smothered with insects. I also pulled up a quantity of Jerusalem artichokes, which has, I presume, been planted for the appearance of shrubs.
19 Dec. Fencing the Moat."

Mr. Joseph Roe died 23 Dec. 1815, and lies buried at All Saints. His widow, Mrs. Elizabeth Roe, died in 1838. Mr. Thomas Roe, a member of the Stationers' Company, the son of Mr. Joseph Roe, resided here till his death, which occurred 19 May 1873. About five years ago the house was taken by Mr. Frank Boyton, of the firm of Boyton, Pegram and Buckmaster, auctioneers, who conferred upon it the appropriate name of "The Retreat."

The house, which is the largest in the Row, was originally two tenements, converted by Mr. Thomas Roe into one. It was this gentleman who built the present large hall and staircase, four rooms being cleared away for this purpose. He also greatly enlarged the garden, which is now about three-quarters of an acre. Like most of its neighbours, it runs back to the Bishop's Moat, but, unlike them, it enjoys the distinction of possessing a little flight of steps at the far end leading down to the water's edge. In the garden is a noticeable old mulberry tree, which still yields abundantly. The grounds once boasted a fine walnut tree, said to have been planted in the year in which Mr. Thomas Roe was born. Singularly enough, it died of decay in 1873, the year of his death.

Mr. Roe largely added to the house at the back, which was extended out some 25 feet. In the old part of the house the principal feature is the noble well staircase. The rooms in this portion are somewhat low and most of the oak floors have a slight list. The old oak joists are a noticeable characteristic.

At No. 6 resided Mr. Henry Bunnett, senior, surgeon, who died 17 May 1827. On his death the business was continued under the style of Bunnett and Holmes. Mr. W. F. Wolley, on quitting

Pryor's Bank, retired to No. 6, which he renamed Egmont House. Here he died in 1896. It is believed to have been at No. 6 that Robert Limpany died in 1735. In the iron scroll-work over the garden gate in front of this house are entwined the initials "R. L." At the end of the garden, under cover of a trellis porch, stands a quaint stone figure. It is that of a dwarf, habited as a general. On his breast-plate is depicted the double-headed eagle of Russia. On the top of his helmet is a sphynx, the head of which has gone. In the general's right hand is a gun, with metal fittings.

Mr. William Howard, son of Mr. William Howard, of Walham Green, died at No. 5, Church Row, 27 Oct. 1835. The house continued in the occupation of the family down to the death of Mr. Frederick Howard, which occurred 18 Oct. 1876. Three of the four Misses King, on giving up their school at Fulham House, returned, in 1876, to their old home, No. 5, Church Row.

At No. 4 lived, in 1804, Captain Macnab.

An eccentric lady, a Miss Etherington, resided at No. 3 for some time, sharing her domicile with 30 or 40 cats. Here the late Dr. Henry Laumann came to live after leaving the Rectory House. He eventually moved to No. 6, Middleton Road, Wandsworth, where he died, 12 Nov. 1883.

Miss Marianne Emma Thackeray, niece of the first wife of the Rev. R. G. Baker, and daughter of the Rev. J. R. Thackeray, M.A., Mr. Baker's successor at Hadley, died at No. 2, 7 Dec. 1872.

At No. 1, for upwards of forty years, lived "Honest" John Phelps, the Waterman. The Phelpses bear the reputation of being one of the oldest families in Fulham. In the Church Registers there are scores of entries referring to the family, the first one being for 1675, the year when they commence. It reads:

1675 John Phelpes agricol. mort 19 . . . sepult 21 die Aprilis.

The family, though an industrious one, never rose above the humblest of occupations. They were mostly watermen or water-bailiffs, who, in the person of "Honest" John, lived to see their trade gradually decay. John and his father William obtained considerable distinction in the aquatic world.

John Phelps was born at No. 10, Bridge Street, 24 May 1805. As far back as the year of the Queen's accession [1837], his achievements had gained for him the title of "the hero of Fulham." Indeed, he first made his mark when only twelve years of age by rowing second to John Kelley, the father of Harry Kelley, the ex-champion. At the age of fourteen he was apprenticed to the river. Having served his time, he rowed for Doggett's Coat and Badge in 1827, being second to Voss, of Fountain Stairs. It was his straightforward conduct in acting as judge at the inter-University contests which won for him the sobriquet of "Honest" John. After the memorable dead-heat in the Oxford and Cambridge Boat race, in 1877, he ceased to act as judge. For many years he was always ready to ferry persons across to Putney, and was a constant figure on the river down to within a few months of his death. He was waterman to Theodore Hook when that celebrated wit resided at Egmont Villa.

It is related that when the late Rev. William Rogers resided at Fulham, he used to hire John Phelps for a row up the river. "John, I'm thirsty," Mr. Rogers would remark after they had been out for a time. "So am I, Sir," was the sure echo of John. "Pull in then," Mr. Rogers would say, and at the "Crabtree" or at Mortlake the natives would be astonished to see a parson walk in and call for half a gallon of ale and not leave much behind. It was at No. 1, Church Row that Mrs. Phelps died, 26 Oct. 1888. Subsequently "Honest" John moved with his daughter to No. 6, Dolby Road, Hurlingham, where he died, 5 Dec. 1890.

Before we leave Church Row we must not omit to mention the quaint little nursery garden at the rear of the Row, reached by a path at the side of No. 1. For some years it was conducted by Thomas Brazier, for thirty years deputy sexton of this parish. He died 2 Aug. 1862. His son, Frederick Brazier, who was for some years parish sexton, died from the effects of a fall from a walnut tree at Rosebank, 8 Oct. 1875. The nursery is still occupied by the family.

Church Row. From a photograph by Mr. J. Dugdale, 1895.

CHAPTER XXII: FULHAM CHURCH

When the first church was built by the water side at Fulham, there are no memorials to tell. There is, however, no doubt that the quaint old edifice, which was pulled down in 1880-81, was not the original church.

The Domesday Survey furnishes no evidence that, in the Conqueror's time, the village possessed a church. The first known rector was appointed in 1242, at which date a church must, of course, have existed.

In the Old Church. From an oil painting by Miss Jane Humphreys

The most ancient portion of the Church, demolished in 1880-81, was certainly not older than the fifteenth century. About the Church which is known to have preceded this edifice, little can be said. In December 1880, in the course of digging for the south buttresses of the present building, about two feet west of the then existing south porch, the remains of an old foundation were discovered. An examination showed that an earlier church had extended somewhat further in a southern direction. This was not, however, the only trace of a pre-existent building. Among the rubble walls of the old Church were found many stones which had evidently formed portions of some earlier structure. The most noticeable of these was a stone which had on one side the bottom of the shafting of a window jamb of the Early English period (circa 1150). The stone had, apparently, next been used in a Perpendicular church (circa 1400), for another face of it was cut to the distinctive mouldings of that style. This interesting old stone, with a history of, perhaps, seven centuries, might well have been preserved in the present Church. Unfortunately, it was mislaid at the time of the rebuilding, and now lies hidden from view among some ferns in the Vicarage garden.

Other evidence of this earlier Church is forthcoming. In 1361 we find a reference made to the Church in the will of a London goldsmith, one Robert de Norwich, who, among other bequests, left the sum of forty pence to the altar of the Parish Church of Fulham for masses to be said for the repose of his soul. <u>The bequest stands</u>:

"Item: Lego summo altari ecclesie parochialis de Fulham xl^d."

Other ancient testamentary bequests occur among the wills preserved at Somerset House. By his will, dated 19 July 1459, John Lok, citizen and mercer of London, left "to the reparation of the Church of ffulham, xl^s." John Norman, Alderman of the Ward of Chepe, left, by will dated 13 May 1468,

"to the reparation of the parish church of ffulham in County Middlesex and to the emending the goods and ornaments of the same church, 5 marcs."

John Sutton, citizen and mercer of London, by will dated 9 Sept. 1479, bequeathed

"to the sustentacon of the pish church of ffulhm vli [£5]."

The earliest writer to describe the old Church was John Bowack. In his "Antiquities of Middlesex" (1705) he writes:

"This church, standing a small distance from the waterside, is built of stone and does not seem to be of very great antiquity, the Tower, at the west, being in very good condition as well as the body of the church; it has not been patch'd up since its first erection so as to make any considerable alteration in the whole building, nor has (sic) there been any additions made, as is usual in ancient structures (except of a small building for a school, etc., at the north door) but both Tower and church seem of the same age and manner of workmanship. We were in hopes, whatever imperfect accounts have been left of the foundation of other churches, yet that here we should not have wanted light, since 'tis situated so near the Bishop of London's seat which appears to be much ancienter, but after the most inquisitive search, we could discover nothing at all, nor so much as gather to whom 'twas dedicated. However, from a very careful examination of the building, we concluded it was built about the beginning of the 15th century."

Bowack's description is not altogether accurate. He speaks of the old Church as of "stone," whereas the chief element in the composition of its walls was a curious mixture of brick and flint. That the old Church had not been considerably "patch'd up," is another misstatement, for probably no church ever underwent more continuous mending. Bowack's failure, also, to discover the particulars of the dedication shows that his investigations did not go far, for John Thorley or Chorley, in his will (1445), describes it by the name of All Saints. Newcourt, in his "Repertorium Ecclesiasticum Par. Lond." (1708), speaks of the Church as dedicated to All Saints. In most old documents, however, the Church is not described according to its dedication, but simply as the Parish Church of Fulham. In the Parish Books the earliest employment of the name "All Saints" is in the minutes of a Vestry held 6 May 1779.

The Tower, or Steeple, as it was formerly termed, is the only portion of the old Church now remaining. It is in the Perpendicular style of architecture which prevailed in England between the time of Edward III and Richard III. It is constructed of Kentish ragstone and rises to a height of 96 feet. It is square in shape, and consists of five stages, terminating in a battlemented parapet, with a small turret at its south-west corner. The date of its erection was, as we have seen, surmised by Bowack to have been "about the beginning of the 15th century." Lysons conjectures that it was built "in or near the 14th century." Its architecture would, of course, suggest this period, but fortunately the exact date of its erection is set at rest by a document preserved among the Privy Seals at the Public Record Office. The text is as follows:

"A° xix. Hen. vj.
To the King oure Souerain Lord.
Please it unto youre benigne Grace for to graunte unto the people and parochiens of the paroisshe of Fulham your l'res of protection under your Grete Seal that noone (none) of yr Officers lette (hinder) the cariage of stone by lande or by water ordeined to come from Maideston in Kent at there cost to Fulham, in perfourmyng the werk of the Steple there, which by your Grace they may with Goddis help fully complische, And also to graunte by ye said l'res that noon of yr said ministers do tak unto any of your werks, during the making of the said Steple, Richard Garald nor Piers Chapel, the which hath taken the same Steple to make, and they shall pray God for you.
[Minuted]. "The King hath granted [it] at Shene (Richmond) the v day of May A° xix [1440].
(Signed) "T. Bekinton."

It is thus placed beyond a doubt that the Tower was built in 1440, the nineteenth year of the reign of Henry VI. The petitioners, it will be observed, make two requests of the King:

(1) that none of the royal officers should be allowed to hinder the transport of the stone, and

(2) that they should not be suffered to employ, on any royal works, the two skilled artificers who were engaged in the erection of the Tower of the Church.

In the far-off days of which we write, it was no unusual thing for the King's officers to "impress" workmen. In 1359 William of Wykeham was appointed surveyor of the royal castles (Windsor, Leeds, Dover, Hadleigh, etc.) "with power to appoint and dismiss all workmen." In the following year the great architect is recorded to have "impressed" workmen to carry out the new buildings at Windsor for the Knights of the Garter, and issued writs in the Kings name to the Sheriffs of London and the twelve adjoining counties ordering them to send "360 of their best diggers and stone-hewers," to be employed as long as was necessary.

In 1440, the year of the building of the Tower of Fulham Church, Henry VI founded Eton College, and it is therefore not improbable that it was in connection with this great undertaking that the misgivings of the good folk of Fulham were aroused. It is satisfactory to note that the weak-minded monarch granted the prayer of the parishioners. Beneath the royal minute is the signature "T. Bekinton." Thomas Bekinton or Beckington held under Henry VI (whose tutor he had been) several lucrative posts. He was Secretary of State, keeper of the Privy Seal and warden of New College, Oxford. From Rymer's "Fœdera" it appears that, in 1431 and 1432, he acted as one of Henry's ambassadors to the Dauphin of France. For a time he was rector of the parish of St. Leonards, near Hastings. Finally, in 1443, he was made Bishop of Bath and Wells. He lies buried in the south aisle of Wells Cathedral, where a monument is erected to his memory.

Tower of Fulham Church, looking west. From a drawing executed in 1835, signed "A. P.," preserved in the Vicarage "Faulkner."

We will now ascend the Tower, access to which is gained by a small door on the south side. Opening this we ascend a dark and

Fulham Old and New

narrow staircase which winds round a central newel. The steps, which are 120 in number, are here and there much worn away.

The first apartment we reach is the Ringing Chamber or "Loft," through the ceiling of which depend the bell ropes. Against the wall, in one corner, hangs a quaint portrait of John Hudnott, beadle and sexton of Fulham in the reign of Charles II. The picture, which is of no particular merit, represents the beadle as an elderly man, in a red coat with broad yellow cuffs. In his right hand he holds a quart pot, containing, doubtless, his favourite beverage, and in his left is a typical "churchwarden," which he is in the act of smoking. The inscription reads:

> "John Hudnett, Beadle and Sexton of the Parish of Fulham, Middlesex, 1690."

The picture, as to the history of which nothing is known, was possibly an original gift to the steeple.

Around the walls of the Ringing Chamber are framed records of famous peals which have been rung on the old bells. The oldest one reads:

> "January the xxvi 1735. The Society of Fulham Youths rang in this Steeple a compleat peal of ten thousand and eighty bob major in six hours and forty minutes. Tho. Warland treble, Edw. Hudnott second, Iohn Farlar third, Miles Dent fourth, Henry Dennis fifth, Willm Hudnott sixth, Hen. Holland seventh, Sam. Walton tenor. Wm Souch, Churchwarden."

In this apartment is kept a beautifully illuminated peal book, in which the peals rung are regularly entered. This was the gift, in May 1890, of Mr. Norman Edward Snow. There is little to be noted with respect to the history of the Ringing Chamber. Here, sometimes, the meetings of the Vestry were held. At a Vestry held on 12 July 1727,

> "It was order'd . . . that the belfry stairs and Ringing Loft be repair'd, And that Mr. Clarke, Mr. Gray, Mr. Scott and Mr. Robt. Gray agree with Mr. Hinton to perform the same."

Again, on 2 August of the same year,

"At a Vestry then Assembled, It was Order'd that the Steepl stairs be repair'd with stone and the Ringing Loft new laid with Boards, two shillings and sixpence to be allow'd for each step and thirty shillings p. square yard for the Flowering."

On 17 September 1730,

"It was order'd that the Ringing Loft, call'd the first Loft, be forthwith glazed, plaister'd, ceiled and whitewashed."

At its base the walls of the Tower are about 5 ft. 6 ins. thick. In the Ringing Chamber the thickness is 4 ft. 6 ins. Upwards the walls are proportionately thinner.

The Ringing Chamber.
From a photograph by Mr. J. Dugdale, 1894

Proceeding up the staircase, we next reach the Clock Room or Closet, in which now stands the great clock, manufactured by Messrs. Gillett and Bland, of Croydon. The earliest reference to any clock at Fulham Church occurs in the accounts of the

Churchwardens for 1637, where we find,

> "Pd. the Clockman for his yeare 6s. 0d."

- the annual charge for winding the clock.

In 1638 the Churchwardens

> "pd. the Clockeman for his yearely payment and for wyer 7s. 8d."

And so on down to 1643, when the Churchwardens purchased a new clock:

> "Paid the Clockmaker for a new Clocke £3. 6. 2."

From this date the entry for winding ceases. Against the last payment (that for 1642-43) the Clerk notes:

> "pd. the clockmaker for a yeare 6s. 0d."
> "This charge to cease for tyme to come, the Clockmaker not to be paid the next yeare."

In the following year we find the Vestry in need of a sum of £18 10s. for sundry repairs to the Church, including "repayring or exchange of the Clocke."

In 1649 there is a further assessment for various repairs, including the mending of the Church Clock. The disbursements of the Churchwardens included:

> To Bastian the Smith for mending the Church Clock £2. 5s. 0d.
> For Deal boards to mend the Clock house to keep out the Dust 3s. 0d.
> For spikes and nayles vsed about it 1s. 0d.
> To Jonathan for workmanship about the Clockhouse 2s. 0d.
> For a new lock and key to the Clockhouse doore 2s. 6d.

In 1655 John Drake, the sexton, was appointed "keeper of ye Clocke." At a Vestry, 4 Sept. 1656:

> "It is . . . ordered that the psent Churchwarden doe pay the arreares dew to Bastin for keeping the pish Clocke and that the sd Bastin be ordered

by the Churchwarden to put the Clocke into repaire forthwth & that the Churchwarden doe continue to pay the qterly sallery for the keeping of the same as formerlie hath beene paid."

Tower of Fulham Church, looking south, before the restoration of 1845.
From a water colour drawing in the Vicarage "Faulkner."

By dint of sundry repairs, the "new Clocke" lasted till 1664, when the Vestry determined to replace it by a better one. It so happened that in this year one Richard Gosling had been elected an Overseer of the Poor. To refuse, when elected, to serve this office is an indictable offence. In olden times the only method by which service could be evaded was by the payment of a fine, which the Vestry usually fixed at ten guineas. This penalty carried exemption from service during the whole period of residence in the parish. Richard Gosling, to avoid the burdens of office, agreed to give the parish a clock not under the value of £12. The gift is thus recorded in the minutes of a Vestry, held 14 Aug. 1664:

> "It is ordered at this Vestry yt Ricd Goslinge of this pish brickmaker bee and is from this day forward (duringe his abode in this pish) acquitted from bearing any office or service off and belonginge to the pish of Fulham, vpon condition yt the said Richd Goslinge doe att his owne proper costs and charges giue an able and substantiall Clock not vnder the vallue of 12li [£12]; and yt the old clock be giuen vnto the said Ricd Goslinge; wch new clock is the volluntary gift of him the said Ricd Goslinge, in consideracon of the previlidges aforesaid."

The contract for the new clock was given to Edmond Stevenson of Hammersmith for the sum of £7 10s., or £4 10s. under the price which the old brickmaker promised to pay. At a meeting of the Vestry, held on 27 Nov. 1664, it was ordered:

> "That Mr. Edmond Stevenson of Ham'smith clockmaker bee allowed and paid seaven pounds tenn shillinges for a new clock by the Churchwarden and the said Stevenson is to find lynes and all other materialls thereunto belonginge and to keepe the said Clocke one whole year, vizt from the 25th of December next ensuinge vntill the 25th of Decembr 1665, gratis, and to have tenn shillinges p. ann. duringe his life to keepe the said Clock in good repair after."

Mr. Stevenson appears to have attended to the clock down to 1670 when his name ceases:

> "Paid Edm. Stevenson locksmith a yeares wagges for lookinge to the Clocke 10s. 0d."

Judging from the entries in the Parish Books the clock appears, in early times, to have had but one face or dial, which was probably on the south side of the Tower. Thus, in 1642-43, the Churchwardens

> "Pd. for mending the church wall and dyall 2s. 4d."

In 1689, however, a clock face was added to the north side of the Tower. This was the gift of Mr. John Fitter, and, like the 1664 clock, was presented to the parish in consideration of exemption from service in the office of Overseer. The gift is thus minuted in the Parish Books:

> "We whose names are hereunder written doo promise to excuse Mr. John Fitter from being any parish officer vpon this condition yt the said Mr. Fitter doe at his owne costs and charge erect and set vpon a hand diall at the north side of the Steple and keepe it in order during his life at his owne charge betwixt this and Michas. Witness or hands this 17 day of January 1689."

Stevenson's clock appears to have gone satisfactorily for many years. On 11 February 1726, the Vestry ordered:

> "That Mr. Chubb do continue to look after the repair and winding up the clock and that he be allow'd four pounds per annum for the same, to commence Midsummer last."

Interior of the Clock. From a photograph by Mr. J. Dugdale, 1894

In 1730 the "Clock Closett" was again repaired. The old clock lasted for a period of about 218 years. The present clock was purchased by private subscription at a cost of £200. The clock, which is provided with apparatus for striking the "Cambridge quarters" on the 4th, 5th, 6th and 9th bells, was set going at 5 p.rn. on Saturday, 14 April 1883.

Bell Loft Of Belfry

A further ascent of the old staircase brings us to the Bell Loft or Belfry proper. Here, among beams, black with age, hang the old bells, ten in number.

In the good old days, when the Thames was really the silvery stream it has been pictured by the poet, and when the quiet little village of Fulham nestled in undisturbed peace upon its shore, the bells of All Saints had a reputation second to none along the river. Mr. J. T. Smith, in his interesting "Book for a Rainy Day," (pp. 285-86) tells a story of George Heath, of Strand Lane, a famous waterman who used to be taken off by Charles Mathews as "Joe Hatch." The old man had himself been a noted ringer. He fell into conversation with a "fare" he was rowing on the river one day. "You like bells, then," observed the gentleman." Oh, yes, sir," replied George, "I was a famous ringer in my youth at St. Mary Overies. They are beautiful bells, but, of all the bells, give me those of Fulham, they are so soft and sweet. St. Margaret's are fine bells, so are St. Martin's, but, after all, Fulham for my money." And the Thames Waterman was not far wrong.

The first mention of any bells occurs in the Inventory of the Church effects made by the Royal Commissioners in 1549, just over a century after the building of the Tower. We learn that there were then

"V greate belles and a lyttell bell in the steple and iij hande belles."

The three hand-bells, as we learn from the Inventory, were subsequently sold along with other goods belonging to the Church. The Commissioners accordingly report as remaining

"In the steple v greate Belles and a saunce Bell."

The "saunce" or saints' bell was doubtless that previously spoken of as a "lyttell bell." The Churchwardens' Accounts contain many entries relating to repairs, etc., to these bells. Among others are:

1638. pd. for a sett of bellropes 18s. 6d.

1638. pd. Mott and Sherecroft for mending the bell Wheeles 6s. 0d.

1639. Pd. for trussing the Clappers of the bells 1s. od.

1640. pd. for a set of bellropes £1. 2s. 8d.

1641. Pd. the Smith for rounding the clappers and other worke about the church 4s. 0d.

1642. pd. for mending the great bell wheele 2s. 6d.

1648. To Jonathan Harris for makeing of Wedges and other worke about the Bells 3s. 0d.

1649. To Bastian of Hammersmith for a new Clapper for the great Bell, the ould one being unserviceable and indangering the Bell 18s. 0d.

1649. More to him six moneths after for mending the eye of yt Clapp wch was broken 6s. 0d.

1650. To Robert Turner bellhanger ffor Taking downe and new Hanging ffower of the Bells (the brasses googions and Baldricks being decaied and worne out) and for new casting the sd. Brasses and Googions and adding to them five pounds more of mettall and for new head (?) Baldricks and Poolls and other worke appearing by Bill £4. 12s. 6d.

1650. To him more for Taking downe and new Hanging the second Bell over throwne by the Soldiers and for locks and Nayles 6s. 8d.

The above entry is the only direct allusion, in the Parish Books, to the mischief wrought in the Church by the soldiery during the Civil War.

1651. To a bell-founder for his paines and advice about a Broken Bell 1s. 0d.

The old bells, which had by this time fallen into a state of general decay, were, in 1652, recast. The original intention was, apparently, merely to repair the bells out of the proceeds of a fine paid by Col. George Langham, a republican soldier who lived at Parson's Green, and a great friend of Col. Edmund Harvey, then the owner of the Bishop's Manor. Langham had been elected to the office of Churchwarden, but, like Gosling and Fitter, he was desirous of being excused. The transaction is thus recorded among the minutes of a Vestry, 19 April 1652:

"Coll. George Langham elected Churchwarden for the yeare ensuing. After the election it was resolved that Coll. Geo. Langham, being elected Churchwarden, shall be excused vpon a voluntary fine & Mr. Thomas Crooke be Churchwarden for the yeare ensuing. At the sd. Vestry Coll. George Langham did voluntarily giue to the parish of ffulham on ffulham side the somme of fiue pounds and the inhabitants did consent to excuse the said Col. langham from all offices for the repaire of ye Bells wch are now in decay."

Tower of Fulham Church, as restored by Mr. G. Godwin.
From a drawing in the "Builder" for 4 Oct. 1852

The "decay" of the bells seems to have been the first subject to which Mr. Thomas Crooke, on entering on his office, paid attention. It was eventually decided that the whole of the six should be recast, one Bryan Eldridge, bell-founder, of Chertsey, being entrusted with the work.

In connection with this recasting, a very curious story is recorded in the Parish Books. Briefly, the facts were these: Mr. Thomas Crooke, by the authority of the Vestry, and in his capacity as Churchwarden, entered into a bond with Eldridge, "in ye penall sum of 120li," for the payment of the contract amount of £60. Of this £60, Crooke paid off £40 and John Sherecroft, the succeeding warden, discharged the remaining sum, £20. Eldridge, however, failed to return to the Churchwarden the bond which had been honourably satisfied. The dishonest bellfounder put the bond "in suits." The case went against poor Crooke, who had judgment passed against him for £127 1s., and was himself "taken in execution." The Vestry, after investigating the matter, ordered an assessment to be at once made for the indemnification of the wronged warden. The following is the full account of the affair as recorded in the minutes of a Vestry, held 24 Nov. 1657:

> "Mr. Thos. Crooke late churchwarden for ye said parrish aquaintinge ye said Vestry that Whereas in ye yeare of his churchwardenshipp the bells belonging unto ye said parish were new cast and yt hee in ye discharge of his office and with the consent of divers inhabitants requesting the same, he did not onely vndertake ye care and charge thereof But also as churchwarden and by ye name of Churchwarden of ye said parrish in ye behalf of ye parishioners thereof ingadged and became bound unto Bryan Eldridge of Chersey in ye County of Surrey, Bellfounder, for ye casting and new making of ye said Bells, By one obligation in ye penall sum of 120^{li} wth condition for ye paymt of 60^{li}; of wch 60^{li} he ye said Mr. Thos. Crooke had paid and satisfied vnto ye said Eldridge 40^{li} and caused the same to bee endorsed on ye said bond and that afterwards in full satisfaction thereof By John Shercroft ye succeedinge Churchwardn ye sum of 20li was paid unto ye said Eldridge And hee therevpon engadged to deliver vpp ye said Bonde to bee cancelled in a short tyme after (then alleadging it was not in his custody) yett neverthelese some tyme afterwards ye said Eldridge putt ye aforesaid Bond in suits And all though ye said Thomas Crooke made a legal defence and proofe of ye aforesd sums paid, yett in Trinity Terme last judgmtt past against him for 127^{li} 1^s. for costs and damages and by Vertue thereof on Munday ye 16 of this Instant November he the said Tho. Crooke was taken in execution and therevpon necessitated to pay downe forthwth 50^{li} in pte thereof and giue his Bonde for further satisfacon All wch ye said Vestry haueing duely examined and findinge ye premises to bee true (as aboue alleadged), doe Order yt An Asseasmtt bee made forthwth to rate & assease all ye Inhabitants of ye said Parrish on ffulham side as well for ye new makeinge castinge & workmanshipp & charges of and concerninge ye said Bells, as also for other necessary repaires of & belonginge to ye said Parrish church ffor ye sum of 60^{li} and that ye said sum bee asseased by a pound rate

accordinge to ye forme last agreed vpon for ye releife of ye poore And it is further Ordered that Mr. Thomas Crooke & ffrancis Larkin bee Collectors & doe collect ye aforsd. asseasmtt And lastly it is Ordered By ye Vestry for ye Better incouragmtt of all such as hereafter shall heare office or bee publiquly imploy'd by ye said parrish That hee ye said Tho. Crooke shall out of ye first money wch shall bee collected by ye said asseasmtt bee paid and satisfied ye said sum of 50^{li} by him disbirsed as aforesaid vnto ye said Bryan Eldridge in ye behalfe of ye said Parrish of ffulham on ffulham side."

Bowack merely notes of the bells:

"In the Church tower is a very good ring of six bells."

In 1728 the six old bells, which had become broken and out of tune, were ordered to be recast. The entry in the Parish Books stands:

"At a Vestry held ye 24th day of July Anno Domini 1728, pursuant to due and legall notice for that purpose, it was unanimously agreed and order'd that the whole peal of six bells be recast, it appearing that the Tenor was broke, the third crack't, and ye rest untunable, and that a rate should be made and levied at four pence in ye pound to defray ye expences of recasting and hanging ye said bells and other necessary repairs in and about ye same."

But the resolution proved impracticable. Enquiry showed that an eight-penny, if not a ten-penny, rate would have to be levied. At a Vestry, held in the summer of the following year,

"It was Resolved that the six bells of the Parish Church of Fulham which wants (sic) to be new cast, shall be weighed and a compensation (sic; 'computation' apparently intended) made of the value thereof and what the old bells are worth, and the expense of new casting and hanging them, and that Mr. Francis Conyers churchwarden, Reginald Marriott, Mark Frecker, William Skelton, Esqrs., Mr. Christopher Gray, senior, Mr. Robert Gray, Mr. Peter Osgood and Mr. Thomas Hinson be desired to take an account of the same as also to contract with any bell founder to new cast and make them Tuneable, as also to get estimates of the carpenters, mason, and other works and repairs necessary to be done about the Steeple and Bells for which wee the several Inhabitants of the said Parish whose names are hereunder Written do promise to

mak a pound rate of eight pence and levy it on the several inhabitants in order to defray that Expence and that if this rate of eight pence in the pound is not sufficient, that a further rate shall be made on the said inhabitants not exceeding two pence in the pound to which we have hereunto set our hands the day and year before mentioned.
(Signed): Fran. Conyers (Churchwarden), R. Marriott, M. ffrecker, W. Skelton, Peter Osgood, Christop. Gray, Rob. Gray, Tho. Gray, Tho. Hinson, John Carr, Joseph White, John Poole, Richard Acres, John Brassett, Alexr Wells, Samuel Milles, Patrick Allen and Francis Hutchinson (clerk)"

The Committee, not content with the mere recasting of the six bells, matured a more ambitious scheme. The Tower of the Parish Church was strong and capacious enough for eight bells; why not, by private subscription, collect funds for two more? The year 1729 was a memorable one in Fulham, for it witnessed the erection and opening of the first permanent bridge across the river. Enthusiasm ran high. The Committee, in anticipation of collecting the funds required for the two additional bells, at once petitioned the Bishop of London for a license to recast the old peal and to increase the number to eight. On 22 July 1729, Bishop Gibson granted the following faculty:

"Edmund by Divine permission Lord Bishop of London to all Christian people to whom these psents. shall come or shall or may in anywise concern and more especially to the Vicar, Churchwardens, Parishioners and Inhabitants of the Parish of ffulham in the County of Middlesex and diocese of London SENDETH GREETING in Our Lord God Everlasting.
Whereas it hath been set forth unto us by a petition under the hands of the Vicar, Churchwardens, Parishioners and Inhabitants of the said Parish That the Bells belonging to the said parish church consist of six in number, That the great bell is broke, the third cracked and the rest untunable, and that the tower of the said church is a strong, handsome ffabrick and capable of containing a peal of eight Bells, That the said Vicar, Churchwardens and Parishioners of the said parish in Vestry lawfully assembled have agreed to have the said Bells recast and made tunable, and have also made a Rate for that purpose and agreed to add more Mettle to them and to make a peal of eight Bells in case they can raise a sum sufficient by voluntary contributions which they are in great hopes of effecting and have therefore humbly craved our licence or ffaculty to recast the said old Bells and also to make them a peal of

eight Bells by adding mettle thereto in case there shall be contributions sufficient to compleat the same as in and by the said petition now remaining in our principall registry, relation being thereunto had, it doth and may more fully appear We therefore the Bishop aforesaid, well weighing and considering the premisses do by Vertue of our power ordinary and episcopall and as far as by the ecclesiasticall laws of this Realm and temporall Laws of the same We may and can, give and grant to them the said Vicar, Churchwardens, Parishioners and Inhabitants of the parish of ffulham aforesaid our Leave and Licence or ffaculty to recast the said old Bells and also to make them a peal of eight bells by adding mettle thereto in case there shall be contributions sufficien to compleat the same in manner as by them desired. In witness whereof we have caused the seal of our Chancellour which we use in this behalf to be fixed to these psents. dated the twenty-second day of July in the year of our Lord one thousand seven hundred and twenty nine and in the seventh year of our translation."

Tower of Fulham Church. From a water-colour drawing, signed "C. Howard, 1858," in the Vicarage "Faulkner."

At the next meeting of the Vestry, 13 Aug. 1729, Mr. Skelton presented the parish with "ye Bsps. Licence for ye new Bells," which was read and "thanks return'd him." At a further meeting, on 12 Mar. 1729-30,

"Upon a motion made by ye gentlemen of ye Vestry yt persons be appointed to assist Mr. Conyers ye Churchwarden to collect ye rate made for ye paying for ye bells at ye request of ye said gent. Mr. Robert Gray, Mr. Tho. Scott and Mr. John Poole were pleas'd to consent to their being appointed to assist in ye said affair."

The contract for the recasting of the old peal of six and for the provision of two additional bells was given to Mr. Abraham Rudhall, of Gloucester, bellfounder.

Mr. William Skelton appears throughout to have been the prime mover in the matter and to have made himself practically responsible for the cost of the additional two bells. Unfortunately no statement has been preserved showing the amount of Abraham Rudhall's contract, the sum realised by the special rate or the amount which the voluntary subscriptions produced. Probably the deficit was a large one, for, on 17 Mar. 1731-32, the Vestry resolved that the

"fourescore pounds secur'd to be paid by the inhabitants of Hammersmith shall, when received, be apply'd towards the debt due for bells and be paid into the hands of Mr. Skelton for that purpose."

Mr. Skelton's generosity in the matter was recognised by the Vestry, who directed the two additional bells to be inscribed " EX dono Gvlielmi Skelton, Gen." (the gift of William Skelton, gentleman).

The Bell Loft. From a photograph by Mr. J. Dugdale, 1894

The recast bells met with a curious mishap before they reached the Belfry of All Saints. From Gloucester they were conveyed to Fulham by water. Off Fulham the barge sank. The bells were, however, recovered and found to be little the worse for their immersion.

The eight bells were tuned by John Harrison, the inventor of the timekeeper for ascertaining the longitude at sea.

The trial of the enlarged peal was made an occasion of much rejoicing among the townsfolk. The ringing was attended by several professors of music. Some of the company went on the towing path at Putney, some along the Bishop's Walk, while others took up positions in the Town where they could hear the bells. After the ringing, a dinner was held at the "King's Arms," when an opinion was generally expressed that the peal, for the size of the bells, was one of the finest in England.

The erection of the eight bells in the Tower was followed by the appointment of an official styled the "belfry keeper."

In 1746 the Belfry received a further addition through the munificence of The Mr. Theodore Ecclestone, of Mortlake. The details of this gift are not quite clear. According to tradition the donor intended to give two bells to the tower of the old church at Mortlake, but, as it was found, after they were made, that the belfry would not hold them, he determined to offer them to Fulham. But, be this as it may, we find that, at a Vestry held 29 Jan. 1745-46, to consider a proposal which had been made to hang two more bells to the then existing peal of eight,

> "Mr. Henry Holland declared that Theo. Ecclestone, Esq. of the parish of Mortlack, in the County of Surrey, had commissioned him to make the offer of the said two bells, with the framework, wheels, ironwork and other necessaries for the said bells, and the Rev. Mr. Blomberg declared that Mr. William Skelton likewise promised to hang the said bells and to procure a lycense for the same. It was thereupon unanimously agreed to accept this kind donation."

It was further decided

> "that leave be given to, hang the said bells and put the others in tune provided the parish is at no expense whatsoever for the same or any part thereof."

The two new bells, which were apparently smaller than the smallest of the bells recast in 1729, were found, on being brought to Fulham and tried, to require re-casting. Consequently, at a meeting of the Vestry, held 26 May 1746, it was agreed,

> "That the Churchwarden do deliver the two new small bells to Mr. Robert Catlin, the bellfounder, to be new cast, Mr. Theodore Eccleston by letter, dated 15 instant, having desired the same and Mr. Holland (present at this Vestry, as well as Mr. Eceleston by letter), having engag'd to redeliver the same with all convenient speed as the property of this parish."

Tower of Fulham Church, looking west.
From a pencil sketch by Miss Lucy E. Blomfield (Mrs. A. C. Bather), now in the possession of Sir Arthur W. Blomfield

On being recast, the two bells were hung in the Belfry, thus completing the peal of ten.

In 1760 Mr. Ecclestone's bells were exchanged for two others with the firm of Rudhall who supplied, in lieu, two bells which are said to have once belonged to St. Martin's church. One of these had been recast by Abraham Rudhall in 1759. The other bore the words, "The gift of the Vestry, by Subscription, 1727," an inscription which, as it now reads on the bell in the Tower of All

Saints, is somewhat misleading, as it was certainly not subscribed for by the Fulham Vestry. The following entry, in the Churchwardens' Accounts for 1761, refers to this exchange:

"Pd. Mrs. Ruddal for exchange of 2 bells as p. bill £12. 15. 9."

We append a copy of the inscriptions on the ten bells as they now hang in the Tower. The original six bells, which, as we have seen, have been twice recast, are Nos. 5, 6, 7, 8, 9 and 10. The two bells which were added to complete the peal of eight are Nos. 3 and 4, inscribed as being the gift of Mr. William Skelton; and lastly, the two so-called St. Martin's bells, which were received in exchange for Mr. Theodore Ecclestone's gift, are Nos. 1 and 2.

Bell.	Key.	Inscription.	Date.	Diameter of Mouth.	
1st, or Treble Bell	G	RECAST BY AB: RUDHALL	1759	28½ inches.	(a)
2nd	F	THE GIFT OF THE VESTRY BY SVBSCRIPTION	1727	28 ,,	(b)
3rd	E	EX DONO GVLIELMI SKELTON GEN	1729	30 ,,	
4th	D	EX DONO GVLIELMI SKELTON GEN	1729	30 ,,	(c)
5th	C	PEACE AND GOOD NEIGHBOVRHOOD A ⚜ R	1729	33 ,,	(d)
6th	B	ABR: RVDHALL OF GLOCESTER CAST VS ALL	1729	34½ ,,	
7th	A	PROSPERITY TO THE CHVRCH OF ENGLAND	1729	37⅝ ,,	
8th	G	PROSPERITY TO THIS PARISH	1729	39 ,,	
9th	F	FRANCIS CONYERS CHVRCHWARDEN	1729	43 ,,	
10th, or Tenor Bell	E	I TO THE CHVRCH THE LIVING CALL AND TO THE GRAVE DO SVMMON ALL A ⚜ R	1729	48½ ,,	

(a) All the cannons broken off.
(b) One cannon broken off.
(c) Two cannons broken off.
(d) All the cannons broken off.

The above particulars were taken by Mr. Henry Wilson, campanologist, on 24 Jan. 1872. The present ten bells are pitched in the key of E, the same as those of Magdalen College, Oxford.

By permission of the author, Mr. W. E. Harland-Oxley, we reproduce the following pleasant verses, composed in eulogy on the "Bells of Old Fulham":

Bells of old Fulham! Old Fulham bells!
Proudly ye ring a bright natal peal
That of joy and gladness tells;
Into this world of want and woe
Born is the child, for friend or foe,
May't be for the common weal !

Charles James Fèret

God bless the infant born this day,
Is what the bells all seem to say,
He's set on thee *His* seal !
Old Fulham bells ! Sweet Fulham bells !
How oft across our pleasant meads
Thy rhythmic music swells
Sweet, clear, and bright,
Morn, noon and night,
And tho' thy music from us speeds
Its mem'ry with us dwells !

Bells of old Fulham ! Old Fulham bells !
Blithely ye ring a gay nuptial peal
That of hope and peace foretell !
Together joined for good or ill,
The twain can make life what they will,
If they but its duties feel !
Straight from the bells, borne on the air,
Come notes of joy to the wedded pair,
As trustingly they kneel !
Old Fulham bells ! Sweet Fulham bells ! etc., etc.

Bells of old Fulham ! Old Fulham bells !
Sadly ye ring a deep fun'ral peal
That of grief and sorrow tells !
Gone from a world of strife and care,
To blissful realms, to regions fair,
Where ills of earth shall heal !
The dear one sleeps in trust and faith,
Is what the sombre peal now saith,
From death there's no appeal !
Old Fulham bells ! Sweet Fulham bells ! etc. , etc.

Bells of old Fulham ! Old Fulham bells !
Whatever the tale told by thy peal,
Rare harmony grandly swells !
For if mid strife thou'rt wildly swung,
Or in sweet peace thou'rt blithely rung,
Thy melodies o'er us steal !
Be't low weird wail as ye wildly whirl,
Or jocund sound as ye twist and twirl
Ye sweetest voice reveal !
Old Fulham bells ! Sweet Fulham bells ! etc., etc.

The old accounts of the Churchwardens are crowded with entries relating to the ringing of the bells. Accession day, Coronation day, the King's birthday, the Prince of Wales's birthday, Gunpowder Treason day, or the days when the king chanced to pass through the Town on his way to Hampton Court, were sure to find the ringers ringing out a merry peal. The following are a few samples of the entries:

1578 Paid for the Queen's Majesties being at Putney for vyttels for the ringers 2s. 8d.

1588 To the ringers at the Queen's return from Barnelms 6d.
(Barn Elms was, at that time, the seat of Sir Francis Walsingham.)

1592 When the Queen went from Chelsey 14d.

1597 When the Queen went to Lord Burleigh's house at Wimbledon 14d.

1597 When the Queen went to the Lord Admiral's and so back again 2s. 8d.

1602 28 July. At the remove of the Queen from Greenwich to Chiswick 12d.

1623 Payed to the ringers upon the king's rout through to Hampton Court 1s. 6d.

1636 To the King's footmen for not ringing 10s. 6d
(This would seem to have been a fine for failing to ring when the King passed by.)

1637 Pd. for ringing ye 5th of nouember and for ye king's birth and two other daies £1. 6s. 2d.

1638 Pd. for ringing at the King's passing by and other times apointed £1. 8s. 6d.

1639 Pd. for ringing five daies for the king's comming by 15s. 0d.

1640 pd. for ringing powder treason daie, the king's birthdaie and for his retourne fro[m] Scotland 18s. 0d.

1642 pd. for ringing coronation daie 9s. 0d.
Not to be allowed for tyme to come.

1643 Pd. for ringing the king's birthday the 19 of Nouember 1643 5s.

At a Vestry, held 6 May 1672, it was decided to limit bell-ringing expenses as under:

> "for ringing on Gunpowder Treason tenn shillinges and no more. And on the King's Coronacon tenn shillings and on the Kings Birthday the like sum of tenn shillings and not to exceed more in the pteculers aforesaid."

1713 Paid to the Ringers when Peace was Proclaimed 5s. 0d.
(This was the War of the Spanish Succession closed by the Treaty of Utrecht in 1713)

1715 Pd. for Ringing the restorn of King Charles the Second 10s. 0d.

1715 Pd. for Ringing for the King's accession to the Throne 10s. 0d.

1715 Pd. for Ringing his entry into London 10s. 0d.

1715 Pd. for Ringing Queen Anne's Birthday 10s. 0d.

1716 Paid the Ringers for Ringing the Prince and Princess through the Town 5s. 0d.

1723 Paid to the Widow Smith one day's ringing (9 May) 10s. 0d.

On 5 March 1730-31 the Vestry limited more closely these occasions of public rejoicing, the following being the order given:

> "That for the future the Churchwarden for the time being do pay to the ringers for ringing on the several days following and no other, the sum of ten shillings each day and not more, viz on Christmas day, Easter day, the King's birthday, the Queen's birthday, the Prince of Wales' birthday, the King's accession to the Throne, the King's Coronation, the Restauration and the Gun Powder Plott."

On occasions, however, of general public rejoicing, Fulham rarely failed to set her bells going. Thus:

1759 29 Nov. Gave the Ringers for ringing on the news of taking Quebeck 10s. 0d.
(This was General Wolfe's magnificent victory over Montcalm on the heights of Abraham.)

1800 Paid the Ringers on account of Nelson's victory £1. 1s. 0d.
(This was the battle of the Nile, fought 1 Aug. 1800)

1801 Paid for Ringing for the joyful news of the return of Peace £2. 2s.
(This is in reference to the preliminary articles of peace signed in London in Oct. 1801. The definite treaty was concluded at Amiens in the following year)

1813 Gave the Ringers when the French Army was defeated 10s. 6d.

1813 Gave the Ringers on Bounaparte's defeat at Moscow £1. 11s. 6d.

1817 Paid the Ringers for a Leg of Mutton for Ringing when the Queen breakfasted at the Bishop's (2 Aug.) 9s. 0d.
(This was Queen Charlotte, the Consort of George III)

By virtue of a time-honoured custom, the ringers at All Saints annually claimed and received a shoulder of veal, on which they feasted on Easter Tuesday.

1820 Paid Hudnott for Ringing when the Queen arrived at Brandenburgh House £1. 11s. 0d.
(This was Queen Caroline, the hapless Consort of George IV)

In Fulham the ancient custom of ringing on Gunpowder Treason day dropped on the occasion of the Prince of Wales's birthday in 1841, when the ringing was deferred from 5th to 9th November. The bells are now rung at the greater festivals, such as Christmas and Easter, on New Year's Eve and the Queen's Birthday. They are also rung when the Bishop comes into residence, when the Vicar returns from his annual holiday, etc.

Knell tolling, after death, took the place of "the passing bell" of pre-Reformation times, rung as the spirit ebbed away, a sign whereby watchers might know what was occurring, and might pray for the soul of the dying. In Fulham the knell for the dead was often sounded, and brought a considerable sum annually into the coffers of the Churchwardens. The following are a few instances in the Accounts for 1638:

> Recd. for a knell great bell Earsbey 2s. 6d.
>
> Recd. for a knell with the great bell, a nursse child 5s. 0d.
>
> Recd. for a knell, great bell 2s. 6d.
>
> Recd. for a knell, litle bell 6d.
>
> Recd. for buryall a nurse child in the Church and knell great bell double dues 18s. 4d.
>
> recd. for bells and <u>hearse cloath</u> Clacknell 6s. 0d.
>
> recd for knell Powell 6d.
>
> recd for bells and knell Mr. Juxon's child 5s. 0d.
>
> recd for knell my L. Mortons man 2s. 0d."

The charge for a knell is now 2s. 6d.; in the case of a non-parishioner, double this fee is payable. In tolling the ending is three times three for a man; three times two for a woman, on the tenor bell: the same, on a smaller bell (the 5th), for children. Hence it is always known whether a man or a woman, or a male or female child, is being tolled for.

A quaint custom long lingered in Fulham in respect to the ringing of a bell each day, a survival of the times when the curfew warned the parishioners to put out their lights.

In olden times, when clocks were possessed by few besides the municipal authorities and the wealthy, the curfew bell served several purposes. The ringing of a bell or the blowing of a horn at stated times really constituted the only means by which the people could, apart from general observation, tell the hour of the day. In Fulham the practice was to ring the bell at 5 a.m. and 8 p.m. Formerly it was the custom to rise much earlier than we do in these degenerate days. The hour at which it rang in the evening was that at which it sounded in most towns and parishes, though in some, seven and, in others, nine, was the time. In days when there were no effective police, the roads at night were extremely dangerous. The bell, therefore, warned law-abiding citizens of the hour when they should return to their homes, extinguish their fires and retire to rest.

Tower of Fulham Church. From a photograph by Mr. H. Ambridge, 1869

Anciently in Fulham the bell was rung all the year round, the duty of ringing falling on the parish clerk. Subsequently it was rung during the winter half only, from 29 Sept. to 25 March. In 1647 the Churchwardens

"pd Thomas for ringing the Eight a clocke Belle 5s. 0d."

And in 1648:

"To Thomas Earsbie for Ringing the eight a Clocke Bell 10s. 0d."

In the minutes of a Vestry, for 26 March 1655-56, is the following entry:

> "It is ordered that whosoever shalbe elected from time to time by ye inhabitants to ring the eyght o clocke bell (wch is ordered to be from the 29th of September to ye 25th of March) at eyght of ye clocke att night and five of ye Clocke in the morning and to keepe ye clocke in good temper shall receive for his paines for ye qrter begining from ye 25 of March and ending ye 24th of June ye summe of vs and also for ye qter ending the 29th of September and for ye two winter qrters ye summ of vs for each qrter and it is ordered that John Drake shall be keep(er) of ye Clocke and the Bell ringer as aforsaid and receive the aforsaid sallery vntill further order be taken by ye inhabitants at their meeting in ye Vestrie."

Leaving the old Belfry, we ascend some more steps and emerge on the roof through a door beneath the little turret. From this coign of vantage, on a fine day, the visitor may obtain a splendid View all over Fulham and across the river as far as Sydenham. The battlemented stonework surrounding the parapet has been graven over and over again with the names and initials of persons who have adopted this method as the only possible one by which to hand down their memory to posterity. In some cases the letters are merely scratched, but in others they are cut deeply into the stone.

The Tower has been more or less extensively repaired on numerous occasions. In 1637 the Churchwardens:

> "Pd. for bords and worke for the steeple, windowes and churchgates to Coxe 17s. 6d."

> "Pd. the smith for worke done in the steeple, gates of the churchyard and other in ye church £1. 3s. 2d."

The disbursements of 1638 include:

> "pd. for mending the weather-cocke and setting it vpp 13s. 8d."

The receipts for 1645 include:

> "More for old lead taken of (sic) the Crosse 2s. 6d."

In 1719 a flag-staff was erected. On 6 March of that year the Churchwardens

> "Paid for a flagstaff and putting it up, etc. £1. 3s. 6d."

In 1724, when it was blown down, there was paid

> "For raising the Flagg pole 2s. 0d."

In the following year it again came down in a storm:

> "To money paid for hoisting the flag when blown down 2s. 6d."

On 2 Aug. 1727, it was ordered:

> "that the lead upon the Steeple be mended and all other necessary repairs be done likewise."

In 1731 the Churchwardens

> "paid for ten yards of Crape to mend the Flagg 10s. 0d."
> "paid for mending the same 5s. 0d."

In 1732 the lead of the roof had to be taken up and fresh lead laid. In 1750 numerous repairs were done to the Tower, the work including new steps of Portland stone. Several stones of the battlements were renewed and fresh lead placed on the "parpet wall." The 1787 disbursements include:

> "Paid for a flag for the church as per Bill £5. 10s. 0d."

> "Paid Robt. Buckland for going to Wapping Wall to order the flag and bringing it home when ready 2s. 0d."

> "Paid for a bag to keep the flag in 5s. 6d."

At a general repair of the Church in 1797 the original battlements of the Tower, some of which were thrown down by a storm, were replaced by the existing range. A new flag-staff was erected, and the lead on the steeple was re-laid "17 lb. to the foot."

The Tower of All Saints was long disfigured by an unsightly octagonal spire of wood, popularly known as "the pepper-box," through the centre of which rose the flag-staff. In 1845 a Committee was appointed by the Vestry to look into the state of the Tower. On 24 April, in the course of a detailed statement of needful repairs, they reported:

> "Your Committee then proceeded to the summit of the Tower and found some of the weather boarding enclosing the flagstaff in a defective state, but would strongly recommend the entire removal of the same, not on account of the repairs that are necessary, but because they consider it not in character with the style of the building."

The suggestion to remove the ugly structure was very wisely adopted by the Vestry. Under the superintendence of Mr. George Godwin, F.R.S., the Tower was entirely refaced and thoroughly repaired. The work was carried out by Mr. Cundy, at a cost of £396. 13s.

The Old Church Prior to Demolition

We will now take a glance at the old Church as it appeared just prior to its demolition.

Old All Saints was an irregular, barn-like structure, with a low, red-tiled roof, terminating, at its western end, in the handsome Gothic Tower which we have just visited. The Rev. J. Norris Brewer, describing the Church in 1816, speaks of it as "destitute of uniformity." Mr. E. Walford writes in "Old and New London,"

> "It has been well described as 'little else than a collection of high pews and deep galleries, contained within four walls, pierced at intervals with holes for the admission of light; in fact, one of the worst specimens of suburban churches which have of late years so rapidly and happily disappeared before the growing taste for a purer and more devotional style of church architecture."

The judgment is a severe one, but it is, in the main, perfectly true. The east end of the north aisle, added so recently as 1840-41, was really the only portion of the old building which could lay claim to any architectural beauty.

The Church consisted of a nave and two aisles. There was no chancel, properly so called, but merely a recess for the communion table. At the south-east corner, forming an incongruous annexe, was the Vestry, a tall and well lighted room. The "south transept" was merely a portion of the south aisle, <u>with a row of free pews facing north</u>. The north transept extended a little further back than the north aisle, and had a continuous row of free pews facing south. The vaulted semicircular roof, which was lighted with attic-like windows, was of wood, coloured blue.

A deep broad gallery extended along the north and south sides and across the west end of the Church. Affixed to the front of this gallery were numerous benefaction tablets, preserved in the north porch of the present Church. In the north-west corner was a large, square pew, over the door of which was <u>some curious twisted ironwork</u>. It was generally known as the "Limpany" pew, or chapel, from the large Limpany monument, now in the north porch, which entirely covered the north wall of this corner. At the east end of the south aisle was formerly the Great or Vicar's Pew, immediately behind the pulpit. This pew is many times mentioned in the Churchwardens' Accounts. Thus, in 1753,

> "Recd. of Mrs. Mary Hatton for seating her in the Great pew next the Reading Desk 10s. 6d."

On entering the north porch the visitor passed a broad wooden staircase, which led to the North and West Galleries and the Organ. At the top of this staircase, on the north side of the Organ, was a rising gallery set apart for the girls of the National Schools. On the south side of the Organ was a similar gallery for the boys. From here another flight of stairs led to the south aisle. The Organ stood in the centre of the West Gallery: in front of it were two rows of seats. In the North and South Galleries were similar rows of seats, then an aisle, and then further rows of seats. At the east end of the North Gallery (but entirely separated from it) was the Bishop's Gallery, approached by a stone staircase just north of the chancel. The Bishop's pew was in front at the east end. The seats behind were for the use of the servants from the Palace and others.

The chancel wall, under the east window, was covered with oak panelling. On each side of the window were canopied painted boards with the Decalogue, etc., with panelling beneath. These are now placed in the Mission Hall, Parson's Green.

The pillars supporting the galleries were of wood, with the exception of those belonging to the eastern extension, which were of stone.

The Limpany Pew. From an oil painting by Miss Jane Humphreys

The old Church had five doors. The West door, under the Tower, was seldom used, except for weddings and funerals. Glass and baize doors separated the Tower chapel from the Church. The North and South porches faced each other near the west end. The fourth door communicated with the Vestry at the south-east corner. The fifth, at the north-east corner, led to the Bishop's Gallery and the north transept.

The floor of the Church was somewhat (1 ft. 9 ins.) below the level of the ground.

The West Door.
From a water-colour drawing by Miss Jane Humphreys

We will now deal with the history of some of the principal features of the old Church.

To Dr. Thomas Edwardes, chancellor to John King, Bishop of London, the parish was indebted for several benefactions. The most substantial of these was a legacy of "fower scoore poundes to the Church of ffulham" which he left in a codicil, appended on 13 Jan. 1618-19, to his will, bearing date 9 January of that year.

Little is known about Dr. Edwardes. He was descended from an old Berkshire family. In 1579 he became a Fellow of All Souls College, Oxford, in which University he took his B.A. degree on 26 March 1582-83. He proceeded B.C.L., 19 Nov. 1584 and D.C.L. on 17 Dec. 1590. He died circa 1618-19. The following is an extract from his will (dated 9 Jan. 1618-19) together with its codicil (dated 13 Jan. 1618-19), proved 21 April 1619 (P.C.C. 40 Parker), by Sir William Bird, kt., sole executor:

"I Thomas Edwardes of London doctor of lawe and chauncellor of the Dioces of London. To be buried in decente fitt and convenient manner without anie greate worldlie pompe and ceremoney in the parish Church of ffulham in the countie of Middlesex where I nowe dwell. To my wife ffrances Edwardes my nowe dwelling house in ffulham for her life or widowhood. Remainder to <u>Ravis Edwardes</u> my eldest sonne and heirs for ever. To said wife furniture, etc., and £5,000; to said son Ravis, £500; to John Edwardes my sonne, £1,000; to William Edwardes my sonne, £500; to my daughter Alice Edwardes, £600; to my daughter ffrances Edwardes, £600; to my daughter Elizabeth Edwardes, £500; to my daughter Anne Edwardes, £400; to my daughter Dorothie Edwardes, £400, all payable at 21, or, in case of daughters, at 21 or marriage.

I give and bequeathe to the poore of the parish of ffulham aforesaid the some of twentie poundes of lawfull money of England.

Codicil, 13 Jan. 1618-19.

A codicill to be annexed to the last Will and Testamente of the said Thomas Edwardes as followeth vizt. Memorandum that uppon Wednesday the thirtenth of January one thousand six hundred eighteene the right Reverende ffather in God John Lord Bishopp of London repayringe to visit the said Deor Edwardes his Chauncellor after many Speeches passed betweene them which his Los used for his comforte beinge in that bodilie weaknes the said doctor Edwardes beinge of perfecte mynde and memory said as followeth or to the lyke effecte, there is three hundred pounds yt is due to me or will shortlie be due to me but yt shall not be received to be parte of my other estate, but disposed thus one hundred pounds to the poore of ffulham to buy them Land one hundred poundes to the Scholes at Oxford to be delivered into yor Lorps handes, fower scoore poundes to the Church of ffulham and twentie poundes to my poore kinsman Mr. Harris whome he lykewise said he would have to take his dyet with his wief untill he weare otherwise provided for, his Lordshipp further sayinge that he doubted not, but that hee had alreadie ordered and disposed of his worldlie estate for the good of his wife whoe had beene a loving wife to him and of his sweete children his annsweare was that this was out of the worlde, meaninge (as was conceived) that this three hundred poundes was noe parte of that worldlie estate which he had formerlie disposed All which wordes were spoken the day and yere aforesaid in the pnce of the said Right Reverend ffather, Mr. Henry Kinge his sonne one of the Cannons Residentiarie of the Cathedrall Church of Saincte Paule London Mrs. ffraunces Edwardes wife of the said Testator and others."

It does not appear from the codicil to the will that Dr. Edwardes specified in what way the £80 should be spent, but from the old "Register Book" we learn that it was "imployed about making of a Gallerye in the sayd Churche, new casting the lead of the Steeple of the sayd Churche, new seeting of the Bodie of the sayd Churche, & about other necessaries for the said Churche."

From this entry it is clear that the Church had not heretofore possessed a gallery. The galleries were erected piecemeal. The first, which was built by the aid of Dr. Edwardes' legacy, was the one at the west end. The actual date of its erection is unknown. The earliest allusion to it occurs in the Parish Books under date 1646, when, at a Vestry held on January 11th of that year, it was

"Agreed that Mr. Stisted (one of the Churchwardens) doe pay unto Havell Page, in regard of his Attendaunce vpon the West Gallery on sabbath dayes, after the rate of six pence a Sabbath day henceforward, soe long as he shall continew in the same imployment, and, in consideration of his paines past, the twenty shillings formerly lent to him shall be remitted to him."

Poor old Page held his post as janitor down to 1655. On 4 Nov. of this year the Vestry "Order'd that henceforth the fforty shillings formerly paid to Havell Page for his attendance at the gallery be forborne to be paid."

The South Door. From a Water-colour drawing by Miss Jane Humphreys

The West Gallery is again referred to in the minutes of a Vestry, held 11 May 1687, when permission was given to Mr. Samuel Gee to lay a gravestone, to the memory of his wife, "at ye ffoot of ye stayers goeing vp the West Gallery." (See "Epitaphs") In the time of Bishop Compton five new pews were built in the West Gallery by Dr. George Clarke for

> "the use of such of the Inhabitants and Parishioners and to such of the Youth as had or should hereafter learn to sing the Psalms after the method now in use."

On 29 August 1722:

> "At a Vestry then held it was order'd that John Corder be allowed ten shillings p. an. for looking after the children in the West Gallery as the former Beedle had."

These were the Charity School children. In 1732 the Organ was erected in the West Gallery. In 1771 the Hon. Richard Fitzpatrick presented to the Church the old clock which was fixed against the centre of the West Gallery. It was replaced, in recent times, by the clock now in the Vestry.

The North Gallery was added about the end of the 17th or the beginning of the 18th century. Some light was thrown on this matter when the old Church was pulled down. On 30 April 1880, a discovery of special interest was made. On taking down the face of the galleries, it was found that the three western pairs of pillars had assumed the form which they presented by two stages of growth. Originally they had been simple baulks of timber, marbled in paint, with a plain bead ornament at the four corners, thus:

These primitive columns were subsequently altered by having a deep groove cut in each face and the corners rounded, thus:

The columns were now painted white in imitation of stone. The last form which we have described must have been assumed by the columns just about the time when the North Gallery was raised in level. This fact was made clear by the added portions being found, on the demolition of the old Church, to have been cut away to allow of the insertion of the fronts of the gallery. By these means the original form of the columns was ascertained.

On one of these columns - the north-west one - where the North and West Galleries met, on the east face of the original square column, at a point hidden by the galleries, was rudely cut,

1707
W. B.

a circumstance which proves that, when the columns had their original form, there must have been a north gallery extending further east than the old West Gallery and at a lower level.

In 1768 the North Gallery, as we shall presently see, was altered to bring it into uniformity with that on the south side of the Church. The addition at the north-east end of the North Gallery, known as the Bishop's Gallery, was not made till 1840.

The South Gallery, as it existed in modern times, was erected in 1769-70. The first mention of a proposed gallery in the south aisle occurs in the Churchwardens' books as early as 1714:

> "Recd of Mrs. Drew towards building the Gallery in the South Ile . . . £4. 6s. 0d."

Though the project was evidently thus early contemplated, it was probably not carried out for some years. The first reference to a south gallery, as actually existing, is in 1735. At a Vestry, held 13 April of that year, it was

> "Order'd . . . that the Gallery erected in the South Isle of the church and now occupied by Mr. Lloyd's scholars, be for the future (in consideration of the sum of six pounds six shillings paid by Mr. Robt. Lloyd) kept for the use of the scholars belonging to the School of Mr. Robt. Lloyd aforesaid during his residence in the parish as an inhabitant and parishioner."

The wording of this resolution seems to suggest that the South Gallery referred to was then of recent erection. This was probably only a small erection, for the old South Gallery, which was taken down with the Church, was, as we have said, not built till 1769. In 1766 the Vestry took into consideration the question of providing further accommodation in the Church. Accordingly, on 1 Nov. 1766, it was resolved that

> "The several particulars of repair, alteration and erection, hereinafter mentioned, are necessary for making the said church as well more decent as more convenient for the inhabitants of the said parish (to wit) to pull down and clear away the Pew in the south aisle in order to make room for a gallery on that side, to erect a gallery on the south side, to be made of ffir timber," etc.
>
> "That an alteration shall be made in the North Gallery to correspond with the gallery on the south side," etc.

In 1768 the Churchwardens obtained the necessary faculty. The license, which is dated 24 Nov. 1768, states that the South Gallery

> "is intended to be of the dimension of 30 feet in length and 16 feet in breadth."

It was not till 1798 that the three galleries were brought into some measure of uniformity of appearance and level. At a Vestry, held on 29 May 1798,

> "Mr. Ward produced a plan and estimate of the intended alteration in

the organ gallery, and the Vestry are of opinion that it will not only be the means of accommodating a number of respectable parishioners who are in want of pews, but will on the whole have the effect of rendering the 3 Gallerys in some degree uniform; they are therefore unanimously of opinion that the Churchwardens do give him directions to carry the said plan into execution."

Geometrical Elevation of Fulham Church, south side, from measurements by Mr. Upsden, Surveyor. Drawn by P. B. Cotes, Jan. 1797.
The original drawing, in the possession of W. J. Harvey, Esq., F.S.A., was executed apparently to a scale of 10ft. to the inch

The following are the details of Mr. Ward's plan and estimate:

"Take down the present pews in front of the organ, alter do. according to plan; alter the floors agreeable to do.; frame and fix new wainscot where necessary and 3 partitions with leaved trusses to answer the trusses on the side gallery pews; hang doors; put on new latches; to use all the old wainscot and other materials in the above alterations. Will amount to the sum of £20.
(Signed) F. WARD."

To Dr. Thomas Edwardes, whom we have mentioned in connection with the West Gallery, the parish was also indebted for the nucleus of the fund with which a quaint little building, known as the School-house and Vestry, was built over and about the north porch of the old Church.

In his "life-tyme," we gather from the "Register Book," he gave

> "Sixteene poundes towardes the building of the house over the Church Porche for a Vestrye, and Schoole-house, and lodging for the schoole-Mr and Clerke."

The Vestry and School-house appear to have formed a small building consisting of two principal rooms, the upper one being the Vestry chamber and the lower one the School-room for the use of the village children and also for the meetings of the <u>inhabitants in Vestry</u>. The building was erected about 1630. In 1635 the Churchwardens paid

> "For mending the curate's room 5s. 6d."

In 1637 they

> "Pd. for mending Mr. Walpoles roomes and glass windowes at severall times £1. 0s. 4d."

During a great storm which occurred in 1639, the premises were severely injured. The parish clerk records for this year:

> Payd for Mr. Viner the curate for his house rent during the time of his displacement and fro[m] the scholehouse and lodging by reason of a great winde wch blew it downe the sume £1. 6s. 8d.

> pd. the Carpenter for a stile, a planke and shoring the Church porch and his worke 11s. 7d.

> pd. the smith for worke about the Schoolehouse 6s. 6d.

> pd. the bricklayer for worke about the same 10s. 7d.

In 1645 the Vestry and School-house were again repaired:

> Pd. Goodm Smith ye bricklayer for worke done about the Vestry

Chamber ouer the Schole and tyling the church hee finding all materialls £2. 6s. 6d.

pd. Mr. Viner for ye materialls of his studdie in ye Vestry Chamber and setting up the table 11s. 2d.

In 1646 the Churchwardens

"Pd. for a Table for ye Vestry 13s. 0d."

In this year some of the parishioners assisted the Vicar to furnish the Vestry room. The entry of these gifts thus stands in the "Register Book":

"Theire was giuen by ye Parrishoners herevnder named in ye yeare 1646 for & towards ye furnishinge of the Vestry ouer ye Churche Porche of Fulham wth necessaries vsefull in ye said Roome:

Mr. Thomas Hill one Carpett of stript stuffe.
Mr. William Raylton two red Leather Chaires.
Mr. William Stisted one red Leather Chaire.
Mr. Henrie Dewell one Wainscott Chaire.
Mr. Adoniram Byfeild 4s. 6d. & a standish
Mr. Wm. Yeo 5s. 0d.
Mr. Andrewe Arnold 4s. 6d.
Mr. Wm. Earsbie 4s. 6d.
Mr. Wm. Hinson 4s. 6d.
Mr. Peter Nurse 4s. 6d.
Mr. Symon Wilmott 4s. 6d.
Mr. Thomas Upfman 2s. 6d.
Mr. George Saris 5s. 0d.
Mr. Henry Marsh 4s. 6d.

In 1648 the Churchwardens

Paid for a paire fire Irons for the Vestry 3s. 0d.
More for firesholue tongs and Bellowes for the Vestry 4s. 0d.
More for Bookes for the Vestry laid out by Mr. Byfield 6s. 7d.

In 1653 the building was assigned to the use of Samuel Clarke, who was that year appointed to the threefold office of public registrar, parish clerk and schoolmaster. Clarke's election is thus quaintly entered in the minutes:

> "At a Vestry held 28 Aug. 1653:
> It is ordered, that in psuance of a late Act of this prsent prlamt publicke notice shalbe giuen the next lordes day in the pish church of fulham and the Chappell of Hamersmith That the Inhabitants of both places doe meet on Thursday come seuennight att Two of ye Clocke in the afternoone att the Vestrie howse att fulham. To choose a parish Register for this pish of fulham.
> Att the Vestrie howse of fulham September 8th 1653
> It is . . . orderd That wheras in p'suance of a late Act of Parliamt the pishoners did meet this psent day att the Vestrie after publicke notice giuen in the pish Church and Chappell att Hammersmith And at their meeting did elect and choose Mr. Samuel Clarke to be publicke Register for the same pish. of fulham That the said choyse shalbe entred accordingly and thervnto haue sett their hands.
> Att this psent Vestrie the before menconed Mr. Samuell Clarke was also elected for pish Clarke for the pish of fulham and it is also consented unto and agreed vppon that the said Mr. Clarke shall haue libertie to Teach Schoole in the psent Vestrie howse wth the vse of the additionall and adjoyning Roome reserving to the pish the vse thereof as often as occasion shall seeme meet."

Fulham Church, circa 1800, from the north-west. From a pencil drawing, signed E. M. N., in the possession of the Author.

Clarke proved an unworthy servant, deserting his post within a few days of his election. The Parish Books record:

> "Att a Vestrie September 21th 1653
> It is ordered That wheras in p'suance of a late Act of p'liamt att the last Vestrie the pishoners did meet and did elect Mr. Samuell Clarke to be publicke Register for the pish And ffor that the said Mr. Clarke did desert the said Imploymt as the pishonrs were informed   The said pishonrs whose names are hervnder written did elect and choose Mr. Thomas Crooke to be publick Register for the said pish of fulham, publicke notice being giuen both att the pish Church of fulham and Chappell of Hammersmith.
> The choyce ahoue I doe aprooue of
> (Sd.) EDM° HARVEY
> ISAAC KNIGHT Rector
> GEO. LANGHAM
> JNO. VICKERS."

The vacant parish clerkship was filled up at a Vestry meeting, held 5 Feb. 1653-54, when Mr. John Gee, who was elected, was given permission to teach the children in the "psent Vestrie" the same as accorded to Clarke. In 1657 he also received the post of registrar.

In 1656 the lower room adjoining the porch was again used for the School-house. At a meeting of the Vestry, held on 28 Sept. 1657, it was

> "Ordered that ye Churchwarden doe cause ye schoole house to bee glazed forthwth."

Gee held his offices of parish clerk, registrar and schoolmaster for nearly thirty years. In the Church Registers is the following:

> 1682. John Gee pish Clerke of Fulham bu. 20 of Novemb.

In the troublous days of the Revolution the parishioners appear to have been unable to find a suitable person to conduct the school, for,

> "At a Vestry held 13 March 1688,
> It is order'd (by the consent of the right honourable and right reverend

father in God Henry Lord Bishop of London) and by and wth the consent of the parishoners he under written that Willm Terrey haue the vse of the two roomes aboue staires in the Vestry to liue in vntil such tyme as any fitt pson yt may be thought fitt to keepe schoole shalbe admitted to liue in the same pmises and then the said Wm Terry is to depart and leave the same vpon a moneths notice given to him by the parishoners."

Fulham Church, south side, 1812.
From an engraving in Faulkner's "Fulham."

We hear little more of the ancient Vestry and School-house till the days of Dr. Philip Dwight, Vicar of Fulham, the son of John Dwight, the founder of the famous Pottery in the New King's Road. When an infant, Philip Dwight had been brought by his father from Wigan to Fulham. As the whole of his life had been spent in our parish, he was naturally regarded as a good and wise counsellor, while his repeated signature in the Vestry minute books shows that he must have taken a very keen interest in the affairs of the place. At a Vestry, held on 7 Mar. 1722-23, when the good doctor, though only 51, had grown infirm, the parishioners showed their appreciation of his services by passing the following resolution:

"Whereas It is represented unto us by Mr. Justice Marriott That the Vestry Room in our Parish Church is in a very Ruinous condition and unfit for use and so damp that it spoils the books and everything else that's laid in it And that the Reverend Doctr Dwight, our Vicar, being very Lame and much out of Order in his health, cannot go up stairs into the Old Room where the Inhabitants sometimes meet (to do the business of the parish) to give them his kind assistance for the Reasons before mention'd,

We therefore by and with the consent of Mr. Alexander Wells the present churchwarden do order that the said Vestry be forthwith made more useful and convenient at the charge of the parish but in as frugal a manner as may be (vizt.) the room to be flour'd with Boards upon the Tiles the Rotten Wainscott to be taken down and new put and Painted, a Chimney to be built, a fireplace made and the Window altered."

Fulham Church. From an engraving signed "H. West, *del.* J. *sc.*" circa 1820

On 5 Mar. 1723-24, the Churchwardens and Overseers of the poor were ordered to buy "a dozen strong leather chairs for the use of the parish" in Vestry.

On 1 Feb. 1725-26, the Vestry

"Order'd that Mr. Paul be admitted to have the use of the Vestry room and the room adjoyning to it upon condition that the Charity Children have the liberty to lay their cloathes there as usual."

Mr. John Paul was the parish clerk. This is the first mention of "charity children." Probably in very early times the school served for the children of the parishioners generally without class distinction. As the population increased and private schools came to be established for the children of better-to-do residents, the village school would naturally merge into an institution for training those of the poorer classes.

On 3 July 1728, the Vestry's order of 1 Feb. was "revers'd," and

> "'twas order'd That Thomas Johnson and his wife haue the said Vestry room and the room adjoyning to live in They keeping them clean and the Charity Cloathes to lie therein."

On 24 Mar. 1729, it was

> "Ordered yt Alexander Wells have ye key of ye Vestry room & yt He keep ye said Room clean & fit for ye reception of ye gentlemen of ye said parish, & yt ye other room adjoining to it be kept lockt."

Alexander Wells had then recently been chosen "Vestry Clerk," an office which he held for many years.

A proposal was, in 1750, made for the pulling down of the Vestry and School-house. A Committee of the Vestry, appointed to consider what repairs to the Church were needful, presented, on 26 Mar. 1750-51, their report. After detailing the repairs they considered necessary, they added:

> "But if the School building on the north side of the Church, which is most decayed and of no use to ye church be pulled down, then the repairs to be done there are not to be proceeded in and future repairs thereof will be prevented.
> We have no objection to this alteration, but the pulling down of the charity school, which cannot be replaced in any other part of the buildings contiguous thereto; but there is a convenient place on the south part of the Church to erect a room against, which will make a more compleat charity school and this will make an additional charge to the repairs about £26. 10s."

The Vestry, on considering the report, came to the opinion

"that the School building adjoining to the Church ought not to be pulled down."

But the respite was not to last for many years. At a Vestry, held 7 Feb. 1782, the parishioners "took a survey of the Great Vestry Room and other buildings adjoining to and over the Church Porch" which they found in a very decayed and ruinous condition. It was accordingly resolved that it would be for the benefit of the parish to take down the whole of the buildings and to erect in lieu

> "a decent portico or entrance into the Church as they are of opinion it will be attended with much less expence than repairing the present building."

A Committee was appointed to carry out the scheme. At its first meeting, on 12 February, a resolution was passed to immediately take down the premises, and in lieu thereof to erect a portico or entrance

> "nearly similar to the portico of Wandsworth Church, the pillars to be of stone, if it is not found to be attended with too great an expence."

On 21 Mar. 1782, the Committee announced that the materials of the old buildings had been sold to the following persons:

				£.	s.	d.
Lot	1	Old Tiles	Mr. Chasemore	2.	2.	0.
,,	2	Five Doors	,, King	2.	5.	0.
,,	3	A Window	,, Preedy		12.	0.
,,	4	Old Iron	,, Willson		13.	6.
,,	5	Timber	,, Chasemore		17.	0.
,,	6	,,	,, ,,	2.	2.	0.
,,	7	Fire wood	,, Mackinder		18.	0.
,,	8	Stone	,, Gray	1.	1.	0.
,,	9	,,	,, ,,		14.	0.
,,	10	,,	,, Webb		14.	0.
,,	11	,,	,, ,,		10.	6.
				12.	9.	0.

It does not seem that the stone portico was then erected, for the views of the Church subsequent to this date show merely a tumbledown building on the site of the original structure. This second building was itself taken down when the Church was restored in 1840-41.

The windows of the old Church were, until 1840, chiefly of ordinary glass. There is, however, no doubt that in ancient times All Saints did possess some stained or painted glass. Nicholas Charles, Lancaster Herald *temp*. James I, in his "Church Notes," mentions four coats of arms as then existing in the windows. Of these, three were "In ye Chauncell in glass." Of each of these he gives carefully executed drawings with the following blazons:

> (1.) Arms of the see of Canterbury impaling three garbs (sheaves of wheat). [Evidently the impalement of Archbishop Kemp, who was Bishop of London from 1421 to 1426.]
> (2.) Lozengy sa. and erm., on a chief of the first three lilies slipped arg. [Over this shield the herald has written the name "Waynfleet," doubtless supposing it was intended for William Waynfleet, Bishop of Winchester, but more probably the arms were those of John Waynfleet, who was Rector of Fulham from 1465 to 1476.]
> (3.) Sa., a talbot sejant within a bordure engrailed arg. [These were the arms of Simon Sudbury, Archbishop of Canterbury, whose name the herald has written above his drawing of the shield, but it is very probable that the coat also belonged to John Sudbury alias Crall, who was Vicar of Fulham from 1439 to 1451. Simon Sudbury, before his translation to Canterbury, was Bishop of London from 1362 to 1375.]
> (4.) The fourth coat the herald merely describes as "In a Window." The blazon is: Three birds' heads erm. in a bordure. - [We have been unable to identify these arms.]

These coats were probably lost during the Commonwealth. Three others, however, have survived those unsettled times. Lysons remarks:

> "In the east window of the south aisle are the royal arms, the arms and quarterings of Cecil and those of Sir Wm. Billesby, Knt. It is probable that he and the Earl of Exeter, who married Sir Thomas Smith's widow, contributed toward the repairs of that aisle, which seems to have been considerably raised with brick about the beginning of the last century."

Subsequently these shields were transferred to the window of the Vestry of the old Church, where they remained down to the demolition of 1880-81, when they were inserted in their present position in the window of the north porch of the new Church. Lysons' identification is not entirely accurate. They are as follows:

> No. 1. - Quarterly, France-Modern and England, over all, on a cross of St. George, arg. a saltier sable.

These arms, which have never before been identified, are those of the Carthusian Priory of Jesus of Bethlehem beside Sheen. As a probably unique representation of the arms of this ancient priory, the coat is of surpassing interest and value, whether considered from a heraldic or an ecclesiological point of view. The only seal of this community, now known to be extant, is in the British Museum and is so very indistinct that it is quite impossible to say in what manner the arms of the Royal Founder were differenced. Fortunately, however, this old piece of glass at Fulham settles the question, as it is in a state of perfect preservation. The only point of doubt is whether what we have above described as a saltier should not, in reality, be the Greek letter *Chi* [χ].

A slight undulation in Richmond Park is all that remains to mark the site of what is said to have been the resting place of James IV's body after the battle of Flodden, while the seal at Bloomsbury and the pane of glass at Fulham Church are the sole surviving examples of the arms of these Carthusian Priors. The presence of this coat in Fulham Church is easily accounted for. As we shall see when we come to speak of the ancient Rectory House at Parson's Green, Bishop Clifford, in 1420, licensed the priors of the House of Jesus of Bethlehem to appropriate Fulham Church to their priory. As the priors farmed the rectory only for about two years, it is clear that this interesting coat must be not far short of 500 years old.

> No. 2. - Quarterly, I. and IV. Barry of ten arg. and az. over all 6 escutcheons three, two, one, sa., each charged with a lion ramp. of the first (Cecil). II. Sa., a plate between three towers triple turreted with portes desplayed arg. (Caerleon). III. Arg. three fleurs-de-lis or (Williams?).

These are, as Lysons observes, the arms of a member of the

Cecil family, in all probability those of Thomas, 1st Earl of Exeter, who, on his own marriage with Lady Smith, came to reside at Parson's Green.

> No. 3. - Quarterly, I. Arg., a chevron between the sinister halves of three Lozenges [*i.e.* bill-heads] sa. (Billesbie of Billesbie, co. Lincoln.) II. Broken or obliterated at the date of Lysons' visit, but since wrongfully filled up with the quarter next following. III. Arg., 2 bars engrailed sa. and in chief a file of three of the last (perhaps intended for Steynes). IV. Gu., an eagle desplayed or (for Kevremond alias Kermermond or else Goddard). *Crest*: On a wreath of the colours a panther's head erased at the neck affrontèe arg. An esquire's helmet mantled gules doubled or.

The mantle and surrounding diaper work have been somewhat damaged either by time or restoration. This shield evidently represents the achievement of Sir William Billesbie, but, judging from the form of the helmet, is probably anterior to 14 Mar. 1603-04, when he received the honour of knighthood.

Cole states in his manuscript, 1758:

> "In the east window of the chancel are the arms of Bishop Compton impaled with the see of London, supported by two angels, and ensigned with a mitre in beautiful painted glass, and underneath this motto: *Nisi Dominus*."

These arms probably disappeared in the restorations of 1840-41.

In olden times the services of the glazier were in such constant request that the accounts of the Churchwardens are seldom without an item for window mending. For instance, in 1637, the Churchwardens

> "Pd. for mending . . . the glass windowes at severall times £1. 0s. 4d."

In 1639

> "Pd. the glasier for a yeare for ye church windowes £1. 0s. 0d."

In 1642 the Churchwardens paid

"Richard Kirbey glasier for halfe a yeare 10s. 0d."

A note appended to the above entry runs:

"The glasier not to be paid vntill the windows be mended."

In 1646 the Churchwardens,

"pd. the Carpenter for makeing newe puese and boarding the South windowe £1. 11s. 0d."

In 1649, when the Church was robbed, one of the windows was "broken downe," doubtless for the purpose of effecting an entry. The glazier's bill for mending this "and other windowes of ye Church at severall tymes," amounted to £1. 1s. 0d. In 1650 the glazier was paid

"for mending the West window and Vestry window p. bill 16s. 0d."

In 1658 the "glasse windows" were again reported to be "much broken." In 1750 a Committee, which was appointed to consider what repairs to the Church were needful, recommended, in respect to the windows, that

"The ironwork of the great window over the belfry door being all decayed be taken down, and instead thereof a new oak frame to be made, to fit the present opening, but the inside stone jaumbs and arch, being good, to remain.
The 2 east windows of the north aisle being crippled to be reduced to one window about 8 feet wide with an oak frame, a space to be added with solid brick work at the body of the church to strengthen that part. The W. window of the great Vestry to be taken down."

Faulkner, writing of the repairs effected in the Church in 1770, remarks:

"The curious Gothic windows of the south ile were destroyed in the great repair of this church, *anno* 1770. Those ignorant contractors chose rather to put in new wooden frames than to endeavour to restore the antique stonework which might, however, have been easily effected. Only one window has escaped the hands of the barbarians. This is in the north-east end of the nave and is a very fine specimen of Gothic and well worthy of the notice of the antiquary."

In 1840 Bishop Blomfield presented to the Church the fine East window over the communion table. It now lights the south transept. In 1855 the Daniel family erected a memorial window in the Church. It was placed in the north window of the east end extension of 1840. It now lights the north transept.

The Blomfield and Daniel windows will be found described in our account of the new Church.

Church Plate, Ornaments, Vestments, Etc.

The first account we possess of the Church plate, ornaments, vestments, etc., is contained in the Inventory taken by the Royal Commissioners in 1549.

We may perhaps add a few words in explanation of the circumstances under which this return was made. From the commencement of the reign of Edward VI, the government lost no time in pushing forward the reformation of the Church. Cranmer, to use the words of Bishop Burnet, "being now delivered from that too awful subjection that he had been held under by King Henry, resolved to go on more vigorously in purging out abuses." In this course the Archbishop had the support, not only of the youthful King, but also of the Protector Somerset and of most of the members of the Council. The frequent robbery, too, of churches, was another matter which demanded and received attention. Fuller tells us that private men's halls were hung with altar cloths, their tables and beds covered with copes, while chalices were used as drinking cups at meals. Perry, in his "Church History," referring to this desecration of the churches, observes (p. 216, s. 24):

> "So scandalous did this become that a commission was issued (10 June 1552) to enquire after all the valuables that had been embezzled from monasteries, chantries, and colleges, and to take possession of them for the use of the Crown. The Commissioners were to leave in every church one, two or more chalices and cups and such other ornaments as by discretion should seem requisite for divine service. A very large

amount of valuables was recovered by this agency, the sale of which produced much money for the exchequer."

Fulham Church, east end, 1836.
From a water-colour drawing preserved in the Vestry

The Inventory relating to Fulham Church is entered in "Miscellaneous Book," vol. 498, pp. 8-10, in the Public Record Office.

The document, which we append, *in extenso*, contains (1) the presentment of the jury, (2) a complete inventory of the goods existing in the Church at the time of the visit of the Commissioners (1549), (3) a list of certain goods which, savouring of the old régime, the parishioners were induced to sell, (4) a list of certain goods stolen from the Church subsequent to the preparation of the inventory, (5) a list of the goods which remained after the sale and the theft (1552), and (6) a valuation of the Church Acres. Finally, a note is appended respecting a brotherhood which had existed in the reign of Henry VIII.

Certificate of Church Goods, Middlesex. *tempo* Edward VI.
ffulham.

We the Jury Doo present and sertyfy the goodes plate Ornamentes Jewelles And belles belongynge and apertenynge to the Churche of ffulham in the Countie of Midd as Well wtin the Inventory takyn by the kynges maiestes Comissioners as also other goodes belongynge to the same churche not beynge in the kynges Inventory wt Rerages and other Deptes belongynge to the same Churche as aperythe hereafter more playnly sertyfyed by us the same jury the fyft Daye of Awgoost in the yere of owr Lorde god a thowsande fyve houndryth fifty and two And in the Sexte yeare of the Reigne of owr sovereigne Lorde Edwarde the Sext by the grace of god of Ingland ffraunce and Ierlande kynge Defendor of the faithe and of the Churche of Inglande and Ierland the suprem hede Emedyatly under god.

This Inventory made the tenth Daye of Marche in the thurde yere of the Reigne of owr Dread sovereigne Lorde Kynge Edwarde the Syxt of all suche goodes as Remaynyth in the church of ffulham in the countie of Midd sertyfyed then unto the Commessioners by Nycholas Smythe curate there John Nycholes and John Kyppyng churche wardens John burtton and Willim Holden consentynge to the same.

(1) **Imp'm's** three Challices of sylver wt pattentes whereof to of them parsell gylte and a lyttell pyxe of sylver psell gylte

(2) **It'm** one Crosse of copper and gylte And two owlde Crosses of Latten two payre of sensors of latten and a shype and a spone of latten

(3) **It'm** two lyttell basons of pewter and vj lyttell candellstyckes of Brase

(4) **It'm** iiij greate Candelstyckes of of [sic] latten and two basons of latten and a Ewer of latten and a holly watter Stocke of latten

(5) **It'm** fyve Coopes one of Crymessen vellett one of whytt satten one of blacke Chamblett one of grene sarsnet and one of whytt fustyan

(6) **It'm** a vestment of grene vellett (wt) a Deakon and subdekon of grene Damask

(7) **It'm** a vestment of whytt satten wt a Deakon and subdekon of the same

(8) **It'm** a vestment of blacke Chamblett wt a Deakon and a subdekon of ye same

(9) **It'm** a vestment of blacke Damaske and one vestment of Dyu'es colered sylkes

(10) **It'm** one vestment of Russett satten of brydges and one vestment of Redd satten of brydges and a vestment of grene sarsnet And one vestment of whytt bustyan and one vestment of Redd vellett

(11) **It'm** one frount for an aultor of vellett yellow and Redd And two frountes of tawny satten of brydgges And two trountes of whytt satten of brydgges And three owlde frountes of taw'ey sylke of Dyvers collers

(12) **It'm** one Hearse Clothe of blacke vellett

(13) **It'm** a vestment of bustyon wtowt amas or albe and a vestment of

sanguyne satten of brydgges wtowt albe or amas

(14) **It'm** a vestment of taw'ey Chamblett wtowt albe or amas And a vestment of Dornex wtowt albe or amas

(15) **It'm** vj Aultor clothes of lenen clothe And one owld vestment of blacke saye wtowt albe or amas

(16) **It'm** xxti pecyes of owld paynted clothes that Dyd kever the Images in ye church

(17) **It'm** a clothe cawlled a Cannapy clothe of Redd and grene satten of brydgges And tenn owlde banner Clothes some of them of sylke and the Reast of Lynen clothe And two Crosse clothes of sylke And fyve banner poles iij cruyttes of pewter and v Dyeper towelles

(18) **It'm** xiij Candelstyck bosses of latten And one old Candelstycke And a bason to holde the pascall And a bason for a lampe

(19) **It'm** xij greate bowkes sum of paper and other some of parchment

(20) **It'm** iiij sorpleses and two Rotchettes And two Cortens of sylke to hange at the aultors eandes

(21) **It'm** v greate belles and a lyttell bell in the steple and iij hande belles And a vayle of whytt and Blewe lynen clothe

(22) **It'm** two clothes that hangeth over the sakaramente one of Changable sylke and one of lynen clothe

(23) **It'm** a payre of Orgayns that lyeth all to broken And a qwesshyon of Redd and grene sylke

(24) **It'm** a Hangynge for an Aultor of whytt sylke & a nother of Dornex.

I I Serten goodes sowde by thomas wilkockes and george Burtton Churche Wardens aforesayd wt the consent of the hole parrysshoners the parselles as aperythe hereafter.

Sowlde. Imp'm's sowlde to thomas Read Dwellynge in the pryssh of saynte Mychaelles in wood streat gerdelar two owlde Crosses of latten two payre of sensors of latten a Shype and a Spoune of latten vj littell Candellstyckes of bras and iiij greate Candellstyckes of latten & two basons & a ewer of latten And a holly watter stocke of latten xiij bosse candelstyckes for the Roode lyght and one owlde hollow candelstyck and a Bason to holde the paskall and a bason for a lampe of latten And three hande Belles sowlde for — j˘s

It'm sowlde to Robertt Madder marchaunt taylor Dwellynge in saynte Mychaelles parryssh in wood streat the pselles as followeth :

It'm a Coope of crymessyn vellett and one of blacke chamblett And one of grene sarsnett

It'm a vestment of grene vellett w^t a Deakon and a subdekon of grene Damaske And a vestment of Blacke Chamblett w^t a Deakon and a subdekon And a vestment of Blacke Damaske and a vestment of Dyvers colored sylkes

It'm a vestment of Russet satten of Brydgges And a vestment of grene sarsnett And a vestment of Redd vellett

It'm two frountes of tawney satten of brydgges and iij olde frountes of tawne sylke w^t Dyvers other colors a vestment of bustyan [sic] And a vestment of sangwyn satten of brydgges w^towt albe or amas a vestment of tawny Chamblett w^tout albe or amas And a vestment of black saye w^tout albe or amas — xi^li

It'm tenn owlde banner clothes sum of sylke and sume of lynen clothe And two cross clothes of sylke sowlde to one Robertt Maddar marchaunt tayllar Dwellynge in saynt mychaelles parryssh in woodstreat and all the olde parchement bowkes in the Churche

Some totalle — xiij^li x^s

Stolen. Serten goodes stowln and the churche brokyn the parselles as followeth hereafter A challys wt a pattent parsell gylte And a herse clothe of black vellett two sorplesses a carpett and a commyon table clothe And a clothe a boute the founte wt other suche lyke payntyd clothes

These Be parselles of the goodes plate Ornamentes and Jewelles Remanynge in the Churche beynge parselles of the Inventory taken by the kinges Highnes Commessioners in the thurd yere of his moost Gracyous Reigne unsowlde

Imp'm's two Challices of Sylver w^t pattentes parsell gylte

It'm a lyttell pyxe of sylver parsell gylte

It'm a Coope of whytt satten And a Coope of whytt fustyan

It'm a vestment of whytt satten w^t a Deakon and subdekon to the same

It'm a vestment of Redd satten of brydgges

It'm a vestment of grene sarsnett

It'm a vestment of Dornex

It'm a fronnte for an aulter of vellett Redd & yellow

It'm two fronntes of whytt satten of brygges

It'm a Cannapy clothe of Redd and grene satten of brydgges

It'm a Hangynge for an Aultor of whytt sylke

It'm two clothes that hangythe over the Sakaramentt one of Changable sylke thother of lynen clothe

It'm two Corteyns of sylke to hange at the Aultors endes

It'm iiij Aultor clothes of lynen clothe

It'm fyve towelles of Dyeper And two Sorplesses

It'm two Rotchettes And a Qwesshion of Redd & grene sylke

It'm iij Cruyttes of pewter And a Bason of pewter

It'm a payre of Orgayns that lyethe all to brokyn

It'm in the steple v greate Belles and a saunce Bell

Londe. Alsoo we Doo present and sertyfy that ther Doithe belonge and apertayn to the Churche of ffulham two Akars of medow grownde to the yearly vallew — xiij^s iiij^d

a Brothered. Also ther hathe byne a Brotherd Cawled Saynt peters brothered at the Dyssolucyon of the whiche brothered wasse wardens Edward Lathar and other three men of the same parryssh hauying the goodes and stocke in ther handes the c'teyne some the whiche we cannott knowe Ther wass bothe money and kyne.

An analysis of the foregoing return yields the following results (following pages):

Item.	Articles.	Sold by Church-wardens.	Stolen from Church.	Unaccounted for.	Remaining in Church.
1.	3 Chalices of silver (two silver gilt)[1].		1		2
	1 Pyx, silver gilt[2]				1
2.	1 Cross of copper and gilt.			1	
	2 Old Crosses of latten	2			
	2 Pairs of Censers of latten	2			
	1 Ship[3]	1			
	1 Spoon of latten	1			
3.	2 Little Basins of pewter.			1	1
	6 Little Candlesticks of brass	6			
4.	4 Great Candlesticks of latten.	4			
	2 Basins of latten	2			
	1 Ewer of latten	1			
	1 Holy Water Stock[4] of latten.	1			
5.	5 Copes,[5] vizt:				
	1 crimson velvet	1			
	1 white satin				1
	1 black camlet[6]	1			
	1 green sarsnet.	1			
	1 white fustian[7]				1
6.	1 Vestment of green velvet with a deacon and a sub-deacon of green damask.	1			
7.	1 Vestment of white satin with a deacon and a sub-deacon of the same				1
8.	1 Vestment of black camlet with a deacon and a sub-deacon of the same	1			
9.	1 Vestment of black damask	1			
	1 Vestment of divers coloured silks.	1			
10.	1 Vestment of russet satin of Bruges[8].	1			
	1 Vestment of red satin of Bruges				1
	1 Vestment of green sarsnet	1			
	1 Vestment of white fustian			1	
	1 Vestment of red velvet.	1			
	[We are told (a) that the vestment of green sarsnet was sold and (b) that it remained in the Church. In one of these instances the vestment of white fustian was doubtless intended.]				
11.	1 Front for altar of velvet of yellow and red				1
	2 Fronts of tawny[9] satin of Bruges.	2			
	2 Fronts of white satin of Bruges.				2
	3 Old Fronts of tawny silk of divers colours	3			

Notes to Table:

1. Chalice, Lat. calix, Fr. *calice*, a cup. The cup used to administer the wine in the celebration of the Holy Eucharist. Chalices are usually of silver, but sometimes of gold or gilt.

2. Pyx, Gr. *puxis*, a box, from puxos, a box tree. In the Roman Catholic Church it denotes the covered vessel used for holding the sacred host.

3. Ship, a dish or utensil, formed like the hull of a ship, for holding incense.

4. Holy Water Stock, perhaps another form of stoup, a vessel.

5. Cope, a modification of cape, a vestment resembling a cloak, worn in processions and other sacred functions.

6. Camlet or chamlet, a stuff originally made of camels' hair; now generally

a mixture of goats' hair and wool or silk.
7. Fustian, Old Fr. *fustiane*, from Fostat, a suburb of Cairo, where this material was first made.
8. Bruges, or Bridges, called after Bruges in Belgium.
9. Tawny, Old French, tané, tanned, of a yellowish dark colour resembling goods tanned.

Item.	Articles.	Sold by Church-wardens.	Stolen from Church.	Unaccounted for.	Remaining in Church.
12.	1 Hearse Cloth[1] of black velvet.		1		
13.	1 Vestment of fustian without alb[2] or amas[3].	1			
	1 Vestment of sanguine satin of Bruges without alb or amas.	1			
14.	1 Vestment of tawny camlet without alb or amas.	1			
	1 Vestment of Dornex[4] without alb or amas				1
15.	6 Altar cloths of linen.			2	4
	[The two cloths unaccounted for were perhaps among the painted cloths stolen.]				
	1 Old Vestment of black saye[5] without alb or amas	1			
16.	20 pieces of old painted covering cloths for images[6].		20		
17.	1 Canopy Cloth[7] of red and green satin of Bruges.				1
	10 Old Banner Cloths[8] of silk and linen	10			
	2 Cross Cloths[9] of silk	2			
	5 Banner Poles[10].			5	
	3 Cruets[11] of pewter.				3
	5 Diaper Towels[12].				5
18.	13 Candlestick bosses[13] of latten for rood light.	13			
	1 Old Candlestick	1			
	1 Basin to hold the paschal[14]	1			
	1 Basin for a lamp	1			
19.	12 Great books of paper and parchment[15].	12			
20.	4 Surplices.		2		2
	2 Rotchetts[16]				2
	2 Curtains of silk to hang at the ends of the altar.				2

Notes to Table:
1. Hearse Cloth, already explained.
2. Alb, Latin *albus*, white. A long linen robe hanging down to the feet worn by the officiating minister, etc.
3. Amas or Amice, a white veil or oblong piece of fine linen, with strings, worn over the shoulders like a collar and tied in front, a Eucharistic vestment like the alb.
4. Dornex, Dornick, Dornic, etc., the Flemish name for Tournay in Flanders where the stuff so-called was first made for table cloths.
5. Saye or Say. From French *saye*, Lat. saga=sagum, a coarse woollen mantle or blanket. Halliwell describes it as a "delicate kind of serge or woollen cloth."

6. Painted Cloths. Perhaps included with the painted cloths stolen.
7. Canopy Cloth, probably a cloth placed over the chalice.
8. Banner Cloths, probably banners.
9. Cross Cloths, coverings when not in use.
10. Banner poles. Most likely sold with the Banner Cloths.
11. Cruets are the two vessels used for the wine and water for supplying the chalice.
12. Diaper. From French *diapre*, pp. of *diaprer*, to variegate. It is a fabric composed of linen and cotton, upon the surface of which a figured pattern is produced by a peculiar mode of twilling.
13. Candlestick bosses, candlestick stands. They were usually of iron or latten. They stood out from the rood.
14. Paschal, Heb. *pascha*, a passage, from *pasach*, to pass over. Pertaining to the Passover.
15. Great Books, probably ancient mass books, missals, etc.
16. Rotchetts, or rochets, short frocks like a narrow surplice, made of lawn, with light sleeves.

Item.	Articles.	Sold by Church-wardens.	Stolen from Church.	Unaccounted for.	Remaining in Church.
21.	5 Great Bells and a little (or saints') bell[1] 3 Handbells 1 Veil of white and blue linen cloth[2]	3		1	6
22.	2 Cloths over Sacrament, one of silk and one of linen.				2
23.	1 Pair of Organs[3] 1 Cushion of red and green silk.				1 1
24.	1 Hanging for altar of white silk. 1 Hanging of Dornex.			1	1

Notes to Table
1. Bells, already dealt with.
2. Veil of white and blue linen cloth. Perhaps this was identical with the "cloth about the font" which was stolen.
3. Organs, elsewhere dealt with.

The Inventory of the Commissioners affords us a very fair idea of the character of the furniture of the old Church in the reign of Henry VIII. The articles which were of an obsolete description or were too old to be of further use, were, we see, sold with the consent of the parishioners in two lots, one being bought by Thomas Read, a Wood Street girdler, for £2. 10s., and the other by Robert Madder, also of Wood Street, a merchant tailor, for £11. The purged Church appears to have been left with very little plate.

Of the Church Acres we shall speak in our account of the

Town Meadows. About the St. Peter's Brotherhood nothing is known. It was probably abolished at the dissolution of the monasteries and chantries by Henry VIII. Possibly the St. Peter's Brotherhood owed its origin to the Abbots of Westminster whose church was dedicated to St. Peter. The Abbots, as elsewhere stated, once owned Sandford Manor at Sands End.

From the old "Register Book" we gather that Dr. Edwardes, who died circa 1618-19, gave, in his "life tyme," the following:

> 1. Item. The said Dr. Edwardes did bestowe a fayre gilden bowle covered with a case for the Communion Table.
> 2. Item, a fayre embroydered Pulpit Cloth, with two embroydercd Quissians for the preacher.

From the same record we learn that

> "Mrs Joane Hill wife of Mr Thomas Hill of Fulham in her lifetime gave unto the Church of ffulham one silver plate for the minister to carry the Bread about in at the Communions and after her death Mr Thomas Hyll her husband gave another of the same fashion and equall weight the two weighinge twelve ounces fower penny wt Anno Domi. 1632: and these to remaine to the Church for ever."

In 1641 the Churchwardens

> "pd. for two fflagons for ye commn 16s. 8d."

In 1643 Mrs. Elizabeth Manwaring or Mannuring, gave:

> "one table cloath of Damaske, for the Communion table: against Christmas in the same yeare of our Lord god 1643."

In 1649 the retiring Warden, Mr. William Raylton, delivered to his successor:

> "One bond dated 20 October 1646 from Willm Hare and Thomas Ball in fifty pounds to discharge the Parish of the Issue of the said Thomas Ball."

> "One bond dated 27 October 1647 in twenty pounds from Ferdinando Smart, James Taylor and John Best, to saue the Parish harmles

concerning the education of William Goodwin the son of Thomas Goodwin deceased."

"One bond dated 3 November 1647 in twenty pounds from Willm Preist, John Shercroft, Thomas Harding and Thomas Holdernes for discharging the Parish of the childe that Martha Clarke goeth withall."

"Parcells in the lower vestry now delivered vp by the said Willm Raylton:
One great Bible; A pulpit Cloth of velvet; Two velvet Cushions; One Cup of Silver and guilt, with a Couer; One Silver bowle; Two Silver plates wth feete; Six Pewter Flaggons; Two Pewter Dishes or Basins for Collections; A Church cloth; A Deale Chest with lock and key to it; a Table; a Green cloth-carpet; An Elme Chest with three Locks and Keys to it."

"Parcells in the Vestry Chamber."

"A drawing Table; Nine red Leather Chaires; One wainscot Chaire; Six green Cloth Cushions; One stript Stuff Carpet; A paire of Fire Irons; Tongs and Fire Shouell; A paire of Bellowes."

In 1649 thieves broke into Fulham Church and carried off sundry valuables. In May of that year an assessment was levied on the parish to raise £20 for certain work to the Church, etc., including

"Mending the Stone worke, Iron barrs and Glasse of one of the windowes which was broken by Theeves."

Among the disbursements of the Churchwardens this year there was paid

"To a free mason for stone and workmanship to mend one of ye church windowes wch was broken downe when the Vestry was robbed £1. 5s. 6d."

"For eight pounds of lead to fasten the Iron Barrs 1s."

"To the Glasier for worke done about that and other windowes of ye Church at severall tymes £1. 1s."

"To judere the Smyth for mending the Barrs and for other work about the Church 10s. 4d."

"For printing sevrall bills to have found out the Basins wch were stollen 1s."

"To a Bedell for dispersing them to severall shops in London 1s."

"For two new pewter dishes to be vsed for collections instead of the Basins wch were stollen 5s."

"For grauing on them an Inscription for Fulham Church 2d."

In 1663 Mrs. Katharine Hues gave the Church two silver flagons, which form the oldest (dated) portion of the plate still in use. The vessels are inscribed:

"The gift of Katharine Hues Gentlewoman and made in the Year 1663, Henry Marsh being Churchwarden."

These are most probably Nuremberg drinking vessels brought over by churchmen returning to England after the Restoration. Enclosed in a heart shaped shield is the maker's mark G.D. with a cinquefoil beneath.

In the Parish Books is the following further inventory of Church plate and furniture, circa 1670:

"Bonds and Plate and goods belonginge to the Church and pish delivd to me _____ succeeding churchwarden.
Mr. Willimotts 2 bonds att interest.
Mr. Yardlies bonde, money lent gratis.
Plate namely:
    Two silver flaggons weighing 200 ounces beinge the gift of Mrs. Catherine Howse deceased.
    One challice Bowle gilt;
    One bowle and couer gilt.
    Two silver Salvers for bread att the Communions.
    One dammaske Table Cloth. One holland surplice.
    One greene Table Cloth, carpitt for the Communion table.
    One large folio Bible, Two common prayer books in Fol.
    One booke of Homilies.
    One booke of Cannons.
    A table of Degrees of marriages.

A pulpitt cloth and cushion of violett coullered velvett.
Another new pulpitt Cushion given by Mr. Hickes.
One old cushion of tissue worke.
One table in the Vestry below.
One deale chest.
7 Bundles of Matts.
A hearse cloth given by Nath. Dauncer.
One Elmne Chest wth 3 lockes and keyes to keepe the pish writinges in.
3 keyes to the poores box.
A Church Bier.
9 Bucketts.
One long lather (i.e. ladder).
One spade.
One bushell.
One half bushell.
One shovell (these last menconed are in the Colehouse). In the roome on the church porch:
One drawinge table, one old stript stuff carpett (not fitt to lay vpon the table 7 yeares since).
One wainscott chaire.
9 leather (chairs) broken and whole.
Six very old cushions of greene baze not fitt to vse.
One paire of old fire irons and one paire of tonges of the largest size."

In 1676 Mr. Peter Nourse, brewer, gave a new altar piece ornamented with the figures of Moses and Aaron and the Ten Commandments, surmounted with carving. This piece of work cost £60.

In 1684 Mrs. Anne Winter presented to the Church a large silver paten which is still among the Church plate. This is inscribed on the edge

"The guifte of Mistresse Anne Winter to ye Church of Fulham."

In the centre is the date "24 June 1684." In the old "Register Book" is the following entry regarding it. It will be observed that there is a discrepancy in date:

"Edward Chubb, Church Warden. A peece of plate given by Mrs Ann Wynter to the Parish Church of Fulham for the Collecting of Mony at the Saccrament the 24th day of June in the year of our Lord 1685: as is exprest upon the peece of plate. Edward Chubb, Church Warden, 1685."

It is a common silver plate with a piece in the centre beaten out and engraved.

In 1684 two smaller patens were also presented to the Church. The more interesting one was the gift of Bishop Compton. The "Register Book" records,

"The Rt Honble Rt Revd Father in God, Henry, Lord Bisp of London did give to the Parish Church of Fulham A peece of plate for the Administring or searveing the Bread at the Saccrament in the yeare of our Lord God, 1684, as is exprest upon the peece of plate."

This paten is inscribed:

"The guift of Henry Lord Bishopp of London to the Parish Church of Fulham 1684."

The second small paten is inscribed:

"Belonging too the Parish Church of ffulham 1684."

These patens took the place of the one given by Mrs. Joan Hill, which was probably stolen in the robbery of 1649. Both the patens bear the date mark for 1683. The maker's marks are not distinguishable.

In 1689 Mr. Benjamin Allben presented a silver gilt harrop which still exists. It is inscribed

"The guift of Benjamin Allben, Esqre, to the Parish Church of Fulham. John Webb Churchwarden 1689."

It bears the Nuremberg mark N in a circular stamp and the maker's mark TW (Tobias Wolff) in monogram in an oval stamp.

The Church plate now consists of the following:

1 Silver gilt Harrop, the gift of Mr. Benjamin Allben [already described].

2 Chalices with lids. One of these has the date mark for 1615, and a maker's mark A B in linked letters in a shaped shield: the other has no marks. There is no record as to date of gift.

2 Silver flagons, the gift of Mrs. Katharine Hues [already described].

1 Large Paten, the gift of Mrs. Anne Winter [already described].

2 Small Patens, one the gift of Bishop Compton [already described].

2 Alms dishes. One of these is a silver dish with the letters I H S inscribed in the centre. It bears the date mark for 1770, and the maker's mark S C over I C (Septimus and James Creswell) with a mullet between the letters, in a square stamp. There is no record as to when it was given to the Church. The other dish is of brass and is inscribed, "All Saints Church, 1878, J. S. Hodgkins, W. H. Weaver, churchwardens."

1 Staff. This is a beadle's staff with an ornamental silver top surmounted by the figure of a man holding a stick. It is inscribed, "The gift of Mr. Barry Picker, Mr. Thomas and Mr. Limpany for a beadles staf on Fulham side for ever." There is no record as to when this silver top was given to the Church.

1 Silver figure of "Faith" to match the Beadle's Staff.

1 Chalice, silver gilt, jewelled with garnets, presented by the Rev. W. C. Muriel, M.A., to whom it was given by Mr. W. F. Wolley.

1 Paten, silver gilt, the gift of the Rev. W. C. Muriel, M.A.

1 Wine Strainer, inscribed "All Saints Church, Fulham, Easter, 1861, from R. G. Baker."

1 Spoon. This is a silver Apostle's spoon inscribed at the bottom "By thy Cross and Passion, Good Lord, deliver me. In Memoriam H.M.B." It has two marks (1) two hatchets or flags in saltier under S and over the figure 13, in a quartrefoil stamp, the 17th century mark of Schemnitz in Hungary, and (2) the capital letter D. This was a private gift in 1879.

1 Wine Decanter Glass or Wine Cruet in mounted silver.

1 Processional Cross, presented by the Rev. W. C. Muriel, M.A., 1891.

1 Mace presented by Mr. B. T. Wright in 1898.

1 Pair of Brass Altar Candlesticks (date about 1600), presented by the Rev. W. C. Muriel, M.A.

Mr. E. H. Freshfield, to whom we are indebted for some of the foregoing details, observes of the All Saints plate, in "The Communion Plate of the Churches in the County of London":

> "This is an extremely fine and very interesting collection of church plate. The flagons are tankards of the usual type. The large cup [is] a magnificent piece of plate . . . The two smaller cups are magnified editions of the pretty 'grace' cups, of which there is but a single specimen in the City Churches, at St. Giles', Cripplegate."

In 1899 a handsome pair of wrought iron side screens to chancel was presented by the Rev. W. C. Muriel, M.A., in memory of the late Mrs. Muriel.

Despite the numerous robberies which occurred at the old Church, the parish officers appear to have taken very inadequate precautions to ensure the safety of the valuable plate, etc., of which they were the custodians. In the inventory of 1649 the only receptacles for the plate were, as we have seen, a deal chest with lock and key and an elm chest with triple locks and keys. The latter appears to have been used for keeping the parish treasure generally, including the "poor's stock." At a Vestry, held 4 Sept. [1656?], we find

> "It is . . . ordered that Mr. Viccars be desired to suffer the Chest belonging to the pish for the keeping of the Treasure of the sd. pish to be and remaine in his howse and that the three keyes belonging thervnto doe remaine in the Custodie of these psons following, vizt. one of them wth the minister of the pish for the time being, one other wth the Churchwarden for the time being and one other key wth Mr. Viccars; and that also such sunnnes of money as are now in stocke be forthwth put into the said Chest and that noe pte thereof or of any summe of money that shall at anie time thereafter be put into the same shalbe taken forth or disposed of wthout a consent had and agreed vpon in the Vestrian."

It was not till 1736 that an iron safe was thought of. On 13 June of that year the Vestry

> "Ordered that an Iron Chest be forthwith provided at the charge of the parish in order to deposite the Church plate by Mr. Wm. Gray the present Churchwarden and that the same be fixt down to the floor of the little Vestry."

In the days of the Rev. R. G. Baker it had disappeared, for the Church plate was then kept in an old oak chest, lined with baize, with no divisions to protect the contents. The Rev. F. H. Fisher had the plate transferred to a strong oak box, and, for greater safety, removed to the Vicarage, where it is still kept.

Church Plate. From a photograph by the London Stereoscopic Co., Ld., reproduced by permission of E. H. Freshfield, Esq.

Extracts from Parish Books

In the Parish Books are numerous entries relating to the purchase and sale of sundry books for the Church. From the Inventory of the Commissioners of 1549, we learn that there were then in Fulham Church

"xij greate bowkes sum of paper and other some of parchment."

These, as we have seen, the Churchwardens disposed of. In the Churchwardens' Accounts for 1637 are the following entries:

Rec. for the old Bible and two seruice bookes £1. 2s. 0d.
Pd. for this new booke for accounts 3s. 6d.
Pd. for bookes for the church as bible and service books the sume of £3. 7s. 8d.

In 1695 Mr. Robert Limpany presented the Church with three volumes of Foxe's "Book of Martyrs." Faulkner, in a manuscript note in his "History" added about 1840, remarks, "Two of these books still remain but in the last stage of decay." One of these volumes, some twenty years later, was at the School House, having been given to Mr. J. Hutchins, who was then Master, by the Rev. R. G. Baker. Dr. Jewell's "Apology for the Church of England," given to the Church by the Rev. Richard Stevenson (1666-91), was in existence in Faulkner's time. These books were kept in a niche beneath the monument to the memory of "Baby Limpany" at the west end of the north aisle.

The Churchwardens' Accounts for 1733 record:

"Pd. Mr. Chubb for putting clasps, screws and chains to eleven prayer books in ye Gallery £1. 7s. 6d."

This is the only allusion, in the Parish records, to chained books. In 1738 there was:

"Pd. for advertizing the Common Prayer Books that were stoln from the Church 2s. 6d."

The Churchwardens' Accounts for 1805 record:

"Pd. Mr Rivington for a Church Bible as per Bill £5 10s. 0d."
"Pd. Mr Thomas for hand bills etc. as per bill when the old Bible was stolen £1 0s. 0d."

Fulham Church, east end, circa 1850.
From a drawing by Miss Sulivan

And for 1813:

"Pd. Scratcherd and Co for books for the Faculty Pew £2 7 0"

A highly interesting volume preserved in the Church chest is entitled

"A Register Booke for the perpetuall remembrance of all those worthie benefactours, who ether whiles they lived or when they Deceased this world were beneficiall ether to the poore or for the repaire and adorning of the Church of Fulham."

The book appears to have been commenced in 1622, and to have been continued, with more or less care, down to 1785. Faulkner saw it in 1812. The book, after having been mislaid for many years, was, in 1877, found in a cupboard in the offices of Mr. Park Nelson, in Essex Street, Strand. Mr. Charles Griffin, his confidential clerk, who fortunately discovered the missing volume, at once communicated with the Rev. F. H. Fisher, the Vicar, who lost no time in reclaiming it. In 1879, Mr. Fisher published, with notes and additions, the entire work. The original book has parchment leaves. It has wood covers and is bound in calf. The boards are much worm-eaten. Its brass clasp is broken. Underneath, on its lower edge, is a portion of the fastening by which it was once chained to a shelf. The date of the disappearance of this book is unknown, except that it must have occurred between the years 1812 and 1834. Mr. W. Skirrow, who of course did not see it, remarks in his "Report on the Fulham Charities" (1867):

> "This Benefaction Book or some copy thereof or extracts therefrom must have been in the hands of Faulkner when he wrote, but no traces of such Book now exist and neither the present Vicar (Rev. R. G. Baker) inducted in 1834 nor any one else who attended the inquiry had ever seen it. Indeed, there is no evidence to show that the original book was ever consulted by the Commissioners for inquiring concerning charities or by a Parochial Committee appointed on 9 July 1835 by the Vestry of the Parish of Fulham to inquire into the charities of that parish and report thereon."

In the chests, in the Church and Vestry, are preserved the Registers of Baptisms, Marriages and Burials. These form an unbroken series from 1675 to the present time. The oldest volume (1675 to 1735) is on the *recto* inscribed

> "A Register Booke for the pish of ffulham of all Baptismes, Marriages and Burialls wch have beene since the xxvth of March 1675."

The corresponding *verso* contains a list of twenty-one marriages which were solemnized in Fulham Church between 26 April 1674 and 28 February 1674-75.

The front of the fly-leaf is scribbled over with the name "William Law," several times repeated, and the date "20 Feb, 1757." William Law, who died in 1778, was the parish clerk and sexton. It is a thick volume, bound in old calf, and measures 17½ inches by 11 inches. The Fulham entries extend half way through. At what is properly the end of the book, the Hammersmith Register begins, the first entries being for 1680, the two sections meeting in the middle, at the year 1735. A similar arrangement is adopted in those of the subsequent volumes containing Hammersmith entries.

Fulham Old and New

The second volume (1736-1754) is inscribed:

"Fulham Side in the County of Middlesex. Register Book of Burials and Baptisms Commences in the Year one Thousand seven Hundred and thirty six."

North East view of Fulham Church. After a pencil drawing, dated 22 Dec. 1837, in the Vicarage "Faulkner."

This book is smaller than the preceding. It was originally bound in calf, but nearly the whole of the leather is now worn away. The book has brass corners. The Clasps are broken off. The Marriages for this period are also included.

The third volume (1755-1789) is inscribed:

"The Register for Baptisms and Burials for the Parish of Fulham on Fulham side in the County of Middx. for 1755. Henry Holland Churchwarden."

In 1754 a separate Register for Marriages was commenced, only the Baptisms and Burials still being entered in the same book. It is inscribed:

"Fulham Register of Banns and Marriages. Mr Peter Reynold Churchwarden 1754."

On the fly-leaf is written

"A Register book for the registering of all banns and marriages published or solemnised in the parish church of Fulham in the county of Middlesex provided by the Ch'dns of the said parish, in pursuance of the statute of the twenty seventh year of His present Majesty King George the Second Intituled an *Act for the Better Preventing of Clandestine Marriages*, which act commenced from the twenty fifth day of March in the year of Our Lord one thousand seven hundred and fifty four. London Printed for and sold by J. Coles, Stationer, in Fleet Street. MDCCLIV."

Old Fulham Church, east end.
From a photograph by Messrs. W. Field & Co.

The 1790-1812 volume also includes both Baptisms and Burials. It is inscribed:

"A Register of Baptisms and Burials for the parish of Fulham on Fulham side in the County of Middlesex 1790. Wm. Griffiths Churchwarden."

From 1813 the Baptisms and Burials are entered in separate books. The following is a synopsis of the volumes:

The Baptisms, Marriages and Burials, on Fulham side.

BAPTISMS	MARRIAGES	BURIALS
1675 to 1735	1674 to 1735	1675 to 1735
1735 to 1754	1736 to 1754	1736 to 1754
1755 to 1789	1754 to 1768	1755 to 1789
1790 to 1812	1768 to 1785	1790 to 1812
1813 to 1828	1785 to 1803	1813 to 1829
1828 to 1843	1803 to 1812	1829 to 1844
1843 to 1880	1813 to 1822	1844 to 1863
1881 to —	1822 to 1831	1863 to —
	1831 to 1837	
	1837 to 1847	
	1847 to 1857	
	1857 to 1867	
	1867 to 1878	
	1878 to 1885	
	1886 to —	

The Baptisms, Marriages and Burials, on Hammersmith side.

BAPTISMS	MARRIAGES	BURIALS
1680 to 1735	1680 to 1735	1680 to 1735
1736 to 1755	1738 to 1754	1735 to 1755
1755 to 1789		
1790 to 1811		

The subsequent Registers for this parish are deposited at St. Paul's, Hammersmith, constituted a parish church by the Act separating Hammersmith from Fulham, 27 June 1834.

There is no doubt there was a Register of Baptisms, Marriages and Burials for Fulham earlier than the one which commences in 1675, but it has long since been lost.

The more ancient minute books of the Churchwardens and Overseers of Fulham have perished. Lysons, in his "Environs of London," written in 1796, quotes extracts from the Parish Books covering the years 1578 to 1623, none of which now exist. In Faulkner's time, the volumes for these years had already disappeared, for, in a manuscript note, inserted at page 139 of his own copy of his "History," he writes : "I cannot find any parish book of this date (i.e. 1578)." The whole of the existing parish records, including the accounts of the Churchwardens and Overseers, Vestry minutes, Poor Rate assessments, etc., are, with the exception of the volume of the Churchwardens' minutes for years 1721-39, now kept in the Muniment Room of the Fulham Town Hall, in the custody of the Vestry Clerk. The dates of the volumes are as follows:

1625 to 1648, 1649 to 1691, 1711 to 1739, 1739 to 1765, 1776 to 1798, 1798 to 1815, 1815 to 1836, 1836 to 1855, 1855 to 1865, 1865 to 1870.

The records subsequent to 1870, are, by order of the Vestry, in the custody of the Clerk to the Vestry.

The Churchwardens' minute book for the years 1721-39 is now at the Fulham Public Library, to which, in 1895, it was given by the Vicar, the Rev. W. C. Muriel. This valuable book was "lost" for upwards of 150 years. On 13 Sept. 1894, the Vicar received a letter from a gentleman stating that a relative of his wife, residing at Hounslow, had found among his books, the volume in question, and, thinking it would be of more interest to the Vicar than to any one else, had sent it for his acceptance. Thus it was that the book found its way back to Fulham.

It was long the custom to enter, in certain books kept in the Church Chest, details as to the number of the cattle which the copyholders were allowed to pasture on the Commonable Lands of the Manor. At a Court General, in 1648, it was ordered:

"No person whatsoeuer to put any cattle into any comon of this Mannor more then their accustomed stint and Nomber entered in the Church Books of ffulham on paine to forfeite to the Lord of this Mannor for eury offence the some of vjs viijd."

The Special Army Assessments were also entered in the Church Books. Thus:

"Att the Vestrie howse of fulham September 8th 1653:
It is ordered that the Churchwarden doe desire Mr. Eaursbie to deliver to the Churchwarden the coppies of all such assessmts as haue beene made for the Army by himselfe and the other assessers from the yeare

1648 to thend that the same may be entred into the Church Books according to a former order made touching the pish and Mr. ffrazer."

The earliest notice of a collection in the Church occurs in the receipts of the Churchwarden for 1626, vizt.:

"It. rec. by a Colection in the Church 12s. 0d."

Other early entries of the kind are:

1637. Rec. in the bason at Whitsontide commu: 7s. 4d.
1637. Rec. in the bason at three seurall commons £1. 16s. 3d.
1639. Recd in the bason at fower severall communions £1. 8s. 9d.

Money was often collected upon the authority of "briefs." These documents were letters patent, issued by the Court of Chancery, under the Privy Seal. When a town or village was visited by a calamitous fire, other places, under the authority of these briefs, were called upon to render pecuniary assistance. Occasionally they were issued in the interest of Protestants suffering persecution abroad. The following are a few typical examples from our old Parish Books:

"Collected in the parish of Fulham on Fulham side the 17th June 1655 for the relief of the Deare Brethren the Protestants of Lucern Angora and other places in the dominions of the Duke of Savoy being under persecution for the Gospell of Christ as followeth, etc."

In all, £104. 14s. 10d. was collected; not a bad sum for those days. Another entry reads:

"Collected in ffulham Parrish on ffulham side the sixth day of June 1658 By vs the Minister (Isaac Knight), Churchwarden and ouerseers of the poore in aid of the inhabitants of Endfield in consideration of their great loss and damage by fire the summe of 40s. 0¾d."

In 1658 the claims of the Polish sufferers were heard in Fulham, the collection on behalf of "the poore of Losna and other places in Poland" amounting to £33. 7s. 3d. From the Parish Books we learn that, for this collection,

"The Declaration of his Highness the Lord Protector 1658 was published according to Order ye 25 Aprill in ye yeare aforesaid in the Parish Church of ffulham for a collection for ye Persecuted Protestants in Polonia wch Collection was made accordingly ye second of May ffollowinge in ye Parrish of ffulham on ffulham side as ffolloweth," etc.

But, besides briefs directing collections in aid of persecuted Protestants and burnt-out townsfolk, the good folk of Fulham were sometimes asked for help to enable the inhabitants of other places to build their churches. For instance, in 1658, Fulham was called upon to assist a town so far away as Oswestry. In 1670 the Parish Books record

"Collected upon a Breife for the Redemption of Captives in Turkish Slavery By his Majesties speciall Command Together wth the Names of all such psons as Contributed their Charity for the vse aforesaid in the pish of Fulham on fulham side Anno dom. 1670."

Another minute reads:

"Collected upon a Breife relating to ye distressed condicon of the poor persecuted French Protestants," etc.

It bears no date, but it was during the vicariate of the Rev. Richard Stevenson (1666-91). In 1670 the Churchwarden notes among his disbursements,

"Paid Rich. Coles for carrying a returne to the high constable of wt monie was collected in Fulham Church for the Losse by fire in London 6d."

At the end of one of the Parish Books is preserved a list of all sums collected upon briefs for fires from 1690 to 1730 The following are a few examples:

1690. Colected upon A Brief for A great Losse by fier at St. Ives in the pish of Fulham one ffulham side the sum of one pound thirteene shillings and three pence on the 31 day of August and lying in the hands of Mr. Rich. ffullwood, Churchwarden.

1690. Another collection £1. 5. 7. raised for a fire at St. Georg southwark.

1690. Another coll: fire at St. Botolph in East Smithfield £1. 1. 7.
1690. Another coll: fire at Bishops Lavington in Wiltshire 14s. 4½d.
1690-91. Another coll: fire at Morpeth in Northumberland £1. 0. 1. (15 Mar.)

1691. Coll: fire Teingmouth and Shaldon £1. 2. 8.
1691-2. Coll: fire Northriding of our County of York 13s. 10d.
1691-2. Coll: fire Beult in County of Brecon £1. 4. 4.

Old Fulham Church, west end.
From a photograph by Messrs. W. Field & Co.

In 1718 there was

> "Collected upon His Majies Letter for the Propagation of the Gospel in foreign parts, on Fulham side of the parish, £19. 5. 4."

From very early times it was the custom to distribute the "sacrament money" to the poor in the Churchyard. At a meeting of the Vestry on 15 Feb. 1721-2,

> "It was ordered that the sacrament money shall not be distributed in the churchyard as formerly, that for the future all such money as shall be so collected shall be divided into 3 equall parts, one of which to be distributed as the Reverend Dr. Dwight shall think fitt, one to go towards the use of the Charity Children and the other third part to be kept by the Churchwarden for the time being to be disposed of as he shall be directed."

The first reference to a Font occurs in the Inventory of the Commissioners of 1549. Among the goods therein described as stolen was "a clothe aboute the founte." When the old Church was demolished in 1880 this Font was discovered. It was brought to light on 6 May of that year, being found at a point eight feet from the west wall and ten feet from the south wall. Its upper surface was only a few inches below the level of the soil. It was of rude-construction and octagonal in shape, each of its faces measuring eleven inches. It was reburied, and now lies Just beneath the present Font.

The ancient octagonal Font, which still exists at All Saints, was the gift of Mr. Thomas Hill, of Passor's. The old "Register Book" records:

> "Mr Thomas Hill of the parishe of Fulham Gent; erected and beautified at his owne propper coste and charge the Fonte in the sayd parishe Churche _____ 1622."

An inscription upon the Font reads:

> This Fonnt was
> erected at the
> charge of Tho.
> Hyll chvrch-
> warden.
> 1622.

The Font. From a water-colour drawing, dated 1794, in the possession of the Author

The original position of this Font is unknown. In 1646 there was

> "pd. for setting vpp the ffount and paueing about it 16s. 0d."

In 1805 it was again moved. In the Churchwardens' Accounts, under 4 March 1806, is the following:

> "Paid James Willson for a Carved Wainscot Cover for the Font made by order of Mr. Meyrick (by order of the Vestry) £26."

This cover still exists.

Faulkner, in 1812, describes the Font as then situated at the east end of the south aisle. In the view of the interior of the

Church, which we reproduce, executed in 1836, the Font is represented as standing immediately in front of the altar steps, at the end of the middle aisle. In 1840 it was placed in a more prominent position in the same aisle. In 1872 it was moved to the west end of the middle aisle. In 1881, when the Church was rebuilt, it was re-erected, in its present position near the door of the North Porch.

In the summer of 1896 an ancient cauldron-shaped basin, supposed to have originally belonged to Fulham Church, was erected on a brick base in the Churchyard, on the south side of the Church. Its story is a curious one. About the year 1827 Mr. William Quinton purchased a plot of land in the High Street, on which had stood three very ancient cottages, and erected on it the house No. 11. In digging out the foundations, the font, of which we are speaking, was discovered, buried only a few feet below the soil. The builder appears to have thought little of his "find," for, partly sinking it in the ground, he used the basin to receive the water from a pump. Thus, with a wooden plug in the hole at the bottom, the ancient font now served the menial purpose of a trough out of which the horses drank. It remained in this position until about 1867, when, being no longer required, it was taken up and filled with flowers. Mr. George Quinton, the son of Mr. William Quinton, on a visit to Fulham shortly after the conversion of the "trough" into a "flower-pot," was much struck by the similarity it bore to the font in Chester Cathedral. It continued, however, to be used as a receptacle for flowers until 1877, when the house and premises were let to the late Mr. C. Humphrey, in whose possession it continued to remain. About the commencement of 1896 it was brought under the notice of the Rev. H. S. Beard, then curate at All Saints, by Mr. W. T. Humphrey. This circumstance led to the ancient font being presented to the Church by Mr. Thomas Quinton, brother of Mr. George Quinton. It probably dates from early in the 12th century. It is, of course, impossible to say with certainty that it ever belonged to Fulham Church, but its discovery almost within a stone's throw of All Saints, suggests the possibility that it may have done so.

The earliest reference to the Pulpit occurs in the Churchwardens' Accounts for 1645:

Pd. Goodm Johnson for ye Canopie for the pulpitt and mending the Churchyard gate £3. 3s. 6d.

Pd. for making a scaffold for ye Canopie ouer the pulpitt and makeing a hole through the wall, stuff and laboure 3s. 4d.

pd. for the pulpitt cushion £1. 13s. 0d

In the old "Register Book" it is recorded that the Lady Elizabeth Mordaunt gave to Fulham Church

"A Pulpitt Cloth and Cushon of Purple cullered silk Camlett embrodered wth a peece of the same for the Pulpitt doore."

In 1771 the thanks of the Vestry were returned to the Hon. Mr. Fitzpatrick,

"for his gift of a Crimson velvet Cushion fring'd with gold for the pulpit."

The "Hon. Mr. Fitzpatrick," who made many gifts to the Church, was [Richard Fitzpatrick](), second son of Richard, first Lord Gowran, and brother of John, second Lord Gowran, who was created Earl of Upper Ossory, a title which became extinct on the death of the second earl.

On Sunday, 16 Jan. 1780, an announcement was made in the Church, stating that the parishioners were desired to meet in Vestry

"on Wednesday next at 10 o'clock in the morning to take into consideration the expediency of removing the pulpit from its present position."

Unfortunately, we are not told what the "present position" was. Most probably, in conformity with the custom of the time, the Pulpit had stood somewhere near the centre of the middle aisle. At a subsequent meeting of the Vestry it was ordered:

"That Mr. Neave be desired to begin the work on Monday next which he promises to do and engages that the church shall not be shut up more than one Sunday, and that he will finish the business for the church to be opened on Friday, 4 Feb., being the Fast Day."

In 1840 the Pulpit was again removed, this time to a position on the south side of the middle aisle just in front of the Communion table.

The old Pulpit was a ponderous tripartite arrangement, consisting of the pulpit proper, the reading desk and the clerk's desk. The occupants of this type of pulpit, etc., Cowper amusingly satirizes:

> "Sweet sleep enjoys the curate in his desk,
> The tedious rector drawling o'er his head;
> And sweet the clerk below."
> - *The Task*.

The old "Three-Decker." From a sketch, signed R. R. Wood, *del.*, preserved in the Vicarage "Faulkner."

Above this "three-decker," as it was popularly called, was a weighty sounding board, not improbably identical with the "canopie" of 1645. When the Church was altered in 1840, this board was taken down and cut in halves. One portion was converted into a communion table by having its rounded corners filled in with deal. The other half found its way to Wardour Street. In December 1872, the reading desk and clerk's desk, the two lower stages of the erection, were removed, and the original Pulpit, to which they had been attached, was transferred to the north side of the chancel. On the rebuilding of the Church in 1880-81 the panels of the old Pulpit were turned into a screen for the organist's seat, and in this capacity they still do duty. Of the four panels, which are now extended in a straight line, three are of oak, beautifully inlaid. The fourth is painted in imitation of the others. The last-named formed the door to the Pulpit, to which it was added in recent times.

The hour-glass was a familiar adjunct to the Pulpit. In 1643 the Churchwardens

> Pd. for an houre glass and a quire of paper 2s. 0d.

In 1646 there is a similar entry:

> "pd. for ye houre glasse 6d."

Fulham Church, south side. From a photograph taken circa 1879

Among the references to the Communion Table may be noted the following:

1637 Pd. for two hassocks for ye Cornmō table 2s. 6d.

1638 pd. Howler for a matt and Wadmore for mending the frame about ye communion table. 6s. 6d.

1648 (Recd) of Henry Brooks for A peece of the rayles yt were about the Communion table 8s. 0d.

From the "Register Book" we learn that:

"The Lady Eliz. Viscountess Mordaunt did in her life time (she died in 1679) give unto the pish church of Fulham a hanging for the east end of the church, wth a Carpitt for the Comunion Table."

"Sr John Elwes of the Parish of Fulham Kt did of his owne cost and Chargis erect the Railes and Banisters about the Communion Table in the Parish Church of Fulham in the yeare of our Lord God 1683."

At the rebuilding of the Church these rails were preserved and were placed between the pillars north and south of the chancel. In 1899 they were brought into more prominence by being fixed on either side of the front of the chancel arch constituting a sort of low chancel screen.

In 1787 the Churchwardens

"Paid for a set of cushions to surround the rails of the Communion table £6. 10s. 0d."

Of the Communion Table of 1840 we have already spoken in our account of the Pulpit. It was covered with a red velvet cloth, on the front of which was a crown of thorns with the letters "I H S" worked in gold.

Standing against the east wall, in the north-east corner of the chancel, stood the Bishop's Chair. During the time of the Rev. R. G. Baker, <u>a second chair was added</u>, for the Vicar's use. This was placed on the opposite side of the Communion Table, in the south-east corner.

There was formerly an old sedile or stone stall in the chancel.

Near it was a piscina. These were probably destroyed in the improvements of 1840.

The old Organ, which was taken down when the Parish Church was rebuilt, was erected by Mr. Benjamin Jordan in 1732.

Little is known in regard to the music provided in early times. When, in 1549, the Commissioners of Edward VI prepared their Inventory of the furniture, etc. in Fulham Church, they found "a payre of Orgayns that lyeth all to broken," which they allowed to remain. This "payre of orgayns" had, in all probability, been used in rendering the mass in the days of Bishop Bonner. During the Puritan period, probably no organ was used in Fulham Church. From the "Diary" of Samuel Pepys we learn that organs reappeared in Westminster Abbey in 1660. From 1625, when the existing records of the Fulham Churchwardens begin, down to 1732, there is no reference whatever to an organ in the Church. Down to the latter year the singing was most likely led by the usual apology of wind and string, as it was in many village churches till quite recent years.

The faculty for the erection of an organ was granted by Bishop Gibson, 31 Jan. 1732-33. It reads:

"ffulham ffacultas pro erecco organi, etcc.
Edmund, by Divine permission, Lord Bishop of London, to all Christian people to whom these presents shall come, or shall or may in any wise concern, and more especially to the Churchwarden, parishioners and inhabitants of the parish of ffulham in the county of Middlesex and diocese of London, SENDETH GREETING in our Lord God everlasting.
Whereas it hath been set forth and alledged before the worshipfull Edward Kinaston, doctor of laws, surrogate of the right worshipfull Humphrey Henchman, also doctor of laws, our Chancellor, on the part and behalf of the Churchwarden and severall of the parishioners of the said parish That they have by voluntary subscriptions obtained a sufficient sume of Money for the purchasing of an organ which they are desirous of erecting in the West Gallery of the said parish church and That there is a large Beam lyeing cross the roof near the West end of the said church which will be very incommodious and obstruct the view of the said organ when erected and That the said Beam may be taken away without prejudice to the roof or ffabrick of the said church as appears by a certificate under the hands of able and experienced workmen who have viewed the same now remaining in our principal

Registry and they, the said Churchwarden and parishioners have by their proctor humbly prayed our License or ffaculty for erecting the said organ in the said Gallery and for taking away the said Beam and likewise for stopping up the Arch at the West end of the said Church next the belfry and making a new window in the roof of the North side opposite to the window on the South side of the said church in order to supply the light that will be taken away by stopping up the said arch, and Whereas the said Dr. Edward Kinaston surrogate aforesaid rightly and duely proceeding did at the petition of the said proctor decree the Vicar, parishioners and inhabitants of the said parish in special and all others in general, having or pretending to have any right title or interest in the premises, to be cited to appear before our sd. Chancellour, his surrogate or some such competent Judge in that behalf at a certain competent time and place then and there to show cause (if they or any of them had any) why license or ffaculty should not be granted to the said Churchwarden and parishrs in manner as they desire with intimation that if they did not appear at the time and place aforesaid, or appear and not show good and sufficient cause to the contrary, our said Chancellour, his surrogate, or some other competent Judge in his behalf did intend and would proceed to grant to them the said Churchwarden and parishioners our license or ffaculty for erecting the said organ in the said Gallery and for taking away the said Beam and likewise for stopping up the said arch and making a new window in the roof on the north side opposite to the window on the south side of the said church, and whereas our said Chancellour rightly and duely proceeding on the due execution and return of the said citation with intimation and calling All persons as well in speciall as in general so cited to appear and none of them appearing hath pronounced them to be in contempt and on pain of such contumacy hath decreed our license or ffaculty to be granted to the said Churchwarden and parishrs for the purpose aforesaid (justice so requiring) as in and by the proceedings thereupon had and now remaining in our principal Registry it doth and may more fully appear.

We therefore the Bishop aforesaid, well weighing and considering the premises, do by virtue of our power ordinary and episcopal and as far as by the ecclesiasticall laws of this realm and temporal laws of the same We may and can ratify and confirm whatsoever our said Chancellor hath done or caused to be done in the Prmises and do hereby give and grant to the said Churchwarden and parishioners of the parish of ffulham aforesaid our leave and license or ffaculty for erecting the said organ in the said West Gallery and for taking away the said Beam and likewise for stopping up the said arch at the West end of the said church next the belfry and making a new window in the roof on the north side opposite to the window on the South side of the said Church in manner as by them desired. In witness whereof we have caused the seal of our Chancellor (which we use in this behalf) to be fixed to these presents. Dated the thirty-first day of Janry in the year of our Lord one thousand seven hundred and thirty two and in the tenth year of our translation."

At a meeting of the Vestry, 23 June 1740, it was resolved that the Organ, "which, at present, is out of tune, shall be put in tune"; and it was further agreed to entrust the work to

"Mr. Jordan or Mr. Bridge, the expenses whereof to be defrayed at the charge of the parish."

On 16 June 1748, the Vestry ordered,

"That the organ be repaired at the discretion of ye Churchwarden, ye charge whereof not to exceed ten pounds and kept in repair at the charge of the parish."

About 1865 the Organ was reconstructed by Messrs. Jones and Co. of the Fulham Road, when the old keyboard, which went down to GG, was curtailed to CC. On this occasion some very fine old diapason pipes were removed from the lower notes. The additions included several new stops and a new pedal board and bellows.

In the centre of the Organ was a bishop's mitre in gold. On the top was an ancient coat of arms, lost during the re-erection in 1880-81. With the new Organ we deal further on.

The Reredos in the old Church was erected to the memory of the Sharps. On the rebuilding, it was removed to the Mission Hall, Parson's Green. The brass tablet which it originally bore was, a few years ago, restored to All Saints. The inscription reads:

"This reredos was erected in 1845 to the honor of God and in memory of William Sharp of Fulham House, Surgeon to King George, III., Catherine his wife, daughter of Thomas Barwick, Granville Sharp, his brother, and Mrs. Elizabeth Prowse, his sister; these three children of Dr. Thomas Sharp, Archdeacon of Northumberland, and grandchildren of Dr. John Sharp, Archbishop of York, are, together with the said Catherine Sharp, buried in a vault near the Western side of the adjoining churchyard. 'If we believe that Jesus died and rose again, even so them also which sleep in Jesus, will God bring with Him.' I Thess. IV. xiv."

This brass is now placed against the east wall of the north transept. The words preceding "To the honor," etc. have been removed from the plate.

Repairs to the Old Church

The history of the old Church is one of continuous mending. The Parish Books teem with entries about the "decays" of the Church. Space compels us to limit our quotations to a few of the more interesting:

1638

> pd. Chapman for mending the Church tyling 11s. 0d.
> pd. for a locke and keye for the church and cleaning ye gutters 1s. 8d.
> pd. for mending the keye of the church dore 10d.

1639

> "Pd. for a dynner when the workmen came to view the decaies of the Church 3s. 6d."

In 1641 the Churchwardens

> Pd. the plumber for mending the church leades £1. 5s. 8d.
> Pd. Edward Limpany for fagots for ye plumber 1s. 10d.
> pd. for mending the church and laying new tiles when it was sunke 9s. 4d.

In 1650 the Churchwardens paid

> "To Mr. Lilly Plumber for mending the Leades and gutters of the Church where it raine'd in and for fire soder and Labor p. Bill £1. 10s. 1d."

In 1652 the pews were altered. A minute reads:

> "Att a Vestrie September 30th, 1652.
> It is . . . ordered Vppon View of the Vnseemelienes and Vnserviseablenes of Certeine pewes in the Middle Ile That ye psent

Churchwarden shall forthwth cause the said pewes to be repaired and made vniforme on both sides of the said Ile and sutable to the vpp pewes next the Chauncell and aceasemt to be forthwth made aswell for the pulpitt as the said pewes and a Report (vppon view of the said pewes) to be brought att the time of the Asment (?) making of the charges therof."

In the Parish Books is the following report on the condition of Fulham Church in 1658:

"At a Vestry the 3 of January 1658,
We the inhabitants there mett haueing o'selves with the workmen taken a veiw of the decayes of the said Church of ffulham and finding the pauements of the said church are sunck and much broken as also decayes in the leads to the indaingering by the fall of some part of the church, as also that the glasse windowes are much broken, after finding that the eighth part of the late asessment for the poore wch was ordered to that vse at ye last meeting will not suffice to repaire the said church, it is therefore ordered the day and yeare aboue written That an aseassment be made to inable the churchwarden to repair the said church and the said asessment to be one third part of the last yeares assesment for the poore."

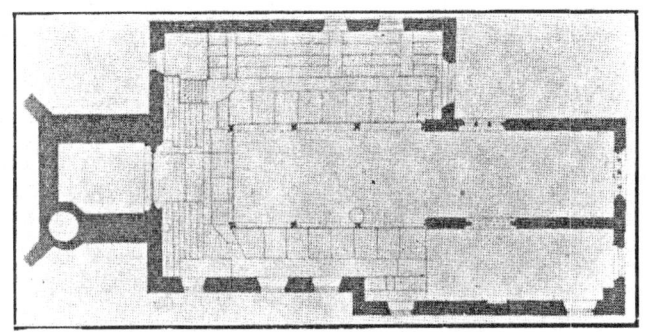

Fulham Church. Gallery plan,
from a survey made by E. H, Browne, 1837

In 1686 the old Church was "new roofed, beautified, enlightened and rendered more commodious" at a cost of about £160. The roof was a continual source of expense, for a storm at all violent was sure to carry away a portion of the tiling. In the winter of 1734-35, the Church suffered considerably. On 13 January of this year the inhabitants met to "consult what method to take relating to the repairs of the said church, a view having been taken by prope workmen."

Eventually it was agreed,

"That, in consideration of the extravagant price of tiles at this present juncture caused by the late tempest the roof of the church be for the present boarded over."

In 1735 a special church rate of sixpence in the pound was levied for repairs. The Church underwent numerous repairs in 1742, 1746 and 1748. In 1749-50 miscellaneous repairs cost £162. 13s. 7½d. A Committee, which had been appointed by the Vestry in 1750, presented a long report recommending that the decayed ground floor of the steeple should be taken up and paved with Purbeck stone

"and reset from the outward door step with a descent to the step into the church . . . the floor of the pews to be repaired, the floors of the allys, except where there are gravestones, to he mended."

- together with sundry repairs to the Tower, etc. The Vestry adopted the report with the exception of the Tower pavement: this they decided should be "new floored with oak." The work was carried out at Easter 1750.

In 1770 the Church was completely overhauled at a cost of £1,002. 19s. In 1797 repairs, costing £493. 6s. 1½d, were carried out. These included the re-tiling of the roof. In 1800 the sum of £1,010. 10s. 8d. was spent upon the old edifice.

The repeated thefts of lead from the Church induced the Vestry, in 1802, to substitute slates as a covering. In 1820 the Church was, for the first time, heated by steam instead of by fire. In 1838 gas was substituted for candles for lighting purposes. In the same year an abortive scheme was devised for a new church.

On 13 July 1839, a meeting was called to consider the expediency of enlarging the Church which had grown too small to adequately meet the needs of the population. It appears, however, that the estimates prepared for the work were so expensive in proportion to the proposed increased accommodation, while the difficulty of removing many of the "inconveniencies" of the old building found to be so great that the general opinion of the meeting was adverse to the measure. It was therefore agreed that an attempt should be made to raise a fund adequate to the erection, on the same site, of a new church, retaining the old and handsome Tower.

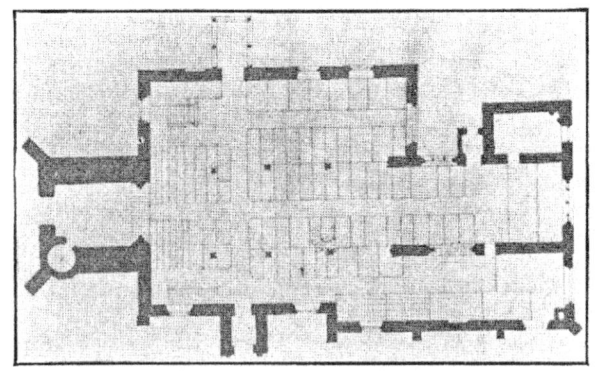

Fulham Church, ground plan, from a survey made by E. H. Browne, 1837.

The project to rebuild the Church was unsuccessful, and so the parishioners again turned their attention to the question of enlarging the old one. This time a workable scheme was arranged, and, in 1840-41, the Church was much improved and its seating accommodation increased. We cannot, perhaps, better describe the alterations than by quoting from the report, dated 1 March 1841, issued by the Committee appointed to superintend the work:

"The Committee was appointed at a Vestry meeting of the Parishioners, held 6th February 1840, and proceeded forthwith to obtain tenders from the principal Builders of the Parish, for the execution of the work proposed by Mr. Lapidge, and sanctioned by the Vestry. The lowest of the four tenders which were sent in, being that of Messrs. Dawson and Potter, and amounting to £1,523, was accepted. But in order to give effect to the resolution adopted by the Vestry, and to afford a complete indemnification against any injury or risk, which, in the progress of the work, might affect the security of the Building, an addition of £227 was subsequently made to the amount of the contract, and a clause of more than ordinary strictness was annexed to it, imposing on the Contractors the whole liability that could possibly arise, either from any defects in the existing Building, or from any casualty attending the alteration of it.

The works thus contracted for were commenced early in March, and prosecuted, without any interruption to the Sunday Services, until the 3rd August, when it became requisite to close the Church for about two months. On the 18th of October, being completely finished, it was again opened for Divine Service. The improvements effected were these:

1st. The removal into the Tower of those monuments and tablets by which the South Eastern extremity of the Building was chiefly occupied, and the consequent addition of that space to the available means of accommodation. In their new situation these monuments, being brought into one view, and in a space which had hitherto been nearly useless, contribute to form a commodious and handsome entrance into the Church, from the West.

2nd. An addition to the area of the Building at the North Eastern end, with an elevation given to it, according not only in its material, but in its character and design with the oldest and more interesting parts of the Building.

3rd. The removal of the Vestry to the space hitherto occupied by the Font and the Steam Boiler, the latter being re-erected on the outside, and the former brought into a more conspicuous and appropriate position in the middle aisle. The expense of moving and replacing the Boiler, as well as that connected with colouring and painting all that portion of the Church which remained unaltered, was defrayed by the Churchwardens from the payments made for the new seats.

4th. The removal of the Desk and Pulpit, from the inconvenient place before assigned to them, to the front of the Communion Table, by which arrangement a much larger number of the congregation are brought within the sight and hearing of the officiating clergy.

5th. The alteration of the double pews throughout the Church, those in the aisles having an uniform aspect given them towards the east and those above being made parallel with the front of the galleries.

6th. As the result of all these improvements, 261 new seats have been gained, of which 172 are free and unappropriated, while many of those which existed before have been made far more commodious."

The alterations carried out by Mr. Edward Lapidge, the architect, very materially enhanced the appearance of the old Church. The dedication of the lower portion of the Tower, which had hitherto been used as a lumber room, to the purposes of a "mortuary chapel" at once turned it to an appropriate use, while it freed the other portions of the old Church which had been cumbered by the memorials to its dead. Besides the floor space thus gained, the galleries were enlarged. To the north of the chancel the Bishop's Gallery was, as has already been stated, erected in a line with the North Gallery. By the removal of the South wall of the chancel, the South Gallery was also increased in length. Before 1840 there were not more than 85 free seats in the whole Church. The total cost reached nearly £2,000, of which sum £1,600 was obtained by voluntary contributions.

In 1860 the Church was again thoroughly cleaned and repaired.

Fulham Church. Elevation showing the addition to the North Front.
From a drawing signed E. Lapidge, January 1840,
preserved in the Vicarage "Faulkner."

The New Church

The enlargement and restoration of 1840 sufficed for the next forty years. In 1869 the sum of £8,000 was offered to the Vicar (the Rev. R. G. Baker) to rebuild the Parish Church, and, in accordance with instructions, the late Sir Gilbert G. Scott prepared plans for a Gothic edifice. Unfortunately his estimate amounted to

£15,000. The scheme had therefore to be abandoned and the generous offer declined. About 1877 the decayed state of the old fabric made demolition a matter of absolute necessity, for the Church showed signs of collapse. The Vicar, the Rev. F. H. Fisher, took the initiative in the matter, and, before many months had passed, a good deal of preliminary work was accomplished. On 10 July 1878, a Building Committee was appointed. Tenders were invited, the lowest offer received being that of Messrs. Goddard and Sons, £7,980. By some judicious omissions this sum was eventually reduced to £7,774 13s. 3d.

The faculty for rebuilding the Church (except the Tower, which it was not proposed to touch), was granted by the Bishop of London, 4 July 1879. The old Church was finally closed 18 April 1880.

During the work of demolition some very interesting discoveries were made.

On 27 April 1880, Bishop Henchman's tomb was discovered in the south aisle. The fine black marble stone was found to be in a good state of preservation.

On 30 April the discovery respecting the galleries, to which we have already referred, was made.

On 1 May 1880, an arch, or head of an old window, was found in the west wall, behind the gallery, to the south of the Tower arch on the inside. It was a pointed arch with simple bead moulding.

On 4 May nine old glazed encaustic tiles were unearthed among the loose rubbish under the seats in the north aisle. They were mostly in a good state of preservation. In the same place, about nine to twelve inches beneath the surface, the workmen came upon the remains, apparently, of an old tiled floor with gravestones.

On 6 May the font, of which we have already spoken, was found.

On 13 May, in taking down the gable of the east end, portions of an old window were found. These we have already described. A few more tiles were found on this date.

On 14 May the workmen came upon the very handsome bases of the west arch. The floor of the Limpany pew was found to be composed of black and white marble. A remarkable discovery on this date was the digging up of a perfect jaw-bone with all its teeth.

It was found set in the masonry of the east gable.

On 15 May another strange relic was brought to light. This was a human heart, highly spiced, enclosed in a lead cover. It was found about two feet below the surface, at a point near Sir F. Child's vault. On the ceiling of the north aisle being removed, an old one of oak was exposed to view. This had, at one time, been whitewashed.

On 18 Dec. two more tiles, but of a different pattern, were found in digging for the south buttresses.

The work of removing and replacing the ancient monuments, etc., was performed under the supervision of the Vicar. Such was the care displayed that, as far as possible, every stone was put back in the same place, while only two were actually lost.

On 10 July 1880, Dr. Tait, Archbishop of Canterbury, laid the corner stone of the beautiful Perpendicular Church which the parish now possesses.

Fulham Church, south side. From a photograph by Mr. T. S. Smith, 1895

The new Church, which was built from the designs of Sir Arthur Blomfield, was consecrated by Dr. Jackson, Bishop of

London, 9 July 1881, when the sermon was preached by the Archbishop of Canterbury. Inclusive of the furniture, the total cost was £8,855. 19s. 6d. Of this sum £1,593. 16s. 7d. was raised by mortgage on the Church Houses, while no less than £6,085. 1s. 3d. was obtained by voluntary effort. The largest contributors were Miss Palmer, £1,500, the Ecclesiastical Commissioners, £750, the Rev. F. H. Fisher, Vicar, £500, and the Bishop of London, £500. In addition to financial assistance, the parishioners and others also made a number of special gifts. Among these may be mentioned the Organ, the Pulpit, and most of the stained glass windows. Particulars of these gifts will be found under their respective heads.

The new Church is a light and handsome building, consisting of a nave, north and south aisles, north and south transepts, choir and chancel. The Vestry is attached to the north transept. In it is preserved a "Plan of the Parish of Fulham in the County of Middlesex, from Surveys made between the years 1824 and 1838 by W. S. Leonard, York Place, Queen's Elm, Chelsea." The walls are also covered with drawings, etc., relating to the Church.

The Organ is erected against the east wall of the south transept, on the site of the vestry of 1840. With one or two important exceptions, which we shall presently notice, it is an entirely new instrument. It was the gift of the Palmer family, erected as a souvenir of their fifty years' residence in the parish. On one of the panels of the case is a brass tablet, inscribed:

> "To the Honor and Glory of God and in memory of John Horsley Palmer of Hurlingham, Elizabeth his wife, their sons and daughters deceased, This Organ is presented to the Parish Church of All Saints Fulham by the members of their family, *Anno Domini*, 1881."

The Organ was, in 1881, reconstructed throughout by Messrs. J. W. Walker and Sons. It was opened at Christmas, 1882. The main portions of the Jordans' original organ, which were preserved, were the case, the swell open and the swell stopped diapason, and the pedal 16 ft. open. At the time of its reconstruction, it contained only two manuals and pedals with twenty-one stops, four couplers and five composition pedals. The first improvement, the provision of a trumpet stop consisting of 56 pipes CC to G, was made in 1883. In 1888 it was again enlarged by

Messrs. Walker and Sons, when a choir organ of seven stops and the necessary couplers were added, and four additions made to the swell organ. In 1890 some further additions were made, including the insertion of a violone CCC to F, 16 feet, to form a frontage to the south chancel arch, and the erection of a Melvin hydraulic motor engine for blowing. In 1894 extensive improvements in the Organ were carried out by Messrs. Hill and Sons. The following is a specification of the Organ at this date. The stops which have been added since 1882 are marked with an asterisk (*) and those which can be identified as belonging to the Jordans' organ are indicated by the letter "J". The improved Organ was re-opened 1 Nov. 1894:

GREAT ORGAN
1* Open Diapason   8 feet
2 Open Diapason No. 2   8 feet
3 Horn Diapason   8 feet
4 Wald Flute (Stopped Bass)   8 feet
5 Principal   4 feet
6 Flute   4 feet
7 Fifteenth   2 feet
8 Mixture   3 Ranks
9* Trumpet   8 feet

SWELL ORGAN
10 Open Diapason   16 feet
J11 Open Diapason (old)   8 feet
J12 Stopped Diapason (old)   8 feet
13 Echo Gamba (C) grooved   8 feet
14* Vox Angelica (C)   8 feet
15 Principal   4 feet
16 Mixture   3 Ranks
17 Vox humana   8 feet
18 Horn   8 feet
19 Oboe   8 feet

CHOIR ORGAN
20* Violin Diapason   8 feet
21* Lieblich Gedact   8 feet

22* Dulciana	8 feet
23* Clear Flute	4 feet
24* Gemshorn	4 feet
25* Harmonic Piccolo	2 feet
26* Clarionet	8 feet

PEDAL ORGAN

27 Open Diapason	16 feet
28 Bourdon	16 feet
29* Violone	16 feet
30* Trombone	16 feet

Manuals CC to G, 56 Notes
Pedals CCC to F, 30 Notes

31* Violoncello	8 feet

ACCESSORIES
32 Swell Lo Great Unison
33 Swell to Great Sup. Octave
34* Swell Sub Octave on its own manual
35* Swell to Choir
36 Swell to Pedals
37 Great to Pedals
38* Choir to Pedals
3 Composition Pedals to Great
2 Composition Pedals to Swell
*Tren1ulant
Swell Pedal
* Pedal to control Octave to Pedal Coupler

Front Pipes of Best Spotted Metal. Blown by a Melvin Hydraulic Motor controlled by a stop at Organist's right hand.
Pneumatic Action to Great Organ and Couplers.
Tubular Pneumatic Action to Pedal Organ (5 stops).

On different parts of the old case the following initials have been cut: "T. H. 1751" and "R. W. 1764." In the centre, Where the Bishop's mitre was originally placed, the Royal Arms have been fixed.

The present arcaded Reredos, which for design and execution

is much admired, was completed in 1885. When the Church was rebuilt, no funds were available for the decoration of this portion of the sacred edifice. At the suggestion of the architect, the panels were filled in with Japanese paper. In 1884, a special fund was raised to complete the decoration. The late Dr. Egan, at that time Churchwarden, suggested, as a suitable design, the figures of Moses, Aaron and David, to which Isaiah was added. Messrs. Heaton, Butler and Baynes were accordingly instructed to carry it out. The figures of the four saints are painted on zinc. Moses, the law-giver, holds two tables of stone, on which the Ten Commandments are legibly written; David, the musician king, crowned, carries his harp and sceptre; Isaiah, the Messianic prophet, is distinguished by the tongs holding a live coal (Isaiah vi. 6); while Aaron, the high priest, is robed in his vestments, which are portrayed with great accuracy in accordance with Exodus xxviii. The decoration was carried out at a cost of £230.

The Pulpit, which stands in the north-east corner of the nave, was given in 1881, in memory of the Rev. R. G. Baker, by the members of his family. It is beautifully carved, very light and of costly design.

The brass eagle Lectern was placed in the Church by the family of the late Bishop Jackson. It is inscribed:

"In loving and thankful memory of John Jackson, D.D., Bishop of London, this lectern is dedicated to the glory of God by his children and other members of his family, July 12th 1885."

The Church is particularly rich in its stained glass. The windows have, in most instances, been the free gifts of parishioners. They have been arranged on a definite plan, the leading motive of which has been to illustrate the dedication of the Church to All Saints.

The magnificent East Window, which is in five compartments, is devoted to scenes connected with the life of our Lord, the King of Saints, including the Last Supper and the Crucifixion. It was the gift of Sir A. W. Blomfield, the architect of the Church, and was erected by him in memory of his father, the late Bishop Blomfield, and other members of his family.

The North Window of the chancel, which illustrates the

Ascension, was the gift of the family of the late Mr. Jonas Turner. The brass tablet is inscribed:

> "To the Glory of God and in loving memory of Jonas Turner of Churchfield House, this window is erected by his sorrowing children, 1881."

In the east wall of the north transept are two windows. The right hand one has for its subject the Adoration of the Magi. It was the gift of the sons-in-law of the late Mrs. Jackson. The tablet is inscribed:

> "Ad Gloriam Dei et in piam memoriam Mariæ Annæ Frith Iohannis Iackson, D.D., episcopi Londinensis dilectissimæ vxoris qvae die festo Epiphaniæ A.D. 1874 in Christo obdormivit. Generi eivs amoris erga se vere materni havd immemores hanc fenestram exornandam cvraservnt, A.D. 1881."

The left hand window depicts the Annunciation. It was the gift of the Rev. B. Gore-Browne, in memory of his wife. The brass tablet is inscribed:

> "To the Glory of God and in memory of Helen Mackenzie the beloved wife of Barrington Gore-Browne, daughter of John Bishop of London and Mary Ann Frith Jackson, who was born on Novr 8th 1852 and was laid to rest in the Island of Madeira having fallen asleep in Christ Sept. 1st 1879."

The north end of the north transept is adorned by a three-light window, which was, as already stated, erected in the old Church in 1855 by the family of the late Mr. John Daniel of Parson's Green. The subjects are the Magi, the Nativity, the Shepherds, and three lesser subjects. The tablet is inscribed:

> "In memory of John Daniel, Sybella his wife, John their Son, and Sybella Gertrude Hammet their Granddaughter, A.D. MDCCCLV."

In the north aisle there are five windows. The first (proceeding from East to West) is erected to the memory of Mrs. J. Passman Tate, sister of the late Mr. Park Nelson. The subject is the

Confession of St. Thomas. The tablet is inscribed:

> "To the Glory of God and in affectionate memory of Julia the beloved wife of John Passman Tate of Lee and youngest sister of Park Nelson of this parish; born 15 March 1812; died 20 June 1875."

The second Window was erected by Dr. R. Roy in memory of his father, the Rev. Robert Roy, M.A. The subject is the Charge to St. Peter. The tablet reads:

> "To the Glory of God and in memory of the Rev. Robert Roy, M.A., of Sidney Svssex College, Cambridge, and of this Parish, who died Janvary 1st 1863."

The third window, also the gift of Mr. J. P. Tate, perpetuates the memory of Mr. and Mrs. Park Nelson. It depicts the Martyrdom of St. Stephen. The tablet is inscribed:

> "To the Glory of God, and in memory of Park, and Catherine Anna Maria Nelson, for 44 years residents of this parish."

The fourth window was erected to the memory of Mrs. Weiss, the wife of Mr. F. F. Weiss of the firm of Messrs. Weiss and Son, of Oxford Street. Mrs. Weiss was the daughter of Mr. Thomas Roe of Church Row. The subject is the "Massacre of the Holy Innocents." The tablet is inscribed:

> "To the Glory of God and in memory of Mary Elizabeth Weiss This Window is placed here by her affectionate husband Frederic Foveaux Weiss and her brother Matthew Thomas Roe, obiit Jan. 21, 1886."

The fifth window is a memorial subscribed for by the children of All Saints. It represents Christ blessing little Children. The tablet reads:

> "To the Glory of God in grateful commemoration of their own Baptism and the rebuilding of the Church of their Childhood this window was here placed by the Children of this Parish 1881."

In the south aisle there are six windows. The first (proceeding from East to West) was erected by the late Mr. W. H. Lammin of

Holcroft's, to the memory of his father and mother. The subject is Timothy brought to St. Paul by his mother Eunice and his grandmother Lois. At the bottom, the window is inscribed:

> "To the Glory of God & in loving memory of James & Harriot Lammin for many years Inhabitants of this Parish: He died 16th Augt 1846. She died 30th Decr 1853."

Beneath is a tablet bearing the arms of the family and adding,

> "Also to the dear memory of their only son William Henry Lammin. Born June 22nd 1814. Entered into rest, January 21st, 1890. 'In hope of eternal life.'"

The second window was the gift of Mr. James Wray of Arragon House, and was erected in memory of his wife and daughter. The subject is the Preaching of John the Baptist. The tablet is inscribed:

> "To the Glory of God and in memory of Emily davghter of James Wray of Parsons Green, Fvlham. Died Dec. 7th, 1876 and of Anna Maria his wife died Nov. 3rd 1878."

The third window was erected in memory of the late Bishop Jackson. The subject is the Conversion of St. Paul. The tablet, at either end of which are the arms of the sees of Lincoln and London, impaled with the Bishop's domestic coat, is inscribed:

> "To the Glory of God and in reverent Memory of the Right Reverend Father in God John Jackson, D.D. Bishop of Lincoln 1853-1869, Bishop of London 1869-1885, who rested from his labours on the Feast of the Epiphany 1885 this Window is here placed by his neighbours, friends and others connected with the Parish of Fulham."

The fourth window recalls the memory of the late Mr. James English of Colehill House. The subject is the Descent of the Holy Ghost on the Day of Pentecost. The tablet is inscribed:

> "To the Glory of God and in loving memory of James English of Colehill House, Fulham. Born 18th Novr 1821. Died 4th April 1887."

The fifth window was erected by Lieut. A. E. Bassano of Elysium Row in memory of his father and mother. It represents St. Barnabas laying the money at the Apostles' feet. On the lower portion of the window is this inscription:

"To the Glory of God and in memory of Maior General Alfred Bassano, C.B., yovngest son of F. M. Bassano, Esqre Army Med. Dept. Born 25th Ivne 1826, Died 12th September 1882; also of Mary wife of the above, eldest davghter of G. W. Dvmbell, Esqre of Belmont Isle of Man. Died Octr 13th, 1860. This window was erected by their only child Alfred Ernest Bassano Lievtenant 32nd Cornwall Light Infantry in which corps his father served with distinction for 27 years, 1883."

The Blomfield Window, now in the South Transept.
From a photograph by Mr. H. Ambridge

The sixth Window, which is placed in the west wall of the south aisle, was, in 1883, erected by the parishioners of Fulham to the memory of Archbishop and Mrs. Tait. The subject is St. Andrew bringing his brother, St. Peter, to Christ. The tablet is inscribed:

"To the Glory of God and in reverent memory of Archibald Campbell Tait, D.D., Bishop of London 1856-1868, Archbishop of Canterbury 1868-1882, and Catherine Tait, his wife, This Window is here placed by the Parishioners of Fulham. They entered into rest, Catherine Tait Advent Sunday 1878, Archibald Campbell Tait Advent Sunday 1882."

Of the eleven windows in the two aisles, eight are three-light and three are two-light.

The south transept window was, as previously stated, originally at the east end of the old Church, whence it was transferred to its present position during the rebuilding of 1880-81. It was, as we have also stated, the gift of Bishop Blomfield in 1840. It has four figures of the Evangelists, bearing their emblems. The lower portions of the lights illustrate the Annunciation, the Epiphany, the Crucifixion and the Resurrection. In the upper tracery are scenes in the life of Our Lord. The window was the work of Mr. W. Wailes of Newcastle-on-Tyne. In the lower left-hand corner of the glass are the initials of Bishop Blomfield and the date 1840 [MDCCCXL].

The large West Window in the Tower Chapel is of much historical interest. It has five lights, containing the following twelve shields of arms:

1. Or, a greyhound courant between two bars sa., for difference a mullet arg. Robt Geo. Baker A.M. huius Ecc. Vic.
2. Gu., a dolphin embowed arg. and chief ermine. Fred. Hor. Fisher hujus Ecc. Vic.
3. *Dexter* [right]: The see of London. *Sinister* [left]: Quarterly per fess indented arg. and az., a bend gules. Caro. Jacob. Epus. Londin. (Blomfield as Bishop of London).
4. *Dexter:* The see of London. *Sinister:* Sa., a cross patonce between four pheons arg. (Jackson as Bishop of London).
5. *Dexter*: The see of London. *Sinister*: Or, a chevron between three henchman's bugle horns sa., on a chief gules as many lions ramp. of the field (Henchman as Bishop of London).
6. A small shield encircled with the garter, containing, quarterly (1) and (4), Gu., three lions passant gardant in pale (England); (2) and (3) Az., three fleur-de-lis (France-Modern).

This shield of the Royal Arms, as borne by our Sovereigns from Henry V. to Elizabeth, has this peculiarity, *vizt* that the English coat precedes the French, whereas the opposite was the use. Possibly the glass is inserted backwards, which would account for what is otherwise unexplainable.

7. *Dexter*: Az., our Lady statant crowned, the child Jesus on her dexter arm, a sceptre in the sinister hand all or (See of Sarum). *Sinister*: Or, a chevron between three henchman's bugle horns sa., on a chief gules as many lions ramp. of the field (Henchman as Bishop of Salisbury).
8. *Dexter*: The see of London. *Sinister*: Quarterly (1) and (4), Or, an eagle desplayed sa. (2) and (3) Arg., on each of two bars sa., three martlets of the first. Fred. Temple, Epis: Lon: (Temple as Bishop of London).
9. *Dexter*: The see of Canterbury. *Sinister*: Az., an eagle desplayed erminois, on his breast a cross flory gules. Gulielmus Archiepus. Cantuar. (Howley as Archbishop of Canterbury).
10. *Dexter*: The see of Canterbury. *Sinister*: Quarterly (1) and (4) Arg., a saltier and chief engrailed gu. (Tait); (2) and (3) Arg., two ravens suspended by the neck from one arrow in fess sa. (Spooner) Archibaldus Campbell Archiepus. Cantuar. (Tait as Archbishop of Canterbury).
11. Arg., in the dexter chief and sinister base a tree vert and in the sinister chief and dexter base a boar's head erased sable armed of the first. Gul. Wood S.T.P. hujus Ecc. Rec.
12. Or, on a bend gu. a crescent arg., in base of the field a crosslet of the second. *Crest*: On a wreath of the colours a boar passant. Gul. C.

Muriel A.M. hujus Ecc. Vic:

By far the most interesting of these arms are the two Henchman shields, composed of a curious kind of enamelled glass. They were originally in the centre window on the west side of the Hall of Fulham Palace. Bishop Blomfield presented them to All Saints, probably that they might form a memento to Dr. Henchman, the only occupant of the see of London known to have been buried within the Church. It will be noticed that the four shields on either side of the Henchman arms are those of the Vicar, Bishop, Archbishop and Rector, when (in 1840-41) the Tower Chapel was arranged, while in the second row are those of the Vicar, Bishop and Archbishop, when (in 1880-81) the Church was rebuilt.

The West Window, it may be added, was reconstructed by the Rev. R. G. Baker when the Tower Chapel was opened up in 1840-41.

The clerestory is lighted by twenty windows, ten on each side. These, in accordance with the plan before mentioned, are intended to be filled with single figures of the Saints, etc., of All Ages, but, thus far, only five in the south clerestory have been completed. The following are the subjects with the inscriptions on the accompanying brasses. We take them from east to west:

(1) Subject: Noah and Melchisedek.
[Brass: "To the Glory of God this Window was placed in this Church by R. V. Tomlinson A D. 1899."]

(7) Subject: S. Agnes and S. Mary Magdalen.
[Brass: "To the Glory of God and in loving memory of Agnes Jeune, wife of Frederic Horatio Fisher, sometime Vicar of this Parish, who fell asleep at Debden, in the county of Essex, 19th April, 1898."]
This window was the gift of the Rev. F. H. Fisher.

(8) Subject: S. Lawrence (martyr) and S. Jerome (confessor and doctor).
[Brass: "To the Glory of God, and in pious memory of the Reverend Edmund Fisher, M.A., sometime Rector of Chipping Ongar, Essex, who fell asleep in Christ at Putney on May 8th, 1881, in his 80th year."]
This window was the gift of the Rev. F. H. Fisher, his son.

(9) Subject: S. Hugh (bishop) and S. Edmund (king and martyr).
[Brass: "To the Glory of God, and in loving memory of the Venerable Edmund Henry Fisher, M.A., first Archdeacon of Southwark, and Vicar of Kennington, Surrey, who rested from his Labours on May 6th, 1879, aged 44 years."]
This window was the gift of the Rev. Edmund Fisher, in memory of his son.

(10) Subject: George Herbert and John Keble (poets of the Church).
[Brass: "To the Glory of God, the gift of Frederic Horatio Fisher, Vicar, and Agnes Jeune, his wife, in grateful memory of the blessings of mingled joy and sorrow in this parish, 1871-90."]
This window was erected by the late Vicar of Fulham as a memorial of his nineteen years' ministry in this parish.

All the memorial windows, except the two given by Mr. P. Tate (which were made by Messrs. Cox, Buckley and Co., of Southampton Street, Strand) and the two which were in the old Church, are the work of Messrs. Heaton, Butler and Baynes, of Garrick Street, W.C.

In 1896 the walls above the arches, at the east and west ends of the nave, were spirit-painted. The painting over the chancel steps represents the Saviour seated, with an open book, and, in the underneath panel, a company of angels. It is inscribed

"Te Gloriosvs Apostolorvm Chorvs Te prophetarvm Lavdabilis nvmervs."

The painting over the arch of the Tower Chapel depicts the Lamb, on either side of which are the Greek letters A and Ω. Beneath are, in the centre, a figure on which are the words "Ecce Agnus Dei," and, to the left and right, figures bearing the names "Abel," "Melchisedek," "S. Peter" and "S. Pavl." Round the edge of the arch runs the inscription,

"Make us to be numbered with thy saints in glory everlasting."

The eight shields on the clerestory walls have also recently been embellished in colour. They represent S. Paul, S. Peter, S. Matthew and S. Andrew, S. Thomas and S. Bartholomew, S.

Simon and S. Jude, S. Philip and S. James Minor, S. John and S. James Major.

The Church is seated with low benches. All the seats are free and unappropriated.

CHAPTER XXIII
FULHAM CHURCH: IT'S MONUMENTS AND EPITAPHS

Fulham Church was once particularly rich and interesting in its mural monuments. Bowack, who wrote nearly two centuries ago, tells us that

> "this church has been the repository of the ashes of many considerable persons and there are some monuments now standing that appear very stately (the inscriptions of which time hath depriv'd us of) which evince this."

But even before Bowack's day many of its monuments had perished, and since his time there have, we regret to say, been custodians to whose carelessness must be ascribed the loss of several others. Of the many valuable brasses which the Church once possessed, only one now remains. Doubtless, during the troublous days of the Civil War, when the soldiery ravaged the old Church, many of the monuments were injured or destroyed. Some, naturally, have perished from sheer decay. The brasses, however, have, we fear, mostly disappeared at the hands of relic-hunters.

Fortunately, some of the more important inscriptions have been preserved by Weever, an antiquary to whom almost every old parish church in the country is under a debt of obligation.

John Weever lived in the reign of Charles I. Noticing the neglect with which the memorials of the dead were, in his day, everywhere treated, he determined to perambulate the country for the purpose of recording such epitaphs of interest as still existed. The result of his labours he has enshrined in his "Antient Funerall Monuments," which was published in 1631, the year before his death.

Weever, on his visit to Fulham Church, noted eleven inscriptions, two only of which - those of Butts and Svanders - now exist. From Bowack, who wrote only seventy four years later, we gather that the whole of the inscriptions quoted by Weever, with the two exceptions mentioned, had already disappeared, a circumstance which shows how seriously the Church must have suffered during the Great Rebellion. In respect to the inscriptions which have perished, Weever's testimony fortunately finds support from other quarters. In a large volume, forming No. 874 of the Lansdown Manuscripts at the British Museum, is preserved a collection of "Church Notes," mainly in the handwriting of Nicholas Charles, Lancaster Herald. He visited several churches, including those of Fulham, Chelsea, Lambeth, etc. On one fly-leaf is the signature

"Nich. Charles
Lancaster
Anno Dni. 1610."

A defaced Monument formerly in Fulham Church.
From an engraving published by John Simco in 1794

The portion relating to Fulham appears to be in the handwriting of this herald. Other fly-leaves are signed by different members of the College of Arms.

The date of Charles's visit to Fulham is not given, but, as his "Notes" include the Bonde monument, which is dated 1600, it must have been subsequent to that year. Probably 1610 is about correct. The Fulham section of the manuscript occupies two pages (folio 82), the notes being divided into fourteen compartments, which contain sixteen coats of arms, twelve relating to monuments and four to shields in the windows of the Church. The herald's object appears to have been not so much to take full copies of the epitaphs as to obtain correct drawings of the arms. These are beautifully executed.

Harleian Manuscript No. 6072, in the British Museum, is another source of information regarding some of the non-existent inscriptions. The manuscript is a large volume containing miscellaneous entries of Church Notes, lists of knights, etc. The Fulham portion occupies two sides of a page (fo. 86^b). Against these notes is neither date nor signature, but, judging from internal evidence, they were doubtless written before 1600. On an otherwise blank page, at the end of the volume, is the following:

"The names of all the pishe Churches wthin London and the suburbes thereof as the(y) Remayne at this daye 1597 May 25."

In point of date, the last epitaph mentioned is that of Thomas Cleybroke, who died in 1587. Fulham Church must therefore have been visited by the herald between 1587 and 1597. The inscriptions given in the Harleian Manuscript are fuller than those in the Lansdown Manuscript, and agree pretty closely with Weever. The heraldry is meagre and poorly executed.

We will first take the inscriptions quoted by Weever and in the two manuscripts in the order of their dates.

The earliest recorded epitaph known to have existed in Fulham Church was one to the memory of John Sherburne or Shirebourne, who died in 1434. The tomb, according to Weever, was inscribed:

"Hic iacet Iohannes Sherburne Bachalaureus vtriusque Legis, quondam Archidiaconus Essex; qui ob. 1434."

(Translation: "Here lies John Sherburne, Bachelor of both Laws (i.e. Civil and Canon), formerly Archdeacon of Essex, who died 1434.)

In an Avisage Roll of the Manor of Fulham, 1401, occurs the name of John Archedēn. This John Archedēn (or Archdeacon) was doubtless John Sherburne.

We have already spoken of John Sherburne or Shirebourne in our account of Fulham House.

The second epitaph was to the memory of John Thorley. The inscription is recorded in the Harleian Manuscript as follows:

> "Orate pro anima Johis Thorley armigeri qui obijt penultimo die Mensis februarij Ao. Dni. 1445."
> (Translation: Pray for the soul of John Thorley, esquire, who died the last day but one in the month of February in the year of our Lord, 1445.) [i.e. 27 Feb. 1445-46.]
> Arms: *Dexter*: Arg., on a bend flory counter flory sa. 3 mullets pierced of the field. *Sinister*: Az., 2 bars gemelles or in chief a mullet; a chief charged within an armlet.

Nicholas Charles's "Notes" afford the following information:

> "John Thorley, Esquire, died in An° 1445."
> Arms: *Dexter*: Arg., on a bend flory counter flory sa. 3 mullets of the first impaling. *Sinister*: Az., 2 bars gemelles or surmounted of a mullet of the last a chief of the same.

Weever's copy of the inscription reads:

> "Orate pro anima Iohannis Thorley, Armigeri, qui obiit penultimo die men. Febr. Ann. Dom. 1445."

Little is known respecting John Thorley beyond the information furnished by his will. From this he appears to have been a man of considerable wealth, possessing property at Windsor, Putney, Fulham and Uxbridge. Three children are mentioned, Elizabeth, John and Thomas. In the registered copy of the will at the P.C.C. the name is written Chorley. It also appears in this form in the original index, though, in that lately printed, it is corrected to Chorley alias Thorley. The agreement of the Harleian and Lansdown manuscripts and Weever as to "Thorley" makes it evident that the copyist of the will must have blundered in writing "Chorley."

John Thorley's will, which is written in Latin, is dated 21 Dec. 1445 (P.C.C. 30 Luffenam). The date of proof is obliterated, but it was probably circa 1446. The following is an extract:

> "I John Chorley of sane mind and good memory, etc. My body to be buried in the Church of All Saints at Fulham if it fortune me from this infirmity there to depart this life, and if it fortune me to die in the suburbs of Wyndesore (Windsor), then to be buried in the Church of St. Andrew of Clyver (Clewer). If it fortune me to die at ffulham and there to be buried, I bequeath to the Vicar of the same church xx^s of good money and to the works of the church of ffulham xx^s and if in the parts of Wyndesore, to the Church of Clyever and to the works of the same xx^s.
>
> To my wife all my lands in ffulham co. Middlesex, which lately I acquired of John Sudbury, clerk.
>
> To my wife all my houses and lands in the Town of Wyndesore to put my son John to school while he live and if he die to dispose for my soul, the souls of my relations and the souls of my benefactors. To Elizabeth my daughter c^s in money, ij cups of silver, vj spoons of silver, one napkin holder and one book according to the discretion of my wife. To Thomas my son c^s in money, ij cups of silver, vj spoons, and one napkin holder and one book. To John my son c^s in money, ij cups of silver, vj spoons, etc., as to his brother."

Next we have the epitaph of John Fischer. Weever gives it:

> "Hic iacet Iohannes Fischer quondam Thesaurarius Domini Cardinalis Sancte Balbine et postea Hostiensis et Cantuariensis Archiepiscopi qui obijt 27 Aug. 1463."
>
> (Translation: Here lies John Fischer, at one time Treasurer to the Lord Cardinal of Santa Balbina and afterwards of Ostia [i.e. St. Ruffina] and Archbishop of Canterbury, who died 27 Aug. 1463.)

The allusion in the epitaph to John Fischer's connection with the household of John Kemp, Bishop of London and afterwards Archbishop of York and Canterbury, is interesting. In December 1439, Kemp, at that time Archbishop of York, was made by the Pope cardinal-priest of (with the title of) Santa Balbina. This explains the allusion, "Sancte Balbine," the common mediæval form of Sanctæ Balbinæ. When, in 1452, Kemp was translated to the see of Canterbury, he was made by the Pope cardinal-bishop of (with the title of) Santa Ruffina. His nephew, Thomas Kemp, Bishop of London, thus summed up his uncle's preferments: "Bis primas, ter præsul erat, bis cardine functus." To which old Fuller adds: "Et dixit legem bis cancellarius Angles."

The inscription on Archbishop Kemp's monument at Canterbury describes him as "tituli S^{ce} Rufine sacrosancte ecclesie Romane Episcopus Cardinalis," etc. Santa Ruffina was the titular church which (so far) belonged to the cardinal-bishop of Ostia, close to which town it lies. This explains the allusion in the Fulham epitaph to "postea Hostiensis" or Ostiensis.

In the Harleian Manuscript the herald writes:

"Hic Jacet Johes Fisher quondam thesaurarius dni. Cardinalis Sci. Balbini et postea Hostiensi in Cantuarens Arch. qui obijt 27 August 1452."
Arms: Arg., on a chevron between 3 demi-lions issuant gu. 5 bezants.

Nicholas Charles in the Lansdown Manuscript writes:

"John ffisher Tresorer to ye L: Cardinal Archbishopp of Canterbury, who died in An° 1452."
Arms: On a chevron between 3 demi-lions rampant, 5 roundels.

It will be noticed that Weever gives the date of Fischer's death as 1463. In the Harleian Manuscript the date, though "overwritten," is clearly intended for 1452. Charles also gives this date, which is shown to be correct by the will, which was proved in November 1453.

The will of John Fischer, dated 27 Aug. 1452, is preserved in the Library of Lambeth Palace (Reg. Kemp 259a). Its presence here is doubtless accounted for by his connection with the household of the Archbishop. It is partly in Latin and partly in English. The following is an extract:

"On Sunday the 27th day of August in the year of the reign of Henry the Sixth after the Conquest the 30th, I John ffissher make this my present testament in this manner. In the first place I will that my body be buried in the Church of Fulham. I bequeath to the Church aforesaid for breaking of the ground where my body should have sepulture vj^s

viij^d. and to the lights in the Church aforesaid vj^s. I leave to the (Easter) sepulchre in the said Church vj^s viij^d. I will that my executors ordain in the day of my sepulture for my sepulchre £4 sterling in wax (i.e. tapers)."

The will was proved before John Stoke, chancellor to Archbishop Kemp.

It is a somewhat singular fact that, out of all the rectors and vicars of the parish, only six are known to have been buried at Fulham. The epitaph to William Harvey or Hervey, as copied by Weever, read:

"Hic iacet Magister Willelmus Harvy nuper vicarius istius Ecclesie qui ob. 5 die Nouemb. 1471."
(Translation: Here lies Master William Harvey, sometime vicar of this church, who died 5th day of November 1471.)

In the Harleian Manuscript the inscription similarly reads:

"Hic Iacett rnagister Willmus Harvy nup vicarius istius ecctie qui obiit 5° die Novembris Anno Dni 1471."

The arms are blazoned:

Or., a chev. between three leopards' faces gules, within a bordure azure.

Down to about the end of the last century there existed at Fulham Church a mutilated brass, representing a priest, supposed to be William Harvey.

The fifth epitaph refers to Lora, daughter of Sir John Blount, third Baron of Mountjoy of Thurston. As the Court Rolls of the Manor are silent with regard to the name, it seems improbable that the Blounts lived at Fulham.

Sir John, who died in 1485, was Governor of Guisnes. He married Lora, daughter of Sir Edward Berkeley, of Beverstone Castle, co. Gloucester. His issue were William, his heir, Rowland, who died *s. p.* 1509, Lora, who died 6 Feb. 1480-81, and was buried at Fulham, and Constantia, who married Sir Thomas Tyrrell of Heron Hall, Essex.

Supposed brass to the Rev. William Harvey.
From an engraving published by John Simco in 1794

The epitaph, as copied by Weever, read:

> "Hic iacet Lora filia Iohannis Blount, militis Domini Mountioy, & Lore vxoris eius, que obiit 6 die mens. Febr. Ann. Dom. 1480. Cuius anime Deus sis propitius."
> (Translation: Here lies Lora, daughter of John Blount, Lord Mountjoy, and Lora his wife, who died the 6th day of the month of February 1480. To whose soul God be merciful.)

The text in the Harleian Manuscript reads:

> "Hic jacet Lora filia Johis Blunt, militis Dni Mountioy et Lora uxoris eius que obijt 6° die mensis ffebruarij Ano. Dni. 1480."

The shield for the arms the herald was left blank.
The earliest English epitaph belonged to the year 1503. Weever gives it:

> "Pray for the sowls of Iohn Long gentylman, Katherin and Alice his wyfs. Who died the x of March on thowsand fyve hundryd and three. On whos sowls and all Christen sowls Iesu haue mercy.

<u>Fili redemptor mundi Deus miserere nobis</u>
Sancta Trinitas vnus Dens miserere nobis
Spiritus Sanctus Deus miserere nobis."

Translation:
O God, the Son, Redeemer of the world; have mercy upon us.
O Holy Trinity, One God; have mercy upon us.
O God, the Holy Ghost; have mercy upon us.

Perhaps the most important of the monuments which have perished was that which recorded the memory of Sir Sampson Norton. As copied by Weever the inscription ran:

"Of your cherite pray for the soul of Sir Sampson Norton knyght, late Master of the Ordinance of warre with kyng Henry the eyght, and for the soul of Dame Elysabeth hys wyff Whyche Syr Sampson decessed the eyght day of February on thowsand fyve hundryd and seuentene."

Nicholas Charles gives the following details:

"In the Quyre on ye North side:
Sr Sampson Norton, knight, and Dame Elizabeth his wiffe, basse D: to . . . L. Zouche, who died 1517. He was M^r [Master] of ye Ordinance of Warre to K. H. 8."

The arms as blazoned by Charles were:

I. Gu., three swords arg. their pomels meeting in fess point or, on a chief or a lion passant gu. between two maunches ermine. *Crest*: On a wreath a demi-dragon holding a sword. II. The same impaling gu. twelve bezants and a canton erm. over all a bend sinister az.

In the Harleian Manuscript the epitaph reads:

"Of your chaitye pray for the soule of Sampson Norton knight Late M^r of the ordinance of Warre wth king Henry the eight and for the soule of Dame Elisabeth his Wife, w^h Mr Sampson deceased the 8 of february 1517."
Arms: Per pale, *Dexter*: Az., on a chief of the last a talbot stat. between 2 water bougets erm. *Sinister*: Semèe of roundels a bend sinister and a canton ermine.

The first we hear of Sir Sampson Norton is in the reign of Edward IV. He was engaged in Brittany under Lord Brooke about 1483. On 6 Aug. 1486, he was appointed a commissioner to enquire what wool was exported from Chichester without the royal license. Subsequently he became serjeant porter of Calais. From the Chester "Recognizance Rolls" it appears that Sir Sampson was appointed Constable of Flint Castle on 10 April 1495. During the reigns of Henry VII and Henry VIII he held the post of Surveyor of the Ordnance, a position of much importance. At Arras, in 1512, Sir Sampson was taken prisoner and was liberated only after much difficulty. In Feb. 1514-15 he was made marshal of Tournay. While in this position, he was nearly killed by a mutiny of the soldiery, who wanted their pay.

Sir Sampson, as stated by Nicholas Charles, married Elizabeth, an illegitimate daughter of John, 7th Baron Zouche. He resided at Hore's tenement, Parson's Green, which he left to his cousin, John Norton.

Bowack writes:

> "On the left hand (of the chancel) is a very ancient monument against the wall . . . with oak leaves, flowers and other Antique ornaments, and within a large nitch in Brass, plates and the effigies of a man and woman kneeling with an Inscription which is defac'd."

This, there can be little doubt, was the Norton tomb. Lysons also mentions it.

Next we come to the epitaph on George Chauncey, Receiver-General to Bishop Fitzjames. Weever gives it:

> "Hic iacet Georgius Chauncy quondam Receptor generalis Reuerendi Patris Domini Ric. Fitz Iames Londin. Episcopi, qui obiit decimo nono die Decembris, Ann. Dom. 1520."
> (Translation: Here lies George Chauncey, formerly receiver general to the Rev. Father in God, Richard Fitzjames, Bishop of London, who died 19th day of Dec. in the year of Our Lord 1520.)

Nicholas Charles writes:

> "George Chauncey Receiver Generall to the late Reverend Ric. Fitz James Bishopp of London who died 9 December 1520."

He blazons the arms:

> I. A cross moline, on a chief a lion passant impaling a bend compony cotised. II. The former coat, the cross charged with an annulet, impaling a lion ramp. debruised by a bendlet.

Charles incorrectly gives the date of Chauncey's death as 9th, instead of 19th, December, 1520.
The Harleian Manuscript reads:

> "Hic Jacet Geoigius Chauncy quondam Receptor Generalis Reuerend Patris Dni. Ric. Fitz James Lond. Ep. qui obijt decimo nono die Decembris Ano. Dni. 1520."
> Arms: *Dexter*: A cross flory on a chief a lion passant. *Sinister*: A lion rampant or, debruised by a bendlet gules.

Supposed brass to Sir Sampson Norton.
From an engraving published by John Simco in 1794

The will of George Chauncey, dated 13 Dec. 1520, was proved 4 May 1521 (P.C.C. 9 Maynwaring). The following is an extract:

"I George Chauncy of ffullhm in the Countie of Mydd. hoole of mynde and syke in bodye make my testament and last will in thise wis ffirst I bequeth my Soule to almyghty god to our lady seint Mary Virgine and to all the holly company of heyven and my body to be buryed before the Image of the Crucifix in the parissh Churche of ffulhm and to the reparacions of the said Church I bequethe vj^s viij^d aboue all ffunerall and necessarie expences I bequethe to the highe aulter at Pevensay for tythes necligently forgoten or to lytill paid ten shelinges To Seint Richard Schryne of Chychestre x^s To Saint Arkenwold Shryne in pawlis Church iij^s iiij^d To thold warkes of paules vj^s viij^d I will incontynent after my dethe be said for my soule at Scali Celi at Westm xxx masses whereof xv masses to be said by ten of the blaeke frieris and xv by x of the whyte ffriers in fflet strete and those frieres to be assigned by theire priors or in theire absence by the priors deputies of the said places and euery prior to haue xij^d and of theire Charite to say masse for me when it shall please them and euery of the said x and x friers to have v^d for eu'y masse. I bequeth toward the Repacion of euery housse of frieris in London vj^s viij^d; to euery o my lord of london doctors chaplayn iij^s iiij^d to euery other chaplen of his xij^d apece To Maister Penitanciary of Paules iij^s iiij^d [i. e. the prebendary of St. Pancras to whose stall was annexed the office of Penitentiary]. I bequethe to Maister John broke of Oxforde to syng for my soule iij yeris next following the daye of my dethe xviij^{li} that is to say euery yere vj^{li}. To the Vicar of ffulhm for tythes forgoten x^s.

The next epitaph was to a member of a well-known Fulham family, the Stourtons of Fulham Hall. Weever gives it:

"Hic iacet Anna Sturton filia Iohannis Sturton Domini de Sturton, & Domine Katherine vxoris eius. Que quidem Anna obiit in Assumptionem beate Marie Virginis, Ann. Dom. 1533."
(Translation: Here lies Anne Stourton, daughter of John Lord Stourton and the Lady Katherine his wife. This same Anna died on the Feast of the Assumption of the Blessed Virgin in the year of Our Lord 1533.)

Nicholas Charles has the following:

"Anne, D. to John Lord Stourton and of Katherine his wiff: died 1483.

He blazons the arms:

Sa., a bend or between six fountains; imp. gu. an escutcheon within an orle of martlets arg. (Chidiok).

The Harleian Manuscript reads:

> "Hic Jacett Anna Sturtō filia Johis Sturtō dni. de Sturtō et Dne. Katherine uxore eius Quæ quidem Anna obijt in Assunpcon beate Marie Virgine 1533."
> Arms: *Dexter*: A bend between six fountains. *Sinister*: An escutcheon in an orle of eleven martlets.

There is some doubt as to the correct date of Anne Stourton's death. The Harleian Manuscript and Weever agree in fixing it on the Feast of the Assumption of the Virgin Mary 1533 (i.e. 15 Aug. 1533), while Nicholas Charles writes 1483. The latter date appears to be the more probable, for the Stourtons ceased to be connected with Fulham, circa 1518. Further, the absence of any mention of her name in the will of her father, dated 18 Aug. 1484, suggests that she predeceased him. The arms given in the Harleian and Lansdown Manuscripts, as those of Anne Stourton, are those of her grand parents, William second Lord Stourton and Margaret Chidiok.

The Harleian Manuscript gives the following:

> "Heere lyeth buryed the body of Thomas Claybroke sonne of Steven Claybrooke gent. wh. Thomas dyed the 24 of August 1587."
> Arms. Arg., a cross formèe gu. *Crest*: Issuant out of a ducal coronet an ostrich's head erm. winged or, holding in the beak a horse-shoe.

Nicholas Charles writes:

> "Thos Claybrooke sonne to Steven Claybrooke, Esq., died . . ."

He blazons the arms:

> Arg., a cross patèe gu. *Crest*: On a coronet or a demi-ostrich arg. holding in its beak a horseshoe az.

"Cross patèe" is an error for "Cross formèe." The date of Thomas Cleybroke's death, as recorded in the Harleian Manuscript epitaph, must be wrong, as his will was dated 2 Sept. and proved 13 October 1587.

During the Tudor period the Cleybrokes held extensive

possessions in Fulham and Hammersmith. Of the former we shall speak under Cleybroke House.

To Nicholas Charles we are indebted for the following fragment:

"Sr Thomas Morgan of . . . in . . . died 159 . . . married . . . "

This refers to Sir Thomas Morgan of Aston, co. Hereford, who died at Fulham 22 December 1595. The arms, as blazoned by Charles, were:

I. Quarterly of nine, I. Or, a griffin rampant sa.; 2. Arg., three bucks' (bulls') heads caboshed sa. (Morgan of Tredegar); 3. Arg., a lion rampant gu. (Morgan ap Meredith); 4. Sa., a cross engr. between four spears' heads arg. (Prosser); 5. Or, a lion ramp. regardant sa. (Gwaethroed); 6. Sa., a lion rampant arg. (Odwyn ap Teith Walch); 7. Gu., three chevronels arg. (Llewellyn ap Tror or Morgam Gam); 8. Gu., fretty arg. a fess az. (Norris); 9. Sa., billetty and a cross flory arg. (Norris). *Crest*: On a wreath a stag's head couped or. *Motto*: "Noli altum sapere." II. The same impaling; Paly or and gu. a bordure engr. az. (Merode.)

The will of Sir Thomas Morgan, dated 18 Dec. 1595, was proved 3 March 1595-96 (P.C.C. 18 Drake). The following is an abstract:

"I Thomas Morgan, knight, being weake in body, *etc*. To my wife Dame Anna de Merode generallie all such goodes, *etc*., as remaynes in the handes of the Lady Merode and Petersom her mother and Christopher Kennell. To my daughter Anne Morgan all somes due unto me from her Maiestie for her marriage portion and if she die under 16 or before marriage her said portion to my sonne Morrice Morgan and if he be not then living said portion to my wife. To Edward Morgan my sonne my sorrell gelding and fifteene poundes to be given oute of my armes in his purse and my shorte clothe shagg cloake. To my servaunte William Powell fortie shillinges in his purse wth the gelding and nagge he hath alreadie in his custody. To my nurse twentie nobles condiconallie that Medlicote and my nurse carrie over my child and goodes not at theire charg. To Lynkine my maide servant fortie shillinges in her purse and to be transported over.

My said wife my executrix and my Lord Hunsdon Lord Chamberleyne of her princelie maiesties most honorable houshould my Overseer wth

Robert Horseman and Spero Pottingarre my good and trustie frendes."

At the date of his will, Sir Thomas was probably in Holland, hence the allusion to the conveyance of his child, maidservant and goods to England. In the Probate Act Book is the following:

"1595-96 Mar. 3, Probate of the will of Sr Thomas Morgan, knight, late of ffulham co. Midd^x to Thos. Iles Notary Public, Proctor for Lady Anne de Merode ats Morgan relict of said deceased and executrix."

"Late of ffulham" suggests that the testator's death occurred at Fulham, probably at Brightwell's, Parson's Green. The Burial Registers of St. Michael, Wood Street, record:

1596-97 Jan. 22. Thomas s. of Sr Thomas and the Ladie Morgan buried att ffulham.

Anciently there existed at the upper end of the chancel a noble monument, to the memory of Sir William Billesbie. The inscription as recorded by Stow read:

"Hic situs est Gulielmus Billesby Eques Auratus, Fisci Regii ostiarius, cum Anna Uxore, è Familia Brogravia quæ illi peperit duas Filias, Franciscam & Margaretam todidemque Filios, qui infantes objerunt.
Obiit ille 25 Martii 1607.
Illa 27 Maii 1608.
Francisca Filia primogenita, primum nupta Joanni Madocks Armigero, postea Thomæ Walker Armigero Fisci Regii ostiario. Obiit die 6 Nouembris 1607, & hic parentibus tumulatur. Margar. altera Filia enupta Hugoni Parlor de Plumsted Armigero. Obiit & in Ecclesia Sanct. Margaretæ Westmonasterii . . . Requieseit."

(Translation: Here lies Sir William Billesbie, knight, doorkeeper of the royal treasury, with Anna his wife, of the family of Brogravia, who bore to him two daughters, Frances and Margaret, the same number of sons who died in infancy.
He died 25 March 1607.
She died 27 May 1608.
Frances, the elder daughter, married, first, John Maddocks, gentleman, afterwards Thomas Walker, gentleman, doorkeeper of the royal treasury. She died 6 Nov. 1607, and was here buried with her parents. Margaret, the other daughter, married Hugh Parlor, of Plumstead,

gentleman. She died and lies interred in the church of St. Margaret, Westminster.)

Bowack quotes the above inscription from Stow, a circumstance which shows that, although he wrote only a century after the death of Sir William Billesbie, the inscription had already become illegible. Indeed, further on, Bowack tells us that he found in the chancel a large stone, the inscription of which was gone, with the effigy of an armed man. At each corner of this stone were cut the arms. "Probably," he adds, "this may be the gravestone of Sr William Billesby before mention'd, taken notice of by Stow." The epitaph is quoted in Strype's Stow, 1754.

Sir William Billesbie's will, dated 24 Dec. 1607, was proved 7 April 1608 (P.C.C. 37 Windebank). From it we take the following:

"I Sr William Billesbie of ffulham, knight, *etc.*, To Anne my wife my two crofts called Ores Crofts situate neere Parsons Green for life and at her death the same and also my two closes called Proffits feild in the parish of ffulham to my sonne in lawe Thomas Walker of Warfeilde co. Berks., Esq., and to my daughter Frances his now wife and heirs male of their two bodies and in default to Wm. Parlor my grandchild and his heirs for ever. To my grandchild Wm. Maddocks and his heirs for ever a messuage, one orchard and one garden which I purchased of Sr Thomas Knowles, kt. To Anne Maddocks my grandchild £200. To Margaret Maddocks and Marie Maddocks my two grandchildren £100 each. To the poore people of the pishe of ffulham aforesaid, £3. 6. 8."

Sir William Billesbie was a member of the ancient family of Billesbie of Billesbie, co. Lincoln, his great grandfather being Sir Andrew Billesbie of Billesbic, knight. He was knighted by James I, 14 March 1603-04.

According to Harleian Manuscript 1551, the arms of Sir William Billesbie were:

Arg. a chevron sa. between 3 castles of last fined proper.

Lady Billesbie's will, dated 12 May 1608, was proved 30 May 1608 (P.C.C. 39 Windebanck). From it we take the following:

"I Dame Anne Billesbie of Westminster, widowe. To be buried at discretion of executrix. To my two grandchildren William Madox and

William Parler my best chaine of goulde. To my grandchild Anne Madox my best jewell, and to her, to Margarett Madox, Marie Madox, Thomasine Parlor, and Anne Parler to each of them a chamber reddie furnished. To Marie Bowghton one basonne and ewer. To Thomas Madox my grandchild a chambre reddie furnished and £20. To Edward Parler £10. To ffraunces Parler £10 at full age. To my nephew Jerome Brograve one Ringe with a Deathes heade and to Christian his wife a Sarianntes Ring. To my sister-in-lawe Jane Brograve one Ringe of Golde. To the poore of the parrishe of ffullham £5. Residue to my daughter ffraunces Walker, and she sole executrix.

PEDIGREE OF THE BILLESBIE FAMILY

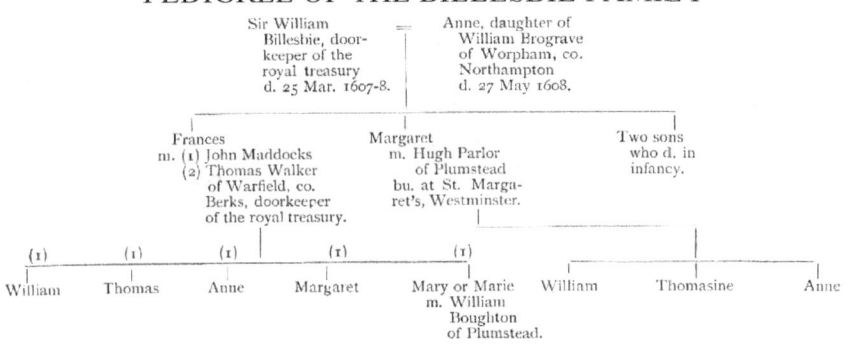

```
        Sir William           =   Anne, daughter of
        Billesbie, door-          William Brograve
        keeper of the             of Worpham, co.
        royal treasury            Northampton
        d. 25 Mar. 1607-8.        d. 27 May 1608.
        ┌─────────────────────────┼─────────────────────────┐
     Frances                   Margaret                  Two sons
  m. (1) John Maddocks       m. Hugh Parlor             who d. in
     (2) Thomas Walker          of Plumstead             infancy.
        of Warfield, co.        bu. at St. Marga-
        Berks, doorkeeper       ret's, Westminster.
        of the royal treasury.
 (1)   (1)   (1)    (1)         (1)
William Thomas Anne Margaret  Mary or Marie  William  Thomasine  Anne
                              m. William
                              Boughton
                              of Plumstead.
```

The following are a few other notices of monumental inscriptions now non-existent. Bowack states that, in the middle of the north aisle, there was a small marble monument which was inscribed:

> "Near this place lyes Interr'd the Body of Abraham Downing, Esq., Serjant Skinner to his Majesty Charles II. He married Anne, the daughter of Wm. Prew, rector of Ditton in Kent, and had by her four children, Richard now surviving, and William, Prudence and Anne, buried near this place. He departed this life January the 19th, 1676, aged 59 years."

No trace of it was found during the rebuilding of 1880-81.

Administration of the goods, etc., of Abraham Downing, described as "late of the parish of St. Clement's Danes, co. Middlesex, deceased," was granted to Anne Downing, his relict, 27 Jan. 1676-77.

> "Alexander Marshall | ex honesta familia oriundus | Dorotheam | filiam Francisci Smith generosi | uxorem duxit | Prolem non reliquit | at | probitate et ingenio | longior huic facta est quam data vita fuit | . Obiit Decembris 7 | A.D. 1682."

(Translation: Alexander Marshall, descended from an honourable family. He married Dorothea, daughter of Francis Smith of noble birth. He left no issue, but, by reason of his integrity and gifts, he will live longer than the life which was vouchsafed him. He died 7 Dec. 1682.)

This stone fell to pieces on the demolition of the Church in 1880.

An old stone in the floor of the north aisle recorded the memory of Mrs. Katherine Gee. It was inscribed:

> "Here lyes the Body of Mrs. Katherine Gee wife of Samuel Gee of London who departed this life the viii day of April Anno Dom . . . "

The year was illegible. The Church Registers record:

> 1686 The wife of Mr. Sam. Gee bu. 15 of Apl.

In the minutes of a Vestry held 11 May 1687, is the following:

> "At a Vestry held the day and yeare aboue written we whose names are vnd^r written doe giue leave y^t Mr. Samuell Gee may haue liberty to lay a graue stone of black marble vpon his wife's graue being at ye ffoot of ye stayers goeing vp the West Gallery and there be continued and remain in consideracon whereof the said Mr. Gee doth p^{r}mise to giue to the psent Churchwarden Mr. Robert Limpany fiue guineas to be by the said Churchwarden layd out at his discreccon in or about the church."

In 1880 the stone fell to pieces upon removal.

> "Thomas Gilbert, Esq., | died Friday August 20 | 1750 Aged 62 years | Likewise Miss Martha | Gilbert his daughter | died June 2 1759 | Aged 25 years."

This stone fell to pieces upon its removal in 1880.

Faulkner states that next to the Carlos stone there was one inscribed:

"Samuel Lancelot Jarvis, Esq.; a distinguished officer in North America, d. Dec. 11, 1795, aged 59 years."

This stone was not found during the rebuilding of the Church in 1880-81.

"Here lyeth | the Body of Mary, | Daughter of W. Miller, Esq., | who departed this life | v of D . . . | ye 29th year of her age."

This stone fell to pieces when the Church was pulled down in 1880.

The following noteworthy persons have been buried at Fulham, though no epitaphs to them are recorded.

In the Commissary Court of the Bishop of London (vol. I, 1374-1400) is preserved a copy of the will of Richard Colman, dated 12 Kalend July 1376, and proved 5 Kal. Aug. 1376. In it he directs that he shall be buried in the churchyard of "All Saints of ffulham." To the High Altar of the same Church he left "xij^s"; to the "works" of the said Church, "xl^s," and to the "clerk" of the same, "vj^d." He also left "To the lights burning above the bodies deceased in the said church, xij^d." The Colmans were an old Fulham family. They are mentioned in the Court Rolls down to 1422.

Near the grave of his patron, Bishop Compton, was once a stone to the memory of the Rev. Richard Fiddes. The Church Registers record:

1725. The rev^d Richd Fiddes D D bu. 11 July.

The Rev. Richard Fiddes, D.D., was born in Yorkshire in 1671. He is chiefly known as a religious writer. His principal works are "Theologia Speculativa" (1718); "Theologia Practiva" (1720); and "Life of Cardinal Wolsey" (1724). He has been described as ingenious rather than learned, a clever rhetorician but an inaccurate thinker. His "Life of Cardinal Wolsey " is by far his best known work.

The following note occurs in the manuscripts of Peter Le Neve:

"Lady Frazier buried at Fulham Sunday Dec 22. 1695. Dr Frazier her son mad."

The Church Registers record:

1695. The Lady Fraisior bu. 22 Dec.

William Grene, a distinguished musician, in his will, dated 14 Jan. 1546-47, describes himself as "late of Whaplode in Holland in the countie of Lincoln, gentilman." He directed that his body should be buried in the Church of Fulham, and gave to the "high aulter" there "iij^s iiij^d." To Sir Robert Kyrkham, kt., he gave his "fiue vyalls," and to the parish church of Whaplode his "regalls." One of the witnesses to his will was "William Beck, singingman."

An epitaph formerly existed to the memory of Robert Powlett, who died in 1723. In his will, dated 12 Mar. 1710-11, proved 14 Nov. 1723 (P.C.C. 241 Buckingham), he describes himself as of "Clement's Inn in the county of Middlesex, gentleman." To his son William he left all his "written books of Precedents." He married Alice, daughter of Matthew Thorpe. He had two nieces, Margaret Jones, who married Edmund Gibson, Bishop of London, and Elizabeth Jones, who became the wife of Dr. John Bettesworth.

Bowack's "Supplement" (1706) contains the following:

"Under the Communion table, in the Chancel, lie interr'd in a small Vault made about Four Years Ago the Bodies of the Honourable the Lady Katherine Seymour, grandmother of his Grace the present Duke of Sommerset, and also of Sir John Elwes, of Grove House, Sands End."

The Church Registers record:

1700. The Lady Catherin Seaymor barroness St. Martens ffeilds bu. 5 Mar.

She was the daughter of Sir Robert Lee, of Billesley, co. Warwick, and second wife of Sir Francis Seymour, created, in 1641, Baron Seymour of Trowbridge, and died in 1671.

Of Sir John Elwes we shall speak under "Grove House."

Richard Zouch, LL.D., the eminent English jurist, was born at Ansley, in Wiltshire, about 1590. He was the. son of Francis Zouch by his wife, Philippa, daughter of George Ludlow of Hill Deveral, Wilts. He was descended, through his ancestors, the Lords Zouche, from the Dukes of Brittany. He was educated at Winchester and Oxford. He became Fellow of New College in 1609, D.C.L. in 1619, and regius professor of civil law in the following year. He was M. P. for Hythe in 1621. He became Chancellor of the diocese of Oxford, principal of St. Alban Hall and Judge of the High Court of Admiralty.

Dr. Zouch was the author of "The Dove," a short and uninteresting poem, published in 1613, and of several treatises on law, on which he was regarded as the highest authority of his time. One of his daughters, Katherine, married William Hinson alias Powell, afterwards Sir William Powell, of Fulham.

Dr. Zouch died in his lodgings at Doctors' Commons, 1 March 1660-61, and was buried in Fulham Church near the grave of his daughter Katherine. His will, dated 16 Oct. 1660, was proved 25 April 1662. From it we take the following:

> "I Richard Zouch judge of the Admiralty. To be buried without needless ceremonies and expences. My estate to be divided into 3 parts, one to my wife Sara Zouch, another to my son Richard Zouch and the third to my daughters Anne Zouch and Sara Zouch. My wife and son Richard to be joint executors."

The Fulham Church Registers contain several entries relating to the Zouches.

Fulham Church Monuments Still Extant

We will now pay a visit to the monuments which still exist in Fulham Church, commencing with the Chancel.

Against the north wall of the chancel is an elaborate mural monument, about ten feet in height, to the memory of Sir Thomas Smith, of whom we shall speak in our account of Brightwell's.

This large monument is in a good state of preservation. In the centre of the pediment, on a black marble slab, supported by two Corinthian columns, is the following inscription:

"D.O.M. | Thomas Smitho Eqviti Avrato Regiæ Ma^ti | A supplicvm Libellis et ab epistolis Latinis | Viro Doetrina Prvdentiaq. singvlari | Franeisca Gvil: Baronis Chandos filia | Opt. Marito conivx Mœstiss. | Plorans posvit | Obiit xxviii die Novr MDCIX."
(Translation: To the Glory of Almighty God. To Sir Thomas Smith, knight, Master of Requests and Latin Secretary to the King's Majesty, a man of remarkable learning and foresight, Frances, daughter of William, Baron Chandos, his most disconsolate wife, weeping, has erected [this monument] to her excellent husband. He died 28th day of Nov. 1609.)

The monument is surmounted by the following arms:

Dexter: Az., a lion rampant or, langued gu., on a chief arg., three torteaux (Smith). *Sinister*: Quarterly, (1) and (4), Arg., on a cross sa., a leopard's face or (Brydges); (2), Or, a pile gu. (Chandos); (3), Arg., a fess between three martlets sa. (Berkeley); over all a crescent gu., for difference.

The monument originally stood on the south side of the chancel. During the alterations of 1840-41, it was moved to a position similar to that which it now occupies. In 1842 it was restored by Charles, Duke of Richmond, a descendant of Margaret, the only surviving child of Sir Thomas Smith.

On the south side of the chancel is a marble monument to the memory of Lady Margaret Legh, wife of Sir Peter Legh, of Lyme, Cheshire.

The monument, which is about twelve feet in height, is remarkably fine. In an arch is the effigy of Lady Legh rather less than life size. She is seated, habited in stiff Elizabethan costume. On her right arm she holds an infant. Her left hand is pressed against her breast. She wears a ruff, and from her hair, which is "curled, frizzled and crisped," depends a hood. On a pedestal, to the right is a second child, and to the left is an hour-glass. On either side of the monument are Corinthian columns, terminating in gilt capitals. Above are the following arms:

Dexter: Quarterly of nine, (I), Sa., in an orle of ten mullets or, a man's arm couped at the shoulder, in armour proper, the hand clenching a standard to the sinister gu.; (2), Gu., a cross engrailed arg. (paternal coat of Legh); (3), Or, three lozenges az. (Baguley); (4), Az., a chevron arg. between three crowns or (De Corona); (5), Arg., a pale lozengy sa. (Daniers); (6), Arg., a cross sa. in the first quarter a fleur-de-lis of the second (Haydock); (7), Vert, a chevron between three cross crosslets or (Writington); (8), Arg., a mullet pierced sa. (Aston); (9), Lozengy sa. and arg. (Croft). *Sinister*: Quarterly of ten, (I), Arg., a saltier gu. (Gerard); (2), Az., a lion rampant arg. crowned or (Byrn); (3), Az., a lion rampant arg. (Windle); (4), Arg., two bendlets az. enclosing three torteaux (Ince); (5), Arg., a bend engrailed sa., in chief an escallop gu. (Radcliffe); (6), Az., a cross patonce between four martlets arg. (Plessington); (7), Arg., a lion rampant gu. (Balderston); (8), Arg., a cross raguly gu. (Lawrence); (9), Arg., two bars gu., in chief three mullets of the second (Washington); (10), Az., a chevron between three covered cups or (Butler).

Monument to Sir Thomas Smith.
From a photograph by Mr. T. S. Smith, 1896

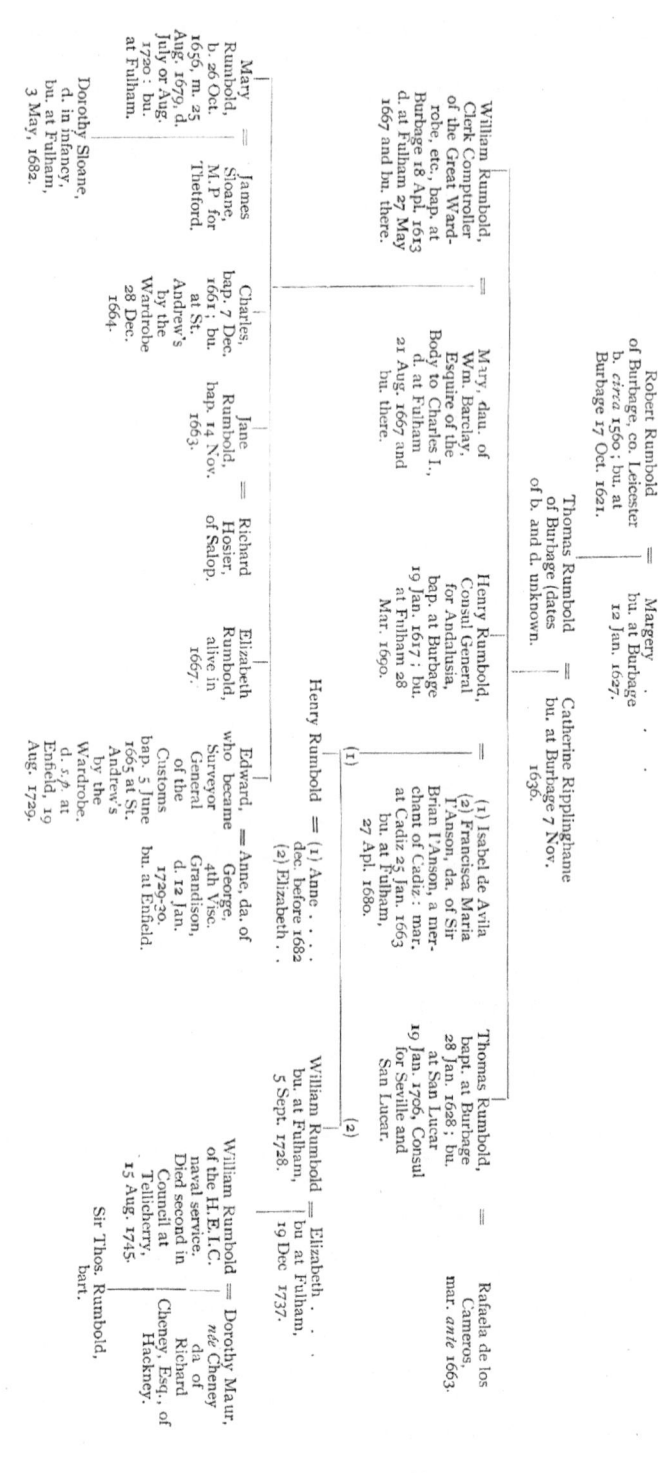

PEDIGREE OF RUMBOLD FAMILY.

Robert Rumbold of Burbage, co. Leicester, b. circa 1560; bu. at Burbage 17 Oct. 1621. = **Margery** bu. at Burbage 12 Jan. 1627.

Children:

- **William Rumbold**, Clerk Comptroller of the Great Wardrobe, etc., bap. at Burbage 18 Apl. 1613, d. at Fulham 27 May 1667 and bu. there. = **Mary**, dau. of Wm. Barclay, Esquire of the Body to Charles I., d. at Fulham 21 Aug. 1667 and bu. there.
- **Henry Rumbold**, Consul General for Andalusia, bap. at Burbage 19 Jan. 1617; bu. at Fulham 28 Mar. 1690. = (1) **Isabel de Avila** (2) **Francisca Maria I'Anson**, da. of Sir Brian I'Anson, a merchant of Cadiz; mar. at Cadiz 25 Jan. 1663, bu. at Fulham, 27 Apl. 1680.
- **Thomas Rumbold** of Burbage (dates of b. and d. unknown). = **Catherine Ripplinghame** bu. at Burbage 7 Nov. 1636.

Children of William Rumbold and Mary Barclay:

- **Mary Rumbold**, b. 26 Oct. 1655, m. 25 Aug. 1679, d. July or Aug. 1720; bu. at Fulham. = **James Sloane**, M.P. for Thetford.
- **Charles**, bap. 7 Dec. 1661; bu. at St. Andrew's by the Wardrobe 28 Dec. 1664.
- **Jane Rumbold**, bap. 14 Nov. 1663. = **Richard Hosier, of Salop.**
- **Elizabeth Rumbold**, alive in 1667.
- **Edward**, who became Surveyor General of the Customs bap. 5 June 1665 at St. Andrew's Wardrobe, bu. at Enfield. = **Anne**, da. of George, 4th Visc. Grandison, d. 12 Jan. 1729-30.
- **Henry Rumbold** = (1) **Anne . . . .** dec. before 1682 (2) **Elizabeth . .**

Child of Mary Rumbold and James Sloane:
- **Dorothy Sloane**, d. in infancy, bu. at Fulham, 3 May, 1682.

Children of Henry Rumbold (Consul General):

(1)
- **Thomas Rumbold**, bapt. at Burbage 28 Jan. 1648; bu. at San Lucar. = **Rafaela de los Cameros**, mar. ante 1663.

(2)
- **William Rumbold**, bu. at Fulham, 5 Sept. 1728. = **Elizabeth . . .** bu. at Fulham, 19 Dec 1737.

Child of Thomas Rumbold and Rafaela:
- **William Rumbold** of the H.E.I.C. Died second in Council at Tellicherry, 15 Aug. 1745. = **Dorothy Maur**, née Cheney da. of Richard Cheney, Esq., of Hackney.

Thomas Rumbold, Consul for Seville and San Lucar. 19 Jan. 1706.

- **Sir Thos. Rumbold, bart.**

382

A black marble slab at the foot of the monument is inscribed:

"To ye Memory | or | what else dearer remayneth of yt Verteovs Lady La: Margaret Legh | Davghter | of him, yt sometimes was Sr Gilbet gerard Knight & M^r of ye | Rolles in ye High Co: of Chancery | wife | To Sr Peter Legh of Lime in ye Covntie of Chester, K. & by him ye | mother of 7 | sones, Peirce, Fravnces, Radcliffe, Thomas, Peter, Gilbert, | Iohn, wth 2 davghters Anne & Katherine of w^{ch} | Radcliffe, Gilbert, Iohn | deceased infants ye rest yet svrviving to ye happye increase of ther hovse, | Ye yeares ye she enioyd ye world were 33, y^t her hvsband enioyd her 17 | at wch period she yeelded her sovle to ye blessednesse of long rest | & her body to this earth Ivl. 23. 1603 | This inscription in ye note of piety & love | by her sad hvsband is here | devotedly placed."

Stow and Bowack describe the monument.

During the alterations in 1840-41, the monument, which originally stood on the north side of the chancel, near the north door, was taken down and built into the south wall of the sacrarium. In 1842 it was completely restored by Mr. Thomas Legh of Lyme, a lineal descendant of Lady Legh. Originally iron rails protected the base.

Lady Margaret Legh was the daughter of Sir Gilbert Gerard, Master of the Rolls, by his wife, Anne, daughter and heiress of Thomas Radcliffe of Wilmerley. Her grandparents were James Gerard, second son of William Gerard of Ince, and Margaret his wife, daughter of John Holcroft of Holcroft. She was born in 1570. When only sixteen, she was married to Peter Legh, grandson and heir of Peter Legh, of Lyme and Bradley. Sir Peter succeeded his grandfather in 1590, inheriting from him artistic tastes, a great knowledge of forestry, and much sound business capacity. He was Member of Parliament for Wigan, Forester of Macclesfield Forest and Captain of the Isle of Man under the Earls of Derby. From Beamont's "History of the House of Lyme," we find that his wife was a "help-meet" for him in the best sense of the word, and her name is found, joined with his, on the old house at Bradley, which was restored and repaired by them in 1597. Peter Legh was knighted in 1598. There is no evidence to show that Sir Peter and Lady Legh ever lived at Fulham or were in any way connected with the parish.

Monument to Lady Margaret Legh.
From an engraving published by John Simco in 1794

At Lyme Park, Disley, Cheshire, the seat of Lord Newton, the present head of the family, there is preserved a good contemporary portrait of Lady Legh in the style of Jansen. Sir Peter married, as his second wife, Dorothy, Widow of Richard Brereton of Tatton. There were no children of the second marriage. The second Lady Legh lies buried in Eccles church by the side of her first husband. Sir Peter Legh died in 1635 and was buried at Warrington. At Lyme Park is a portrait of Sir Peter and his second wife painted by Jansen.

In the floor of the choir are laid five stones. The inscription on one is almost entirely obliterated. The others are:

"The Right Honorable | Lady Sophia Margaret | wife of | Sir Charles Egleton Kent, Bart. | obiit 16 Novernbris 1834 | Ætatis 45 | Also | Sir Charles Egleton Kent | Bart. | obiit 5 Decembris | 1834 | Ætat. 50 | And

Sir Charles William Kent | Bart. I son of the above | obiit 8 Aprilis 1848 | Ætat. 29."

Sir Charles Egleton Kent, bart., who was born, 4 Mar. 1784, was the only son of Sir Charles Kent, bart., formerly of Egleton, by his wife, Mary, daughter and co-heiress of Josias Wordsworth of Wadsworth. He married the Lady Sophia Margaret Lygon, daughter of William, first Earl Beauchamp. They had issue one son, Sir Charles William Kent, bart., born in 1819 and died 1848, and three daughters, Mary, Sarah Ann and Louisa Elizabeth.

The Church Registers record:

1834 Lady Sophia Margaret Kent, Peterborough House. bu. 22 Nov. aged 45 years. Buried in the Chancel.

1834 Sir Chas. Egleton Kent, Bart. Peterborough House. bu. 11 Dec. 50 years. Buried in the Chancel.

1848 Sir Chas. Wm. Kent, Bart. The Barracks, Regent's Park. bu. 15 Apl. 29 years.

Monument to Lady Margaret Legh.
From a photograph by Mr. T. S. Smith, 1895

This interesting stone reads:

"Here lyeth ye Body of | Wm Rvmbold, Esq. Clarke | Comptroller of his Maj^{tis} | Great=Wardrobe & Svrveyor | Gen^{ll} of all ye Cvstomes of | England who dyed ye 27th | May 1667 | and also ye Body of Mary | his wife only davghter of Berclay (Esq. of ye Body to his | late Maj^{tye} of Blessed Memorie | King Charles ye first |. She died ye 21th of Avg^t following."

The arms are:

Dexter: On a chevron engrailed 3 cinqucfoils ermine, a canton charged with a leopard's face (Rumbold). *Sinister*: A chevron between 3 crosses formèe, a mullet for difference (Barclay).

In the old Church the stone was situated in the floor in front of the Communion Table. The sunken coat of arms had apparently been found to wear out the Communion carpet, for, at the rebuilding of the Church, it was found entirely filled in with cement.

The Rumbolds were originally seated in Essex, where there are traces of them among the landed gentry as far back as the time of Richard I. The branch, to which the Fulham Rumbolds belonged, had, however, in the time of the Comptroller, been established at or near Burbage, in Leicestershire, for two or three generations.

William Rumbold was born at Burbage in 1613, and was baptized in the parish church, 18 April 1613. He was the eldest of three brothers, the sons of Thomas Rumbold of Burbage, by his wife Catherine Ripplinghame. The second son, Henry, was baptized at Burbage, 19 Jan. 1617. His life was chiefly spent in commercial undertakings in Spain. At the Restoration, Henry was appointed to the office of Consul General for Andalusia. The third son, Thomas, was baptized at Burbage, 28 Jan. 1628. He was also a merchant in Spain and filled the office of Consul General at Seville and San Lucar, at which latter place he was buried 19 Jan. 1706.

In 1629 William Rumbold, then a youth of 16, entered the office of the Great Wardrobe.

A few years ago, the late Mr. Charles Bridger, the well-known genealogist, discovered at the British Museum, a highly interesting document entitled "A Particular of the Services performed by me Henry Rumbold for his Majesty."

The paper is not dated, but was evidently written about 1674. In this document Henry Rumbold informs us:

> "That from King Charles the Firsts goeing from London my Brother William Rumbold attended his Majesty, and after by his Majesty Comand returned for London and brought away the Standard, that was Lodged in the Great Wardrobe of Which my Brother was then Clarke, and all along from that time followed his Majesty till after the Battle of Nasbey, in which both my father and Brother were engaged, and my father soone after taken from his owne house in Lecestershire and made Prisoner in Lecester by Colonel Gray, and my Brother gott out of England and came to me to Spaine, untill better security (in disguise as a Marchant) hee returned for England, and after the late kings murder, he was soe farr concerned in his present Majestys Service, that therein he spent a good Estate of his owne and mine also, to assist him therein."

In 1653 Henry Rumbold tells us that he came from Spain to London,

> "Where I found my Brother wholly engaged in his Majestys Concernes, as being a Secretary to his Councill and Cheife Agent for supplying his Majesty with Moneys, with whom I joined my endeavours to my best capacity and Particularly contriveing with my Brother how I might be Serviceable to his Majesty in Spaine (which commerce kept England flourishing) and whither I was returning to my partner, Anthony Vpton, Merchant," etc.

Cromwell kept watch on the brothers Rumbold, with the result that William was lodged in the Tower of London and examined to see whether he held any communication with Henry. The Protector tried by offers of "enlargement" to induce William to get his brother over to England, "But," adds Henry, "he was not a subject to be so wrought upon." On the Restoration of Charles II, William Rumbold was installed in the offices of Comptroller of the Great Wardrobe and Surveyor General of the Customs.

On his return from Spain, Henry Rumbold was sworn in as a Gentleman of the Privy Chamber Extraordinary, 14 Dec. 1663, by his brother the Comptroller, a somewhat paltry recompense for his loyal services. On 25 Oct. 1664, we find Henry, who had ceased to hold his consular appointment in Spain, writing a curious letter to Secretary Bennet. He tells him that he has heard of the death of Col. Dan O'Neale, who held the patent for gunpowder for 21 years, and begs that he and his brother William may succeed in the management of it, "as the profits will naturally be considerable if well managed." Sir Horace Rumbold, in his "Notes" on the foregoing paper, observes:

> "William Rumbold was unquestionably one of the worthies of the small and faithful band who successfully laboured to bring the King back to his own, and, notwithstanding Pepys's sneer at the 'courtiers and pomp' attending the christening of his child at the Wardrobe ('Diary,' Dec. 8th, 1661), is spoken of with great affection by Lord Mordaunt, Colonel Henry Norwood, Andrew Newport, and others, who had worked with him, and, with him, shared captivity and persecution. One interesting trace of him I recently came across in his signature in the Vellum Book of the Honourable Artillery Company, entered among those of other guests entertained at a banquet in September 1663."

William Rumbold spent the last three or four years of his life at Fulham. His bold signature, "Will Rumbold," first appears in the Parish Books attached to the minutes of a Vestry held 14 Aug. 1664.

The quaint "Diary" of Elizabeth, Viscountess Mordaunt, which she kept while residing at Parson's Green, makes mention of William Rumbold. On 1 June 1664, her ladyship enters the following "thanksgiving" for the restoration of her friend to health:

> "My God, to whome I adres my prayers and my voues, in all my aflicktions, I now apeare befor thee to performe a vow mayd for the reeouery of Mr. Rumbell; Whoses being restored to perfitt helthe by thy mercy, bringes me now apon my knees to returne thanks to thee my God, and to performe my promas mayd vnto thee in his behalfe."

To this illness William Rumbold himself refers in a letter, dated 19 April 1664, to Samuel Pepys, Secretary of the Admiralty, asking for payment of an order on the Commissioners left by his brother Henry, when Consul at Cadiz, at his departing. In this letter he reminds Pepys that he wrote about it "six months ago, but had been prevented by sickness from renewing his suit." (Admiralty Papers.)

With William Rumbold's estate at Parson's Green we shall deal later on.

Not much is known about "Berclay," the father of Mrs. Rumbold. No Christian name or initial can be seen on the stone, but from other sources we know that it was William. Among the receipts of the Fulham Churchwardens for 1642 is an entry which probably refers to the interment of this William Barclay; it reads:

"Rec^d for buriall of Barkley in ye Church 7s. 8d."

In 1649 a Mrs. Barclay, possibly the widow, was assessed for a house at Sands End, a district not very far from William Rumbold's house. The mother of Mary Rumbold was still alive when the latter made her will, 15 July 1667.

By his wife, Mary, William Rumbold left four surviving children. The eldest daughter, Mary, married James Sloane, M.P. for Thetford, elder brother of Sir Hans Sloane. She was born 26 Oct. 1656, and died in July 1720. Jane, the second daughter, was baptized 14 Nov. 1663. She married Richard Hosier of Salop. The dates of the birth and death of Elizabeth, the third daughter, are unknown. According to the Registers of St. Andrew's by the Wardrobe, a son named Charles was there buried on 28 Dec. 1664. This was, doubtless, the child whose great christening "yesterday at Mr. Rumbell's" Pepys mentions in his "Diary." Rumbold's youngest and only surviving son, Edward, was baptized at St. Andrew's by the Wardrobe on 5 June 1665. He eventually succeeded his father in the post of Surveyor General of Customs. He married, 13 April 1687, Anne, daughter of George, 4th Viscount Grandison, and died, 'without issue, in 1729.

William Rumbold died at his house at Parson's Green on 27 May 1667. On his deathbed he made a nuncupative will, dated 17 May. It was proved 10 June 1667 (P.C.C. 82 Carr). It reads:

"Memorandum That on or about the seaventeenth day of May in the year of our Lord one Thousand Six Hundred Sixty Seaven William Rumbold of Parsons Greene in the parish of ffulham and County of

Middlesex, Esquire, being sicke and weake in body but of sound and perfect mind memory and understanding with a serious intent and resolution to make his last will and Testament nuncupative and to dispose of his estate did utter nuncupate and declare the same in these words following or to the same effect, (*vizt*.):

I haue had a greate happines in a good and loueing wife And then (speaking to his wife, Mrs. Mary Rumbold then present) said I giue you all that I have not doubting but you will be just to my children which words or the like in effect he then spake and uttered for and as his last will and Testament in the presence of the Right Honourable John Lord Mordaunt and Elizabeth Lady Mordaunt his wife James Halsell, Esquire, Mrs. Elizabeth Waldron and other credible witnesses."

Administration of the goods, etc., of the deceased was granted at London, 10 June 1667, to Mary Rumbold, the sole executrix. On 11 Dec. 1667, a further administration of goods, etc., of William Rumbold, deceased, was granted to James Halsall and Andrew Newport, two of the testamentary guardians in the will of Mary Rumbold, deceased, for the use of Mary, Jane, Elizabeth and Edward Rumbold, the children, during their minority.

The will of Mrs. Mary Rumbold, who survived her husband barely three months, is dated 16 July 1667. It was proved on 7 Nov. 1667 and 3 Jan. 1667-68 (P.C.C. 158 Carr). From it we take the following:

"I Mary Rumbold widow the relicte of William Rumbold Esquire. To be buried at Fulham so nere the place where the body of my said late husband lyeth interred as may bee. I haue granted all my goodes and personall estate unto my loveing friends James Halsall Esq. and Thomas Niuill Cittizen and Merchant taylor of London for performance of this my will. To my Mother £50 per an. for life. To the poor of Fulham £10. All my plate and household goods to be divided into 5 parts, 2 whereof I give to my eldest daughter Mary and the other 3 parts equally between Jane and Elizabeth my 2 younger daughters. All the residue of the goods of my late husband and the profitts of one share of the office of Surveyor Generall of the Customes and all other things of my late husband of which I haue power to dispose (excepting my howse and lands which I desire should descend to my only son) into 6 parts 2 parts whereof I give to my said daughter Mary Rumbold and 2 to my said son Edward Rumbold and the other 2 between my youngest daughters Jane and Elizabeth.

I appoint my Honourable friend The Right Hon[ble] John Lord Mordant

Henry Norwood Esq. Andrew Newport Esq. James Halsall Esq. Thomas Armstrong Esq. my brother Henry Rumbold and Thomas Kynaston gent. my Executors and also Guardians of my Children but desireing they may live with my mother of whose care and love to them I haue greate experience and assurance."

On 5 June 1668, an order was made granting a petition of Andrew Newport and James Halsall, the executors of William Rumbold,

"That his salary as Surveyor General of Customs, with the arrears already due thereon, may be paid for the benefit of his children, with the proviso that this case be not drawn into a precedent."
(State Papers, Dom. "Entry Book" 18, P. 309).

Two months later the King signed a warrant to pay Andrew Newport and two others an annuity of £250 for the use of the children of William Rumbold,

"to continue during the suspension of the salary of £500 a year, payable from the Customs " (Docquet, vol. 23, No. 254).

In the Church Registers are the following entries:

1680. Mrs. Rumbold uxor bu. 27 Aprill.

The omission of the husband's name after "uxor" [wife of] is unfortunate, but there is little doubt that the entry refers to the wife of Henry Rumbold, the Comptroller's brother.

1682. Dorothy Sloone infant d. of Mrs. Mary Rumball bu. 3 May.

This was the infant daughter of Mary, the eldest daughter of William Rumbold, and wife of James Sloane. "Mrs. Mary Rumball" is, of course, an error for "Mrs. Mary Sloane."

1690. Henry Rumbell, Esq. bu. 28 Mar.

This was Henry Rumbold, the Comptroller's brother.

1728. Mr. William Rumbold bu. 5 Sept.
1737. Elizabeth W. of Wm. Rumbald bu. 19 Dec.

These were the grandparents of Sir Thomas Rumbold: see pedigree chart earlier in this chapter.

Mrs. Mary Sloane, the eldest daughter of the Comptroller, was also buried at Fulham Church, "as near her dear parents as might be." Her will, dated 29 July 1720, was proved 9 Aug. of the same year.

Another interesting epitaph is that to the memory of Thomas Carlos. On a black marble slab at the foot of the lectern is the following inscription:

"Here lyeth interred the Body | of Thomas Carlos sonn of Co | lenell William Carlos of | Stafford sheire who departed | this Life in the 25th yeare of | his age on the 19 Day of May 1665.
    Tis not bare names that noble fathers giue
    To worthy sonnes, though dead, in them they liue
    For in his progeny 'tis Heauen's decree
    Man onely can on Earth immortal bee
    But Heauen giues soules wch grace doth somtimes bend
    Early to God their rice and soueraigne end
    Thus whilst that earth concern'd did hope to see
    Thy noble Father liueing still in thee
    Carelesse of earth to Heauen thou didst aspire
    And wee on earth Carlos in thee desire."

At the head of the stone are these arms:

An oak tree fructed, debruised by a fess, charged with three regal crowns: *Crest*: On an esquire's helmet surmounted of a wreath a garland of oak fructed, interlaced by a sword and sceptre in saltier. *Motto*: "Svbditvs fidelis regis regni salvs." [A faithful subject of the King is a preserver of the Monarchy.]

These arms recall an incident of historic interest. The flight of Prince Charles after the memorable rout at Worcester, on 3 Sept. 1651, was accompanied by some exciting episodes, not the least noteworthy of which was the one which resulted in the bestowal of these arms on the Carlos family. To elude Oliver's troopers, Charles was forced to hide for a whole day among the branches of a friendly oak. His companion on this occasion was Colonel William Careless, of Bromhall, Staffordshire, a village near Boscobel, a brave soldier who had fought for the Prince's father in the Civil War. From the "Boscobel Tracts" we learn that, in recognition of the services and fidelity of Colonel William Carlis (as the name is there spelled),

> "His Majesty has been pleased, by letters patent, under the great seal of England, to give him by the name of William Carlos (which in Spanish signifies Charles) this very honourable coat of arms *in perpetuam memoriam*, as 'tis expressed in the Letters Patent."

This special grant of arms was made in 1658.

The cracked and decayed condition of the Carlos stone in Fulham Church led, in past years, to some confusion. For instance, Mr. J. Hughes, M.A., who edited "The Boscobel Tracts" in 1830, writes:

> "With respect to Col. William Carlos, the companion of King Charles during his temporary occupation of the royal oak, it appears that he not only survived the Restoration, but lived to see the family for which he had exerted himself, again expatriated. His will, dated in 1688, was proved in the Prerogative Office, Doctors' Commons, in the October of the following year. By its contents we may presume that, although he had once possessed a son named after himself, William, who died at the age of 25, twenty years before his father (as is proved by a tablet erected to his memory at Fulham), yet at his decease he left no surviving legitimate issue, inasmuch as he bequeaths the whole of his property to his 'adopted son, Edward Carlos,' then of Worcester, apothecary, and his issue."

Faulkner gives the name as the editor of the "Boscobel Tracts" appears to have read it:

> "Here lieth William Carlos of Stafford, who departed this life in the 25th yeare of his age the 19th day of May 1668 (*sic*)."

If Mr. Hughes followed this reading, it would account for his calling the Colonel's son William, instead of Thomas, and for speaking of him as predeceasing his father twenty, instead of twenty-three years.

The fracture of the stone through the second line of the epitaph probably accounts for the confusion which has arisen. The correct wording is fortunately set at rest by the preservation of the inscription in Strype's edition of Stow's "Survey of the Cities of London and Westminster," 1754 (vol. ii., App. 1), where it reads:

> "Here lyeth interred the Body of Thomas Carlos, son of Colonel William Carlos of Staffordshire, who departed [this life in] the 25th year of his age, the 19th of May, 1665."

On the rebuilding of the Church in 1880-81, the slab was neatly repaired, when the arms and the first part of the epitaph were recut. A fresh piece of stone, bearing the words "of Thomas Carlos," was inserted. The Thomas Carlos buried at Fulham is believed to have been the Colonel's only son. The relationship of his "adopted son" Edward, is not stated in the Colonel's will, though he was probably a nephew. This large black stone is inscribed:

> "Here lyeth interred the Body of | Captayn Iohn Saris of Fvlham in | the Covnty of Middlesex, Esq. who | departed this Life the 11 day of | Decem. A° Dni. 1643, Age 63 years. | He had to wife Anne, the | davghter | of William Migges | of London, Esq. She departed this life the second day of | February A° Dni. | 1622 | and lieth bu | ried in the Parishe Chvreh of St. | Botolph in Thame-Street | being aged 21 yeares."

The following are the arms:

> *Dexter*: A chevron between three saracens' heads couped at the neck (Saris). *Sinister*: A chevron engrailed between three mascles, on a chief a greyhound courant (Migges or Megges).

In the Churchwardens' Accounts is the following reference to the burial of Capt. Saris:

> 1643 "Rec[d] for the buriall of Captaine Saris the 19 of Decem. 1643 . . . 2s. 6d."

Captain John Saris, who spent the last years of his life at Fulham, was a distinguished traveller. He went out to the East

Indies in 1604 in the fleet commanded by Captain (afterwards Sir) Henry Middleton, and was left at Bantam as a junior factor. He remained there until 1609, when he returned to England. In April 1611 he conducted an expedition, one of the principal objects of which was to make an effort to open up communication with Japan. After spending some time in the Red Sea, Saris reached Bantam, the head-quarters of English trade, in October 1612. In the following January he sailed for Japan in the "Clove." On 11 June he arrived at Firando (now Hirado). A journey was then made to the Court of the Emperor, who gave Saris a favourable reception and granted the necessary privileges for English trade with Japan. He returned to Firando, and, after establishing an English factory under Richard Cocks, sailed to Bantam. In September 1614 Saris arrived safely at Plymouth. His original journal of the voyage to Japan is preserved in the records of the India Office. An account of the expedition is also printed in the first volume of "Purchas His Pilgrimes."

The name of "Captaine John Sayer" first appears in the Poor Rate assessments for 1629 and continues till his death in 1643. He resided, as we have seen, in Church Row. His property apparently passed to a nephew, George Sayers. In the Calendar of the "Proceedings of the Committee for the Advance of Money," a body whose duty it was to find the sinews of war for the Parliamentary party, this George Sayers or Sairs, described as of Bassieshaw Ward, was assessed (28 Feb. 1644-45) at £400. On 23 May 1645, he was ordered to be brought up in custody to pay his assessment, but on 4 July his liability was discharged "for the £75 5s. 4d. lent by his uncle Captain John Sayers of Fulham and £124 14. 8. now paid, being his proportion on oath."

The old "Register Book" records:

> "Captaine John Saris of Fulham by his last will and testament gave thirtie pounds to be distributed by the Churchwarden of Fulham on Fulham side to such poore on the same side being parishioners as he shall see fitting."

In a different hand is the following addition:
> "And it is to be given in bread weekcly every Sunday to 30 poore people to every one a two penny Loafe after Sermon untill the said

thirtey pounds be fully disposed of; which said sume was payd unto Nathaniell Dancer then Churchwarden and hee began the first distribution thereof to the said poore on Sunday the last day of December 1643: being within one moneth after his death according to his will."

PEDIGREE OF SARIS OR SAYERS FAMILY

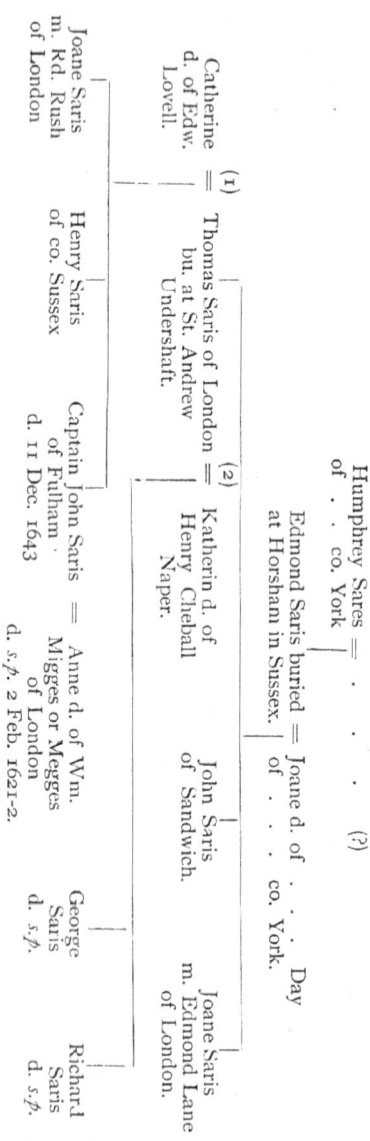

Humphrey Sares of . . co. York = . . . (?)

Thomas Saris of London, bu. at St. Andrew Undershaft
- (1) = Catherine d. of Edw. Lovell.
- (2) = Katherin d. of Henry Cheball Naper.

Joane Saris m. Rd. Rush of London

Henry Saris of co. Sussex

Captain John Saris of Fulham, d. 11 Dec. 1643 = Anne d. of Wm. Migges or Megges of London, d. s.p. 2 Feb. 1621-2.

John Saris of Sandwich.

Edmond Saris buried at Horsham in Sussex. = Joane d. of . . . co. York.

Joane Saris m. Edmond Lane of London.

George Saris d. s.p.

Richard Saris d. s.p.

The above pedigree is taken chiefly from Harleian Manuscript 1551, fo. 101.

North Transept Floor

The first stone on which we tread, on entering the Church by the north door, is one to the memory of John Chasemore (d. 1787) and his wife Hannah (d. 19 Mar. 1801). The date of John Chasemore's death is quite obliterated, but the Church Registers record:

> 1787 John Chasemore bu. 12 Sept.

The next is to Thomas Doughtie, etc.:

> "Here lyeth ye Body of | Thomas Doughtie, Gent., of this | Parish who departed this life ye | 31st of August 1706 Ætat. Suæ 80. | Also ye Body of Mrs. Mary Doughtie his Wife who departed | this life ye 6th day of April 1705 Ætat. Suæ 67."

Above are the Doughtie arms. The Church Registers record:

> 1706 Mr. Thomas Doughty, Gent. bu. 4 Sept.

The Marriage Alligation Books of the Bishopric of London record an application, made by "Tho. Doughtie" of Fulham, 5 July 1705, for a license for marriage between his daughter Mary and Arthur Simpson of Fulham.

The next stone records the memory of Isaac Cooke:

> "Here lyeth the Body of | Mr. Isaac Cooke who was one | of the gentlemen to ye Right Hon. | the Lord Bishop of London . . . years | and was Groome of his Majest: | Chappel Royal at Whitehall | and Departed this life ye 16 of | March Anº 1697, Aged 53 yeares."

The date quoted is New Style. The Church Registers record:

> 1696 Isaac Cook from the Bishop of London bu. 18 Mar.

> "Samuel Ashhvrst | Esqr | Died Nov. 7th 1753 | Aged 71 | Sarah wife of the above | Samuel Ashhurst | Died August the first 1769 Aged 73."

The Church Registers record:

1753 Samuel Ashhurst Esqr bu. 14 Nov.

"Henry Garforth the son of I the Revd Edmund Garforth I and Elizabeth his wife I Died Nov. 1799."

This family was related to that of Bishop Gibson.
A black stone is inscribed:

"Inter alios I Ejusdem Familiæ I Hic I Requiescit I Johannes Ashhurst, Armiger, I Erga Amico justus et Suavis I Erga Pauperes I Admodum Munificens I Obiit Junii die decimo 1792 Ætat. suæ 67."
(Tranlation: Here, among others of his family, lies john Ashhurst, gentleman, just and pleasant towards friends, always munificent towards the poor. He died 10th day of June, 1792, aged 67.)

The Church Registers record:

1792 John Ashhurst Esqre (in the Church) bu. 18 June.

North Transept Wall

Against the east Wall of the north transept is an interesting monument to the memory of William Payne, Lord of the Manor of Paddenswick, Hammersmith.

The monument, which formerly stood against the wall of the south aisle, near Lord Mordaunt's statue, is thus described by Bowack:

"A Monument of Alabaster about 8 Foot High Gilded, Painted and Adorn'd with Antique Embellishments, having the Effigies of William Payne, Esq., and his wife kneeling before an altar."

The two kneeling figures are finely carved. The husband is to the left and the wife to the right of a desk, on which lies an open book. The hands of the female figure are now gone. The monument is supported at the sides by black marble columns. At the top are the following arms:

"Quarterly, (I) and (4) Arg., on a fess engrailed gu. between 3 martlets sa., as many cinquefoils of the first; (2) and (3), Or, 3 pellets, on a chief embattled az. as many bezants (Payne's ancient coat?) *Crest*: On an esquire's helmet a griffin passant. Below, *dexter*, the same quarterings as above; *sinister*, gules guttèe d'eau, a fess nebulèe arg. (Doreland or Dryland?).

Monument to William Payne and Jane his wife.
From an engraving published by John Simco in 1794

A great deal of the ornamentation has been broken off, but the effigies are not much damaged. Beneath the figures is a black marble tablet, inscribed:

"William Payne of Pallenswick, Esqvier, hath placed this Monvment | To the memory of himselfe and Iane his wife who lyved with | him in Wedlock XLIIII yeares, and dyed the first daye of Maye | in An° Dn^i 1610; and the sayd William Payne the . . . daye of . . . | An° Dn^i . . . | The sayd William Payne hath geven forever after | his decease an Ilande in the ryver of Thames caled Makenshawe | to the vse of the poore of this Parrish on Hamersmyth side."

At the bottom of the monument are the usual cross bones and there is a space for a skull which is now missing.

The blank spaces in the inscription clearly show that William Payne intended to be buried at Fulham by the side of his wife, but nothing is known as to the place of his sepulture. He died 9 Jan. 1625-26.

The little "Ilande," which he bequeathed to the poor of the parishes of Fulham and Hammersmith, is situated in the Thames just above Kew Bridge.

The earliest notice of the gift is the following memorandum in the Parish Books for 1626:

> "On account of Mr. Wheatlye the Kings Ma^{ts} Basket maker the gift of William Payne Esqre. a twighate neere Brainford within the Hamlett or parishe of Richmount ouer vnto Hamersmith syde . . . iij^{li}"

From a deed of trust, dated 10 Oct. 1626, and also from an abstract of title, now in the possession of Messrs. Park Nelson and Co., of Essex Street, Strand, it appears that the twig ait or eyot, was copyhold of the Manor of Richmond. By deed, dated 22 Oct. 1613, enrolled in Chancery 17 Dec. 1613, Payne, without first obtaining from the Lord a license to alienate it, conveyed the property to Trustees in trust for himself for life and afterwards for certain charitable uses. The eyot was, therefore, nominally forfeited to the Lord. On Payne's death it was found that six of the Trustees were also deceased. The survivors therefore applied, 22 Oct. 1626, for themselves and six others to be admitted as a new trust.

The gift was a curious one. The Trustees were to pay, in the first half year following the death of William Payne, thirty shillings to twelve of the poorest men and women on Hammersmith side, being lame and blind, and, in the second half year, a further similar payment was to be made, each person receiving half a crown. In the second year the sixty shillings were to be employed in apprenticing a boy of upwards of twelve years of age, to be chosen from Hammersmith side, or, if there should be no such boy, then one from Fulham side. Each two years these methods of distributing £3 of the income arising from the island were to be alternately repeated. If the income from letting the island any year exceeded the £3 the surplus was to be bestowed upon the poor of Fulham side. The surplus, in early times, generally amounted to a few shillings only.

In 1811 the island was leased by the Trustees to Mr. Robert Hunter, for the use of his Majesty George III, for a period of 21 years at a rent of £20; the lessee covenanting to lay out £200 within two years in substantial repairs of a house erected upon it many years before. This lease, which expired in 1832, is described in the "Report" of the Commissioners on Charities, as "very advantageous to the charity." It was doubtless for the purpose of planting poplars, in order to shut out the view of Brentford, that George III took the island. As late as 1840, we find her Majesty's Commissioners of Woods and Forests continuing the yearly payment of £20, £3 of which went to Hammersmith side. In 1823 the Fulham Trustees commenced, out of this charity, a subscription of two guineas per annum to St. George's Hospital, entitling the parish to send two in-patients and any number of out-patients. The residue used to be distributed in bread, coals and money.

On 21 Dec. 1836 the Trustees and Vicar resolved that, as far as concerned Fulham side, the proceeds of the charity should, in future, be expended in the purchase of knit or flannel waistcoats, to be given annually to certain poor men. In 1875 the property was sold and the proceeds invested in Consols which produce £13. 3s. 8d. a year for Fulham and £3 for Hammersmith. The island is variously called Mattingshaw, Matting Shawe, Makan Shawe, Maken Shawe, Mattings hawe alias Macke a shawe, etc.

William Payne's name, in the Court Rolls, is first mentioned in the minutes of a Court Baron held in 1573. Some account of the Payne family occurs in W. P. Courtney's "Parliamentary Representation in Cornwall."

Charles James Fèret

PEDIGREE OF PAYNE FAMILY
See Berry's "Genealogies" (Sussex Families)

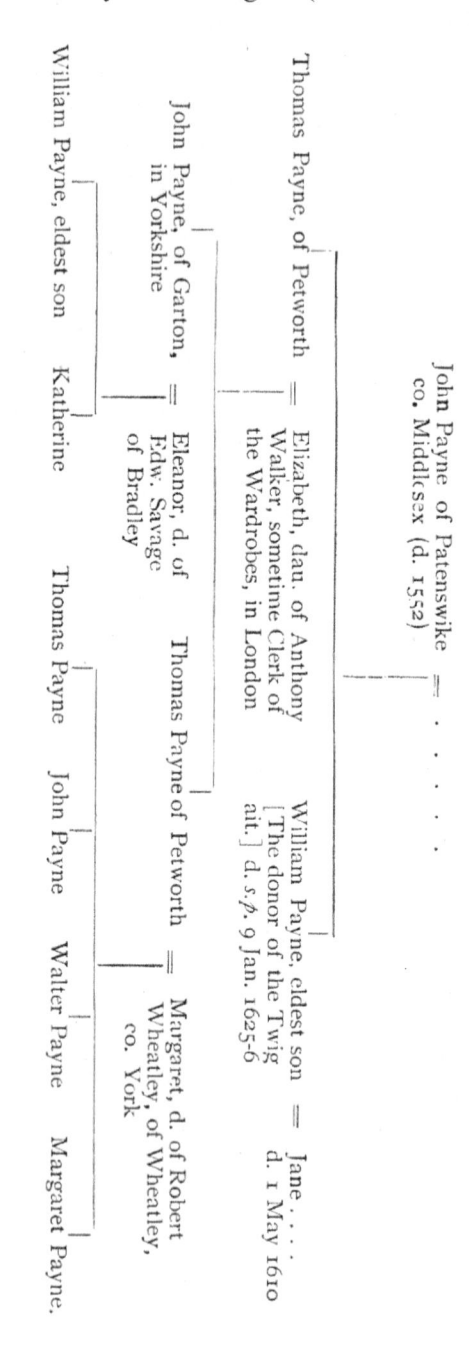

John Payne of Patenswike, co. Middlesex (d. 1552) = ...

Thomas Payne, of Petworth = Elizabeth, dau. of Anthony Walker, sometime Clerk of the Wardrobes, in London

William Payne, eldest son [The donor of the Twig ait.] d.s.p. 9 Jan. 1625-6 = Jane . . . . d. 1 May 1610

John Payne, of Garton, in Yorkshire = Eleanor, d. of Edw. Savage of Bradley

Thomas Payne of Petworth = Margaret, d. of Robert Wheatley, of Wheatley, co. York

William Payne, eldest son

Katherine

Thomas Payne

John Payne

Walter Payne

Margaret Payne.

The oldest monument against the east wall of the north transept is a square tablet, with a gilt sculptured border. Anciently it was affixed to the piece of return wall at the north-west end of the south aisle, but, during the alterations of 1840-41, when the Bishop's Gallery was added at the north-east corner, it was, with the other monuments in this portion of the Church, removed into the Tower Chapel. The tablet was placed against the left side of the walling which filled in the Tower arch. At the rebuilding in 1880-81 the monument was placed in its present position. It is inscribed:

> At Earth in Cornwell was my firste begininge
> From Bondes and Corringtons as it may apere,
> Now to earth in Fvlham, God dyspos'd my endinge,
> In March the thovsand & six hvndred yere,
> Of Christ in whome my body here doth rest,
> Tyll both in body & sovle I shalbe fvlly blest.
> Thomas Bonde
> Obijt A° Æ^{tis} svæ
> 68."

The tablet is surmounted by a shield bearing the following arms:

> "Quarterly, (I), Arg., on a chevron sa. three bezants (Bonde); (2), Arg., three stags' heads couped sa. collared and armed or (Earth); (3), Arg., a chevron az. between three sinister hands couped and erect gu. (Maynard); (4), Arg., a saltier sa. (Coriton). *Crest*: A demi-pegasus az., semèe of estoiles or."

Thomas Bonde was the second son of Richard Bonde of Earth *juxta* Saltash, co. Cornwall, by his wife Elizabeth, daughter and co-heiress of Thomas Corrington, Coryton or Coriton, of Saltash. In "Magna Britannia," Lysons notes:

> "Earth, of Earth, in St. Stephen's, near Saltash, in the reign of Edward III. (1327-77). The heiress married Bond."

From this it appears that Earth was the original family name, as well as the name of the place whence the family sprang. The play on the words "Earth" in Cornwall and "earth" in Fulham will doubtless have been noticed by the reader, but the above extract suggests the existence of a double pun including "begininge" in the epitaph.

PEDIGREE OF BONDE FAMILY

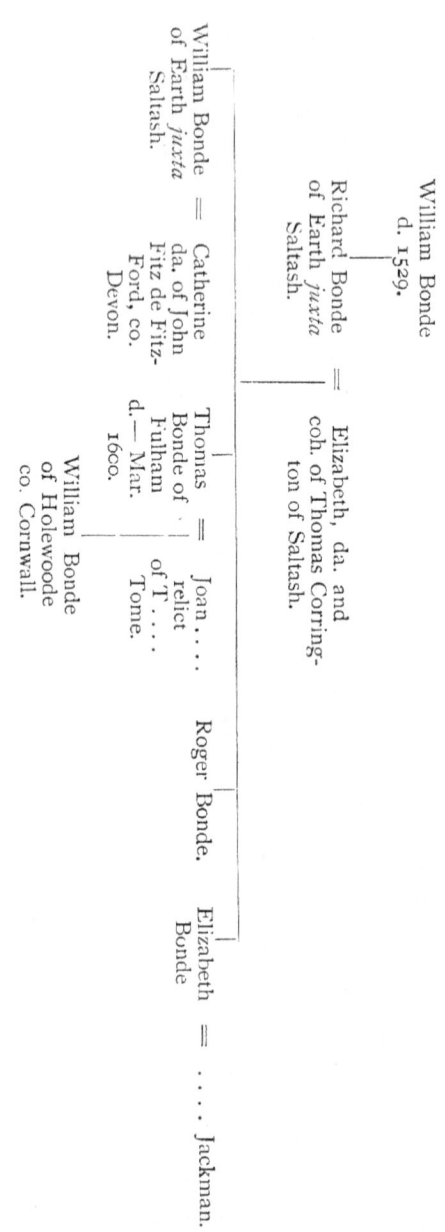

```
William Bonde
d. 1529.
├── William Bonde of Earth juxta Saltash.
└── Richard Bonde of Earth juxta Saltash. == Elizabeth, da. and coh. of Thomas Corrington of Saltash.
    ├── William Bonde == Catherine da. of John Fitz de Fitz-Ford, co. Devon.
    └── Thomas Bonde of Fulham d.—Mar. 1600. == Joan .... relict of T.... Tome.
        ├── William Bonde of Holewoode co. Cornwall.
        ├── Roger Bonde.
        └── Elizabeth Bonde == .... Jackman.
```

The pedigree is in part compiled from that given in Harleian Soc., ix., 14, 15.

The will of Thomas Bonde, dated 20 March 1599-1600 was proved 12 April 1600:

> He left to Margaret Meredith, widow, "two acres and a rode of ffreland . . . in a certain ffeild in ffulham called Austen's ffeild to hold to her Heires for ever," charged, however, with the payment of twenty shillings yearly for ever to the collectors or other officers of the poor of Fulham. In default, the land was to vest in the Churchwardens of Fulham for the use of the poor. For distribution among the poor of Fulham, on the day of his funeral, he left twenty shillings.

Monument to Thomas Bonde.
From a photograph by Mr. T. S. Smith, 1895

The charge on the two acres and one rood of land was for some years duly paid. How the legacy lapsed there are no means of saying. Had it not been lost, it would now be one of the most valuable charities in the parish.

The Court Rolls show that Thomas Bonde held property in several parts of Fulham, including a part of Windmill Shot and land near the Fulham Road between Stamford Bridge and Walham Green. In these records his name frequently occurs between 1566 and 1600. In the first named year he, in common with some other tenants, was fined twelve pence, because he had no bows. The

Court inflicted this fine under a statute passed in the reign of Philip and Mary. In the same year Thomas Bonde and some of his neighbours were ordered to "lop the boughs of their trees where they overhang a part of the road leading from 'Sandeyende' towards Waname Grene before Pentecost next."

In 1569 he was again required to cut and lop his trees overhanging the Queen's highway, between "Standford Bridge" and "Wendon Grene" "before St. John Baptist next or xii^d per perch." His residence appears to have been at Sands End.

Katharine Hart. The monument to the memory of Katharine Hart is now affixed to the east wall of the north transept. Originally it was placed in the south aisle over the vault of Dr. Samuel Barrow, whence, in 1840-41, it was removed to the north wall of the Tower Chapel.

Katharine, who was the wife of John Hart, was the eldest daughter of Mr. Edmund Powell of Fulham, and therefore sister to Sir Edward Powell of Munster House.

The large square monument, which is noticed by Bowack, represents Mrs. Hart with ruff and hat, kneeling. Her four children, two in front and two behind, are similarly postured. The mother rests her right hand on the head of the child immediately in front of her. The left arm, which hangs at her side, has lost its hand. The upper part of the head has been broken in two and mended. The first child behind the mother has the greater part of its head and the whole of one hand broken off. The child in front of the mother holds a skull to indicate that it had predeceased her. Beneath the figures is a black marble tablet inscribed:

> "Here lieth Katharine Hart late wife of Iohn Hart, gent. & | eldest davgher of Edmond Powell of Fvlham, gent. who Lived w^h | her said hvsband ye space of 8 yeres & had by him 2 sones & 2 | davghters. she lived vertvovslie & died Godlie, ye 23 daie of Octo: | 1605, in ye 24 yere of her age in constant hope of a ioyfvll Resvr | rection wth elect children of God."

Above the head of Mrs. Hart, on a small marble tablet, are the following touching verses:

"Iohanes Hart dilectissimæ svæ conivgi | Katharinæ Hart hoc monvrnentvm, | Amoris testimonii ergo posvit.

Qvæ potvi lachrymans persolvi fvnera conivx
Qvæ lvbens volvi non dare, dona, dedi,
Dona dedi qveis si everint (*sic*) pia nvmina votis
Concessvra meis tecvm ego spero frvi.

Interea pro te mihi fas sit amare relicto,
Tres liberos casti pignora chara tori,
Qvotq. mihi & natis, qvot charo tristia patri
Loqvisti, totidem det tibi laeta Devs."

Translation:

"John Hart has erected this monument as a token of affection for his most dear wife, Katharine Hart.

What rites I could, I've paid, while tears have flow'd,
And gifts which fain I would not have bestow'd;
Gifts which, if heaven my earnest prayer shall hear,
Consigned to this tomb, I hope to share.

Three cherish'd pledges of our chaste desire
Now claim th' affection of their widow'd Sire;
Oh, may the sorrow, which thy death has given,
To you be equalled in the joys of heaven."

This elegant translation we quote from Faulkner, for whom it was made by the Rev. G. Savage, M.A., vicar of Kingston, Surrey. Two small skulls surmount the top. Between them is a damaged shield bearing these arms:

Arg., 3 lozenges sa. each charged with an escallop or (Hart). Below, the same arms repeated singly and also impaling this coat: Per fess vert and or, three escallops arg. (Powell).

As to John Hart, little is known. In the 1625 assessments he is rated for a house in "ffulham streete" (see Chapter XVII: High Street (East Side) In 1648 the Churchwardens received "for buriall of Hart vj^{d}" In 1628 John Hart was granted a lease of six acres of land in Fulham Fields, "in the Shott comonly called the Windmill

Shott," formerly in the tenure of Thomas Bonde. The following entry occurs in the Bishop of London's Registry:

"Mr. John Hart, of Fulham, gent., and Katherine Powell, maiden, daughter of Mr. Edmond Powell of Fulham, gent., about 17, her father's consent, at Fulham aforesaid 20 Dec. 1597."

Monument to Katharine Hart.
From an engraving published by John Simco in 1794

The child whom we see in effigy, to the extreme left of the monument, rose to be a doctor of laws and a man of considerable consequence in the parish. If we may judge from a curious petition of one John Bumsted, a lime merchant, to Laud, Archbishop of Canterbury, dated 22 Feb. 1639-40, honest dealing was not a prominent trait in the character of Dr. Richard Hart. Poor Bumsted, a prisoner in the King's Bench, tells a pitiful story. He complains that Richard Hart, LL.D., had sold him certain timber trees at Fulham, valued at £86, and had sealed a bond of £300 penalty that he should enjoy his bargain. The petitioner goes on to say that he paid £6 on account when he discovered that the timber, in the felling of which he had expended £30, did not belong to Hart at all, but to the executors of one Richard Richards, to whom the property had previously been mortgaged. Though it was plain that Richard Hart had sold that to which he had no right, and though the bond for £300 was forfeit, yet, for the non-payment of the £80, he had cast the petitioner into prison, where he had been detained since New Year's Day, thus throwing forty of his labourers out of work and ruining him, "unless his Grace vouchsafe some relief speedily." The result of the petition is not known, but it appears to have been referred to Sir john Lambe, Dean of the Arches, "to see that the petitioner receive satisfaction or else that he may have leave to sue him at law" (S. P. Dom. 446, No. 10).

Monument to Katharine Hart.
From a photograph by Mr. T. S. Smith, 1895

In the Calendar of the "Proceedings of the Committee for Advance of Money" is an "information," dated 18 June 1649, in which Dr.

Hart is described as "late of Fulham, advocate of the Prince's Fleet." He and his wife, Diana, "recusant," are stated to possess lands worth "£80 a year at Fulham." The enquiry showed that he had been

> "against Parliament all through the wars; that he had been in the service of the rebels in Ireland before and since 1648, and was with Prince Rupert in his ships at sea."

Against the west wall of the north transept is a large marble monument to the memory of William Townsend. Originally this stone was fixed against the wall of the chancel over the monument of Sir Thomas Smith. It is inscribed,

> "To the memory of | William Townsend, Esquire, | Fulham House, Middlesex, | who died June 30th. 1823, Aged 82 years.
>
> How drear the hearts he gladden'd with his worth !
> How dark the circle where his friendship shone !
> What sterling virtues have we lost on earth !
> What social happiness with Townsend gone !
>
> His generous bosom sickness could not chill
> Age cast no shadow on his brilliant mind
> Still could his converse yield delight, and still
> His Christian charity exalt mankind.
>
> Tho' long, blest spirit, was thy sojourn here,
> And mild as Heav'n's own music thy recal;
> Well might that precious term too short appear !
> Well might that summons give a pang to all.
>
> How calm thy parting hour ! How soft the breath
> Which bore thee homewards from thy earthly shrine,
> And, oh ! may all who prize so sweet a death,
> Secure its comforts by a life like thine.
>
> Erected by his affectionate sister."

This sister was Mrs. Mary Barnard, of Fulham House. By her will, dated 2 Aug. 1837 she gave £50 in trust to the Vicar and Churchwardens, the dividends on which were to be applied to the repair of the monument, any surplus to go to the poor of the parish. It was invested in the purchase of £55. 3s. 5d. Three per cent. Consols.

Against the west wall of the north transept is a white marble slab. Above is an urn, partly covered with drapery. The inscription reads:

> "Sacred to the Memory | of Elizabeth, late wife of John Hatsell, Esqre | Clerk of the House of Commons, | She was the second daughter of | the Revd Jeffrey Ekins, Rector of Barton, in Northamptonshire, | Born on the 26 October, 1735: died on the 2^d December, 1804: | and was, at her own request, buried in | this chancel, near to her brother, the Dean of Carlisle. | She was first married to Major Newton Barton, | by whom she had two sons, John and Newton; | the latter only survived her. | Her most exemplary piety, | Conjugal affection, Maternal kindness, | And universal charity and benevolence, |Attended by the mildest and most engaging manners, | Will be long remembered and her death lamented by all who knew her. | She lived in most affectionate union for near 27 years, | with her husband John Hatsell, | who has directed this Marble to be erected | to her Memory: 1805."

This memorial was formerly fixed over the door leading from the chancel to the south aisle and near the slab to the memory of her brother, the Rev. Jeffrey Ekins, Dean of Carlisle. The space for the arms is blank. The Church Registers record:

> 1804. Elizabeth Wife of John Hatsell Esq. (in chancel) bu. 8 Dec.

Under the Daniel Window in the north transept is a curious monument about ten feet in height, composed of alabaster, inlaid and ornamented with various coloured marble. It was erected by Mrs. Elizabeth Plumbe to the memory of her husband, William Plumbe.

William Plumbe was the son of John Plumbe, of Eltham, in Kent, where he was born in the year 1533. It is not known when he first settled in Fulham, but he was here in 1575, when John Norden published his "Speculum Britanniæ," for, in his list of "Noblemen and gentlemen, for the most part haueing houses or residences within this shire" (Middlesex), he mentions "Plumbe at Northende by Fulham."

In the centre of the upper part of this monument is an oblong slab of black marble, bearing an inscription in Latin. The marble columns at the sides, with gilt capitals, support a superstructure, above which are portions of the arms, namely those of Gresham impaling Dormer. These we shall presently describe. The Plumbe arms are lost.

We are indebted to Nicholas Charles for the earliest allusion to this monument. His notes are as follows:

> "Wm. Plumbe sonne to John Plumbe of Eltham, mar. to his I. wyffe Margaret D. and sole heire to S[r] Thos. Neuell knight, Speaker of ye p'liment, and widow to S[r] Rob Sowthwell M[r] of ye Rolles, by whom he had ffrances his only sonne; and, secondly, he maried Elizab. only D. and heire to Edw. Dormer of ffulham in ye Co. of Midd. youngest sonne to Geffrey Dormer of Thame in Oxon. and widow to John Gresham of Mayfeld in ye con [county] of Sussex, second sonne to Sr John Gresham of London, by ye wch John Gresham she had issue Thos W[m] and Edw. The said Wm Plumbe deceased the 9th. day of February An° Dni. æt 60."

He blazons the arms:

> (I.) Erm. on a bend vaire coticed sa. (Plumbe), impaling, quarterly of five, (I) Neville, (2) Warren, (3) Clare, (4) Despenser, (5) Beauchamp differenced by a crescent. (II.) "Plumbe," as before, with crest on a wreath a talbot sejant gu. impaling quarterly of four, (I) and (4), Az. 10 billets or, on a chief a demi-lion issuant sa. charged with a martlet (Dormer); (2), Gules on a chev. bet. 3 chubs naiant arg. as many martlets sa. on a chief indented of the second three escallops of the field (Dorre als Chobbs); (3), Arg., 3 fleurs-de-lis az. (Collingridge). Crest of impalement, on a wreath a wolf statant between 2 wings sa. charged with a martlet or. (III.) Arg., a chevron erminois [should be "ermines"] between 3 mullets pierced sable (Gresham); impaling Dormer quarterly as before.

The Dormer and Gresham arms are displayed on three shields:

> In the middle, Gresham impaling Dormer, *Dexter*: A chevron ermines between 3 mullets pierced (Gresham); *Sinister*: Quarterly, (1) and (4), Ten billets 4, 3, 2, 1, on a chief or, a demi-lion issuant (Dormer); (2), A chevron between 3 fishes naiant on a chief indented as many escallops; (3), Three fleurs-de-lis. This shield is surmounted by two helmets on

the *dexter* of which is a dog sejant, and on the *sinister* a beast statant. On either side of this shield is an escutcheon of Gresham impaling Dormer quarterly as above recited.

The only part of Nicholas Charles's blazon which agrees with that given above is III and the crests in II. Since Charles's time the blazon has apparently been purposely altered.

Stow is the first topographer to fully describe the Plumbe monument, which, curiously, he locates in Chelsea Old Church. Bowack, who also describes it, speaks of it as situated

> "in the south Isle or south chancel on the Right Hand against the wall, a neat monument of Alabaster with black and red Marble, adorned after the Ancient Manner."

Faulkner speaks of it as at the north end of the south aisle. From this situation it was removed during the alterations of 1840-41, when it was erected on the north side of the Tower Chapel. In 1898 it was unwisely removed to its present position. The inscription reads:

"Sacrvm memoriæ Gvlielmi Plvmbe Armigeri | Et Elizabethæ vxoris eivsdem | Gvlielmvs Plvmbe filivs et hæres Iohanis Plvmbe de Eltham Ar | migeri, dvas vxores dvxit, priorem Margaretam Filiam et vnicam [hæredem Thomæ Nevil Eqvitis, qvam Robertvs Sovthwell Eqves | vidvam reliqverat, ex qva nvllam prolem genvit, alteram Elizabe | tham, ex qva vnicvs ei filivs natvs est, Franciscvs Plvmbe. Elizabe | tha, vnica filia et hæres Edvardi Dormer de Fvlham armigeri filij | natv minimi Galfridi Dormer de Thame armigeri priorem conivge habvit Iohanem Gresham de Mayfield in Comitatv Svssexiæ armi | gerv' et secvndv' filiv' Iohis Gresham Eqvitis (qvonda maioris Londo) cvi tres peperit filios Thoma Gvlielmv' et Edvardvm Gresham, eo | defvncto Gvlielmvm Plvmbe prædictvm conivgem accepit. | Gvlielm Plvmbe Obijt 9° die Feb. Ano Dni. 1593 A°q ætatis svæ 60 | Elizabetha Plvmbe Obijt . . . die . . . A° Dni . . . A°q Ætatis svæ . . . "

(Translation: "Sacred to the memory of William Plumbe, Esquire, and Elizabeth his wife. William Plumbe, son and heir of John Plumbe of Eltham, Esquire, married two wives, the first, Margaret, daughter and sole heiress of Thomas Nevil, gentleman, whom Sir Robert Southwell, knight, left a widow, by whom he had no issue; the other, Elizabeth, by whom he had an only son, Francis Plumbe. Elizabeth was the only daughter and heiress of Edward Dormer of Fulham, Esquire, youngest son of Geoffrey Dormer of Thame, Esquire. She had for her first husband John Gresham, of Mayfield, in the County of Sussex, Esquire, and second son of Sir john Gresham (once Lord Mayor of London), to whom she bore three sons, Thomas, William and Edward Gresham. After his death, she married the above mentioned William Plumbe. He died 9th day of February Anno Dom. 1593 and in the 60th year of his age. Elizabeth Plumbe died . . . day of . . . Anno Dom. . . . and in the . . . year of her age).

The will of William Plumbe, dated 20 July 1593, was proved on 1 Mar. 1593-94 (P.C.C. 24 Dixey). The following is an extract:

"I William Plumbe of ffulham in the Countye of Middlesexe gentleman knowinge that I was borne to dye and that the tyme thereof may be soe shorte a momente w^{the} twynckling of an eye, and fynding by daylie experience the manyfolde and intricate suytes and questions in lawe which doe arise for lacke of Disposing and advisinge of such havior as yt pleaseth the allmyghtie to commytt unto us haue thought very meete and convenyent in this contagyous tyme of infecton whilest it pleaseth almightie God of his greate mercye and goodnes to gyve me perfect remembraunce of mynd and reasonable health of bodye, etc.
To be buried at discretion of executrix without pompe or Worldly glory, onely £5 amongst the poor present at my funeral and £2 to the poor mens box of the parish where I shall fortune to decease. To my son Frauncis £2,000 to be bestowed in land for his use. To my said sonne ffrauncis all my Jewelles of golde as well Ringes as browches buttons bracelettes and tablettes sett wyth stones or otherwise excepte such as are in the possession of Elizabeth my wife. To said sonne ffrauncis all my apparell of silke or cloth wyth sylke or trymed with gold or syluer lace or furred. To said sonne ffrauncis all my bookes as well lattyne as Englishe and all manner of thinges in my closett as yt nowe standeth excepte all manner of coyne of syluer or golde. To Thomas Gressham my wives eldest sonne three hundred poundes of lawful Englishe money to be Deliuered unto him at the age of one and twentye yeres and in the meane tyme to remayne in the hands of his mother.
To William Gressham my wives seconde sonne three hundred poundes of lawful Englishe money to be Deliuered unto him at the age of one and twentye years and in the meane tyme to remayne in the hands of his mother hopeing that hereby and by theire educacon and preferment in service which hath bynn very chardgeable to me I have made full satisfaction for three hundred and ffiftye poundes which I receyued of Sr John Goodwyn as was allotted unto theire mother and them of the goodes of the Lady Gressham their grandmother. And if yt happen

that any of the two sonnes Thomas or William to Decease before the age of one and twenty yeres then I will that the porcon of him soe dyinge shall remayne unto him that shall survive. And yf yt shall happen that they both dye before the age of one and twenty yeres then I will that both their porcons of three hundred pounde apeice be equally divided between Elizabeth my wife and ffrauncis my sonne.

To poore of ffulham 40s. to be distributed at discretion of executrix.

Residue to Elizabeth my wife and she sole executrix and my freindes Mr. William Lambert of Kent Mr. Richard Williams and Mr. Henry Thornton my overseers most earnestly praying them in the bowells of Jesus Christ to take some paynes herein and to be ayding and assisting unto my poore wife whoe is an ignorant body in these cases and therfore shall haue greate neede of theire helpe and for theire paynes herein to each a piece of plate vallewe fyve markes to be made of purpose for them and my name to be ingraved upon each of them. I have written this wyth myne owne hand and hereunto subscribed my name as a testimony that yt is my full intencon and last will conteyned in thre sheetes of paper which I pray God may take effecte according to my meaninge soe as yt may be most to his glory and my salvacon Amen."

Monument to William Plumbe.
From a photograph by Mr. T. S. Smith, 1896

Charles James Fèret

PEDIGREE OF DORMER, PLUMBE AND GRESHAM FAMILIES

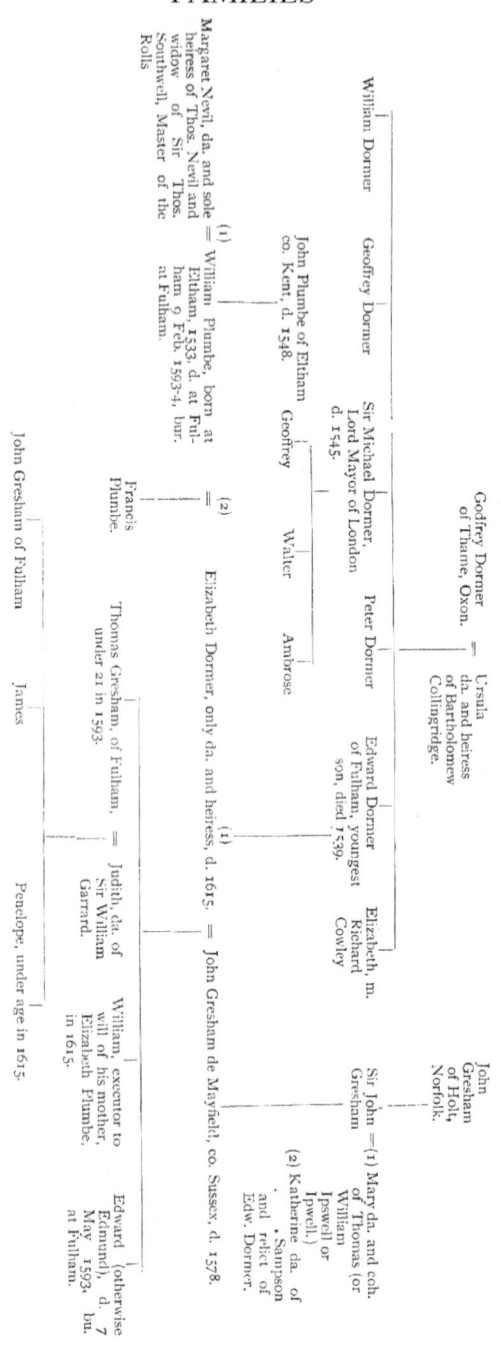

Geoffrey Dormer of Thame, Oxon. = Ursula, da. and heiress of Bartholomew Collingridge.

William Dormer

Geoffrey Dormer

Sir Michael Dormer, Lord Mayor of London, d. 1545.

Peter Dormer

Edward Dormer of Fulham, youngest son, died 1539.

Elizabeth, m. Richard Cowley

John Gresham of Holt, Norfolk.

John Plumbe of Eltham co. Kent, d. 1548.

Margaret Nevil, da. and sole heiress of Thos. Nevil and widow of Sir Thos. Southwell, Master of the Rolls = (1) William Plumbe, born at Eltham, 1533, d. at Fulham, 9 Feb. 1593-4, bur. at Fulham.

Geoffrey   Walter   Ambrose

Francis Plumbe.
= (2)

Elizabeth Dormer, only da. and heiress, d. 1615. = (1) John Gresham de Mayfield, co. Sussex, d. 1578.

Sir John = (1) Mary, da. and coh. of Thomas (or William Ipswell or Ipswell).
(2) Katherine da. of . Stampson and relict of Edw. Dormer.

John Gresham of Fulham

James

Thomas Gresham, of Fulham, under 21 in 1593.

Judith, da. of Sir William Garrard.

William, executor to will of his mother, Elizabeth Plumbe, in 1615.

Edward (otherwise Edmund), d. 7 May 1593, bur. at Fulham.

Penelope, under age in 1615.

416

The son, Francis Plumbe, mentioned in the will, was educated at Oxford. He proceeded B.A. on 8 July 1596. He entered as a student at Gray's Inn in 1598. In the Gray's Inn Register he is described as "of Fulham, Mid., gent." On 24 June, 1620, the Bishop of London granted license to Francis Plumbe to marry Jane, daughter of Sir Richard Ogle, knight.

There is some doubt as to whether Mrs. Elizabeth Plumbe was buried at Fulham. Bowack thinks she was not. His inclination to this belief appears to be based on the circumstance that the blanks in the epitaph were never filled in. As, however, she died at Fulham in 1615, and left money to the poor of the parish to be distributed at her funeral, it seems far more likely that she was interred here. Her will, dated 2 Sept. 1615, was proved 22 Nov. 1615 (P. C. C. 95 Rudd).

South Transept Floor

Under the organ steps is a stone inscribed:

> "Frances Elizabeth Garforth, | wife of Will[m] Garforth, Esq., | eldest son of the Rev[d] Edmund Garforth | and Elizabeth his wife: | died January 8th 1800, aged 40 years. | Also Mrs. Frances Asthigh, aunt of Mr. Garforth, | who died 9th December 1815, aged 77."

In the floor of the south transept is a large black marble stone recording the memory of Dr. Samuel Barrow. The epitaph runs:

> "P.M.S. | Samuelis Barrow, M.D. ex vetusta | In agro Norfolk: prosapia | Carolo II° edicim ordinarij | Exercitui Anglicano | Advocati Generalis & Iudicis Martialis | Per Annos, plus minus viginti | Quæ munera, jussu regio suscepit | Quod Albemarlium secutus | Optatum Caroli reditum | Suis rnaturavit consilijs | Uxorem duxit unicam | Relictam Gul. Clarke, Eq. Aur. | Cujus felicissimi paris | (Cum sexdecim, annos rarum | Amoris conjugalis exemplum exhibuisset) | Quæ sola potuit, mors fregit Consortium | xii. Kal. Aprilis A.D. [MDCLXXXII] | Infracto adhuc manente superstitis amore. | Ob. Æt. LVII.
> (Translation: Sacred to the pious memory of Samuel Barrow, M.D., descended from an ancient family in the county of Norfolk, Physician in Ordinary to Charles II and above twenty years Advocate General and judge Martial to the English Army; which offices he undertook by the King's command, having followed Albemarle and, by his counsels,

expedited the return of Charles. He married, once, the widow of Sir William Clarke, knt. Of this most happy pair, Death broke the union, which it alone could, after they had, for sixteen years, exhibited a rare example of conjugal love 12 Kal. Apl. 1682 (i.e. 21 Mar. 1682-83). The affection of the survivor remains unbroken. He died aged 57).

Above are the following arms:

Dexter: Barrow. *Sinister*: Hyliard. [See the Clarke-Barrow monument. later in this chapter] *Crest*.' A fawn's head erased.

The original site of this stone was at the east end of the south aisle. In a vault here, on 25 Mar. 1682-3, the remains of Dr. Barrow were interred. On the death, in 1695, of his wife, Lady Dorothy Clarke, relict of Sir William Clarke, that lady's son, Dr. George Clarke, erected to the memory of his mother and step-father the elegant monument now in the Tower Chapel. This monument was originally placed by the side of the 1682 stone, the whole being protected by iron rails. In 1840-41, the monument was removed into the Tower Chapel, where it now stands. In 1880, when the old Church was taken down, the Barrow stone was found under the boarded floor of the old vestry, added in 1840. On the erection of the new Church the stone was placed in its present position.

"Here lieth the Body | of Elizabeth late Daughter of | Simon and Elizabeth Horner | of Hull, | died 16: May 1793 | in the 17th year of her age."

South Transept Walls

On a white marble slab, on a black stone, is the following epitaph:

"Sacred | to the memory of | John Goldsborough Ravenshaw, Esqre | twenty two years | a Director of the East India Company | obiit 6th June A.D. 1840 | Ætatis 63 | And of his wife | Hannah, | who died on the 30th of November 1862 | aged 78. | This monument is erected by the surviving family, | as a tribute of affection | to their highly respected and lamented parents."

Above the inscription is the following impaled coat:

Dexter: Quarterly as in arms of T. W. Ravenshaw [see later in this chapter]. *Sinister*: Barry wavy of seven arg. and az. on a chief sable two lions passant gardant between as many anchors erect argent. *Crest*: as in monument to T. W. Ravenshaw.

A small brass tablet records the sad end of the third son of the late Francis Bishop Blomfield:

"In memory of | Francis | third son of | Charles James Blomfield, D.D. | late Bishop of London | who was lost in the wreck of | the Northerner off Cape | Mendocino, North America | January V Anno Domini MDCCCLX | In the thirty-third year of his age | This tablet is erected by his mother, | brother and sisters. | 'Thy way is in the sea | and thy path in the great waters | and thy footsteps are not known.' | Psalm LXXVII. xix."

Above the foregoing, in a canopied niche of marble, is a memorial brass to Bishop Blomfield; it reads:

"To the memory | of the Right Rev. Charles James Blomfield, D.D., | late Bishop of London. | This monument is erected | by his personal friends and neighbours, | long resident in this parish, as a tribute of their admiration of | his abilities, his munificence, & his kindness; | and with a grateful estimate of the manner | in which they were devoted, | during a period of twenty-nine years, | to advance the welfare | and to relieve the distress of all around him here. He died 5th August 1857, Aged 71 years."

This memorial was originally erected in the Tower Chapel.

Sir Charles Egleton Kent, bart., etc.
"Sacred to the Memory of | the Right Honorable Lady Sophia Margaret | wife of Sir Charles Egleton Kent | of Fornham in the County of Suffolk, Baronet, | Obiit 16 Novembris, A.D. 1834. | Also of Sir Charles Egleton Kent, Baronet, | Obiit 5 Decembris, A.D. 1834 | whose remains are deposited in vault beneath.

When heaven recalled the spirit pure and kind
Whose sweet affection solaced life's decay
The manly breast that ne'er till then repined
In grief's lone dwelling found it hard to stay.

The tie was broken but the widowed heart
To Mercy's throne was lifted not in vain
Joined sacred ashes never more to part
For Death unites the severed Nuptial chain."

Thomas William Ravenshaw
"Sacred | to the Memory of | Thomas William Ravenshaw, Esq[re] | many years | Colonel of the Royal Berkshire Regt. of Militia: | Eldest son of | John Goldsborough Ravenshaw, Esq[re] | of Old Bracknell, Berks. | and of Elizabeth, only daughter of | William Withers, Esq[re] | He departed this life August 14th 1842, | aged 66 years. | As a tribute of her sincere love, | regard and respect for the memory | of the most affectionate of husbands | and kindest of friends, | this monument is erected | by his faithfully attached Widow."

Beneath are the arms impaled:

Dexter: Quarterly, (1) and (4), Arg., a chevron between three ravens' heads erased sa. (Ravenshaw); (2) and (3), Arg., a chevron between three crescents gu. (Withers). *Sinister*: Az., a chevron or, guttèe gules between three mullets pierced of the second. *Crest*: On an esquire's helmet a cap of maintenance proper surmounted by a lion statant gardant arg.

PEDIGREE OF RAVENSHAW FAMILY

The Ravenshaw family was from very early times settled in the neighbourhood of Cheshire and Shropshire, and claims descent from the ancient Saxon family of the name.

In Domesday Book their holding of land in Shipley and other places in Yorkshire and other counties is mentioned. The name occurs in ancient records of Lancashire and Cheshire, Plea Rolls, etc., all the way down to the present time.

The following page shows the Ravenshaw family chart.

From the Ravenshaws, of Sansaw Hall, Shropshire, descended

Richard Ravenshaw, living 1781.

Thomas Ravenshaw, of Sunbury, Middlesex, and Old Bracknell, Berks, buried at East Hampstead, Berks, 1788.
= (1) Sarah, d. of Thos. Barnes, Esq., of Guildford, Surrey, d. 1759.
(2) Anne Wilmot, d. 1104, without issue.

John Ravenshaw, of The Mount, Whitchurch, Salop. Will proved at Lichfield, 1783, by Susannah, his widow.

Elizabeth Ravenshaw. = Harry Monteith.

Mary Ravenshaw.

John Goldsborough Ravenshaw, of Old Bracknell and Bath, buried at Walcot Church, æt. 73. Anno 1824
= Elizabeth, d. of William Withers, of Dummer and Fulham. (v. *Withers' Pedigree*.)

Geo. Ravenshaw, R.N. d. 1812.

William Ravenshaw, Captain of Engineers, E. I. Co., Madras Est. d. 1825.

Rev. Edw. Ravenshaw, M.A., Rector of West Kington, Wilts; ed. at Eton and B.N.C. Oxon, b. 1782; d. 1854.
= (1) Elizabeth, d. of Chas. Purvis, of Dagshaw, Suffolk, J.P., D.L., High Sheriff 1794;
(2) Jemima Charlotte, d. of John Ibbetson, of Ealing, d. 1854.

John Goldsborough Ravenshaw, D.L. of Harley St., London, Chairman and Director of the Honble. East India Company. d. 1840 bu. at Fulham.
= Hannah, d. of Chas. John Bond.

Thos. Wm. Ravenshaw, Colonel Berks Militia bu. at Fulham.

John Hardis Ravenshaw, of Derby Lodge, Richmond.
(2) Edw. Cockburn, E.I.C.S., Bengal Est., b. 1804; d. 1877 s.p.
(3) Henry Thomas, Civil Service of China, b. 1807; d. s.p.
(4) Holden Shepherd, E.I.C.S., Bengal Est.; b. 1814; died s.p
(5) Charles Alexander, E.I.C.S., Bengal Est.; b. 1820; d. 1843. s.p

Adelaide, m. Edgar Delacour Je Labilliere, Bar.-at-Law of Harrow.

Rev. Thomas FitzArthur Porrin Ravenshaw, M.A., Rector of Pewsey, Wilts.; ed. Oriel College, Oxon, b. 1829; died s.p.

Emma Caroline.

Annie, m. Donald Baynes, C.E., and son of Sir Wm. Baynes, Bart., of Harvfield Place, co. Midd.

(8) Elizabeth Augusta, m. Chas. McCarthy, Director of the Bk. of England
(9) Caroline Finistrina, m. Thos. Carpenter, Commander R.N
(10) Charlotte, m. Jas. Murray, C.B., Assistant Under Secretary, Foreign Office
(11) Hester, m. (1) to Thomas Dowler, M.D., and (2) to the Rt. Honble. Sir Jasper Selwyn, Q.C., M.P. afterwards Lord Justice of Appeal, and a brother of Bishop Selwyn of Lichfield, and had issue Capt. Selwyn, late M.P. for Wisbeach division of Cambs.
(12) Amelia Hannah, m. Wm. Price. of Ryde. I. of W.
(13) Rose Sarah, m. Charles Fountaine, Capt. of 52 Regt.

Edw. Cockburn Ravenshaw, Cornet 1st Regt. Light Cavalry, died in East Indies, s.p.

Geo. Chandler Ravenshaw, E.I.C.S. Home Dept. b. 1830; d. 1879; m. Eliza, 2nd daughter of Sir Hy. Willock, Chairman of East India Co.

John Henry Ravenshaw, E I.C.S., Bengal Est., b. 1833; d. 1874; m. Caroline, d. of Col. W. J. Thompson, C.B. s.p.

(1) Rose Milly, d. of John Thuillier, Baron de Malaperte, of Geneva, and sister of General Sir Henry Thuillier, Surveyor General of India
(2) Harriet Lalande, d. of Lewis James Biggs, of the Admiralty

Hardis Secundus Lalande Ravenshaw, Capt. in Devonshire Regt. b. 1869; m. younger d. of Colonel Sir Hy. Ravenshaw Thuillier. K.C.I.E. late Surveyor General of India and granddaughter of Gen. Sir Hy. Thuillier, kt.

Thos. Edw. Ravenshaw, J.I., C.C. late E.I.C.S., Bengal Est., of South Hill, Worth, Sussex. b. 1827; m. Susannah, d. of Alex. Symonds, of Ombersley, Worcester.

Capt. Herbert Edw. Ravenshaw, b. 1853; d. 1880.

Harold Alexander Ravenshaw, Major Indian Staff Corps, b. 1856.

Henry Willock Ravenshaw, b. 1858.

Rose Melley, b. 1861.

Caroline Annie, b. 1862.

Chas. Withers Ravenshaw, Lt.-Col. Indian Staff Co. and I C.S. b. 1851.

North Aisle Walls

Against the west wall of the north aisle, over the door leading to the North Porch, are the following two marble slabs:

"To the memory | of | Jhn Thomas Bigge | of the Inner Temple, Esquire, | Barrister at Law | formerly Chief Justice of Trinidad | third son of Thomas Charles Bigge of Benton House | in the county of Northumberland, Esquire, | This monument is erected | by his surviving brother and sister | Born 8th. March 1780 | Died 22nd. December 1843."

"Sacred | to the Memory of Jemima | relict of the late | Thomas Charles Bigge, Esqr | of Benton House, Northumberland | who died November 25, 1806 | Aged 58 years. | Her remains were deposited at her own | request near this place. | In the same grave with her mother | are deposited the remains of | Eliza | their fourth daughter; | who died May 19th, 1819 | in the 38th year of her age."

Against the east wall are the following:

"Sacred | to the Memory of | Mary Barnard | Relict of the Revd Benjamin Barnard | Prebend of Peterborough | who departed this life 16th. April 1842 | in the 90th. year of her age. | Her remains are deposited | in conformity with her own desire | by the side of her brother | William Townsend, Esq. | in a vault at Kensington. | This Tablet is erected in the Church of this Parish | (where her charities and benevolence are well-known) | by her nephew | Chaloner Bisse Challoner, Esqre | as a token of affection and gratitude | to whom she was at all times a kind and liberal benefactress."

"Sacred | to the Memory of | Sir Charles William Kent, Bart., | Captain in the first regiment of Life Guards | who died April 8th. 1848 | Æt. 28, | to the deep regret of his family | and numerous friends. | His remains are deposited in the same vault in this church | with those of his deceased parents."

South Aisle Walls

The first stone against the south aisle walls is inscribed:

"Sacred | to the Memory of | Francis Matthias Bassano | Apothecary to

H.M's. Forces | who died 7 June 1869 aged 83 years | and of | Charlotte his wife, | who died 30 July 1855, aged 69 years. | Also of Francis Richard Bassano | Eldest son of the above | who died 19 April 1825, aged 9 years, | Christopher Bakewell Bassano, | M.R.C.S. Eng, Staff Surgeon Late H. M.'s. 70th. Reg^t | fifth son of the above, | who died in the Crimea 1 February 1856 | aged 31 years, | Melinda Bassano, | younger daughter of the above, | who died 31 July 1874, aged 44 years | and | Thomas Bromsall Bassano, | fourth son of the above, | who died at Havre 9 February 1876 | aged 54 years: | He was interred with his family | in the Churchyard, | and by his desire this tablet was erected."

The oldest and, in many respects, the most interesting memorial in the Church is the Flemish brass, 23 inches square, now fixed against the east wall of the south aisle. Weever gives a corrupt copy of the inscription in which he spells the surname "Suanden." During the Civil War, it has been supposed, the brass was, for the sake of greater security, buried beneath the ground. In 1705 the brass was certainly missing, for Bowack copies the inscription as he found it in Weever with the false spelling "Suanden." The inscription in Strype's Stow's "Survey" (1754) is also taken from Weever. From Lysons' "Environs" we learn that the brass was discovered in 1770, "in digging for the foundation of a column when the church was repaired." As Lysons wrote in 1796, he doubtless stated this fact from living testimony.

The recovered brass was erected against the east wall of the north aisle where it was in Faulkner's time. In 1840-41 it was placed in the Tower Chapel. In 1858 it was once more removed in order to make room for the Blomfield monument, when it was assigned a position similar to that which it now occupies.

The brass consists of a half-length effigy, evidently a portrait, in a hood or veil, marked with a Maltese cross above the forehead, and with a cloth passing under the chin. Beneath the effigy is the following inscription in a frame supported by an angel on each side:

"Hic Jacet domicella Margareta Svanders nata Ganda in | Flandrie que ex magistro Gerardo Hornebolt Gandauensi | Pictore nominatissimo peperit domicellam Susannam | uxore magistri Johannis Parcker Archarij Regis que | obijt anno dni. MCCCCCXXIX xxvi Nouebris: orate p' aia."

(Translation: Here lies Dame Margaret Svanders, born at Ghent in Flanders, who, by Master Gerard Hornebolt, a most renowned painter of Ghent, bore Dame Susanna, the wife of Master John Parker, keeper of the king's 'wardrobe, who died Anno Dom. 26 Nov. 1529. Pray for her soul.)

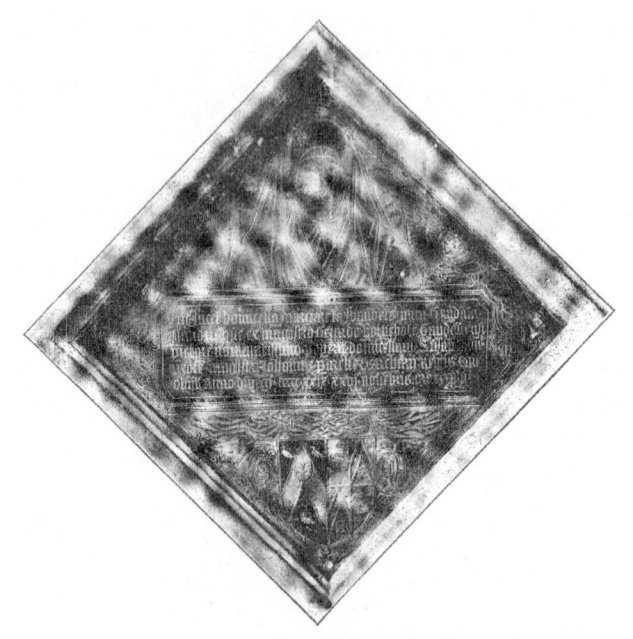

Monumental brass to Margaret Svanders.
From a photograph by Mr. T. S. Smith, 1896

Beneath this inscription is placed a shield of arms, and the initials G.O. supposed to be for Gerard Hornebolt or Ornebolt. The arms appear to be reversed, those on the dexter half being Svanders, Swinders or Swinters of Flanders, and the escutcheon and the quarterly impalement those of her two husbands, Jan van Heerweghe and Gerard Hornebolt, a somewhat peculiar arrangement. The coat is, apparently:

Dexter: A chevron between 3 martlets. In a fess point an escutcheon charged with a cross moline between 4 crescents. *Sinister*: Quarterly, (1) and (4), A winnowing fan surmounted of a crescent; (2) and (3), A chevron between 3 men's heads couped.

Gerard Hornebolt, Hornebaud, Horenbout, Hoorenbault, Horebout, etc., was born at Ghent about 1480. The first reference to him occurs in the communal accounts for 1510-11, being a payment for a plan or map of the city of Ghent and its environs. Hornebolt was regarded as one of the best illuminators of his day, and, between 1516 and 1521, he was largely employed in working for the Princess Margaret of Austria, regent of the Netherlands. In December 1517, he was already married to Margaret Svanders, daughter of Derick Svanders, and widow of Jan van Heerweghe.

In 1528 Gerard Hornebolt came to England, accompanied by Luke Hornebolt. According to some authorities, Luke was a son of Gerard, but others state that he was a brother or a cousin. Soon after Gerard's arrival, we find him appointed Court Painter to Henry VIII. He died in 1540.

Susanna Hornebolt, named in the inscription, was born in 1503. She is first mentioned by Albrecht Durer as being with her father at Antwerp in 1521. She appears to have come to England with her parents and to have married one John Parker, who is described in the brass as "Archarij Regis," i.e. the keeper of the "arca vestiaria" or wardrobe. Parker seems to have been a Fulham man, for, in a grant of exemption from service as sheriff, escheator or other officer or commissioner in England, Wales, Calais or the Marches, he is described as "yeoman of the wardrobe of robes *alias* of Fulham, Middlesex" (State Papers, Pat. p.1 m.23, 20 Oct. 25 Henry VIII.)

The following tablet records the memory of Sir John Beckett, bart., and his brother, the Rev. George Beckett:

"Sacred to the Memory of | the Right Hon[ble] Sir John Beckett, Baronet, | of Stratford Place, London, | and Somerby Park, Lincolnshire, who died at Brighton, on the 31st. of May 1847, | in the 73rd. year of his age | Also sacred to the memory of | The Reverend George Beckett, | Prebend of Lincoln, Rector of Epworth, | and vicar of Gainsborough, | who died in London, on the 13th. of April 1843 | in the 51st year of his age. | Their remains are deposited in the adjoining vault of their ancestor | Edmund Gibson, Bishop of London."

A small oval slab bears the words:

"Near this spot lie | the | remains of | Madame de Stark | who | died A. D. 1805."

In Faulkner's time there existed in a window in the south aisle a small octagonal brass plate inscribed:

> "Near this spot | are deposited the remains | of | Martha Ogle Baroness de Stark, | of the Holy Roman Empire | Youngest daughter of | Nathaniel Ogle of Kirkley in the County of Northumberland, Esquire. | She was born on the 9th. day of May, A. D. 1719 | And died on the 20th. day of January, A. D. 1805 | Aged 85 Years and 8 Months.
>
> If virtue boasts a triumph in our love,
> And filial tears are seen by Saints above,
> She, at whose sepulchre this Verse is laid,
> O spotless innocence ! O Holy Shade !
> Shall know that she was lov'd - well pleas'd shall see
> Her Children's grief record her Memory;
> And grateful for life past, His pow'r adore,
> Who call'd her hence, the spoil of death no more."

The Church Registers record:

> 1805. Martha Barroness De Starck in South Ile from London bu. 27 Jan.

Beneath the above is a plain marble monument, with the arms (a cross, between four pheons) blazoned above and the motto "Cœlitus mihi vires." It is inscribed:

> "Under this tablet, in a vault the property of | the Right Honorable Thomas, Lord Viscount Ranelagh, | lie the bodies of | Caroline Elizabeth Viscountess Ranelagh, | his late wife, Daughter of Sir Philip Stephens, Baronet, | who died in child-bed on the 17th of June, 1805, aged 33 years. | And of his Infant daughter, the Honorable Caroline Jones, | who lived one day | Also Sir Philip Stephens, Baronet, | who died the 20th of November 1809, aged 87 years. | Also the Right Honorable Thomas, Lord Viscount Ranelagh, | Baron Navan, &c. | who died at Fulham on the 4th of July 1820, aged 58 years. | And also the Honorable Arthur Jones, | who died on the 28th of June, 1820, aged 2 years and 2 months."

The vault here described was purchased by Lord Ranelagh on the occasion of the death of his first wife, Caroline Elizabeth, in 1805. Of the Ranelagh family we shall speak in our account of

Ranelagh House. The Church Registers record:

> 1805. The Right Honble. Lady Caroline Elizabeth Wife of Thomas Lord Viscount Ranelagh . . . bu. 24 June.

> 1809. Sir Philip Stephens Bar^t . . . bu. 28 Nov.

> 1820. The Honorable Arthur Jones son of Viscount Ranelagh, Fulham, aged 2 years and 4 months bu. 1 July

> 1820. The Honorable Thomas Jones Viscount Lord Ranelagh, Fulham, aged 58 years . . . bu. 12 July

All that remains of the once lovely monument to the memory of this Fulham worthy is a faded tablet surmounted by two winged heads with shield of arms. The inscription reads:

> "Here lies the Bodie of Sr Thomas Kinsey | Knight and Alderman of the City of London | who died the third day of Ianuary in the | Yeare of our Lord one thousand six hundred | ninety and six and in the Sixtieth Yeare of | his age."

Lower down on the stone is this addition:

> "In the same graue lie also the Bodies of | Robert and Elizabeth Atkyns his | Grandchildren by his only child Mary the | wife of Richard Atkyns, Esquire."

Bowack, who states that this monument cost £100, speaks of it as

> "A Beautiful Monument of Marble of several colours about 10 Foot in length. From an urn above hang neat Festoons, etc. Over the inscription is Two Cherubs' heads supporting the arms."

The arms, now nearly obliterated, are:

> *Dexter*: Arg., a chevron between three squirrels at browse proper (for Kinsey as borne by a family of that name in co. Chester). *Sinister*: Sa., a chevron between three fleurs-de-lis and a canton or. [The field was originally azure.]

Sir Thomas Kinsey was a member of the Vintners' Company, and served the office of Sheriff in 1685. He was elected Alderman of Dowgate, 27 Oct. 1685. He was suspended in 1688, but restored before the close of the year. He was knighted at Windsor on 24 Aug. 1685. According to Le Neve, "he kept the Crown Tavern in Bloomsbury after the building of that square, and there got his estate." Sir Thomas died intestate, 3 Jan. 1696-97, administration of his goods being granted to his relict, Mary Kinsey, 13 Feb. 1696-97.

The space left in the epitaph, below the inscription to Sir Thomas Kinsey, was doubtless intended to be filled upon the death of his wife, whose remains were interred in the vault in 1717. Her will, dated 22 Mar. 1716-17 (codicil 16 Aug. 1717), was proved 9 Jan. 1717-18 (P.C.C. 13 Tenison). It contains the following request:

> "My will and desire is to be decently and privately buryed in the Parish Church of ffulham in the County of Middlesex where my dear Husband lyes Interred and as near him as conveniently may be."

The Church Registers record:

> 1696. Sr Thomas Kincy Knight Bart. bu. 9 Jan.
> 1717. Dame Mary Kensey from London bu. 3 Oct.

Inserted against the wall of the south aisle, in a handsome marble frame, with mosaic border of blue and gold, bearing the family arms, etc., in the upper corners, is a tablet inscribed:

> "In memory of | Alfred Bassano | Major General, C.B., Formerly of the | 32nd Cornwall Light Infantry with which | regiment he served in the 2nd Sikh War, 1848-9 | being present at the siege of Mooltan | and the battle of Goojerat. | Also during the Indian Mutiny 1857-9 | including the ever memorable defence | of the Residency of Lucknow. | He died Sepr 12th 1882 aged 56 years. | This tablet is erected by his comrades, | past and present, of the above regiment in token of their esteem and regret. - 'I will give you rest.' "

Against the return wall at the west end of the south aisle is another quaint and highly interesting monument. It is to the memory of William Earsby, a well-known market gardener. Bowack speaks of it as situated at the west end of the south aisle, a position similar to that which it still occupies. The monument, which is of plain alabaster, bears, on a black marble slab, the following inscription:

> "In Memory of William Earsby of northend, Gent. | who departed this Life the 18th of October 1664 | and in the 73rd year of his age.
>
> Neare to this place his aged corpes doeth lye
> Who whilst hee lived was not afraide to dye
> his pantinge sovle in hopes of heavenly rest
> imbraced death as his most wellcome guest
> hee did that worke whilst time and strength did last
> which many shun tell both be ouerpast
> vnto good workes his mind was euer prest
> yet on gods grace throvgh christ his faith did rest
> he rvn the race and hath obtain'd the prize
> that which remayns for us to doe likewise."

Monument to William Earsby.
From a photograph by Mr. T. S. Smith, 1896.

Of the Earsby family we shall speak in an account of North End.

Floor Of Nave

John Longley, d. 3 Dec. 1726; Mrs. Martha Longley, widow of John Longley, d. 7 Jan. 1736.

Susanna Duncombe, d. 6 Sept. 1748, widow of the Hon. Col. Duncombe, an ancestor of the Earl of Feversham.

Anthony Hammond, d. 28 Jan. 1810; Rebecca Hammond, his widow, d. 11 Dec. 1815.

"Here lies ye Body of | Elizabeth Wimberley | late wife of Bartholomew | Wimberley of y^s Parish who | departed y^s Life Jan^{ry} ye 12th | 1733. Aged 53 years. | Here also lies the Body of | Elizabeth Wimberley | the Daughter of Bartholomew | and Elizabeth Wimberley | who died the 21st of September | 1737 Aged 21 years. | Mr. Bartholomew Wimberley | was buried here 17 June 1755, | Aged 82 Years."

In the Churchwardens' Accounts for 1733 is the following entry:

"Rec^d of Mr. Wimberley for laying a Stone in the Church over his wife's grave £3. 3s. 0d."

The Church Registers contain these entries:

1733. Elizabeth Wife of Bartholomew Wimberly bu. 17 Jan.
1737. Eliz. D. of Bartholomew Wimberly bu. 29 Sept.
1755. Bartholomew Wimberley Esq. bu. 7 June.

Bartholomew Wimberley resided at Wimberley House, latterly known as Holy Cross House, Fulham Road.

Joseph da Cunha Pareira de Neyva, d. 9 Oct. 1826; Harriet Maria Henrietta de Neyva, his widow, d. 16 Apl. 1833.

M. de Neyva was a resident of Hammersmith.

The next stone recalls the memory of Robert Blanchard, goldsmith, who, with Sir Francis Child, carried on the bank now known as Child and Co.'s. The inscription reads:

> "Mr. Robert Blanchard | Late of This Parish | Was Buried June X | MDCLXXXI."

At one time, however, there must have been another stone, for Bowack gives the following:

> "Here lyeth the body of Robert Blanchard citizen and goldsmith of London and an inhabitant of this parish who Dyed the 6th day of June Annoque Domini 1680 Ætatis Suæ 57."

The date "1680" was doubtless Bowack's error for "1681." Of Robert Blanchard we shall speak in our account of Hollybush House. A clause in his will, dated 17 August 1680, contains the following instructions as to his burial:

> "My Will alsoe is that my Body be decently Buryed in the Parish church of Fullham in the sayd Countie of Middlesex and that it may there quietly remaine, I desire to bee layd as deepe in the Ground as conveniently may bee: I give therefore forty shillings yearly and euery yeare for ever vizt. Tenne shillings to the Minister or Vicar five shillings to the Churchwarden three shillings to the Clarke and two shillings to the Sexton for the time being: the remayning Twenty Shillings to be layd out in good Bread and given to twenty poore people on Fulham side that have been honest, laborious, and of good report The first payment and distribution thereof to be made on first Lord's day next ensuing (one) yeare from my decease and soe every yeare for Ever at the discretion of the Minister and Churchwarden Allways provided and it be understood that it be so long continued and payd and noe longer then the place of my Enterrment (except for the Buriall of a relation or the repayre of what covers the ground) remayne undugg or undisturbed: the fforty shillings I will to be payd out of my house in or neere Parsonage green in the parish of Fulham aforesaid."

The Rev. R. G. Baker states in his "Benefactions":

> "The premises charged with this annuity, consisting at present of three small houses, and being the property of J. P. Powell, Esq., the payment is duly made by him. 'The sum of 5s. is paid to the Parish Clerk, who

fills the several offices of Clerk and Sexton. And as the Minister and Churchwarden decline their respective portions, the whole residue of £1 15s. is applied to the augmentation of the Bread and Beef Fund' (*Report of the Commissioners*, p. 175). The income is still applied in the same manner."

From Skirrow's "Report" on the Fulham Charities, we learn that the money had been paid for several years by the Vestry Clerk, but was not collected by him, and that the present owner of the property declined to pay. The charity has been allowed to lapse.

> Urcilla Thomas, wife of Louis Thomas, rector of Upton Lovell, Wilts, and eldest daughter of Sir Thomas Woodcock, d. 31 July 1716.

A black marble stone is inscribed to Joan Burton. Nothing beyond the words "Here lieth . . . Joane Burton" can now be deciphered.

A stone is simply inscribed "R. E. 1778." The Church Registers, however, supply the name:

> 1778. Mrs. Rachael Eckley in the Church bu. 9 Sept.

A small stone is inscribed:

> "Jeffery Ekins | Dean of Carlisle | died Novr 20 1791 | Aged 60 years."

Dean Ekins resided at Hollybush House. The Church Registers record:

> 1791. The Revd Jeffery Ekins, D.D. Dean of Carlisle bu. 25 Nov.

Following the foregoing is a coat of arms, the owner of which we have been unable to identify. The blazon appears to be a fess and in chief two annulets.

Bowack, speaking of the monument of William Earsby, at the west end of the south aisle, adds:

> "And in the pavement under a black stone lyeth John Earsby his son, of the same place, gent, who Dyed September 9th, 1687, aged 47 years, also Mary his wife, who Dyed Jan. 11th, 1690, aged 47."

In the middle aisle of the present Church this black stone may still be seen, but almost every trace of its inscription has disappeared. Near the top of the stone, and let into it, are two small pieces of white marble, the upper one of which still bears the arms of the wife of John Earsby. On the stone itself the only letters which can be faintly made out are the first and the last of his name - J(ohn) (Earsb)y. Faulkner quotes the inscription thus:

> "Here lieth interred the Body of John Earsby of this Parish who departed this life in September MDCLXXXVII aged XLVII."

The Church Registers record:

> 1687 John Earesby of North End bu. 13 September.

The stone which now marks the Daniel vault bears simply the initials of the six members of the family buried there; F. D. 1815, H. D. 1818, S. D. 1827, J. D. 1838, S. G. H. 1848, and J. D. 1853. These stand for Frances Daniel, Henry Daniel, Sybella Daniel, John Daniel, Sybella Gertrude Hammet, and John Daniel.

"Squire" Daniel, who was buried 17 Oct. 1853, was the last person interred inside Fulham Church. The original stone was replaced by the present one in 1880-81. Of the Daniel family we shall speak in our account of East End House.

A large stone records the memory of Samuel Heather, an apothecary, son of John Heather, of Mortlake:

> "Integer vitæ Scelerisq. purus | Non timet Mortis Jaculum neq. Arcum | Hic situm est | Quantum mortale fuit | Samuelis Heather | Operis Pharmaceutici practici | Londinensis | Vir cum et Arte & moribus | Integerrimus | (Nec erga Amicos Fide incorrupta) | minus spectabilis | Haud mirum fuerit si vel desiderium | Maximum omnibus quibus innotuerat | Reliquierit | Vxorem duxit Fideliam Iohannis Aikeroyd de Folkerthorpe com. Ebo. | Armiger Filiam natu quartam cui peperit | Liberos Octo viz. Elizabetham, Gulielmum, | Em . . . delciam, Fideliam, Samuelem. | Natus Eboraci A.D. 1651 Denatus Londini A.D. 1714 Ætatis Suæ lxij."
>
> (Translation: The man, blameless in life and pure of crime, fears neither the spear nor the bow of Death. Here is sown so much as was mortal of Samuel Heather, apothecary of London. Since he was most sound in his art, nor less remarkable for his unwavering loyalty to his friends, it was

little wonder that he left behind him the greatest regret among all to whom he was known. He married Faith, the fourth daughter of John Aikeroyd of Folkerthorpe, county York, gentleman, who bore him eight children, namely Elizabeth, William, Em . . . delcia, Faith, Samuel. Born at York A.D. 1651. Died at London A.D. 1714, aged 62).

This stone in the old Church was in the south aisle, eastwards of that of Billingsley. Administration of the goods, etc., of Samuel Heather, described as "of the parish of St. Paul's, Covent Garden," was granted to Faith Heather, his relict, 16 Aug. 1714. Administration of the goods, etc., of Faith Heather, described as of St. Giles-in-the-Fields, widow, deceased, was granted to Samuel Heather, her son, 28 April 1725. The Church Registers record:

1714. Mr. Samuel Heather from London bu. 2 June.

The following is from the "Marriage Allegation Books" of the Bishop of London:

"1709 June 6: Licence for John Heather of Fulham co. Mid^x, gent., a Bachelor, aged 35 and Mary Jane Baron of the same, Spinster 30. To be married in the Parish Church of Fulham or the Lord of London's Chappell there."

Peter Brames stone:

Peter Brames, d. 16 Mar. 1834.

The Brames family resided at Elysium Row, in the New King's Road.

Sir Thomas Kinsey stone: a stone, on which only a few words are now legible, doubtless formerly marked the site of the vault of Sir Thomas Kinsey.

Elizabeth London stone:

Elizabeth London, d. 20 Apl. 1732

George London, her husband, was also buried in the Church.

Viscountess Ranelagh, etc. stone, which marked the site of the Ranelagh vault:

> "The Right Honorable Caroline | Elizabeth Viscountess Ranelagh | who died in childbed on the 17th | June 1805 Aged 33 years | is buryed in this vault | Also her infant daughter | the Honorable Caroline Jones | who lived one day | Also Sir Philip Stephens, Bart. | who died the 20th of Novr 1809 | Aged 87 years."

William Stevenage, etc. stone:

> "Here lies the Body of Liev^t Col. Will. Steuenage late Capt. of a | Companie in her Majesties | Coldstream Regement of Foot | Guards, who departed this life | the 14th. day of October 1709 in | the 46 year of his age. | Here also lies the body of Mr. | William Steuenage the only | child of him and Lucy his wife, | Daughter of Henry Beaufoy | Esq. of Guyscliff, Warwickshire. | He was ensign to his fathers Comp. | and died just 5 weeks after him | aged 16 years (to) whose beloued mamorie this | marble stone was laid by the mournful widdow and Mother | of the Deceased. | Here also lies the body of Mrs. Lucy | Steuenage widdow & Mother of | The aboue mentioned who | departed this life the 1st. of Aprill 1713."

The Church Registers record:

> 1709. William Stevenidg Gent. from Sandy End bu. 16 Oct.
> 1709. William Stevenidg Gent. from London bu. 20 Nov.
> 1713. Mrs. Lucy Stevenage bu. 11 Apl.

Cary Eleanor Hamilton stone:

> Cary Eleanor Hamilton, b. 5 Nov. 1692; d. 28 Mar. 1725.
> Arms: On a lozenge three cinquefoils (Hamilton).

Hon. Elizabeth Mordaunt stone:

> "Here rests the Body | of the Honble Elizabeth | youngest Daughter of S^r In° D'Oyly | In the County of Oxon, Baronet | married | to the Honble George Mordaunt | youngest son of In° Ld Visc^t Mordaunt | Deceased | March ye 20 1718 | Aged 31 years | She had issue three daughters | Sophia, Anne & Margaret | whereof ye two eldest only surviv'd.

> Fair vertuous, kind, in whose embrace I past
> Four years each minute happier than the last
> No peevish word, nor discomposing frown;
> But constant peace did all my blessings crown."
> Arms: Mordaunt (Arg., a chevron between three estoiles sa.) impaling D'Oyly.

The Church Registers record:

> 1718. Elizabeth the wife of the Hono^ble George Mordaunt bu. 24 Mar.

Of the Mordaunts we shall speak in our account of Peterborough House.

John Batchellor stone:

> "In a vault beneath this stone | are deposited the Remains | of an affectionate Husband, Parent, and Brother | Mr. Iohn Batchellor Merchant | who died August the 8th. 1766. | He possessed every requisite for business | except Health & Strength of Constitution | and by his Prudence Industry Attention | above all by an inviolable Integrity | He assisted in the successful management | of an extensive Commerce. | Lament, reader, | with the widow & the Fatherless | that a Life so dear to his Friends | so useful to the Publick | was limited to thirty eight years | and reflect | with awe and Improvement | That this night thy soul may be required of thee."

The Church Registers record:

> 1766. John Batchelor, Esq. . . . bu. 16 Aug.

Henry Shelley stone:

> Henry Shelley, d. 26 Sept. 1722; Robert Shelley, brother, d. 1 July 1729.

Lucy Van stone;

> Lucy Van, of Hammersmith, widow of Thomas Van, of Monmouth, d. 7 Aug. 1825.

Dowager Countess of Lonsdale stone:

> "Underneath lies interr'd | waiting her Saviour's call | Mary, | Countess of Lonsdale, | Widow of James Earl of Lonsdale | and Eldest Daughter of | John Earl of Bute, | by Mary Wortley his wife, | She died April 5th 1824. | Aged 86."

The Church Registers record:

> 1824. The Right Honorable Mary Dowager Countess of Lonsdale, Broomhouse, Fulham bu. 13 Ap. aged 86.

Of the Countess of Lonsdale we shall speak in our account of Lonsdale House.

Eleanor Ramus, etc. stone:

> Mrs. Eleanor Ramus, d. 19 Sept. 1804; George Ramus, husband of Mrs. Eleanor Ramus, d. 1 May 1808.

Susannah Leigh, etc. stone:

> Susannah Leigh, d. 2 Sept. 1819; John Leigh, her husband, d. 6 Apl. 1822.

Sarah Carlton, etc. stone:

> Sarah Carlton, d. 17 June 1826; Thomas Carlton, her husband, d. 30 Nov. 1850; Mary Ann Carlton, their daughter, b. 26 July 1797, d. 5 Nov. 1854, bu. at Dallington, Northamptonshire.

Frederick George Lenthall stone:

> "In Memory of | Frederick George, | youngest son | of William John and | Frances Mary Lenthall | Born January 14 1812 | Died January 1 1830."

The Church Registers record:

> 1830. George Frederick Lenthall, Fulham . . . bu. 8 Jan. aged 17.

John Meyrick stone:

> "Died November 27th. 1805 | Aged 52 | John Meyrick, Esqr. | of Peterborough House | Whose Virtues were beyond all Praise."

The Church Registers record:

> 1805. John Meyriek, Esq. . . . bu. 6 Dec.

Of Mr. John Meyrick we shall speak in our account of Peterborough House.

David Steers, etc. stone:

> David Steers, d. 8 Jan. 1830; William Steers, his son, d. 11 Aug. 1831.

Ann Titley stone:

> Ann Titley, wife of Edward Titley, d. 26 June 1810.

[The next stone is illegible]

Elizabeth Frecker, etc. stone:

> Mrs. Elizabeth Frecker, d. 18 Sept. 1727; Katherine Frecker, daughter of Elizabeth Frecker, d. 15 Nov. 1731; Mark Frecker, d. 29 Nov. 1738.

Elizabeth Osborne, etc. stone:

> Mrs. Elizabeth Osborne, d. 16 Feb. 1820; William Osborne, her husband, d. 19 Apl. 1824; Susannah Osborne, d. 18 July 1841.

Of the Osbornes we shall speak in our account of Osborne's Nursery.

Floor of Church, West End

Humphrey Henchman epitaph:
In the north-west corner is a very large black marble stone, with the following arms at the top, deeply cut:

Dexter: The see of London; *Sinister*: A chevron between three henchman's bugle horns, on a chief as many lions rampant (Henchman). The Whole is surmounted of a mitre.

Humphrey Henchman is the only Bishop of London buried within the walls of Fulham Church. The epitaph reads:

"P.M.S | Sub certa spe Resurgendi repostæ | Hic jacent Reliquiæ | Humphredi Henchman Londinensis Episco. | Et gravitate & pastorali Clementia (Quæ vel in vultu elucebant) | Et vitæ etiam sanctitate venerabilis | Spectata in ecclesiam afflictam Constantia | Singulari in Regem Periclitantem fide | Quo feliciter restituto | Cum Sarisburiensi Diæcesi duos Annos | Londinensi duodecim p'fuisset | Regi etiam ab Eleemosynis et Sanctioribus conciliis | Plenus Annis et Cupiens dissolvi. | Obdormivit in Domino | Octobr. 7° Anno Dni MDCLXXV Ætat. suæ LXXXIII. Redemtor meus vivit."
(Translation: Sacred to Pious Memory. In assured hope of the Resurrection, here lie the remains of Humphrey Henchman, Bishop of London, venerable alike for his gravity and for his pastoral clemency (legible in his very countenance), and also for the sanctity of his life. He was of well-tried constancy to the oppressed Church, of singular loyalty to the King when in the greatest hazards, upon whose happy restoration he was first made Bishop of Salisbury, where he remained two years. Afterwards he was translated to the see of London, where he remained twelve years. He was also the King's almoner and Privy Councillor. Full of years and longing for his dissolution, he fell asleep in the Lord the 7th Oct. 1675, aged 83. My Redeemer Liveth.)

The stone was, for a great number of years, obscured from view. Bowack, in 1705, speaks of it as then situated "in the pavement about the middle of the (south) Isle," and he gives a copy of the inscription. It is also quoted at length in Strype's Stow's "Survey," 1754. When, in 1758, Cole inspected it, it was enclosed with an "Iron Palisado." In 1795 it had disappeared. It was missing down to the demolition of the Church in 1880, when it was found under the flooring of the free pews in the recess of the wall in the south aisle.

The Church Registers record:

1675. Humphrey Henchman Lord Bishopp of London departed this life at his house in Aldersgate Street, London, on the 7th. day of October and lyes buried in the south Ile of Fulham Church under a black marable stone. bu. 13 Oct.

Benjamin Harvey, etc. stone:

Benjamin Harvey, d. 6 Mar. 1718; William Harvey, son of Benjamin Harvey, d. 31 Mar. 1769; Mrs. Jane Wigan, d. 14 Dec. 1776; Benjamin Harvey, d. 10 June 1785; Charles Wigan, d. 23 May 1802.

John Elliot, etc. stone:

"Here lies the Body of John Ellio^t, Gent, of | the Parish of St James, Westminster, who Departed | This Life the 19th day of June 1722 in the 49th year | of his Age. He married the Daughter of Iohn | Burnett, Gen^t, of this Parish by whom he had | Sixteen Children.
Nere this place lieth ye Body of Iohn Burnett | Gen^t. who departed this life Octo. 15th. 1689, aged 38 | Here lyeth also the Body of Mrs. Sarah Burnett | wife of Mr. Iohn Burnett who departed | this Life Septr ye 5th 1726 in the 84 year of her age."

The Church Registers record:

1722. John Elliott bur. 23 June.
1689. John Burnett, Sandy End bu. 17 Oct.

Cordelia Longley stone:

Cordelia Longley, daughter of John and Martha Longley, d. 26 July 1720.

William Earsby stone: the only words now legible on this stone are "William Earsby." It originally marked the position of the vault in which the remains of William Earsby were interred in 1664.

Philip Laurents, etc. stone:

"The Revd | Philip Laurents, A.M. | died Novr 10th 1787 | aged 56 years. | Also his Widow | Mrs. Elizth Laurents, | died Jan^{ry} 18th 1796 | Aged 75 years."

The Rev. Philip Laurents was for many years curate at Fulham

Church. On leaving Fulham, Mr. Laurents, who was a native of Jersey, became master of Bury School. The Church Registers record:

> 1787. The Rev. Mr. Philip Laurents (from Bury in Suffolk) bu. 17 Nov.

Martha Billingsley stone:

> "Here lyes the Body of Martha | the truly loving and as truly | beloved wife of | Edward Billingsley | of Westminster, gent. | She was eldest Daughter of Mr | John Earsby of Northend in this | Parish and Martha departed this life ye | 26 day of November 1698 | Ætatis Suæ 26."

The Church Registers record:

> 1698 Martha wife of Edward Billingsley, Gent. from St. Martins in St. James Street at ye Countis of Northumberleyns . . . bu. 30 Nov.

George Dunnage, etc. stone:

> George Dunnage, d. 4 Aug. 1823, Elizabeth Dunnage, widow of George Dunnage, d. 27 Nov. 1824.

Floor of Church, East End

An epitaph, now almost obliterated, reads:

> "To the memory of | John Alleyne | from the Island of Tobago | West Indies | died September 30 1822 | Aged 13 years. | He was an amiable & interesting youth."

Thomas Green, etc. stone:

> Thomas Green, d. 11 Feb. 1806; Mrs. Elizabeth Green, his widow, d. 18 Oct. 1833.

Elizabeth Tipping stone: a black marble stone is inscribed,

> "Here lyeth interred the body of | Elizabeth Tipping | Daughter of Edward Cosyn of Hillesley | in ye County of Gloucester, Esq., by his | wife, Frances eldest Daughter of William | Trye of Hardwick court in

Hardwick in | ye same County, Esq[re] Descended of one | of ye coheiresses of S[r] Charles Brandon | K[t] Duke of Suffolk & K[t] of the most | Noble Order of ye Garter haveing Issue | Lucretia one onely Daughter by Her | Husband | Deceased 29th July 1686 Aged 22 years."

A cut will be observed across this stone near the top. The upper part having become broken, the late Vicar, the Rev. F. H. Fisher, had a piece removed from the bottom of the stone to match the mutilated portion. This was inserted at the top, and the required portion of the inscription engraved upon it.

This stone is first mentioned by Bowack, who speaks of it as "in the pavement of the middle Isle." The deeply-sunk arms, somewhat mutilated, are:

> On a bend engrailed 3 pheons (Tipping) impaling a chevron between 3 hinds' heads erased (Trye).

The Church Registers record:

> 1686 Mrs. Eliz. Tipping the Wife of Mr. Geo. Tipping . . . bu 31 July.

Robert Hickes stone: on a large black stone, bearing the arms of the Hickes. family, is the following:

> "MS. | Here lyeth the Body of Robert | Hickes, Esq., who died the 23 | day Ivne 1669 | Ætatis Svæ 56. Resurrecturus."

In the "Register Book" is the following:

> "Robert Hickes Esq. late of this p[ish] did by his last will & Testament give & bequeath to the poore of this parish on Fulham-side the sum of five pounds to buy them a stocke of sea-coles yearely for ever: wch said sum was paid by me John Needler & me John Holman Executors of the said Rob[t]. Hickes to Mr Richard Stevenson Vicar & Mr Thomas Willett Churchwarden of ffulham the first day ot August 1670."

Of the Hickes or Hicks family we shall speak under Parson's Green and North End.

Daniel Leckie, etc. stone:

> "Beneath this Marble | Rest the remains | of | Daniel Leckie, Esq[r] | Descended from an ancient Family | In Scotland | As the Husband, Father, Friend | He was Exemplary | Just Humane and Charitable; | the Poor he pitied and relieved | Generous without Ostentation, | Hospitable with ease and Chearfulness, | he Distinguished for his Guests | the men of merit | from the opulent and undeserving | as he Lived Esteemed | he Died Lamented | in the Seventy Second Year | of his Age | 1783 | Also Mrs. Jane Leckie his Wife | who died Oct. 8th 1808, Aged 75 Years."

The Church Registers record:

> 1783 Daniel Leckie (in the Church) . . . bu 12 Feb.

Judith Laurence stone: an ancient black stone is inscribed,

> "Here lyeth ye Body of | Mrs. Ivdeth Lav | rance Davghter of | Thomas Francis | the elder Gent. | wife of Edmond Lavrance who li | ved in Wedlock | . . . ty years & 6 | months: she | deceased ye . . . "

The rest of the stone is broken off. Of Edmund Lawrence we shall speak in our account of Grove House.

Tower Chapel: South and West Walls

By far the most magnificent monument in Fulham Church is that to the memory of **Lord Mordaunt**, which now stands against the south wall in the Tower Chapel. This monument originally stood in the south aisle near that of Lady Dorothy Clarke and Dr. Samuel Barrow, but was removed to its present site in 1840-41. In 1842 it was restored by Charles, Duke of Richmond, a lineal descendant of Lord Mordaunt.

The monument consists of a white marble statue of Lord Mordaunt, rather larger than life. His lordship is habited in a Roman dress. In his right hand he holds a baton as Constable of Windsor Castle. The statue stands against a large slab of black polished marble. It rests on a table of black marble, which is itself supported on a pedestal of white marble. In front are two stands, the one to the left bearing the gauntlets and the one to the right the coronet of the deceased. At the back, on each side of the statue, is an oval tablet.

Monument to John, Viscount Mordaunt.
To the right are two other memorials:
the upper one to Bishop Gibson,
and the lower one to Bishop Wilson.
From a photograph by Mr. T. S. Smith, 1896

The tablet to the left is inscribed as follows:

"H. S. I. | Nobilissimus heros *Iohannes Mordaunt* | Iohannis Comitis Petroburgensis | Filius Natu Minor | ex | Mordauntiorum stemmate quod ante sexcentos annos | Normannia traductum | Serie perpetua, deinceps hic in Anglia floruit | Qui | Acceptum a parentibus decus | Rebus gestis auxit et illustravit | Opera egregia posita | In restituendo Principe ab avitis Regnis pulso | Mille aditis periculis | et | Cromwelli rabie sæpius provocata sæpe etiam devicta | a | Carolo Secundo feliciter reduce | In laborum mercedem et renevolentiæ tesseram | Vicecomes de Aviland est renunciatus | Castri etiam Windesoriæ et Militiæ Surriensis | Præfecturæ admotus | ex | Nuptiis cum lectissima Heronina *Elizabetha Carey* | Comitum Monumethæ stirpe oriunda | Auspicatissime initis | Suscepta prole numerosa | Filiis septem Filiabus quatuor | Medio ætatis flore annorum 48 Febre. correp^{tus} | Vir immortalitate dignus animam | Deo reddidit | V | Die Iunii Annoque Domini | MDCLXXV."

(Translation: Here lies interred the most noble hero, John Mordaunt, younger son of John, Earl of Peterborough, of the family of the Mordaunts, which, coming from Normandy more than 600 years ago, has flourished in England in an unbroken line ever since; who, by his deeds, has enhanced and adorned the fame he derived from his ancestors. He performed eminent services in the restoration of the King when driven from his hereditary dominions. He encountered a thousand dangers, very often provoking and frequently overcoming the wrath of Cromwell. As a reward for his labour, and a mark of royal benevolence, he was, by Charles II, on his happy return, created Viscount Aviland, and was also appointed Constable of Windsor Castle and Lord Lieutenant of Surrey. By his most auspicious marriage with that excellent heroine, Elizabeth Carey, descended from the Earls of Monmouth, he was blessed with a numerous progeny, seven sons and four daughters. Being seized with a fever in the flower of his age, 48, this man, deserving of immortality, returned his soul to God, 5th day of June in the year Of Our Lord 1675.)

On the tablet to the right is the following pedigree of the Mordaunt family:

"Stemma Gentilitium | Mordauntiorum | qui | per annos sexcentas primum in Normannia | deinceps in Anglia floruerunt."

(Translation: Pedigree of the Mordaunt family who flourished through a period of 600 years, first in Normandy (and) afterwards in England.)

Osbertus Mordaunt
Miles Normannus
||
Osmanus Mordaunt-Balwinus
||
Eustachius Mordaunt-Robertus
||
Gulielmus Mordaunt-Agnes
||
Gulielmus Mordaunt-Richardus
||
Nicholas-Robertus Mordaunt-Gulielmus-Richardus
||
Edmundus Mordaunt
||
Robertus Mordaunt
||
Robertus Mordaunt-Cassandra
||
Matilda-Gulielmus Mordaunt-Elizabetha
||
Gulielm'-Iohannes Mordaunt-Elizabetha
Miles
||
Gulielm'-Iohan. Baro. Mordaunt-Ioanna-Robert
||
Winif-Etheld-Geor-Guliel-Edmu-Iohan Bar0. Mordaunt-Edit-Anna-Margar-Dorot-Elizab
||
Margareta-Elizabet-Ludovic' Baro. Nordaunt (*sic*)-Anna-Ursula
||
Katherina-Henric' Baro. Mordaunt-Maria-Elizabet
||
Anna-Eliza-Iaco-Iohan Comes Petrobur.-Ludo-Fra-Marg
||
Iohan-Henric' Comes Petrobur-Elizabet

The name of John, Lord Mordaunt, whose monument we are describing, figures first in the last line of the "Stemma," he being the younger son of John, first Earl of Peterborough. Above the statue of Lord Mordaunt is a shield containing the following arms:

Dexter: Arg., a chevron between 3 estoiles sa (Mordaunt). Sinistra: On a bend 3 roses (Carey).

This handsome monument was the joint work of John Bushnell and Francis Bird. Bowack, who has left us the earliest description of it, remarks:

> " 'Tis done with abundance of Spirit by the late celebrated English Statuary Mr. Bushnel, and cost near £250. . . . The whole performance is extraordinary fine and is computed at £400."

Bird, who sculptured the statue, carved the "Conversion of St. Paul" on the pediment over the west door of St. Paul's and the original statue of Queen Anne in front of the cathedral. Bushnell, who was the sculptor of the statues of Charles I and Charles II, in the old Exchange, and of the Kings on Temple Bar, designed the so-called ornaments. The monument is also described by Strype and Lysons. John Evelyn, a great friend of the Mordaunts, notes in his "Diary" under date 16 Mar. 1675-76:

> "The Countess of Sunderland and I went by water to Parson's Green to visit my Lady Mordaunt and to consult with her about my Lords Monument. We returned by coach."

Christopher Wilson, etc. To the right of the Mordaunt monument is a marble slab to the memory of Dr. Christopher Wilson, Bishop of Bristol. His remains lie interred in the vault of Bishop Gibson, whose daughter he had married. Beneath the arms is the following inscription:

> "Sacred | to the Memory of | Christopher Wilson D.D. | Ld Bishop of Bristol; | who died on the 28th. (*sic*) of April 1792 | aged 77 years. | Anne, his wife daughter of | Edmund Gibson, D.D. Ld Bishop of London | who died on the 16th. of May 1782 (*sic*) | aged 61 years | And of their sons | Richard Wilson, | who died on the 12th. of May 1787 | aged 35 years | and Christopher Wilson, | who died on the 25th. of May 1842, | aged 78 years | Also of | Sophia, his wife | who died October 18th. 1848, | aged 75 years | whose several remains | are deposited in the Tomb of | Edmund Gibson, D.D. Ld Bishop of London, | in the Church yard adjoining."

The 28 April 1792, is an error for 18 April 1792; and the 16 May 1782, is an error for 16 May 1789.

The arms are:

Dexter: A wolf rampant, in chief three estoiles (Wilson). *Sinister*: A fess humette between three birds. *Crest*: A demi-wolf issuant.

The Church Registers record:

1787 Richard Wilson, Esq. bu. 26 June.
1789 Anne wife of Christopher Lord Bishop of Bristol bu. 23 May.
1792 The Rt. Rev. Christopher Willson Lord Bishop of Bristol bu. 26 Apl.

Christopher Wilson, who was born in 1715, was educated at Cambridge, where he graduated in 1736, and M.A. in 1740. He became Proctor and afterwards Fellow of Catharine Hall, Cambridge. He was appointed rector of Halstead, Essex. In 1745 he was made prebendary of St. Paul's, a position which he held till his death. In 1748 he was installed prebendary of Westminster, but resigned in 1758. In 1753 he obtained the degree of D.D., and, in the following year, he was selected to preach the annual sermon before the House of Commons at St. Margaret's, Westminster, on 30 January, the anniversary of the execution of Charles I. In 1783 he was advanced to the see of Bristol. He was chaplain in ordinary to George II. Christopher Wilson, who died in 1842, was popularly known in his day as the "Father of the Turf."

Edmund Gibson. Above the Wilson memorial is a stone of various coloured marbles inscribed to the memory of Bishop Gibson, who is buried in the adjacent Churchyard. In Lysons' time this stone was fixed against the north wall of the nave near the chancel. In 1840 it was removed to the Tower Chapel. At the top are his official arms, viz.:

Dexter: The see of London; *Sinister*: Az., 3 storks rising arg.

The stone bears this panegyric:

"To the Memory of | that excellent Prelate | Doctor Edmund Gibson | Lord Bishop of London, | Dean of His Majesty's | Chapels Royal | And One of the Lords of | His Majesty's most Honble | Privy Council | In Him | This Church and Nation lost an Able and Real Friend, | and | Christianity a Wise, Strenuous, and Sincere Advocate | His Lordship's Peculiar Care and Concern for the Constitution and Discipline of the | Church of England were eminently distinguished; not only by his Invaluable | Collection of Her Laws, but by his prudent and Steady Opposition to every Attack made upon Them. | His Affection for The State and Loyalty to His Prince were founded on the best Principles | And Therefore were upon all Occasions Fixd and Uniform and his Zeal | To establish the Truth and spread the Influence of the Christian Religion | Display'd in That most Instructive Defence of It, His Pastoral Letters | Will ever remain as the Strongest Testimony of the Conviction of his own Mind And | Of his Affectionate Attention to The most Important interests of Mankind | Thus Lived and Dyed this Good Bishop | A Great and Candid Churchman, | A Dutyfull and Loyal Subject, | An Orthodox and Exemplary Christian | Obijt Septr. 6th. 1748 Ætat. 79."

Beneath are sculptured a crozier, palm-branch and book.

Beilby Porteus. To the right of the Gibson epitaph is a plain stone tablet with a black marble border. It is inscribed:

"In Memory | of | The Rt. Revd Beilby Porteus, D.D. | late Bishop of London, | and | Dean of His Majesty's Chapels Royal. | He died on the 13th. of May 1809; | aged 78 years."

This stone was originally fixed against the upper wall south of the nave, over the Bishop's pew. In 1840 it was removed to its present position. As Bishop Porteus lies buried at Sundridge, in Kent, the above tablet is somewhat misleading.

"Edmund" Gresham. Beneath the Porteus memorial, and just above the closed door which formerly led to the Tower, is a very small marble tablet, painted and gilded, recording the memory of "Edmund" Gresham. It is inscribed:

"Monvmentv Edmvndi Gresham filij natv | minimi Iohannis Gresham dc Mayfield Ar | migeri qvi obijt 7° die Maij Anno Domini | 1593

Annoq. Ætatis svæ 16."
(Translation: The monument of Edmund Gresham, youngest son of John Gresham de Mayfield, gentleman, who died 7th May 1593, and in the 16th year of his age.)

It is surmounted by the following arms:

Quarterly, (1), Arg., a chevron ermines between 3 mullets pierced sa. (Gresham); (2), Az. ten billets 4, 3, 2, 1, or, on a chief of the second a demi-lion issuant sa., a martlet for difference gu. (Dormer); (3), Gu., on a chevron arg. between 3 fishes naiant or, as many martlets sa. on a chief indented of the second, 3 escallops of the field (Dorre ats Chobbs); 4), Arg., 3 fleurs-de-lis az. (Coulrich ats Cailridge, or Collingridge). *Crest*: On a wreath a grasshopper proper.

Nicholas Charles, who blazons the arms as already given, notes:

"Edward Gresham youngest sonne to John Gresham of Mayfield in Sussex. Died 1593 æt. 16."

This youth was, as the tablet records, the youngest son of John Gresham, of North End and of Mayfield, Sussex, citizen and mercer of London, by his wife Elizabeth, daughter of Edward Dormer, of North End, citizen and haberdasher of London. This lady married, as her second husband, William Plumbe, of North End, who died 9 Feb. 1593-94, only three months before the death of her youngest son by her first marriage.

As the reader will observe, a discrepancy occurs in regard to the Christian name of the subject of the epitaph. The stone at All Saints gives "Edmund," and the Add. Manuscript 14311, fol. 73-79, compiled by Le Neve and James Gresham, circa 1590, gives the third son of John Gresham as "Edmundus." On this authority, apparently, Mr. Leveson-Gower has so inserted it in his "History" of this family. The evidence is, however, in favour of "Edward" being the correct name. Our reasons are these:

(1) In the Plumbe monument, which was erected in the year in which young Gresham died (1593), the three sons of John Gresham are given as Thomas, William and *Edward*.

(2) Nicholas Charles, in his "Church Notes," calls him "Edward." Charles was a contemporary writer.

(3) The boy's grandfather was Edward Dormer.

(4) "Edward" Gresham, of Oxon, gent., matriculated at Queen's College, Oxford 2 Mar. 1591-92, then aged 16.

There can be little doubt that this entry refers to the youth who is buried at Fulham, for it will not "fit" any other Gresham. If, as is probable, Nicholas Charles copied the name from the epitaph, it is evident that the inscription must have been since (incorrectly) restored.

Bridget Holland. On the west wall of the Tower Chapel is a stone to the memory of Mrs. Bridget Holland, the wife of Henry Holland, the celebrated architect who designed Park House and Colehill House, Fulham, old Drury Lane Theatre, etc. The inscription reads:

"To the Memory of | Bridget | widow of Henry Holland, Esq., | whose earthly remains are deposited in the same vault with those of her husband | in the adjoining Churchyard | She was daughter of Launcelot Brown, Esq., | A name well known to every lover of rural beauty for the taste | with which he improved and embellished the face of Nature | as her husband was not less distinguished for his skill and genius | in the profession of architecture. | She died on the 14th. Sept. 1828 in her 78th. year respected and beloved | Rich in every Christian and Domestic virtue | Having preserved in an uncommon degree to the latest period of life | The natural graces and animated feelings of her powerful mind | She resigned her soul to her Creator in full assurance of a resurrection, | and committed to the divine care, in her last tender expressions, | the family she was leaving, | with a fervent prayer that they might become joint partakers with her | of a joyful meeting hereafter."

Philip Daniel Castiglione Maurelli. Beneath is a plain stone slab inscribed:

"Near this place lyeth the Body of | Philip Daniel Castiglione Maurelli | Descended from an Ancient Family | in the Kingdom of Naples. | He was educated in the Church of Rome, | But for the sake of the Gospel and a good Conscience | having left his Native Country and Relations | and become a sincere Convert to the Protestant Religion, | and a true Member of the Church of England, | He was entertained in the Familys of | two successive Bishops of London | Dr. Iohn Robinson and Dr.

Edmund Gibson | In the service of whom he lived | with great piety and fidelity | upwards of twenty years, | and dyed January the 1st. 1737-38 Aged 53 years."

At a Vestry held 20 June 1738, it was

"Ordered . . . that the executor of Mr. Castiglione have power to fix a stone in the wall for his memory not exceeding three feet in length and two and half in breadth, nor six inches in thickness he paying as an acknowledgment to the Churchwarden the sum of half a guinea."

The Church Registers record:

1737 Philip Daniel Castiglione Maurelli . . . bu. 4 Jan.

Tower Chapel: North and West Walls

Robert Richard Wood. Against the west wall, on the north side of the Tower door, is the following tablet:

"Sacred | to the Memory of | Robert Richard Wood, Esq., | the third son of | Thomas and Mary Wood | of Littleton in this County. | He died 1st November 1857 | aged 77 years, | Having been | during forty eight years | a resident parishioner of Fulham. | Respected and Beloved by | all its inhabitants | and a most liberal promoter | of every work which contributed | either here or elsewhere | to advance the Glory of God | and the welfare of mankind. | Job xxiv. 11-13, Revelation xiv. 13."

Mr. Wood left £2,000 to the Waste Land Almshouses. He also gave his library to the Vicarage.

Thomas Winter. One of the finest monuments in the Church is that to the memory of Thomas Winter, of Fulham House, erected by his wife, Anne Winter. Bowack describes it as

"A very Beautiful tho' Plain Modern Monument of black and white Marble, Rais'd near 12 Foot from the Ground. The Ornaments are fine Foldage (sic), Festoons, etc. very well done with a Neat Urn at the Top and over it the Arms. Upon a loose separate Drapery finely Polish'd hanging upon the Base this Inscription following. The whole secur'd with Iron Spikes wash'd with Gold is a curious piece of Workmanship, and cost £150," etc.

The monument is also noticed in Strype's Stow's "Survey," 1754, and in Lysons' "Environs of London," 1796, when it stood against the north wall of the nave. Faulkner, in 1812, states that "the urn is gone," but that the iron rails were still existing. The rails have long since disappeared, but, curiously enough, the urn is still in situ. The inscription, recording the achievements and the sufferings of Thomas Winter, is as follows:

"H.S.I. | Thomas Winter, Armiger, | inclyti illius Winteri Pronepos | Qui Hispanorium Classem | (Quæ vinci non potuit) fudit | Bello dein Paci obstetricante, | Hic Pacis filius, in Indos Mercator navigat | ubi Messalapatamiæ Præfecturam gessit & adornauit | Vigessimo plus minus anno elapso | Patri cognatisque | (ob fidelitatem optimo Regu a pijs fœderatoribus) | ad inopiam redactis | Velis et Rebus secundis, | Plane Alter Joseph Deo mittente, redijt | Omnibus tandem Boni Viri functus officijs, | Postquam trigenta quatuor annos, | Mira patientia acri laboraverat morbo, | In Domino moriens, a laboribus requievit | Mœstissima Coniux | hoc qualecunq. Μνημοσυνου | Amoris ergo Posuit | Obijt Jan. 15 salutatis MDCLXXXI Ætatis LXVI.
Here also lyeth | Anne, daughter of Richard Swinglehurst of | London, Gent., Relict of Tho. Winter above s[d] | Shee dyed wife to Charles eldest sonne of | S[r] Tho. Orby of Lincolnshire, Bar[nt] | 15 Martii Ann. Dom. 1689 Ætatis suæ 54."
(Translation: Here lies buried Thomas Winter, Esquire, the great-grand child of that famous Winter who defeated the Spanish Fleet, styled the Invincible. The war at last being succeeded by peace, this son of Peace, goes as a merchant to the Indies, where, with great honour, he discharged the duties of governor of Masulipatam. After the lapse of about twenty years, he returned, after a successful voyage, like another Joseph, sent by God, to his father and relations, who, on account of their fidelity to the best of Kings, were reduced by the Pious Covenanters, to poverty. At length, having fulfilled all the offices of a good man, and after having, for thirty-four years, suffered from a painful disease, borne with admirable patience, dying in the Lord, he rested from his labours. His sorrowing wife, as a mark of her affection, erected this monument to his memory. He died 15 January in the year of our salvation, 1681, aged 66.")

The arms are:

Sa., a fess ermine (Winter). *Crest*: Issuant out of a ducal coronet a beast's head.

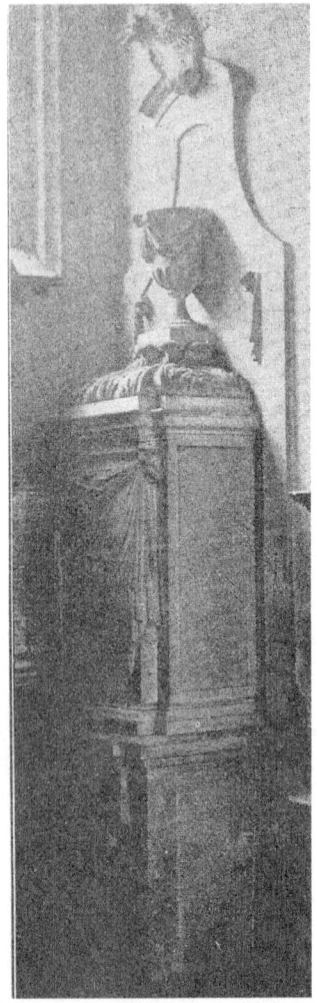

Monument to Thomas Winter.
From a photograph by Mr. T. S. Smith, 1896.

Bowack, speaking of Thomas Winter, tells the following quaint story:

"This gentleman was descended from a Family very remarkable for their great Bravery and Valour; his great grandfather was very famous for the great services done to his Country in destroying the Spanish

Armado as before mentioned, his Grandfather and Father were much esteem'd for their Strength and Courage, and his brother, Sir Edward Winter, who liv'd at York Place near Battersy, the later part of his Life, in his younger years (when a Consol in India) kill'd a Tyger with his own Hands without any weapon. The Story is so well known that we need not add the Particulars."

In Le Neve's "Knights," p. 153, the story of the tiger is thus mentioned:

"Sr Edward Wintour of the East Indies a sea captain Governor of fort St. George: he lived at battersea in Surr. he killed a tyger in the east Indies. he dyed at battersea . . . day of . . . and lyes buried there."

The Church Registers record:

1681. Thos. Winter, Esq. bu. 30 Jan.
1688. Charles Orby Esqr and Mrs. Ann Winter married p. Lycens Aprill ye 26.
1689. Ann Orby ye wife of Charles Orby Esq. bu. 22 Mar.

The following is an extract from the will of Thomas Winter, dated 28 July 1679, and proved 3 Feb. 1681-82 (P.C.C. 28 Cottle):

"I Thomas Winter of ffulham in the County of Middlesex Esq. To my wife Mrs. Anne Winter my house wherein I now dwell in Fulham for life and all my furniture and my stocke in the East India and African Companies and one bond for £3500 due from said East India Company. To my brother Sr Edward Winter knight £20. To my nephew Edward Winter his son £2000.
After death of my wife my house and lands in Fulham to my Nephew Edward Winter and heirs and if he die without issue male same to my brother Francis Winter and heirs male and in default to my sister's son Mr. Robt. Pennington injoining whosoever shall liue in the aforesaid house after my decease to pay or distribute yearly the sume of Tenn pounds of good and lawfull money of England or to its worth in what they shall thinke best for the benefitt of the poore belonging to this side of the said parish of ffulham which is comonly called or Termed ffulham side or ffulham division To comence or begin on St. Thomas his day That shall next happen after my decease and soe to continue on that day yearly for ever in such manner and forme as is hereafter menconed," etc.

Mrs. Ann Winter, who on 26 April 1688, married, as her second husband, Charles Orby, died in March 1689-90. Administration of the goods, etc, of Ann Orby alias Winter, was granted to Charles Orby, her husband, 26 April 1690.

It was long the custom to distribute the Winter gift in half-crowns to 80 poor women, the distribution taking place, after service, in the Vestry on December 21.

The greater part of the site of Fulham House, the residence of Thomas Winter, is now covered by the approach road to Putney Bridge. This property was acquired on the erection of the present Bridge, when the rent-charge was extinguished by the investment of a sum sufficient to produce £10 per annum in Consols. The funds are now administered under the scheme of the United Charities.

Anthony Nourse, etc. Against the same wall is a handsome marble tablet to the memory of Anthony Nourse, of Walham Green, and Katherine his wife. It is richly ornamented. At the top are the following arms:

> *Dexter*: Gules, a fess between two chevrons arg. (Nourse); *Sinister*: Sa., on a bend engrailed or, three human hearts gu. (Tooker?). *Crest*: An arm embowed entwined by a viper.

The inscription reads:

> "To the Memory | of Anthony Nourse Gent. | and Katherine, his wife, of | this Parish, who both depart'd this life | in the year of our Lord 1704. | This monument was erected by Mrs. Katharine Sanderson; their only daughter as a | Small Testimony of her duty & of | the sincere affection She bears | to their memory."

The Church Registers record:

> 1704. Anthony Nourse Gent. bu. 31 Jan.

The will of Anthony Nourse, dated 24 October 1704, was proved 31 January, 1704-5 (P.C.C. 13 Gee).

Sir William Butts. To the right of the Nourse memorial is a small stone tablet to the memory of Sir William Butts, knight, chief physician to Henry VIII. The tablet, which is set in a marble framework, surmounted by a skull, is inscribed:

"Epitaphiv D. Gvlielmi Bvtij Eqvitis Avrati | et Medici Regis Henrici Octavi qvi | Obiit A° Dni. 1545 17° Novemb.

Quid medicina valet, quid honos, quid gratia Regum
Quid Popularis Amor, mors vbi sæva venit ?
Sola valet. Pietas quæ structa est auspice Christo
Sola in morte valet, cætera cuncta flvunt
Ergo mihi in vita fuerit quando omnia Christus,
Mors mihi nunc lucrum, vitaq. Christus erit.

Epitaphiv hoc primitvs inscriptvm pariete et | sitv iam pene exesvm sic demvm restitvit | Leonardvs Bvtts, Armiger, Norfolciensis | Oct. 30, 1627. Amoris G°."

(Translation: Epitaph to Sir William Butts, knight, and physician to King Henry the Eighth, who died 17 November 1545.

Physic or honour, flatt'ry, wealth, or pow'r
To Man of What avail in death's dread hour ?
Then Christian piety alone can save
Our only firm assistance in the grave.
Since Christ in life has been my only joy
Death will bring happiness without alloy.

This epitaph, originally inscribed on the wall, and by reason of its position now nearly eaten away, thus at length Leonard Butts, of Norfolk, Esquire, has restored as a mark of love, Oct. 30, 1627.)

We give the translation of the Latin elegiacs as it stands in Faulkner, for whom it was made by his friend, the Rev. C. G. Savage, M.A., vicar of Kingston. A more literal rendering would be:

"Of what worth is medicine, honour, royal favour, the love of the people, where cruel death comes? Piety, which is built on Christ the Founder alone helps us. It alone in death avails: all other things pass away. Therefore, when Christ has to me been everything in life, death, for me, will be a gain, and Christ will be life."

A noble monument, originally standing within the chancel, against its south wall, formerly existed to the memory of Sir William Butts. The earliest notice of it occurs in the Harleian Manuscript. This reads:

> "Here lyeth buryed the bodye of Sr Raufe Butts knight and phisition to our Soueraigne Lord King Henry the Eighth who died the 18th of Nouemb. A° Dni. 1545."

The use of "Raufe" for "William" is difficult of explanation. The "18th Nov." for "17th Nov." is another discrepancy. The arms are identical with those given by Charles in the Lansdown Manuscript, a document which comes next in point of date. Charles notes:

> "In the Quyre on ye South side
> Sr Wm Buttes, knight, phisition to K. H. 8. maried Margret Bacon of Cainbridgshire and died ye 17 Nouember 1545."

The arms as blazoned by Charles were:

> I. Az., on a chevron betw. three estoiles or, three lozenges gu. *Crest*: On a wreath, two hands conjoined holding a caduceus. II. The same impaling, gu., a boar passant or, differenced by a martlet sa.

Next we have the following inscription, given by John Weever, written only 86 years after the decease of the famous physician:

> "Here lyeth buryed the body of Syr Raufe Buts, knight, and Phisitian to our Soueraigne Lord Henry the viii Who decessyd 1545 on whose sowl, etc."

To this evidently incomplete quotation Weever appends the Latin verses above quoted. The substitution of "Raufe" for "William" is a repetition of the curious error which we have already noted in the Harleian Manuscript. The retention of the old spelling affords, however, evidence that Weever must have copied from the original inscription, which was apparently in English, and not from the epitaph as restored by Leonard Butts in 1627, which is in Latin. Weever's book, which was published in 1631, was many years in course of preparation. We may fairly assume that his visit to Fulham Church was paid before the restoration of the epitaph in 1627.

Our next notice of the Butts monument is that by Bowack. This writer, who refers to Weever's error of "Raufe" for "William," gives the inscription precisely as it now stands, except that he reads "erasum" for "exesum" in the last line but two. After quoting the tablet by Leonard Butts, Bowack proceeds to describe the tomb of the physician:

> "Underneath is his tomb rais'd above Two Foot from the Ground, upon which in brass is represented an armed Knight (the inscription being taken away) and at his left hand a Death's Head with these words, 'Myn Advantage.' At each corner of the stone his Arms."

The epitaph, as it now stands, is also given in Strype's Stow's "Survey," 1754. The Rev. Wm. Cole, who visited Fulham Church on 20 April 1758, describes the monument as it existed in his day. After speaking of Sir Thomas Smith's monument, he proceeds:

> "A little below this monument of Sir Thomas Smith and touching the two steps up to the Altar, is a low Alter Monument of English Marble, close against the South wall and the Head of it touching a Door or Entrance into the South chapel parellel to the chancel, under which lies entombed Sir Wm. Butts, Knt., and Cheif Phisitian to King Henry the 8th, having his Portraiture in brass in Armour, as a Knight, and his Arms at the four Corners of the Stone, only one of which is lost. . . . The inscription at his feet in brass is erased; but a Scrole of Brass on one Side of Him has this imperfect Inscription," etc.

Lysons (1796) quotes the Leonard Butts tablet, which he describes as on the south wall of the chancel, near the monument of Sir Thomas Smith. Faulkner's account (1812) is almost identical with Cole's. In 1840 the Leonard Butts tablet was removed to the Tower Chapel. The monument was probably taken down, and not replaced, during the alterations of 1840-41.

Supposed brass to Sir William Butts.
From an engraving published by T. Simco in 1794

    The epitaph is said to have been the composition of Sir William Butts' great friend, Sir John Cheke. Strype quaintly observes, "And what if I should think that this was the issue of Cheke's pious fancy in his last respects to this man for which he had so high and deserved a veneration." Of the beautiful epitaph, the Rev. R. G. Baker truly observes, "It is, in fact, nothing else than an amplification of those expressive words addressed by St. Paul to the believers at Philippi, where, he declares, 'To me to live is Christ and to die is gain.' " It was through the influence of Sir William Butts that Sir John Cheke was appointed tutor to Prince Edward, afterwards Edward VI.

    Leonard Butts, who, in 1627, restored the epitaph in Fulham Church, was Sir William's first cousin twice removed. Thomas Butts, the father of the physician, had a brother, William Butte of Garbesthorp, who married Margaret Coningsby. Their son, a second William Butts of Garbesthorp, married Ursula Tindall and died in 1567-8. Their son, a third William Butts, married Jane Cockett. He died in April 1585. Leonard Butts of Bromley was the second son of this third William Butts. He died 18 Dec. 1633.

Sir William Butts was a native of Norfolk. The date of his birth is unknown. He was educated at Caius College, Cambridge, and, in 1528, became domestic physician to Henry VIII. Among the distinguished patients whom he is known to have attended were, besides the King, his Queens, Anne Boleyn and Jane Seymour, the King's daughter, the Princess Mary, Henry Fitzroy, Duke of Richmond, a natural son of Henry, Cardinal Wolsey, the Duke of Norfolk, Sir Thomas Lovell, Sir Geo. Boleyn and Lord Rochford. In his capacity as physician to the King's eldest daughter, he received a livery of blue and green damask for himself and two shillings and cloth for an apothecary. His wife, Lady Margaret Butts, was one of the gentlewomen to the Princess Mary.

Sir William Butts, in 1529, joined the College of Physicians which had been founded the preceding year. His influence at Court was considerable and his power was always exercised for a worthy purpose. When the great Wolsey fell under the King's displeasure, Butts endeavoured to bring about a reconciliation. His good offices in favour of Archbishop Cranmer have been immortalized by Shakespeare in his play of *Henry the Eighth* (act v. sc. ii.).

There is some doubt as to the correct date of the death of Sir William Butts. His epitaph, as quoted by Nicholas Charles, circa 1610, gave 17 Nov. 1545, and Leonard Butts, when he restored it in 1627, repeated this date. The Harleian Manuscript gives 18 Nov. In two inquisitions, however, taken at the death of Sir William Butts, the date is given 22 Nov. 1545. In the State Papers (Foreign and Domestic, Henry VIII. xi. 59) is the following curious communication from Secretary Paget to a Mr. Mont:

> "Mr. Mownt I commende me hartelie unto youe Signifying unto the same, that the Kinges Majeste, the Quenes Grace, and my Lord Prince, with all the rest of your frendes and acquayntaunce be, thankes be to God, in good health and prosperitie, except Mr. Butt, who, after a longe and grevous sikenes of a dooble febre quartane, is departed in an honest and godly sorte to God, where I trust he resteth in peac."

The minute is endorsed "To Mr. Mownte from Mr. Secretarie Paget xxv° Februarij 1545" (i.e. 25 Feb. 1545-46), rather over three months after Sir William's death.

Sir William Butts' residence at Fulham was the Rectory House which he rented from his friend, Dr. Simon Heynes. The inquisitions taken at his death show that he possessed houses at various places, including Fulham and Whitefriars (London), the Manors of Thornage, Thornham, Edgefield, and Melton Constable in Norfolk, and Panyngton in Suffolk. His will, dated 8 Nov. 1545, was proved on 28 Nov. 1545 (P.C.C. 45 Pynning). The following is an extract:

> "I comitte my soul to the great mercy of God wherein I chefely trust and my body to the earth to be buried where God shall call me from this lyfe at the which buriall I gewe fyve pounds to be geven to poure men and to be bestowed at my burriall to such as shall take payne at the same. I wille that my Wyfe shalhave thoccupacon and profits of all suche landes and tenements as I have by lease for terme of yeres in ffulham during her lyfe And if she fortune to dye before thende and expyracon of the said yeres, Then I will that Edmund Butt my nevewe shall enioye the Rest of the said yeres yf he be then lyving, yf not Then I will that my nevewe Martyn shalhave and enioye the Rest of the said yeres. To my son Edmund my interest in the Manor of Thornham, to hym my bedde w^t all things thereunto belonging in the Toure Chamber in ffulham. To Doctor Haynes a ring and he one of my executors."

By his wife, Lady Margaret Butts, Sir William had three sons, William, Thomas and Edmund. These three brothers, curiously enough, married three sisters, daughters of Henry Bures of Acton, Suffolk. Edmund Butts alone had issue. His daughter, Anne, married Nicholas Bacon, eldest son of Sir Nicholas Bacon of Redgrave, co. Suffolk, Lord Keeper of the Great Seal.

From Col. Chester's "London Marriage Licences" (1521-1869), it appears that "Edmund Buttes, gent," a nephew of Sir William, obtained license, dated 23 April 1563, to marry "Thomasine Bedell, puella, of Fulham." The Bedells were one of the oldest families in the parish, deriving their name from the office held by some of their ancestors - that of "The Lord's beadle."

Lady Margaret Butts was the daughter and coheiress of john Bacon of Cambridgeshire. On her husband's death she retired to Milton in the parish of Egham, where she died in 1547. She was buried at Fulham.

Monument to Lady Dorothy Clarke and Dr. Samuel Barrow.
To the left are three memorials; the top one to Anthony Nourse,
the next to Sir William Butts, and the bottom one to William Plumbe.
The last named was removed from the Tower Chapel in 1898.
From a photograph by Mr. T. S. Smith, 1896

Lady Dorothy Clarke and Dr. Samuel Barrow. The last monument to be noticed in the Tower Chapel is that to the memory of Lady Dorothy Clarke and Dr. Samuel Barrow. It originally stood against the south wall, towards the east end of the south aisle. Bowack thus describes it:

> "A Most stately Monument of black and white Marble secur'd with Iron rails, in all about 14 Foot from the Ground, done after the Modern Manner, with several very Elegant Profusions in Carving, has a neat Drapery, a large Vase at the Top, from whence hang Festoons, etc., and the arms supported by Two wing'd Genii, the whole being an excellent

piece of Workmanship perform'd by that great Master, Mr. Grinling Gibbons, cost £300."

Lysons and Faulkner give similar accounts. In 1840 it was re-erected in its present position but without the iron railings.

The most striking feature of this monument is the elegantly shaped urn. The festoons of flowers, mentioned by Bowack, which were in existence down to Faulkner's time, have long since entirely disappeared. Behind the monument is a stone slab, bearing the arms, supported by the two angels, mentioned by Bowack.

On the sarcophagus is the following inscription:

D.O.M.S.

Beatam hic expectat Resurrectionem	Dein
DOROTHEA CLARKE	SAMVELI BARROW
Filia et ex Cohæredibus	Ejusdem illustrissimi Principis
THOMÆ HYLIARD Hantoniensis	Medico Ordinario,
Et	Nec non, pro Exercitu Anglicano,
ELIZABETHÆ KYMPTON :	Et Advocato et Iudici
Nupsit primum	cum quo
GVLIELMO CLARKE, Equiti Aurato	ut vixit,
Serenissimo Regi Carolo Secundo	Ita subtus in pace requiescit.
A rebus bellicis Secretario.	

Illa obijt VI. Kal : Aug :	Charissimæ Matri, a cujus uberibus pependit,	Ille obijt XII. Kal : Apr :
A.D. MDCXCV.	Et vitrico optimo multumq. de se merito.	A.D. MDCLXXXII.

GEO CLARKE
Filius unicus et privignus
P.

Translation:

In the name of Almighty God.

Here, in the expectation of a blessed
resurrection, lies Dorothy Clarke,
daughter and one of the
coheiresses of Thomas Hyliard,
of Hampshire, and Elizabeth Kympton.
She married, first,
Sir William Clarke, knt., Secretary at
War to His Majesty Charles II.
She died 27 July 1695.

Secondly,
Samuel Barrow, physician in
ordinary to the same most illustrious
prince, and furthermore
Advocate and Judge to the English

Army, with whom,
as she lived,
so underneath she rests in peace.
He died 21 March 1682.

To his most dear mother, at whose breasts
he hung, and to his excellent and
most affectionate step-father, George Clarke,
their only son and stepson, erected
this monument.

Arms:

On a lozenge for Lady Dorothy and her two husbands: *Dexter*: On a bend between 3 roundels, as many swans; on a canton a leopard's jamb (Clarke). In pale a chevron between 3 mullets (Hyliard); *Sinister*: Two swords in saltier between 4 fleurs-de-lis (Barrow).

The Church Registers record:

1682. Samuel Barrow, Esq. one of his Ma^{ts} Physicians in Ord sepult 25 Mar.

1695. The Lady Dorathy Clarke buried 31 July.

Sir William Clarke, knight, the first husband of Lady Dorothy Clarke, was born about 1623. In 1645 he was admitted a student of the Inner Temple and eight years later was called to the Bar. He also acted as secretary to General Fairfax and afterwards served General Monk in a similar capacity. From the Calendar of State Papers (Domestic, 1660-61), we gather that he was in that year appointed Secretary at War and knighted. In his official capacity he attended Monk on board the *Royal Charles* in the expedition against the Dutch in 1666. The fight off Harwich, which began on 1 June, lasted four days. On the second day Sir William's leg was shattered by a cannon ball. He bravely bore his injuries, which proved to be mortal, expiring on 4 June, the last day of the engagement. The body was brought to Harwich and interred near the south door of the chancel of the parish church of that town, where his widow erected a monument to his memory.

Lady Dorothy Clarke, as the monument in Fulham Church

records, was the daughter of Thomas Hyliard of Hampshire by his wife Elizabeth (Kympton). She had, by her first husband, Sir William Clarke, one son, George.

Dr. Samuel Barrow was, as his own tombstone records, descended from an ancient Norfolk family. He was appointed chief physician to the Army of Monk in Scotland, and, by his counsels, is recorded to have assisted that leader in bringing about the return of Prince Charles. After the Restoration, Charles II made him his physician in ordinary and Advocate General and Judge Martial to the English Army. He was a great friend of John Milton. A copy of some Latin elegiacs, written by Dr. Barrow, was prefixed to the second edition of "Paradise Lost" (1674). His marriage with Lady Dorothy Clarke took place in 1667. His will, dated 23 June 1676, was proved 22 May 1682 (P.C.C. 54 Cottle).

Dr. George Clarke, who erected the monument which we are describing, was born in 1660. He was educated at Oxford where he graduated B.A. on 27 June 1679, M.A. on 18 April 1683, B.C.L. on 28 April 1686 and D.C.L. on 12 July 1708. He was a man of courtly manners, and was respected for his architectural taste and for the zeal he displayed in enriching the University in which the greater part of his life was spent. On 23 Nov. 1685, he was elected a member of Parliament for the University of Oxford, but he never sat, the House being shortly afterwards prorogued. At the General Election of 1705, he was returned for the borough of East Looe. After this Parliament, he retired into private life, but, at a by-election on 4 Dec. 1717, he was again elected as member for the University of Oxford. His death occurred 22 Oct. 1736. From 1684 to 1705, Clarke held the post of Judge Advocate General and from 1692 to 1704 he was Secretary at War, the office once filled by his father. He was also secretary to Prince George of Denmark, the consort of Queen Anne. From May 1702 to Oct. 1705, he was joint Secretary to the Admiralty. He was buried in the Chapel of All Souls, Oxford.

By his will (the last codicil of which is dated 1736), Dr. Clarke left his property to Worcester College, Oxford, which is required to pay to the Vicar and Churchwardens of Fulham £5 per annum on receipt of a certificate as to the good condition of the monument.

In the last Report of the Historical Manuscripts Commission (1899) is a highly interesting "Autobiography of Dr. George Clarke" (manuscripts of F. W. Leyborne Popham, Esq.) In it Dr. Clarke gives an account of the monument which he erected in Fulham Church to the memory of his mother and father-in-law.

North Porch

Edward Limpany. In the North Porch are two memorials to the Limpany family. The first, a small stone, reads:

> "Here Lyes the body | of Edward Limpany | who departed this Life | ye 23 day of april 1662 | aged 58 years | and Margery his wife | who departed this Life | ye 8 of december 1675 | aged 72."

Elizabeth Limpany. The second and more important monument was erected by Robert Limpany to the memory of his infant daughter, Elizabeth. It originally stood against the north wall at the west end of the north aisle, immediately over the large old-fashioned pew which occupied the north-west corner of the Church. Bowack describes it as "a very handsome Monument of white Marble, Secur'd with Iron Rails beautified with a neat border of carving, fruit, flowers, etc.," and adds that it cost £100. It is inscribed:

> "Here lies Elizabeth | The Daughter of Robert | and Isabel Limpany | who dyed | October the 10th, 1694 | In the third year | of her age."

The Church Registers record:

> 1694. Elizabeth, dau. of Robert and Isabella Limpany bu. 14 Oct.

The monument bears the following impaled coat:

> *Dexter*: Per pale gu. and sa. a lion passant gard. or, between three roses arg. seeded of the third (Limpany). *Sinister*: a chevron embattled or between three roses arg. seeded of the second (Cornish).

A board in the Porch is inscribed:

"1881. The Parish Church of All Saints, Fulham, having lapsed into a state of decay and being subject to floods from the River Thames, was pulled down and rebuilt. In the construction of the present church, stones belonging to three previous churches, the oldest of which apparently dated from the 12 century, were discovered. The east end has been carried 9 feet and the south wall 5 feet beyond the limits of the previous church, while the floor of the nave has been raised 2 feet 9 inches and the roof 13 feet above the former levels. The corner stone at the east angle of the north transept was laid by Archibald Campbell Tait, Archbishop of Canterbury, on 10 July 1880, and the church was reconsecrated by John Jackson, Bishop of London, on 9th July 1881. F. H. Fisher, Vicar, James Wray and William H. Weaver, Churchwardens."

Monument to Elizabeth Limpany.
From a photograph by Mr. T. S. Smith, 1896

Fulham Old and New

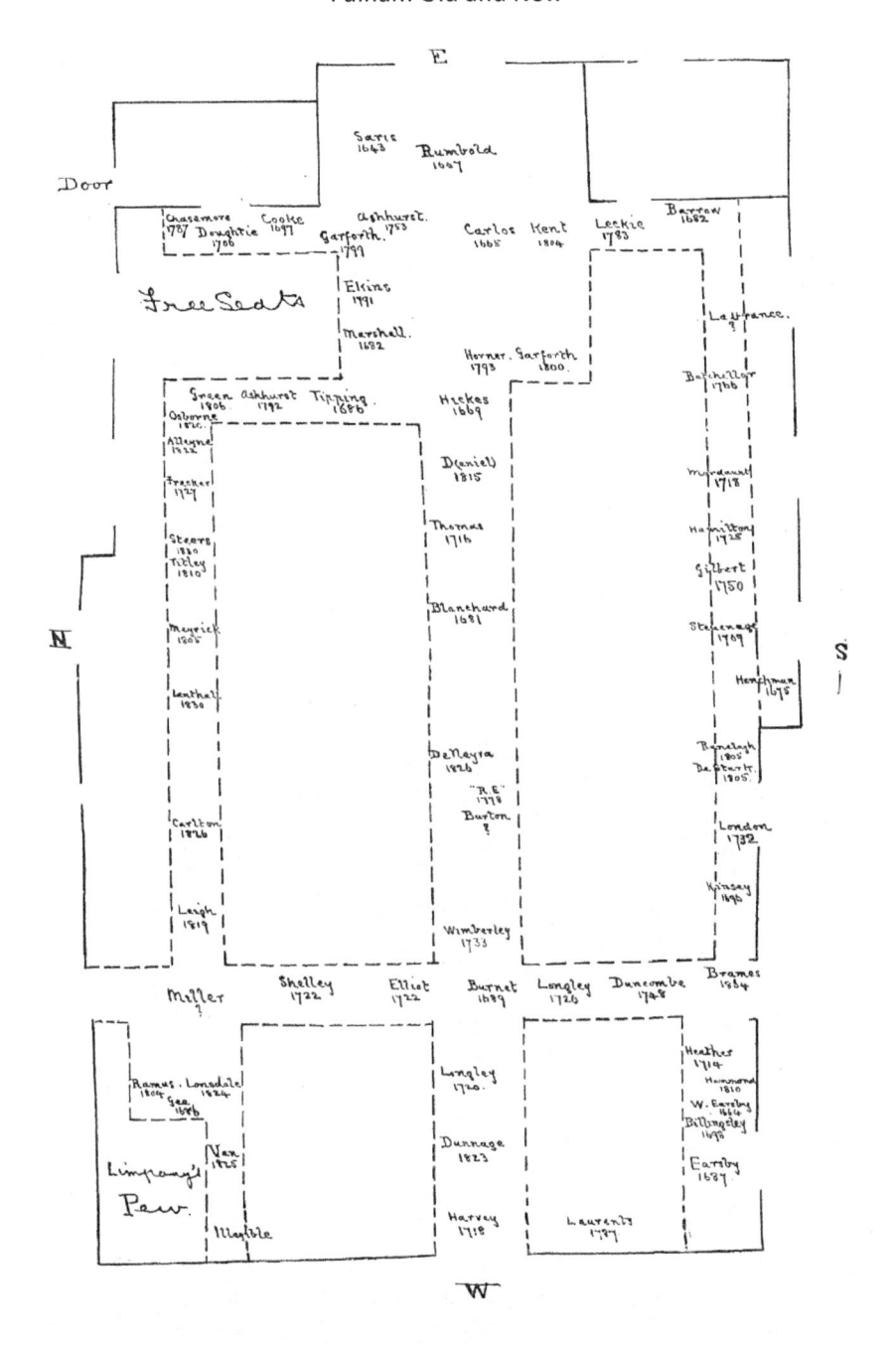

Plan Showing the Positions of the Grave Stones in the Old Church,
Before the Rebuilding of 1880-81

CHAPTER XXIV: FULHAM CHURCHYARD

The pretty little God's acre at All Saints is one of the most picturesque spots to be found in Fulham. Its principal approach is that from Church Row, whose quaint old houses lend the place an air of quiet dignity in marked contrast to the busy High Street at the eastern end.

Entering the iron gates, we observe a notice board containing the laconic instructions:

Do no harm,
Pluck no flowers,
Walk not on the grass,
Suffer no one to play.
The place whereon thou standest is holy ground.

Pathway through the Churchyard.
From a water-colour drawing by Miss Jane Humphreys

The Churchyard is crossed from east to west by a path which divides it into two almost equal portions. It is bounded on the east by the Vicarage grounds and the approach road to Putney Bridge, on the west by the Moat, on the south by John's Place, and on the north by Sir Wm. Powell's Almshouses. Its area is now 2a. 0r. 12p., but originally it could hardly have exceeded half this extent. In Rocque's Map (1741-45), the Churchyard does not reach either to the Moat on the west or to Church Lane (John's Place) on the south.

In the Court Rolls the earliest allusion to the Churchyard occurs in the minutes of a Court General in 1392. The first known burial was that of Richard Colman in 1376.

The following curious order was made at a Court General in 1611:

> "That all the inhabitants of ffulham streete yf after the publishinge of this order any of them shall <u>suffere their hoggs or hoggerells to come and goe into the pishe Churcheyarde</u> of ffulham they shall forfeit to the lorde for each hogge or hoggerell so founde vj^s viij^d."

The Churchwardens in 1640:

> "Pd. for cleansing the Churchyard of Rubish 1s. 0d."

In 1646 there was

> "Pd. for makeing ye Causey in ye Churchyard and two graues for poore people 2s. 8d."

The "causey" or "causeway," which generally took the direction of the present path, appears to have at one time been a thoroughfare sufficiently wide for coaches and carriages, which, when the Church bridge was not barred by posts, were wont to cause much annoyance to the worshippers.

In 1650 the Churchwardens paid

> "To Richard Blackman carpenter for mending ye Churchyard Gates and for Nailes and Workmen, etc. 4s. 6d.

> "To the Smith for a pair of Crosse Garners for ye Churchyard gates and for mending ye old cross garne^{rs} and for nailes, p. bill 19s. 0d."

Formerly the graveyard was surrounded by a low brick wall. At a Vestry, held 28 Feb. 1680-81, we find

> "Itt is ordered that there be a brick wall built att the entering into the churchyard from the grate to the next neighbouring wall (ye gateway excepted) and that the present churchwarden, Mr. Storer, do defray the charge thereof and place it to his account."

This wall was on the south side of the Churchyard.

Anciently a piece of waste ground existed on the north side of the Churchyard, adjoining the residence of William Skelton. In 1699 Skelton obtained from Bishop Compton a license to enclose the site for his own use conditionally on his paying the Rev. Vincent Barry and his successors the sum of two shillings and sixpence a year. The faculty is dated 20 February 1699-1700.

For the next fifty years we hear little more of the Churchyard, except payments by the Churchwardens for clipping trees, laying gravel, etc.

Curious as it may seem, it was no unusual thing in the early years of the last century for the graveyard to be turned into a drying or airing ground. A resolution passed by the Vestry on 8 September 1738, reads:

> "It was unanimously agreed that if any person hereafter shall hang Cloaths to dry in the churchyard they shall be prosecuted for a Nuisance, and that Curtis the sexton do give notice to the several persons concern'd and likewise to Francis Reynolds to keep his Hog out, otherwise It will be pounded, and himself prosecuted for the same."

At a Vestry, held 11 July 1754,

> "It was agreed that the steps in the east part of the Churchyard be taken away, that rails be placed instead of those next Mr. Skelton's and a door instead of those next the Rev. Mr. Knight's."

The first recorded enlargement of the Churchyard was in 1781. On 5 June of that year

> "The Churchwarden reported to the Vestry his having agreed with Mr. Bedell for the tenement and land adjoining to the churchyard late in the occupation of John Goldfinch in order to enlarge the churchyard."

This land was on the south side of the Churchyard.
In 1783, another addition was made on the south side, by the inclusion of a piece of land which had just reverted to the Bishopric. The site, which contained about 2,900 square feet, now

forms the southern portion of the Churchyard near its west end. The following minute occurs in the Parish Books:

> "At a Vestry held 25 July 1783, the inhabitants present, having taken a view of the ground to be added to the churchyard and also having examined two plann produced to them of the intended inclosure, are of opinion that the ground should be inclosed immediately at the expense of the parish with a wall two bricks thick in the foundation and a brick and a half above, leaving a sweep for the accommodation of the neighbourhood sufficient for a coach and a pair of horses to turn with ease."

The site was the gift of Bishop Lowth, who consecrated the ground. The following details of the consecration we extract from the Vicar-General's books in the Bishop's Registry:

> "On Friday 9 July 1784 the Rt. Rev. Father in God, Robert Lord Bishop of London went to the house of the Rev. Graham Jepson, Vicar of the parish of Fulham, accompanied by the Rev. Stephen Eaton, clerk, chaplain to Robert Lord Bishop of London, at which place were before come the worshipfull Wm. Macham, doctor of laws, surrogate of the worshipful Wm. Wynne, also doctor of laws, Vicar General of the Rt. Rev. Father in God, Robert, by divine permission, Lord Bishop of London, . . . Mark Holman, notary, deputy registrar of the Court and the Lord Bishop of Bristol. Having taken some refreshment they proceeded to the church, attended by the churchwarden and others of the parish and went to the Vestry Room where the Bishop put on his episcopal robes after which morning service was performed in the church."

The petition read at the consecration states that the piece of land to be added to the Churchyard

> "contains from East to West on the north 98 feet or thereabouts and from North to South on the west 39 feet or thereabouts and from East to West on the south to the sweep 49 feet or thereabouts and from South to North on the east from the sweep 20 feet or thereabouts and is more particularly delineated in the plan in the margin hereof."

South side of Fulham Churchyard, showing the old boundary wall. From a drawing published by R. Wilkinson, 1 Feb. 1824.

In the above view of the Church, a portion of the "sweep" or bend is clearly indicated. The old wall was taken down in 1888, when the new railings were put up. Through the exertions of Dr. T. J. Woodhouse a piece of the brickwork was preserved, and may still be seen in the Churchyard.

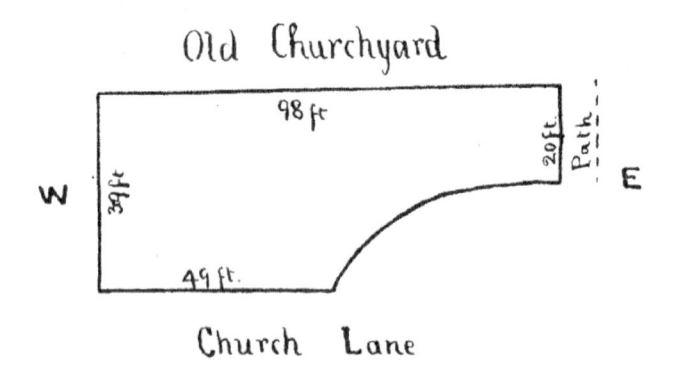

Plan of addition to Churchyard made in 1783

The following memoranda of the expenses of the Churchwardens in connection with the consecration are of interest:

Paid Mr. Holman's bill for the consecration of the ground added to the churchyard and given to the parish by the Bishop of London £23. 2s. 4d.

Paid the Apparitor his fee for attending the consecration 10s. 6d.

Paid the Organist for attending on that day £1. 1s.

Gave the Ringers 10s. 6d.

Gave Mrs. Petteward's servants for bringing and putting up a markee in the churchyard for the Bishop and his tenants to repair under in case the weather proving unfavourable at the consecration 5s.

Paid Mr. Lucas his bill for refreshments for the servants of the Bishop and others attending on him at the consecration £1. 6s.

In 1792 the Vestry purchased for £300 from the heirs of Mr. Kender Mason a piece of land westwards of the last extension, thus bringing the Churchyard up to the Moat boundary. Dr. Beilby Porteus consecrated this extension, the ceremonial being similar to that adopted on the previous occasion. In 1802 the Churchwardens

"Paid for making the New Walk in the Churchyard £5. 15s. 0d."

This was most likely the continuation of the path through the newly acquired site.

In 1817 and 1818 the old men from the Parish Workhouse were extensively employed in laying out the Churchyard, which had fallen into a ruinous state. Among the disbursements of the Churchwardens for 1824 are the following:

Paid Flood for helping to dig cesspools in various parts of the churchyard to drain the walks 18s.

Men for making several cesspools in the churchyard and making drains round the church to take the water into the cesspools from off the church and turning and gravelling the main walks leading to the church £5. 10s. 0d.

In 1843 the fourth enlargement of the Churchyard was made, this addition being on the north side. The site, which was this year acquired, actually included the piece of waste land which William Skelton, in 1699, obtained a license to enclose. On 9 April 1843, a meeting of the Vestry was held

> "To consider the expediency of accepting from the Lord Bishop of London a grant to the Commissioners for Building Churches in populous Parishes, of a Piece of Ground, containing a quarter of an Acre, or thereabouts, to be added to the Churchyard of this Parish, on condition that all expences of making out the Title, and of the Conveyance, are defrayed by the Parish, and that some effectual measures are adopted, either by Fencing, or otherwise, to prevent the frequent <u>injuries now done to the Tomb Stones and Graves, by Boys and others</u> assembling in the Churchyard to play; and further on condition that the proposed addition is enclosed on the North East side by a neat and strong Iron Fence, to be kept in constant repair by the Parishioners."

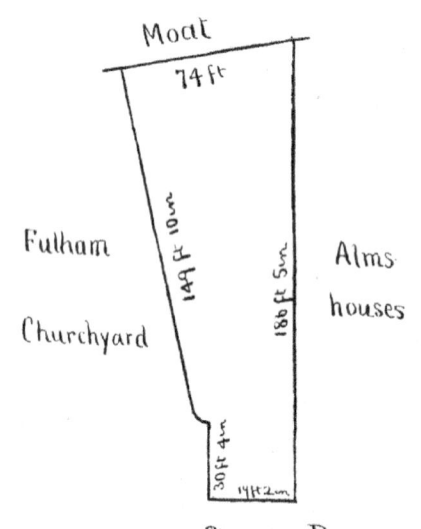

Plan of addition to Churchyard made in 1843

On 18 April the Vestry accepted the offer. The consecration was performed by Bishop Blomfield on 1 Nov. 1843, in the presence of the Vicar, the Rev. R. G. Baker, the Churchwardens and many of the leading residents. The accompanying plan shows the dimensions of the site added.

Consequent on this addition to the Churchyard, an

improvement was in the same year (1843) effected at the entrance by the erection of a pair of iron gates, which were brought forward to the new boundary houses line.

In connection with this enlargement, it may be mentioned that Bishop Blomfield reserved a piece of the ground, sufficient for about four vaults, contiguous to the Moat, for the exclusive use of himself and his successors in the see of London. The site, which is marked off by two stone posts, lettered "B^{P}L.," is occupied by the graves of Bishop Blomfield, Col. Tait, brother of Bishop Tait, and Bishop Jackson.

The Churchyard, after having been in use for something like six hundred years, was closed by an Order in Council, dated 20 March 1863. For some time before it had become evident to the authorities that it was in a very crowded state. The Medical Officer of Health for Fulham, in examining, in 1862, some well water in the immediate locality of John's Place, found it impregnated by filtration from the soil of the graveyard, and that the interments amounted to no less than 280 a year. It became, therefore, imperative to take early action for the closing of the ground. The Order provided that the whole of the older portion of the Churchyard should be forthwith closed, with the exception of the then existing vaults and graves, in which there should be interred only the bodies of husbands, wives, parents, unmarried children and brothers and sisters of persons already buried therein. In regard to the then newly added portion, the Order provided that burial should be conducted in accordance with the official regulations for new burial grounds.

The Churchyard is not remarkable for its trees. Near the centre there were, some thirty years ago, a few fine old yews. Faulkner mentions two which, in his day, grew on either side of the principal entrance, and another, much decayed, on the north side.

There formerly existed, in addition to the main footpath, of which we have spoken, another and narrower path, which led from it at a point just opposite to the west door, across nearly to the south-west corner of the Churchyard. As the way was practically useless, the necessary order was, in 1869, obtained for its closing.

In the Churchyard once stood a sundial. The Parish Books record:

1647. "pd. Mr. ffrazer for . . . a cocke for the sun diall, etc. 4s. 6d."

1650. "For mending the Diall in the Churchyard 6d."

1670. "Pd. Wm. Williams bricklayer for worke and stuff about the Dyall post 19s. 7d."

1670. "To Wm. Ludwell carpenter for a dyall post and other worke done about the Church 13s."

In 1638 the Churchwardens

"Pd. for a petition touching buryalls 9s. 6d."

Fulham Churchyard, showing the path stopped up in 1868.
From a photograph by Messrs. C. G. and A. C. Wright, 1897.

During the Commonwealth the payment of burial fees was so frequently evaded, that the Vestry found it needful to pass the following resolution:

"Att the Vestrie howse of ffulham September 8th. 1653.
It is . . . ordered that from henceforth the Saxton nor anie other pson belonging to ye Church shall breake open anie ground in church or churchyard ffor anie pishoners or other pson to be buried Vntill all such dues and duties to the pish (menconed in a certeine table now

remaining in the Vestrie) shall be first paid and satisfied: And if anie officer apeyteining to the Church shall not observe the Tenor of this order, shall forthw[th] be dismissed of his Imploymn[t] in or about the church and Provided this order shall not extend to anie psons that shall he penconers."

At Doctors' Commons is preserved a copy of a table of fees "made and agreed upon by the Vicar, Churchwardens, parishioners and inhabitants of the parish of Fulham in Vestry assembled 2 Aug. 1727." This table includes:

Item For the benefit of the Charity Children at Fulham:
For the great Velvet pall 7s. 6d.
For the cloath pall 5s. 0d.
For the little Velvet pall 2s. 6d.

The legality of these fees was called in question, and the Trustees of the Charity Schools were sued for the recovery of charges so made. A test case showed that these fees for the use of the pall could not be enforced.

John Dwight, the son of the Vicar and grandson of the founder of Fulham Pottery, was shortly afterwards brought into dispute with the church authorities respecting the heavy burial fees charged in connection with the interment of his little daughter, Millicent, who, according to the Church Registers, was buried on 3 May 1733. Dwight beat the Vestry, which had to pay the following costs:

1733. 20 Apl. Pd. Expenses at attending at the trial of Law between A. Wells (the Vestry Clerk) and John Dwight £1. 12s. 6d.

17 Oct. Pd. Mr. Dwight for recovery and costs £16

17 Oct. Pd. Mr. Hall the attorney 10s.

Dwight appears to have borne the church authorities a grudge to the day of his death, for a clause in his will, dated 3 Oct. 1745, reads:

"To be decently buried upon my father's corps being first wrapt in a sheet of Lead and one shilling only to be paid for fees to the priest who officiates for that purpose (in remembrance only) to shew they impose upon the poor parishioners of ffulham."

In 1783 Dr. Robert Lowth interfered with the scale of fees charged for burials. At a Vestry, held 10 June of that year, the Rev. Graham Jepson announced that the Bishop considered that the fees paid for building vaults in the Churchyard were

> "very large and unreasonable for parishioners; also that the fees received by the Churchwarden for burial in general were not applied in such manner as his Lordship wished them to be."

The Vestry agreed with the Bishop. The minute runs:

> "The Vestry taking the same into their consideration are of opinion with his Lordship that the sum of £60 (£30 to the Vicar and £30 to the parish), the present fee for a vault is a very extravagant sum for a parishioner to pay and they are of opinion and do hereby order, with the consent of the Vicar, that the sum be reduced to £40 (£20 to the Vicar and £20 to the parish) for parishioners only; and the more effectually to keep the churchyard for the use of the parishioners they are of opinion and do also hereby order, with the consent of the Vicar, that the fees for other persons (non-parishioners) be advanced to £80 (£40 to the Vicar and £40 to the parish)."

In 1831 some quaint "Orders and Regulations to be observed respecting Funerals" were put into operation. One of these reads:

> "And for the obtaining a punctual attention to the time fixed, if the Funeral does not arrive at the Church Gates within ten minutes after the hour appointed, which is to be ascertained by the Church Clock, an additional Fee of Two Shillings must be paid to the Officiating Minister, to be disposed of in the same manner as the Sacrament Money. If not within twenty minutes after the hour appointed, an additional Fee of Four Shillings must be paid. If not within half an hour, Six Shillings, and an additional Shilling for every five minutes after the half hour.
> The time in the latter cases also to be determined by the Church Clock."

Against a copy of these "Regulations," preserved in the Vicarage "Faulkner," the Rev. R. G. Baker, in 1858, aptly appended the following query: "If the 'Officiating Minister' should prove unpunctual, what was to happen then? *Audi alteram Partem.*"

West side of Fulham Churchyard.
From a drawing by C. Sulivan, published circa 1849

In the early years of this century this quiet little graveyard was frequently visited by body snatchers, who would come here in the dead of night, break open a grave, where an interment had recently taken place, wrench open the coffin and carry off the corpse in a sack or other convenient covering. Lying so near, as the Churchyard did, to the river, these "resurrection men," as they were termed, found the silent highway a very convenient means for the deportment of their gruesome wares. Chiswick, Putney, and other burial grounds adjacent to the river, suffered similar desecration. Sometimes the body snatchers would prefer the road. On one occasion a couple of resurrectionists drove the corpse of a man, which they had snatched from its grave, along the Fulham Road. Arriving at the "Admiral Keppel," the driver and his friend (who had ridden inside with the body, which they had fully habited) stopped for a drink. The two men, in turn, kept watch at the tavern door to see that no one tampered with their "fare," but, in spite of their vigilance, an ostler from the inn, seeing, as he thought, an old gentleman asleep in the vehicle, went up to him. "This is a house for refreshment, Sir," he observed, but before he could proceed further with his invitation, the pair of resurrectionists rushed out in affright, placed a piece of silver in the hand of the officious stableman, and, with a nod more significant than words, drove off as fast as they could.

In by-gone times in Fulham, it was a common expression to hear people say, when they saw a funeral, "Oh, if they don't mind, it'll go to Blenheim Steps," meaning that the body would be stolen. Blenheim Street, it may be explained, is a thoroughfare running from Great Marlborough Street to Oxford Street, terminating, at its northern end, in a flight of steps - Blenheim Steps - just facing the Princess's Theatre. Close to these steps was a famous anatomical school, kept, about the beginning of this century, by Joshua Brookes, a well-known London surgeon. From Fulham and other churchyards, bodies were spirited away to supply the anatomical needs of this and similar schools and the hospitals of London.

So much were the people of Fulham terrorized by these body snatchers that it was once the custom for the friends of a deceased person, buried at All Saints, to guard the grave for some time after the interment. In the early years of this century, William Tomlin got a frugal living by minding the Churchyard at night. On one occasion, about the year 1825, some boys were commissioned to "watch" a grave. "Billy" Tomlin, not relishing the idea of his "business" thus passing out of his hands, donned a white sheet and, making some hideous gesticulations, swooped down on the group of amateur grave-watchers, who, for dear life's sake, fled before the awful vision. "You make a pretty set of watchmen," cried old Billy as he cast aside his ghostly attire and revealed his identity to the boys. From that time forth, William Tomlin is said to have encountered no further competition in his office of grave-watcher.

The body snatchers, after having secured their booty, would make off for their "market." To Brookes's school they generally went. Arriving at Blenheim Steps in the early morn, the resurrection men would wheel the body up in a truck and deliver it through a trap-door in the wall, something like the door in a baker's oven. This done, the "party" then went round to the front, where payment was made. It was a point of strict etiquette between doctors and snatchers that no questions should be asked. On one occasion there was a dearth of corpses. The resurrection men, being at their wits' end, determined to sew up in a sack a "live" corpse in the shape of a drunken man. The "body" was duly delivered through the oven-like door at Blenheim Steps and paid for at the "front," but when the sack was cut open the ten guineas' worth woke up and calmly asked for "another pint." After this, Joshua Brookes determined that he would never purchase another corpse until he was certain it was a corpse. The Blenheim Steps Anatomical School is erroneously said to have been superintended, at one time, by no less a person than Sir Astley Cooper, but, though a generous friend to the body snatchers, Sir Astley never had any connection with this establishment. In the grim ballad of "Mary's Ghost," that lady deplores her posthumous misfortunes and appeals to her "William," an anonymous lover:

> The body-snatchers they have come,
> And made a snatch at me;
> It's very hard them kind of men
> Won't let :1 body be!
>
> The cock it crows - I must be gone!
> My William, we must part!
> But I'll be yours in death, altho'
> Sir Astley has my heart.

The Fulham Parish Books contain numerous entries relating to expenses incurred in connection with watching the Churchyard at night. On 11 Dec. 1814, the Churchwardens

> "Paid a man for watching 5 nights in the churchyard 15s. 0d."

and again, on 17 Dec.,

> "Paid a man for 7 nights watching in the churchyard £1. 1s. 0d."

On 8 March 1823, the Churchwardens:

> "Paid Callaway and Hawkins for watching the churchyard, the Resurrection Men being expected down 5s. 0d."

It may be interesting to note that the last body snatched from Fulham Churchyard was that of a man named Brown. The occurrence took place in 1828. The body was taken from its grave, near the Bishop's fence, and placed in a cart belonging to Chambers, the father of "Bobby," the noted water-carrier, and taken to Dr. Rouse's, Berwick House, Walham Green. A very old resident of Fulham, an eye-witness of the incident, furnished us with the following narrative:

> "I was going to the Bishop's about 7.30 one morning. When going through the Churchyard, I saw two coffins broken open and empty, while the tombstone was pulled up and broken in halves. One of the bodies was that of 'Pippy' Brown, a North End man, and the other that of a child. I ran and fetched the grave-digger. It was found that the man who took the bodies was Chambers. As late as 1846 I have known people to watch bodies for a month. One grave-digger I remember used to steal the lead coffins. Then old lead fetched two or three guineas a hundredweight. He used to say, 'What is the use of letting them lie there when you want money?' I always knew when he had sold a lead coffin, because he would always stand an extra quartern of gin."

Churchyard Tombstones, Memorials, Etc

Considerations of space forbid our noticing more than a small proportion of the epitaphs in the Churchyard. According to the calculations of Dr. Woodhouse, there still exist 648 stones or other monuments. These, added to the 101 memorials which are within the Church, make up a total of 749 inscriptions containing not far short of two thousand names. It is, of course, absolutely impossible even to guess at the number of the dead who have been interred in the Church and Churchyard, from, perhaps, the twelfth century down to 1863, when the ground was, except in special cases, closed against further interments.

Before we proceed with our selection of the more important inscriptions to be found in the Churchyard, we must express our indebtedness to the patient labours of Dr. Woodhouse, who, in 1885-87, devoted his spare hours to the difficult and dreary task of copying the whole of the epitaphs both within and without the Church.

The manuscript volume, which he compiled and presented to

the Vicarage, is entitled a "Registry of the Tombs and Tombstones in Fulham Church and Churchyard." This useful work of reference we have taken as the basis of the order of our own selection of epitaphs in the Churchyard. The graveyard was divided by Dr. Woodhouse into nine sections, lettered from A to I, as shown in the rough plan below.

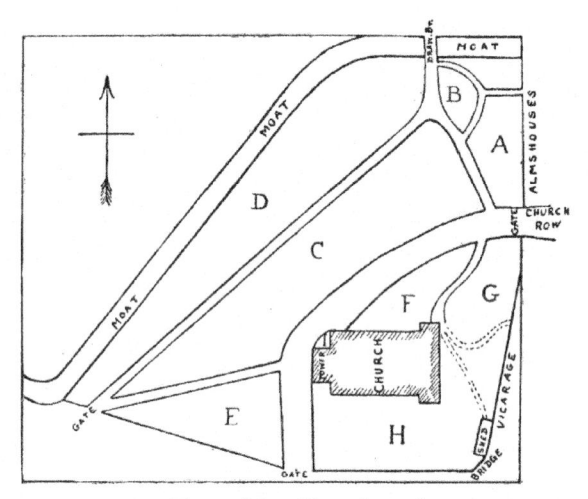

Plan of the Churchyard

Of the older epitaphs at All Saints there now exist four of the 16th century and forty of the 17th century.

In 1861 Mr. Walter Rye commenced to copy the inscriptions on the tombstones in Fulham Churchyard. His transcript, which consists of 254 epitaphs, contains several inscriptions which had perished or become illegible when Dr. Woodhouse made his Register.

PLOT A

RANELAGH. On our right hand, facing the main path, as we enter the Churchyard from Church Row, is a massive grey granite obelisk to the memory of the last Viscount Ranelagh. On the base is the word "Ranelagh," and, above, the late nobleman's arms (a cross, between four pheons), accompanied by the motto, *Cælitus mihi vires*. On the sides are the following inscriptions:

> "Colonel | Thomas Heron | Viscount Ranelagh | K.C.B. | Commandant | 2nd (South) Middlesex | Rifle Volunteer Corps | Born January 12th 1812 | Died November 13th 1885."

> "Erected by | the 2nd (South) Middlesex | Rifle Volunteer Corps | in memory of | their first commanding officer | who raised the regiment in 1859 | and commanded it until his death."

There is an unfortunate error in this inscription. The date of Lord Ranelagh's birth was 9 Jan., not 12 Jan. 1812. The Church Registers record:

> 1885. Thomas Heron (Viscount Ranelagh), Albert Mansions, St. Margaret's, Westminster bu. 21 Nov.

RECHBERG. A little to the rear of this monument is the grave of the Countess de Rechberg, the last of the Ranelagh family. It is inscribed:

> "In loving memory | of | Barbara M. C. de Rechberg, | born | 8th June 1813, | died | 27th May 1894."

Barbara Marianne Caroline, Countess de Rechberg, was the last surviving sister of the late Lord Ranelagh. She was the eldest daughter of Thomas, sixth Viscount Ranelagh. She married Count John Bernard de Rechberg, formerly prime minister to the Emperor of Austria. The Church Registers record:

> 1894. Rechberg, Comtess de, Barbara Marianne Caroline, 80, Ebury St. aged 81 years bu. 1 June.

HACKMAN. A plinth tomb inscribed:

> "Erected | by the vicar and | parishioners of Fulham, | to the memory of | Mr. Thomas Hackman | their late | Vestry Clerk | In testimony of their sense | of his official services | During a period | of thirty one years, | He died on the 18th day of November 1844, | Aged 61 years."

In this grave are also interred Elizabeth (d. 27 Apl. 1845), wife of Thomas Hackman; Henry (d. 22 Oct. 1865), son of Thomas

Hackman; and Mary (d. 20 July 1885), relict of Henry Hackman. Of Henry Hackman it is added:

> "He succeeded his father | in the office of | Vestry Clerk | of this Parish, | and faithfully | discharged his duties | for a period of | twenty one years."

MALTZAN. An upright stone, with cross fleury, is inscribed:

> "Sacred | to the Memory of | Baron Ernest Maltzan | Born at Dresden October 8th 1827 | Died at Fulham September 21st 1854."

The Church Registers record:

> 1854. Ernest von Maltzen 26 yrs. bu. 25 Sept.

Baron Ernst von Maltzan was the second son of Baron Heinrich von Maltzan by Julia, fifth daughter of John Thomson of Waverley Abbey, Surrey. He married, in 1852, Baroness Ottilie von Barsse. There were no children. His widow married Reginald John Corbet, third son of Sir Andrew Corbet, bart., of Moreton-Corbet, co. Salop. The Maltzan family is a very numerous one in Mecklenburg and Pomerania.

SULIVAN. The family grave of the Hon. Laurence Sulivan is surmounted by an inlaid marble slab, in the shape of a church window, with side pillars. Beneath the letters I.H.S. is an eagle on a crown. Below are the family arms, bearing the Irish motto, "Lamb Foistineach an Uachtar" (What we gain by conquest we secure by clemency). A horizontal railed slab is inscribed:

> "Sacred | to the Memory of | The Right Hon[ble] Laurence Sulivan, | Born at Calcutta, | the 7th | January, 1783: | and died the 4th January 1866, | in his 83rd year, | at Broom House, Fulham, | where he had resided 42 years. | He founded the Elizabethan Schools, | and Almshouses, in this Parish, | in memory of his wife, | the Hon[ble] Elizabeth Sulivan, | youngest daughter of | Henry, second Viscount Palmerston, | She died 13th November, 1837 | aged 47. | 'Blessed are those Servants whom the | Lord when he cometh shall find watching.' | St. Luke xii. chap. 37 v."

BAKER. Beneath a raised horizontal railed slab lie the remains of Emma (d. 8 Jan. 1864) and Mary (d. 20 Oct. 1871), wives of the Rev. R. G. Baker, M.A., Vicar of Fulham, Marianne Emma Thackeray, daughter of the Rev. J. R. Thackeray, M.A. (d. 7 Dec. 1872), and the Rev. R. G. Baker, M.A. (d. 21 Feb. 1878).

KEMPE. Beneath a horizontal stone with Celtic cross lie the remains of Alfred John Kempe (d. 21 Aug. 1846) and Anna Eliza Bray (d. 21 Jan. 1883). The stone is inscribed simply "Brother and Sister."

Mr. A. J. Kempe, who lived at 3, Stamford Villas, Fulham Road, was a well-known antiquarian writer and a Fellow of the Society of Antiquaries. He was descended from the Kempes of Ollanligh, Kent. He married at Leyton, Essex, Miss Mary Prior, by whom he had eleven children.

TAIT. In a grave covered with a grey granite stone lie the remains of Col. Thomas Forsyth Tait, C.B., and A.D.C. to the Queen, third son of Craufurd Tait of Harviestoun, Clackmannanshire, who died "in the house of his youngest brother, the Bishop of London," 16 Mar. 1859. The epitaph tells us that

> "He served with much distinction in India | for nearly 30 years and commanded his | regiment the 3rd Bengal Irregular Cavalry | (known by his name as 'Tait's Horse') in the | avenging expedition to Cabul and in the | hard fought campaigns of the Sutlej and | of the Punjab."

JACKSON. Adjacent is the grave of Bishop Jackson. The tomb consists of a grey granite horizontal stone, at the head of which is a plain white marble cross on a granite plinth. The inscription reads:

> "Mary Ann Frith Jackson, | the beloved wife of | John Bishop of London, | born Feb. 4th 1818. | Died on the Feast of the Epiphany | 1874 | 'Waiting for the manifestation of the | sons of God.' | John, Bishop of London | son of Henry and Lucy Jackson | Born February 22nd 1811 | Rector of St. James', Westminster 1846 | Bishop of Lincoln 1853 | Bishop of London 1869 | Entered into rest | on the Feast of the Epiphany | 1885."

The Church Registers record:

1885. John D.D. bishop of London, Fulham bu. 10 Jan.

BLOMFIELD. By the side of Bishop Jackson rests the body of Bishop Blomfield. In his "Memoir" of his father the late Bishop of Colchester Writes:

> "A simple tombstone of white marble, designed by one of the Bishop's sons, has since been erected over the grave. The centre of the headstone displays the cross, with the crown of thorns, and the monogram I.H.S. Upon the tomb itself is sculptured the episcopal crosier, interlaced with a ribbon bearing the Bishop's favourite text (which he had chosen as the motto to accompany his arms in the windows of the palace chapel), *'Vigilando et orando.'* "

The tomb, which is railed, is inscribed:

> "In memory of | Charles James Blomfield D.D. | Born May 29; 1786, Died August 5; 1857. | Consecrated Bishop of Chester; June 1824. | Translated to the see of London; August 1828 | Also In Memory of | Dorothy | Wife of Charles James Blomfield D.D. | Born March 11; 1794, Died February 12; 1870."

Around the edges of slab:

> "Blessed are the dead which die in the Lord: for they rest from their labours; and their works do follow them."

The Church Registers record:

> 1857. Charles James formerly Bishop of London, Fulham Palace bu. 11 Aug.

PLOT B

JOHNSON. Beneath an altar tomb lies Joseph Johnson, the well-known publisher. The inscription runs:

> "Here lie the remains of | Joseph Johnson, late of St. Paul's London, | who departed this Life on the 20th day of | December 1809, Aged 72 Years | A man, | Equally distinguised by probity, industry and |

disinterestedness in his intercourse with the Public and | every domestic and social Virtue in private Life, | beneficent without ostentation, ever ready to produce | merit and to relieve distress; unassuming in prosperity, | not appalled by misfortune, inexorable to his own, | indulgent to the wants of others & resigned and cheerful | under the torture of a malady which he saw gradually | destroy his Life."

The Church Registers record:

1809. Joseph Johnson bu. 28 Dec.

JEPSON. A coffin-shaped stone covers the remains of the Rev. Graham Jepson, B.D., Rector and Vicar of Fulham. The headstone is inscribed:

"Here lie interred the Remains of the | Revd Graham Jepson, B.D. | formerly Fellow of King's College; | afterwards Rector of Milton in | Cambridgeshire, for 35 Years Vicar of | this Parish, & in 1790, was presented | to the Rectory by the Right Rev^d | Beilby late B^p of this Diocese. His | obligation for this mark of his Lord- | -ship's favor, he ever strongly felt & | gratefully acknowledged, and directed | it might be here recorded. He died | 24th May 1811, in the 77th Year of his Age."

The Church Registers record:

1811. The Revd Graham Jepson bu. 31 May.

SHARP. Beneath an altar tomb with rails are interred Elizabeth Prowse of Wickin Park, Northamptonshire (d. 23 Feb. 1810), William Sharp (d. 17 Mar. 1810), her brother, Catherine Sharp (d. 9 Feb. 1814), wife of William Sharp, and Granville Sharp (d. 6 July 1813), brother of William Sharp.

ANSTED. This stone records the memory of a centenarian:

"Henry Ansted, | Born 26th September 1808 | Died 2nd August 1828 | Also Mary Ansted *of Pear Tree Cotiage, Fulham,* | Aunt of the above; | Born 28th February 1762, | Died 2nd March 1863."

PLOT C

MURR. An upright stone, facing the main path, contains the following eccentric inscription:

> "Sacred | To the Memory of | Isabella Murr | of this Parish, | who departed this Life | the 29th of November 1829, | in the 52nd Year of her Age.
>
> Ye who possess the highest charms of life,
> A tender friend, - a kind indulgent wife;
> Oh, learn their worth! In her beneath this stone
> These pleasing attributes together shone.
> Was not true happiness with them combin'd?
> Ask the spoil'd being she has left behind.
> He's Gone Too."

The Church Registers record:

> 1829. Isabella Murr, Fulham bu. 6 Dec.

Joseph Murr, her husband, was a schoolmaster, who resided in Elysium Row.

NUSSEN. A thick upright stone, bearing a winged figure holding a cloth, under which are a skull and thigh bone, is inscribed:

> "Here | lies the Body of | Frederick Nussen Esqr | of this Parish | One of His Majesties Musicians | And Many years Steward to the | late Earl Brooke; Warwick. | A Friend to all, Foe to none | He lived Respected, died lamented | on the 19th day of March 1779 | In the 64th Year of his Age."

The Church Registers record:

> 1779. Frederick Nussen bu. 23 Mar.

Frederick Nussen was a staunch friend of Oliver Stocken, founder of the brewery at Walham Green, to whom he is said to have given £3,000.

DUNDONALD. This is a brick tomb, inscribed with a long and inflated panegyric (written by Dr. Symmonds of Chiswick Square) to the memory of Anna Maria, Countess of Dundonald, who "finished her course upon Earth," 18 Sept. 1822. She was the wife of Archibald Campbell Cochrane 9th Earl of Dundonald, and daughter of Francis Plowden, a distinguished member of the Irish Bar, and historian of Ireland. The inscription, which is now almost illegible, is given in full in Faulkner's "Hammersmith," 1839, in which parish the Countess died.

SCOTT. Beneath an altar tomb with iron rails lie the remains of Hannah Lucy Scott (d. 1 June 1816) and her husband, George Scott (d. 28 March 1859) of Ravenscourt, Hammersmith.

George Scott, who was a well-known philanthropist, bought the estate of Paddenswick, or Ravenscourt, of the Dorville family in 1812. He was a Justice of the Peace for Middlesex, and owned a large amount of land in and around Hammersmith. He married first Miss Hannah Stoe, daughter and heiress of Harry Stoe of Chiswick. She died, as above stated, in 1816. Secondly he married Miss Hannah Gibson, who died in 1884 at an advanced age.

NADEN. On an upright stone, in memory of Miss Ann Naden (d. 17 July 1770), is the following neat epigram:

> "The Poor, the World, the Heavens and the Grave
> Her Alms, her Praise, her Soul, and Body have."

CLEAVER. Within an altar tomb with rails are buried Euseby Cleaver, D.D., Archbishop of Dublin (d. 10 Dec. 1819), Marianne Cromie (d. 13 May 1819), wife of John Cromie of Cromore and daughter of the Archbishop, Catherine Cleaver (d. 1 May 1816), wife of Archbishop Cleaver, and the Rev. Henry Owen Cleaver (d. 4 June 1837), his second son, incumbent of Hawkhurst, Kent.

ORD. Beneath an altar tomb with rails lie the remains of John Ord, Master in Chancery (d. 6 June 1814), his wife Eleanor (d. 21 Feb. 1818), and Mrs. Anne Simpson, sister of Mrs. Ord (d. 20 July 1824).

BOWDEN. This altar tomb with rails contains the remains of Marianne Bowden (d. 31 May 1819), daughter of John and Mary Anne Bowden of Mulgrave House, Jane Roberts (d. 21 Feb. 1841), Mary Anne Bowden (d. 27 Dec. 1836), wife of John Bowden, John Bowden (d. 25 June 1844), Emma Bowden (d. 22 Feb. 1836), wife of Captain Henry Bowden of the Scotch Fusilier Guards, and John William Bowden (d. 15 Sept. 1844).

John William Bowden, who was the eldest son of John Bowden of Mulgrave House, and subsequently of Grosvenor Place, London, was born 21 Feb. 1798, and educated at Harrow and Trinity College, Oxford. In 1819 he was admitted to Lincoln's Inn, and, in 1826, received the appointment of Commissioner of Stamps. He resigned this office in 1840. He married, 7 June 1828, Elizabeth, the youngest daughter of Sir John Edward Swinburne, bart., of Capheaton, Northumberland. He took a great interest in the revival of the ecclesiastical principles of the 17th century. He was a most intimate friend and one of the earliest supporters of John Henry Newman. He was, with him, joint author of "Saint Bartholomew's Eve " (1821). He also wrote "Lyra Apostolica," poems (1836), "The Life and Pontificate of Gregory the Seventh" (1840), "A Few Remarks on Pews" (1843), and "Thoughts on the Work of the Six Days of Creation" (1845). He died at Grosvenor Place, and was buried at Fulham, which had been the home of his childhood and youth. His widow, Mrs. Elizabeth Bowden, was the foundress of St. Thomas's Roman Catholic Church, in the graveyard attached to which she lies buried.

Captain Henry Bowden of the Scotch Fusilier Guards, who was born in 1805, was Mr. John Bowden's youngest son. He was the father of the Rev. Father John Edward Bowden, formerly of the Oratory, who died in 1874, and of the Rev. Fathers Charles Henry and Sebastian Bowden also both of the Oratory.

ROBERTSON. Here are buried, as recorded on an upright stone, the Rev. Duncan Robertson, D.D., founder of the London Gaelic chapel (d. 21 March 1825), Mrs. Jane Hope (d. 11 April 1831), his sister-in-law, and Sarah Armstrong (d. 10 October 1832), relict of Dr. Robertson and wife of R. A. Armstrong, LL.D.

Dr. Robertson was a Highlander who had risen by his education. At one time he was a tutor in a gentleman's family of some consideration. He founded, and was, for some years, Gaelic preacher at the Scotch Chapel in Hatton Garden, where the celebrated Irving subsequently preached. At Chelsea Dr. Robertson kept a seminary for young gentlemen. Dr. Armstrong was the author of a "Gaelic Dictionary" (2 vols. 4to, London, 1825).

RENCH. One of the most noteworthy epitaphs in the Churchyard is the following on an upright stone to the memory of Nathaniel Rench, of whom we shall speak in connection with Southfield Farm, Parson's Green:

> "Under this Stone | Are deposited the Remains of | Nathaniel Rench | late of this Parish, Gardener, | who departed this *Transitory* life | January 18th 1783 | Aged 101 Years | Added to this remarkable instance | of Longevity, he enjoyed unimpaired | the full Powers of his Faculties | until a Short period of time | previous to his Dissolution; | Possessing in an eminent degree | the Social Virtues | it may justly be Applied to him that | An honest Man is the Noblest work of God. | Also Elizabeth his Wife | who died April the 21st 1800 | Aged 72 years."

The Church Registers record:

> 1783. Nathaniel Rench bu. 26 Jan.

DELATTRE. This is an upright stone inscribed:

> "Sacred | to the memory of | Mrs. Ann Delattre, | who died 13th July 1834 | aged 84 years. | Also | Mr. John Marie Delattre, | husband of the above; | who departed this life | 21st June 1843, in his 98th year. | Also | Charlotte Mary Delattre, | Eldest Daughter of the above; | who departed this life | on the 30th of August 1851 | Aged 71 years."

MAXWELL. Beneath an altar tomb lie the remains of William Pearson Low Maxwell (d. 23 June 1806), William Henry Maxwell (d. 25 Jan. 1808), and Mrs. Mary Low, late of Lincoln, who died at Parson's Green, 23 April 1824. According to Faulkner the following lines, on a plain headstone, addressed to the memory of William Pearson Low Maxwell, who died in infancy, were in existence in his day:

> "Piercing the Grief when Parents lose a Son,
> More piercing still to lose an only one;
> But when that one, in heavenly form combined
> Such angel features with so sweet a mind,
> What words can paint, what eloquence declare,
> The heartfelt pangs those Parents long must bear."

Certainly an extraordinary panegyric on a babe of seventeen months.

DE LA BIGNE. Of a stranger, F. J. H. de la Bigne de Bella Fontaine (d. 14 Oct, 1811), it is observed:

> By Foreign Hands thy dying Eyes were clos'd
> By Foreign Hands thy decent Limbs compos'd
> By Foreign Hands thy Humble Grave adorn'd
> By Strangers honoured and by Strangers mourned.

These four lines of verse have now all but perished.

CADOGAN. Beneath a brick tomb lies the remains of that once fashionable physician, Dr. William Cadogan, of whom we have spoken in connection with Hurlingham House. The brief inscription reads:

> "M S. | Gulielmi Cadogan | Oxoniæ et Lugduni Batavorum | alumni et M.D. | Coll. Reg. Med. Lond. | Socii | Ob. xxvi. die Feb. A.D. MDCCXCVII | æt suæ LXXXVI."

The Church Registers record:

> 1797. William Cadogan, Esqr bu. 6 Mar.

DOUGLAS. In an altar tomb with rails lie the remains of Sir Andrew Snape Douglas, of whom we shall speak in connection with Mulgrave House. The inscription reads:

> "Within this Vault are Deposited | the Remains of | Sir Andrew Snape Douglas Knight, | late Captain of his Majesty's Ship Queen Charlotte, | and Colonel of Marines; | who was born the 8th day of August 1761, | and died on the 4th of June 1797. | Of a Life so short in Duration, | but

full of Public Usefulness and Glory | Seventeen Years were spent in the Station | of a Captain in the British Navy. | Among various most essential Services | which Signalized his Zeal and Abilities in his Profession, | His Valour and Conduct on the First of June 1794, | and the Twenty Third of June 1795, | Two of the Proudest Days | which the Naval History of Britain has to record, | were equally Conspicuous and Important; | his Ardour and Bravery as an Officer, | were tempered by those gentler Virtues | Mildness, Affection, Benevolence, and Piety | which distinguished his Character as a Man. | His memory will long be cherished | Amidst the Affliction and tender Regrets | of his Family and Friends. | It will live in the Gratitude and Applause of his Country."

The Church Registers record:

1797. Sir Andrew Snape Douglas knight bu. 12 June.

Captain Douglas was knighted for his conduct in the command of the *Queen Charlotte* in the engagement under Lord Howe off Ushant, 1 June 1794. To commemorate this great victory many medals were struck. One of these was punningly inscribed, "May the French ever know Howe to rule the Main."

BELSHAM. An upright stone is inscribed:

"William Belsham, Esqr | Author of a History of England &c., | died November 17th 1827 | Aged 75 Years. | His cultivated mind was ever ardently | employed in the search of truth as his writings | testify, and he may be added to the list of | celebrated men who have lived and died under | the influence of a thorough conviction of the | truth of Christianity which enabled him to | bear with fortitude the trials allotted him here, | in the hope of a happy futurity."

The Church Registers record:

1827. William Belsham, Portland Place, North End bu. 27 Nov.

PLOT D

HAMILTON. An upright stone reads:

"Sacred | to the Memory of | Mrs. Margaret Hamilton | who was born at

Geneva the second of June 1727 | and died at Fulham | the eleventh of June 1840. | This tribute of Gratitude is respectfully | inscribed to Departed worth."

No record of her interment can be found in the Church Registers. This is one of the most remarkable cases of alleged centenarianism on record, Mrs. Hamilton's age, according to the epitaph, being no less than 113 years.

PLOT E

GRAY. Beneath a coat of arms is the following inscription:

"Here lyeth the Body of | Mr. Christopher Gray, | who Departed this Life | the 20 of March 1741-2 | in the 76 Year of his Age | Also the Body of Alice | the Wife of the abovesaid | Mr. Christ^r Gray who died | Septr 3rd 1749 in the 87th Year of her age | Also the Body of Mr. Thos | Gray son of ye above Chris^r and | Alice who died Jan. 15th 1769 | In the 67th year of his age."
Arms: Within a bordure engrailed a lion ramp. *Crest*: A scaling ladder.

PLOT F

WYCHE. A small upright stone reads:

"Here | Lyes the body of Mr. | Benjamin Wyche | Citizen and Apothe - | - cary of London | who departed this | life the 8th of Sept. | 1686, Aged 55 years."

The Church Registers record:

1686. Benjamin Widch bu. 10 of Sep.

NAMELESS. Upon a small upright stone, bearing a skull, hourglass, spade, pickaxe and ribbon, is a faded epitaph. The complete inscription formerly ran:

"Under this Stone | Lies William & Joan | Y wraig o Wilt Shire | A'r gŵr o Fôn | She died in March | He in November | All that Pass by | Pray them Remember | 1706."

The third and fourth lines, which have all but disappeared, are Welsh. They may be Anglicised: "The Wife of Wiltshire, and the husband of Anglesea."

This singular epitaph is rendered the more remarkable by the absence of any surname. The Church Registers for 1705-7 afford no clue. A Joane Thomas, widow, was buried in Nov. 1706. The Registers for this period contain no other Joan and no William.

PLOT G

DWIGHT. The tomb of Dr. Philip Dwight, Vicar of Fulham, and Jane his wife, consists of a flat stone, surrounded by iron rails. At the top are the following arms:

Dexter: A chevron, ermine, between 3 leopards' faces (Dwight).
Sinister: A lion ramp., a canton [of the last] (Owen).

Beneath is the inscription:

"Hic | Resurgendi spe salutari | Requiescunt Corpora | Philippi Dwight S. T. P. | Hujus Parochiæ Vicarii | Ianæq. etiam Vxoris ejus, | Qui Intra Quadriduum morientes, | Una sub hoc Marmore sepulti sunt | Ejusdem Ætatis, | Annos nempe octo et quinquaginta nati | Obierunt.
   Illa Christi die Natali
   Ille Innocentium festo   }   1729
Uterq. | In Vita amabilis, | Nee vel in Morte separatus."

(Translation: Here, in the hope of a blessed resurrection, lie the bodies of Philip Dwight, S.T.P., Vicar of this parish, and also of Jane, his wife, who, dying within a space of four days, were buried beneath this stone. They were of the same age, namely, 58. They died
   She on Christmas day
   He on the Feast of the Innocents }   1729
Both loving in life; nor in death divided.)

Mrs. Dwight, as the epitaph records, died on 25 Dec. and her husband on 28 Dec. 1729. Both were interred on 2 Jan. 1729-30.

ROACH. An upright stone, to the memory of Charles Roach (d. 28 Mar. 1838), contains the following lines:

"Reader here resteth one," says human Pride,
"Who lived respected and lamented died."
"Reader" says holy Hope, "here resteth one
Who at the Cross has laid his burden down;
Whose end was peace; for, mid his mortal strife,
Faith bade him view in Death the Gate of Life."
"Let then his tomb this solemn warning give,
So learn to die that thou may'st hope to live."

The Church Registers record:

1838. Charles Roach, 35 years bu. 5Apl.

In this grave are also interred Charles Bethell Roach (d. 21 Feb. 1837) and William Jamison (d. 13 July 1857), the son and the brother-in-law, respectively, of Charles Roach.

QUINTON. An upright stone records as under it:
William Quinton (d. 17 Nov. 1820), Eleanor Quinton (d. 11 Nov. 1822), his wife, Harriot Quinton (d. 4 Oct. 1842), granddaughter of William Quinton, William Quinton (d. 11 Mar. 1847), son of William and Eleanor Quinton, William Quinton (d. 10 Oct., 1847), son of the second William Quinton, Mary Quinton (d. 2 Jan. 1876), widow of the second William Quinton, and Robert Quinton (d. 1 May 1877), son of William and Mary Quinton.

According to tradition this family originally came from Holland, and settled, in the first instance, at Hammersmith, probably about the time of the persecution of the Protestants in the Netherlands under Philip of Spain. In the Hammersmith Church Registers is the entry of the burial of a William Quinton in 1684. This is the earliest occurrence of the name.

POOPE. A small upright stone with rounded top, to the memory of Edward Poope, is noticeable as the oldest existing epitaph in the Churchyard. It reads:

"Heare | Lyeth intere(d) | the Body of | Edward Poope | Who departed | This lief, Aparel | the 2 1664."

Edward Poope or Pope was a brickmaker, living at Crab Tree, in one of a group of houses built by Sir Nicholas Crispe in the "Six Acres" near Cockbush. The Church Registers mention other members of this family.

WOOD. A headstone with rails marks the vault of the Rev. William Wood, B.D. Here lie six of his children (three boys and three girls), three of whom he lost by fever shortly before he left Fulham. Their names are not recorded on the stone. The Church Registers give them as follows:

> 1833. Matilda Wood, Vicarage, Fulharn, aged 18½ years bu. 22 Nov.

> 1833. Maria Elizabeth Wood, Vicarage, Fulham, aged 4 10/12 [four years, ten months] years bu. 22 Nov.

> 1833. Emily Mary Wood, Vicarage, Fulham, aged 11 11/12 [eleven years and eleven months] years bu. 22 Nov.

The following elegiacs, which are by no means devoid of beauty, occur on the stone. They were, we believe, composed by Mr. Wood, evidently in imitation of those in the Tower Chapel to the memory of Sir William Butts:

> "Funera natorum tria mors distantia fecit
> Tres eheu natas telo simul obruit uno
> Nil medicæ juvere manus nil forma vel ætas
> Nil pietas moresve sui ceu lilia quondam
> Candida crescebant stravit ceu lilia turbo
> Nee querimur dedit ipse Deus Deus abstulit idem
> At vos relliquiæ gelido sub marmore tristes
> Dum tuba magna sonet cari caræque valete
> Felices animæ terrena labe remota
> Morte dolore procul jamnune sua regna capessunt
> Lucis et eternæ cœlestia regna Diei."

> (Translation:
> Three brothers there were, who had sisters three.
> The first at various times met Death's decree;
> But those three sisters at one blow he took:
> Nor leech's care nor youth nor beauty's look,
> Virtue nor right affection made him spare.
> As lilies fair they grew, as lilies fair

The storm has laid them low, nor dare we say
'Tis hard: God gave, and God has ta'en away.
But ye, wan ashes, resting in the ground
'Neath the cold stone, waiting the fateful sound
Of the last trump, farewell, beloved, farewell:
Blest souls are ye, freed from the painful spell
Of this sad world, who now have won your way
To your own homes of light and lasting day.)

The remains of the Rev. William Wood also lie in this vault. His epitaph reads:

"William Wood, B.D. | of Ch : Ch : Oxon | Prebendary of the Cathedral Churches | of | St. Paul's, London, and Ch : Ch : Canterbury | and for xxiii years | Rector and Vicar of this Parish. | He was born vi August | A.D. MDCCLXIX | and died on Easter Day xi April | A.D. MDCCCXLI æt: LXXII."

FOSTER. A railed altar tomb marks the grave of Thomas Foster (d. 6 Dec. 1815), a great benefactor to this parish. He was the owner of the old house which formerly faced Fulham Vicarage. His wife, Margaret Foster (d. 10 Mar. 1788), is buried in the same grave.

By a codicil to his will, dated 7 Feb. 1815 (proved in the P. C. C. 8 Jan. 1816), Thomas Foster left £100, on trust, the interest on which was to be laid out in keeping the above-mentioned monument in repair, the residue to be applied in providing the Charity Children of Fulham with an annual dinner, or in such other manner as might appear most proper for their benefit. In 1816 the legacy was invested in the purchase of £161. 5s. 10d. 3 per cent Reduced Annuities, producing £4. 16s. 8d. per annum. The maintenance of the tomb is still the first charge on this charity. Any surplus is devoted to treats for the children of the Fulham National Schools.

ROE. A flat marble stone marks the grave of Joseph Roe (d. 23 Dec. 1815), sergeant of His Majesty's Chapels Royal. His children, Eliza, Mary, George and Joseph, are also buried here. The last named died 15 Nov. 1824. There are also buried in this vault Elizabeth Roe (d. 19 Sep. 1838), widow of Joseph Roe, Catherine

Roe (d. 30 Dec. 1831), and Thomas Roe (d. 19 May 1873), her husband.

LOWTH. In this section of the Churchyard, near the chancel, cluster the tombs of no less than eight Bishops of London. Taking them in the order of the dates of their deaths they are:
Compton, 1713, Robinson, 1723, Gibson, 1748, Sherlock, 1761, Hayter, 1762, Terrick, 1777, Lowth, 1787, and Randolph, 1813, exactly a century intervening between the death of the first and the last of the group. The graves are in two rows. Those immediately outside the chancel are six in number. Taking them in the order in which the monuments stand these are: Lowth, Terrick, Sherlock, Compton, Hayter and Robinson. Near the wall adjoining the Vicarage are the other two, also side by side, namely, Randolph and Gibson. The first to which we come is that of Bishop Lowth.

The tomb, which stands near the present Vestry door, consists of an elegant monument of white marble, enclosed within iron rails. It bears on the north side the following inscription:

"Robert Lowth D.D. | Lord Bishop of London | Died November the III^D MDCCLXXXVII, | In the LXXVIIth Year of his Age. | Mary Lowth his Wife | Daughter and Heiress of | Lawrence Jackson of *Christ Church* | Hants Esqr | died March XIVth MDCCCIII, | in the LXXIVth Year of her Age."

The south side is inscribed:

"Thomas Henry Lowth, | Fellow of New College, Oxford, | And Rector of Thorley, Herts, | Died June the VIIth MDCCLXXVIII. | In the XXVth year of his Age. | Frances Lowth, | Died July the XXIst MDCCLXXXIII, | In the XXVIth Year of her Age. | Martha Lowth, | Died March the XIIth MDCCCXII, | In the LIIND Year of her Age. | Robert Lowth, M.A. | Prebendary of St. Pauls and Chichester, | And Rector of Hinton Ampner, Hants, | Died August XVIIIth, MDCCCXXII. | In the LXIst Year of his Age. | Margaret Lowth, | Died March the Xth MDCCLXIX, | In the VIth Year of her Age. | Charlotte Lowth, | Died May the XXIXth MDCCLXVIII, | In the III^D Year of her Age."

On a tablet, which has been affixed at the west end, is inscribed:

"George Thomas, | Fifth son of the Revd Robert Lowth, | of Hinton, Hants and Grove House Chiswick and Grandson of | Robert Lowth D.D. Lord Bishop of London, | Born June 25th 1807, Died December 31st 1893."

At the west end are the arms of the Bishopric of London, and at the east end the domestic coat of Dr. Robert Lowth, vizt:

> Sa., a. wolf saliant arg. (Lowth). On an escutcheon of pretence quarterly, (1) and (4), on a chevron az. between three eagles' heads erased, as many cinquefoils pierced (Jackson): (2) and (3), five lozenges conjoined in fess, each charged with an escallop (Plumpton?). *Crest*: On a wreath a wolf's head couped.

The foregoing epitaph tells a story which is full of pathos; the passing away of the children before the parents. While Dr. Lowth was still Bishop of Oxford, he lost his two young daughters, Charlotte and Margaret, who were interred in a vault in the church of St. James, Piccadilly. The year following his promotion to the see of London witnessed the death of a young and promising son, the Rev. Thomas Henry Lowth, who, like his father, was a Fellow of New College, Oxford. The grief which Dr. Lowth experienced at this heavy loss may be gathered from the fact that it led to the erection of the beautiful tomb of which we are speaking, and which he evidently designed as the family mausoleum. With this object in view, he obtained a faculty for the removal of the bodies of his two little daughters from St. James's to All Saints. On 13 June 1778, the triple funeral took place at Fulham. The Church Registers record:

> 1778. The Reverend Mr. Thomas Henry Lowth son of The Lord Bishop of London bu. 13 June.
> Margaret and Charlotte two of his Lordship's Daughters who had been buried at St. James's Church were brought from thence and deposited in the same vault with Mr. Lowth 13 June.

On 21 July 1783, Dr. Lowth suffered a still further bereavement in the sudden death at Fulham of his second daughter Frances, then in her 26th year. She was presiding at the tea table at Fulham Palace in company with Bishop Newton. Whilst in the act of placing a cup of coffee on the salver, she called out to the Bishop, "Take this." The cup fell from her hand and she immediately expired. The Church Registers record:

> 1783. Miss Frances Lowth D^r of the Lord Bishop of London bu. 28 July.

It may be added that Bishop Lowth's eldest daughter, Mary, died in 1768, aged 13. She lies buried at Cuddesdon. On her grave is a beautiful Latin epitaph, composed by her father.
The following extracts are of interest:

> "Monday died suddenly Miss Lowth, eldest daughter of the Right Rev. Lord Bishop of London, at Fulham Palace."
> - (*London Chronicle*, July 22-24, 1783, vol. 54, p. 83.)

> "Dr. Lowth has been singularly unfortunate in his family losses; a few years since he was deprived of three daughters in the course of twelve months; soon after he lost a most accomplished and admired son, and now the only remaining daughter but one."
> - (*London Chronicle*, July 26-29, 1783, vol. 54, p. 102.)

The vault was next opened for the interment of Dr. Lowth. His lordship expired on 3 Nov. 1787, and in the forenoon of Monday 12 Nov. he was buried, with great privacy, in accordance with his express wish. The Church Registers record:

> 1787. The Rt. Rev^d. Father in God Robert Lowth Lord Bishop of London bu. 12 Nov.

Mrs. Lowth, who died 14 March 1803, is also buried here. The Rev. Robert Lowth, the Bishop's only surviving son, died in 1822. The Church Registers record:

> 1822. The Rev. Robert Lowth, Chiswick, 60 years bu. 26 Aug.

Dr. Robert Lowth, who was a student of Christ Church, Winchester, died at The Grove, Chiswick. The last interment in the vault was on 6 Jan. 1893, when George Thomas Lowth, of Kenegie, Ascot, aged 86, was buried. This monument was restored in 1814, in 1838 and in 1878.

TERRICK. This monument, which is in a fair state of preservation, lies between those of Lowth and Sherlock. It is composed of Portland stone and is of a plain and heavy character. At the west end are the official arms of Terrick, vizt:

> Gu. three tirwits (Terrick, a pun on the name) impaled with the see of London.

At the east end is his domestic coat impaled:

> *Dexter*: Terrick as before; *Sinister*: Apparently three bars azure on a canton in chief three orles (Stainforth).

On the north side is the following inscription:

> "Here lie the Remains of Richard Terrick, late Bishop of London, *Dean of the Chapels Royal*, and One of the | King's most honourable *Privy Council*. He was consecrated | *Bishop of Peterborough* in July 1757, and translated to | the *See* of London in June 1764. Having discharged the | Sacred Duties of his Functions as became a virtuous and able | Prelate, during a Period of twenty years, his great Experience, | and sound Judgement, his Christian Moderation, and Benevolence, | would have raised him to a Rank still more exalted, But, though | happy in such a Testimony of his Sovereign's Approbation, | He suffered no Inducement to tempt him, at so late an Hour, | to change his Sphere of Publick Action; well satisfied with | the Consciousness of having so spent his Days as to have | secured to himself, and to his Memory, that highest and | most lasting of all earthly Rewards, the Esteem of Good Men. | He died March the 31st 1777, Aged 66."

The south side is inscribed:

> "Under this Tomb are interred the Remains of | Mrs. Tabitha Terrick, Widow of Dr. Richard | Terrick, late Bishop of London. | She died February ye 14th 1790 in the 78th | year of her Age."

The Church Registers record:

1777. The Right Revd Father in God Richard Terrick, Lord Bishop of London bu. 8 Apl.

SHERLOCK. The cumbrous altar tomb to the memory of Bishop Sherlock bears, at the west end, his official arms, vizt:

Three fleurs-de-lis (Sherlock), impaled with the see of London.

and, at the east end, his domestic coat impaled,

Dexter: Sherlock as before; *Sinister*: A fess between three elephants' heads erased (Fountayne).

On the north side is the following epitaph:

"In this Vault is deposited the Body of | The Right Reverend Father in God Doctor Thomas Sherlock, | late Bishop of this Diocese, formerly Master of The Temple, | Dean of *Chichester*, and Bishop of *Bangor* and of *Salisbury*, | Whose beneficent and worthy Conduct in | the several high Stations which he fill'd, intitled Him to the | Gratitude of Multitudes, and to the Veneration of All. | His superior Genius; His extensive, | and well applied Learning, His admirable Faculty, and | unequal'd Power of Reasoning, as exerted in the Explanation | of Scripture, in Exhortations to that Piety and Virtue, of which | He was Himself a great Example, and in Defence especially of | Reveal'd Religion; need no Encomium here, they do Honour | to the Age wherein He liv'd, and will be known to Posterity, | without the Help of this perishable Monument of Stone. | He died the 18th Day of July in the Year | of Our Lord 1761, and the 84th of His Age, | The Powers of His Mind continuing unimpair'd | through a tedious Course of Bodily Infirmities, | which He sustained to the last with a most chearfull | and edifying Resignation to the Will of God."

The inscription was drawn up by Dr. Nichols, Dr. Sherlock's successor at the Temple.
The south side is inscribed:

"Iudith Fountayne | Was Married to Dr. Thomas Sherlock | Master of The Temple August 8th 1707 | Died Iuly 23^d 1764 | Aged 77."

The Church Registers record:

1761. The Right Revd Father in God Dr Thomas Sherlock Lord Bishop of London bu. 25 July.

In a letter, dated 27 July 1764, John Fountayne of York, writing to his brother-in-law, Edward Weston, after stating that he is the executor of his aunt, Mrs. Sherlock, widow of the Bishop, adds briefly the contents of that lady's will, and, in a postscript, dated next day, notes, "Mrs. Sherlock bury'd this morning early at Fulham."

Cole, the antiquary, under date 18 June 1764, thus records his visit to the tomb shortly after its erection:

> "I had a desire to see Bishop Sherlock's tomb, as he had formerly been my patron in giving me the Rectory of Hornsey. Accordingly I was rowed over (from Putney) . . . and made the following observations. At the east end of the north Vestry of Fulham Church, at about 8 or 12 feet from the same, inclosed within an iron palisado, is erected in the Churchyard in a line with the other Bishops' tombs, a very clumsy and heavy altar tomb of Portland stone and black marble, on which is placed a most monstrous and awkward kind of sarcophagus in no sort of taste, or in the very worst. At the head of the tomb on black marble is engraved the arms of the see of London, mitred, and at the foot those of Sherlock impaling Fountayne."

On the tomb is the sculptor's name, "Iohn Vardy *Delin.*"

COMPTON. The grave of Bishop Compton is surmounted by a railed table monument, on the top of which are his official arms, vizt:

> *Dexter*: The see of London. *Sinister*: A lion passant gardant between three esquires' helmets (Compton).

and the following inscription, now almost illegible:

> "H. London | ΕΙ ΜΗ ΕΝ | ΤΩ | ΣΤΑΥΡΩ | MDCCXIII."
> (Translation: H. London. "Except in the Cross" (Gal. vi. 14), 1713.)

The tomb, which lies immediately under the East Window of the Church, was, in 1835, repaired by Spencer, second Marquis of Northampton. It was also repaired in 1879.

The Church Registers record:

> 1713. Henry Compton, Lord Bishop of London departed this Life at Fulham House the seventh day of July, and was interd the 14 day in a valt in ye Churchyard at the Chansel end 14 July.

In the same vault are buried the remains of Sir Francis Compton, a brother of the Bishop. Bowack writes:

> "At the head of this tomb (i.e. Bishop Compton's) upon the ground lyes a black marble stone over the body of the said Bishop's brother."

The Church Registers record:

> 1716. S^r ffrancis Compton, knight bu. 28 Dec.

The inscription on the stone of Sir Francis, which is now lost, is thus given by Faulkner:

> "Here lies the Body of the Honble Francis Compton 5 son of Spenser Earl of Northampton, died Dec. 20, 1716. Aged 87."

Sir Francis Compton was a distinguished soldier. He fought in the Civil War in the reign of Charles I, and, after the Restoration, he had a command in the Horse Guards. He became Lieutenant General of the Horse and Lieutenant Colonel of the Royal Regiment of Horse Guards. He was engaged in the action at Sedgemoor against the Duke of Monmouth. In 1661 he was elected M.P. for Warwick. He was several times married. By his wife Jane, daughter of Sir John Trevor, he had two sons, James and John, both of whom died unmarried, and three daughters, Mary, the wife of Sir Barrington Bourchier, of Benningborough Park, in Yorkshire, knight, and Frances and Anne, both of whom died unmarried. At the time of his death he was the oldest officer in the military service.

HAYTER. An elegant altar tomb of stone, covered by a large marble slab, marks the vault of Bishop Hayter. At the west end are the arms of the see of London, surmounted by a mitre and ensigned with crosier and pastoral staff saltier-wise. At the east end are the arms of Bishop Hayter, vizt:

> Three bulls' heads couped, surmounted by an esquire's helmet thereon, on a wreath a bull's head pierced with a spear to the sinister (Hayter).

On the north side is the following inscription, now fast becoming illegible:

> "In this Vault lie the Remains of | Thomas Hayter, D.D., | Lord Bishop of London, | Whose amiable Character | And | Conspicuous Abilities | Raised him to the See of Norwich, | In the year 1749. | After having filled that See | With Dignity and Reputation | Twelve years | He was, in October 1761, translated | To London, | Where the Expectations of him were | General and Great. | But | Such was the Will of God | they were soon disappointed, | For he died, | Universally lamented, | January 9, 1762 Aged 59."

The above epitaph was composed by Dr. Sandford, rector of Hatherop, Gloucestershire, cousin of the Bishop. The Church Registers record:

> 1762. The Right Revd Father in God Dr. Thomas Hayter Lord Bishop of London bu. 16 Jan.

ROBINSON. The altar monument to the memory of Bishop Robinson lies just south of that of Bishop Hayter, and is the last of this row of six bishops. It faces the east window of the south transept. The sides are of Portland stone and the top is of black marble. The whole is surrounded by iron railings, once gilded. It has recently been repaired. At the west end are the Bishop's official arms, vizt:

> *Dexter*: The see of London; *Sinister*: On a chevron between three roes trippant as many cinquefoils (Robinson). The whole is surmounted of a mitre.

At the east end is the following domestic coat of the Bishop and his two wives:

> *In pale*, Robinson, as before; *Dexter*: Three chevrons (Langton); *Sinister*: A lion rampant (Charlton); an esquire's helmet and mantle

surmounted on a wreath thereon a roe trippant. The coat bears the motto "Propter et Provide."

The monument has, on the north side, the following inscription:

"Hic Situs est JOHANNES ROBINSON, S.T.P. | Natus apud Cleasby in agro Eboracensi A.D. 1650 7° Nov^{ris} ubi Scholam extruxit et Dotavit; | Collegij Orielensis Oxon. Socius Cujus ædificia ampliavit et Scholarium numerum auxit. | Legati Regij Vices obijt Stockholmiæ ab anno 1683 usq. 1708. Anno 1692 Causam PROTESTANTIUM | strenue asseruit, labantem Regis Suecici animu confirmavit, et ne consilijs Gallicis de nono | Electoratu immergeret, effecit anno 1700 Regem Suecicia in itinere periculoso Comitatus | Conjunctionem classium potestatum Fœderatum fœliciter expedivit Navigationem | Maris Borealis liberam suis et Europæis conservavit | 1711 Privati Sigilii Custodiam ei Commisit ANNA PIÆ MEMORIÆ nuper Regina | a qua Legatus et Plenipotentiarius Regius constitutus, Ultrajectæ PACEM | inter Europtæs omnes diu optatam ipsam qua HODIE FRUIMUR | et de qua ETIAMNUM GLORIAMUR Stabilivit."

(Translation: Here lies John Robinson, S.T.P., born at Cleasby in the county of York, 7 Nov. 1650, where he built and endowed a school. He was a Fellow of Oriel College, Oxford, of which he enlarged the buildings and augmented the number of scholars. From 1683 to 1708 he undertook the duties of Ambassador at Stockholm. In the year 1692 he strenuously supported the cause of the Protestants, strengthened the wavering mind of the King of Sweden, and diverted the influence of French counsels regarding the Ninth Electorate. In the year 1700, having gone with the King of Sweden on a dangerous journey, he happily accomplished the conjunction of the fleets of the Allies: he established free navigation for his own and other European countries in the North Sea. The late Queen Anne of blessed memory, in 1711, made him Keeper of the Privy Seal, and appointed him Ambassador Extraordinary at Utrecht, where he signed the Treaty of Peace, among all European nations so long wished for, and which to-day we enjoy and glory in.)

It is somewhat strange that the epitaph - most likely composed by the Bishop himself - makes no mention of the deceased's ecclesiastical preferments. The probable explanation is that Robinson did not think that his life work was that of the Church.

The tomb has been well preserved, thanks to Miss Laetitia Cornwallis, the Bishop's beloved stepdaughter, who, by her will, dated 2 May 1733 (P.C.C. proved 3 Feb. 1740-41), left

> "The sum of £50 the interest whereof to be forever annually paid on the 7th day of November to such poor person for the time being of the Parish of Fulham in Middlesex as the Minister of the said Parish for the time being shall see fit on condition that such poor person doe constantly keep the said Bishop's Tomb in the Churchyard there cleane and preserve the same and the Railes about it as much as may be from damage or spoyle, and doe once in euery three yeares new paint the said railes."

When not required, the income from this legacy was to be devoted to the poor. The investment of this legacy and its accumulations amounted to £179. 6s. 11d. New Consols. The tomb was, until recent years, repaired out of this income, but the fund is now absorbed in the United Charities Scheme.

Mrs. Robinson, the Bishop's second wife, died at her house near Westminster Abbey, 29 Dec. 1747, and was interred in her husband's vault at Fulham, 26 Jan. 1747-48.

The Church Registers record:

1723. Dr. John Robinson Lord Bishop of London bu. 19 Apl.

RANDOLPH. Beneath an altar tomb of Portland stone, enclosed with rails, adjacent to the Vicarage garden, lie the remains of Bishop Randolph. On the west side is the following inscription:

> "Under this stone lies deposited | all that is Mortal of that eminent Prelate | John Randolph | Who was born July 17, 1749, and died July 28, 1813. | Too soon for the Church & his Country and lamented by all who | have any respect for high resplendent Talents & Qualities. | It was his lot to be placed in various & arduous Stations, | But he shone conspicuous in all. His learning was deep and | accurate, his Taste correct, his judgment sound, his Industry | indefatigable, his Piety sincere, his Firmness unshaken, his | integrity uncorrupt. | At Oxford, where he filled the Chairs of Poetry, the Greek | Language and Divinity, his Name has long been enrolled amongst | the most illustrious of her sons, his Theological Lectures especially | were so admirable, that if the laborious discharge of his other | sacred Duties, had not deprived him of leisure to revise them | for Publication, they would have constituted the most durable | Monument of his Fame. | At the age of 50 being raised to the bench, he governed in | succession the

Sees of Oxford, Bangor & London, having declined | a still more exalted station in Ireland, Nor did he disappoint the | <u>great and general Expectations that were formed of him</u>. No Man | knew better than himself the Doctrines, the Discipline, the Rights | and the whole Constitution of the Church of England, & no Man in | these Times was more watchful, more courageous, or more able | to defend them. In him therefore the Church has prematurely lost | an undaunted Champion of Orthodoxy and one of her firmest | Bulwarks against innovation & Change, such was the Divine will. | May those who were directed and animated by his Counsels | whilst he was alive, persevere in the same principles and still | reverence his Example & Authority now that he is dead."

On the north side is the following:

"Also Sacred to the Memory of Henrietta, | Daughter of the above named John Randolph, | Bishop of London; | who died 14th August 1860 Aged 68 years."

Above the inscription to Dr. Randolph are carved his official arms, vizt:

Dexter: The see of London; *Sinister*: On a cross five mullets pierced (Randolph).

The Church Registers record:

1813. John Randolph Bishop of London, Fulham, aged 64 bu. 5 Aug.

The Rev. W. Wood, on 23 Mar. 1820, invested a sum of £42 Navy Five per cents, the first charge on which was the annual payment of £1. 1s. for the maintenance of the tomb of Bishop Randolph. Subsequently, by a writing, dated Apl. 1834, he increased the sum to £1. 5s., for the cleaning of his own tomb, in addition to that of Dr. Randolph.

GIBSON. The table monument to Bishop Gibson lies just southwards of that of Bishop Robinson. On a flat stone which surmounts the tomb, which is enclosed with rails, is the following:

"Edmundus Gibson D.D. | Londinensis Episcopus | Obiit 6 Sept. Anno Dom. | 1748 | Ætat 79."

At the west end are the official arms of Bishop Gibson, as on his monument in the Church. At the east end is his domestic coat, vizt:

> Three storks rising (Gibson), on an escutcheon of pretence a lion rampant (Jones).

The Church Registers record:

> 1748. The Rt. Rev. Father in God Edmund Bishop of London bu. 17 Sept.

In this vault are also interred the bodies of the Rev. Christopher Wilson, Bishop of Bristol (d. 18 Apl. 1792), Anne Wilson (d. 16 May 1789) his wife, daughter of Bishop Gibson, Richard Wilson (d. 12 May 1787) and Christopher Wilson (d. 25 May 1842), sons of Bishop Wilson, and Sophia Wilson (d. 18 Oct. 1848), wife of Christopher Wilson.

Bishop Gibson's tomb was repaired in 1836 at the expense of the family of the Rev. N. Hill, of Snailwell, near Newmarket, a descendant of the Bishop. It was again restored in 1898.

HOOK. A small upright stone bears the following brief inscription to the memory of Hook, the renowned humorist:

> "Theodore Edward Hook, | died 24th August 1841, | in the 53rd year of his age."

The Church Registers record:

> 1841. Theodore Edward Hook, Fulham, aged 52 bu. 30 Aug.

One or two unsuccessful efforts have been made to raise a fund for the erection of a more imposing monument to Hook's memory.

LISLE. Fixed against the east wall of the Church is a small stone inscribed:

"Here lyeth the bodey of | Richard Lisle gent who | Departed this lif one the | 24 daye of Ivly 1665 | in the 62 yeares of his age | Anno Domini."

In a list of recognizances to the Council of State, 29 May 1650 (Calendar of State Papers) appears the name of Richard Lisle of Fulham, gent., bound in the sum of £500 to appear when required and to be of good behaviour. In 1659 he was fined £2 for suffering "vnlawfull games in his howse."

CORNWALLIS. On the same wall of the Church is a tablet containing a long inscription to the memory of Thomas Cornwallis, who died 16 July 1703, aged 33, son of Sir Francis Cornwallis and Elizabeth his wife. He married Emma, daughter of Sir Job Charlton, kt. and bart. This lady married, as her second husband, Dr. John Robinson, whose vault is close at hand. In the Cornwallis vault are also interred the remains of two of his children, Emma, who died in 1714, and Laetitia (Letitia) who died in 1740. It was this Laetitia Cornwallis who left a legacy for the repair of the tomb of her stepfather, Bishop Robinson. The body of Thomas Cornwallis was originally interred in the Parish Church of St. Giles in the Fields, but, on the rebuilding of that structure, it was removed to Fulham. The inscription is given in full by Faulkner. When, in 1861, Mr. Walter Rye copied the epitaph, only a part of it could be read. Mr. Rye notes:

> "Exactly over this slab a water pipe has been placed that drains the roof of the church, and owing to the continual passage of water, the inscription has become nearly illegible."

WITHERS. Near the monument to the memory of Bishop Robinson is the railed altar tomb of the Withers family, containing the remains of Sir William Withers, knight, to whom there is the following epitaph written on the top slab:

> "Hic jacet quod reliquum est | Gulielrni Withers Militis | Qui Municipalibus Urbis Londini singulis | Perfunctus Honoribus Prætorium munus | Tandem capesivit Anno 1707 | Quod tanta sibi cum Laude | Et Reipublicæ Emolumento gessit | Ut merito audiret Vir

probus I Et idem Civis optimus I Obijt 31° Jan. 1720 I Ætatis 70 I Juxta avi Relliquias poni voluit suas I Gulielmi Withers Armigeri qui obijt I 29° Octobris Anno Domini 1768 Ætatis 52."

(Translation: Here lies what is mortal of William Withers, knight, who, having discharged the duties of several civic offices of the City of London, at length attained the Mayoralty in the year 1707: which office he carried out with as great credit to himself and benefit to the State as an honest man and withal an excellent citizen could do. He died 31 Jan. 1720, aged 70. William Withers, gentleman, who died 29 Oct. 1768, aged 52, desired that his own remains might be laid beside those of his grandfather.)

Above this inscription are the following arms:

A chevron between three crescents (Withers). *Crest*: On an esquire's helmet a dem-hare issuant.

The coat is repeated, in colour, on the rails on either side of the grave.

There are also buried in this vault Lady Margaret Withers (d. 1711), wife of Sir William Withers, kt., Col. William Withers (d. 18 Nov. 1772), his son, Mrs. Elizabeth Withers (d. 1727), wife of Col. Wm. Withers, and William Withers (d. 29 Oct. 1768), grandson of Sir William, etc.

Col. Withers, as we have elsewhere stated, by his will, dated 1722, left a rent charge of £5 for keeping clean and in repair the monument which he erected to the memory of his father, Sir Wm. Withers. When not required, the testator directed that the money should be distributed among the poor of Fulham.

In this vault are also buried some of the Ravenshaw family connected by marriage with the Withers family. On the north side of the tomb is the following:

"In this vault I are deposited the Remains of I Thomas William Ravenshaw, Esqre, I eldest son of John Goldsborough Ravenshaw, Esqre, I and of Elizabeth, I only daughter of William Withers, Esqre. I He departed this life August 14th 1842, I aged 66 years."

And on the south side:

"Hic jacent Reliquiæ | Joannis Goldsborough Ravenshaw, | qui obijt Jun. 6 A.D. 1840, | Ætatis 63. | Itemque uxoris eius Hannæ, | quæ obiit xxx Nov. MDCCCLXII, I Annos nata LXXVIII."
(Translation: Here lie the remains of John Goldsborough Ravenshaw, who died 6 June 1840, aged 63: also his wife Hannah who died 30 Nov. 1862, aged 78.)

And on the west side:

"Sarah, | widow of | Colonel | Thos W. Ravenshaw, | June 15th, | 1878, | Aged 89 | R.I.P."

John Goldsborough Ravenshaw was Chairman of the Court of Directors of the East India Company. Thomas William Ravenshaw, who was a Colonel in the Berks Militia, was his brother. They were two of the five sons of John G. Ravenshaw, of Old Bracknell and Bath, by Elizabeth, only child of William Withers, of Dummer, co. Hants, and Fulham.

PLOT H

CHILD. Beneath a railed altar tomb of marble is the vault of the Child family. On the south and north sides of the tomb are sculptured, as the insignia of his mayoralty, the civic cap, sword, mace and chain of Sir Francis Child the elder. At either end are his arms, vizt:

(At the east end) A chevron engrailed ermine between three birds; on an escutcheon of pretence a chevron between three leopards' faces.
(At the west end) On a knight's shield a bird (headless, perhaps a chough) perched on a piece of rock.

On the top of the tomb is the following inscription:

"In a Vault under this Tomb is | Deposited the Body of | Sr Francis Child K[nt] & Alderman | and President of Christ Church Hospit. | in London who departed this life Oct. | ye 4 1713 Ætat. 71. He was Lord Mayor | in the year 1699 & in 1702. He was Chosen | One of the Four Citizens to Serve for the | Said City in the first Parliament of the | Reign of Queen Anne. | He married Elizabeth the only daughter & | Heiress of William Wheeler, Goldsmith, By | whom he had twelve sons and three daughters. | The Bodies of his sons James and William | and of his daughter Martha, wife of Anthony Collins | Esq. are removed from the church into | this vault."

This tomb was repaired in 1841 by the Countess of Jersey, a lineal descendant of Sir Francis Child. It was also repaired by Child's Bank in 1882.

VASLET. A flat stone by the south wall of the Church is inscribed:

"Hic jacet Ludovicus Vaslet | Gallus gente, Anglus Lege atque Animo. | Qui cum multam juventuti erudiendæ operam | Per annos Quadraginta quinque Dedisset | Tandem ex hac vita migravit | Anno Dni 1731, 12 Junii Die ætatis 65. | Hic Duas Uxores Duxerat | Primo Mariam Claudii Barachini Filiam | 10 Januarii [1704-5] Denatam | & Londini Sepultam | In Coemeterio Templi | Quod Divi Ægidii in Campis nomen habet | Secundo Catharinam Caroli Testardi Filiam | Quæ morti occubuit 29 Aprilis 1730 æ. 56. | & in hac Camera una Cum Patre | Filio Testardo Ludovico | Qui obiit 21 Martii [1730-31] æt. 25 | et Marito requiescit | Hic jacet etiam Catherina Edwards | Filia supra dicti Lodovici Vaslet | et Vidua Johannis Nodes | Et Oliveri Edwards Armigerorum | Obiit 10 Septembris . . . et anno ætatis 90 | . . . (pr)obitatis pietatis et urbanitatis | . . ."

The last two lines of the epitaph are now nearly obliterated.

(Translation: Here lies Louis Vaslet, of French descent, an Englishman by naturalization and by sympathy, who, after having bestowed great pains upon the teaching of the young through a period of 45 years, at last departed this life on 12 June in the year 1731, aged 65 He had two wives: first Mary, daughter of Claude Barachin, who died 10 Jan. 1704-5, and was buried in the churchyard of the church which bears the name of St. Giles in the Fields; secondly, Catharine, daughter of Charles Testard, who died 29 April 1730, aged 56, and who rests in this vault with her father, her son Testard Louis, who died 21 Mar. 1730-I, aged 25, and her husband. Here lies also Catherine Edwards, daughter of the above named Louis Vaslet, and widow of John Nodes and Oliver Edwards, esquires. She died 10 Sept. . . . at the age of 90 . . . probity, piety and urbanity . . .)

At the bottom, interposed between the last seven lines, are the arms of Vaslet, vizt:

An anchor erect in pale; on a chief 3 mullets.

The Vaslet stone was originally on the top of a large table monument, at one end of which was the following:

"Here lies also the Body of | Sarah Wake | Elder daughter of | J. & S. N. Wildman | who died on the 20th day of December 1856 | in the 49th year of her age."

The sides were inscribed:

"In this Tomb lie the Remains of | John Wildman who died July 15th | 1824, aged 66 years | also of Sarah Nodes his Wife | Great grand daughter of Louis Vaslet | who died October 8th 1853 aged 80 years | also of George Nodes | their eldest son | who died Decr 22nd 18 . . aged 22 years. | This Tablet is raised to their memory | by the two daughters of | J. and S. N. Wildman, April 1854.

Within this tomb rest the remains of Richard Price, Esq., of Michael's Place, Brompton, ob^t Jany 22nd 1807 Ætat. 71. From an early love of his Maker he led a life of Piety and Benevolence, and felt in his last hours what is expressed in his Essay, page 125.

'O Innocence, what language can express
Thy worth. Those heavenly comforts in distress
What tongue! What tongue of Seraph can define
To human thought thy excellence divine?
Pure source of Happiness without alloy;
Thou life of life, and soul of every joy,
When o'er creation shines thy cheering light,
We feel existence with sincere delight;
From bitter draughts the cup of life's refin'd,
And bliss eternal draws upon the mind.'

This marble is inscribed to his memory by his relict, Margaret Mary, daughter of John Nodes, Esq."

The stones round this grave are now lost.

WODEHOUSE. A brick tomb records the name of Philip Wodehouse (d. 21 Jan. 1838), Vice-Admiral of the White, second son of John, first Lord Wodehouse, of Kimberley, co. Norfolk.

The Church Registers record:

> 1838. Vice Admiral The Honble Philip Wodehouse, Chelsea, aged 65 bu. 27 Jan.

PLOT I

NUTKINS. An upright stone, carved with a winged head, records the names of James Nutkins (d. 1 Feb. 1745) and of Robert and Elizabeth Nutkins, father and mother of James Nutkins.

END OF VOL. I

Charles James Fèret

NOTES

Chapter I: The Name "Fulham"

<u>Fulla</u>: In Norse mythology we hear of one Fulla, an attendant on Friga, whose treasure-casket and slippers she is said to carry. She is also acquainted with the secret counsels of the mother of the gods. As Friga represents the earth's fertility, Fulla would seem to typify the abundance which follows it.

Chapter II: The Manor of Fulham

<u>Translation</u>: The "translation" refers to the canonization of Earconuald, whose body, on 14 Nov. 1148, was removed to a spot near the high altar of St. Paul's.

<u>Norman French</u>: The word "manor" reaches us from the Old French *manoir*, from the Low Latin *manerium*, a dwelling-place, mansion. The original root is the Latin *maneo*, to stay, to dwell.

<u>Fishery</u>: In Mediæval Latin "gurges" is often used in the sense of a fishing ground.

<u>The earliest existing Rolls of the Manor of Fulham are of the time of Richard II</u>: Until the affairs of the Bishopric of London were taken over by the Ecclesiastical Commissioners, the Court Rolls were kept at Fulham Palace. The major part is now preserved at the Ecclesiastical Commission, Whitehall Place, S.W. Unfortunately, at the time of the transfer, a large number of the Rolls, mainly the older ones, were, for some unknown reason, sent to the Principal Record Office. This priceless collection of local records is thus sundered in twain.

<u>Translation of Dr. Tait to the see of Canterbury</u>: Bishop Tait retained the *title* of Lord of the Manor of Fulham because, until the avoidance of the See by his translation, the lands, etc., of the Manor were vested in him as Bishop of London. Dr. Tait was appointed in 1856. On 28 Aug. 1860 an Act (23 and 24 Vic. c. 124) was passed entitled "An Act further to amend the Acts relating to the Ecclesiastical Commissioners, and the Act concerning the management of Episcopal and Capitular estates in England," the second sect. of which reads:

"II. Upon the first avoidance of the See of an Archbishop or Bishop in England, after the passing of this Act, all the lands, Hereditaments or Emoluments of or belonging to such See (except Rights of Patronage or Presentation and the Residences of the Archbishop or Bishop, and such lands necessary for the enjoyment of such Residences as shall be attached thereto by any Scheme sanctioned by Order in Council) shall become vested absolutely in the Ecclesiastical Commissioners for England, for the Purposes and subject to the Provisions applicable to other Hereditaments vested in the said Commissioners.''

Fixed incomes for bishops appointed after 1 Jan. 1848 were provided for by 13 and 14 Vic. c. 94, s. xvii. (14 Aug. 1850), and under this Act Bishop Tait came as far as concerned income.

Chapter IV: The River
From Hamersmith Land's End to the Laystall: The "Land's End" at Hammersmith was doubtless the western limit of that parish. "Laystall" means a place where dung is laid or where milch cows are kept. The Laystall was at the eastern end of the Town Meadows near Chelsea Creek.

Varying in depth from ten to thirty feet: In Dawes Road the bed of gravel was found to be 27 ft. deep.

Chapter VI: Population
Paid rent to the Bishop: Pannage rent in Fulham was payable on the Feast of St. Martin the Bishop (11 November). The tenants paid per annum:

	d.
For a full-grown pig of one year and upwards (*porcus*)	2
For a ¾ year old pig or under one year (*porculus*)	1½
For a ½ year old pig or under ¾ year (*porcellus*)	1
For a ¼ year old pig or under ½ year (*porcellus*)	½

A population of about 3,510: The Diocese Book at Fulham Palace, for 1790, gives only 521 dwellings, viz., "Houses taxed, 418; Cottages not taxed, 103."

Chapter VII: Amusements
Gourd: Gourds were dice in which a secret cavity had been made.

Chapter VIII: Punishments
Lords Pareter: i.e. The Bishop's apparitor.

Chapter X: Wintering of the Danes at Fulham
Anglo-Saxon Chronicle: "Anglo-Saxon Chronicle," ed. by Edmund Gibson, 1692, pp. 85-6.

An. DCCCLXXIX: It will be observed that the date of the settlement of the Danes at Fulham is given in the so-called "Anglo-Saxon Chronicle" as 879, while we have mentioned 880 as the year. Our reason for assigning the latter year is this: the "Chronicle" mentions the fact that, in the same year as the landing of the Danes at Fulham, there was an eclipse of the sun for one hour. From "L'Art de Verifier les Dates," it appears that in 879 there was but one very small eclipse of the sun visible only in the north of Scotland, while on 14 Mar. 880 there was a central eclipse visible all over the west of Europe. It seems therefore pretty certain that 880 is correct. The old chroniclers follow, of course, the inaccuracies of the "Anglo-Saxon Chronicle." Stubbs fixes the year as 880.

Gives no sense: The hieroglyphics in the manuscript for "in fulanhame" (a name with which Roger of Hoveden may not have been familiar, not unlikely bore a resemblance to "infula(m)hame," hence the error.

Chapter XI: Fulham Ferry
Rot. de Lib. ac de Misis et Præstitis: Ed. by T. D. Hardy, 1844, p. 155.

Translation: Household Estab. of Edward I published by the Antiquarian Society, p, 51-54.

Quinzaine: "the 14th day after a feast" - Bond.

Cheife rent: Chief rent, synonymous with quit-rent, was the rent paid by the freeholder and copyholder of a manor in discharge or acquittance of other services.

fferme: ferme or ferm, an old word for rent, especially of farms, etc., French *ferme*, a farm.

Hithe: Putney, *i.e.*, Putten-hithe.

Chapter XIII: Old Fulham or Putney Bridge
Debates: "Debates of the House of Commons," by the Honourable

Anchitelle Grey, published in 1769.

Member for London: John Jones, one of the four members for the City, elected 13 Charles II (1661).

Mr. Love: Alderman William Love, another of the City members.

Sir Robert Walpole in connection with this matter: The origin of this story, handed down through several generations, we have been unable to trace. William Chasemore (b. 1790), John Phelps (b. 1805), and the people connected with the Bridge, all told this anecdote.

This Bill was read, for the first time, on 22 March 1724-25: "Journals" of the House of Commons, vol. 20, p. 631.

Mr. John Price: Mr. Price published "Some Considerations for building a bridge over the Thames from Fulham to Putney," with a design, 8vo. 1726 ; also a second letter of the same date, 8vo. 1726.

Hold votes for the counties of Surrey and Middlesex: in 1846 the freehold votes possessed by the shareholders were disallowed.

Exemption from toll: Legally, only members of the Bishop's household were allowed to use this password, but workpeople and others having business at the Palace sometimes got through with it.

Mr. Castilione: Philip Daniel Castiglione Maurelli, buried at Fulham.

Thirty-four persons: The number of adults mentioned is really 38.

Loss of the Sunday ferry: Sunday was the watermen's busy day. The week day ferry was apparently not taken into account.

These two bells: A date on the bells showed that they were cast in 1739. If a person "shot the bridge," *i.e.*, passed the toll house without paying, the bell was instantly rung and the gate at the opposite end closed till the toll was paid.

Giving power to the late Metropolitan Board of Works to purchase: The price paid by the Metropolitan Board of Works to the shareholders was £58,000.

The work of demolition: This work was carried out by Messrs. John Waddell & Sons, the builders of the new bridge.

Threw his coat to the tollman: The coat was used by the night tollman till worn out. The stable at Putney where the murder was committed still stands.

Wharf belonging to the Fulham Vestry: In 1888 the Vestry purchased this site, comprising about 940 square yards, of the

Board of Works. On payment of a fine to the Thames Conservators, the Vestry were allowed to erect a boundary wall 40 feet further out in the river. This increased the area of the wharf to over 1,500 square yards. The Conservators further required the Vestry to construct a causeway and steps down to the river bed in lieu of the steps they removed.

Chapter XIV: New Putney Bridge
Aqueduct of the Chelsea Waterworks Company: Watermains are now laid under the footways of the new Bridge, two mains being placed beneath each, thus obviating the need for a separate aqueduct.

Chapter XVI: High Street (General)
The name High Street, which came into vogue: Singularly enough, in the minutes of a Court General, held in 1514, the thoroughfare is called the *alta strata*, or High Street.
The "r" was already influencing the vowel-change: Compare Clerk, Clark, Derby, Darbyshire, etc.
The voidance of the grant: In later times in lieu of the service of scouring, the Bishop was accustomed to charge a Moat rent.

Chapter XVII: High Street (East Side)
Family of the name of Passor who were living in Fulham in the time of Edward III: The surname Passor was due to the occupation of the *passator* or ferryman.
St. Swyth's Church in Cheapside: St. Swithin's, now united with St. Mary Bothaw, London Stone.
He died in 1736: In the Fulham Church Registers are the two following entries of the burial of the children of Jacob Tonson:

    1726. Martha. Daugh. of Jacob and Mary Thomson   bu. 15 Aug.
    1728. John son of Jacob Tomson   bu. 30 Apl.

In the Parish Books the usual spelling is Tomson or Thomson.
Almshouses which he had founded in Back Lane: See "Burlington Road."
Manuscript "List of Taverns in London and Westminster and 10 miles round: Now in the possession of W.]. Harvey, Esq, F.S.A.,

to whom we are indebted for the information.

<u>His Royal Highness the Duke</u>: William Augustus, Duke of Cumberland, son of George II.

<u>Giuseppe Baretti</u>: Baretti, between 1752 and 1755, visited the Fulham Manufactory on several occasions. See details given by Montaiglon in the "Bulletin de la Société de l'Art Francais," 3 année, Jan. 1877, p. 95.

<u>Playhouse</u>: Possibly by "playhouse," Faulkner means some place for games such as skittles, bowls, *etc.*, perhaps in connection with the "Golden Lion."

<u>Bequeathed Goodriche's to the Principal of Hertford College, Oxford</u>: The Rev. T. Vere Bayne, Keeper of the Archives, Christ Church, possesses no records showing that Goodriche's was ever given to Hertford College.

<u>The site was acquired for the extension of the Fulham National Schools</u>: On one of the benefaction tablets, still in the porch of All Saints, is the following:

> "1861. The Rev. R. G. Baker, Vicar, by a deed enrolled in the Court of Chancery, May 14th, gave a piece of freehold land in the High Street containing 1r. 4p. [1 rod, 4 pole] as a site for a new National School Room for boys."

<u>Six coats and six pair of breeches, made of good English woollen cloth</u>: The gift of coats, etc., was done away with by the Scheme regulating Sir William Powell's Trust in 1869.

<u>Employment of the inmates of the Workhouse</u>: Hitherto oakum picking had been the chief, if not the only, industry of the House.

<u>Mr. Bunnett</u>: Dr. Henry Bunnett of Church Row. He was for some years "surgeon, apothecary and midwife " to the Workhouse.

Chapter XVIII: High Street (West Side)

<u>Church Houses (Nos. 22 and 50 to 72, High Street) above mentioned</u>: In No. 48 there may still be seen a blocked up window situated in the south wall. This shows that there must once have been an intervening space between it and the old "Poores House " to the south of it.

<u>An entry in the Stourton Manuscript Book is to the same effect</u>: This manuscript (in 2 parts, 23 and 62 pp. respectively) is in the

possession of Lord Mowbray and Stourton.
John Sharp, dean of Norwich: Afterwards Archbishop of York.

Chapter XIX: High Street (Miscellaneous)
John Wynger: Sir John Wynger was Lord Mayor in 1504.
Following order: State Papers, Dom. 372, No. 57.
Holofernes: The word "Holofernes" is an imperfect anagram which Shakespeare coined out of the name "Joh'nes Floreo," omitting the first and last letters, or "J'h'nes Floreo," omitting the first.
Aurelia Molins: Florio's beloved daughter Aurelia Molins, was executrix to her husband, James Molins, barber surgeon, who died at Stoke Newington, 2 Dec. 1638, and was buried at St. Andrew's, Holborn. She left issue six sons and three daughters.

Chapter XX: Burlington Road
Mr. Edmund Day: "late Master of the Academy at Fulham," died suddenly, 1 Sept. 1777.
Consideration of his lease: From Rocque's Map, 1741-45, it appears that the plan of the original Almshouses was precisely similar to that of 1792-93.

Chapter XXI: Church Row
Following terms: In the margin of the Roll, against this entry, occurs the word "Goodriches" in a handwriting *temp.* Eliz. or Jac I, that tenement having subsequently been built on the garden.
Pump Court: These cottages are mentioned in the will of Robert Limpany. See later in this chapter.
Yet another William: "William" was a family name with the Skeltons.
Dr. Ayreton: Dr. Ayrton was "Master of the Boys" at the Chapel Royal.
Three-quarters of an acre: Formerly Nos. 1 to 6 had each a garden reaching to the Moat but intersected with a mews. Of these No. 6 had a large garden. The seventh house had only a narrow yard behind, while the eighth had a fair sized garden, which was spoiled by the large garden of No. 6 coming wholly behind the seventh house and largely behind the eighth. On purchasing No. 6 Mr. Thos. Roe added the larger part of its garden to No. 7, leaving No. 6 the portion it now possesses.

Steps at the far end leading down to the water's edge: Sergt. Roe notes in his "Diary" under date, 27 April 1812: "Began steps to Moat."

Chapter XXII: Fulham Church

The bequest stands: Wills, City of London (Court of Husting), Roll 89 (151).

With power to appoint and dismiss all workmen: "Letters and Papers Illustrating the Reigns of Richard III. and Henry VII." ed. by James Gairdner. (Rolls Series, No. 24.

Small door on the south side: There was formerly a means of communication with the Tower from the Church through a door, now filled up, in the Tower chapel.

The Thames Waterman was not far wrong: The following manuscript note, signed "L. E B." (Lucy E. Blomfield, daughter of Bishop Blomfield), appears in an interleaved copy of "Fulham in the Olden Times," presented to her by the Rev. R. G. Baker in 1856:

> "It was stated, a few years back, in an Article on Bells in the 'Quarterly Review,' that there were 60 peals of 10 bells each in England, and that of these the finest were at Exeter, All Saints, Fulham, and one other place, the name of which I cannot recall."

The payment of the contract amount of £60: It is customary to make bonds for double the amount involved.

Fourescore pounds secur'd to be paid by the inhabitants of Hammersmith: This was a sum which the Hamlet of Hammersmith had, as the outcome of a dispute with Fulham, promised to pay towards the repair of the old Church.

Little the worse for their immersion: The story, as handed down to Richard Kelley, an old bell ringer and waterman of Fulham, was to the effect that, when the barge was off Fulham, it sank with the bells. "They were drownded," he used to say, "but when they were got up, the life of the bells was in them still." John Phelps gave a somewhat similar account of the mishap, but stated that the barge sank as one of the bells was being hauled out. Richard Kelley has left, in writing, a singular account of the bells, now in the possession of the Rev. F. H. Fisher.

The old church at Mortlake: Mortlake Church has a peal of eight bells. No. 2 bears the following inscription:

"Thos. Lester of London made me."
"Theodore Eccleston, Esq, 1746."

Procure a lycense for the same: No license can be traced in the Vicar General's Books at Doctors' Commons for increasing the number of bells from 8 to 10.

Hearse cloath: The hearsecloth was provided for use at funerals. The Commissioners of 1549 mention among the furniture of the Church "one Hearse clothe of blacke vellett." In the minutes of the Vestry, held 9 June 1685, is the following entry:
"It is ordered in Vestry that Mr. Chubb p'sent churchwarden doe buy A Herse Cloth for the vse of the Church for the burials for the future at the value of six pounds and all p'sons that are to mak vse of it being p'ishoners to pay the sum of 2d. and all strangers (*i.e.* non-parishioners) to pay the sum of 4d, for the vsc thereof."

With a row of free pews facing north: The beadle's chair stood against the east wall of the south aisle, behind the Vestry door. The silver-headed staff, carried only before a Bishop, was fixed in a rack between the seat and the Vestry door.

Some curious twisted ironwork: This piece of ironwork, containing the initials "R. L." (Robert Limpany) entwined, now lies in the north porch.

Below the level of the ground: Before the embankment of the river, the Church was frequently flooded when the tides were high. The monuments and Church chests, and their contents, have much suffered from the inroads of the water. On one occasion the late Vicar actually caught a stickleback in the centre aisle !

Ravis Edwardes: Probably christened Ravis after Dr. Thomas Ravis, Bishop of London.

The beginning of the 18th century: The North Gallery is, for the first time, mentioned in the Churchwardens' Accounts for 1723.

By these means the original form of the columns was ascertained: On the removal of the rounded additions to the corners, the original marbling underneath was discovered.

At a lower level: Possibly the level where the date and initials were cut was that of a school gallery rising from the floor rather than a lower level of gallery. It would be close to the Porch School.

The South Gallery, as it existed in modern times, was erected in 1769-70: The south aisle was formerly separated from the body of the Church by Gothic arches and pillars. They were about this time almost entirely removed to allow of the better lighting of the South Gallery.

Inhabitants in Vestry: In more recent times, when the lower room ceased to be used for the purposes of a school, it was known as the Great Vestry Room, the upper one being called the Little Vestry Room.

Standish: A case for pens and ink, cf. "inkstand."

Publicke Register: The Parish Registrar was an officer appointed to keep the record of the baptisms, marriages and burials. Hitherto that duty had been discharged by the incumbent of the living, assisted by the parish clerk.

Teach Schoole: From this entry it would seem that "school" was to be held in the Vestry chamber itself, instead of in the lower room, as heretofore.

Wandsworth Church: The old Church Porch, which many residents may still remember, bore a striking resemblance to that of Wandsworth Church. Its roof was supported on four plain piers.

Church Notes: Lansdown Manuscript 874, Brit. Museum.

Writing of the repairs effected in the Church in 1770, remarks: From manuscript note in Faulkner's own copy of his "History of Fulham," now at the Hammersmith Public Library.

Plate: Mrs Hill's gift of a "plate," instead of a "paten," to "carry the Bread about in," savours strongly of Puritanism in the church.

One great Bible: Probably the Bible purchased in 1637.

Pulpit Cloth of velvet; Two velvet Cushions; One Cup of Silver and guilt, with a Couer: Probably the gift of Dr. Edwardes.

Two Silver plates wth feete: These were the gift of Mr. and Mrs. Thos. Hill.

Two Pewter Dishes or Basins for Collections: These were subsequently stolen.

Vestry was robbed: Robberies of the Church were not of infrequent occurrence. At a meeting of the Vestry on 29 Oct. 1738

> "It was agreed that the Churchwarden should advertize in the *Daily Advertizer* a Reward of five guineas for anyone of the persons concern'd in robbing the church last week that will discover his accomplice or accomplices or to any other person that shall make such discovery to be paid on conviction at the expence of the parish."

In 1670 the poor box at Fulham Church was robbed. The Churchwardens' Account shows:

"Expended att Sessions in proffering a bill against Hawkins about the money he stole out of the poores box by order . . . 14s. 0d."

Church Bier: This appears to have been often used when the parish was "visited" by the plague for the conveyance of bodies to the pest pits at Hurlingharn, Chelsea, Westminster, etc. In 1649 the Churchwardens paid
"For bringing the Church beere from Chelsey being carried thither by the souldiers . . . 6d."

Harrop: A harrop is what is now known as a "ciborium," i.e. a chalice with a lid for the Reserved Sacrament.

Deal chest with lock and key and an elm chest with triple locks and keys: The Churchwardens, in 1641, "pd. for a chest to Wadnmore . . . £1. 5. 0."

Claims of the Polish sufferers were heard in Fulham: Briefs on behalf of the Protestant episcopalians in Poland were issued also in 1681 and 1716. See Mosheim's "History" (III. 234) and Erskine's "Sketches of Church Hist." (II. 147, etc.). Their correct appellation was "Polish Dissidents."

Richard Fitzpatrick: In Little Marylebone Churchyard there is a handsome stone mausoleum, erected by Mr. Fitzpatrick to receive the remains of his wife in 1759. He and his children are also buried there. Mr. Fitzpatrick had a house in Hanover Square and a villa at Fulham. In an old family prayer book, containing a few entries in his handwriting, the baptism of his eldest child "by the Rev. Mr. Croft, of Fulham," is recorded.

Converted into a communion table by having its rounded corners filled in with deal: This quaint table was, after the rebuilding of 1881, given to the Mission Hall at Parson's Green.

A second chair was added: The Bishop's Chair now stands on the north side of the sacrarium. The Vicar's chair, in the new Church, was placed, during the episcopate of Dr. Temple, in what was known as the Clergy Vestry, a portion of the north transept curtained off. This Vestry was recently done away with, when the chair was removed to the Vicarage.

Bishop's mitre in gold: This mitre, which was evidently intended for Bishop Gibson, who granted the faculty for the erection of the Organ, is now placed at the top.

Sir Gilbert G. Scott prepared plans for a Gothic edifice: In the Church Vestry are preserved the original drawings by the architect, showing the proposed edifice as viewed from the north-east.

Glazed encaustic tiles: Some of these tiles are preserved in the new Church on the north side at the back of the choir seats.

A human heart: This relic was again buried in the concrete under the south pillar of the chancel arch. In the same concrete were likewise buried the handsome silver "furniture" of a wooden coffin found in the Mordaunt vault. This was the only wood coffin and was of small size. All the others were of lead. They were re-buried in the Churchyard.

The brass tablet: Explanatory brasses have been added to all the windows, so that the memory of the donors may be preserved.

Christ blessing little Children: The central child in the Children's Window is a portrait of Richard Frederic Fisher, third son of the Rev. F. H. Fisher. It was drawn from life. It was, and indeed still is, a remarkable likeness for painted glass.

South transept window: There are really two windows in the south transept. The second, without stained glass, is entirely blocked from view, on the inside, by the Organ.

In the upper tracery are scenes in the life of Our Lord: One of these, the Adoration of the Magi, is curious, for the crown is represented as being placed on the head of the Blessed Virgin instead of upon that of the Holy Child.

Chapter XXIII : Fulham Church Monuments and Epitaphs

Only six are known to have been buried at Fulham: William Harvey, 1471, Richard Stevenson, 1691, Philip Dwight, 1729, Graham Jepson, 1811, William Wood, 1841 and Robert George Baker, 1878.

Supposed to be William Harvey: Faulkner, in his own copy of his "History of Fulham," has inserted against his reference to the Harvey brass,

> "Gone and sold with Mr. Meyricks books and curiosities at King's Auction Rooms; see Mr. Meyrick's Catalogue," and, further on, against his description of the Norton brass, "These ancient brasses are all gone;

in the late Mr. Meyrick's Catalogue mention is made of 'brasses out of Fulham Church.' Mr. Meyrick was Churchwarden of Fulham in 1800, at which period they were most probably taken away to adorn his museum at Peterborough House, and after his death they were sold by auction as appears by the printed catalogue of the sale."

From a copy of the Catalogue, now preserved in the collections of H. S. Vade Walpole, Esq., of Banstead, it appears that the library, drawings, manuscripts, etc., of Mr. John Meyrick were sold by King and Lochée at their rooms, 38, King Street, Covent Garden. The sale, which lasted twelve days, commenced 21 Apl. 1806. On the last day the following lots were sold:

2536 Monumental Effigy, in Brass, from Fulham Church.

2537 Monumental Effigy and ancient Inscription on the decease of Margaret Cheyne, 1578.

2538 Ancient effigies (4) in Brass.

2538 Ancient effigies (10) and Coats of Arms, Inscriptions, etc., etc.

A note in Mr Walpole's Catalogue shows that these four lots were sold for the paltry sum of £2. 2s. 0d. Unfortunately the names of the purchasers are not given. It would be interesting to learn what became of the three brasses supposed to represent the Rev. W. Harvey, Sir S. Norton and Sir W. Butts, copied by Simco in 1794. Not improbably they were included in the above lots.

Fili redemptor mundi Deus miserere nobis: This is clearly a quotation from an ancient Litany.

Saint Arkenwold: i.e. Earconuald, Bishop of London.

Hour-glass: This hourglass was formerly in the centre on the top; in Faulkner's illustration two hour-glasses are shown on the top.

The hand clenching a standard to the sinister gu.: This was an augmentation granted by Norroy, King at Arms, in 1575, to Sir Piers Legh, or Leigh, in memory of the valiant services rendered at the Battle of Creçy by his ancestor, Sir Perkin Leigh, who bore the standard of the Black Prince.

A Particular of the Services performed by me Henry Rumbold for his Majesty: The paper, with notes by Sir Horace Rumbold, bart., G.C.M.G., was printed *in extenso* in the "Transactions" of the Royal Historical Society, 1892, pp. 145-65.

The little "Ilande," which he bequeathed to the poor of the parishes of Fulham and Hammersmith: The epitaph says Hammersmith side only.

Earth: Earth is, or, rather, was, a house situated in the parish of St. Stephen-by-Saltash. In Norden's "Survey," *temp*. James I, it is marked as the residence of Bond. It also appears in Gough's "Camden."

Double pun including "begininge" in the epitaph: This and the Carlos slab are the only two punning epitaphs at All Saints.

John Plumbe: John Plumbe, or Plume, of Eltham, describes himself in his will, dated 26 May, 1 Ed. VI (1547), as "mayster cook to the Queenes hyghnes." He died soon afterwards, as his will was proved 4 June 1548 (P.C.C. 8 Populwell). He had two surviving sons, William and Roger.

Suanden: The name is said to have originally been Des Vanderes, or Des Vanden, corrupted to Svanders or Svanden.

p' aia: "p' aia" is a contraction for "pro anima."

Purchased by Lord Ranelagh on the occasion of the death of his first wife, Caroline Elizabeth, in 1805: When, in 1880-81, the old Church was pulled down, there were found, below Lord Ranelaghs vault, the coffins of Emily Alice Rendell and Baroness de Stark. It was thus clear that, by dint of a little sharp practice, the Vestry in 1805 had sold to Lord Ranelagh the vault which they had already disposed of to the friends of the Baroness! A stone in the wall bore the annexed inscription (see image below): *i.e.* Martha Baroness de Stark. The Ranelagh vault was found to contain the coffins of Sir Philip Stephens, Thomas, 6th Viscount Ranelagh, Caroline Elizabeth, his first wife and two infants, Caroline, born of the first wife, and Arthur the second son by his second marriage with Miss Louisa Thompson.

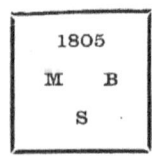

```
   1805
 M    B
    S
```

The field was originally azure: We have been unable to identify this coat.

Renevolentiæ: An error for "benevolentiæ."

He improved and embellished the face of Nature: The impudence of this assertion is noteworthy. "Launcelot Brown, Esq.," is better remembered as "Capability" Brown. He laid out the grounds and lake of Burleigh House, Stamford, the seat of Lord Burleigh.

<u>Buried where God shall call me from this lyfe</u>: From this injunction it seems most probable that Sir W. Butts died at Fulham.

<u>Doctor Haynes</u>: i.e. Dr. Simon Heynes, Rector of Fulham.

<u>Large old-fashioned pew</u>: The ironwork, bearing the initials "R.L.," originally fixed over the door of this pew, stands in the Porch beneath this monument.

Chapter XXIV: Fulham Churchyard

<u>Suffere their hoggs or hoggerells to come and goe into the pishe Churcheyarde</u>: In the olden time it was no uncommon thing for pigs and other live stock to overrun churchyards. In 1623 Lord Francis Russell who owned lands at Chiswick, called Bowles, built a wall around the parish churchyard to prevent swine from profaning the ground. An inscription to this effect may still be seen.

<u>Injuries now done to the Tomb Stones and Graves, by Boys and others</u>: So great was the damage constantly caused by the boys, that in 1822 it was found needful to employ a man to guard the Church and Churchyard. Such entries as the following are of frequent occurrence:

> "28 Sept. 1822. Paid Farr for attending in the churchyard to see that no mischief be done to the church and the monuments by the children 5s. 0d.

<u>Col. Tait, brother of Bishop Tait</u>: Bishop Tait would doubtless have been buried in Col. Tait's grave had he died while Bishop of London.

<u>Ninth Electorate</u>: The Ninth Electorate controversy arose about the creation of the New Electorate of Hanover, which took place in 1692. This was considered a triumph for the Protestant interest.

<u>Great and general Expectations that were formed of him</u>: Perhaps a satirical reference to the inscription on the tomb of Bishop Hayter.

<u>[Blank date]</u>: Faulkner gives the year, now quite illegible, as 1766, but this would make her only ten years younger than her father.

Printed in Great Britain
by Amazon